ALLYN AND BACON'S SERIES OF SCHOOL HISTORIES

THE STORY OF

MODERN PROGRESS

WITH A PRELIMINARY SURVEY OF EARLIER PROGRESS

BY

WILLIS MASON WEST

SOMETIME PROFESSOR OF HISTORY AND HEAD OF THE DEPARTMENT
IN THE UNIVERSITY OF MINNESOTA

ALLYN AND BACON

BOSTON NEW YORK CHICAGO
ATLANTA SAN FRANCISCO

WEST'S HISTORIES

12mo, cloth, numerous maps, plans, and illustrations

THE ANCIENT WORLD

THE MODERN WORLD

HISTORY OF THE AMERICAN PEOPLE

AMERICAN HISTORY AND GOVERNMENT

SOURCE BOOK IN AMERICAN HISTORY

THE STORY OF MAN'S EARLIER PROGRESS

THE STORY OF MODERN PROGRESS

Norwood Press
J. S. Cushing Co. — Berwick & Smith Co.
Norwood, Mass., U.S.A.

FOREWORD

My *Modern History*, of eighteen years ago, and its successor, *The Modern World*, taught insistently, and, for long in rather lonely fashion, the perils in Prussian militarism and autocracy. In 1902, when worship of Bismarckian "efficiency" was at its height in America and England, after presenting details, I ventured to sum up this matter thus (*Modern History*, page 477):

> The story of the making of Germany shows plainly enough that the process was one not merely of "blood and iron" but also of fraud and falsehood. It is hard to tell the story of such gigantic and successful audacity and craft without seeming to glorify it. . . . Bismarck's success has tended too, probably, to lower the tone of international morality; and his policy of fraud and violence has left to Germany a legacy of burning questions which will grieve it long. The rule of the drill-sergeant and of the police officer, the hostility to the Empire felt by the Danes of Sleswig and the French of Alsace-Lorraine, the bitter jealousy between Prussia and Bavaria, and the immense armies of all Europe are among the results of his policy. *It is too early yet to say that that policy is truly victorious.*[1]

Because of this anti-Prussianism, the book suffered heavily in the years before the war from both open and secret pro-German attacks. But when the war came, no hurried revision was necessary to justify the volume to American schools. Nor is any change of attitude on these matters needed now.

[1] July 9, 1918, when the last German drive was still at its high tide of success, and Haig was fighting almost despairingly, "with our backs to the wall," the *Kölnische Zeitung*, in an exultant editorial quoted this paragraph, and added:

"Don't think you are listening to Lloyd George or Wilson delivering one of their speeches dripping with hypocritical morality. No, this stuff is in a *schoolbook* of that country which we believed friendly to us! *Here are the roots of hatred to Germany. . . . We must change all this after the war.*"

But in all history textbooks there *is* now needed a change of emphasis and of distribution of time. The past six years bulk big; and they throw searching light back over earlier years. For purposes of instruction, we must re-inventory all recent history. High-school classes will wish to give to the period since 1871 double the time which has been given heretofore. That means we must cut down somewhere else. The new two-book series, of which this is one volume, meets this need by moving forward several centuries the point at which serious study of Modern history is to begin.

At the same time, the *Story of Modern Progress* is not a revision of the *Modern World.* I have taken glad advantage of the chance to write a new book, better suited, I hope, to elementary high-school students; and I have used the treatment in the *Modern World* only when I have found it simpler and clearer than any change I could make to-day.

Throughout, an unusual amount of space is given to English history. For American students a knowledge of that history is particularly essential. English history gains, however, by being presented, not in an insular way, but in its setting in the history of the continent of Europe. And time consideration makes this method more and more imperative. Seemingly, the high-school course in history must content itself with three years. In that case, one year must go to a background of early human progress, down to the Reformation or later; a second year, to modern progress; and the third, to American history and citizenship. But no such plan can meet the end desired, unless particular stress is placed in the second year upon England's part. With such arrangement, it is possible, I believe, to teach the valuable lessons of English history more emphatically, and with almost as much of detail, as in a separate year upon that isolated subject.

In any course, American history is sure of a place by itself. That is reason enough for omitting it in this volume, except where the connection of events demands its introduction. When touched at all here, it is treated from the viewpoint of world-development, rather than from a restricted American position. The colonization of the seventeenth century is presented as an expansion of Europe, and especially of England, into New Worlds; the "Intercolonial Wars" of the eighteenth century are seen as part of the hundred-year struggle between France and England for world-empire and exclusive markets; American industrial invention in the nineteenth century appears as part of the general Industrial Revolution; the recent advance of America into world-politics is presented as part of the new international relations and new trade relations that followed the partition of Africa and the opening of the Orient in the closing decades of the nineteenth century; while the dominant attention given in these pages to America's part in the World War, both in Europe and at home, corresponds merely to the new significance of our country in world development.

In my *Modern World* I give the first seventh of the book to a brief summary of earlier history. This has proved a popular and, I am assured, a helpful feature, and I use it again here. With the added five hundred years to be covered (including the supremely important Renaissance period), this introductory survey takes a sixth of the volume. It may be omitted, at the discretion of the instructor. If used, it may serve as a review of a first-year study. Or it *may* be used to give at least *some* background in a *two-year* history course concerned only with Modern and American history. Indeed, if high schools do find themselves forced to abandon their three-year history courses (for part of their students), some such feature in the text on Modern history becomes imperative. And even if the introductory survey is not used at all in class, it may perhaps still be justified as a means of convenient reference for the student. I have embodied in it here every historical event to which the later pages make any reference.

Long or short, the high-school course in history must leave no chasm between past and present. It *must* put the student into sympathetic touch with the social movements of to-day. It must give him robust interest in the world-struggle between democracy and reaction, in the "war upon poverty," in the threat of Socialism, and in the promise of labor organization. This volume will achieve its purpose if it helps American youth, in this way, toward better citizenship.

WILLIS MASON WEST

WINDAGO FARM
January 1, 1920

TABLE OF CONTENTS

PART IX. WESTERN EUROPE, 1871–1914

PART X. SLAV EUROPE TO 1914

PART XI. THE WAR AND THE NEW AGE

ILLUSTRATIONS

MAPS

THE STORY OF MODERN PROGRESS

"The chief interest in history lies in the fact that it is not yet finished"

A BRIEF SURVEY OF EARLIER PROGRESS

FIRST PERIOD

FROM STONE AGE TO ROMAN EMPIRE

November 11, 1918, at an early morning hour, the representatives of Germany accepted the terms of armistice dictated by Marshal Foch, commander-in-chief of the Allies. Within three hours, nearly every steam whistle in America was sounding the glad tidings of Germany's surrender. Only a few miles from General Foch's headquarters where the armistice was signed is the city of Ghent. There, about a hundred years before (December 14, 1814), a peace was signed between England and the United States. But almost *four weeks after the signing of that peace,* many gallant lives were sacrificed in the Battle of New Orleans because *the news of Ghent had not reached America.* Indeed, the War of 1812 would not have been fought except for misunderstandings which steamships and electric cables would have cleared up promptly.

Rapid change during the last century

In everyday matters, too, the changes of the last hundred years or so are quite as marked. When George Washington journeyed from Mount Vernon to New York, in 1789, to take up his duties as President, he made the wearisome twelve-day trip on horseback. At Philadelphia he might have taken the slow, jolting stage-coach for the rest of the way; but both for speed and comfort, he chose to keep to his horse. To-day we make that journey in a night, resting in a cosy compartment of a sleeper or reading at ease by brilliant electric lamps.

The tallow candle and the pine-knot fire on the hearth were the best artificial lights in the days of Washington. Abraham Lincoln knew no better light until late in his life, when kerosene lamps came into use. No woman in Lincoln's presidency ever cooked by a gas range, and no woman in Washington's time ever cooked by any sort of iron stove. Washington was one of the leading farmers of his day; but a wooden plow and a clumsy harrow were the only farm machinery drawn by horses that he ever saw. Even the small reapers and threshers of Lincoln's time are now fit only for some museum of curiosities.

Carpenters and masons now work eight hours a day; but until long after Washington's day no laborer ever dreamed of working less than fourteen hours in summer — and he worked for a much smaller wage than our workmen for our shorter laboring day. The palaces of kings a century ago had fewer actual comforts and conveniences than the modest homes of well-paid laborers to-day.

Like change, though slower, during two hundred centuries

At first it is hard to understand that such changes had been going on for long ages before Lincoln and Washington. Twenty thousand years ago no one traveled even in Washington's way. There were no coaches, for no one had found how to make a wheel; and, though the wild horse was hunted for food, no one had tamed it. Indeed there was no need to travel. No man could possibly want to go from the Potomac to the Hudson. If two men living a score of miles apart met at all, the stronger killed and plundered the weaker.

History is the story of human progress from that early savagery to our present civilization.

Early savagery

The first men were more helpless and brutelike than the lowest savages in the world to-day. They had neither fire nor knife — no tools or weapons except their hands, their formidable teeth, and chance clubs or stones. The first marked gain was the discovery by some savage that he could chip off flakes from a flint stone by striking it in a certain way with other stones, so as to give it a sharp edge and a convenient shape for the hand to grasp. This invention lifted man into *the Stone Age.*

STONE FIST-HATCHET found in Suabia.— Now in the British Museum.

Remains in the soil show us that men began to use stone tools at least 100,000 years ago. The earliest remains often lie buried deep under layers of earth deposits that contain the different sorts of tools of succeeding ages. In general, the tools in the upper layers are better than those in the lower ones; and so by studying these relics, from the bottom layers upward, we can trace something of the order of man's development in those uncounted thousands of years in which our forefathers were learning to take the first stumbling steps up from savagery.

SOME STAGES IN FIREMAKING. — From Tylor.

Five gains during the long Stone Age were beyond price: the use of fire; the beginning of language; the taming of the

Gains in the Stone Age

dog, cow, sheep, and other familiar barnyard assistants; the discovery of wheat, barley, rice, and most of our other Old-World food-plants; and the invention of picture-writing.

The Bronze Age in the Orient

Some seven thousand years ago, in the valleys of the Nile and the Euphrates, men learned in some way to replace their stone tools with better *bronze tools*, and soon to improve picture-

SPHINX, WITH PYRAMIDS in the distance; ancient Egyptian works. — From a photograph. The human head of the Sphinx is supposed to have the magnified features of an Egyptian king. It is set upon the body of a lion — a symbol of power. One of the pyramids covers 13 acres and rises 481 feet in height, — the largest and most massive building in the world to-day. It contains two million huge stone blocks, some of which singly weigh more than fifty tons.

writing into the rebus stage so that a picture might stand for a syllable, or for a group of sounds, instead of for an object. Then a connected story could be told in writing — and so true history began.

These Bronze-age Egyptians and Babylonians practiced many arts and crafts with skill of hand that has never been sur-

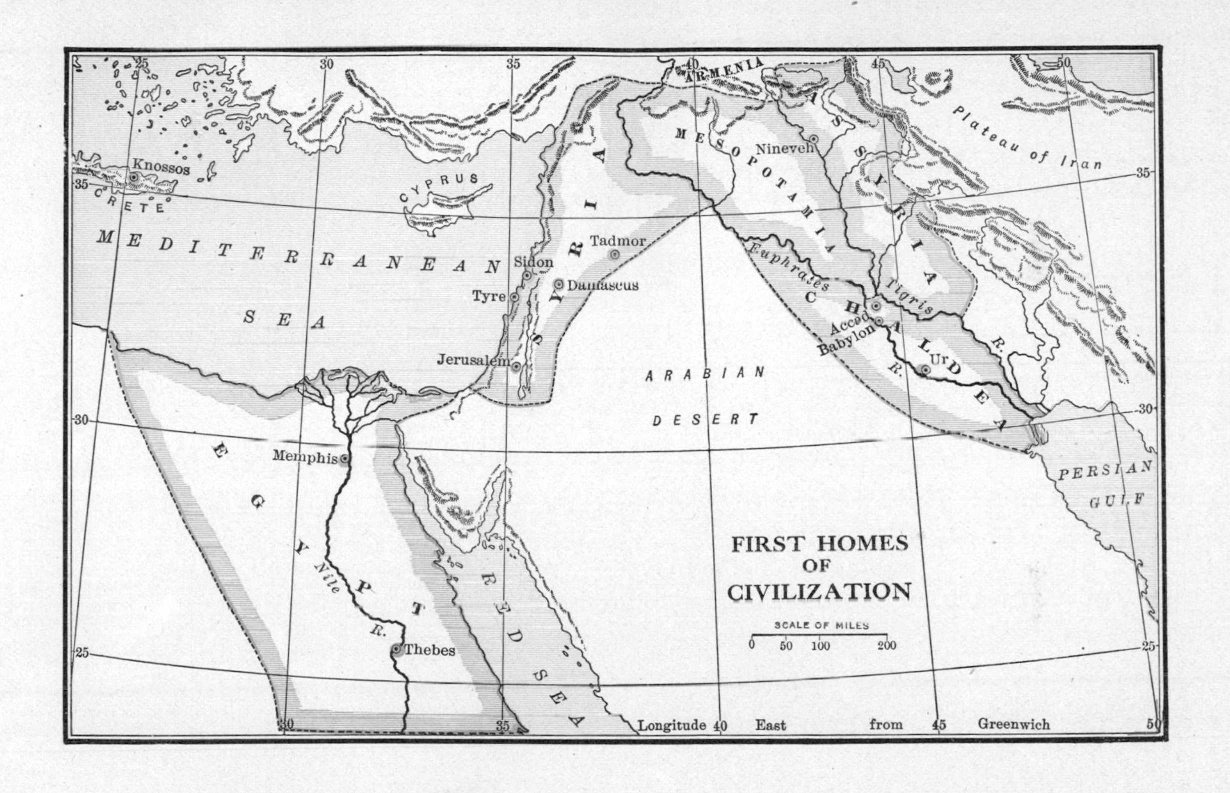
FIRST HOMES
OF
CIVILIZATION
SCALE OF MILES
0 50 100 200
MEDITERRANEAN
SEA
CRETE
Knossos
CYPRUS
SYRIA
Sidon
Tyre
Damascus
Tadmor
Jerusalem
ARMENIA
MESOPOTAMIA
Nineveh
ASSYRIA
Plateau of Iran
Euphrates
Tigris
R.
CHALDEA
Accad
Babylon
Ur
ARABIAN
DESERT
PERSIAN
GULF
EGYPT
Memphis
Nile
Thebes
RED SEA
Longitude 40 East from 45 Greenwich

passed. They built great cities, with pleasant homes for the wealthy and with splendid palaces for their princes. They built, too, roads and canals. With ships and caravans, they sought out the treasures of distant regions; and the wealth they heaped up was spent by their rulers in gorgeous pomp and splendor. Our "year" of 365¼ days, with the division into months, comes to us from the Egyptians through the Romans, as do also the sundial and water-clock. Through

M M M C C C C XX III

EGYPTIAN AND ROMAN NUMERALS.

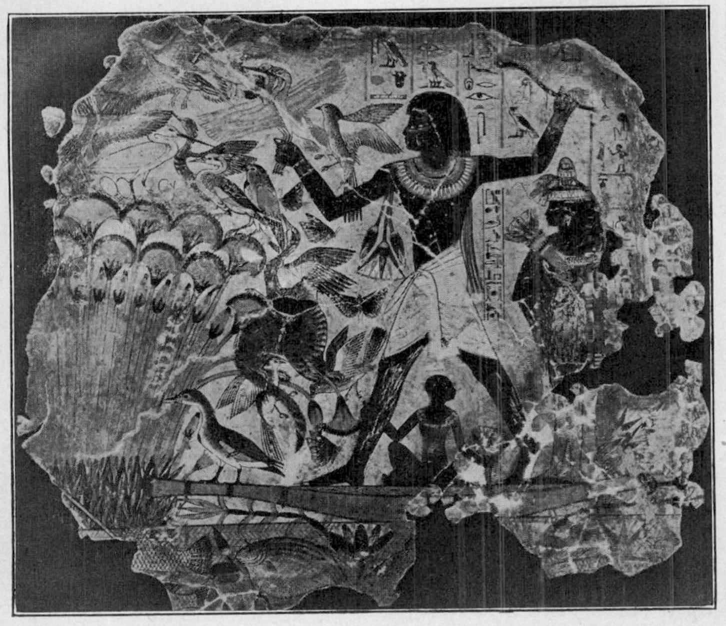

EGYPTIAN NOBLE HUNTING WATERFOWL with a "throw-stick" or boomerang. The wife accompanies her husband, and the boat contains also a "decoy" bird. The wild birds rise from a mass of papyrus reeds. — From an Egyptian tomb painting.

And some of its gains

the Hebrews, the Babylonians gave us the week, with its "seventh day of rest for the soul," and the subdivision of the day into hours and minutes. They invented also an excellent system of weights, and measures based on the length of the hand and foot. They had a system of counting in which they used 12 and 60 as we use 10 and 100. The face of a watch to-day, with its divisions by twelve and by sixty, recalls their work, — as do also the measurement of a circle by degrees, minutes, and seconds; the curious figures on our star maps; the signs of the zodiac in our almanacs; the symbols of our "apothecaries' table," still used by physicians; some of our fairy stories, like that of Cinderella; many of our carpenters' tools; and much of our common kitchen ware.

CRETAN WRITING OF 2200 B.C. — Some of the characters are plainly numerals. Others are much like certain later Greek letters.

Bronze culture spread by Phoenicians

War and trade spread this "bronze" culture slowly around the eastern coasts of the Mediterranean; and, before 1500 B.C., Cretan and Phoenician merchants scattered its seeds widely in even more distant regions with a contribution of their own infinitely important. The commerce of these peoples made it needful for them to keep complicated accounts, and to communicate with agents in distant places; and so, out of the crude earlier systems of rebus writing, both Cretans and Phoenicians developed *real alphabets*.

Persians and Hebrews

About 630 B.C. all these precious beginnings of civilization were imperiled by hordes of savages that poured forth from the frozen plains of Scythia in the North. Persia repulsed the ravagers, and saved the slow gains of the ages. At the same time, she conquered all the civilized East, and united it under *an effective system of government*. And finally, toward the close of these four thousand years of "Oriental history" there grew up among the Hebrews *a pure worship* whose truth and grandeur were to influence profoundly the later world. For centuries more, however, this religion was the possession of one small people.

The scene shifts to Europe

Now, happily, appeared the Greeks, — new actors on a new stage. About 600 B.C., *the center of interest shifted westward from Asia to southeastern Europe.* For two thousand years a

COOKING UTENSILS found in one tomb at Knossos, Crete, belonging about 2200 B.C.

European culture had been rising slowly along the coasts and islands of the Mediterranean, drawing from the East in handicraft, but possessing moral and intellectual traits of its own.

Greek civilization contrasted with Oriental: physical differences

Oriental states had begun in supremely fertile districts where food was almost the free bounty of nature, and where the tropical climate made most men averse to unnecessary exertion. The few with spirit and energy easily made slaves of the multitude. But the sterile soil of Greece demanded more work from all the people; and its temperate climate encouraged more general enterprise. Men lived more on a level with one another than in the East. The benefits of Oriental culture had been for the few only: *the benefits of Greek culture were to be for the many.*

Oriental submission and Greek independence

When an Oriental state had grown by conquest into an empire, it spread over vast plains and was bounded by terrible immensities of desolate deserts. Greece was a land of intermingled sea and mountain, with everything on a moderate scale. There were no deserts. No mountains were so astounding as to awe man. There were no destructive earthquakes, no tremendous storms, no overwhelming floods. Oriental men had bowed in dread and superstition before these terrible and destructive forces: they had feared to inquire, and in all things they accepted slavishly the traditions of their fathers. But in Greece, nature was not terrible. There men began early to search into her secrets. *Instead of bowing to tradition, the Greeks thought for themselves. Instead of submitting to despotism, they governed themselves.*

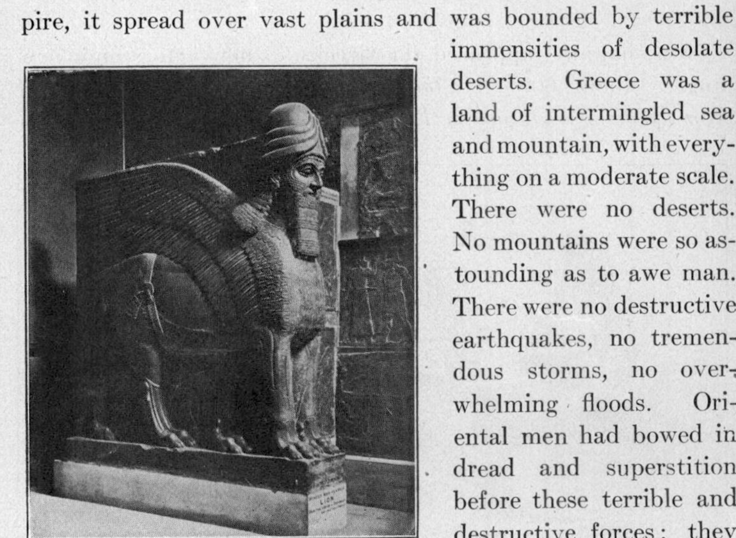

COLOSSAL MAN-BEAST IN ALABASTER. — From an Assyrian palace. (Now in the British Museum. The photograph shows also part of a series of relief sculpture, telling a long story, from the walls of the same palace.)

Oriental sameness and European diversity

Greece was broken up into many small districts. Each division was protected from conquest by its sea moats and mountain walls; and each, therefore, became the home of a distinct political state. Some of these were busied in agriculture; others, mainly, in trade. Some were monarchic in government; others, democratic. *These differing societies, side by side, reacted wholesomely upon one another.*

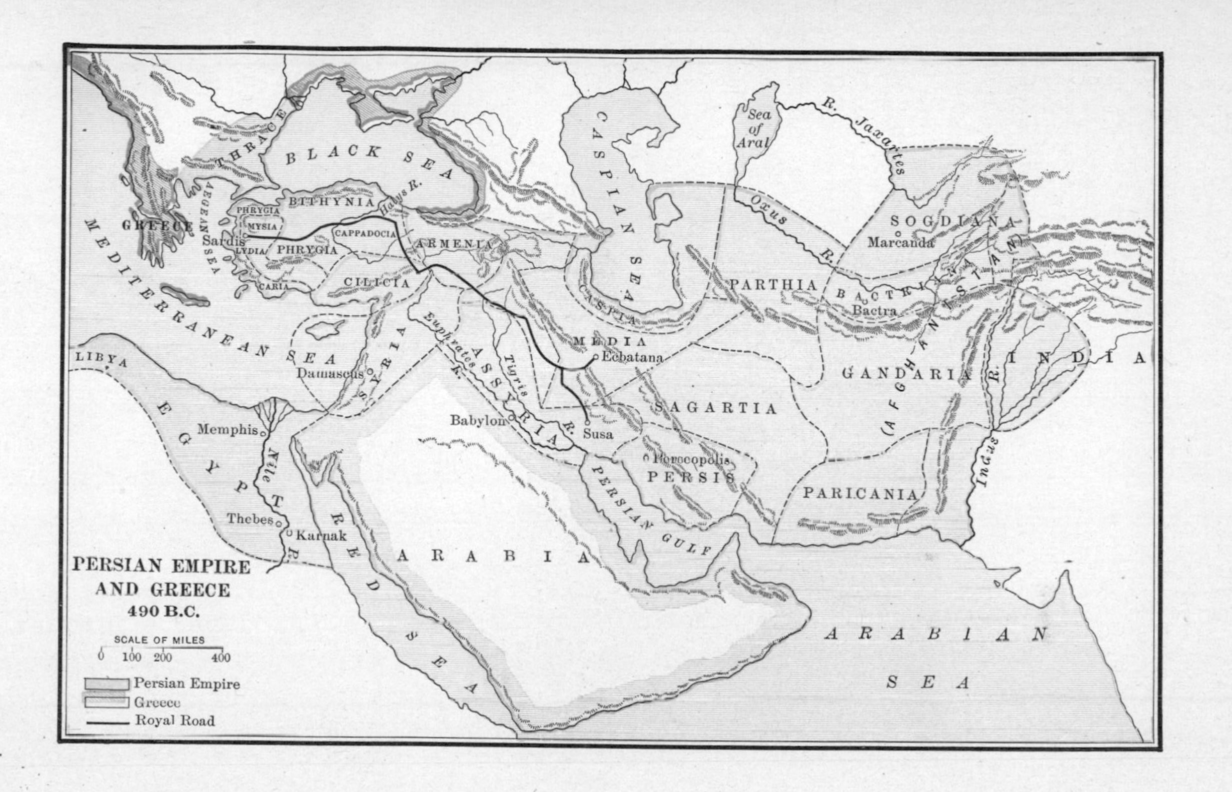
PERSIAN EMPIRE
AND GREECE
490 B.C.
SCALE OF MILES
0 100 200 400
Persian Empire
Greece
Royal Road
BLACK SEA
THRACE
GREECE
AEGEAN SEA
MEDITERRANEAN SEA
PHRYGIA
MYSIA
Sardis
LYDIA
PHRYGIA
CARIA
BITHYNIA
Halys R.
CAPPADOCIA
ARMENIA
CILICIA
SYRIA
Damascus
LIBYA
EGYPT
Memphis
Nile
Thebes
Karnak
RED SEA
ARABIA
Euphrates R.
ASSYRIA
Tigris R.
Babylon
Susa
MEDIA
Ecbatana
CASPIA
CASPIAN SEA
Sea of Aral
R. Jaxartes
Oxus R.
SOGDIANA
Marcanda
PARTHIA
BACTRIANA
Bactra
(AFGHANISTAN)
GANDARIA
SAGARTIA
Persepolis
PERSIS
PERSIAN GULF
PARICANIA
Indus R.
INDIA
ARABIAN SEA

Oriental and Greek art

No doubt, too, the moderation and variety and wondrous beauty of hill and dale and sun-lit sea had something to do with the many-sided genius of the Greek people and with their lively but well-controlled imagination. Oriental art was unnatural; it delighted in placing a man's head upon a beast's body, mingling the monstrous with the human; and in architecture it sought for colossal size rather than for proportion. But above all peoples, before or since, *the Greeks developed a love for harmony and proportion;* and their art sought for beauty in simplicity and naturalness.

THE HERMES OF PRAXITELES. — Praxiteles was one of the most famous Greek sculptors. This statue of the god Hermes is sadly mutilated, but the head and torso are among the finest remains of Greek art.

Greek contributions to our civilization

In sculpture, architecture, drama, oratory, poetry, and philosophy, the Greeks rank still among the world's masters. The Oriental contributions to the future had been chiefly material: *the Greek contributions were intellectual and spiritual.* Above all, the Greeks gave us the ideal of freedom regulated by self-control, — freedom in politics, in religion, and in thought.

Moreover, this Greek civilization is essentially one with our own. The remains of Egyptian or Babylonian sculpture and architecture arouse our interest as curiosities; but they are foreign to us. With a Greek temple or a Greek poem we feel at home. It might have been built or written by an American. Our most beautiful buildings use the Greek columns and capitals; and some, in spite of our different climate, are copied almost wholly from Greek models. Our children still delight in the stories that the blind Greek Homer chanted; and the historian still goes for his model to the Greek Herodotus, "the father of history."

Defects in Greek culture

Four weak points remained in this dazzling Greek civilization: (1) It rested on slavery. (2) It was for males only: at best, the wife was only a higher domestic servant. (3) The moral side fell far below the intellectual side. Religion had little to do with conduct toward men. Some Greek philosophers taught lofty morality; but, on the whole, while no other society ever produced so large a proportion of great men, many societies have produced more good men. (4) Brilliant as was the Greek mind, it did not discover the modern method of finding out the secrets of nature by experiment. Consequently it did little to increase man's power over natural forces, and so could not produce wealth enough to go around.

Greece and Persia

About 500 B.C., the rising Greek culture was threatened with conquest by Persia; but at Marathon and Salamis the little Greek states heroically repelled the huge Asiatic empire, and saved Western civilization. Two centuries later, through the genius of *Alexander the Great*, the Greeks *welded East and West into a Graeco-Oriental world.*

Leadership shifts west to Rome

But in the end the vast sluggish East would have absorbed the small Greek element, had not the latter found reinforcement from another European land. Now, happily, *the leadership in human progress shifts westward once more — to Rome.*

Rome was the central city of Italy, the central Mediterranean land. It began as a village of shepherds and farmers. Partly through advantages in geography, more through genius in war, most of all through a marvelous power of organization, it had grown step by step into the headship of Italy, and was ready now to march on to the lordship of the world. First, it *gave a Latin civilization to the western Mediterranean coasts;* and then, a century before the birth of Christ, it *unified new West and old East into a Graeco-Roman world.*

As Greece stands for art and intellectual culture, so Rome stands for law and government. *The Greeks*, aside from their own contributions to civilization, *had collected* the arts and sciences of the older peoples of the Orient. *Rome preserved this common treasure of mankind, and she herself added legal and political institutions* that have influenced all later time.

Rome's contributions

Still, with all her genius for government, Rome did not hit upon our modern plan of representative government. Until this plan was discovered, government had to be exercised, at best, by those who could meet at one spot. Since this was practicable only for a city or a small district, a large state could not then remain a free state. While Rome was uniting Italy, she was a free city-republic. She succeeded in expanding this form of government so that it met fairly well the needs of united Italy; but it broke down before the needs of a widespread subject world. For a century the government of the ruling city became merely the agent of a selfish moneyed aristocracy which looted the dependent provinces. Then, a little before the birth of Christ, *Julius Caesar* and his successors swept away the outgrown "Republic," and *introduced the "Empire,"* with the emperor as the despotic but beneficent father of the whole Graeco-Roman world.

Failure of the Roman Republic

A "RESTORATION" (by Lambert) OF THE ATHENIAN ACROPOLIS, at first a citadel, later the "holy hill," crowned by statues and temples of gleaming white marble which are still peerless in loveliness.

A Roman Chariot Race. — A modern imaginative painting.

SECOND PERIOD

THE ROMAN EMPIRE

The Roman Empire is the central lake in which all the streams of ancient history lose themselves, and which all the streams of modern history flow out of. — Freeman

Life under the Empire concentrated in "municipia"

The Roman world was a broad belt of land stretching east and west, from the Atlantic to the Euphrates, with the Mediterranean for its central highway. On the south it was bounded by sandy deserts, African and Arabian; on the north, by stormy waters, — the North Sea, the Rhine, the Danube, and the Black Sea. Within its vast territory, about as large as the United States, were 75,000,000 people. They lived mostly in cities (municipia) large and small, throbbing with industry and with intellectual life and possessing some *local* self-government in those municipal institutions they were to pass on to us. Gaul (France) was Romanized late, after Julius Caesar; but in the third century A.D. that district had 116 flourishing cities, with public baths, temples, aqueducts, roads, and famous schools that drew Roman youth even from the Tiber's banks.

Most towns were places of 20,000 people or less, and usually each one was merely the center of a farming district; but there were also a few great centers of trade, — Rome, with perhaps 2,000,000 people; Alexandria (in Egypt) and Antioch (in Asia)

with 500,000 each; and Corinth, Carthage, Ephesus, and Lyons, with some 250,000 apiece.

These commercial cities were likewise centers of manufactures. The Emperor Hadrian visited Alexandria (about 125 A.D.) and wrote in a letter: "No one is idle; some work glass; some make paper (papyrus); some weave linen. Money is the only god." The looms of Sidon and the other old Phoenician

Industry and trade

ROMAN AQUEDUCT NEAR NÎMES, FRANCE: present condition. — From a photograph. This structure was built by the Emperor Antoninus Pius, about 150 A.D., to bring water from distant mountain springs. Some of these Roman aqueducts remained in use until recent days.

cities turned forth ceaselessly their precious purple cloths. Miletus, Rhodes, and other Greek cities of the Asiatic coast were famous for their woolen manufactures. Syrian factories poured silks, costly tapestries, and fine leather into western Europe. The silversmiths of Ephesus were numerous enough (*Acts*, xix, 23–41) to stir up a formidable riot.

The roads were safe. Piracy ceased from the seas, and trade flourished as it was not to flourish again until the days of Co-

Communication by sea and land

lumbus. The ports were crowded with shipping, and the Mediterranean was spread with happy sails. The grand military roads ran in trunk-lines — a thousand miles at a stretch — from every frontier toward the central heart of the empire, with a dense network of branches in every province. Guide-books described routes and distances. Inns abounded. The imperial couriers that hurried along the great highways passed

Remains of a Greek Temple at Paestum in Italy. — From a photograph. Before 800 B.C. many Greek colonies had been established in Sicily and southern Italy, so that these districts were long known as "Great Greece" (Magna Graecia). These Italian Greeks taught Rome much before her rule reached outside of Italy.

a hundred and fifty milestones a day. The products of one region of the empire were known in every other part. Jewelry made in Asia Minor was worn by women in the Swiss mountains; and Italian wines were drunk in Britain and in Cilicia. Private travel from the Thames to the Euphrates was swifter, safer, and more comfortable than ever again until the age of railroads, less than a century ago.

There was also a vast commerce with regions *beyond the bound-*

aries of the empire. As English and Dutch traders, three hundred years ago, journeyed far into the savage interior of America for better bargains in furs, so the indomitable Roman traders pressed on into regions where the Roman legions never camped. From the Baltic shores they brought back amber, furs, and flaxen German hair with which the dark Roman ladies liked to adorn their heads. Such goods the trader bought cheaply with toys and trinkets and wine. A Latin poet speaks of "many merchants" who reaped "immense riches" by daring voyages over the Indian Ocean "to the mouth of the Ganges." India, Ceylon, and Malaysia sent to Europe indigo, spices, pearls, sapphires, drawing away, in return, vast sums of Roman gold and silver. And from shadowy realms beyond India came the silk yarn that kept the Syrian looms busy. Chinese annals tell of Roman traders bringing to Canton glass and metal wares, amber, and drugs.

The universities

Literature and learning flourished. It is impossible here even to mention the great numbers of poets, historians, essayists, philosophers, and other writers who made glorious the Early Empire. The three great centers of learning were Rome, Alexandria, and Athens. In these cities there were universities, as we would call them now, with vast libraries (of *manuscripts*), and with many professorships supported by the government.

Morals under the Empire

Morals grew gentle, and manners were refined. The Letters of the author Pliny reveal a society high-minded, refined, and virtuous. Pliny himself is a type of the finest gentleman of to-day in delicacy of feeling, sensitive honor, and genial courtesy. The Emperor Marcus Aurelius shows like qualities on the throne. The philosopher Epictetus shows them in a slave.

Woman's position improved

Woman secured more freedom and more intellectual culture than she was to find again until the nineteenth century. The profession of medicine was open to her. She became the equal of man before the law, and his companion, not his servant, in the home.

Sympathies broadened. The unity of the vast Roman world prepared the way for the thought that all men are brothers.

Broader human sympathies

Said Marcus Aurelius, "As emperor I am a Roman; but as a man my city is the world." The age prided itself, justly, upon its progress and its humanity, much as our own does. The Emperor Trajan instructed a provincial governor not to act upon anonymous accusations, because such conduct "*does not*

PART OF THE COURT OF A PRIVATE RESIDENCE AT POMPEII — *the House of the Vetii.* The Roman city, Pompeii, was overwhelmed by an eruption of ashes and volcanic mud from Vesuvius in 80 A.D. Recent excavation enables a modern visitor to walk through the streets of an ancient city in almost perfect preservation. The shrubbery in this court, of course, is not "ancient"; but probably the court originally contained shrubbery much like this.

belong to our age." There was a vast amount of private and public charity, with homes for orphans and hospitals for the poor.

More humane law

This broad humanity was reflected in imperial law. The harsh law of the Republic became humane. Women, children, and even dumb beasts shared its protection. Torture was limited. The rights of the accused were better recognized. From the Empire dates the maxim, "Better to let the guilty escape than to punish the innocent." "All men by the law of nature are equal" became a law maxim, through the great jurist Ulpian. Slavery, he argued, had been created only by the lower law, enacted not by nature but by man. Therefore, if one man claimed another as his slave, the benefit of any possible doubt was to be given to the one so claimed. (It is curious to remember that the rule was just the other way in nearly all Christian countries through the Middle Ages, and in the United States under the Fugitive Slave laws from 1793 to the Civil War.)

Peace and prosperity for 200 years

This widespread, happy society rested in "the good Roman peace" for more than two hundred years, — from the reign of Augustus Caesar through that of Marcus Aurelius, or from 31 B.C. to 192 A.D. No other part of the world so large has ever known such unbroken prosperity and such freedom from the waste and horror of war for so long a time. *Few troops were seen within the empire*, and "the distant clash of arms [with barbarians] on the Euphrates or the Danube scarcely disturbed the tranquillity of the Mediterranean lands."

A few of the emperors at Rome, like Nero and Caligula, were weak or wicked; but their follies and vices concerned only the nobles of the Capital. The empire as a whole went on with little change during their short reigns. To the vast body of the people of the Roman world, the crimes of an occasional tyrant were unknown. To them he seemed (like the good emperors) merely the symbol of the peace and prosperity which enfolded them.

Unity of the Roman world

In language, and somewhat in culture, *the West remained Latin, and the East,*[1] *Greek;* but trade, travel, and the mild and just Roman law made the world one in feeling. Briton, African, Asiatic, knew one another only as Romans. An Egyptian Greek of the period expressed this world-wide patriotism in a noble ode, closing, —

> "Though we tread Rhone's or Orontes'[2] shore,
> Yet are we all one nation evermore."

[1] The Adriatic may be taken as a convenient line of division.
[2] A river of Asia Minor.

The dark side

But this picture had a darker side. During some reigns the court was rank with hideous debauchery, and at all times the rabble of Rome, made up of the off-scourings of all peoples, was ignorant and vicious. Some evil customs that shock us were part of the age. To avoid cost and trouble, the lower classes, with horrible frequency and indifference, exposed their infants to die. Satirists, as in our own day, railed at the growth of divorce among the rich. Slavery threw its shadow across the Roman world. At the gladiatorial sports — so strong is fashion — delicate ladies thronged the benches of the amphitheater without shrinking at the agonies of the dying.

The really hopeless feature was the absence of liberty. The Roman world, in this first period, was happy, contented, prosperous, well-governed, but not free; and even its virtues had something of a servile tone. Moreover, great landlords were crowding the small farmers off the land, and that yeoman class were giving way to slave or serf tillers of the soil.

Decline in the third century

And so the third century began a period of swift decline. For a time despotism had served as a medicine for anarchy (p. 11), but now its poison began to show. Weak or vicious rulers followed one another in ruinous succession. The throne became the sport of the soldiery. *Ninety-two years* (193–284 A.D.) *saw twenty-seven "barrack emperors"* set up by the army, and all but four were slain in some revolt.

Reorganization by Diocletian

After this century of misery, the stern soldier, *Diocletian* (284–305), grandson of an Illyrian slave, grasped the scepter with a firm hand, restored order, and re-shaped the government. For more convenient administration, he divided the Roman world into an East and a West, along the dividing lines between the old Greek and Latin civilizations; and each half he subdivided again and again into units of several grades — praefectures, dioceses, provinces. To care for these divisions, he then created a series of officers in regular grades, as in an army. Each was placed under the immediate direction of the one just above him, and the lines all converged from below to the emperor. Each official sifted all business that came to him from his subordinates, and sent on to his superior only the more important matters. The earlier, loosely organized despotism had become a vast centralized despotism, a highly complex machine, which fixed responsibility precisely and distributed duties in a workable way.

Excursus: "Centralization" and "Absolutism"

It is desirable for students to discuss in class more fully some of these forms of government of which the text treats. "Absolutism" refers to the *source of supreme power:* in a system of absolutism, supreme power is in the hands of one person. "Centralization" refers to the *kind of administration.* A centralized administration is one carried on by a body of officials of many grades, all *appointed from above. Absolutism and centralization do not necessarily go together.* A government may come from the people, and yet rule through a centralized administration, as in France to-day. It may be absolute, and yet allow much freedom to local agencies, as in Russia in past centuries.

Under a great genius, like Napoleon the First, a centralized government may for a time produce rapid benefits. But the system always decays. *It does nothing to educate the people politically. Local self-government is often provokingly slow and faulty, but it is surer in the long run.*

Crushing weight of the bureaucratic despotism

The fourth century showed outward prosperity, but this appearance was deceitful. *The system of Diocletian warded off invasion: but its own weight was crushing.* The Empire had become "a great tax-gathering and barbarian-fighting machine." It collected taxes *in order* to fight barbarians. But the time came when the people feared the tax collector more than the barbarians, as the complex government came to cost more and more. About 400 A.D., the Empire began to crumble before barbarian attacks less formidable than many that had been rebuffed in early centuries. *Secret forces had been sapping the strength and health of the Roman world.*

1. Population had ceased to advance, and even fell away. A series of terrible Asiatic plagues swept off vast numbers;

Decline of population: slavery

but the causes of permanent decay were within Roman society. The main cause, probably, was the widespread slave system. The wealthy classes of society do not have large families. Our population to-day grows mainly from the working class. But in the Roman empire the place of free workingmen was taken mainly by slaves. Slaves rarely had families; and if they had, the master commonly "exposed" slave children to die, since it was easier and cheaper to buy a new slave, from among captive barbarians, than to rear one. Besides, the competition of slave labor ground into the dust what free

A German Bodyguard of Marcus Aurelius. — A detail from a column commemorating the campaigns of that emperor against untamed Germans, about 180 A.D.

labor there was; so that free working people could not afford to raise large families, but were driven to the cruel practice of exposing their infants. Year after year, "the human harvest was bad."

Peaceful infusion of barbarians

2. One measure helped fill up the gaps in population. This was the introduction of barbarians from without. The Roman army had long been mostly made up of Germans; and whole provinces were settled by them, *before* their kinsmen from without, in the fifth century, began in earnest to break over the Rhine. Conquered barbarians had been settled, hundreds of thousands at a time, in frontier provinces; and whole friendly tribes had been admitted into depopulated

districts. But all this had a danger of its own: the barrier between the empire and its assailants was melting away.

Approach to a caste system

3. The classes of society were becoming fixed. At the top was the emperor. At the bottom were peasantry, artisans, and slaves, to produce food and wealth wherewith to pay taxes. Between were two aristocracies, — a small imperial nobility of great landlords, and an inferior local nobility in each city.

REMAINS OF THE LIBRARY OF A ROMAN VILLA near Tivoli. Walls so extensive and well preserved are not common, but the *foundations* of such structures are scattered widely over Western Europe, and new finds of this sort are not uncommon even to-day on the scene of new excavations.

"Privilege" of the great lords

The landlord nobles had many special privileges. Through their influence upon the government and by bribery of officials they escaped most of the burden of taxation — which they were better able to bear than the unhappy classes that paid. Besides his town house, each landlord had one or more costly country houses, or villas, with all the comforts of the city — baths, museums, libraries, mosaic pavements, richly gilded ceilings, walls hung with brilliant tapestries, and sideboards beautiful with vases and gold and silver plate. About the house spread extensive parklike grounds, with ornamental shrubbery and playing fountains and with glorious marble statues gleaming through the foliage, and perhaps with fish ponds and orchards.

Commonly a villa was the center of a large farm; and its magnificent luxury found a sinister contrast in the squalid huts, leaning against the villa walls, in which slept the wretched herds of slaves that tilled the soil. Near by, in somewhat better quarters, lived the more skilled artisans — carpenters, smiths, bakers — while troops of household slaves slept on the floors of the large halls or in the open courts of the central mansion.

The smaller nobility

The local nobility (curials) were the families of the senate class in their respective cities. They, too, *had some special privileges*. They could not be drafted into the army or subjected to bodily punishment. They were compelled, however, to undergo great expenses in connection with the offices they had to fill. And, in particular, they were made responsible for the collection of the imperial taxes in their districts.

This burden finally became so crushing that many curials tried desperately to evade it, — even by sinking into a lower class, or by flight to the barbarians. Then, to secure the revenue, law made them an hereditary class. They were forbidden to become clergy, soldiers, or lawyers; they were not allowed to move from one city to another, or even to travel without permission.

The old middle class disappeared

Between these local nobles and the artisan class, there had been, in the day of the Early Empire, a much larger middle class of small landowners, merchants, bankers, and professional men. This middle class had now almost disappeared. Some were compelled by law to take up the duties of the vanishing curials. More, in the financial ruin of the period, sank into the working class.

The artisans

The condition of artisans had become desperate. An edict of Diocletian's regarding prices and wages shows that a workman received not more than one-tenth the wages of an American workman of like grade, while food and clothing cost at least one-third as much as in our time. His family rarely knew the taste of eggs or fresh meat. And now the law forbade him to change his trade.

SERFS IN ROMAN GAUL.

Farm labor grows into serfdom

The peasantry had become serfs. That is, they were bound to their labor on the soil, and changed masters with the land they tilled.

When the Empire *began,* free small-farmers were growing fewer, over much of the realm, while great estates, managed by stewards and tilled by slaves, were growing more numerous. Grain culture decreased, and large areas of land ceased to be tilled. To help remedy this state of affairs, and to keep up the food supply, the emperors introduced a new class of *hereditary* farm laborers. After successful wars, they *gave* large numbers of barbarian captives to great landlords, — thousands in a batch, — not as slaves, but as serfs.

BREADMAKING BY SERFS IN ROMAN GAUL.

The serfs were really given not to the landlord, but to the land. They were not personal property, as slaves were. *They were part of the real estate.* They, and their children after them, were attached to the soil, and could not be sold off it. They had some rights which slaves did not have. They could contract a legal marriage, and each had his own plot of ground, of which he could not be dispossessed so long as he paid to the landlord a fixed rent in labor and in produce.

This growth of serfdom made it still more difficult for the free small-farmer to hold his place. That class more and more sank into serfs. On the other hand, many slaves rose into serfdom.

Lack of money

4. Lack of money was one of the great evils. The empire did not have sufficient supplies of precious metals for the demands of business; and what money there was was steadily drained away to India and the distant Orient (p. 15). By the fourth century this movement had carried away hundreds of millions of dollars of coined money. Even the imperial officers were

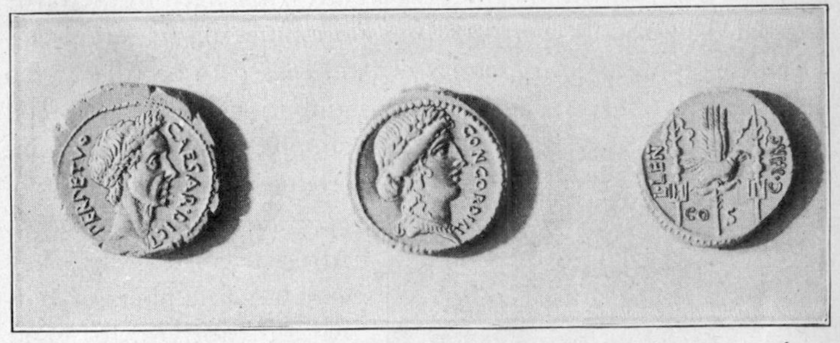

Roman Coins of the Empire. Many such coins have been found in the Orient.

forced to take part of their salaries in produce, — robes, horses, grain. Trade began to go back to the primitive form of barter; and it became harder and harder to collect taxes.

In the third and fourth centuries there were no more great poets or men of letters. Learning and patriotism both declined. Society began to fall into rigid castes, — the serf bound to his spot of land, the artisan to his trade, the curial to his office. Freedom of movement was lost. Above all, *there was dearth of money and dearth of men. The Empire had become a shell.*

The Empire no longer able to resist outside barbarians

For five hundred years, outside barbarians had been tossing wildly about the great natural walls of the civilized world. Commonly they had shrunk in dread from any conflict with the mighty Roman legions, always on sleepless ward at the weaker gaps — along the Rhine, the Danube, the Euphrates. Sometimes, it is true, the barbarians had broken through for a moment, but always to be destroyed promptly by some Roman Marius or Caesar. In the fifth century they broke in to stay.

But the Empire gave time for Christianity to win the world

But meanwhile Christianity had come into the world. The supreme service of the dying Empire was to foster this new force for human progress.

For three centuries, it is true, the Empire had despised or persecuted the sect of Christians; but still the unity of the Roman world made it far easier for the new moral and spiritual teachings to spread than if the world had been broken up into a multitude of petty, disconnected, hostile states, with little communication and with unintelligible dialects. *Then, early in the fourth century* (313 A.D.), under the Emperor Constantine, Christianity became a tolerated and even a favored religion. Before the close of that century it became the state religion; and its victory just at this time enabled it to conquer also the barbarians who were soon to conquer the Empire, but *who were still eager to follow where Rome led.*

The church adopts much from Rome in its government

The church, too, modeled its marvelously efficient government upon the territorial divisions and the political organization of the Empire. As the first missionaries spread out beyond Judea and came to a new province, they naturally went first to the chief city there. Thus the capital of the province became the seat of the first church in the district. From this mother society, churches spread to the other cities of the province, and from each city there sprouted outlying parishes.

At the head of each *parish* was a *priest*, assisted usually by deacons and subdeacons to care for the poor. The head of a *city church* was a *bishop* (overseer), with supervision over the rural churches of the neighborhood. The bishop of the *mother church in the capital city* exercised great authority over the other bishops of the province. He became known as *archbishop* or *metropolitan;* and it became customary for him to summon the other bishops to a central council.

Commonly, one of these metropolitans in a given region came to have leadership over others, and became known as a *patriarch*. Then the patriarchs of a few great centers were

JERUSALEM TO-DAY: GETHSEMANE AND THE MOUNT OF OLIVES.

exalted above the others. Finally all the East became divided among the four patriarchates of Antioch, Jerusalem, Alexandria, and Constantinople, *while all the West came under the authority of the bishop of Rome.*

THIRD PERIOD

MERGING OF ROMAN AND TEUTON, 378–815 A.D.

I. FOUR CENTURIES OF CONFUSION

East of the Rhine there had long roamed many "forest peoples," whom the Romans called Germans, or *Teutons*. These barbarians were tall, huge of limb, white-skinned, flaxen-haired, with fierce, blue eyes. To the short, dark-skinned races of Roman Europe, they seemed tawny giants.

The savage Teutons

The tribes nearest the Empire had taken on a little civilization, and had begun to form large combinations under the rule of kings. The more distant tribes were still savage and unorganized. In general, they were not far above the level of the better North American Indians in our colonial period.

The usual marks of savagery were found among them. They were fierce, quarrelsome, hospitable. Their cold, damp forests helped to make them drunkards and gluttonous eaters. They were desperate gamblers, too, staking even their liberty on a throw of the dice. At the same time, they had all a savage's proud spirit of *individual* liberty, — a spirit that had been lost in the Roman world.

In contrast to this was another trait. Every great chief was surrounded by a band of "companions," who lived in his household, ate at his table, and fought at his side. To them the chief gave food, weapons, and plunder. For the safety of their "lord" they were ready to give their lives. To survive his death, leaving his body to a victorious foe, was life-long disgrace. This "*personal loyalty*" among the Teutons corresponded to the Roman loyalty to the state.

Government of village and tribe

The government of the Teutons is described for us by a Roman historian, Tacitus. A tribe lived in villages scattered in forests. *The village and the tribe each had its Assembly* and its hereditary chief. *The tribal chief*, or king, *was surrounded by his council of village chiefs.* To quote Tacitus:

> "On affairs of smaller moment, the chiefs consult; on those of greater importance, the whole community. . . . They assemble on stated days, either at the new or full moon. When they all think fit, they sit down armed. . . . Then the king, or chief, and such others as are conspicuous for age, birth, military renown, or eloquence, are heard, and gain attention rather from their ability to persuade than their authority to command. If a proposal displease, the assembly reject it by an inarticulate murmur. If it prove agreeable, they clash their javelins; for the most honorable expression of assent among them is the sound of arms."

Invasion of the West Goths

The first Teutonic people to establish itself within the old Empire was the West Goths. These barbarians *in 378* defeated and slew a Roman Emperor at *Adrianople*, almost under the walls of Constantinople, and then roamed and ravaged at will for a generation in the Balkan lands. *In 410*, they entered Italy and sacked Rome, and then moved west into Spain, where they found the Vandals — another Teuton race who had entered Spain through Gaul from across the Rhine. Driving the Vandals into Africa, the West Goths set up in Spain the first firm Teutonic kingdom.

Other Teutonic invaders

Meanwhile, other Teutons had begun to swarm across the Rhine. Finally, after frightful destruction, the East Goths established themselves in Italy; the Burgundians, in the valley of the Rhone; the Angles and Saxons, in Britain; the Franks, in northern Gaul. This "wandering of the peoples" filled the fifth century and part of the sixth.

Slav Europe and Teutonic Europe

These two terrible centuries brought on the stage also another new race, — *the Slavs;* and the opening of the following century brought *Mohammedanism* (pp. 38 ff.). But of these three forces, *we are concerned almost alone with the Teutons.* Mohammedanism, as we shall see, seized swiftly upon all the old historic ground in Asia and Africa; but these countries have had little touch since with our Western civilization. South of the Danube, Slavic tribes settled up almost to the walls of Constantinople, where the Roman Empire still maintained itself. *Southeastern Europe became Slavic-Greek,* just as Western Europe had become Teutonic-Roman. But, until very recently, Southeastern Europe has had little bearing upon the Western World. *The two halves of Europe fell apart,* with the Adriatic for the dividing line, — along the old cleavage between Latin and Greek civilizations (p. 17). In all the centuries since, human progress has come almost wholly from the Western Romano-Teutonic Europe — and from its recent offshoots in other continents.

The invasions overthrow the old civilization

The invasions brought overwhelming destruction upon this Western world, — the most complete catastrophe that ever befell a great civilized society. Civilization, it is true, had been declining before they began; but they tremendously accelerated the movement, and prevented any revival of the old culture in the West.

And when the invaders had entered into possession, and so ceased to destroy, two new causes of decline appeared: (1) *The new ruling classes were densely ignorant.* They cared nothing for the survivals of literature and science. Few of them could read, or write even their names. Much of the old civilization was allowed to decay because they could not understand its use. (2) *The language of everyday speech was growing away from the literary language* in which all the remains of the old knowledge were preserved. The language of learning became "dead." It was known only to the clergy, and to most of them at this period very imperfectly.

The "Dark Ages," 400–800

The fifth and sixth centuries brought the Teuton into the Roman world; the seventh and eighth centuries fused Roman and Teuton elements into a new "Western Europe." For the whole four hundred years (400–800), Europe remained a dreary scene of violence, lawlessness, and ignorance. The old Roman schools disappeared, and classical literature seemed to be extinct. There was no tranquil leisure, and therefore no study. There was little security, and therefore little work. The Franks and Goths were learning the rudiments of civilized life; but the Latins were losing all but the rudiments — and they seemed to lose faster than the Teutons gained.

Survivals of Roman civilization in towns and in the church

But after all, the invasions did not uproot civilization. The conquests were made by small numbers, and, outside Britain, they did not greatly change the character of the population. The conquerors settled among ten or fifty times their own numbers. At first they were the rulers and almost the only large landowners. But *the towns,* so far as they survived, *remained Roman,* and, almost unnoticed by the ruling classes, they preserved some parts of the old culture and handicrafts. *The old population, too, for a long time furnished all the clergy.* From this class — the sole possessors of the art of writing and keeping records — the Teutonic lords had to draw secretaries and confidential officers; and by these advisers they were gradually persuaded to adopt many customs of the old civilization.

Most important of all, *the church itself lived on much in the old way.* Necessarily it suffered somewhat in the general degradation of the age; but, on the whole, it protected the weak, and stood for peace, industry, and right living. In the darkest of those dark centuries there were great numbers of priests and monks inspired with zeal for righteousness and love for men. The church, too, had its own government, with which the new rulers of the land did not much interfere.

A Silver Coin of Justinian.

The "Greek Empire"

The preservation of Roman law we owe mainly to a source outside Western Europe. The Roman Empire lived on in part of eastern Europe and in Asia, with its capital at Constantinople. Cut off from *Latin* Europe, that Empire now grew more and more Greek and Oriental, and after 500 A.D. we usually speak of it as "the Greek Empire."

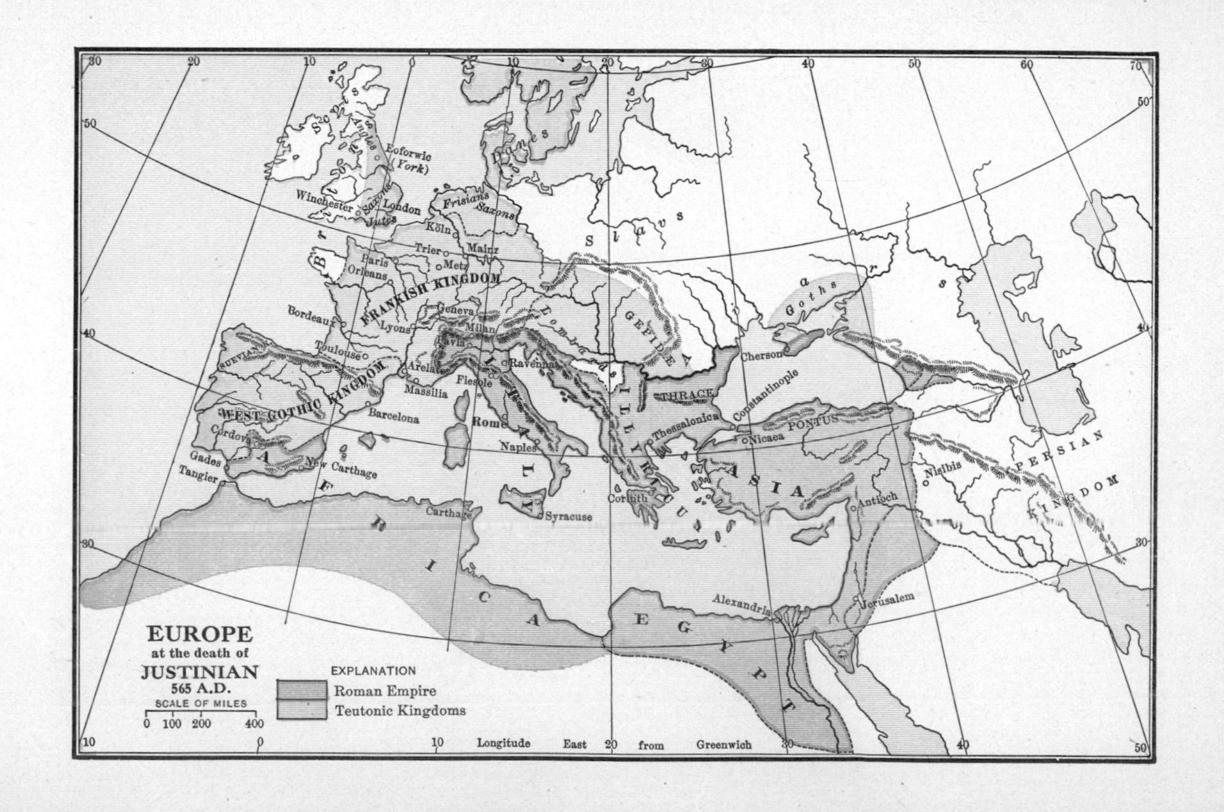

EUROPE
at the death of
JUSTINIAN
565 A.D.
SCALE OF MILES
0 100 200 400
EXPLANATION
Roman Empire
Teutonic Kingdoms
Longitude East from Greenwich
Scots
Angles
Eoforwic (York)
Britons
Winchester
Saxons
Jutes
London
Frisians
Saxons
Danes
Köln
Trier
Mainz
Metz
Paris
Orleans
FRANKISH KINGDOM
Bordeaux
Lyons
Geneva
Milan
Pavia
Toulouse
Arelate
Massilia
SUEVIA
WEST GOTHIC KINGDOM
Barcelona
Cordova
Gades
Tangier
New Carthage
Carthage
AFRICA
Fiesole
Ravenna
Rome
Naples
Syracuse
ITALY
Lombards
Slavs
GEPIDAE
Goths
THRACE
ILLYRICUM
Thessalonica
Corinth
Constantinople
Cherson
Nicaea
PONTUS
ASIA
Antioch
Jerusalem
Alexandria
EGYPT
Nisibis
PERSIAN KINGDOM

The Justinian Code

In the sixth century, after long decline, the Empire fell for a time to a capable ruler, *Justinian the Great* (527-565). We remember him chiefly because he brought about *a codification of the Roman law.* In the course of centuries, that law had become an intolerable maze. Now a commission of able lawyers

CHURCH OF ST. SOPHIA. CONSTANTINOPLE, built by Justinian upon the site of an earlier church of the same name by Constantine. The whole interior is lined with costly, many-colored marbles. This view shows only a part of the vast dome, with eighteen of the forty windows which run about its circumference of some 340 feet. In 1453 the building became a Mohammedan mosque (p. 121). In 1919 it became again a Christian temple.

put the whole mass into a new form, marvelously compact, clear, and orderly.

Justinian also reconquered Italy for the Empire, and so the code was established in that land. Thence, through the church, and some centuries later through a new class of lawyers, it spread over the West.

Justinian's conquest of Italy had another result less happy.

Lombards and Greeks in Italy

His generals destroyed a promising kingdom of the East Goths in Italy. Then (568), immediately after the great emperor's death, a new German people, *the savage Lombards,* swarmed into the peninsula, and soon conquered much of it. Their chief kingdom was in the Po valley, which we still call Lombardy; but various Lombard "dukedoms" were scattered also in other parts. The Empire kept (1) the "Exarchate of Ravenna" on the Adriatic; (2) Rome, with a little territory about it; and (3) the extreme south.

RELIGIOUS PRELIMINARY TO A JUDICIAL COMBAT. Each party is making oath to the justice of his cause. — From a fifteenth century manuscript.

Thus Italy, the middle land for which Roman and Teuton had struggled for centuries, was at last divided between them, and shattered into fragments in the process. No other country suffered so terribly in the centuries of invasion as this lovely peninsula which had so long been mistress of the world.

Teutonic Law

When the barbarians came into the Empire, their law was only unwritten custom. Much of it remained so, especially in Britain. But, under Roman influence, the conquerors soon put parts of their law into written codes. Two common features of these codes throw interesting sidelights on the times.

1. *Offenses were atoned for by money-payments,* varying from a small amount for cutting off the joint of a finger, to the wergeld (man-money), or payment for taking a man's life.

2. When a man wished to prove himself innocent, or another man guilty, he did not try to bring evidence, as we do. *Proof consisted in an appeal to God to show the right.*

Thus in the *trial by compurgation,* the accuser and accused swore solemnly to their statements, and each was backed by "compurgators," — not witnesses, but persons who swore they believed their man was telling the truth. To swear falsely was to invite the divine vengeance, as in the boyish survival, — "Cross my heart and hope to die."

Trial by ordeal

In *trial by ordeal*, the accused tried to clear himself by being thrown bound into water. Or he plunged his arm into boiling water, or carried red-hot iron a certain distance, or walked over burning plowshares; and if his flesh was uninjured, when examined some days later, he was declared innocent. All these ordeals were under the charge of the clergy, and were preceded by sacred exercises. Such tests could be made, too, by deputy: hence our phrase to "go through fire and water" for a friend.

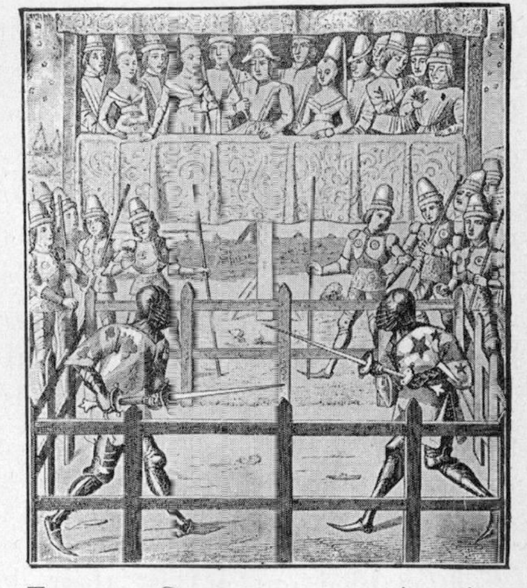

TRIAL BY COMBAT: a companion piece to the preceding cut.

Among the fighting class, the favorite trial came to be the *trial by combat*, — a judicial duel in which God was expected to "show the right."

The Teutons introduced once more a system of *growing* law. Codification preserved the Roman law, but crystallized it. Teutonic law, despite its codes, remained for a long time crude and unsystematic; but it contained possibilities of further growth. The importance of this fact has been felt mainly in the English "Common Law," the basis of our American legal system.

The conquest modified the political institutions of the conquerors in many ways. Three changes call for attention.

The conquest modifies Teutonic institutions

1. *The Teutonic kings became more absolute.* At first they were little more than especially honored military chiefs, at the head of rude democracies. In the conquests, they secured large shares of confiscated land, so that they could reward their supporters and build up a strong personal following. Their authority grew by custom, since, in the confusion of the times, all sorts of matters were necessarily left to their decision. Moreover, the Roman idea of absolute power in the head of the state had its influence. With all its excellences, the Roman law was imbued with the principle of despotism. A favorite maxim was, — "What the prince wills has the force of law."

2. *A new nobility of service appeared.* The king rewarded his most faithful and trusted followers with grants of lands, and made them rulers (counts and dukes) over large districts.

3. *The assemblies of freemen decreased in importance.* They survived in England as occasional "Folkmoots," and in the Frankish kingdom as "Mayfields"; but they shrank into gatherings of nobles and officials: if others came, it was only to hear the king's will.

At the same time, while these assemblies *of the whole nation* died out or lost their democratic elements, they kept much of their old character for various *local* units, as in the counties of the Teutonic kingdoms in England. *Thus the Teutons did carry into the Roman world a new chance for democracy.* It is not correct to say that they gave us representative government; but *they did give the world another chance to develop it.* The earlier peoples had lost their chances; but in England, later, representative institutions grew out of these local assemblies.

Life in Western Europe, 700 A.D.

Everyday life in the seventh century *was harsh and mean.* The Teutonic conquerors disliked the close streets of a Roman town; but the villa, the residence of a Roman country gentleman, was the Roman institution which they could most nearly appreciate. The new Teutonic kings lived not in town palaces, but on extensive farmsteads in the midst of forests. The new nobility, too, and other important men were great landlords and lived in the open country in rude but spacious dwellings of wood.

Population shrunken

Population had shrunken terribly, even since the worst times of the Roman Empire. In the north, most towns had been destroyed. If they were rebuilt at all, it was upon a smaller scale, and from wood. The occupations of town-dwellers had mostly vanished. The town, surrounded by a rude palisade, was valued chiefly for a refuge, and for its convenient nearness to the church or cathedral in its center. In the south, it is true, the old cities lived on, with a considerable degree of the old Roman city life.

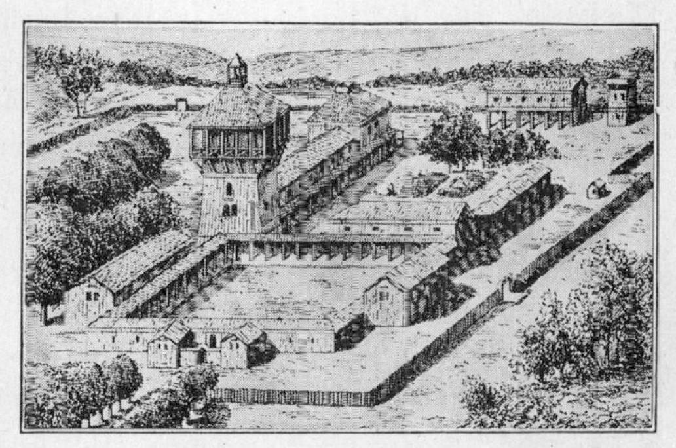

SEVENTH CENTURY VILLA (in wood) IN NORTHERN GAUL. A "restoration," from Parmentier.

Life of the poor

Everywhere, the great majority of the people were the poor folk who tilled the land for neighboring masters. Most of these toilers lived in mud hovels, or in cabins of rough boards, without floors and with roofs covered with reeds or straw. At the best, little more of their produce remained to them than barely enough to support life; and they were constantly subject to the arbitrary will of masters. At frequent intervals, too, they suffered terribly from pestilence and famine.

Monasticism

This picture of ordinary seventh-century life helps us to understand the monastic life which became popular in that day. In the old East, holiness was believed to be related to withdrawal from the world, to contempt for human pleasures, and to disregard for natural instincts, even love for mother, wife, and child. This unnatural, ascetic tendency invaded Eastern Christianity, and, in the Egyptian and Syrian deserts, there arose a class of tens of thousands of Christian *hermits*, who strove each to save his own soul by tormenting his body. In some cases these fugitives from society united into small societies with common rules of life.

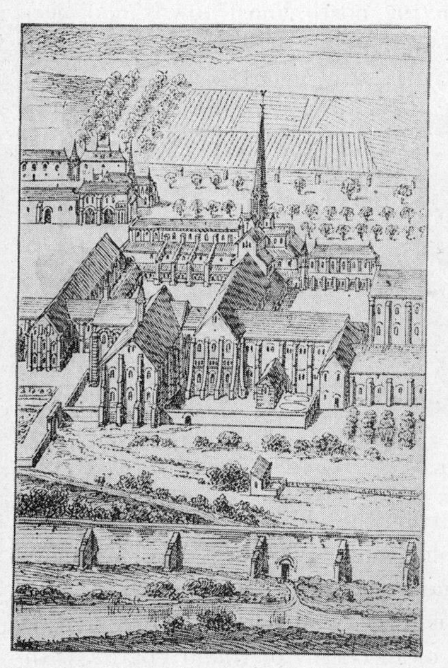

THE ABBEY[1] OF CITEAUX. — From a miniature in a twelfth century manuscript.

In the latter part of the fourth century this idea of *religious communities* was transplanted to the West and the long anarchy following the invasions made such a life peculiarly inviting. European monasticism, however, differed widely from its model in the East. The monks of the West, within their quiet walls, wisely sought escape from temptation, not in idleness, but in active and incessant work. Their motto was, "To work is to pray." *In the seventh century, the majority of cultured and refined men and women in Western Europe lived within monastic walls.* Monks did not go out into the world to save it; but their doors were open to all who came for help. For centuries of violence and brutality, the thousands of monasteries that dotted Western Europe were the only almshouses, inns, asylums, hospitals, and schools, and the sole refuge of learning.

[1] A *large* monastery was an *abbey*, and its elected head was an *abbot* — from the Syrian word *abba*, "father."

II. FRANKS, MOHAMMEDANS, AND POPES

During the two centuries of fusion (p. 29), two great organizing powers grew up in Western Europe — *the Frankish state* and *the Papacy;* and one great danger appeared — *Mohammedanism.*

Rise of the Franks

The growth of the Frankish state was due mainly to *Clovis,* a ferocious and treacherous Teutonic savage of shrewd intellect. *In 481,* Clovis became king of one of the several little tribes of Franks on the lower Rhine. Fifty years later, thanks to a long-continued policy of war, assassination, and perfidy, his sons ruled an empire that was beyond comparison the greatest power in Europe, comprising nearly all modern France, the Netherlands, and much of western Germany.

Monks Busy in Field Work. — From Lacroix, after a thirteenth century manuscript.

This new Frankish empire remained for three centuries not only the greatest power in Western Europe but practically the only power. The Gothic state in Spain was in decay. Italy was in fragments. England (Britain) remained a medley of small warring states (p. 56). Germany, east of the Frankish empire, held only savage and unorganized tribes

The "Do-nothing" kings

For two of these centuries the family of Clovis kept the throne, — a story of greed, treachery, and murder, and, toward the end, of dismal, swinish indolence. The last of these kings were mere phantom rulers, known as "Do-nothings," and all real power was held by a *mayor of the palace.* The Empire of the Franks seemed about to dissolve in anarchy. Austrasia (northeastern France and the lower Rhine region) was the most Frank in blood, and was engaged in war with Neustria (north-

The Frankish state re-united by Martel

western France), which had more of the old Roman character, and was ambitious for supremacy. German Bavaria and Roman Aquitaine attempted complete independence under native dukes. But about the year 700 a great mayor, Charles, known as Martel ("the Hammer"), by crushing blows right and left began to restore union and order.

And none too soon. For the Mohammedans now attacked Europe. Except for Martel's long pounding, there would have been no Christian power able to withstand their onset —

A REPAST IN THE HALL OF A FRANKISH NOBLE. — After a tenth century manuscript.

and Englishmen and Americans to-day might be readers of the Mohammedan Koran instead of the Christian Bible.

Arabia before Mohammed

A century after Clovis built up the empire of the Franks, a better man, out of less promising material, built a mighty power in Arabia. Until that time, Arabia had had little to do with human progress. It was mainly desert, with occasional oases, and with strips of tillable land near the Red Sea. In this coast district there were a few small cities. Elsewhere the Arabs were wandering shepherds, — poor and ignorant, dwelling in black camel's-hair tents, living from their sheep and by robbing their neighbors, and worshiping sticks and stones. The inspiring force that was to lift them to a higher life, and fuse

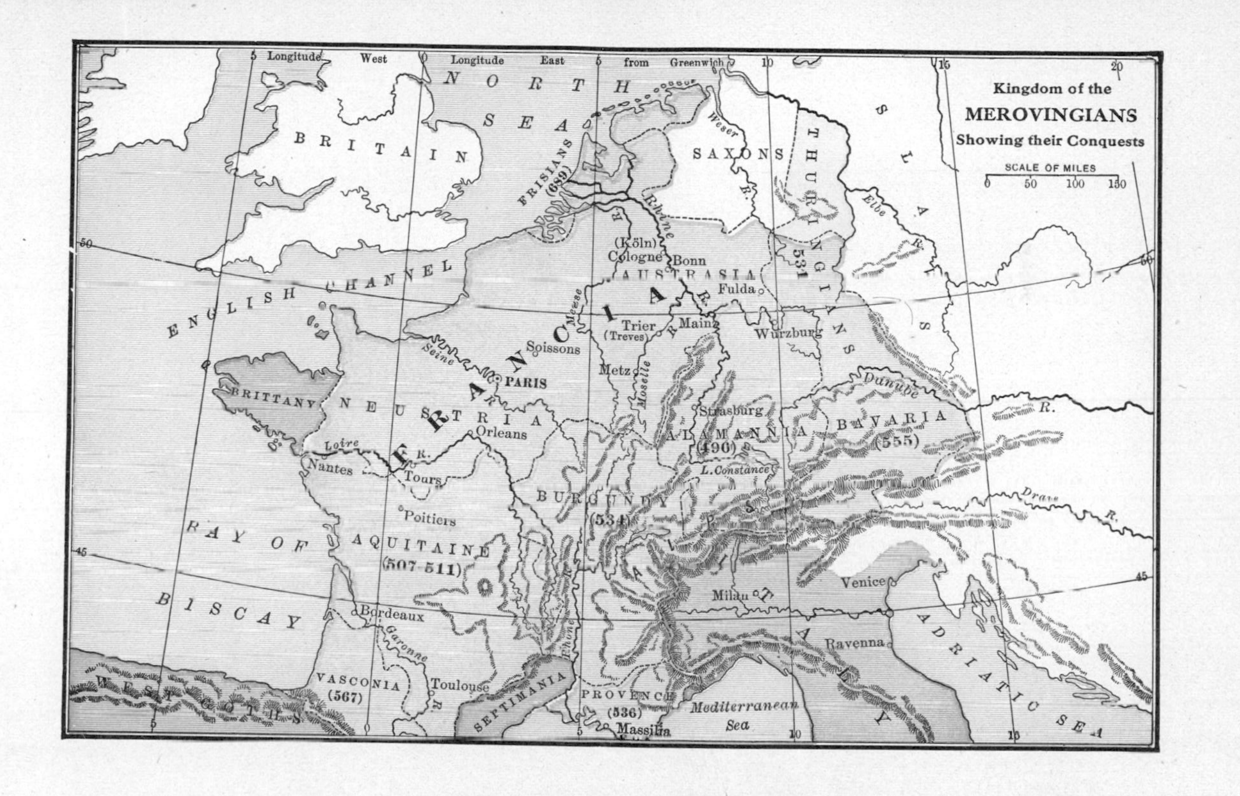
Kingdom of the
MEROVINGIANS
Showing their Conquests
SCALE OF MILES
0 50 100 150
Longitude West
Longitude East from Greenwich
NORTH SEA
BRITAIN
ENGLISH CHANNEL
FRISIANS (689)
SAXONS
THURINGIANS 531
SLAVS
Weser
Elbe R.
Rhine R.
(Köln) Cologne
Bonn
AUSTRASIA
Fulda
FRANCIA
Meuse
Trier (Treves)
Main R.
Wurzburg
Soissons
Seine R.
PARIS
Metz
Moselle
Danube R.
BRITTANY
NEUSTRIA
Orleans
Strasburg
ALAMANNIA (496)
BAVARIA (555)
Loire R.
Nantes
Tours
L. Constance
BURGUNDY (534)
Drave R.
Poitiers
BAY OF BISCAY
AQUITAINE (507-511)
ALPS
Venice
Milan
ITALY
Bordeaux
Garonne
Rhone
Ravenna
VASCONIA (567)
Toulouse
SEPTIMANIA
PROVENCE (536)
Massilia
Mediterranean Sea
ADRIATIC SEA
WEST GOTHS

them into a world-conquering nation, was the fiery enthusiasm of *Mohammed.*

Mohammed, 570–632

Mohammed was born at Mecca, the largest city of Arabia, about 570. He never learned to read; but his speech was ready and forceful, and his manner pleasing and stately. As a youth, he was modest, serious, and truthful, — so that as a hired camel-driver, he earned the surname "the Faithful." He had always been given to occasional periods of religious enthusiasm and ecstasy, watching and praying alone in the desert for days at a time, as indeed many Arabs did. In such a lonely vigil, when he was a respected merchant forty years old, God appeared to him (he said) in a wondrous vision, revealing to him a higher religion and ordering him to preach it to his countrymen. Mohammed really drew the best features of his new religion from Jewish and Christian teachings, with which he had become somewhat acquainted in his travels as a merchant. The two central requirements were *faith* and *obedience.* A "true believer" must accept only the one God, *Allah*, and must offer complete submission (*Islam*) to his will.

Moral teachings of Mohammed

The Koran,[1] the "sacred book" made up of Mohammed's teachings, taught a higher morality than the Arabs had known, — not so very unlike that of the Ten Commandments; but it accepted also certain evil customs of the time, such as slavery and polygamy, and it attracted converts by its sensuous appeals to future pleasures or pains. At the "Last Day," all souls would be gathered to judgment. Then all sinful Mohammedans, together with all "Unbelievers," would be cast into an everlasting hell of scalding water covered with thick clouds of smoke. True believers, on the other hand, were to enter the joys of an eternal Paradise, to recline, in the midst of lovely gardens, on couches of gold and jewels, where they would be served constantly by beautiful maidens ("houris") with delicious foods and wines.

The Hegira 622 A.D.

For twelve years the new faith grew slowly. A few friends accepted Mohammed at once as a prophet; but the bulk of

[1] See extracts in Ogg's *Source Book*, No. 13.

his fellow townsfolk jeered at the claim, and when he continued to order them to put away their stone idols, they drove him from Mecca. This flight is "the Hegira" (*622* A.D.).

THE MOSQUE OF EL AZHAR AT CAIRO. — This view shows only the minarets and dome of the roof.

Mohammed makes converts by the sword

But Mohammed converted the tribes of the desert, and then took up the sword. His fierce warriors proved themselves almost irresistible, conquering many a time against overwhelming odds. They felt sure that to every man there was an appointed time of death, which he could neither delay nor hasten, and they rejoiced in death in battle as the surest admission to the joys of Paradise. "The sword," said Mohammed, "is the key of heaven. Whoso falls in battle, all his sins are forgiven; at the day of judgment his wounds shall be resplendent as vermilion and odoriferous as musk." Before his death, ten years after the Hegira, Mohammed was master of all Arabia. Eighty years later, his followers stood victorious upon the Oxus, the Indus, the Black Sea, the Atlantic, — rulers of a realm more extensive than that of Rome at its height. Within the span of one human life, the Mohammedans had won all the old Asiatic empire of Alexander the Great, and all North Africa besides; and drawing together the sweeping horns of their mighty crescent, they were already trying to enter Europe from both east and west across the narrow straits of the Hellespont and Gibraltar.

Rapid growth of the faith

The most formidable attacks wore themselves away (672 and 717) about the walls of "the City of Constantine," defended by its new "Greek fire"; but in 711 the Arabs did enter Spain and were soon masters of that peninsula, except for remote mountain fastnesses. Then, pouring across the Pyrenees, the Mohammedan flood spread over Gaul, even to the Loire. Now, indeed, it "seemed that the crescent was about to round to the full." *But the danger completed the reunion of the Frankish state* (p. 38).

The Saracens attack Europe

The duke of Aquitaine, long in revolt against Frankish rule, fled to the camp of Charles Martel for aid against the Mohammedan; and, in 732, in the plains near *Tours*, the "Hammer of the Franks" with his close array of mailed Austrasian infantry met the Arab host. From dawn to dark, on a Saturday in October, the gallant, turbaned horsemen of the Saracens hurled themselves in vain against the Franks' stern wall of iron. At night the surviving Arabs stole silently from their camp and fled back behind the shelter of the Pyrenees.

Battle of Tours, 732 A.D.

This Battle of Tours, just one hundred years after Mohammed's death, is *the high-water mark of the Saracen invasion.*

A few years later, the Mohammedan world, like Christendom, split into rival empires. The Caliph[1] of the East built, for his capital, the wonderful city of Bagdad on the Tigris. The Caliphate of the West fixed its capital at Cordova in Spain. The two Caliphates were more or less hostile to each other, and the critical danger to Western civilization for the time passed away. *The repulses at Constantinople and at Tours rank with Marathon and Salamis, in the long struggle between Asia and Europe.*

The Frankish state had saved Europe from Africa. Next it allied to itself the papacy. We must now trace the rise of that power.

Claims of the Roman papacy to headship

In the fourth century, we have seen (p. 26), the leadership of the Christian world was divided among the great bishops of Jerusalem, Antioch, Alexandria, Constantinople, and Rome. Very early the last of these put forth a vigorous claim — as spiritual successor to St. Peter, alleged founder of the church at Rome — to supremacy over all the Christian church.

Rome's advantages in the Western church

Rome had advantages that helped to make good this claim. (1) Men thought of Rome naturally as the world-capital. (2) The Latin half of the Empire had no other church founded by an Apostle; nor did it contain any other great city: Rome's rivals were all east of the Adriatic. (3) The decline of the Roman Empire in the West, after the barbarian invasions, left the pope less liable to interference from the imperial government than the Eastern bishops were. (4) A long line of remarkable popes, by their wise statesmanship and their missionary zeal, confirmed the position of Rome as head of the Western churches.

The name pope ("papa") was at first only a term of affectionate respect ("father"). It did not become an *official* term until 1085.

Even in the West, however, until about 700 A.D., most men looked upon the bishop of Rome only as one among five great

[1] *Caliph* ("successor") became the title of the successors of Mohammed.

patriarchs, though the most loved and trusted one. *But the eighth century eliminated the other four patriarchs, so far as Western Christendom was concerned.* In quick succession, Alexandria, Jerusalem, and Antioch fell to the Saracens; and, soon afterward, remaining Christendom split into rival Latin and Greek churches, grouped respectively around Rome and Constantinople.

THE CHURCH OF ST. JOHN LATERAN AT ROME, on the site of the first papal church. The popes used the adjoining Lateran palace as their official residence until 1377.

The "Great Schism" leaves Rome mistress in the Western church

This "Great Schism" followed the ancient lines of partition between the Latin and Greek cultures; but the occasion for actual separation was a dispute over the use of images (the "iconoclast," or image-breaking question). An influential party in the Greek Empire desired to abolish the use of images, which, they felt, the ignorant were apt to degrade from symbols into idols. A great reforming emperor, *Leo the Isaurian*, put himself at the head of the movement, with all his despotic power, and ordered all images removed from the churches. The West believed in their use as valuable aids to worship; and the pope forbade obedience to the order of the emperor. The result was the separation of Christendom into two halves, never since united.

Thus, Rome was left the unquestioned head of the Latin church, the spiritual lord of Western Europe. At the same

CLOISTERS OF ST. JOHN LATERAN.

The pope becomes a temporal prince

time, too, *the pope was growing into a temporal*[1] *sovereign* over a small state in Italy. In the break-up of that peninsula (p. 32), the imperial governor kept his capital at Ravenna, safe amid the marshes of the Adriatic coast. Thus he was soon cut off, by Lombard states, from Rome, which with neighboring territory still belonged to the Empire. Bishops always held considerable civil authority. This new condition left the

[1] *Temporal*, in this sense, is used to apply to matters of *this* world, in contrast to the *spiritual* matters of the world *eternal*.

bishop of Rome the only lieutenant of the Empire in his isolated district; and the difficulty of communication with Constantinople (and the weakness of the emperors) made him in practice an independent ruler. After the split between Greek and Latin churches, this independence was openly avowed.

Popes and Lombards

At once, however, the new papal state was threatened with conquest by the neighboring Lombards, who already had seized the Exarchate of Ravenna. The popes appealed to the Franks for aid against Lombard attack. The Frankish mayors needed papal sanction for their own plans just then; and so *the two organizing forces of Western Europe joined hands.*

Alliance of Franks and Papacy

The Frankish mayor now was Pippin the Short, son of Charles Martel. This ruler felt that he bore the burdens of kingship, and he wished to take to himself also its name and dignity. Such a step needed powerful sanction. So, in 750, Pippin sent an embassy to the pope to ask whether this was "a good state of things in regard to the kings of the Franks." The pope replied, "It seems better that he who has the power should be king rather than he who is falsely called so." Thereupon Pippin shut up the last shadow-king of the house of Clovis in a monastery, and himself assumed the crown.

A little later, Pope Stephen visited the Frankish court and solemnly consecrated Pippin king. All earlier Teutonic kings had held their kingship by will of their people; but Stephen anointed Pippin, as the old Hebrew prophets did the Hebrew kings. This began for European monarchs their "sacred" character as "the Lord's anointed." On his part, Pippin made Lombardy a tributary state and gave to the pope that territory which the Lombard king had recently seized from Ravenna. This "Donation of Pippin" created the modern principality of "the Papal states" — to last until 1870.

FOURTH PERIOD

CHARLEMAGNE'S EMPIRE

"A patch of light in a vast gloom"

arle- ne, 814

In 768 Pippin, King of the Franks, was succeeded by his son *Karl*, soon to win justly the title of *the Great* — the greatest medieval man. Karl the Great was known in his own day, in the Latin form of his name, as Carolus Magnus, and is best known to us by the French form *Charlemagne*.

SEAL OF CHARLEMAGNE. (This is the nearest approach we have to a likeness of Charlemagne. The so-called "pictures" of Charlemagne in many books are purely imaginative, by artists of later centuries.)

Repulse of barbarian danger: civilization expanded

Charlemagne was a statesman rather than a fighter; but he found his realm still threatened by barbarian Germans on the east and by Mohammedan Moors on the south, and his long reign of a half century was filled with ceaseless border wars. He thrust back the Saracens to the Ebro, redeeming a strip of Spain; and, in a long pounding of thirty years, he subdued the heathen Saxons amid the marshes and trackless wilderness between the lower Rhine and the Elbe. All this district, so long a peril to the civilized world, was colonized by Frankish pioneers and planted with Christian churches. In such bloody and violent ways *Charlemagne laid the foundation for modern Germany.*

Other foes engaged energy the great king would rather have given to reconstruction. The vassal Lombard king attacked the pope. After fruitless expostulation, Charlemagne marched into Italy, confirmed Pippin's "Donation," and at

Pavia placed the Iron Crown of Lombardy upon his own head, as King of Italy. And when restless German Bavaria once more rebelled (p. 38), that district was at last thoroughly and lastingly subdued.

"Buffer" states on the East

Thus Visigoth in northern Spain, Burgund in south Gaul, Lombard in Italy, and the more newly "civilized" Bavarian and Saxon in Germany, along with the dominant Franks — *all the surviving Teutonic peoples* except the Norsemen in the Scandinavian lands and the Angles and Saxons in Britain — *were fused in one Christian Romano-Teutonic state.* Beyond this "Western Europe," to the east, stretched away savage and heathen Avars and Slavs, still hurling themselves from time to time against the barriers of the civilized world. Charlemagne made no attempt to *embody* these inharmonious elements in his realm; but, toward the close, he did attack barbarism in these last European strongholds, reducing the first line of peoples beyond the Elbe and the Danube into *tributary states* to serve as buffers against their untamed brethren farther east.

SERVINGMAN WITH LAMP: time of Charlemagne.

"Emperor of the Romans," 800 A.D.

But no mere "King of the Franks" could hold in lasting allegiance the minds of Visigoth, Lombard, Bavarian, and Saxon, and of the old Roman populations among whom they dwelt. And so *Charlemagne now strengthened his authority* over his empire[1] *by reviving in the West the dignity and magic name of the Roman Empire,* ruling at once from the old world-capital, Rome on the Latin Tiber, and from his new capital, the German Aachen on the Rhine.

There was already a "Roman Emperor" at Constantinople, whose authority, *in theory,* extended over all Christendom;

[1] An "empire," strictly speaking, is a political state containing many substates. A "state," in this sense, does not mean such a unit as Massachusetts or New York, but rather England or the United States. That is, it means a people living in a definite territory, under one government.

but just at this time, Irene, the empress-mother, put out the eyes of her son, Constantine VI, and seized the imperial power. To most minds, East and West, it seemed monstrous that a wicked *woman* should pretend to the scepter of the world; and, on Christmas Day, 800 A.D., as Charlemagne at Rome knelt in prayer at the altar, Pope Leo III placed upon his head a gold crown, saluting him "Charles Augustus, Emperor of the Romans." This deed was at once ratified by the enthusiastic acclaim of the multitude without.

two
[illegible]res

In theory, Rome had chosen a successor to Constantine VI, just deposed at Constantinople. In actual fact, however, *the deed of Leo and Charlemagne divided the Christian world into two rival empires,* each calling itself *the* Roman Empire. After a time men had to recognize this fact, — as they had to recognize that there were two branches of the Christian church; but to the men of the West, *their* Empire, like their church, remained the only legitimate one. Two things must be borne in mind.

1. *Neither Empire was really Roman.* As the Eastern grew more and more Oriental, the Western grew more and more Teutonic. Roman ideas, so far as they remained at all, were worked out by rulers of Teutonic blood.

2. *The new Empire arose out of a union of the papacy and the Frankish power.* In later times the union was expressed in the name, The *Holy* Roman Empire. The Empire had its spiritual as well as its temporal head. The limits of authority between the two heads were not well defined, and dissensions were afterward to arise between them.

Poverty and misery of Europe, 800 A.D.

The glory and prosperity of the old Empire had not been restored with its name. To accomplish that was to be the work of centuries more. *In 800, the West was still ignorant and wretched.* There was much barbarism in the most civilized society. Roads had fallen to ruin, and murderous brigands infested those that remained. Money was little known, and trade hardly existed. Almost the only industry was the primitive agriculture of the serfs. Even Charlemagne could raise

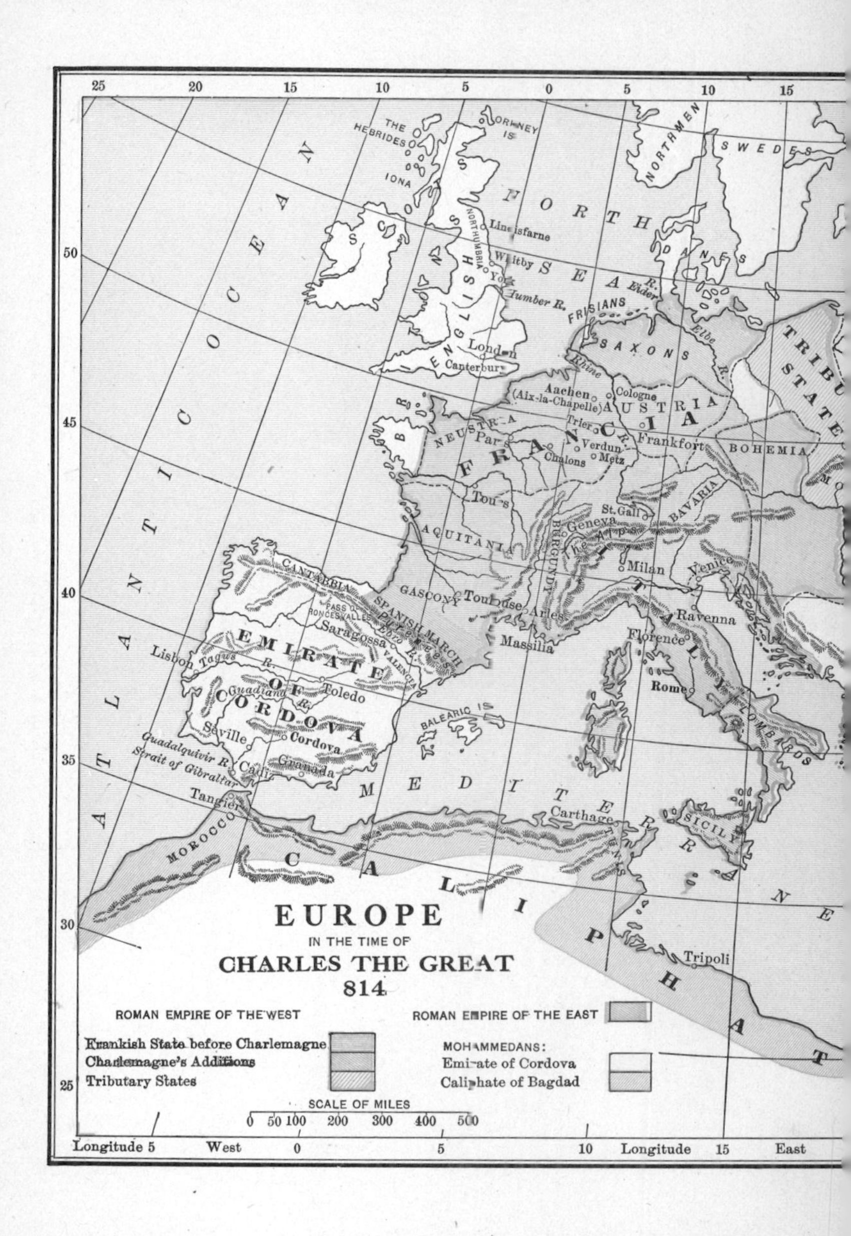
EUROPE
IN THE TIME OF
CHARLES THE GREAT
814
ROMAN EMPIRE OF THE WEST
Frankish State before Charlemagne
Charlemagne's Additions
Tributary States
ROMAN EMPIRE OF THE EAST
MOHAMMEDANS:
Emirate of Cordova
Caliphate of Bagdad
SCALE OF MILES
0 50 100 200 300 400 500
Longitude 5 West 0 5 10 Longitude 15 East
ATLANTIC OCEAN
NORTH SEA
MEDITERRANEAN
CALIPHATE
THE HEBRIDES
IONA
ORKNEY IS
NORTHMEN
SWEDES
DANES
SCOTS
NORTHUMBRIA
ENGLISH
Lindisfarne
Whitby
York
Humber R.
London
Canterbury
FRISIANS
SAXONS
Elbe R.
Eider R.
Rhine
Aachen
(Aix-la-Chapelle)
Cologne
AUSTRASIA
NEUSTRIA
FRANCIA
Paris
Trier
Verdun
Metz
Chalons
Frankfort
BOHEMIA
BAVARIA
Tours
AQUITANIA
BURGUNDY
St. Gall
Geneva
The Alps
Milan
Venice
Ravenna
Florence
Rome
ITALY
LOMBARDS
GASCONY
Toulouse
Arles
Massilia
CANTABRIA
PASS RONCESVALLES
SPANISH MARCH
Pyrenees
Ebro R.
Saragossa
VALENCIA
EMIRATE OF CORDOVA
Lisbon
Tagus R.
Toledo
Guadiana R.
Seville
Cordova
Guadalquivir R.
Cadiz
Granada
Strait of Gibraltar
Tangier
MOROCCO
BALEARIC IS.
Carthage
SICILY
Tripoli
25 20 15 10 5 0 5 10 15
50 45 40 35 30 25

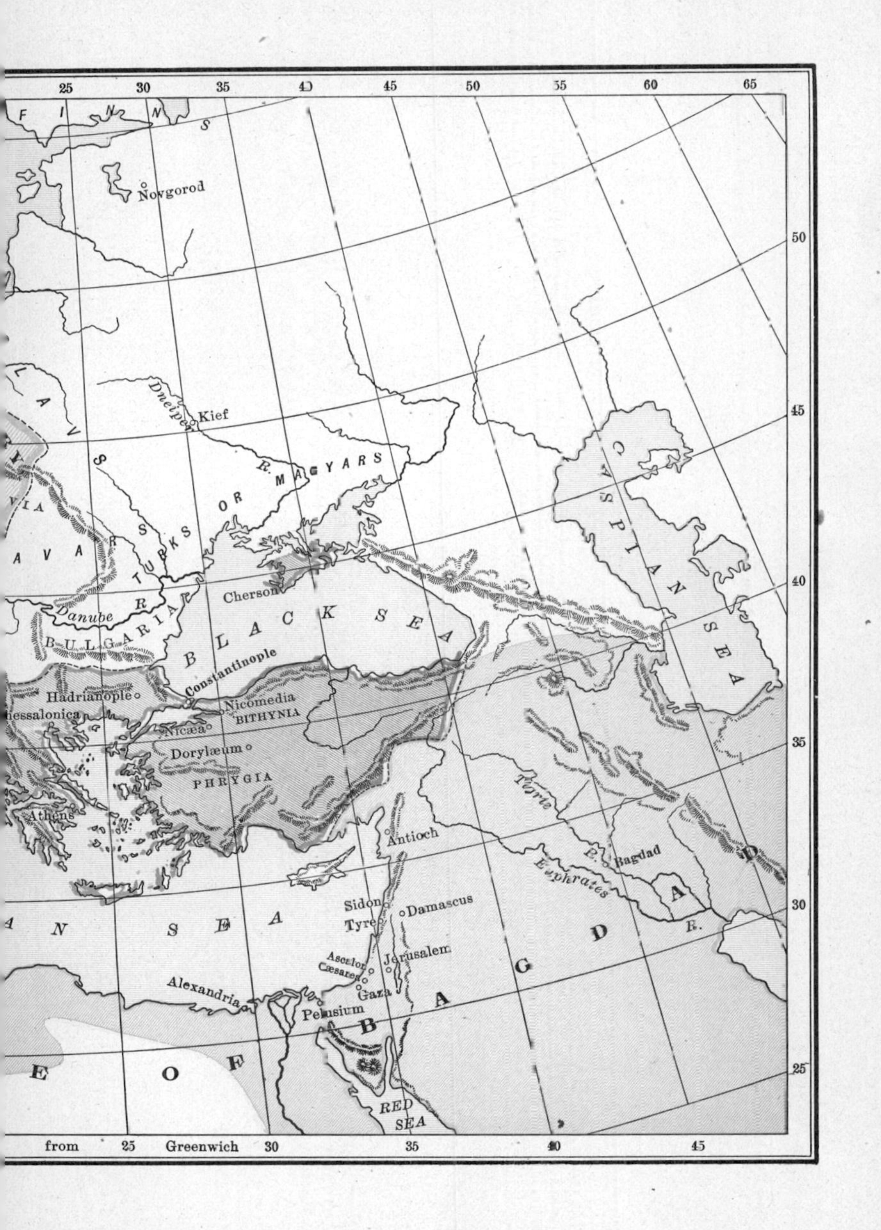

Novgorod
Kief
Dneiper R.
MAGYARS
TURKS OR
AVARS
BULGARIA
Danube R.
Cherson
BLACK SEA
CASPIAN SEA
Constantinople
Hadrianople
Nicomedia
BITHYNIA
Nicæa
Dorylæum
PHRYGIA
Athens
Antioch
Tigris R.
Euphrates R.
Bagdad
Sidon
Damascus
Tyre
Jerusalem
Ascalon
Cæsarea
Gaza
Alexandria
Pelusium
RED SEA
BAGDAD
from 25 Greenwich 30 35 40 45

no "taxes." He exacted "service in person" in war and peace; and the other support of his court came mainly from the produce of the royal farms scattered through the kingdom. Partly to make sure of this revenue in the cheapest way, and more to attend to the wants of his vast realms, Charlemagne and his court were always on the move. No commercial traveler of to-day travels more faithfully, or dreams of encountering such hardship on the road.

The "May-fields" of the Franks

To keep in closer touch with popular feeling in all parts of the kingdom, Charlemagne made use of the old Teutonic assemblies in fall and spring. All freemen *could* attend. Sometimes, especially when war was to be decided upon, this "Mayfield" gathering comprised the bulk of the men of the Frankish nation. At other times it was made up only of the great nobles and churchmen (p. 34).

SILVER COIN OF CHARLEMAGNE. The obverse side shows the Latin form of his name. Note the rudeness of the engraving compared with that of Justinian's coin on page 30.

To these assemblies were read the capitularies, or collections of laws decreed by the king; but the assembly was not itself a legislature. *Law-making was in the hands of the king.* At the most, the assemblies could only bring to bear upon him mildly the force of public opinion. A modern French historian (Coulanges) pictures a Mayfield thus:

"An immense multitude is gathered in a plain, under tents. It is divided into separate groups. The *chiefs* of these groups assemble about the king, to deliberate with him. Then each of them tells his own group what has been decided, perhaps consults them, but at any rate obtains their consent as easily as the king had obtained his; for these men are dependent on him, just as he is on the king. . . . The king's will decided everything; the nobles only advised."

Charlemagne made brave attempts also to revive learning. He never learned to write, but he spoke and read Latin, as well

Attempts to revive learning

as his native German, and he understood some Greek. For his age he was an educated man; and he wished earnestly to make more learning possible for others. The difficulties were greater even than in Russia to-day. Nearly every noble, and many of the clergy, were densely ignorant. The only tools to work with were poor. There seemed no place to begin.

Still much was done. For teachers Charlemagne sought out learned men in South Italy, where Roman civilization best survived, and he opened schools in monasteries and at bishops' seats for the instruction of all children who could come to them — even the children of serfs. Some of these schools, as at Tours and Orleans, lived on through the Middle Ages.[1]

The world of 800 A.D.

In the early part of the eighth century there were four great forces contending for Western Europe, — the Greek Empire, the Saracens, the Franks, and the papacy. By the year 800, Charles Martel and Charles the Great had excluded the first two and had fused the other two into the revived Roman Empire. For centuries more, this Roman Empire was to be one of the most important forces in Europe. Barbarism and anarchy were again to break in, after the death of the great Charles; but the imperial idea, to which he had given new life, was to be for ages the inspiration of the best minds as they strove against anarchy in behalf of order and progress.

Charlemagne himself towers above all other men from the fifth century to the fifteenth — easily the greatest figure of a thousand years. He stands for five mighty movements. He widened the area of civilization, created one great Romano-Teutonic state, revived the Roman Empire in the West for the outward form of this state, reorganized church and society, and began a revival of learning. He wrought wisely to combine the best elements of Roman and of Teutonic society into a new civilization. *In his Empire were fused the various*

[1] The term "Middle Ages" is used for the centuries from 400 to 1500, or from the Teutonic invasions to the Discovery of America. These centuries cover that "Medieval" period which intervenes between the distinctly *Ancient* and the distinctly *Modern* period.

streams of influence which the Ancient World contributed to our Modern World.

The world was divided among four great powers — two rival Christian "Roman" Empires and two rival Mohammedan Caliphates. For centuries *the Western Empire* remained the least polished, least wealthy, least civilized of the four. And yet this rude state, with its fringes in the Teutonic lands of England and Scandinavia, *was the only one of the four great*

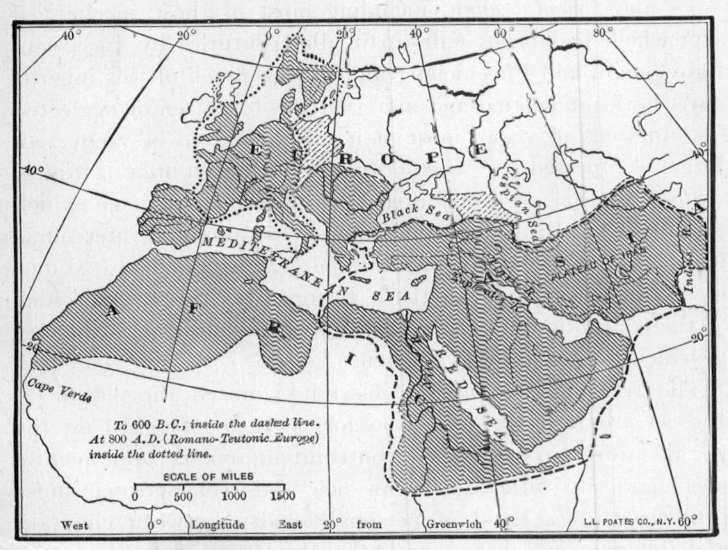

THE FIELD OF ANCIENT HISTORY, TO 800 A.D.

powers that was to stand for further progress, — the only one with which later history is much concerned.

Scene of "history" shifted to "Western Europe"

The scene of history had shifted to the West once more, and this time it had shrunken in size. Some Teutonic districts outside the old Roman world had been added; but vast areas of the Roman territory itself had been abandoned. The Euphrates, the Nile, the Eastern Mediterranean, all Asia with Eastern Europe to the Adriatic, and Africa with Western Europe to the Pyrenees, were gone. The Mediterranean, the center of the old Roman world, had become an ill-defended moat between Christian Europe and Mohammedan Africa; and its ancient place as the great highway of civilization was taken over, as well as might be, by the Rhine and the North Sea.

Western Europe's heritage from the ages

We can now sum up the inheritance with which "Western Europe" began.

Through Rome the Western peoples were the heirs of *Greek mind* and *Oriental hand,* including most of those mechanical arts which had been built up in dim centuries by Egyptian, Babylonian, and Phoenician; and though much of this inheritance, both intellectual and material, was forgotten or neglected for hundreds of years, most of it was finally to be recovered. Rome also passed on *Christianity* and its church organization.

Rome herself had contributed (1) a universal language, which was to serve as a common medium of learning and intercourse for all the peoples of Western Europe; (2) Roman law; (3) municipal institutions, in southern Europe; (4) the imperial idea — the conception of one, lasting, universal, supreme authority, to which the world owed obedience.

The fresh blood of the Teutons reinvigorated the old races, and so provided the men who for centuries were to do the world's work. *The Teutons* contributed, too, certain definite ideas and institutions, — (1) a new sense of personal independence; (2) a bond of personal loyalty between chieftain and follower, in contrast with the old Roman loyalty to the state; (3) a new *chance* for democracy, especially in the popular assemblies of different grades in England.

Out of Roman and Teutonic elements there had already developed a new serf organization of labor; a new nobility; and a new Romano-Teutonic kingship — and now there was to grow out of them a new feudalism (below).

The use of the words *German* and *Teuton* in the above treatment calls for a word of caution. They are the only proper words to use, but they may easily give rise to misunderstanding.

The *mingling* of Teutonic and Roman elements in our civilization took place not in Germany but in the lands we call England, France, Belgium, Italy, and Spain. The people who brought the Teutonic contributions into those lands were not the ancestors of the modern Germans — any more than were other Teutons, like the Danes and Swedes, who never entered Germany: they were, in part, the ancestors of English, French, Spanish, and Italian peoples. They left Germany fourteen hundred years ago; and the civilization which grew up in those Western lands, after these migrations into them, was the civilization of a new "Western Europe." Then, some three or four centuries later, as we have seen, Christianity and armed conquest began, in a measure, to carry this new civilization east from these lands into the forests of savage and heathen Germany.

Caution as to the terms "Teuton" and "German"

FIFTH PERIOD

THE FEUDAL AGE, 800–1300

I. THE NEW BARBARIAN ATTACK

"*From the fury of the Northmen, O Lord, deliver us.*" — PRAYER IN CHURCH SERVICE OF TENTH CENTURY

The division of Verdun, 843 A.D.

Charlemagne died in 814, and his empire did not long outlive him. His brilliant attempt to bring Western Europe into order and union was followed by a dismal period of reaction and turmoil, while his ignoble descendants sought only to see who could grab the largest slices of the realm. The most important of these selfish contests closed *in 843* with the *Treaty of Verdun.*

Beginnings of France and Germany

This treaty *begins the map of modern Europe.* Lothair, Charlemagne's eldest grandson, held the title Emperor, and so he was now given North Italy and a narrow strip of land from Italy to the North Sea — that he might keep the two imperial capitals, Rome and Aachen (p. 47). The rest of the Empire, lying east and west of this middle strip, was broken into two kingdoms for Lothair's two brothers.

The eastern kingdom was purely German. In the western, the Teutonic rulers were being absorbed rapidly into the older Roman and Gallic populations, to grow into France. Lothair's

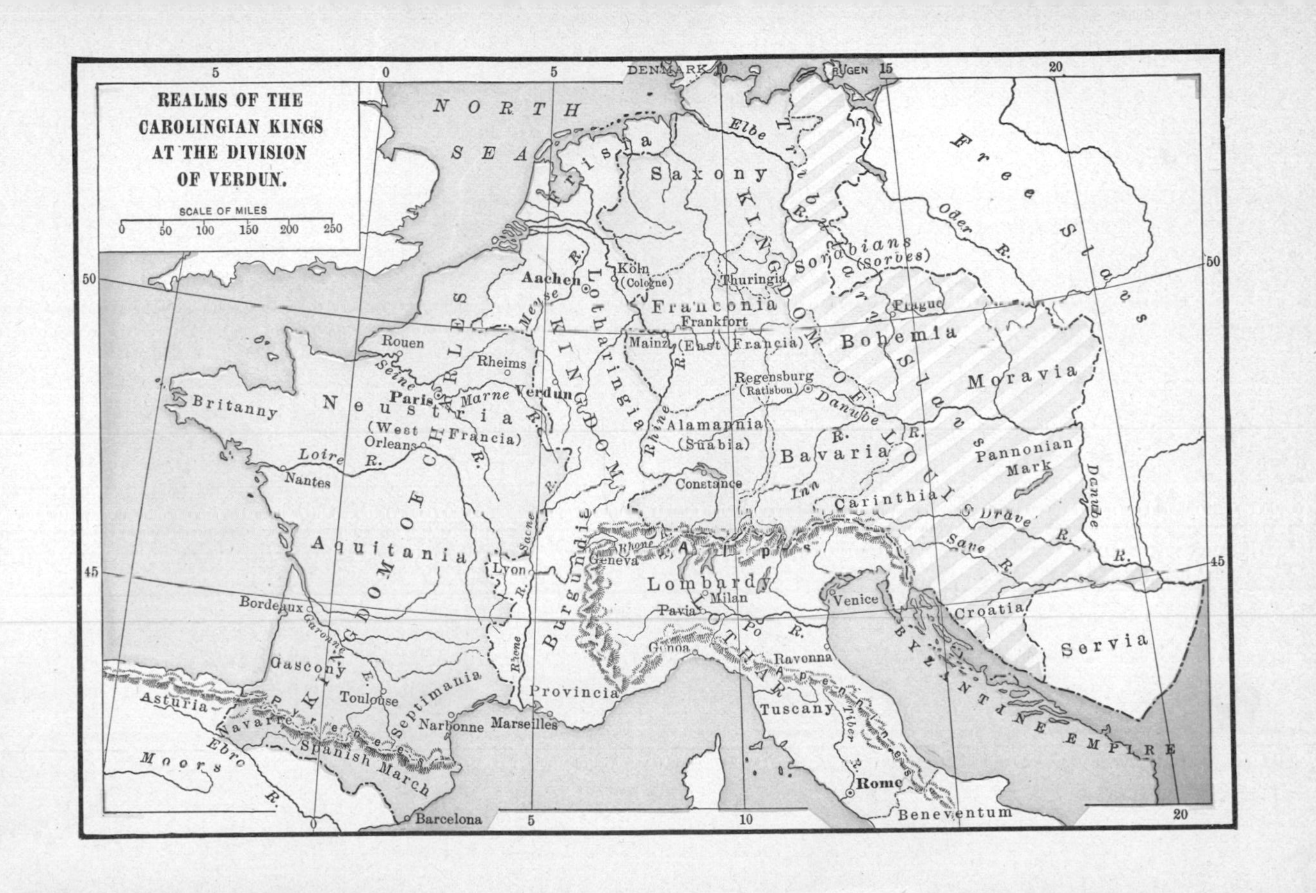
REALMS OF THE CAROLINGIAN KINGS AT THE DIVISION OF VERDUN.
SCALE OF MILES
0 50 100 150 200 250
NORTH SEA
DENMARK
RÜGEN
Frisia
Saxony
Elbe
Tribes
Free Slavs
Oder R.
Sorabians (Sorves)
Thuringia
Köln (Cologne)
Aachen
Meuse R.
Lotharingia
Franconia
Frankfort
Mainz
(East Francia)
Prague
Bohemia
Moravia
Regensburg (Ratisbon)
Danube R.
Rhine R.
Alamannia (Suabia)
Bavaria
Inn
Pannonian Mark
Danube R.
Constance
Carinthia
Drave R.
Save R.
KINGDOM OF LOUIS
Slavs
Rouen
Seine
Rheims
Paris
Marne
Verdun
Neustria (West Francia)
Orleans
Britanny
Loire R.
Nantes
Aquitania
KINGDOM OF CHARLES
KINGDOM OF LOTHAR
Saone R.
Lyon
Burgundie
Rhone R.
Geneva
Alps
Lombardy
Milan
Pavia
Po R.
Venice
Croatia
Servia
Genoa
Ravenna
Apennines
Tuscany
Tiber R.
Rome
Beneventum
BYZANTINE EMPIRE
Bordeaux
Garonne
Gascony
Toulouse
Septimania
Narbonne
Marseilles
Provincia
Asturia
Navarre
Pyrenees
Spanish March
Ebro R.
Moors
Barcelona
50
45
5
0
5
10
15
20

unwieldy "Middle Europe" proved the weakest of the three. Italy fell away at once. Then the northern portion, part French, part German, crumbled into "little states" that confused the map of Europe for centuries. Most of them were finally absorbed by their more powerful neighbors on either side. Four survive as Belgium, Holland, Luxemburg, and Switzerland.

Degenerate Carolingians

For a century after Verdun, political history remained a bloody tangle of treacherous family quarrels, while the descendants of the Hammer and the Great were known as the Bald, the Simple, the Fat, the Lazy. And now distracted Europe was imperiled by a new danger from without. Once more barbarian invasions threatened the civilized world. On the east, hordes of wild *Slavs* and of wilder *Hungarians* broke across the frontiers, ravaged Germany, and penetrated sometimes even to Rome or to Toulouse in southern France. The *Mohammedan Moors* from Africa attacked Italy and Sicily, establishing themselves firmly in many districts and turning the Mediterranean into a Mohammedan lake. Fierce *Norse* pirates harried every coast, and, swarming up the rivers, pierced the heart of the land.

REMAINS OF A VIKING SHIP found buried in sand at Gökstad, Norway. It is of oak, unpainted, 79′ 4″ by 16½′; 6 feet deep in the middle.

New barbarian inroads

The Norsemen

The Norsemen were a new branch of the Teutons, and the fiercest and wildest of that race. They dwelt in the Scandinavian peninsulas, and were still heathen. They had taken no part in the earlier Teutonic invasions; but, in the ninth century, population was becoming too crowded for their bleak lands, and they were driven to seek new homes. Some of them colonized distant Iceland, and set up a free republic there; but the greater number resorted to raiding richer countries. The Swedes conquered Finns and Slavs on the east, while

Danish and Norse "Vikings" ("sons of the fiords") set forth upon "the pathway of the swans," in fleets, sometimes of hundreds of boats, to harry western Europe. Driving their light craft far up the rivers, they then seized horses and ravaged at will, sacking cities like Hamburg, Rouen, Paris, Nantes, Tours, Cologne, and stabling their steeds in the cathedral of Aachen about the tomb of Charlemagne.

At last, like the earlier Teutons, the Norsemen from plunderers became conquerors. They settled the Orkneys and Shetlands and patches on the coasts of Scotland and Ireland, and finally established themselves in the north of France — named, from them, *Normandy* — and in the east of England.

II. BRITAIN BECOMES ENGLAND

The Teuton conquest of Britain, 449–600 A.D.

We must go back to note how Britain had become England. In 408 the Roman legions were withdrawn from Britain to defend Italy against the threatened invasion by the Goths (p. 28). This left the dismayed Romanized Britons to defend themselves as best they could against Teutonic ravagers on the coasts and the wild Celts[1] of the Scottish mountains. The Britons called in the Teutons to beat off the other foe, and (449) these dangerous protectors began to take the land for their own.

Many little Teutonic states were founded by the invaders, and gradually these small units were welded into larger kingdoms, until there appeared seven main Teutonic states: *Kent*, the kingdom of the Jutes; *Sussex, Essex*, and *Wessex* (kingdoms of the South Saxons, East Saxons, and West Saxons); and *East Anglia, Northumbria*, and *Mercia* — kingdoms of Angles, or *English*, who were finally to give their name to the island.

This conquest, unlike that of Gaul and Spain, was very slow. It took the Teutons a century and a half (till about 600) to

[1] *Celt* includes the Highland Scots, the Irish, the Gauls of France, and the native Britons of Britain before the Teutonic conquest. At an earlier period the Celts seem to have covered much of central Europe.

master the *eastern half* of the island. For this there were four reasons. (1) The Angles and Saxons at home were living in petty tribes and therefore could make no great organized attack. (2) *Coming by sea,* they came necessarily in small bands. (3) They were still *pagans:* they spread ruthless destruction and provoked desperate resistance, until, about 600 A.D., Christianity began to win the heathen conquerors.

The conquest slow and thorough

St. Martin's Church, Near Canterbury. — From a photograph. Parts of the building are very old, and may have belonged to a church of the Roman period. At all events, on this site was the first Christian church in Britain used by Augustine and his fellow missionaries, sent out by Pope Gregory. They secured the right to use it through the favor of Queen Bertha, a Frankish princess, who had married the king of Kent. A tomb, said to be Queen Bertha's, is shown in the church.

(4) Britain had been less completely Romanized than the continental provinces were. There was more of forest and marsh, and a less extensive network of Roman roads: hence the natives found it easier to make repeated stands.

Because the conquest was slow, it was thorough. Eastern England became strictly a Teutonic land. Roman institutions, the Roman language, Christianity, even names for the most part, vanished, and the Romanized natives were slain, driven out, or enslaved.

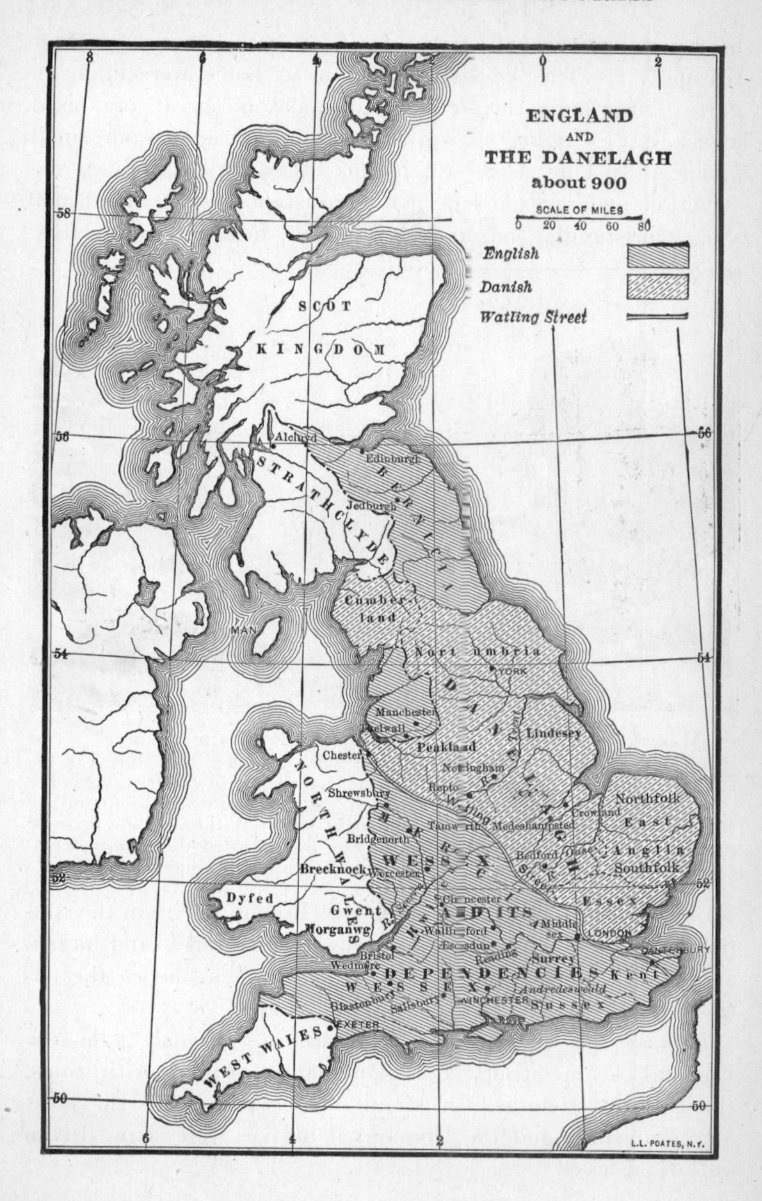
ENGLAND
AND
THE DANELAGH
about 900
SCALE OF MILES
0 20 40 60 80
English
Danish
Watling Street
SCOT KINGDOM
Alcluyd
Edinburgh
STRATHCLYDE
Jedburgh
BERNICIA
Cumberland
MAN
Northumbria
YORK
DANELAGH
Manchester
Thelwall
Peakland
Lindesey
Chester
Nottingham
Repton
NORTH WALES
Shrewsbury
Crowland
Northfolk
East Anglia
Southfolk
Tamworth
Medeshamsted
Bridgenorth
MERCIA
WESSEX
Bedford
Ouse
Watling Street
Brecknock
Worcester
Dyfed
Gwent
Morganwg
Cirencester
Essex
Middlesex
LONDON
Wallingford
Escesdun
Reading
Surrey
Bristol
Wedmore
DEPENDENCIES
CANTERBURY
Kent
WESSEX
Andredesweald
Glastonbury
Salisbury
WINCHESTER
Sussex
EXETER
WEST WALES
L.L. POATES, N.Y.

In the middle of the ninth century *Egbert, king of the West Saxons, brought all the Teutonic parts of the island under his authority*, though he was only head king over jealous tributary kings. Then came the Danish invasions — to shatter this new union, but, in the end, to cement it more firmly. The Danes, who had long harried the coasts, made their first permanent settlement in 850; and, in 871, after a great battle in which the king of Wessex was slain, they became for a time masters of England. The power of Wessex was soon revived however by Alfred the Great (871–901). The Danes were defeated, baptized, and shut off in the northeast, beyond Watling Street (an old Roman road from London to Chester); and all the Teutonic states in South England now willingly accepted the rule of Wessex for protection against the Dane.

The Danes in England

Alfred the Great

Alfred gave the rest of his splendid life to heal the wounds of his kingdom, and, more successfully than Charlemagne, to revive learning in a barbarous age — though at first he found "not one priest" in the kingdom who could understand the church services that he mumbled by rote. His great successors reconquered the Danelaw district, and under Edgar the Peaceful (957–975), his greatgrandson, the island rested in union and prosperity — so that even distant Celtic princes came to Edgar's court to acknowledge his overlordship.

III. FEUDALISM

"*A protest of barbarism against barbarism.*" — TAINE

The anarchy of the ninth century forces Europe into Feudalism

The barbarian invasions of the ninth and tenth centuries did not create a new society in Europe, as those of the fifth century had done; but they did force Europe to take on a new military organization. After Charlemagne, the ninth century on the continent became a time of indescribable horror. The strong robbed the weak, and brigands worked their will in plunder and torture.

But out of this anarchy emerged a new social order. Here and there, and in ever growing numbers, some petty chief —

retired bandit, rude huntsman, or old officer of a king — planted himself firmly on a small domain, fortifying a stockaded house and gathering a troop of fighters under him to protect it. By so doing, he became the protector of others. The neighborhood turned gladly to any strong man as its defender and master. Weaker landlords surrendered ("commended") their lands to him, receiving them back as "*fiefs*." They became his *vassals;* he became their *lord*. The former "free peasants," on the lord's own lands and on the lands of his vassals, saw that they were no longer at the mercy of any chance marauder. They ventured again to plow and sow, and perhaps they were permitted in part to reap. On their part, they cultivated also the lord's crop, and paid him dues for house, for cattle, and for each sale or inheritance. The village became his village; the inhabitants, his *villeins*. Fugitive wretches, too, without the old resident's claim to consideration, gathered on the lord's lands to receive such measure of mercy as he might grant, and usually sank into the class of *serfs* (p. 23), of whom there were already many on all estates.

Entrance to a Feudal Castle. — From Gautier's *La Chevalerie*. The *drawbridge* crossed the *moat*, or ditch, that surrounded a castle. When it was raised, the *portcullis* (whose massive iron teeth can be seen in the doorway) was let fall.

In return for the protection he gave, the lord assumed great privileges, unspeakably obnoxious in later centuries, but in their origin connected with some benefit. The noble slew the wild beast — and came to have the sole right to hunt. As organizer of labor, he forced the villeins to build the mill (*his* mill), the oven, the ferry, the bridge, the highway; then he took toll for the use of each, and later he demolished mills that the villeins wished to build for themselves.

Origin of the feudal privileges of the nobles

Bodiam Castle in England — present condition of a fine medieval structure. Note the water in the moat. The student will find in encyclopedias some interesting history for this castle.

After the Teutonic conquests of the fifth century, most common Teutonic freemen became small farmers. By these changes of the ninth century this free class almost disappeared from France, though it still survived in England.

Finally each district had its body of *mailed horsemen* and its circle of frowning castles. These two features typify the new order — which we call feudalism.

Castles rose at every ford and above each mountain pass and on every hill commanding a fertile plain. At first the

The feudal castle

"castles" were mere wooden blockhouses; but soon they grew into those enormous structures of massive stone, crowned by frowning battlements and inclosing many acres of ground, whose picturesque gray ruins still dot the landscape in Europe.

And the ironclad cavalry

Upon even the early and simple castle, the Norse invader spent his force in vain; and the mailed horsemen kept him from ravaging the open country. The old Frankish infantry had proved too slow to bring to bay the nomad Hungarians on their agile shaggy ponies, or the Danes with their swift boats. But now each castle was ready to pour forth its band of trained men-at-arms (horsemen in mail), either to gather with other bands into an army, or by themselves to cut off stragglers and hold the fords. The raider's day was over — but meanwhile the old Teutonic militia, in which every freeman had his place, had given way to an ironclad cavalry, the resistless weapon of a new feudal aristocracy, which could ride down foot-soldiers (*infantry*) at will — till the invention of gunpowder, centuries later, helped again to make fighting men equal.

KNIGHT IN PLATE ARMOR, visor up. — From Lacroix, *Vie Militaire*. Plate armor came in only about 1300, succeeding a lighter armor of chain mail.

Feudal "decentralization"

In government, feudalism was extreme decentralization. Each petty district was practically independent of every other district. The king had been expected to protect every corner of his realm. Actually he had protected only some central district; but under feudalism each little chieftain proved able to protect his small corner, when he had seized the king's powers there. His territory was a little state. The great nobles coined money and made war like very kings. Indeed *a vassal owed allegiance to his overlords* two or more grades above him *only through the one overlord just above him*. He must follow his immediate lord to war against them and even against his king.

This decentralization was the result not only of military needs but also of economic[1] needs — of the lack of money and the lack of roads. The rich man's wealth was all in land; and he could make his land pay him only by renting it out for services or for produce. "Nobles" paid him for parts of it by fighting for him. Workers paid him for other parts by raising and harvesting his crops and by giving him part of their

Economic causes of feudalism

AN ACT OF HOMAGE. — From a twelfth century manuscript.

own. A man without land was glad to pay for the use of some in one way or the other.

Feudal land-holding

In theory, *the holder of any piece of land was a tenant of some higher landlord.* The king was the supreme landlord. He let out most of the land of the kingdom, on terms of military service, to great vassals who swore fealty to him. Each of these parceled out most of what he received, on like terms, to smaller vassals; and so on, perhaps through six or seven steps, until the smallest division was reached that could support a mailed horseman for the noble's life of fighting.

[1] *Economics* refers to wealth, as *politics* does to government.

Lords and vassals

In practice, there was no such regularity. The various grades were interlocked in the most confusing way. Except for the smallest knights, all landlords of the fighting class were "suzerains" (liege lords); and, except perhaps the king, all were vassals. There was no great social distinction between lord and vassals. They lived on terms of familiarity and mutual respect. The "vassal" was always a "noble," and his service was always "honorable," — never to be confounded with the "ignoble" service paid by serfs and villeins.

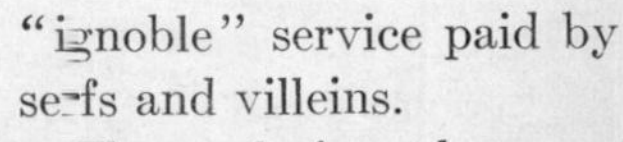

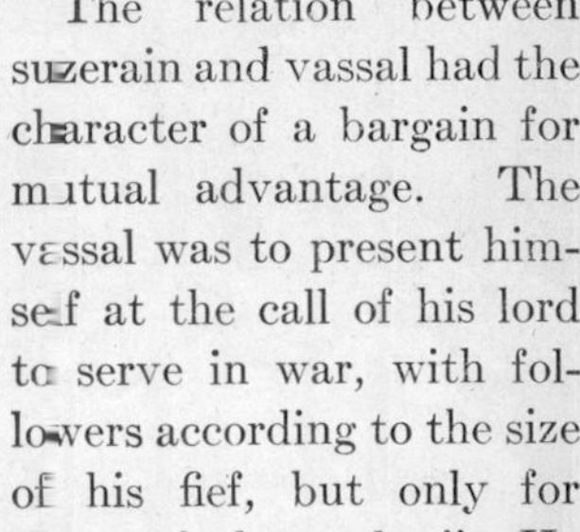

A Baron's Court. — From a sixteenth century woodcut.

The relation between suzerain and vassal had the character of a bargain for mutual advantage. The vassal was to present himself at the call of his lord to serve in war, with followers according to the size of his fief, but only for short terms and usually not to go "out of the realm." He must also serve in the lord's "court" twice or thrice a year, to advise in matters of policy and to give judgment in disputes between vassals. He did not pay "taxes," in our sense, but on frequent occasions he did have to make to the lord certain financial contributions — "reliefs" and "aids." The lord, on his part, was bound to defend his vassal, to treat him justly, and to see that he found just treatment from his co-vassals.

Private war

Feudal theory, then, paid elaborate regard to rights; but *feudal practice was mainly a matter of force.* There was no adequate machinery for obtaining justice: it was not easy to enforce the decisions of the crude courts against a noble offender who chose to resist. War, too, was thought the most honorable and perhaps the most religious way to settle disputes. Like the trial by combat, it was considered an appeal to the judgment of God. Naturally, "private wars," between noble and noble, became a chief evil of the age. They hindered the growth of industry, and commonly they hurt neutral parties quite as much as they hurt belligerents. There was little actual suffering by the warring nobles, and very little heroism. Indeed, there was little actual fighting. The weaker party usually shut itself up in its castle. The stronger side ravaged the villages in the neighborhood, driving off the cattle and perhaps torturing the peasants for their small hidden treasures, and outraging the women.

AN ANCIENT MANOR HOUSE, Melichope, England. — From Wright's *Homes of Other Days*.

The feudal manor

Clergy and *nobles*, praying class and fighting class, were supported by a vastly larger number of "ignoble" *workers*, who were usually referred to only as other live stock might be mentioned. Each noble had to keep some of his land for the support of his own household and for other revenue. This "domain" land was cultivated by the lord's serfs and villeins, under direction of a bailiff, or steward. The peasant workers did not live in scattered farmhouses, each on its own field: they were grouped in little villages of twenty or fifty dwellings, as in Europe to-day. *Such a village, with its adjoining "fields," was a "manor."*

INTERIOR VIEW OF THE WINDOW SHOWN IN MELICHOPE MANOR HOUSE. The wall was so deep that the stairway was cut into it.

Each manor had its church, at a little distance, and usually its manor house — the lord's castle on a hill above the other dwellings, or maybe a house only a trifle better than the homes of the villeins, used by the lord's steward. At one end of the street stood the lord's smithy; and near by, on some convenient stream, was the lord's mill.

Serfs and villeins

As in the last Roman days, the *serf* was bound to the soil by law: he could not leave it, but neither could he be sold apart from it. He had his own bit of ground to cultivate, at such times as the lord's bailiff did not call him to labor on the lord's land. Usually the bailiff summoned the serfs in turn, each for two or for three days each week; but in harvest or haying he might keep them all busy, to the ruin of their own little crops. If the serf did get a crop, he had to pay a large part of it for the use of his land. He paid also a multitude of other dues and fines — sometimes in money, but usually "in kind," — eggs, a goose, a cock, a calf, a portion of grain.

VILLEINS RECEIVING DIRECTIONS. — From a miniature in a fifteenth century manuscript.

The *villein* was a step higher. He was "free" in person. That is, he could leave his land and change lords at will; but he had to have *some* lord. The landless and masterless man was an outlaw, at the mercy of any lord. In profits from labor and in manner of life, there was little to choose between serf and villein.

The peasant homes,[1] serf's or villein's, were low, filthy,

[1] The most graphic treatments of peasant life are in Jessopp's *Friars*, 87–112; Jenks' *Edward Plantagenet*, 46–52; and in Cheyney's *Industrial and Social History of England*, 31–52.

Homes of the peasants

earth-floored, straw-thatched, one-room hovels of wood and sticks plastered together with mud. There was no chimney except a hole in the roof, and usually no other opening (no window) except the door. These homes straggled along either side of an irregular lane, where poultry, pigs, and children played together in the dirt. Behind each house was its weedy garden patch and its low stable and barn. These last were often under the same roof as the living room of the family, — as is still true sometimes in parts of Germany.

A REAPER'S CART GOING UPHILL. — After Jusserand's *English Wayfaring Life;* from a fourteenth century manuscript. The force of men and horses indicates the nature of the roads. The steepness of the hill is, of course, exaggerated, so as to fit the picture to the space in the manuscript.

The house, small as it was, was not cluttered with furniture. A handmill for grinding meal, or at least a stone mortar in which to crush grain, a pot and kettle, possibly a feather bed, one or two rude benches, and a few tools for the peasant's work, made up the contents of even the well-to-do homes.

Cultivation of the land in common

Farming was very crude. *The plowland was divided into three great "fields."* These were unfenced, and lay about the village at any convenient spots. One field was sown to wheat (in the fall); one to rye or barley (in the spring); and the third lay fallow, to recuperate. The next year this third field would be the wheat land, while the old wheat field would raise the barley, and so on. This primitive "rotation of crops" kept a third of the land idle.

Every "field" was divided into a great number of narrow strips, each as nearly as possible a "furrow-long," and one, two, or four rods wide, so that each contained from a quarter of an acre to an acre. Usually the strips were separated by "balks," or ridges of turf. A peasant's holding was about thirty acres, ten acres in each "field"; and his share in each lay not in one piece, but in fifteen or thirty scattered strips.

PEASANTS' MAY DANCE. — From a miniature in the Bibliothèque Nationale in Paris The dress at least is idealized.

This kind of holding compelled a "common" cultivation. That is, each man must sow what his neighbor sowed; and as a rule, each could sow, till, and harvest only when his neighbors did. Serfs were not intelligent or willing workers, and even the lord's stewards did not know how to get good returns from the land. Threefold the seed, or six bushels of wheat to the acre, was a good crop in the thirteenth century.

Small variety in food

Farm animals were small. The wooden plow required eight oxen, and then it did hardly more than scratch the surface of the ground. Carts were few and cumbrous. There was little or no cultivation of root foods. Potatoes, of course, were unknown. Sometimes a few turnips and cabbages and carrots, rather uneatable varieties probably, were grown in garden plots behind the houses. Beer was brewed from the barley.

Well-to-do peasants had a hive of bees in the garden plot. Honey was the chief luxury of the poor: sugar was still unknown in Europe.

The most important crop was the wild hay, upon which the cattle had to be fed during the winter. Meadowland was twice as valuable as plowland. The meadow was fenced for the hay harvest, but was afterward thrown open for pasture. Usually

FALCONRY. — From a medieval manuscript reproduced by Lacroix. A falconer, to capture and train young hawks to bring game to the master, was among the most trusted under-officials of each castle.

there were other more distant but extensive pasture and wood lands, where lord and villagers fattened their cattle and swine.

It was difficult to carry enough animals through the winter for the necessary farm work and breeding; so those to be used for food were killed in the fall and salted down. The large use of salt meat and the little variety in food caused loathsome diseases.

Life in the manor

Each village was a world by itself. Even the different villages of the same lord had little intercourse with one another. The lord's bailiff secured from some distant market the three outside products needed, — salt, millstones, and iron for the plowshares and for other tools. Except for this, a village was hardly touched by the outside world — unless a war desolated it, or a royal procession chanced to pass through it.

This shut-in life seems to us cheerless and degrading and often indescribably ferocious and indecent. Pictures in manuscripts of the time, however, show that it had occasional

THE EXERCISE OF THE QUINTAIN. — This shows an important part of the schooling of noble children. The boys ride, by turns, at the wooden figure. If the rider strikes the shield squarely in the center, it is well. If he hits only a glancing blow, the wooden figure swings on its foot and whacks him with its club as he passes.

festivities; and at least it was a step up from the slavery of earlier times.

Life in the castle

The noble classes lived a life hardly more attractive to us. They dwelt in gloomy fortresses over dark dungeons where prisoners rotted. They had fighting for business, and hunting with hound and hawk, and playing at fighting (in tournament and joust), for pleasures. The ladies busied themselves over tapestries and embroideries, in the chambers. Gay pages flitted through the halls, or played at chess in the deep windows. And in the courtyard lounged gruff men-at-arms, ready with blind obedience to follow the lord of the castle on any foray or even in an attack upon their king.

Hunting

The noble hunted for food, quite as much as for sport, and he did not suffer from lack of fresh meat. The game in forest and stream was his: for a common man to kill deer or hare or wild duck or trout, was to lose hand or eyes or life.

Feasting and story telling

Feasting filled a large part of the noble's life. Meals were served in the great hall of the castle, and were the social hours of the day. Tables were set out on movable trestles, and the household, visitors, and dependents gathered about them on seats and benches with nice respect for rank, — the master and his noblest guests at the head, on a raised platform, or "dais," and the lowest servants toward the bottom of the long line. A profusion of food in many courses, especially at the midday "dinner," was carried in from the kitchen across the open courtyard. Peacocks, swans, whole boars, or at least boar heads, were among the favorite roasts; and huge venison "pies" were a common dish. Mother Goose's "four and twenty blackbirds" had real models in many a medieval pasty, which, when opened, let live birds escape, to be hunted down among the rafters of the hall by falcons.

A Court Fool. — After a medieval miniature in brilliant colors. Many great lords kept such jesters.

At each guest's place was a knife, to cut slices from the roasts within his reach, and a spoon for broths, but no fork or napkin or plate. Each one dipped his hand into the pasties, carrying the dripping food directly to his mouth. Loaves of bread were crumbled up and rolled between the hand to wipe off the surplus gravy, and then thrown to the dogs under the tables; and between courses, servants passed basins of water and towels. The food was washed down with huge draughts of wine, usually diluted with water. Intervals between courses were filled with story-telling and song, or by rude jokes from the lord's "fool," or perhaps traveling jugglers were brought in to entertain the company.

JUGGLERS. — From a thirteenth century manuscript.

IV. THE CHURCH IN THE FEUDAL AGE

The church also a government

The church in the feudal age was not only a religious organization: it was *also a government*. Its officers exercised many powers that have now been handed over to civil[1] officers. Public order depended upon it almost as completely as did private morals. With its spiritual thunders and the threat of its curse, it often protected the widow and orphan, and others in danger of oppression, from brutal barons who had respect for no earthly power.

The priest

All Christendom was made up of *parishes*, — the smallest church units. Commonly, a parish was a farming village (a manor) or a part of a town. At its head was a *priest*, who, in large city parishes, was assisted by deacons to look after the poor.

The bishop

A group of parishes made up the *diocese* of a *bishop*. Nearly every town of any consequence in the twelfth century was a bishop's seat, and so gained the name *city*. The bishop was the mainspring in church government. He was revered as the successor of the apostles, and was subject only to the

[1] *Civil* is used very commonly in contrast to *ecclesiastical*.

guidance of the pope, who was successor to the chief of the apostles. Originally, the bishop's special duty had been to oversee the parish priests; but, with the growth of the church, he had come to have other functions. He was a great feudal landlord, owing military service to one or more suzerains, and holding power over many temporal vassals. He had charge of extensive church property in his diocese, and of the collection of church revenues. And he looked after the enforcement of the laws of the church. This "canon law" had grown into a complex system. To administer justice under it, each bishop held a court, made up of trained churchmen, over which he presided. This court had jurisdiction not merely over matters pertaining to the church: it tried any case that involved a clergyman or any one else under the special protection of the church.

Bishops' courts

To help in these duties, the bishop had a body of assistant clergy called *canons*. On the death of the bishop, this body (the "cathedral chapter") chose his successor, — subject perhaps to the approval of some king or other temporal ruler.

Benefit of clergy

This right of the clergy to be tried in clerical courts was known as "benefit of clergy." The practice had its good side. Ordinary courts and ordinary law partook of the violent and ferocious life of the age. Trials were rude and ghastly punishments were inflicted for trivial offenses, — often, no doubt, upon the innocent. It was a gain when the peaceful and moral part of society secured the right to trial in more intelligent courts and by more civilized codes. Moreover, in the Middle Ages, *all* corporations, even trade gilds, very commonly had courts with considerable power of jurisdiction over their own members. It was natural, therefore, for the church to have like powers over its clergy.

But the church law was too mild to deal with serious crimes. Its advantages tempted men to "take Holy Orders," until, besides the preaching clergy and the monks, the land swarmed with "clerics" who were really only lawyers, secretaries, scholars, teachers, or mere adventurers. Some of these, by their crimes, brought disgrace upon the church and danger to the state.

The archbishop

A number of dioceses made up a province, — which was usually one of the old divisions of that name under the Roman Empire. Over each province, seated in its most important city, was an archbishop, or metropolitan. The archbishop was a bishop also of one diocese, and he had a general supervision, but not a very definite one, over the other bishops of the province. His court, too, heard appeals from theirs.

The pope

At the head of all this church hierarchy stood the *pope*, the spiritual monarch of Christendom. He was *supreme lawgiver, supreme judge, supreme executive.* He issued new laws in the form of *bulls* (so-called from the gold seal, or *bulla,* on the documents), and he set aside old laws by his *dispensations,* — as when it seemed best to him to permit cousins to marry (a thing forbidden by the canon law). His court heard appeals from the courts of bishop and archbishop, and likewise from many of the temporal courts of Christendom. Now and then he set aside appointments of bishops and other clergy, and himself filled the vacancies. At times he also sent *legates* into different countries, to represent his authority directly. A legate could revoke the judgment of a bishop's court, remove bishops, and haughtily command obedience from kings, — quite as Shakspere pictures in his *King John.*

College of cardinals

For aid in his high office, the pope gathered about him a "college[1] of cardinals." At first this body comprised only seven bishops of Rome and its vicinity; but it grew finally to include great churchmen in all countries.

Excommunication

To compel obedience, bishops and pope had two mighty weapons — excommunication and interdict. An excommunicated man was shut out from all religious communion. He could attend no church service, receive no sacrament, and at death, if still unforgiven, his body could not receive Christian burial. Excommunication was also a boycott for all social

[1] "College," in this sense, means merely a "collection" of people.

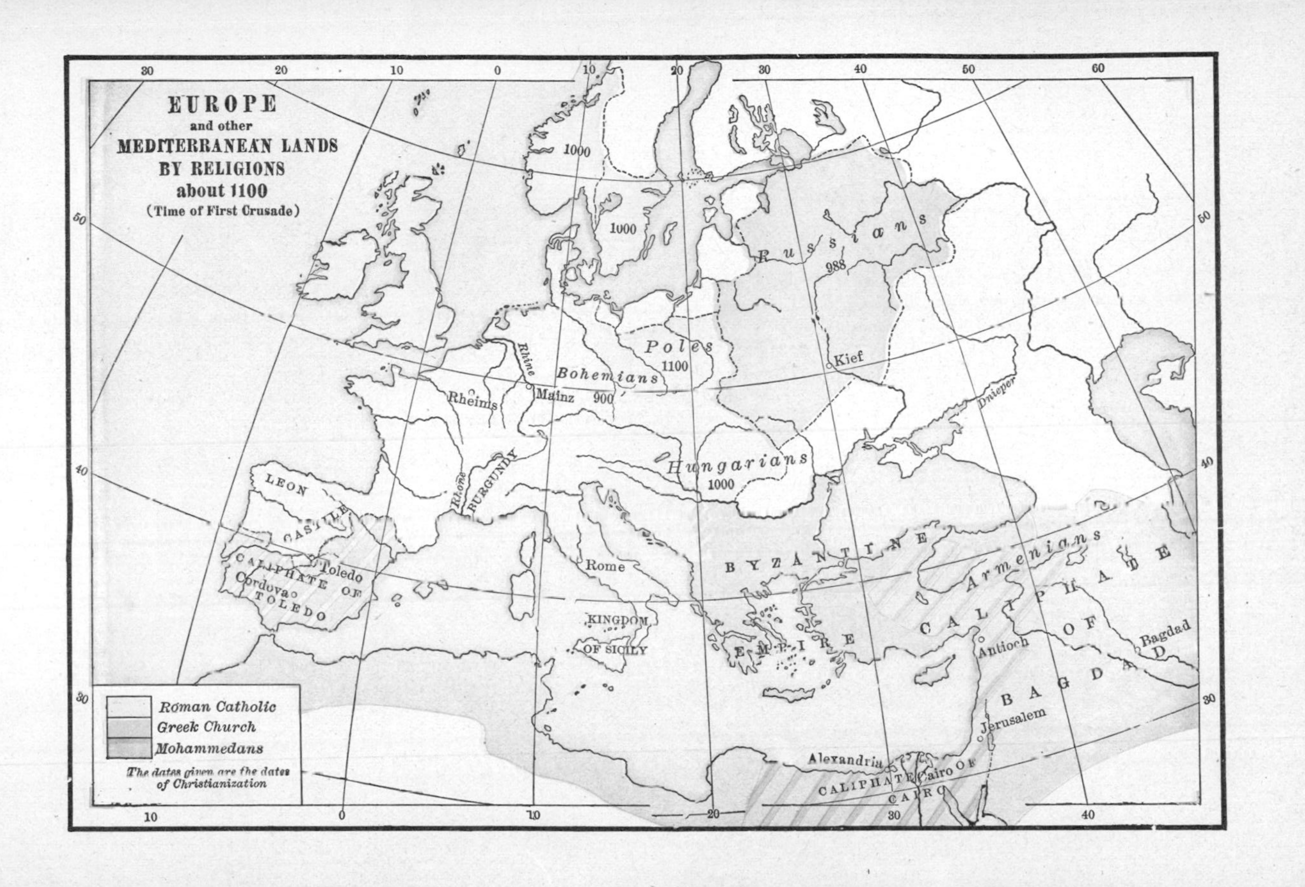
EUROPE
and other
MEDITERRANEAN LANDS
BY RELIGIONS
about 1100
(Time of First Crusade)
Russians
988
Kief
Dnieper
Poles
1100
Bohemians
900
Mainz
Rhine
Rheims
1000
1000
Hungarians
1000
BURGUNDY
Rhone
LEON
CASTILE
Toledo
CALIPHATE OF
Cordova
TOLEDO
Rome
KINGDOM
OF SICILY
BYZANTINE
EMPIRE
Armenians
CALIPHATE OF BAGDAD
Antioch
Bagdad
Jerusalem
Alexandria
Cairo
CALIPHATE OF CAIRO
Roman Catholic
Greek Church
Mohammedans
The dates given are the dates
of Christianization

and business relations. If obeyed by the community, it cut a man off absolutely from all communication with his fellows, and made him an outlaw. No one might speak to him or give him food or shelter, under danger of similar penalty, and his very presence was shunned like the pestilence.

Interdict

What excommunication was to the individual, the interdict was to a district or a nation. Churches were closed, and no religious ceremonies were permitted, except the rites of baptism and of extreme unction. No marriage could be performed, and there could be no burial in consecrated ground. "The dead were left unburied, and the living were unblessed."

Thus the church was a vast centralized monarchy, with its regular officers, its laws and legislatures and judges, its taxes, its terrible punishments — and its promise of eternal reward.

The democracy of the church

And yet this government was more democratic in spirit than feudal society was. Men of humblest birth often rose to its loftiest offices. Gregory VII, who set his foot upon the neck of the mightiest king in Europe, was the son of a poor peasant. The church was the only part of society in the Middle Ages where study and intellectual ability could lift a poor boy to power — and so it was recruited by the best minds.

The priest and the daily life of the village

Of all this mighty organization, the village priest brought the church closest home to the mass of the people. The great ecclesiastics — bishops, archbishops, and abbots — were often from the noble class by birth, and in any case they always became part of the aristocracy. But the rural priest was commonly a peasant in origin, and he often remained essentially a peasant in his life, — marrying in the village (until the eleventh century) and working in the fields with his neighbors. He was a peasant with a somewhat better income than his fellows, with a little learning, a revered position, and with great power for good. He christened, absolved, married, and buried his parishioners, looked after their bodily welfare so far as he knew how, comforted the heart-sore and wretched, and taught all, by word and example, to hold fast to right living.

The church building was also the social center of the parish. Near it, on Sunday, between the sacred services, the people found their chief recreation in sports and games. And from its steps the priest gave to them what news they received from the outside world, reading aloud there, too, any rare letter that some adventurous wanderer might be able to get written for him by some stranger-priest.

The friars and town life

From time to time new organs developed within the church to meet new needs. In the twelfth century, when, as we shall see, towns began to grow up, these did not fit into the old organization of the church. Neither parish priests nor monks took care of the religious needs of the new, crowded populations. The poorer inhabitants were miserable in body, too, beyond all words, — fever and plague stricken, perishing of want and filth and wretchedness such as no modern city knows. But early in the thirteenth century, these conditions, together with the spread of heretical movements, called forth a general religious revival, with the rise of two new religious orders — *the Franciscan and the Dominican brotherhoods.*

These "begging friars" went forth two and two, to the poor and the outcasts, living from day to day in the midst of noisome wretchedness, to act as healers and preachers. They nursed lepers, ministered to the poor, and with short, homely speech, preached to all the love of Christ and the call to turn from sin. They were *missionary* monks.

V. ENGLAND IN THE FEUDAL AGE

Local self-government and the idea of representation in *Saxon* England

The splendid story of England for the thousand years from Alfred the Great to the present day is also, most of it, the story of the foundations of American liberty. And so, even in this brief "survey," that story is told more fully than other topics are.

Long before the year 1000 *the Saxons* in England had *learned to work* many forms of *local* self-government — to manage many of their own affairs at their own doors, not only in village (manor) "courts," but also in courts (assemblies) of the larger units, the hundreds and shires (counties). Moreover, they *had become familiar* with the practice of sending a sort of *representative* from the village to these larger assemblies — since all men could not attend these in person.

Saxon feudalism

True, after the year 900 an irregular Saxon feudalism had been growing up; and these local "courts" had fallen largely under the control of neighboring landlords. Still enough activity among the people themselves survived so that these assemblies, with their representative principle, were to prove the cradle of later English and American liberty.

PLOWING. — From an Anglo-Saxon manuscript in the British Museum.

The Norman Conquest, 1066

In 1066 came the Norman Conquest. In long succession in earlier times, conquering Briton, Roman, Saxon, Dane, had brought in each his peculiar contributions. Now for the last time in history a host of conquering invaders established themselves in the island. A century and a half before, Norse pirates had settled in a province of northern France. In that district of Normandy, they had quickly become leaders in Frankish "civilization," and now they transplanted it among the ruder Saxons of England, along with much new blood and new elements in language.

A more efficient *central* government

For our purpose here, the most important Norman contribution was his contribution in government. Since the time of Alfred, the chief dangers to England had been (1) a possible splitting apart of Danish north and Saxon south, and (2) the growth of feudal anarchy. The Norman crushed the old north and south into one, and built up a central government strong enough to control the feudal nobles and to prevent them from dividing the kingly power among themselves.

Local institutions, in the main, remained Saxon, but the central government gained a new efficiency from the Norman genius for organization.

A thousand-year struggle for liberty

At the same time, the Norman kings were not supreme enough to become absolute despots. This was chiefly because, through dread of the new royal power, conquering Norman noble and conquered Saxon people drew together quickly into *an English nation — the first true nation of Europe.* Then, in centuries of slow, determined progress, this new nation won constitutional liberty.

> "Lance and torch and tumult, steel and gray-goose wing,
> Wrenched it, inch and ell and all, slowly from the king."

Battle of Hastings. — From the Bayeux Tapestry. The Bayeux Tapestry is a linen band 230 feet long and 20 inches wide, embroidered in colored worsteds, with 72 scenes illustrating the Norman Conquest. It was a contemporary work. The scene given here pertains to the close of the battle. Harold, the Saxon king, supported by his chosen hus-carles, is making the final stand, beneath the Dragon standard against the Norman horse.

And not merely by fighting in the field was this liberty won, but, even more, by countless almost unrecorded martyrdoms of heroic and often nameless men, on the scaffold, in the dungeon, or, harder still, in broken lives and ruined homes. Thus did Englishmen, at a great price, work out, first of all peoples for a large territory, the union of a strong central government and of free institutions.

The Conquest drew isolated England back into the thick of continental politics. *Henry II* (1154–1189) was the most

Reforms of Henry II in the law courts

powerful monarch of Europe, ruling not only England but more than half France as well — as a nominal vassal of the French king. Still all the really important results of his long and busy reign came in England. Preëminent stands out the organization

A NORMAN DOOR IN CANTERBURY CATHEDRAL. — Note the massive round arch and the simple but effective ornament.

of the English courts of justice, with *circuit* judges to spread a "common" law throughout the entire realm — in place of the varying local customs found in feudal courts in the continental countries. At this same time came the development

Circuit judges and the Common Law

of our grand jury and also of our trial jury. Henry's reforms, as completed a century later by the great Edward, gave us the English judicial system of the present day in almost every particular.

Between the great Henry and the even greater Edward came three weak, would-be tyrants — Richard, John, and the third Henry. The misrule of John resulted in Magna Carta; that of Henry, in the first true Parliament.

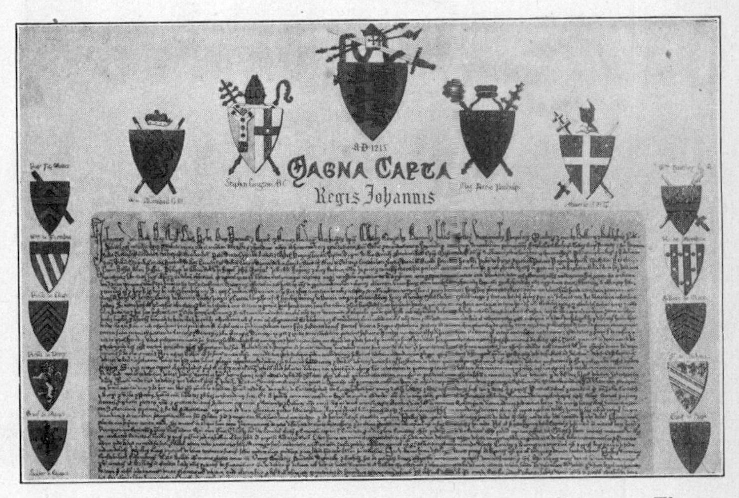

FACSIMILE (REDUCED) OF THE OPENING OF MAGNA CARTA. — The escutcheons in the margin are later embellishments. They are supposed to be the coats of arms of barons who signed as witnesses.

Magna Carta, 1215

1. In *1215*, in a grassy meadow of the Thames called *Runnymede*, the tyrant John, backed only by a few mercenaries and confronted by a people in arms, found himself forced to sign the Great Charter, "the first great document in the Bible of English Liberties."

In the main, the charter merely restated ancient liberties; but the closing provision expressly sanctioned rebellion against a king who should refuse to obey it. That is, *it set the law of the land above the king's will.* True, in some other countries during the Middle Ages, the great vassals extorted charters of liberties *for themselves* from their kings. But the peculiar features of this Charter are: (1) the barons promised to their dependents the same rights they demanded for themselves from the king; and (2) special provisions looked after the welfare of townsmen and even of villeins. The wording, necessarily, belongs to a feudal age; but, as a new society and new needs grew up, men read new meanings into the old language and made it fit the new age. In the next two centuries, English kings were obliged to "confirm" it thirty-eight times; and its principles, and some of its wording, have passed into the constitution and laws of every American state.

And American liberty

The Charter defined precisely the "aids" to which suzerains were entitled, — and so put an end to extortion. It declared that the king could raise no scutage[1] or other unusual "aid" from his vassals without the consent of the Great Council, — and since all vassals of the king had a right to attend this Council, this provision established the principle, No taxation without the consent of the taxed. It declared an accused man entitled to speedy trial, — and so laid the foundation for later laws of "habeas corpus." It affirmed that no villein, by any fine, should lose his oxen or plow, and so foreshadowed our modern laws providing that legal suits shall not take from a man his home or his tools.

The beginnings of Parliament

2. Henry II and Edward I were the two great "lawgivers" among the English kings. But Henry carried his many reforms, not by royal decrees, but by a series of "assizes" (codes) drawn up by the Great Council; and Edward carried his in an even longer series of "statutes" enacted by a new national legislature which we call Parliament.

Some sort of "Assembly" has always made part of the English government. Under the Saxon kings, the *Witan* (or meeting of Wisemen) sanctioned codes of laws and even deposed and elected kings. It consisted of large landowners and officials and the higher clergy, with now and then some mingling of more

[1] A sort of war tax recently introduced in the place of military service.

democratic elements, and it was far more powerful than the Frankish Mayfield.

After the Conquest, the Witan gave way to the *Great Council* of the Norman kings. This was a feudal gathering — made up of lords and bishops, resembling the Witan, but more aristocratic, and less powerful. A king was supposed to rule "with the advice and consent" of his Council; but in practice that body was merely the king's mouthpiece until Henry II raised it to real importance.

Magna Carta prescribed just how the Council should be called together. All who held land directly of the king ("tenants-in-chief," or "barons") were entitled to be present, but only the "great barons" ever came. According to the Charter, thereafter the great barons were to be summoned *individually* by letter, and the numerous smaller barons *by a general notice* read by the sheriffs in the court of each county.

Still the smaller barons failed to assemble; and in the troubles of the reign of Henry III, on two or three occasions, the sheriffs had been directed to see to it that each county *sent* knights to the gathering. *Thus a representative element was introduced into the National Assembly.*

This was a thoroughly natural step for *Englishmen* to take. The principle of representative government was no way new to them. It had taken root long before in *local* institutions. The "four men" of each township present in court of hundred or shire (p. 76) spoke for all their township. The sworn "jurors" of a shire who gave testimony in compiling Domesday Book under William I, or who "presented" offenders for trial under Henry II, spoke for the whole shire. *England was familiar with the practice of selecting certain men from a community to speak for the community as a whole.* The same principle was now applied in a larger, central gathering, for all England.

Then in 1265 the glorious rebel, *Simon of Montfort,* gave us a real "Parliament." He had been leading the people

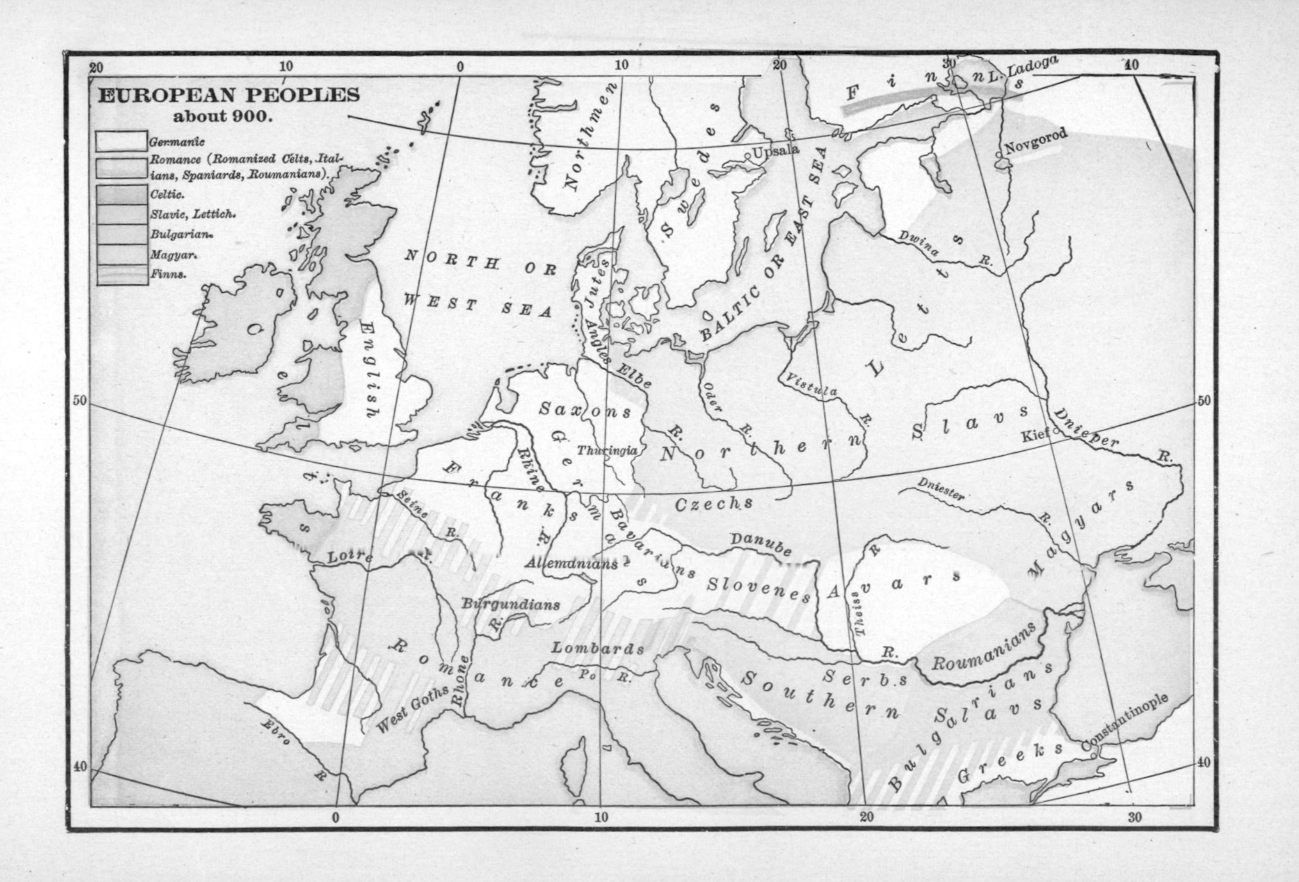
EUROPEAN PEOPLES
about 900.
Germanic
Romance (Romanized Celts, Italians, Spaniards, Roumanians).
Celtic.
Slavic, Lettich.
Bulgarian.
Magyar.
Finns.
Finns
L. Ladoga
Novgorod
Northmen
Swedes
Upsala
BALTIC OR EAST SEA
NORTH OR WEST SEA
Dwina R.
Letts
Celts
English
Jutes
Angles
Elbe
Saxons
Germans
Thuringia
Oder R.
Vistula R.
Northern Slavs
Kief
Dnieper R.
Dniester R.
Magyars
Franks
Rhine R.
Seine R.
Loire
Czechs
Bavarians
Allemanians
Danube
Slovenes
Avars
Theiss R.
Burgundians
Rhone
Romance
West Goths
Lombards
Po R.
Ebro R.
Roumanians
Serbs
Southern Slavs
Bulgarians
Greeks
Constantinople

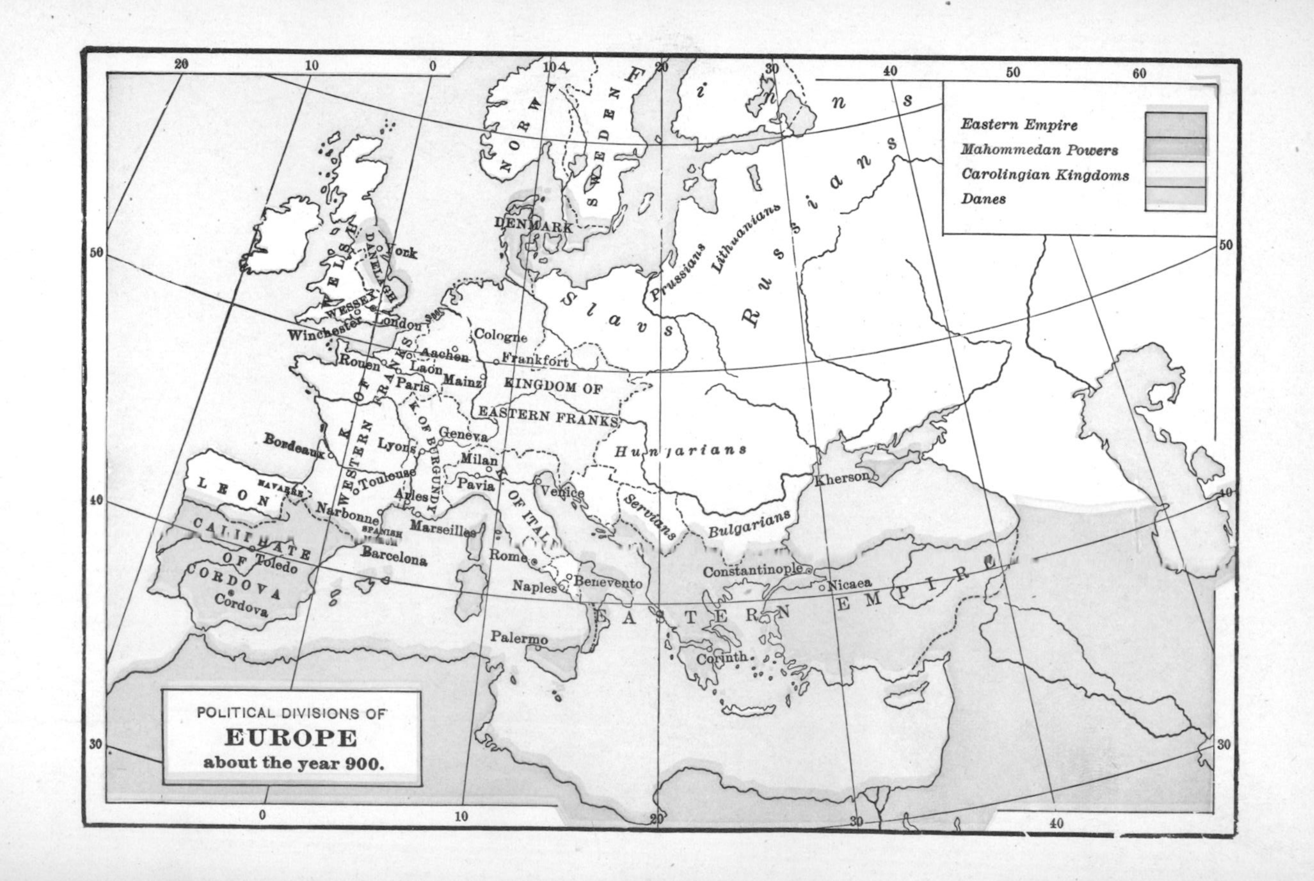

Eastern Empire
Mahommedan Powers
Carolingian Kingdoms
Danes
NORWAY
SWEDEN
Finns
Russians
DENMARK
Prussians
Lithuanians
Slavs
WELSH
DANELAGH
WESSEX
York
London
Winchester
Cologne
Aachen
Frankfort
Rouen
Laon
Paris
Mainz
KINGDOM OF EASTERN FRANKS
WESTERN K. OF FRANKS
K. OF BURGUNDY
Geneva
Lyons
Bordeaux
Hungarians
Milan
Toulouse
Pavia
K. OF ITALY
Venice
Kherson
LEON
NAVARRE
Arles
Narbonne
SPANISH MARCH
Marseilles
Servians
Bulgarians
CALIPHATE OF CORDOVA
Toledo
Barcelona
Rome
Constantinople
Nicaea
Cordova
Naples
Benevento
EASTERN EMPIRE
Palermo
Corinth
POLITICAL DIVISIONS OF
EUROPE
about the year 900.

The Parliaments of 1265 and 1295

against the weak, ill-ruling king, and had made him prisoner, and now he called a national assembly to settle the government. This time not only was each shire invited to send two knights, but each borough (town) to send two burgesses, to sit with the usual lords. Simon wanted the moral support of the nation, to be given by an assembly representing all classes. *The "Great Council of royal vassals" was replaced by a "Parliament" representing the people* of England. Then, *in 1295*, after some variations, *Edward adopted this model of Simon's;* and for the first time in history representative government was firmly established for a nation.

The Hall of Stoke Manor House, a very modest "castle" of the thirteenth century in England. — From Wright's *Homes of Other Days.*

The two "Houses"

Half a century later, Parliament divided into *two* Houses. *Edward's "Model Parliament"* of 1295, like Simon's, *contained* the "*three estates*"[1] — clergy, nobles, and burgesses. The greater nobles and the greater clergy had *personal* summons; the other classes were represented by delegates, — the smaller landholders by the elected "knights of the shire," the towns by their chosen burgesses, and the lower clergy by elected representatives, one for each district.

At first all sat together. Had this continued, the townsmen would never have secured much voice: they would have been frightened and overawed by the nobles. The result would have been about as bad if the three estates had come to sit

[1] "Estate," so used, means a class of people with distinct duties and privileges.

separately, as they did in France and Spain. With so many distinct orders, an able king could easily have played off one against the other. But England followed a different course. The *inferior* clergy, very happily, soon refused to attend Parliament. The *great* spiritual lords (bishops and abbots), with personal summons, were not very numerous by themselves, and so they sat with the great lay lords. Thus, when the different orders

ENGLISH FAMILY DINNER. — From a fourteenth century manuscript. Note the dogs, the musicians, and the barefooted monk, at whom the jester is directing some witticism.

began to sit apart, the great peers, lay and spiritual, who were summoned by individual letters, made a "House of Lords," while the representative elements — knights of the shire and burgesses, who had been accustomed to act together in shire courts — came together, in the national assembly, as the "House of Commons."

The three estates faded into two; and even these two were not distinct. For in England, unlike the case upon the continent, only the oldest son of a lord succeeded to his father's title and

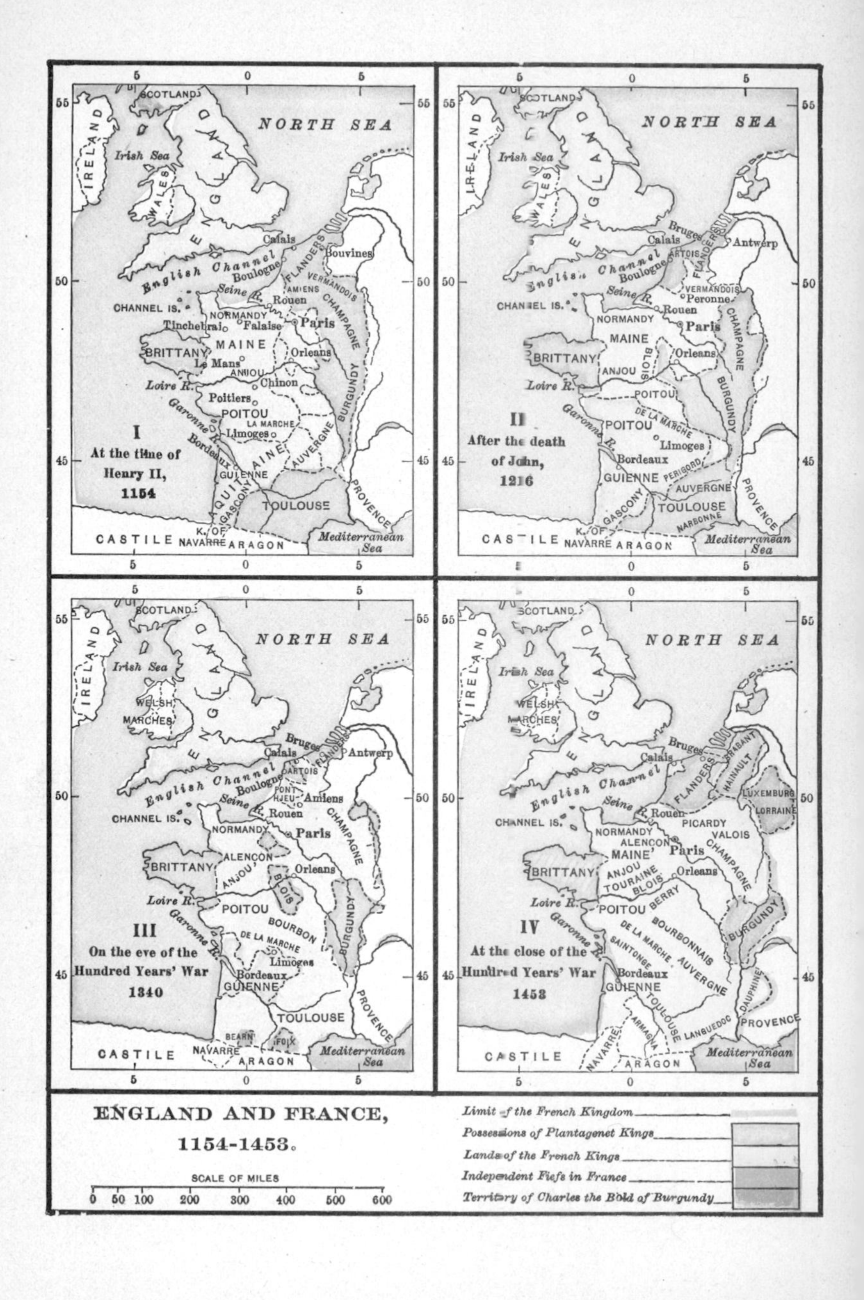

I
At the time of
Henry II,
1154
II
After the death
of John,
1216
III
On the eve of the
Hundred Years' War
1340
IV
At the close of the
Hundred Years' War
1453
NORTH SEA
English Channel
Irish Sea
Mediterranean Sea
SCOTLAND
IRELAND
ENGLAND
WALES
CASTILE
ARAGON
TOULOUSE
BRITTANY
NORMANDY
MAINE
PARIS
ENGLAND AND FRANCE,
1154-1453.
SCALE OF MILES
0 50 100 200 300 400 500 600
Limit of the French Kingdom
Possessions of Plantagenet Kings
Lands of the French Kings
Independent Fiefs in France
Territory of Charles the Bold of Burgundy

nobility, and to the right to a personal summons to the House of Lords. The younger sons — and even the oldest son during his father's life — belonged in the gentry (gentleman) class, and at most were "knights of the shire." As such, oftentimes, the son or the brother of an earl sat for his county in the House of Commons beside the shopkeeper from the town. *The gentry in the Commons formed a link to bind Lords and Commons together.*

The "gentry" a link between "Lords" and "Commons"

VI. OTHER LANDS IN THE FEUDAL AGE

France in the feudal age

In 987 in France the degenerate Carolingian[1] line gave way to Hugh Capet, founder of the long line of *Capetian* kings. Hugh Capet found France broken into feudal fragments. These, in the next three centuries, he and his descendants welded into a new French nation. *It was not the people* here who fused themselves into a nation in a long struggle against royal despotism, as in England: *it was the kings who made the French nation,* in a long struggle against feudal anarchy within and foreign conquest from without.

JUGGLERS IN THE SWORD DANCE.—From a thirteenth century manuscript.

Growth of the king's territory

Philip Augustus (1180–1223) at the opening of his reign ruled directly only one twelfth of modern France — only one sixth as much of it as was then ruled by Henry II of England — and held not one seaport. At the close of his reign Philip ruled directly two thirds of France. The consolidation of the realm was mainly completed by his grandson, *Louis IX* (St. Louis), and by Louis' grandson, *Philip the Fair* (1285–1314).

Growth of royal power

And as the kings won the soil of France piece by piece, so too they added gradually to the royal power, until this *Philip*

[1] The name Carolingian, from Carolus, the Latin form of Charles, is applied to all the rulers of Charlemagne's line.

the Fair and his successors were the most autocratic sovereigns in Europe in their day. France was divided into districts ruled by royal officers. Each such appointed officer, as representative of the king, held vast power, appointing *all* inferior officers in his district, collecting the royal revenues, and controlling the administration in every detail. These royal officers were chosen from men of humble birth — that they might not aspire too much.

The feudal lords had lost all authority except over their serfs and villeins; the small vassals and their townsmen were protected now from their rapacity and capricious tyranny. In England this escape had come, a little earlier, through the courts, the itinerant justices, and the free principles of the common law; and Englishmen grew to have an instinctive reverence for courts and law as the protectors of liberty. In France the like security came through the despotic power intrusted to their officers by the absolute French kings; *and for centuries Frenchmen came to trust autocracy as Englishmen trusted law.*

The Estates General

This contrast is shown, in part, in the history of the French institution which most resembled the English Parliament. Philip the Fair completed his reforms by adding representatives of the towns to the nobles and clergy in the Great Council of France. This brought together all three "estates"; and the gathering was called the *Estates General,* to distinguish it from smaller gatherings in the separate provinces. The first meeting in this form was held in 1302, only a few years after the "Model Parliament" in England. But Philip and his successors used the Estates General only as a convenient taxing machine. *It never became a governing body, as the English Parliament did.* Nor did the French people know how to value it, as the English quickly learned to value Parliament. The kings assembled the Estates General only when they chose, and easily controlled it. When they no longer needed it, *the meetings grew rarer, and finally ceased, without protest by the people.*

In Germany the Carolingian line died out even sooner than in France, and then the princes chose a Saxon duke for King

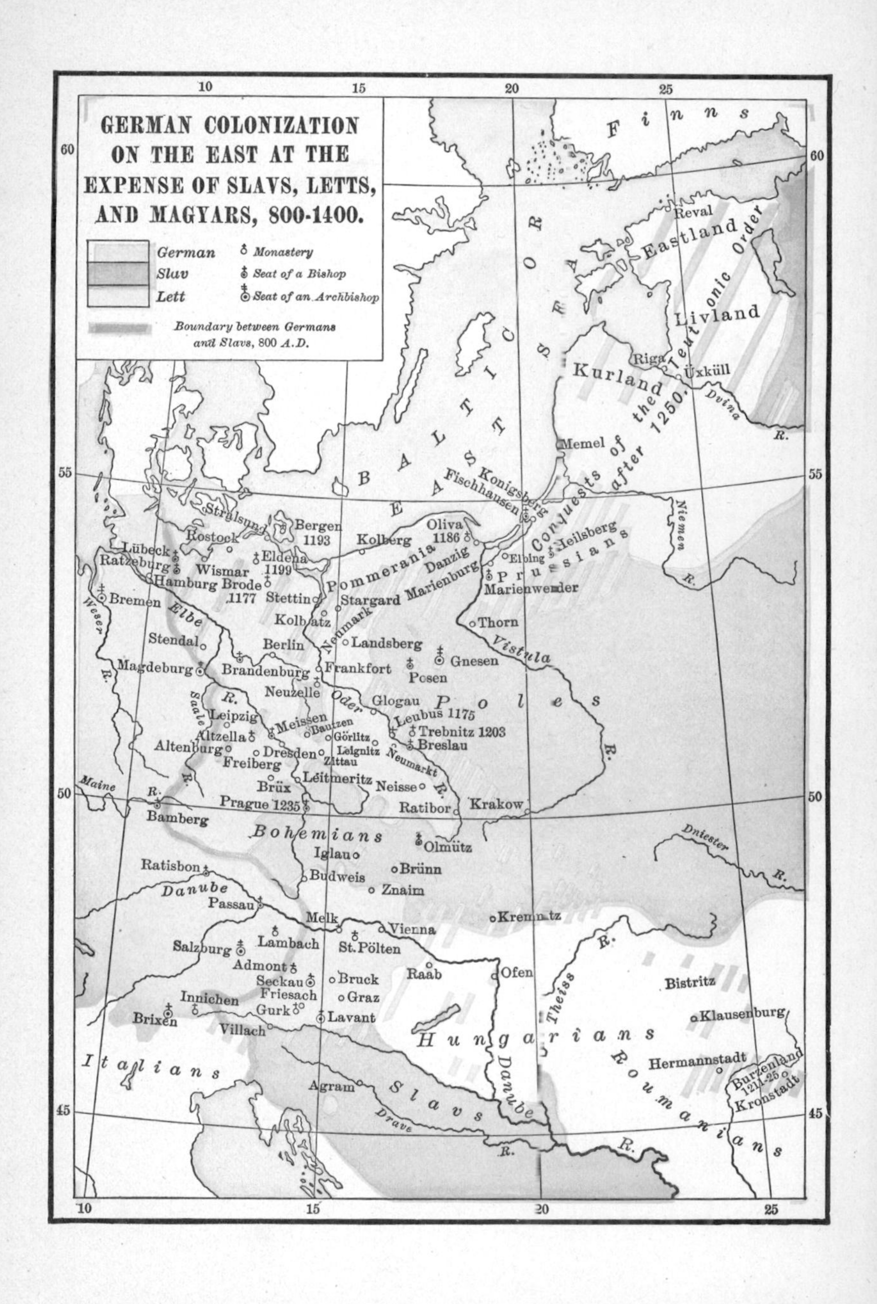
GERMAN COLONIZATION ON THE EAST AT THE EXPENSE OF SLAVS, LETTS, AND MAGYARS, 800-1400.
German
Slav
Lett
Monastery
Seat of a Bishop
Seat of an Archbishop
Boundary between Germans and Slavs, 800 A.D.
Finns
BALTIC SEA
Reval
Eastland
Livland
Teutonic Order
Riga
Üxküll
Kurland
Dvina R.
Conquests of the Teutonic Order after 1250.
Memel
Konigsberg
Fischhausen
Niemen R.
Heilsberg
Elbing
Prussians
Marienwerder
Stralsund
Bergen 1193
Rostock
Kolberg
Oliva 1186
Lübeck
Ratzeburg
Wismar
Eldena 1199
Pommerania
Danzig
Marienburg
Hamburg
Brode 1177
Stettin
Stargard
Bremen
Weser R.
Elbe
Kolbatz
Neumark
Thorn
Vistula
Stendal
Berlin
Landsberg
Gnesen
Magdeburg
Brandenburg
Frankfort
Posen
Neuzelle
Oder
Glogau
Poles
Saale R.
Leipzig
Meissen
Bautzen
Leubus 1175
Trebnitz 1203
Altzella
Görlitz
Breslau
Altenburg
Dresden
Leignitz
Zittau
Neumarkt
Freiberg
Maine R.
Leitmeritz
Neisse
Brüx
Prague 1235
Ratibor
Krakow
Bamberg
Bohemians
Olmütz
Iglau
Brünn
Dniester R.
Ratisbon
Budweis
Znaim
Danube
Passau
Melk
Vienna
Kremnitz
Salzburg
Lambach
St. Pölten
Admont
Raab
Ofen
Seckau
Bruck
Theiss R.
Bistritz
Innichen
Friesach
Graz
Brixen
Gurk
Lavant
Klausenburg
Villach
Hungarians
Italians
Hermannstadt
Roumanians
Burzenland 1211-25
Kronstadt
Agram
Slavs
Drave R.

of the Germans. The second of these Saxon kings was Otto I (936–973). His first great work was to end forever the barbarian inroads. The nomad Hungarians (p. 55) once more broke across the eastern border in enormous numbers. Otto crushed them with horrible slaughter at the Battle of Lechfield. The Hungarians never again attacked Christendom. Soon, indeed, they themselves adopted Christianity and settled down in modern Hungary as one of the family of European nations.

Germany in the feudal age

Otto followed up his success. Year by year he forced further back the Slavs from his eastern borders, and established "marks" along that whole frontier. On the extreme southeast was the Eastmark (against the Hungarians), to grow into modern Austria, while the Mark of Brandenburg on the northeast (against the Slavs) was to grow into modern Prussia. Now, too, began a new colonizing movement which soon *extended Germany from the Elbe to the Oder* and carried swarms of German settlers among even the savage Prussians and the Slavs of the heathen Baltic coast.

Expansion to the east

It should have been the work of the German kings to foster this defensive colonization along their barbarous eastern borders, and to fuse the Germans themselves into a true nation. But Otto and his successors were drawn from this work, so well begun, by greedy dreams of wider empire.

False ambition of the German kings

For half a century the Empire in the West had lapsed. Otto was tempted to restore it — as a mask for seizing upon Italy. That unhappy land had no shadow of union. Saracens from Africa contested the south with the Greek Empire and the Lombards, and the north was devastated by ferocious wars between petty states. Otto invaded Italy, and *in 962* had himself consecrated by the pope at Rome as "Emperor of the Romans."

Otto and the Holy Roman Empire, 962

Popes and Emperors soon quarreled. The restored Empire was "the *Holy* Roman Empire *of the German people*." It did not include all "Western Europe," like Charlemagne's Empire in its day. France was outside, as were the new Christian kingdoms in England, Scandinavia, Poland, and Hungary. As a physical power it rested wholly on "German" military prowess.

Popes and Emperors

And it was "Holy." It claimed to share the headship of Christendom with the papacy, but the relation between Emperors and Popes was not defined. Soon they quarreled; and then followed three centuries of fatal struggle.

Ruin to both Germany and Italy

During these three centuries the history of Germany was bound up with that of Italy. This connection brought to Germany somewhat of the culture and art of the ancient world; but in government and industry it spelled ruin. Otto was merely the first of a long line of German kings who led splendid German armies across the Alps, to melt away in fever beneath the Italian sun. German strength was frittered away in foreign squabbles, and the chance to make a German nation was lost for nine hundred years.

No better were the results to Italy. A German king, however much a "Roman" Emperor, could enter Italy only with a German army at his back. The southern land was a conquered province, ruled by uncouth northern barbarians. True, at last the Popes won, and expelled the Germans; but only by calling in Frenchman and Spaniard, and making Italy for centuries more the battle ground and battle prize of Europe.

The period of "fist-law" in Germany 1254–1273

In 1254 the last German ruler was driven from Italy. *The Empire ceased to be either "Holy" or "Roman." Thereafter it was wholly German. And even the German kingdom seemed extinct.* For twenty years (1254–1273) there was no Emperor, and no king, in Germany. This was the period of "Fist-law." Germany dissolved into more than 300 petty states — "free cities," duchies, marks, counties.

VII. THE CRUSADES, 1100–1300

Mohammedan culture during Europe's "Dark Ages"

For the last two centuries of the feudal age, all Western Europe was deeply moved by one common impulse. To understand this, we must look at conditions outside Europe.

The Mohammedans (pp. 38–42) still ruled from the Pyrenees to the Ganges. They had utilized the old culture of Persia and of Greece. Their governments were as good as the Oriental world had ever known. Their roads and canals en-

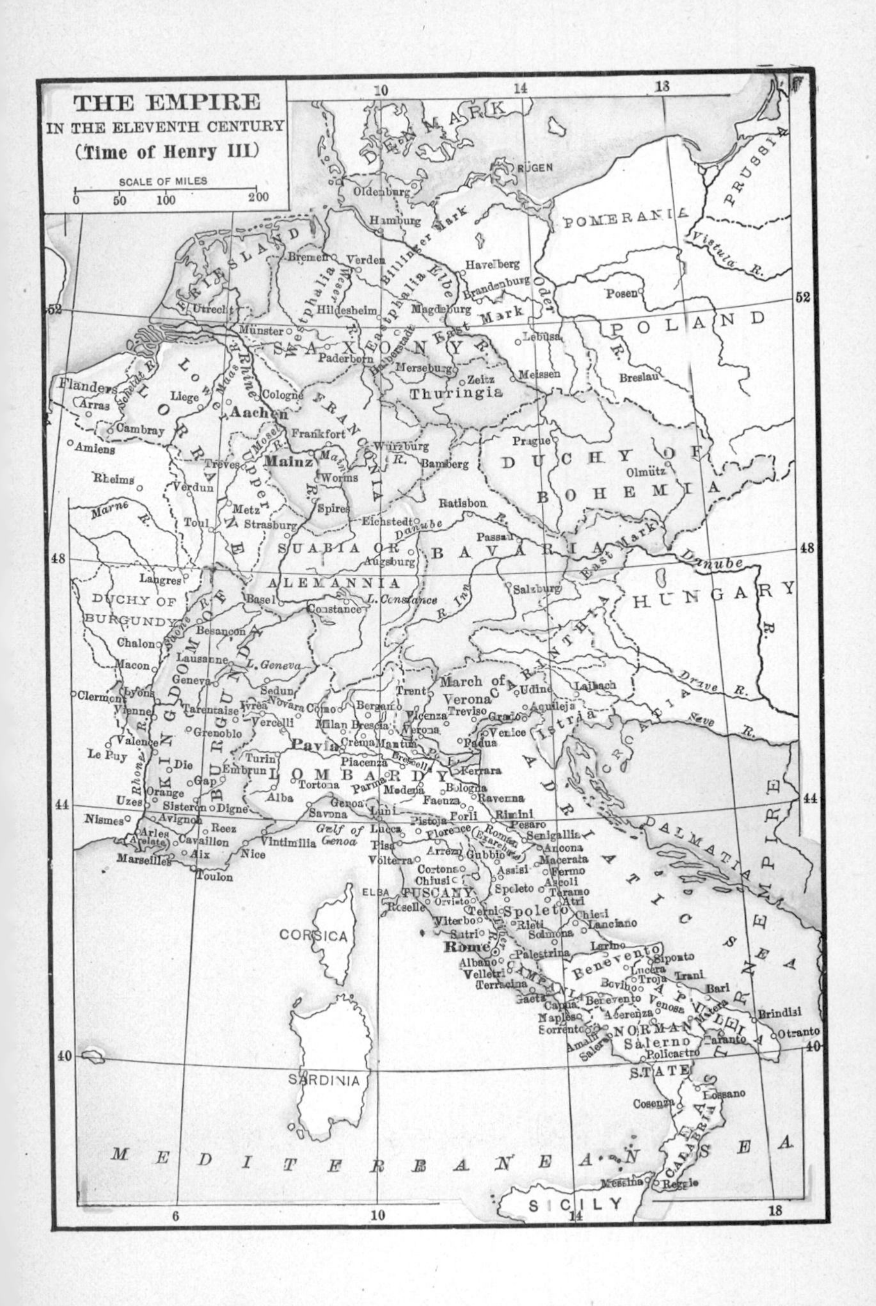
THE EMPIRE
IN THE ELEVENTH CENTURY
(Time of Henry III)
SCALE OF MILES
0 50 100 200
DENMARK
PRUSSIA
POMERANIA
FRIESLAND
SAXONY
POLAND
Thuringia
LOWER LORRAINE
UPPER LORRAINE
FRANCONIA
DUCHY OF BOHEMIA
SUABIA OR ALEMANNIA
BAVARIA
HUNGARY
DUCHY OF BURGUNDY
KINGDOM OF BURGUNDY
CARINTHIA
March of Verona
LOMBARDY
TUSCANY
Spoleto
Benevento
NORMAN STATE
APULIA
CALABRIA
CROATIA
DALMATIA
EMPIRE
ADRIATIC SEA
CORSICA
SARDINIA
SICILY
MEDITERRANEAN SEA
Aachen
Mainz
Pavia
Rome
Cologne
Frankfort
Worms
Spires
Strasburg
Metz
Verdun
Toul
Treves
Liege
Cambray
Arras
Amiens
Rheims
Flanders
Utrecht
Münster
Paderborn
Bremen
Verden
Hamburg
Oldenburg
Hildesheim
Magdeburg
Halberstadt
Merseburg
Zeitz
Meissen
Lebusa
Brandenburg
Havelberg
Posen
Breslau
Prague
Olmütz
Bamberg
Würzburg
Ratisbon
Passau
Eichstedt
Augsburg
Salzburg
Constance
Basel
Besançon
Langres
Chalon
Macon
Lyons
Vienne
Valence
Grenoble
Die
Gap
Embrun
Orange
Sisteron
Digne
Avignon
Arles
Marseilles
Aix
Toulon
Nice
Turin
Milan
Verona
Trent
Venice
Padua
Ferrara
Ravenna
Bologna
Florence
Pisa
Lucca
Genoa
Naples
Salerno
Bari
Brindisi
Otranto
Taranto
Messina
Reggio
Danube R.
Elbe R.
Oder R.
Vistula R.
Rhine R.
Weser R.
Main R.
Moselle R.
Maas R.
Marne R.
Rhone R.
Saone R.
R. Inn
Drave R.
Save R.
L. Constance
L. Geneva
Gulf of Genoa
RÜGEN
ELBA
10
14
18
6
52
48
44
40

couraged commerce and bound together distant regions. Their magnificent cities were built with a peculiar and beautiful architecture, characterized by the horseshoe arch, the dome, the turret, the graceful minaret, and a rich ornament of "arabesque." Their manufactures were the finest in the world, both for beautiful design and for delicate workmanship. Their glass and pottery and metal work, their dyestuffs, their paper, their cloth manufactures, their preparations of leather, all represented industries almost or wholly unknown to the West. We still speak of "Toledo" blades, and "Morocco" leather, while "muslins" and "damasks" recall their superior processes at Mosul and Damascus. Europe was soon to owe to them all these products, with many other things long-forgotten or new, — spices, oranges, lemons, rice, sugar cane, dates, asparagus, sesame, buckwheat, apricots, watermelons, oils, perfumes, calicoes, satins, the cross-bow, the windmill.

A Window in the Mosque at Cordova. See also p. 40 for Mohammedan architecture.

In intellectual lines Arab superiority was no less marked. While Europe had only a few monastic schools to light its "Dark Ages," the Arabs had great universities, with libraries containing hundreds of thousands of manuscripts. In Persia and in Spain they had created a noble literature, both prose and poetry. Philosophy, theology, law, rhetoric, were subjects of special study. The old Chaldean astrology (a sort of fortune-telling by the stars) was becoming true astronomy in the hands of the Arabians of Spain. The heavens still keep proof of their studies in its thick sprinkling of Arabic names, like *Aldebaran*, while common terms in our texts on astronomy (*azimuth, zenith, nadir*) bear like testimony. From India the Arabs brought the "Arabic" notation, while Europe was still struggling with clumsy Roman numerals. Algebra and alchemy (chemistry) are Arabic in origin as in name, and spherical trigonometry was their creation. And while Europe still treated disease from the viewpoint of an Indian "Medicine Man," the Saracens had established, on Greek foundations, a real science of medicine.

A Byzant (Bezant). — A gold coin issued by the emperors at Constantinople in the Middle Ages. This coin had a wide circulation, especially from the eighth to the thirteenth centuries, in the countries of western Europe, when, with the exception of Spain, these lands had no gold currency of their own.

The surviving Greek Empire in the East

Midway in character, as in geography, between Latin Europe and Mohammedan Asia, lay the Greek Empire, living on for centuries a quiet, orderly life. In material prosperity it was unexcelled anywhere in the world, and in intellectual activity it was surpassed only by the Saracens.

It was a civilized state, standing on the defensive against barbarian attack, and waging its wars mainly by Norse mercenaries. The Emperors were often devoted scholars and able authors, as well as great rulers. Constantinople in magnificence and extent and comfort was unapproached by the rude towns of France and Germany; and its wealth, splendor, and comforts, — its paved and lighted streets, its schools and theaters, its orderly police system, its hospitals and parks, — were all amazing to the few visitors from the West. Such little trade as Western Europe possessed was in Greek hands, and the *Byzant*, the coin of Constantinople, was its money standard.

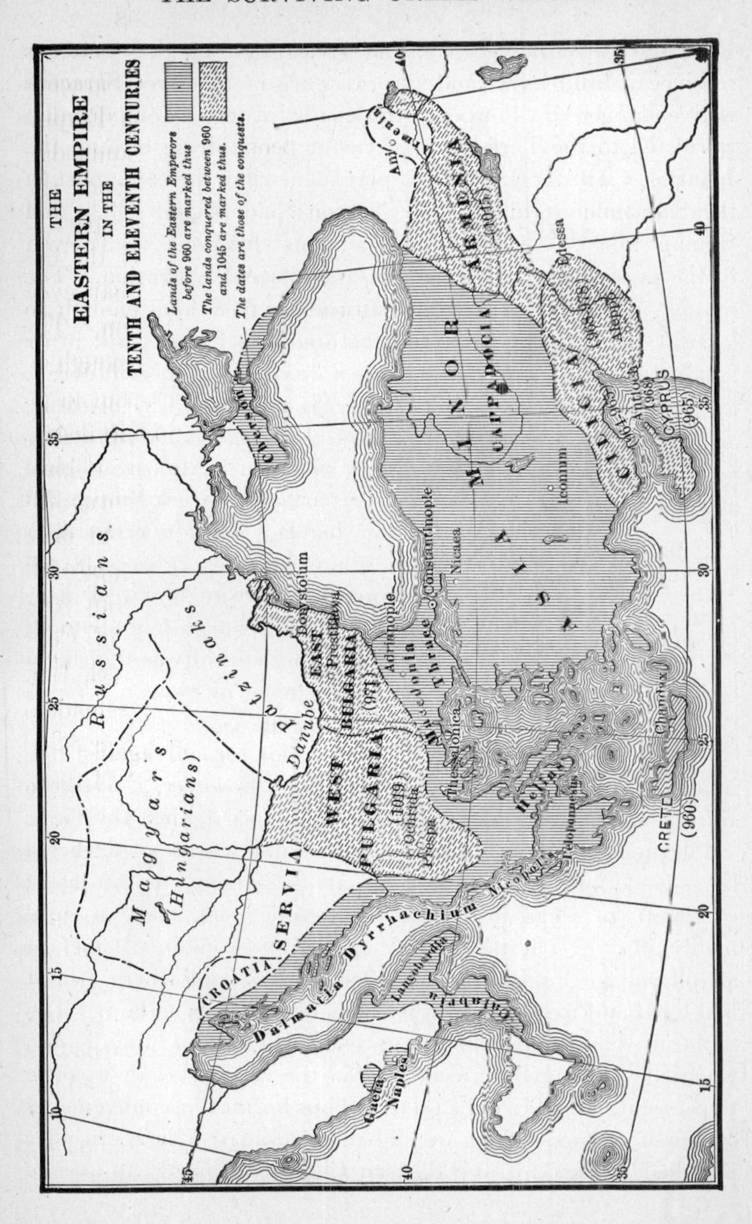
THE
EASTERN EMPIRE
IN THE
TENTH AND ELEVENTH CENTURIES
Lands of the Eastern Emperors before 960 are marked thus
The lands conquered between 960 and 1045 are marked thus.
The dates are those of the conquests.
Russians
Magyars
(Hungarians)
Patzinaks
Cherson
Danube
Dorystolum
Preslava
EAST BULGARIA
(971)
WEST BULGARIA
(1019)
Ochrida
Prespa
Adrianople
Macedonia
Thrace
Constantinople
Nicaea
Thessalonica
Hellas
Peloponnesus
CRETE
(960)
Chandax
ASIA MINOR
CAPPADOCIA
Iconium
CILICIA
Antioch
(968)
CYPRUS
(965)
Aleppo
Edessa
ARMENIA
(1045)
Ani
Armenia
CROATIA
SERVIA
Dalmatia
Dyrrhachium
Nicopolis
Langobardia
Calabria
Naples
Gaeta

The Turkish peril in the East

In the eleventh century, the civilization of the Saracens received a fatal blow, and the existence of the Greek Empire was endangered. Political supremacy in the Mohammedan world fell to the Turks, a new Tartar people from beyond the Jaxartes. The Turks were to play somewhat the same part in the Saracenic world that the Teutons had played in the old Roman world, — with this tremendous difference, that even to the present day they have not assimilated civilization. The Arab culture survived long enough to be transplanted into Europe, but in its own home it was doomed to swift decay.

CRUSADER taking the vow.

The Greek Empire calls on the West to save it from the Turk

The Turks were at least mighty soldiers, and they *began a new era of Mohammedan conquest.* Almost at once the greater part of the Greek Empire fell into their hands. They overran Asia Minor, almost to the gates of Constantinople. In terror, the Greek Emperor turned to Western Christendom for aid; and this appeal was the signal for two centuries of war, "Cross" against "Crescent."

The Turks abuse Christian pilgrims

The Greek call for aid against the infidel would have produced little effect, however, if Western Europe had not had deep grievances of its own against the Turk.

Pilgrimages to holy shrines were a leading feature of medieval life. Good men made them to satisfy religious enthusiasm; evil men, to secure forgiveness for crime; sick men, to heal bodily ills. A pilgrimage was an act of worship. Chief of all pilgrimages, of course, was that to the land where Christ had lived and to the tomb where His body had been laid. The Saracens had permitted these pilgrimages; but the Turks, when they captured Jerusalem from the Arabs, began at once to persecute all Christians there. Thus began those movements of *armed* pilgrims which we call the Crusades. Each crusader marched in part to save Eastern Christians, partly to avenge

The Crusades

pilgrims from the West; and partly to make his own pilgrimage to the holiest of shrines. Mingled with these motives, too, was the spirit of adventure and the greed for gain in land or gold.

From 1096 to almost 1300 there was constant fighting in the East between Christian and Mohammedan. Europe, which in the ninth century had been helpless against plundering heathen bands, had now grown strong enough to pour into Asia for two hundred years a ceaseless stream of mailed knights, with countless followers.

Effigies of Knights Templar, from funeral slabs in the Temple Church, London. The *crossing* of the legs in a funeral sculpture indicated a *crusader*.

For almost the first half of that period the Christians did hold all or most of the Holy Land, broken into various "Latin" principalities, and defended against the reviving Mohammedan power by "Orders" of fighting monks — the Templars, the Knights of St. John, and the Teutonic Order. At the end, the Mohammedans had expelled Europe wholly from Asia.

Importance of the Crusades

This was mainly because Europe had outgrown the crusading movement. The Crusades themselves had created a new Europe. Trade had grown, and society was no longer so exclusively made up of fighters. The *indirect results* of the Crusades were vastly more important than the recovery of Palestine would have been. New energies were awakened; new worlds of thought opened. The intellectual horizon widened. *The crusaders brought back new gains*

Intellectual results

in science, art, architecture, medical skill; and *Europe had learned that there was more still to learn.*

Growth of commerce

Many oriental products (p. 89) became almost necessaries of life. Some of them were soon grown or manufactured in Europe. Others, like spices, could not be produced there; and, in consequence, commerce with distant parts of Asia grew enormously. In the absence of fresh meat in winter and of our modern root-foods (p. 69), spices became of immense importance for the table. For a time, Venice and Genoa, assisted by their favorable positions, monopolized much of the new carrying trade; but all the ports of Western Europe were more or less affected. This commercial activity called for quicker methods of reckoning, and so Europe adopted the Arabic numerals. *Money replaced barter.* Bankers appeared, alongside the old Jew money-lenders; and coinage increased swiftly.

Feudalism undermined

All this undermined both the economic and the military basis of feudalism. Money made it unnecessary for the tenant to pay rent in *service*, and enabled the kings to collect "taxes," so as to maintain standing armies. Moreover the Crusades swept away the old feudal nobility directly. Hundreds of thousands of barons and knights squandered their possessions in preparing for the expedition, and then left their bones in Palestine. The ground was cleared for the rising city democracies and the new monarchies.

And these two new forces at first were allies. The "third estate" wanted order, and the kings could help secure it. The kings wanted money, and the third estate could supply it. Kings and towns joined hands to reduce feudalism to a form. True, a new nobility grew up — but it had only the honors of the old, without its power.

VIII. RISE OF THE TOWNS, 1100–1300

The towns and the feudal lords

From 500 to 1100 A.D. the three figures in European life had been the tonsured priest, the mailed horseman, and the field laborer, stunted and bent. *In the twelfth century*, alongside priest, noble, and peasant *there stood out* a fourth figure — *the sturdy, resolute, self-confident burgher.* The age of the Crusades was also the age of the rise of towns.

Feudalism and the towns were foes by nature. Feudalism had grown out of war, and lived to fight. The new towns could fight stubbornly, when forced to fight; but they grew out of trade and lived for industry, and they shut out the robber-knights by walls and guards.

Origin of the towns

In Italy and southern France, some old Roman towns had lived along, with shrunken population, subject to neighboring

SIEGE OF A MEDIEVAL TOWN: the summons to surrender. — From a sixteenth-century copper engraving.

lords. Under the new commercial conditions after 1200, these districts became dotted once more with self-governing cities, with municipal institutions molded, in part at least, upon those brought down from Roman times. Elsewhere the towns were mainly new growths — from peasant villages. Most were small. Very few had more than four or five thousand people.

Town charters won in two centuries of revolt

At first each inhabitant of a growing town remained directly dependent upon the town's feudal lord. The first advance toward freedom was to change this individual dependence into *collective* dependence. The town demanded the right to have its elected officers bargain with the lord as to services and dues, to be paid by the whole town, not by individual citizens; and after "two centuries of revolt" (1100–1300), by stubborn heroism and by wise use of their wealth, they had won charters guaranteeing this and greater privileges.

THE MEDIEVAL TOWN HALL OF OUDENARDE, BELGIUM.

Town life in the feudal age

Town life showed new wants, new comforts, new occupations. Thatched hovels, with dirt floors gave way to comfortable, and even stately, burghers' homes. Universal misery and squalor among the industrial classes were replaced, for a large part of the population, by happy comfort. There followed a lavish expenditure for town halls and cathedrals and for civic feasts and shows.

Still, the medieval European city fell far behind the ancient Roman city or the contemporary Arabian city. There were no street lights at night, no city water supply, no sewerage, no street-cleaning, no paving. The necessity of inclosing the town within lofty stone walls crowded it into small space, so that streets were always narrow and dark. Dead animals rotted in these streets; loose swine or pigsties obstructed them; and on one occasion in the fifteenth century a German Emperor, warmly welcomed in a loyal city, was almost swallowed up, horse and rider, in the bottomless filth. Within doors, too, the material prosperity was not for all. Says Dr. Jessopp, "The sediment of the town population was a dense slough of stagnant misery, squalor, famine, loathsome disease, and dull despair."

There was no adequate police system, and street fights were constant. At night, no well-to-do citizen stirred abroad without his armor and his guard of stout apprentice lads; and he had to fortify and guard his house at all times. The citizen, however safe from feudal tyranny, lived in bondage to countless necessary but annoying town regulations. When "curfew" rang, he must "cover his fire" and put out lights — a precaution against conflagration particularly necessary because of the crowded narrow streets, the flimsy houses, and the absence of fire companies and of adequate water. His clothing, and his wife's, must be no richer than that prescribed for their particular station. He must serve his turn as "watch" in belfry tower, on the walls, or in the streets at night. And in his daily labor he must work and buy and sell only according to the minute regulations of his gild.

The gild was an institution of old Roman times, modified by medieval conditions. All the *skilled* laborers of one trade, in one place, made up a gild, — bakers' gild, goldsmiths' gild, and so on. The gild was a *social* organization, and a mutual insurance society; and it also minutely regulated the work of its members so as to give each member an equal chance *and to maintain a high standard of work.*

OLD STREET IN ROUEN, present condition. The Cathedral is visible at the opening of the street into the square. Probably the appearance of the street has changed little since the fourteenth century.

The townsmen, from rich merchant down through skilled artisan, were a "third estate" in government, alongside clergy and nobles. They were not as yet "the people." They were only one more "class" risen from the unreckoned mass; and they looked down upon unskilled workmen and farm peasants with contempt as bigoted and cruel as that felt for the burghers by the classes above them.

A "third estate"

For a time it seemed that Europe might be dominated by city leagues, like ancient Greece. More than once, leagues of cities, like the Hanseatic League of north Germany, fought with the mightiest kings, and won. But in Italy by 1350 nearly every city had fallen under the rule of tyrants; in France, they were brought completely under the growing despotic authority of the king; in Germany, the many "free cities" became only one element in the general political chaos (p. 88); and in England they never possessed that extreme independence of the central government which for a time they secured in other lands. *The more advanced countries of Europe moved on toward a national life*, in which city life was soon absorbed.

Leagues of cities

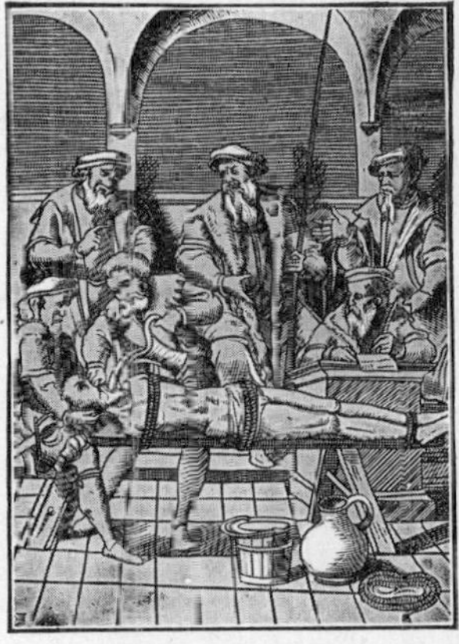

TORTURE BY WATER, a method used in medieval towns, on the continent, in their bitter class strife. This particular form of torture to compel confession survived to recent times in the Spanish Philippines, and was adopted by American soldiers there in the barbarous warfare with the natives.

IX. LEARNING AND ART IN THE FEUDAL AGE

The "Dark Ages" (500 to 1100) saw a gleam of promise in Charlemagne's day, and some remarkable English and Irish schools flourished just before Charlemagne, and again in the day of Alfred. But these were mere points of light in a vast gloom. As a whole, for six hundred years the only schools were

Few schools in the Dark Ages

those connected with monasteries and cathedrals; and these were unspeakably poor — and aimed only to fit for the duties of the clergy.

Rise of the universities after 1100

About 1100, Europe began to stir from this intellectual torpor. Some of the new towns set up trades schools, with instruction in the language of the people, instead of in Latin, to fit education to the needs of everyday life. In leading cities, in France, Italy, and England, the medieval university appeared, with extended courses in "arts" and with other specialties for advanced study, like theology at Paris, medicine at Naples, Roman law at Bologna. By 1400, fifty universities dotted Europe, some of them with many thousand students. *A fifth figure came into European life: alongside peasant, knight, priest, townsman,* there moved now in cap and gown *the lay student or learned "doctor,"* the forerunner of the modern "professional man."

The universities ruled by tradition, not by reason

But the universities did not make good their first promise. The University of Paris, the first medieval university, had grown up about a great teacher, *Abelard.* Abelard was a fearless seeker after truth. Alone among the scholars of his age, he dared to call "reason" the test of truth, even in the matter of church doctrines. *But the church* condemned this heresy, and *forced the rising universities to forswear "reason" for "authority."* This stifled all inquiry. Some garbled fragments of Greek science had been recovered, through Arabian translations from the Greek Aristotle, and soon came to be looked upon with superstitious reverence. For two centuries, "Thus saith Aristotle" was as final in science as "Thus saith the church" in religion. When the intellectual rebirth of Europe finally came, after those two centuries, it came from outside university walls.

The Schoolmen

The method of reasoning used in the universities is called *scholasticism.* It was like the reasoning we use in geometry, — *deducing* a truth from given premises or axioms. This method ignores observation and experiment and investigation, and has no value, by itself, except in mathematics. It has never discovered a truth in nature or in man. The men of the universities (*Schoolmen*) did not use it in mathematics. They tried to use it by turning in upon their own minds, and their arguments were mainly quibbles upon verbal distinctions. Much time they spent in playing with such questions as, How many spirits can dance at one time upon the point of a needle?

The last of the famous Schoolmen was Duns the Scot, who died in 1308. In that day there was no higher praise for a

INTERIOR OF HALL OF MERCHANT PRINCES AT DANTZIG. Originally a Hall of the Teutonic Knights (about 1300). — From Lübke.

young scholar than to call him "a Duns." Before many years, when a new scientific method had come in (p. 178), the term came to be our "dunce."

Medieval science

A very little "science" crept into Europe by 1200 from the Arabs, mainly in astronomy and chemistry. But the astronomy was mostly astrology (p. 90). And chemistry (alchemy) was little more than a search for the "philosopher's stone," which should change common metals into gold, or for the "elixir of life," a drink to make a man immortal. Both astrologers and

SALISBURY CATHEDRAL, from the northwest; one of the finest examples of English Gothic; built 1200–1250. The spire rises 404 feet from the ground.

alchemists mingled their studies with magic incantations and were generally believed to have sold their souls to the Devil in return for forbidden knowledge.

A forerunner of true science

No doubt there were many men, whose names we have never heard, who were trying through those weary centuries really to study into the secrets of nature in a scientific way, by experiment. The greatest man of this kind before 1300 was *Roger Bacon,* an English Franciscan. While the useless Duns Scotus

SALISBURY CLOISTERS, from outside the court, showing only the roof of the Cathedral above them.

was admired and courted by all the world, Roger Bacon was living in loneliness and poverty, noticed only to be persecuted or reviled. He spent his life in trying to point out the lacks of the Schoolmen's method and to teach true scientific principles. Fourteen years he spent in dungeons, for his opinions. When at liberty, he worked devotedly, but under heavy handicaps. More than once he sought all over Europe for a copy of some book he needed — when a modern scholar in like case would need only to send a note to the nearest bookseller. He wrote upon the possibility of reaching Asia by sailing west into the Atlantic. He learned much about explosives, and is said to have invented gunpowder. It is believed, too, that he used lenses as a telescope. Apparently he foresaw the possibility of using steam as a motive power. Certainly he prophesied that in time wagons and ships would move "with incredible speed" without horses or sails, and also that man would learn to sail the air. His "Great Work" was a cyclopedia of the knowledge of his time in geography, mathematics, music, and physics. But Roger Bacon lived a century too soon for his own good, and found no successful disciples.

Literature in the speech of the people after 1200

Latin, a mongrel Latin, too, was the sole language of the university and of learning; and until 1200, except for the songs of wandering minstrels, it was practically the *only* language of any kind of literature. About that time, however, in various lands *popular poetry of a high order began to appear in the language of everyday speech:* the Song of the Cid in Spanish; the love songs of the Troubadours in French and of the Minnesingers in German; the Divine Comedy of Dante in Italian, and, toward 1400, the Canterbury Tales of Chaucer in New English, with Wyclif's translation of the Bible into the same tongue.

Art in the Middle Ages

Classical art was lost, through the Dark Ages, as completely as classical learning. *Medieval painting* existed only in rude altar pieces, representing stiff saints and Madonnas, where even the flowing draperies could not hide the artist's ignorance of how to draw the human body. On a minute scale, to be sure, there was some better work. Monks "illuminated" missals with tiny brushes in brilliant colors, and sometimes with beauty and delicacy.

Architecture, too, was rude until after 1100. But, in the twelfth and thirteenth centuries, the heavy *Romanesque* style gave way to a new French style called *the Gothic*, and the world gained one of its wonders in the Gothic cathedral — "a religious aspiration in stone."

SIXTH PERIOD

THE CLOSE OF THE MIDDLE AGES, 1300–1520

I. ENGLAND AND FRANCE

The Hundred Years' War (1338–1453)

We left the story of England with the great Edward who had the wisdom to adopt and perfect the Parliament of the rebel Simon. In 1327 Parliament deposed the weak second Edward. Then the third Edward began the Hundred Years' War with

ENGLISH LADY ON HORSEBACK. — From a fourteenth-century manuscript in the British Museum.

FRENCH DRESS IN THE FOURTEENTH CENTURY: 1. Middle class; 2. Lower class; 3. Noble lady.

France (1338–1453). On the surface, this war was a struggle between kings for prestige and territory: but at bottom *it was a commercial struggle.* Every country, in that day, shackled foreign merchants with absurd restrictions and ruinous tolls. England wanted to sell her wool freely in Flemish towns and to buy Bordeaux wines freely in the south of France; and the easiest way to get access to these markets seemed to be to conquer France.

France ravaged

The war was waged on French soil. The English won brilliant victories, overran France repeatedly, ravaging crops, burning peasant villages, turning the country into a blackened desert in the usual fashion of warfare in those chivalrous days, and bringing home much plunder — robes, furs, feather beds, kitchen utensils, some rich plate, and some coin from the ransom of "noble" prisoners. The whole century of horrible and meaningless slaughter had just one gleam of promise for the future world. This was given by the Battle of Crécy. An English army was trapped apparently by five times their number. But the English yeomen — men of the six-foot bow and yard-long shafts feathered from gray-goose wings — coolly faced the ponderous mass of French knights, repulsed charge after charge of that gallantest chivalry of Europe, and won back for the world the long-lost equality of the footman with the feudal horseman in war (1346).

Battle of Crécy, 1346

A BOMBARD. — From a sixteenth-century German woodcut. An old chronicler tells us that at Crécy the English had some small "bombards," which, with fire and noise like God's thunder, threw little iron balls *to frighten the horses*. These first cannon were made by fastening bars of iron together with hoops; and the powder was very weak. A century later they began to be used to batter down castles and city walls. It was longer still before firearms replaced the bow for infantry.

The Black Death

For a time, toward 1400, the war languished because pestilence was slaying men faster than steel could. The Black Death, most famous of famous plagues, had been devastating the continent for years, moving west from Asia. At least a third of the population of Europe was carried off by it. Then, in the year after Crécy, the returned victors brought it to England, where, almost at a blow, it swept away half the nation.

And the decay of serfdom in England

This loss fell most heavily of course upon the working classes, but it helped those left alive to rise out of serfdom, — a movement already well under way there. The lack of labor doubled wages, too, and so brought in a higher standard of living.

JOHN WYCLIF

True, Parliament tried, in the interest of the landlords, to keep down the laborers by foolish and tyrannical laws, — forbidding them to leave the parish where they lived or to take more wages than had been customary in the past, and ordering them under cruel penalties to serve any one who offered them such wages. There were many individual cases, too, of bitter tyranny, where some lord, by legal trickery or by outright violence, forced half-freed villeins back into serfdom. Thus among the peasants there was long smoldering a fierce and just discontent.

Wyclif and the Lollards

Another set of causes fanned this discontent into flame. The huge wealth of the church and the worldliness of the greater clergy were becoming a common scandal. Even the gentle Chaucer (p. 104), court poet though he was, wrote in keen raillery of these faults. More serious and less happy men could not dismiss them with a jest. The priest, John Wyclif, a famous lecturer at the University of Oxford, preached vigorously against such abuses, and finally attacked even some central teachings of the church. He denied the doctrine of transubstantiation,[1]

[1] That at the Mass the bread and wine were changed miraculously into the very flesh and blood of Christ.

and insisted that even ignorant men might know the will of God, through the Bible, without priestly intervention. Accordingly, with his companions, he made the first complete translation of the Bible into English; and his disciples wrote out many copies (printing was still a century in the future) and distributed them throughout the land.

These disciples called themselves "poor preachers." Their enemies called them "Lollards" (babblers). Some of them exaggerated their master's teachings against wealth, and called for the abolition of all rank and property. John Ball, one of these "mad preachers," attacked the privileges of the gentry in rude rhymes that rang through England from shore to shore, —

> "When Adam delved and Eve span,
> Who was then the gentleman?"

"This priest," says Froissart, a contemporary chronicler, "used oftentimes to go and preach when the people in the villages were coming out from mass; and he would make them gather about him, and would say thus: 'Good people, things go not well in England, nor will, till everything be in common and there no more be villeins and gentlemen. By what right are they whom we call lords greater folk than we? We be all come from one father and one mother, Adam and Eve, . . . but they are clothed in velvet and are warm in their furs, while we shiver in rags; they have wine, and spices, and fair bread; and we, oat cake and straw, and water to drink; they dwell in fine houses, and we have the pain and travail, the rain and the wind in the fields. From our labor they keep their state. Yet we are their bondmen; and unless we serve them readily, we are beaten.' And so the people would murmur one with the other in the fields, and in the ways as they met together, affirming that John Ball spoke truth."

The Peasant Rising of 1381

In 1377 Edward's grandson, Richard II, came to the throne as a mere boy; and, while the government was in confusion, and England in this seething discontent, Parliament passed a heavy poll tax, bearing unfairly upon the poor. This match set the realm ablaze — in the "Peasant Rising of 1381." With amazing suddenness, from all sides, the peasants, rudely armed, marched upon London; and in a few days the king and kingdom were in their hands.

The special demand of the peasantry was that all labor-rents should be changed into *fixed* money rents. They sacked some castles and manor houses, destroying the "manor rolls," the written evidence of *services* due on the estate; and they put to death a few nobles and their lawyer tools. Women and children were nowhere injured, and there was no attempt at general pillage and massacre, such as usually go with servile insurrections in other lands. *The revolt was marked by the moderation of men who had a reasonable program of reform.*

AN ENGLISH CARRIAGE OF THE FOURTEENTH CENTURY. — After Jusserand's *English Wayfaring Life;* from a fourteenth-century psalter. This carriage is represented as drawn by five horses tandem, driven by two postilions. Such a carriage was a princely luxury, equaling in value a herd of from four hundred to sixteen hundred oxen.

Wat the Tyler

Unhappily the peasants lacked organization. Their chief leader, *Wat the Tyler*, was murdered treacherously, in a conference "under a flag of truce," as we would say. "Kill!" shouted Wat's followers; "they have murdered our captain!" But the young Richard rode forward fearlessly to their front. "What need ye, my masters!" he called; "I am your king and captain." "We will that you free us forever," shouted the peasant army, "us and our lands; and that we be never more named serfs." "I grant it," replied the boy; and by such pledges and by promise of free pardon he persuaded them to go home. For days a force of thirty clerks was kept busy writing out brief charters containing the king's promises.

But when the peasants had scattered to their villages, bear-

The upper-class treachery and revenge

ing to each one a copy of the king's treacherous charter, the property classes rallied and took a bloody vengeance. Parliament declared, indeed, that Richard's promise was void, because he could not give away the gentry's property — the services due them — without their consent. Richard caught gladly at this excuse. Quite willing to dishonor his word to mere villeins, he marched triumphantly through England at the head of forty

A FOURTEENTH-CENTURY BRIDGE IN RURAL ENGLAND, near Danby. — From Jusserand's *English Wayfaring Life.*

thousand men, stamping out all hope of another rising by ruthless execution of old leaders. Seven thousand men were put to death in cold blood. The men of Essex met him with copies of his charters, declaring that they were free Englishmen. "Villeins you were," answered Richard, "and villeins you are. In bondage you shall abide; and not your old bondage, but a worse."

History has preserved a splendid story of one of the martyred heroes. Early in the rising, the peasants of St. Albans (in

Essex) had wrung charters from the monastery which had previously owned their town — in so legal a way that now even the royal courts could not ignore them. The leader of the St. Albans' villagers, *Grindecobbe,* was now condemned to death, however, for his part in the rising, and was then offered his life if he would persuade his townsmen to give up the charters. Grindecobbe turned to his fellows only to bid them take no thought for him but to hold firm their rights. "I shall die for the freedom we have won, counting myself happy to end my life by such a martyrdom. Do then as if I had been killed in battle yesterday."

The peasant cause wins

Such steadfastness was not in vain. Soon the movement toward the emancipation of villeins began again with fresh force; and, *by 1450, villeinage had passed away from England forever.*

Growth of Parliament's power

The growth of Parliament during the Hundred Years' War was almost as important as the rise of the peasants out of bondage. Constant war made it necessary for Edward III and his successors to ask for many grants of money. Parliament supplied the king generously; but it took advantage of his needs to secure new powers.

(1) It established the principle that "redress of grievances" must *precede* a "grant of supply" and at last transformed its "petitions" for such redress into "bills." (2) In the closing years of Edward III the *Good Parliament* (1376) "impeached" and removed his ministers, using the forms that have been common in impeachments ever since in English-speaking countries. And (3) *when Richard II tried to overawe Parliament with his soldiery,* England rose against him, and the Parliament of 1399 deposed him, electing a cousin (Henry of Lancaster) in his place. (4) In the first quarter of the fifteenth century, under the Lancastrian Henrys (IV, V, VI), the House of Commons made good its claims that all money bills must originate with it, and (5) secured the right to judge of the election of its own members. (6) Parliament repeatedly compelled the king to dismiss his ministers and appoint new ones satisfactory to it, and (7) sev-

eral times fixed the succession to the throne. (8) Freedom of speech in Parliament and freedom from arrest, except by the order of Parliament itself, became recognized privileges of all members.

Thus under the Lancastrians there was established in the breasts of the English middle classes a proud consciousness of English liberty as a precious inheritance. With right they believed it superior to that possessed by any other people of the

THE GOOD PARLIAMENT OF 1399, which deposed Richard II. — From a contemporary manuscript. Some of the faces are probably portraits.

time. Wrote Sir John Fortescue, Chief Justice under Henry VI, in his *In Praise of the Laws of England,* for the instruction of Henry's son: —

"A king of England at his pleasure cannot make any alteration in the laws of the land without the consent of his subjects, nor burden them against their wills with strange impositions. . . . Rejoice, therefore, my good Prince, that such is the law of the kingdom you are to inherit, because it will afford both to you and to your subjects the greatest security and satisfaction. . . . [The king] is appointed to protect his subjects in their lives, properties, and laws. For this end *he has the delegation of power from the people,* and he has no just claims to any other power."

Then came the ruinous Wars of the Roses in England. This civil war was not, despite Shakspere's pictures of it, merely a struggle for power between rival lords: in large measure, it was the final battle between the old feudal spirit, strong in the north of England, and the towns, strong in the south. The towns won. The remnants of the old nobility were swept away in battle or by the headsman's ax. But the middle classes were not yet ready to grasp the government, and *the fruits of victory fell for a time to the new Tudor monarchs,* Henry VII and Henry VIII. These rulers were more absolute than any preceding English kings. England entered the modern period under a "New Monarchy."

The Wars of the Roses, 1454–1471

A MEDIEVAL BATTLE. — From a sixteenth-century woodcut.

The "New Monarchy" of the Tudors

Still these Tudors were not "divine-right" monarchs; and they were shrewd enough to cloak their power under the old constitutional forms — and so did not challenge popular opposition. True they called Parliament rarely — and only to use it as a tool. But the occasional meetings, and the way in which the kings seemed to rule through it, saved the forms of constitutional government. At a later time, we shall see, life was again breathed into those forms. Then it became plain that, in crushing the feudal forces, the New Monarchy had paved the way for a parliamentary government more complete than men had dreamed of in earlier times.

The *forms* of free government saved

French monarchy strengthened

France came out of the Hundred Years' War, after unspeakable suffering among the poor and after vast destruction of property, with territory consolidated, with a new patriotism binding her people into one (a patriotism that had blossomed in Joan of

Joan of Arc at the Relief of Orleans. — From a modern imaginative painting.

Arc, the peasant girl liberator of her country), and with her kings stronger than ever. Her industrious peasantry, not for the last time, amazed Europe by their rapid restoration of prosperity in a wasted land. *Louis XI* (1461–1483) kept a small but efficient standing army, with a train of artillery that could easily batter the castle of any feudal rebel about his ears. Louis left France the richest, most orderly, and most united country on the continent. *Under Francis I (1515–1547), France plainly had stepped into the first place in Europe* — among single states — with only the widely scattered, conglomerate Hapsburg power to challenge her supremacy.

II. THE PAPACY AT THE END OF THE MIDDLE AGES

Struggle in England between the government and the pope

The thirteenth-century struggle between popes and emperors (pp. 88, ff.) left the popes victors. But at once England and France challenged that papal overlordship. Neither country questioned the pope's authority in religious matters; but they did demand that he should not interfere with government.

The conflict was hastened by the Hundred Years' War. The kings needed money, and were trying to introduce systems of national taxation in place of the unsatisfactory feudal revenues. The clergy had been exempt from feudal services; but they owned so much of the wealth of the two countries that the kings insisted upon their paying their share of the new taxes. *Pope Boniface VIII* (1296) issued a bull forbidding any prince to impose taxes on the clergy without papal consent, and threatening excommunication against all clergy who paid.

But when the English clergy, trusting in this papal decree, refused to pay taxes, Edward I outlawed them. To outlaw a man was to put him outside the protection of the law: he could not bring suit to recover property or damages, and offenses against him were not "crimes." It became plain at once that, in comparison with this practical "excommunication" by the state, the old clerical excommunication was stage thunder. The clergy submitted.

The conflict in France

France was the scene of a sharper contest. As it progressed, Pope Boniface set forth the old claims of papal supremacy over princes. "Whoever resists this power," said one of his bulls, "resists the ordination of God . . . Indeed we declare . . . that it is altogether necessary to salvation for every human creature to be subject to the Roman pontiff." Philip treated these claims with contempt, and the Estates General (1302), *even the clerical Estate,* denied the pope any control over the state, and pledged their lives to defend the "ancient liberties of the French nation." Philip forbade the payment of any revenues from his realm to the pope, and arrested the papal legate. Boniface threatened to depose the king. A few days later, a company of French soldiers made Boniface prisoner; and the chagrin of the old man at the insult probably hastened his death (1303).

"The Babylonian Captivity"

Philip then secured the election of a French pope, who removed the papal capital from Rome to Avignon, in southern France. Here the popes remained for seventy years (1309–1377), in "the Babylonian Captivity of the church."

Of course the papacy lost public respect. It was no longer an impartial umpire. Politically it had sunk into a mere tool of the French kings, and the enemies of France could not be expected to show it reverence. In Italy, too, the Papal States themselves fell into anarchy, and there was danger that the popes might lose that principality.

In 1377, to save the papal territory, Gregory XI visited Rome. This act brought on a greater disaster even than the exile itself. Gregory died while at Rome. The cardinals were obliged at once to choose a successor. They were Frenchmen (as all high church offices had been given to Frenchmen during the scandal of the Captivity); but even French cardinals did not dare disregard the savage demands of the people of Rome for an Italian pope, and so chose Urban VI. Urban established himself in the old papal seat at Rome; but, a few months later, the cardinals assembled again, declared that the choice of Urban was void because made under compulsion, and elected a French pope, Clement VII, who promptly returned to Avignon.

Rival "popes"

Urban and Clement excommunicated each other, each devoting to the devil all the supporters of the other. Which pope should good Christians obey? The answer was determined mainly by political considerations. France obeyed Clement; England and Germany obeyed Urban. Two such heads for Christendom were worse than no head at all.

The Lollard heresy

This sad condition of the papacy brought with it danger to the church itself. *The Wyclif movement* in England (p. 107) took place toward the close of the exile at Avignon. The church declared Wyclif a heretic; but he was protected during his life by one of King Edward's sons. Soon after Wyclif's death, however, the Lancastrian monarchs began to persecute his followers. In 1401, for the first time, an Englishman was burned for heresy, and the Lollards finally disappeared. But meantime, the seeds of the heresy had been scattered in a distant part of Europe. Richard II of England married a princess of Bohemia, and some of her attendants *carried the teachings of Wyclif to the Bohemian University of Prague.* About 1400, *John Hus,* a professor at Prague, became a leader in a radical "reform" much after Wyclif's example, and the movement spread rapidly over much of Bohemia.

The Hussite heresy

Great and good men everywhere, especially in the powerful universities, began now to call for a General Council as the only means to restore unity of church government and doctrine; and finally one of the popes called the Council of Constance (1414). Five thousand delegates were present, representing all Christendom. With recesses, the Council sat for four years. It induced one pope to resign his office, and it deposed the other claimants. Then it restored unity by electing a new pope, Martin V, to rule from Rome.

The Council of Constance, 1414

Next the Council turned its attention to restoring church doctrine. John Hus was present, under a "safe conduct" from the Emperor. His teachings were declared heresy; but neither persuasion nor threats could move him to recant. "It is better for me to die," he said, "than to fall into the hands of the Lord by deserting the truth." Despite the Emperor's solemn pledge for his safety, Hus was burned at the stake, and his ashes were scattered in the Rhine (1415). Then Wyclif's doctrines, too, were condemned; and, to make thorough work, his ashes were disinterred from their resting place and scattered on the river Swift.

The Council was made up of earnest reformers, — good men for their age, — who believed that in this work they were serving God and saving the souls of future generations of men from eternal torment. But their vigorous measures did not wholly succeed. Hus became a national hero to Bohemia. That country rose in arms against the church. A crusade was preached against the heretics, and years of cruel war followed; but some survivals of Hussite teachings lasted on into the period of the Reformation a century later.

The last popes of the Middle Ages

The papacy never regained its earlier authority over kings. Nicholas V (1447) showed himself a learned scholar, eager to advance learning, as well as a pure and gentle man. Pius II (1455) strove to arouse a new crusade against the Turks, who had at last captured Constantinople; but his complete failure proved (in his own words) that Europe "looked on pope and emperor alike as names in a story." Some of the succeeding popes, like the notorious Borgia (Alexander VI, 1492–1503), were busied mainly as Italian princes, building up their temporal principality by intrigue and craft such as was common at that day in Italian politics.

III. OTHER STATES, 1300–1520

Germany and the Hapsburgs

The "Holy Roman Empire," it has been explained (p. 88), had come to mean merely *Germany*. The anarchy of the "Fist-law" period was checked in 1273 by the election of Rudolph of Hapsburg as Emperor. Rudolph was a petty count of a rude district in the Alps ("Hawks' nest"), and the princes had chosen him because they thought him too weak to rule them. The king of Bohemia, indeed, refused to recognize him as Emperor. Rudolph attacked Bohemia, and seized from it the duchy of Austria, which, until just now, has remained the chief seat of the Hapsburgs. In other ways he showed the now-familiar Hapsburg zeal to widen his personal domain.

GERMANY AND ITALY
During the Interregnum
1254-1273
SCALE OF MILES
0 50 100 200
NORTH SEA
DENMARK
JUTLAND
LAALAND
FALSTER
HOLSTEIN
Lübeck
Hamburg
SLAVINIA
Königsberg
POMERLIA
Danzig
Teutonic
PRUSSIA
Territory
CAMMIN
POMERANIA
Stettin
FRISIA
Bremen
Oldenburg
Elbe
BRANDENBURG
Brandenburg
Zuyder Zee
HOLLAND
Brunswick
Wittenberg
Posen
CUJAVIA
MAZOVIA
LAUSITZ
SAXONY
Meuse
Rhine
POLAND
LOWER SILESIA
Breslau
CRACOVIA
FLANDERS
LOWER
Aix-la-Chappelle
HESSE
THURINGIA
Meissen
UPPER SILESIA
LORRAINE
Mainz
Prague
TREVES
BOHEMIA
MORAVIA
Bouillon
FRANCONIA
Luxemburg
Nuremburg
Brunn
UPPER LORRAINE
Baden
AUSTRIA
Vienna
BAVARIA
Augsburg
Munich
SUABIA
Danube
UPPER ALSACE
LOWER ALSACE
Buda
Pest
Besancon
Constance
Salzburg
HUNGARY
FRANCHE COMTE
LITTLE
STYRIA
TYROL
MERAN
CARINTHIA
BURGUNDY
AQUILEIA
Drave R.
BRESSE
TRENT
Aquilea
GORITZ
CARNIOLA
SLAVONIA
Save R.
Treviso
Trieste
FRANCE
SAVOY
Milan
MARCH OF VERONA
Venice
VENETIAN REPUBLIC
VIENNE
LOMBARDY
Po R.
Parma
Modena
Ferrara
Pola
CROATIA
MONTFERRAT
SALUZZO
Genoa
Bologna
Ravenna
BOSNIA
ROMAGNA
Pesaro
DALMATIA
Rhone R.
KINGDOM OF ARLES
Gulf of Genoa
Florence
MARCH OF ANCONA
THE CHURCH
PROVENCE
Nice
Pisa
TUSCANY
Ancona
ADRIATIC SEA
SERVIA
Gulf of Lyons
Sienna
ELBA
Aquila
CORSICA
Civita Vecchia
Rome
Ajaccio
STATES OF THE CHURCH
Troia
Naples
Tarento
Brindisi
Gulf of Tarento
TYRRHENIAN SEA
SARDINIA
Cagliari
KINGDOM OF SICILY
Palermo
Syracuse

"Sit firm on Thy throne, O Lord," prayed one bishop, "or the Count of Hapsburg will shove Thee off."

After Rudolph's death, the princes of the Empire (the Electoral College) passed the throne from family to family — until, in 1438, after a long line of Bohemian rulers, the imperial dignity came back to the Hapsburgs by the election of Albert, Duke of Austria. From this time, so long as the title endured, *the "Emperor of the Holy Roman Empire" was of the House of Austria,* and election became a form only.

The last medieval Emperor was Maximilian I (1493–1519), the one romantic hero of the Hapsburg race. He made a noble effort to bring Germany abreast of England and France. In the end he failed utterly, because of the selfishness of the German nobles and his own haughty willfulness; and *Germany entered the Modern Age a loose confederacy of many petty sovereign states grouped about Austria.*

Spain at the close of the Middle Ages

The Mohammedan invasion of 711 (p. 41), separated the development of *Spain* from that of the rest of Europe. For centuries, "Africa began at the Pyrenees."

The wave of Moorish invasion, however, left unconquered a few resolute Christian chiefs in the remote fastnesses of the northwestern mountains, and in these districts several little Christian principalities began the long task of winning back their land, crag by crag and stream by stream. This they accomplished in eight hundred years of war, — a war at once patriotic and religious, Spaniard against African, and Christian against Infidel. The long struggle left the Spanish race proud, brave, warlike, unfitted for industrial civilization, intensely patriotic, and blindly devoted to the church.

During the eight centuries of conflict, the Christian states spread gradually to the south and east, — waxing, fusing, splitting up into new states, uniting in kaleidoscopic combinations by marriage and war, — until, before 1400, they had formed the three countries, Portugal, Aragon, and Castile. Nearly a century later, the marriage of Isabella of Castile and

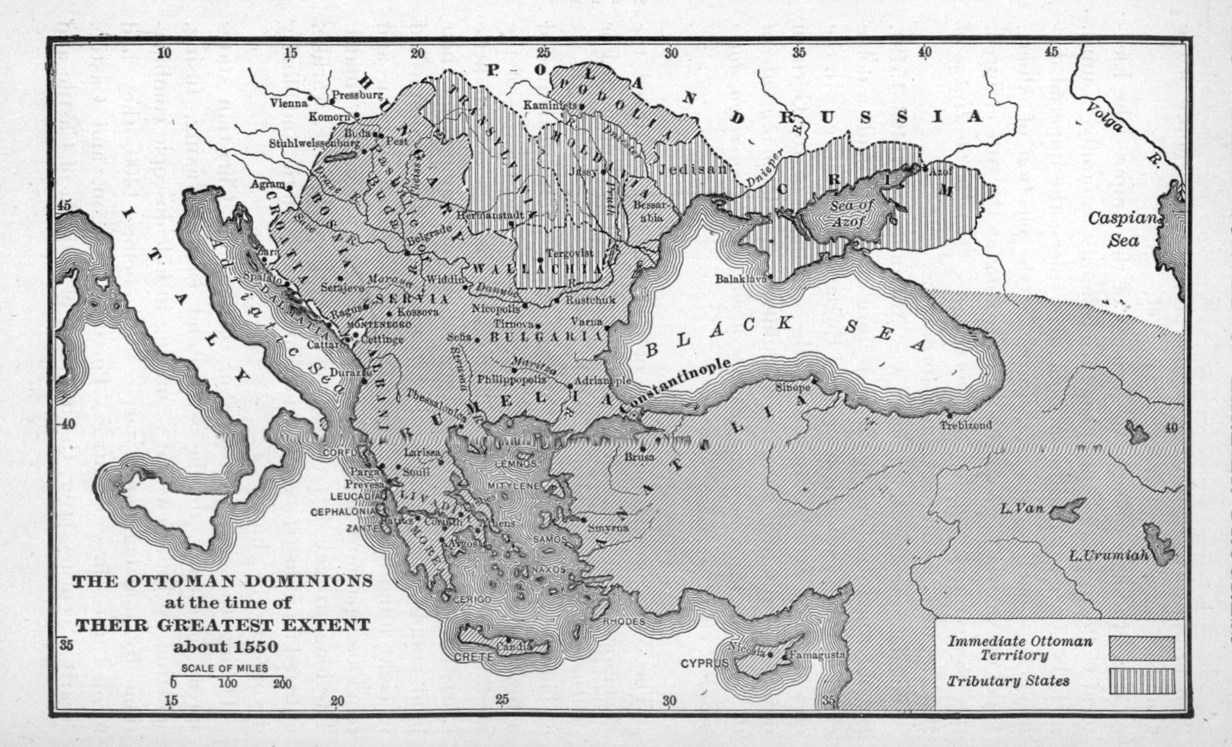

THE OTTOMAN DOMINIONS
at the time of
THEIR GREATEST EXTENT
about 1550

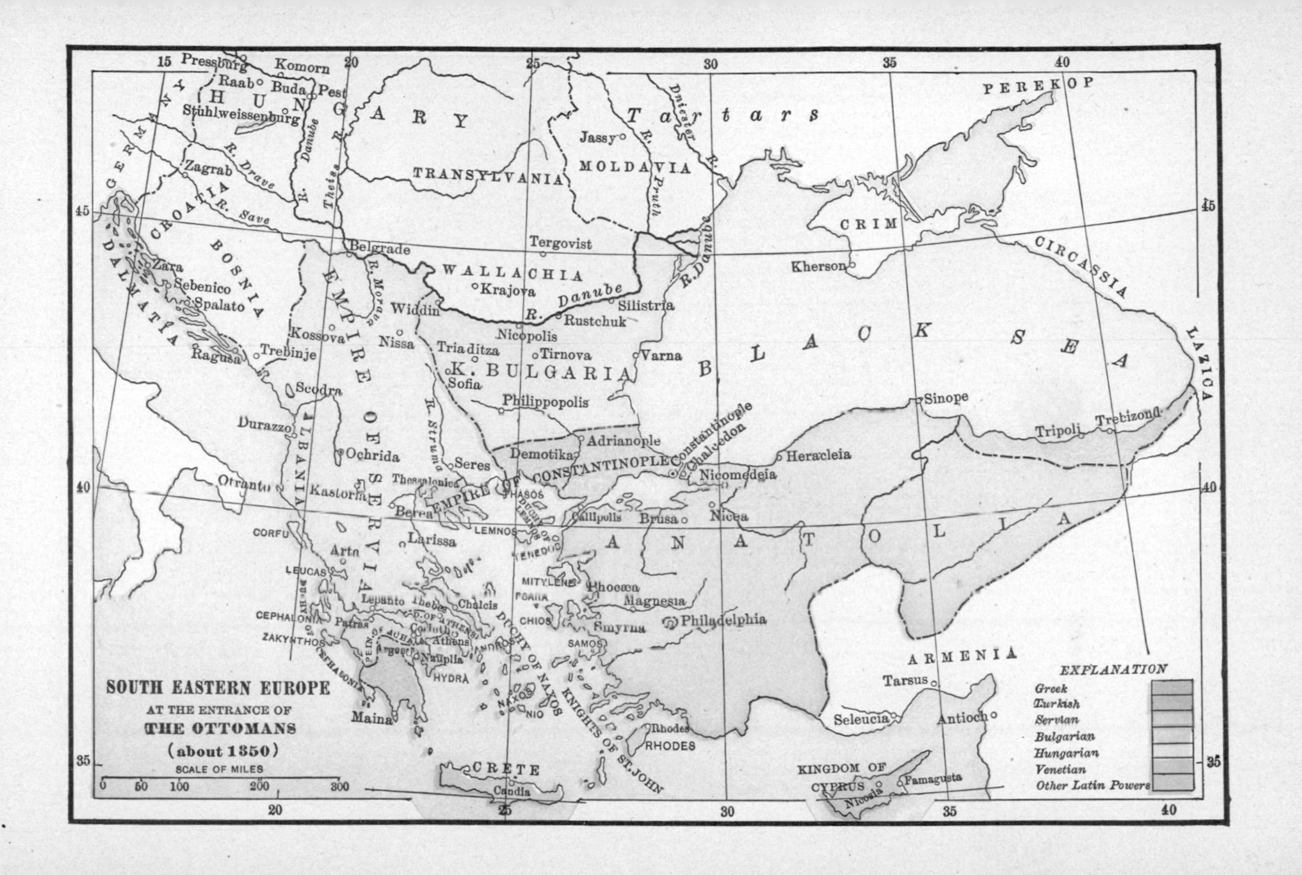

SOUTH EASTERN EUROPE
AT THE ENTRANCE OF
THE OTTOMANS
(about 1350)
SCALE OF MILES
0 50 100 200 300
EXPLANATION
Greek
Turkish
Servian
Bulgarian
Hungarian
Venetian
Other Latin Powers
HUNGARY
GERMANY
Tartars
PEREKOP
CRIM
CIRCASSIA
LAZICA
BLACK SEA
TRANSYLVANIA
MOLDAVIA
WALLACHIA
K. BULGARIA
EMPIRE OF SERVIA
EMPIRE OF CONSTANTINOPLE
ANATOLIA
ARMENIA
CROATIA
BOSNIA
DALMATIA
ALBANIA
DUCHY OF NAXOS
KNIGHTS OF ST. JOHN
KINGDOM OF CYPRUS
CRETE
RHODES
Pressburg
Komorn
Raab
Buda
Pest
Stuhlweissenburg
Zagrab
Zara
Sebenico
Spalato
Ragusa
Trebinje
Scodra
Durazzo
Otranto
Belgrade
Kossova
Nissa
Widdin
Ochrida
Kastoria
Tergovist
Krajova
Jassy
Kherson
Silistria
Rustchuk
Nicopolis
Tirnova
Varna
Triaditza
Sofia
Philippopolis
Adrianople
Demotika
Seres
Thessalonica
Berea
Larissa
Arta
Lepanto
Thebes
Chalcis
Athens
Corinth
Patras
Argos
Nauplia
Maina
Constantinople
Chalcedon
Nicomedeia
Heracleia
Sinope
Tripoli
Trebizond
Gallipolis
Brusa
Nicaea
Phocaea
Magnesia
Smyrna
Philadelphia
Tarsus
Seleucia
Antioch
Famagusta
Nicosia
Candia
Rhodes
CORFU
LEUCAS
CEPHALONIA
ZAKYNTHOS
LEMNOS
THASOS
TENEDOS
MITYLENE
PSARA
CHIOS
SAMOS
HYDRA
ANDROS
NAXOS
NIO
R. Danube
R. Drave
R. Save
R. Theiss
R. Morava
R. Struma
R. Pruth
R. Dniester

Ferdinand of Aragon united the two larger states, and in 1492 their combined power captured Granada, the last Moorish stronghold. In the year that Columbus discovered America under Spanish auspices, Spain at home achieved national union and national independence. During the next two reigns, *the Spanish monarchy,* financed by the treasures of Mexico and Peru, *became the most absolute in Europe.*

The Turks and south-eastern Europe

While the civilized Mohammedan Moors were losing Spain, barbarous *Mohammedan Turks were gaining southeastern Europe.* They established themselves on the European side of the Hellespont first in 1346. Constantinople held out for a century more, a Christian island encompassed by seas of Mohammedanism. But at *Kossova* (1389), the Turks completed the overthrow of the Serbs, and a few years later a crushing defeat was inflicted upon the Hungarians and Poles. Then in, 1453, *Mahomet the Conqueror* entered Constantinople through the breach where the heroic Constantine Palaeologus, last of the Greek emperors, died sword in hand.

The Turks, incapable of civilization, always remained a hostile army encamped among subject Christian populations, whom their rule blighted. From 1453 to 1919, Constantinople remained the capital of their empire. That empire continued to expand for a century more (until about 1550), and for a time it seemed as though nothing could save Western Europe. *Venice on sea, and Hungary by land, were long the two chief outposts of Christendom,* and, almost unaided, they kept up ceaseless warfare to check the Mohammedan invaders. For a time, Hungary was conquered, and then Austria became the bulwark for Western Europe.

Switzerland in the Middle Ages

Switzerland began to grow into a political state just before the year 1300. The brave and sturdy peasantry, in their mountain fastnesses, had preserved much of the old Teutonic independence. Some small districts (cantons) in the German Alps had belonged to the Hapsburg counts. When Rudolph of Hapsburg became duke of distant Austria (p. 118), he left

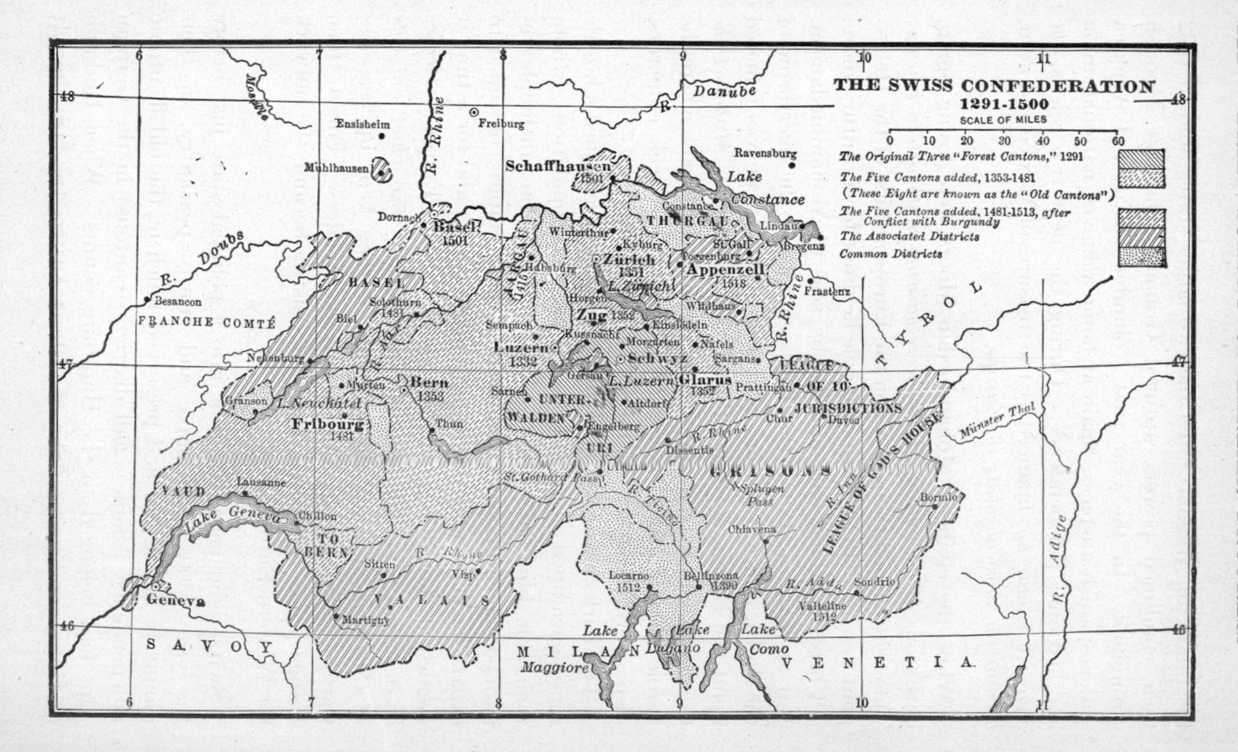
THE SWISS CONFEDERATION
1291-1500
SCALE OF MILES
0 10 20 30 40 50 60
The Original Three "Forest Cantons," 1291
The Five Cantons added, 1353-1481
(These Eight are known as the "Old Cantons")
The Five Cantons added, 1481-1513, after Conflict with Burgundy
The Associated Districts
Common Districts
Danube
Lake Constance
Ravensburg
Freiburg
Ensisheim
Mühlhausen
R. Rhine
Schaffhausen 1501
Basel 1501
Dornach
BASEL
Solothurn 1481
Biel
Zürich 1351
Appenzell 1518
Zug 1352
Luzern 1332
Schwyz
Glarus 1352
Bern 1353
Fribourg 1481
UNTER-WALDEN
URI
THURGAU
Kyburg
Winterthur
Constance
Lindau
Bregenz
St.Gall
Toggenburg
Frastenz
L. Zürich
Habsburg
Horgen
Sempach
Kussnacht
Einsiedeln
Morgarten
Näfels
Sargans
Wildhaus
L. Luzern
Gersau
Sarnen
Altdorf
Engelberg
Thun
Murten
L. Neuchâtel
Neuenburg
Granson
R. Doubs
Besancon
FRANCHE COMTÉ
VAUD
Lausanne
Lake Geneva
Chillon
Geneva
TO BERN
Sitten
Visp
VALAIS
Martigny
SAVOY
St. Gothard Pass
Dissentis
Chur
Davos
Prattingau
LEAGUE OF 10 JURISDICTIONS
GRISONS
LEAGUE OF GOD'S HOUSE
R. Inn
Splugen Pass
Chiavenna
Bormio
Sondrio
R. Adda
Valteline 1512
Bellinzona 1390
Locarno 1512
R. Ticino
Lake Maggiore
Lake Lugano
Lake Como
MILAN
VENETIA
TYROL
Münster Thal
R. Adige
Moselle

these possessions to subordinate officers. These agents oppressed the Swiss by extortion and tyranny; and, *in 1291*, the three "Forest Cantons" — *Uri, Schwyz,* and *Unterwalden* — formed a "perpetual league" for mutual defense against tyranny.

For two centuries, from time to time, the Hapsburgs invaded Switzerland with powerful armies, in order to reduce the mountaineers to subjection; and very soon the league against oppression by the lord's agents became a league for independence, against the lord himself. Freedom was established by two great victories, — *Morgarten* (1315) and *Sempach* (1386), — struggles to which belong the myths of William Tell and of Arnold of Winkelried. Between these two battles, other cantons rebelled against their lords and joined the alliance. The new members — among them Bern, Zurich, and Luzern — were small city states, wealthier and more aristocratic than the original union.

Soon after Sempach, the constitution of the league was revised. Each canton kept complete control over its own internal affairs, and the "Diet," or central congress of representatives, was hardly more than a meeting of ambassadors to manage foreign war and divide the plunder. The union kept this loose form until the French Revolution.

The Netherlands

The Netherlands (Low Countries) did not form an independent state in the Middle Ages. They were made up of a group of provinces, part of them fiefs of the Empire, part of them French fiefs. The southern portion has become modern Belgium; the northern part, modern Holland. The land is a low, level tract, and in the Middle Ages it was more densely packed with teeming cities than any other part of Europe.

The inhabitants were a sturdy, independent, slow, industrious, persistent people. Ghent claimed eighty thousand citizens able to bear arms, while Ypres is said to have employed two hundred thousand people in the weaving of cloth. Wealth so abounded that the "counts" of this little district excelled most of the kings of Europe in magnificence.

Many of the cities, like Rotter*dam* and Amster*dam*, were

Trade and manufactures

built on land wrested from the sea by dikes, and they took naturally to commerce. In their markets, the merchants from Italy and the south of Europe exchanged wares with the Hansa merchants of the Baltic. And the Netherland towns were workshops even more than they were trading rooms. "Nothing reached their shores," says one historian, "but received a more perfect finish: what was coarse and almost worthless, became transmuted into something beautiful and good." Matthew Paris,[1] a thirteenth century English chronicler, exclaimed that "the whole world was clothed in English wool *manufactured in Flanders.*"

HALL OF THE CLOTHMAKERS' GILD AT YPRES, BELGIUM; begun, 1200; finished, 1364. Cf. p. 96.

The need of English wool for the Flemish looms made Flanders the ally of England in the Hundred Years' War. During this period the dukes of Burgundy became masters of Flanders. When Louis XI of France (p. 114) seized the rest of Burgundy from its last duke, Charles the Bold, the Flemish towns wisely chose to remain faithful to Mary, the daughter of Charles.

In return for their fidelity, an Estates General of the provinces secured from Princess Mary a grant of *The Great Privilege,*

[1] The name, Matthew of Paris, signifies that this English monk had studied at the University of Paris.

the "Magna Carta of the Netherlands" (1478). This document promised (1) that the provinces might hold Diets at will — composed, as before, of nobles and elected burgesses; (2) that no new tax should be imposed but by the central Diet, the "Estates General"; (3) that no war should be declared but by the consent of that body; (4) that offices should be filled by natives only; and (5) that Dutch should be the official language.

Mary married the young Maximilian of Hapsburg (p. 119), and *the Netherlands passed to the House of Austria.*

IV. "EUROPE" AT THE END OF THE MIDDLE AGES

The "New Monarchies" in Europe

The rise of "monarchic states" is the political change that marks the close of the Middle Ages. At the moment it seemed a disaster to many great and good men, like the Italian Dante, who had their minds fixed on the old ideal of a united Christendom. But, since the days of the old Roman empire, Europe had never known a true union. "Latin Christendom," in its best period, had contained several *layers* of society, — nobles, burgesses, artisans, priests, peasants. These *horizontal* lines of cleavage between classes had been far more disastrous to union than the new cleavage into nations was to be. One class had been more foreign to another in the same land than France to England. French noble and German noble were always ready to make common cause against peasants or townsfolk of *either* country.

The real mission of each of the new monarchies, whether the monarchs saw it yet or not, *was to weld all the classes within its land into one people with a common patriotism.* While this was being done, some old liberties were lost. But, unconsciously, the monarchs were paving the way for a new freedom, a few centuries later, broader and safer than the world had ever known.

We have noted the rise of new powerful monarchies in England, France, Spain, and Austria. Like governments had appeared in Hungary, Bohemia, Sweden, Denmark, and Poland. Two small lands, Switzerland and the Netherlands, were loosely connected with the Austrian Hapsburg monarchy. Two great

France and Spain in Italy

lands had no part in the movement: until 1250, Germany and Italy had been the center of interest; but their claim for universal rule had left them broken in fragments. Not for centuries were they to reach this new form of united monarchic government. *Leadership, therefore, passed from them to France, Spain, and England,* — the three countries in which the new movement was most advanced. Germany and Italy became little more than battle grounds for these other states.

In Italy, in 1250, as a final blow at German dominance (p. 88), the pope had invited a *French* prince, Charles of Anjou, to become King of Sicily. Soon afterward, the city republics of North Italy (p. 99) fell under the rule of "tyrants," and by 1450 the many petty divisions of the peninsula had been brought under one or another of "Five Great States," the Kingdom of Sicily in the south, the Papal States in the center, and Milan, Florence, and Venice, in the north.

This movement toward unity, however, had not gone far enough to make Italy safe. In 1494, as heir of the House of Anjou, Charles VIII of France claimed the crown of Sicily, crossed the Alps with a mighty army, and marched victoriously from end to end of the peninsula, regulating at will not only the southern kingdom but the northern states as well. But behind him gathered insulted Italian foes; Ferdinand of Aragon advanced a claim to Sicily; and Venice joined the anti-French party. Charles secured his retreat into France by a desperate battle; but Spain was left mistress of Sicily and Naples.

The danger of a world-monarch

Now swift steps brought the Hapsburg power within sight of a world-monarchy. Ferdinand of Aragon had married one daughter to the young English prince soon to become Henry VIII, and another to Philip of Hapsburg, son of the Emperor Maximilian and Mary of Burgundy (p. 119). From this last marriage, in 1500, was born a child, Charles.

Philip, father of Charles, had been ruler of the rich provinces of the Netherlands through his mother, Mary; and his early death left those districts to Charles while yet a boy. In 1516 Charles also succeeded his grandfather, Ferdinand, as king

Illustration from a Fifteenth Century Manuscript, showing in the foreground Maximilian of Austria, Mary of Burgundy, and their son Philip. The original is in colors.

of Sicily and Naples and as king of Spain, with the gold-producing realms in America that had just become Spain's. Three years later he succeeded his other grandfather, Maximilian, as the hereditary ruler of Austria, with its many dependent provinces. Then, still a boy of nineteen, Charles became a candidate for the title of Emperor, which Maximilian's death had left vacant; and his wealth (or that of his Flemish merchants) enabled him to win against his rivals, Francis of France and Henry VIII of England.

Thus Charles I of Spain, at twenty, became also Charles V, Emperor of the Holy Roman Empire. This election gave him a claim to lordship over Germany and the rest of Italy. His hereditary possessions made it seem possible for a while that he might make his claim good — and so more than restore the empire of the first great Charles (Charlemagne).

Compact France, at first, was his only obstacle (p. 115); and no time was lost by Charles and the French Francis in joining battle. The battle of Pavia left Francis a captive, and France apparently at the Hapsburg's feet. *But just then* (1520) *an obscure monk in Germany* burned a papal bull and started a movement which split Germany and Europe at once into opposing camps, and *rendered forever vain the dream of restoring the old imperial unity of Christendom.* This was the political situation when Europe entered the new age of the Protestant Revolt. We must turn back once more to note the intellectual change that had prepared the way for that revolt.

V. THE RENAISSANCE, 1300–1520

The periods within the feudal age

The Age of Feudalism (pp. 54–104) covered five hundred years — from 800 to 1300. The first three centuries (800–1100) were a continuation of the "Dark Ages" of the barbarian invasion, after the brief interruption by Charlemagne. In those gloomy three hundred years we noted the grim feudal system at its height, the medieval church, serf labor, the destructive strife between empire and papacy, and, at the close, the Norman conquest of England.

(1) The Dark Ages

The year 1100 was the threshold over which we passed from those centuries of gloom *to two centuries of fruitful progress.* That Age of the Crusades saw also the rise of towns, of universities, of popular literatures, of Gothic architecture in cathedrals and town halls, of the growth of France out of feudal fragments into one kingdom, and of the rise of courts and of Parliament in England.

(2) The Crusades

The year 1300, to which we have now come, *is another mile-stone of progress,* introducing two centuries of still more rapid advance. *The period 1300–1520 we call the Age of the Renaissance, because those centuries are marked by a "rebirth" of a long-forgotten way of looking at life.* That old way had expressed itself in the art and literature of the ancient Greeks. Accordingly, the men of the new age were passionately enthusiastic over all remains of the old classical period. The fundamental characteristic of the Renaissance, however, was not its devotion to the past, but its joyous self-trust in the present. The men of the Renaissance cared for the ancient culture because they found there what they themselves thought and felt.

The age of the Renaissance

Relation to "Ancient" culture

Between those classical times and the fourteenth century there had intervened centuries of very different life — which we have been studying. Those "Middle Ages" had *three marks* on the intellectual side. (1) Ignorance was the general rule; and even the learned followed slavishly in the footsteps of some intellectual master. (2) Man *as an individual* counted for little. In all his activities he was part of some gild or order or corporation. (3) Interest in the future life was so intense that many good men neglected the present life. Beauty in nature was little regarded, or regarded as a temptation of the devil.

The Renaissance and the feudal age

The Renaissance changed all this. (1) For blind obedience to authority, it substituted the free inquiring way in which the Ancients had looked at things. (2) Men developed new self-reliance and self-confidence, and a fresh and lively originality. And (3) they awoke to delight in flower and sky and mountain, in the beauty of the human body, in all the pleasures of the natural world.

The Renaissance begins in Italy

This transformation — one of the two or three most wonderful changes in all history — began first in Italy. It was well over in that land by 1550; while it hardly began in England until 1500, and there it lasted through Shakspere's age, to about 1600. It showed itself, too, at different times in different ways: first in art, then in a revival of learning, and finally in religious reform.

St. Mark's, Venice. This is a famous example of Byzantine architecture, which was based upon the Romanesque, and modified by Gothic and Saracenic influences. Note the minarets and domes. See also the Ducal Palace on opposite page.

Italy was the natural home for a revival in literature and art. Virgil had been read by a few Italian scholars all down the Middle Ages. The Italian language was nearer the Latin than any other European language was, and more manuscripts of the ancient Roman writers survived in Italy than elsewhere in Western Europe. Thus the Italian *Petrarch* (1304–1374) stands out the first great champion of the coming age. His graceful sonnets are a famous part of Italian poetry, but his

real work was as a tireless critic of the medieval system. He attacked vehemently the superstitions and false science of the day; he ridiculed the universities, with their blind reverence for "authority," as "nests of gloomy ignorance." But he did more than destroy. He, and his disciples after him, began enthusiastic search for classical manuscripts and other remains, to recover what the ancients had possessed of art and knowledge. One of those disciples, Boccaccio, wrote the first dictionaries of

THE DUCAL PALACE, VENICE, facing the Square of St. Mark's.

classical geography and of Greek mythology, and brought back the study of Greek to Italy.

The revival of classical learning in Italy *aided* by the fall of Constantinople

After 1400, the knowledge of Greek grew rapidly among the educated. Greek scholars were invited to the Italian cities and were given professorships in the universities. Increasing danger in the Greek Empire from the Turk made such invitations welcome, and the high prices paid by princely Italian collectors drew more and more of the literary treasures of Constantinople to the Italian cities. Many a fugitive scholar from the East found the possession of some precious manuscript the key to fortune and favor. This movement received a sudden, but brief, acceleration when Constantinople fell, in 1453. "Greece did not perish," said an Italian scholar; "it emigrated to Italy." And soon the new enthusiasm for the classics (*humanism*) captured even the universities, which at first had withstood it fiercely.

Renaissance art

Painting and sculpture were reborn, with the rebirth of delight in life. Italian painting culminated in the years from 1470 to 1550. To these eighty years belongs the work of Leonardo da Vinci, Michael Angelo, Perugino, Raphael, Andrea del Sarto, Giorgione, Titian, Tintoretto, Correggio. A little later came the great periods of Dutch and Spanish painting. The new development in this art in all these lands was made possible, of course, by new methods of preparing oil paints, invented by the Van Eycks in Holland, so that it was possible to paint upon canvas, instead of only upon walls and ceilings.

Return toward pagan morals

There was an evil, pagan side to the Italian Renaissance. The men of the new movement, having cast off old restraints and religious beliefs, fell often into gross and shallow unbelief and into shameless self-indulgence. Delight in beauty sometimes sank into gross sensuality. Morals declined; and for a time Italian society sank lower than the old pagan world. The "Men of the Renaissance" were always polished and elegant and full of robust vitality; but many of them went to their goal recklessly by any means, and some of them were monsters of perfidy and cruelty.

This side of the Renaissance was typified by the Italian *Condottieri*, — roving captains of bands of soldiers of fortune. These chieftains sold their services to any city with a price to pay, — and then betrayed it, on occasion, or seized it for themselves, if convenient. Such was the source of most of the Italian "tyrants" (p. 126) of the time. Many of them were generous patrons of art and learning; but their marked characteristics were indomitable will, reckless scorn of danger, powerful minds, and absolute freedom from moral scruple —

which led them to extremes of cruelty and perfidy whenever such measures seemed useful to them. Like traits show a few years later, in the Spanish conquerors of the New World, — Cortez, Pizarro, Balboa, and their fellows. The scores of English sea-kings of the next century — Raleigh, Drake, Hawkins, Gilbert, Grenville (who fought "the fight of the one and the fifty-three"[1]) — belong to the same order of men *except* that in them cruelty is refined into sternness, and perfidy is replaced by lofty honor — because of the moral earnestness of the Renaissance in the North.

The religious and scientific Renaissance in the North

For in the north of Europe the Renaissance was religious and scientific rather than artistic. A little before 1500, the "New Learning" from Italy was welcomed by an enthusiastic group of young scholars in England, known as the "Oxford Reformers." In Italy, Petrarch and his followers had started the new science of "historical criticism," — a careful study of old and corrupted documents to find out their original form and true meaning. The Oxford Reformers developed this science into a means of correcting evils and errors that had crept into religion.

Erasmus, 1466–1536

This was especially true of Erasmus, a Hollander living in England. In 1516 he published the New Testament *in the original Greek*, with a careful Latin translation. The Greek text was prepared much more carefully, and was undoubtedly much nearer the original gospels, than any the Middle Ages had known, and it was accompanied by critical notes. Now, for the first time, ordinary scholars could test the accuracy of the common translation (the Vulgate) in use in the church. Afterward Erasmus edited the writings of many early Christian Fathers, to show the character of *early* Christianity.

In another sort of works, as in his *Praise of Folly*, Erasmus lashed the false learning and foolish methods of the monks and Schoolmen. He has been called "the Scholar of the Reformation." His writings did furnish Luther (p. 135) with much

[1] Read Tennyson's poem of that name.

material ready for use against the old religious system; but Erasmus was not himself a revolutionist. Instead, he worked, with beautiful charity and patience and largeness of view, for reform *within* the great mother church.

Sir Thomas More

Another leader of the Oxford Reformers was Sir Thomas More, one of the noblest Englishmen of any age. He was a distinguished scholar — his learning brightened by a gentle and pervading humor — and a man of great personal charm. In the year that Erasmus published his Greek Testament, More issued his *Description of the Republic of Utopia* ("Nowhere"). He portrays, with burning sympathy, the miseries of the English peasantry, and points accusingly to the barbarous social and political conditions of his time by contrasting with them the conditions in "Nowhere" — where the people elect their government (which accordingly is devoted solely to their welfare), possess good homes, work short hours, enjoy absolute freedom of speech, high intellectual culture, and universal happiness, with all property in common. *Utopia* was the first of the many modern attempts to picture, in the guise of fiction, an ideal state of society.

New inventions change the world

The new intellectual movement was marked by a number of new inventions or by the first practical use of them. *Gunpowder*, known for some time but much improved about 1500, gave the final blow to the already dying feudalism. *Printing*, from movable types (1450) upon cheap *paper* instead of parchment, did more to advance the new order than gunpowder could do to destroy the old. *The telescope* gave knowledge of other worlds. *The mariner's compass* came in time to enable Columbus to double the area of the world.

Cologne Cathedral. — This magnificent structure was begun in 1248. The work proceeded slowly and was halted entirely during the Reformation. It was resumed in 1823 and was finally completed in 1880.

The design was inspired by the Cathedral of Amiens, and all that is best in its architecture is French.

PART I

THE AGE OF THE PROTESTANT REFORMATION, 1520–1648

CHAPTER I

THE REFORMATION UPON THE CONTINENT

LUTHERANISM

The need for religious reform

All the later references to the church, in the preceding survey, have involved some mention of abuses growing up within it. Good Christians lamented those abuses. A few wise, broad-minded, genial men, like Erasmus and More (pp. 133–134), strove earnestly to *reform* them. Less patient, more impetuous men broke away in revolt against the church itself. This revolt divided Western Christendom into hostile camps for centuries. It is called the Protestant "Reformation" or, perhaps better, the Protestant "Revolt." This latter name helps us to keep in mind that the Protestant movement does not include a vast "reform" within the church itself, a reform begun by Erasmus and his associates and hastened of course by the "revolt."

Special abuses in Germany

The revolt began in Germany. That land had a special grievance. It was then a poor country; but, since it lacked a strong government to protect it, its little, hard-won wealth was drained away to richer Italy by extortionate papal taxes of many sorts. A like abuse existed in other countries, but nowhere else in so serious a degree. From peasant to prince, the German people had long grumbled as they paid; and they needed only a leader to rise against papal control.

Martin Luther

Martin Luther (1483–1546), son of a Thuringian peasant-miner, became that needed leader. Luther was a born fighter, —

a straightforward, forceful man, with a blunt homely way that sometimes degenerated into coarseness. Erasmus addressed polite society: Luther spoke to the people. His father had meant him to be a lawyer, and, with great difficulty, had managed to send him to a university; but, seized by terror of hell and fear for his soul, the young Martin suddenly joined the Augustinian friars — an order somewhat like the Franciscans. His scholarship and his effective preaching soon attracted attention, and

ST. PETER'S, ROME. — To the right stands the Vatican, the palace of the popes.

Duke Frederick the Wise of Saxony made him a professor of theology in the new University of Wittenberg. There, at thirty-four, he entered upon his struggle with Rome.

Luther and the sale of indulgences

Luther's revolt *began* in his opposition to the sale of indulgences. To get money to rebuild St. Peter's Cathedral at Rome, a German archbishop had licensed John Tetzel, a Dominican, to sell indulgences. The practice was an old one, arising easily out of the doctrine of "penance." The authorized teaching of the church was, that, in reward for some pious act — or for the gift of money for a pious purpose — a sinner *who had truly repented and who had, so far as possible, atoned for his sins,* might have the punishment due *in purgatory* remitted by the church. "Letters of indulgence" from the pope, — the immediate representative of St. Peter, — were especially valued, and it had become customary to sell them in great quantities as one source of the papal revenues. The ignorant masses, unable to read the Latin documents, often thought that an "indulgence" was an *unconditional* pardon, — contrary to the doctrine of the church, — or even that it was a license to sin in future; and some professional "pardoners," who peddled such "letters," encouraged these gross errors in their zeal to raise money. Tetzel was a special offender in this way. A rude German rhyme, ascribed to him, runs, "The money rattles in the box; the soul from purgatory flies." More than a hundred years before Luther, the bright-souled Chaucer had given the only bitter lines in his *Canterbury Tales* to the Pardoner with his wallet "bret-ful of pardons, come from Rome all hot." Since then, the evil had grown hugely. The gentle Erasmus wrote scathing words against it. Luther had criticized it on more than one occasion. Now a visit of Tetzel to Wittenberg, with a batch of these papal letters, aroused him to more vehement protest.

Luther's theses arouse Germany

On a Sunday in October, 1517, Luther nailed to the door of the Wittenberg church ninety-five "theses" (statements) upon which he challenged all comers to debate. That door was the usual university bulletin board, and it was customary for one scholar to challenge others to debate in this way.

But Luther's act had consequences far beyond the university. The theses were *in Latin*, the regular university language. They accepted the church doctrine about indulgences, but criticized savagely the abuses connected with *the practice of selling them.* Is there not danger, Luther hinted, that poor men may wonder why, if the pope releases souls from purgatory for money, he does not do so for charity's sake? It was these *criticisms* that drew popular attention. The printing press scattered copies of the theses broadcast *in German*, and in a few days they were being discussed hotly over all Germany.

Luther and the pope

At first Luther seems to have had no thought of denying the authority of the pope. Indeed, he asserted that the pope would be the first to condemn Tetzel's practices. And he was honestly amazed, too, at the public attention his theses received. He dedicated a pamphlet in defense of them to Pope Leo (X), and in his letter to the pope he says:

"By what unlucky chance it is that these propositions of mine should go forth into nearly all the earth, I am at a loss to know. They were set forth here for our use alone. . . . But what shall I do? Recall them I cannot; and yet I see that their notoriety bringeth upon me great odium. In order then to soften my adversaries, . . . I send forth these trifles to explain my theses. For greater safety, I let them go forth, most blessed Father, under your name and under the shadow of your protection. Here all who will may see how basely I am belied. . . . Save or slay, call or recall, approve or disapprove, as it shall best please you, *I shall acknowledge your voice as the voice of Christ.*"

The matter of indulgences soon dropped out of sight. The papal legate in Germany reprimanded Tetzel so sternly for his gross mispractice that the offender is said to have died soon after from mortification. At all events, now that the church had its attention called so forcefully to the abuses, they were soon corrected.[1] But, meanwhile, in the heat of argument, Luther passed quickly to a more radical position. He startled all parties by expressing approval of the heretic Hussites; and in 1519 he *denied the authority of the pope and of church*

[1] Catholics to-day admit, of course, that there had been good cause for complaint. One of the greatest of modern scholars, the Catholic Jansen (*History of the German People*, III, 92) declares that "grievous abuses" in the manner of offering indulgences "caused all sorts of scandal." The Council of Trent, which sat at intervals from 1545 to 1563, to reform the church, reasserted the old doctrine in its purity, emphasizing the indispensable need of "contrition, confession, and atonement." It condemned "those who assert that indulgences are useless, or who deny the power of the church to grant them. . . . In granting them, however, the Council desires that . . . moderation be observed. . . . And, being desirous of mending the abuses which have crept in, by occasion of which the honorable name of indulgences is blasphemed by heretics, the Council ordains . . . that all evil gains for the obtaining thereof be abolished." In later times the practice of granting indulgences in return for money has been discontinued.

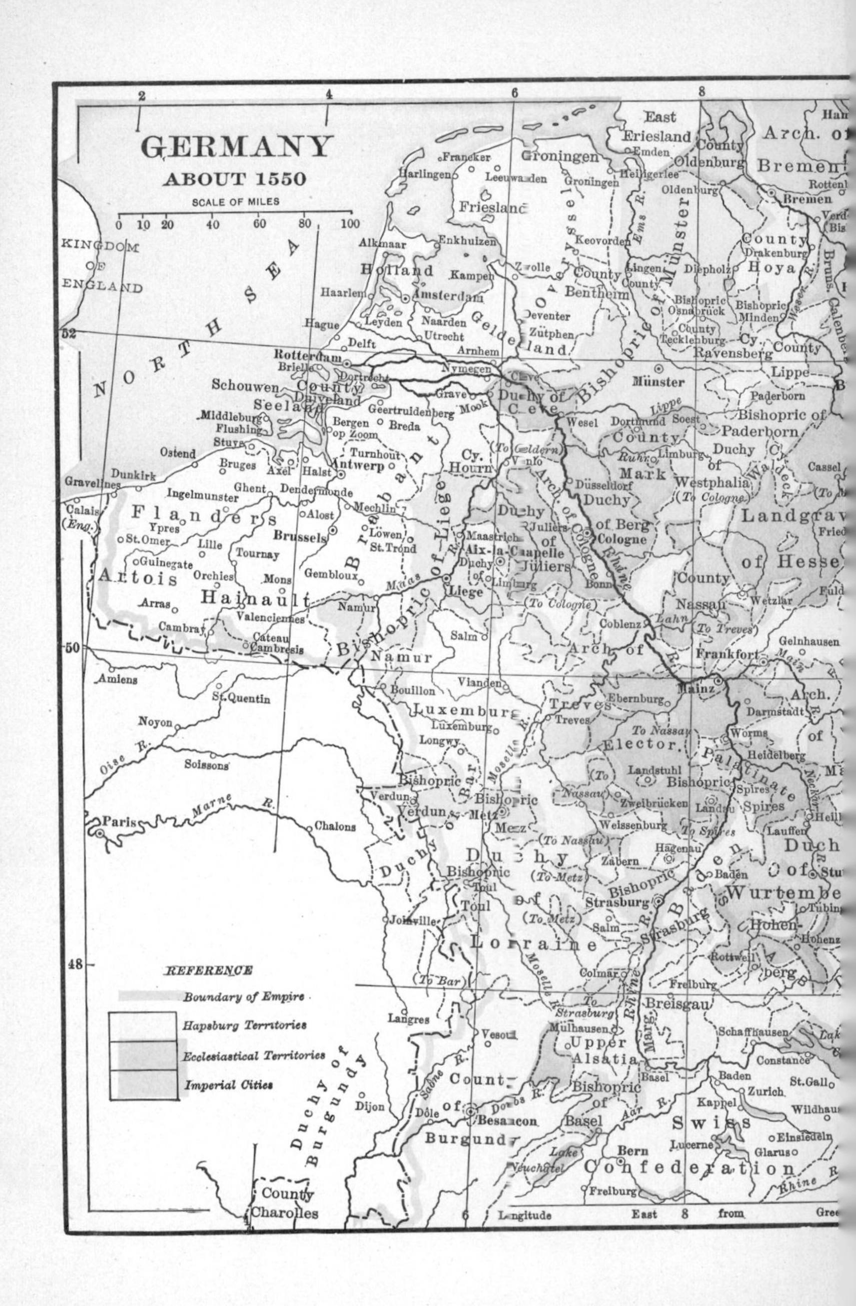
GERMANY
ABOUT 1550
SCALE OF MILES
0 10 20 40 60 80 100
KINGDOM OF ENGLAND
NORTH SEA
East Friesland
Emden
County Oldenburg
Arch. of Bremen
Bremen
Groningen
Franeker
Harlingen
Leeuwarden
Friesland
Alkmaar
Enkhuizen
Holland
Kampen
Zwolle
Amsterdam
Haarlem
Hague
Leyden
Naarden
Utrecht
Delft
Rotterdam
Brielle
Dortrecht
Schouwen
County Duiveland
Seeland
Middleburg
Flushing
Stuys
Geertruidenberg
Bergen op Zoom
Breda
Turnhout
Antwerp
Ostend
Bruges
Axel
Halst
Dunkirk
Gravelines
Ghent
Dendermonde
Ingelmunster
Calais (Eng.)
Flanders
Ypres
St. Omer
Lille
Alost
Mechlin
Brussels
Löwen
St. Trond
Tournay
Guinegate
Artois
Orchies
Mons
Gembloux
Hainault
Arras
Valenciennes
Namur
Cambray
Cateau Cambresis
Bishopric of Liege
Liege
Namur
Brabant
Maas R.
Cy. Hourn
Mook
Grave
Nymegen
Arnhem
Gelderland
Deventer
Zütphen
Overyssel
Keovorden
County Bentheim
Lingen County
Ems R.
Bishopric of Münster
Münster
Diepholz
County Hoya
Drakenburg
Bishopric Osnabrück
Bishopric Minden
County Tecklenburg
Cy. Ravensberg
County Lippe
Paderborn
Bishopric of Paderborn
Cleve
Duchy of Cleve
Wesel
Dortmund
Soest
Lippe
County Mark
Ruhr R.
Limburg
Duchy of Westphalia
(To Cologne)
Waldeck
Cassel
Landgrave of Hesse
Venlo
(To Geldern)
Arch. of Cologne
Düsseldorf
Duchy of Berg
Cologne
Rhine R.
Duchy Juliers of Juliers
Maastricht
Aix-la-Chapelle
Duchy of Limburg
Bonn
(To Cologne)
County Nassau
Wetzlar
Lahn
Coblenz
(To Treves)
Salm
Arch. of Treves
Gelnhausen
Frankfort
Main R.
Mainz
Amiens
St. Quentin
Bouillon
Vianden
Luxemburg
Longwy
Treves
Ebernburg
To Nassau
Elector
Palatinate
Darmstadt
Arch. of
Worms
Heidelberg
Noyon
Oise R.
Soissons
Bishopric Verdun
Verdun
Bar
Bishopric Metz
Metz
Moselle R.
(To Nassau)
Landstuhl
Zweibrücken
Bishopric Spires
Spires
Landau
Neckar R.
Weissenburg
(To Spires)
Lauffen
Paris
Marne R.
Chalons
Duchy of Bar
Duchy of Lorraine
(To Nassau)
Hagenau
Zabern
(To Metz)
Bishopric Toul
Toul
Bishopric Strasburg
Strasburg
Baden
Duchy of Wurtemberg
Tübingen
Joinville
(To Metz)
Salm
Hohenzollern
Rottweil
Colmar
Freiburg
Breisgau
(To Bar)
Langres
To Strasburg
Mülhausen
Upper Alsatia
Marg.
Schaffhausen
Constance
Vesoul
Basel
Baden
St. Gallo
Zurich
Kappel
Wildhaus
Duchy of Burgundy
Dijon
Saône R.
County of Burgundy
Dôle
Besançon
Doubs R.
Bishopric of Basel
Aar R.
Swiss Confederation
Bern
Lucerne
Einsiedeln
Glarus
Lake Neuchâtel
Freiburg
Rhine R.
County Charolles
REFERENCE
Boundary of Empire
Hapsburg Territories
Ecclesiastical Territories
Imperial Cities
Longitude East 8 from Gree
52
50
48
2 4 6 8

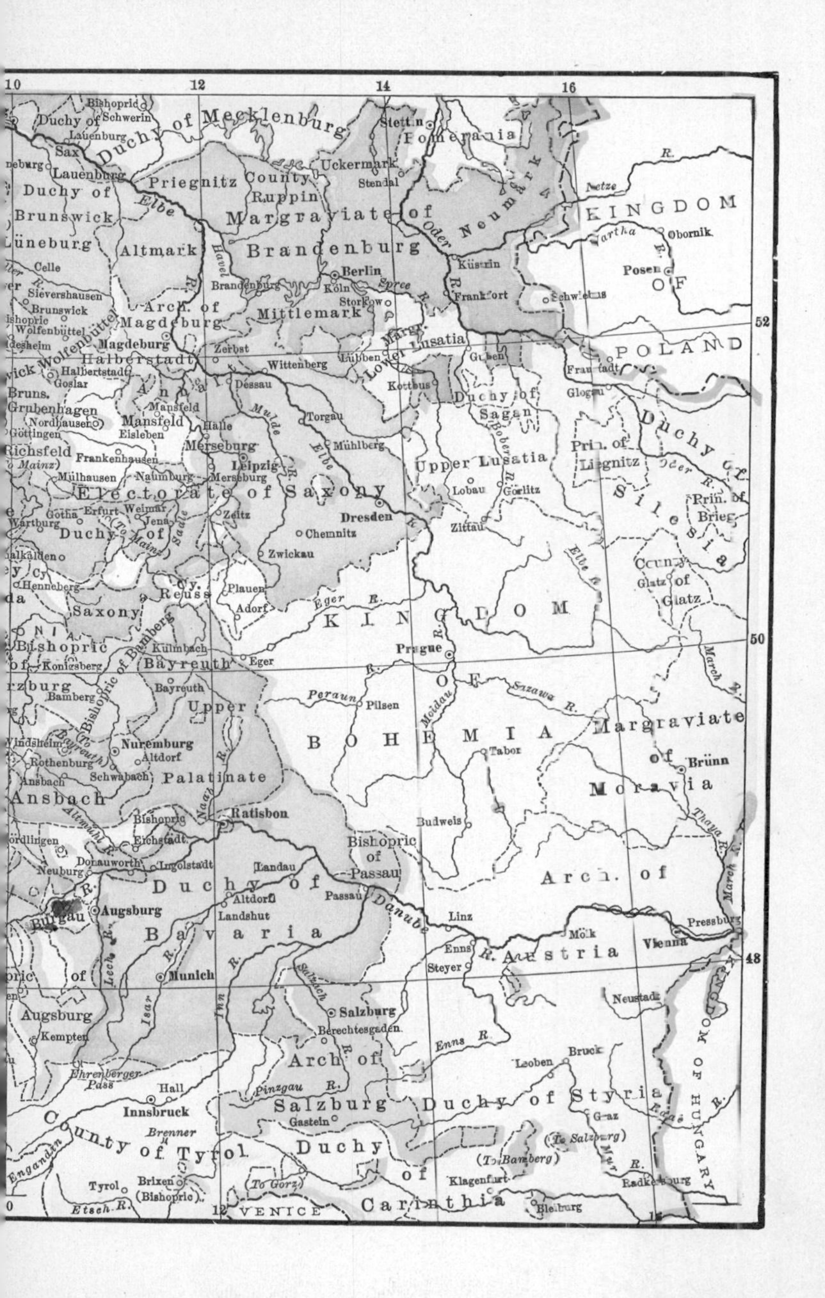
Duchy of Mecklenburg
Pomerania
Uckermark
Neumark
Priegnitz
County Ruppin
Margraviate of Brandenburg
Berlin
Altmark
Mittlemark
Duchy of Brunswick
Lüneburg
Arch. of Magdeburg
Magdeburg
Halberstadt
Lower Lusatia
Duchy of Sagan
Upper Lusatia
Electorate of Saxony
Leipzig
Dresden
Kingdom of Poland
Posen
Duchy of Silesia
Prin. of Liegnitz
Prin. of Brieg
County of Glatz
Kingdom of Bohemia
Prague
Pilsen
Margraviate of Moravia
Brünn
Upper Palatinate
Nuremburg
Ratisbon
Bishopric of Passau
Duchy of Bavaria
Augsburg
Munich
Arch. of Austria
Linz
Vienna
Pressburg
Kingdom of Hungary
Salzburg
Arch. of Salzburg
Duchy of Styria
Graz
Duchy of Carinthia
Klagenfurt
County of Tyrol
Innsbruck
Venice
Danube R.
Elbe R.
Oder R.

councils, appealing instead to the Bible as the sole rule of conduct and belief.

Luther *tried* to substitute one authority for another. He had no intention of advancing freedom of thought. But the Bible is capable of many interpretations. His appeal to the Bible as the sole authority meant Luther's understanding of the Bible. In the mouth of another man, however, the same appeal meant that other's understanding of the book. So, *unintentionally*, the Protestant revolt came to stand for *the right of individual judgment in matters of religion.*

Luther burns the papal bull

Pope Leo, a gentle and good man, tried to bring the rebel back into the church by persuasion and argument; but when this failed, he issued a bull of excommunication against Luther. The document condemned a number of the new teachings, ordered Luther to burn his books, and threatened him and his followers with punishment as heretics unless they recanted within two months. Instead of burning his own books, *Luther burned the papal bull* in a bonfire of other writings of the church, before the town gate *in December, 1520,* while a crowd of students and townsfolk applauded and brought fuel to feed the flames. Open war had begun between the German friar and the church.

Luther at Worms

Luther was protected by his monarch, the Duke of Saxony; and the pope appealed to the young Emperor, Charles V (p. 128), to punish the heretic. Germany was in uproar. A papal legate wrote, "Nine-tenths of Germany shouts for Luther." The Emperor, coming to Germany for the first time, called an imperial Diet [1] at Worms (1521) and summoned Luther to be present, pledging safe conduct.

Friends tried to dissuade Luther from going, pointing to the fate of Hus a century before; but he replied merely, "I would

[1] The German *Diet* in early times contained only nobles. In the fourteenth century, representatives of the "free cities" were admitted. Then the Diet sat usually in three Houses, Electors (the seven great princes), Princes (of second rank), and City Representatives. It never gained any real place in the government of the Empire.

go on if there were as many devils in Worms as there are tiles on the housetops." He found himself confronted with scornful contempt by the great dignitaries of the church and of the Empire, arrayed almost solidly against him. But he boldly answered the haughty command that he recant, — "Unless I am proven wrong by Scripture or plain reason . . . my conscience is caught in the word of God. . . . Here I stand. As God is my help, I can no otherwise."

A German Bible

Charles kept his pledge, and Luther departed in safety. A month later the Diet pronounced against him the "ban of the Empire," ordering that he be seized for execution and that his writings be burned. But the friendly Frederick of Saxony had had him seized, on his way homeward, and carried into hiding in the castle of Wartburg. Here, while for a time most of his followers mourned him as dead, Luther translated the New Testament into strong and simple German.

While he was still in hiding, his teachings were accepted by whole communities. Priests married; nuns and monks left their convents; powerful princes joined the new communion, sometimes from honest conviction, sometimes as an excuse for seizing church lands.

Lutheranism wins the North German princes

In 1522, in spite of dangers, Luther left his retreat to guide the movement again in person and to restrain it from going to extremes that he disliked. Changes in religion, he urged, should be made only *by the governments*, not by the people. He preserved all that he could of the old church services and organization, establishing them on essentially the basis on which they still stand in the Lutheran church. *By 1530, the Lutheran church, under the protection of the rulers of the various states, was in possession of North Germany.*

The peasant rising in in 1525

Meantime the revolt against the old church had led to the rise of some sects of wild fanatics, one of which found sanction for polygamy in its interpretation of the Bible. In 1525, there had been a great rising of the peasants, demanding, "in the name of God's justice," the abolition of serfdom and the right of each parish to choose its own pastor. The peasants in Germany were in a much more deplorable condition than in England, and the new religious teachings had spread among them in connection with new ideas about property, — somewhat as with the Lollard movement in England a hundred years before. So when they rose in arms, in several places they avenged centuries of cruel oppression by massacres of old masters.

Luther preaches a war against the peasants

Luther feared discredit for his new church, and called furiously on the princes to put down this rising with the sword — to "smite, strangle, or stab." The movement was quickly stamped out in blood. The brutal nobles slew many thousands of peasants in merciless battle, and murdered at least ten thousand more in cold blood after the struggle was over, — with ghastly scenes that infinitely surpassed in horror any excesses by the ignorant peasants themselves. The whole peasant class was crushed down to a level far lower than before, — lower than anywhere else in Europe, — where they were to remain helpless for almost three hundred years.

Foreign wars keep Charles V from acting

Charles V, the young emperor, was a zealous churchman, and if his hands had been free, he would have enforced the ban of the Empire promptly and crushed Lutheranism at its birth. But even while the Diet of Worms was condemning Luther, the Spanish towns were rising in revolt and Francis I of France was seizing Italian territory (p. 128). These events called Charles hastily from Germany. He put down the rebellion promptly and crushed the ancient liberties of the Spanish towns; but *the wars against France*, and against the Turk, with only brief truces, filled the next twenty-three years (1621–1644);[1] *and so for a generation the new faith was left to grow strong.*

It is a peculiar fact that the two countries destitute of settled government gave Europe the Renaissance and the

[1] Some features connected with those wars may be assigned for special reports, if the teacher cares to delay upon them. The following topics are especially suitable: The Battle of Pavia; the sack of Rome by Charles' *Lutheran* soldiers; the alliance between Francis and the Turkish Solyman; Solyman's invasion of Germany; the ravages of Turkish pirates.

Reformation. The intense city life in the small Italian states was favorable to the intellectual activity of the Renaissance; and the absence of strong *central* government was the condition which permitted Lutheranism so long to grow unchecked among the princes of Germany.

The "Protestants" and the Augsburg Confession

The first pause in the French wars came in 1529. Charles at once summoned a German Diet at Speier, which reaffirmed the decree of Worms. Against this decision, however, the Lutheran princes in the Diet presented a protest. This act gave the name *Protestant* to their party.

The following year, in a Diet at Augsburg, the Lutherans put forward a written statement of their beliefs, "the Augsburg Confession," which is still the platform of the Lutheran church. Charles, however, prepared to enforce by arms the decrees of Worms and Speier. In defense, the Protestant nobles organized a League; but an open clash was once more postponed, because Solyman the Magnificent, the Turkish Sultan, invaded Germany and threatened the imperial capital, Vienna.

Before Charles was again at liberty to give his attention to his Protestant subjects, Lutheranism had become the religion not only of most of Germany but also of all Scandinavia, while the English church had cut itself off from Rome as an independent Episcopal church (p. 154), and a new Presbyterian heresy had begun to spread rapidly in France.

Peace of Augsburg

Try as he might, Charles did not find himself free to strike in Germany until 1546, the year of Luther's death. Then two brief struggles settled the contest for the time. In the first, Charles seemed completely victorious; but almost at once the defeated princes rallied again, drove Charles in hurried flight from their domains, and forced him to accept the Peace of Augsburg (1555).

According to this treaty, each ruling prince of the Empire was free to choose between Lutheranism and Catholicism for himself and for all his subjects; but if an *ecclesiastical* ruler became a Protestant, he was to surrender his lands to the

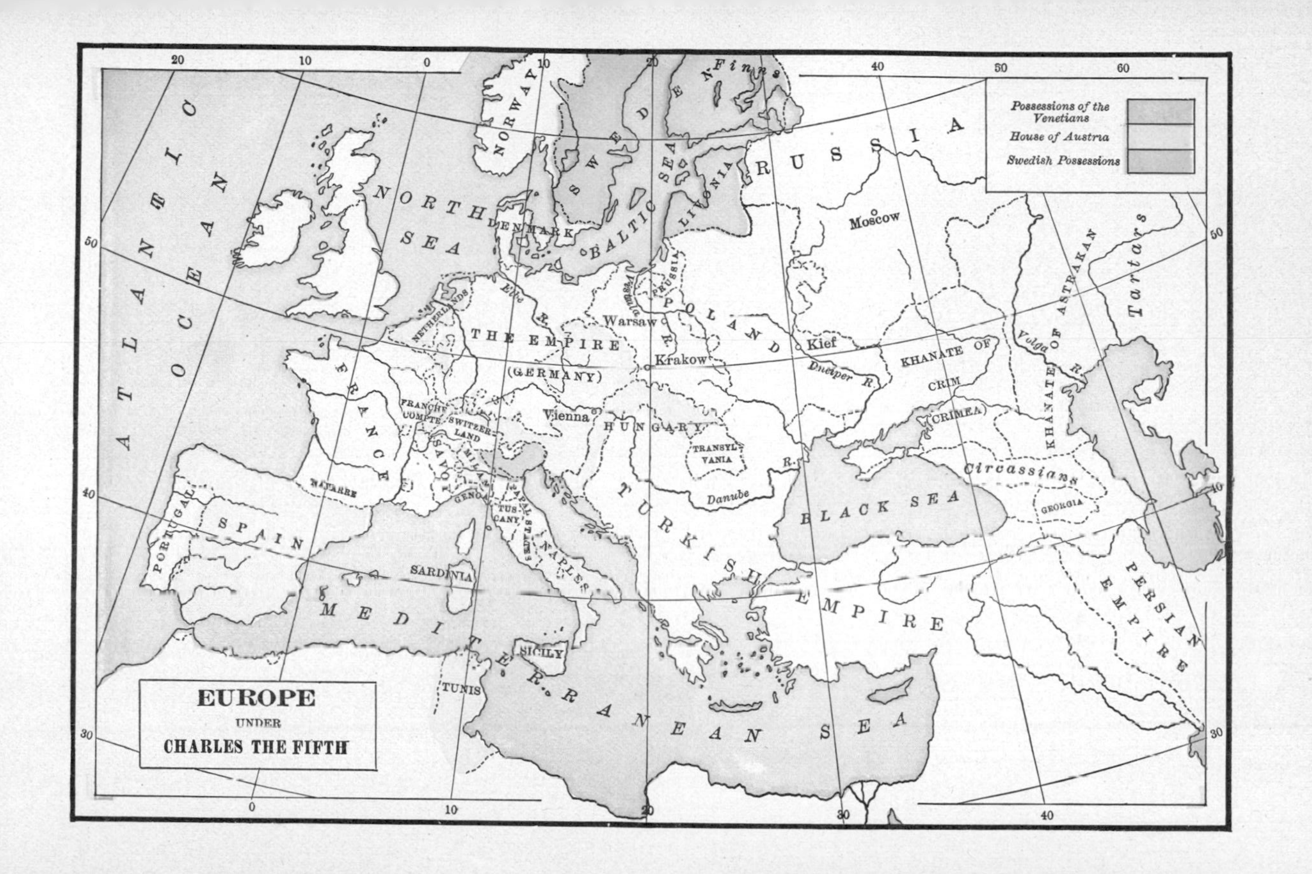
EUROPE
UNDER
CHARLES THE FIFTH
Possessions of the Venetians
House of Austria
Swedish Possessions
ATLANTIC OCEAN
NORTH SEA
BALTIC SEA
NORWAY
SWEDEN
Finns
DENMARK
LIVONIA
RUSSIA
Moscow
Tartars
KHANATE OF ASTRAKAN
Volga R.
PRUSSIA
Vistula
POLAND
Warsaw
Krakow
Kief
Dneiper R.
KHANATE OF CRIM
(CRIMEA)
Circassians
GEORGIA
BLACK SEA
NETHERLANDS
Elbe R.
THE EMPIRE
(GERMANY)
Vienna
HUNGARY
TRANSYLVANIA
Danube
R.
FRANCHE COMTE
SWITZERLAND
SAVOY
MILAN
GENOA
TUSCANY
PAPAL STATES
NAPLES
SARDINIA
SICILY
TUNIS
FRANCE
NAVARRE
SPAIN
PORTUGAL
MEDITERRANEAN SEA
TURKISH EMPIRE
PERSIAN EMPIRE

church, from whom they came. This peace secured *toleration for princes only*, not for their subjects. The people were expected to follow the religion of the ruler.

Abdication of Charles

The Protestants in their last rising had sought aid from Henry II, the new French king; and France for her reward had seized some German districts, including the city of Metz. Chagrined at the loss, and disheartened by the split within the Empire, Charles abdicated his many crowns in 1556. His brother *Ferdinand* became ruler of Austria, and soon after was chosen Emperor, while by marriage he added Hungary to the Hapsburg hereditary dominions. Charles' son, *Philip II*, received the Netherlands, Spain, Naples, and Spanish America.

There were now *two* Hapsburg Houses, one in Spain, one in Austria. *France*, with some reason, *feared that she might be crushed between them*, and was long eager to take advantage of any chance to weaken them, or to seize German lands at their expense.

FOR FURTHER READING. — The opening chapters of Beard's *Martin Luther* picture conditions in Germany. Lindsay's *Luther and the German Reformation* is excellent and brief. Much source material is given in Robinson's *Readings*. The great Catholic histories are too extended and costly for high schools; but, if students have access to the work, they should consult the scholarly *Catholic Encyclopedia* ("Luther," ix, 438 ff.; "Indulgences," VII, 783 ff., etc.).

CALVINISM — IN SWITZERLAND AND FRANCE

While Lutheranism was winning North Germany and Scandinavia, another form of Protestantism, *Calvinism*, was growing up in Switzerland and, for a time, in France and even in the west of Germany.

Zwingli and Luther

This movement was started in 1519 (the year before Luther burned the papal bull), by *Zwingli*, a priest at Zürich, in German Switzerland. Zwingli, like Luther, was of peasant birth, but he too had enjoyed a good education. He was far more radical than Luther. Luther *tried to keep everything of the old worship and doctrine that he did not think forbidden* by the Bible. But

Zwingli *refused to keep anything* of the old *that he did not think absolutely commanded* by the Bible. He also organized a strict system of church discipline which severely punished gaming, swearing, drunkenness, and some innocent sports.

The contrast between Zwingli and Luther appeared clearly in their different attitude toward the Catholic doctrine of *transubstantiation.* Catholics believe that the bread and wine of the communion are turned by the sacrament into the actual body and blood of Christ. Luther tried to hold as much of this doctrine as he could, and to keep to a literal use of Christ's words — "This is my body" (*Mark*, xxiv, 23). He taught that the bread and wine were still bread and wine as they seemed, but that the body and blood of Christ were also present, *along with them* in the communion. "*Con*substantiation" was the term used to signify this doctrine. The followers of Zwingli held that Christ's words were figurative, and that the bread and wine were only *symbols* to remind us of his sacrifice.

Dissensions among the Protestants

This difference prevented a union between the two Protestant movements. Zwingli attempted to secure union, and a conference was arranged in 1529. But Luther stuck stubbornly to his text — "This is my body," and when Zwingli offered his hand in token of amity, *Luther refused to take it* unless Zwingli would first accept those words literally.

This division illustrates the way in which the Protestant appeal to private judgment was to give rise to a multitude of sects. At first, in particular, these sects were scandalously hostile to one another; and, in Germany, the mutual hatred of Lutherans and Calvinists endangered more than once the whole cause of Protestantism. When the Lutheran princes secured the Peace of Augsburg *for themselves,* they did not include Calvinists in the toleration they secured. Catholics, of course, pointed to such dissensions as proof of the necessity of trusting to the collective wisdom of the church, rather than to individual judgments — as conservatives and reactionaries always find argument in the absurdities of progressives.

Zwingli's teachings were accepted rapidly by the rich "city cantons" of Switzerland, both German and French, like Zürich and Berne. But the peasant "forest cantons," the core of the original confederation (p. 123), remained Catholic. In a battle between the two parties, in 1531, Zwingli was killed; but his work was soon taken up — and carried further — by the man whose name has come to stand for the whole movement.

Calvin at Geneva

John Calvin was a young French scholar of sternly logical mind. He is the father of Puritan theology and of the Presbyterian church, with its system of synods and presbyteries. This system of church government and doctrine he built up at Geneva.

Geneva was a French town in the Swiss Alps. It was not yet a member of the Swiss confederation, but it had recently become a free city-republic by rebellion against its overlord. That overlord had been a Catholic ecclesiastic; and so Geneva was now ready to accept the teachings of Zwingli.

In 1536, Calvin, a fugitive from France because of his heresy, found refuge at Geneva, and soon became there an absolute dictator over both the church and the civil government. Indeed, the civil government of the city was absorbed in the church government, and Geneva became a Puritan "theocracy" "with Calvin for its pope."

Calvin took the law of Moses rather than the spirit of Christ for the basis of his legislation. Blasphemy he counted a capital crime, and he once *had a child beheaded* because it had struck its father. The government repressed harshly amusements like dancing, and it tyrannized over the private life of citizens, punishing sternly for absence from church and for luxury in dress. But it did make turbulent and unruly Geneva into a sober, industrious commonwealth, and it furnished many hints for the Puritan colony of Massachusetts a century later.

Calvin and Servetus

One terrible case of persecution, in particular, stains Calvin's fame. *Servetus* was a learned Spanish physician, with intense religious convictions somewhat like those of modern Unitarians. He had had some literary controversies with Calvin; but, to escape from Catholic persecution as a heretic at home, he fled to Geneva. Calvin's government there seized him, tried him in its own way for heresy, and burned him at the stake.

A VILLAGE MERRYMAKING of the sixteenth century, such as Calvin condemned. Compare the earlier Maypole merry-making pictured on page 68.

Incidentally, *this crime put back medical progress for at least fifty years.* The foundation of true medical science lies in a knowledge of the circulation of the blood, as taught in any elementary physiology to-day. But in the time of Servetus, it had been believed for centuries that the bright blood of the arteries and the dark blood of the veins were two distinct systems, one from the heart, the other from the liver. Servetus first discovered that the two were one system. He found out how the dark blood is purified in the lungs, and understood fully the work of the heart. He had just published his medical discovery in the same book that contained his theological opinions. His persecutors sought out and burned this volume so zealously that only two copies (out of the edition of a thousand) have survived, and these were long overlooked. The great discovery in physiology — which would have shown how to save hundreds of thousands of lives — was lost for half a century, until made again, independently, in England (p. 179).

It is worthy of note that Catholic Spain early erected a statue in honor of Servetus; and, in 1903, Calvinists all over the world subscribed a fund for the erection of the noble "expiatory statue," which stands in Geneva to mark the spot where he suffered martyrdom.

Calvinism in Scotland, England, and America

Calvin's writings influenced profoundly his own and future times. Ardent reformers from all Europe flocked to Geneva to imbibe his teachings, and then returned *to spread Calvinism in their own lands.* From Geneva came the seeds of *Scotch Presbyterianism,* of *the great Puritan movement within the English church* (soon to be treated), of *the leading Protestant movement among the Dutch,* and of the *Huguenot church in France.* John Winthrop, the founder of Massachusetts, took his ideas both in religion and in politics from Calvin. It is from the French Calvin, not the German Luther, that modern liberal Protestantism has sprung.

In its original form, the Calvinistic doctrine seems to nearly all men of the present time too somber and merciless. It was, however, sternly logical. It made strong men, and it appealed to strong spirits. True, Calvin did not believe in democracy, and he taught that for "subjects" to resist even a wicked ruler was "to resist God"; but, in spite of this teaching, in the course of historical movements, Calvinism became the ally of political freedom in Holland, England, and America.

CATHOLICISM KEEPS THE SOUTH OF EUROPE

The "Counter-reformation"

For a time, Protestantism promised to win also the south of Europe; but *Spain, Italy, France, Bohemia and South Germany, were finally saved to Catholicism.*

This was *mainly* because the old church quickly purged itself of old abuses. At first Erasmus and other Humanists had been interested in the work of Luther. But when it became plain that that movement was breaking up the unity of Christendom, they were violently repelled by it. Disruption into warring sects, they felt, was a greater evil than existing faults. They continued to work, however, with even greater zeal than before, for *reform within the church.*

Such reform was finally carried out by the *Council of Trent* (1545–1563). That great body did not change Catholic forms; but it defined some doctrines more exactly, pruned away evils (note on p. 140), and infused a greater moral energy into the church.

The new religious enthusiasm within the Catholic world gave birth, also, to several new religious orders. The most important of these was the "Order of Jesus" (Jesuits), founded in 1534 by *Ignatius Loyola,* a gallant Spanish gentleman of deep religious feeling.

The Jesuits

The Jesuits stood to the friars somewhat as the friars stood to the older monks (p. 76). Holding fast like the friars to an intensely religious private life, *they represented a further advance into the world of public affairs.* Their members mingled with men in *all* capacities. Especially did they distinguish themselves as *statesmen* and as *teachers.* Their schools were the best in Europe, and many a Protestant youth was won back by them to Catholicism. In like manner, as individual counselors, they converted many a Protestant prince — especially in Germany, where the religion of the prince determined that of his people; and their many devoted missionaries among the heathen in the New Worlds won vast regions to Christianity and Catholicism.

The Inquisition

Unhappily less praiseworthy forces had a share in the victory of Catholicism. Religious wars, we shall see (p. 166 ff.), in large part kept France, Bohemia, and South Germany Catholic; and elsewhere the final success of the Catholic church in crushing out Protestantism was due in part to *the Inquisition.*

Origin three centuries earlier

The Inquisition dated back to the twelfth century, some three hundred years earlier. At that time the church had suffered one of its periods of decline; and discontent with its corruption had given rise to several small heresies. The most important of these twelfth century heretical sects were *the Albigenses* in southeastern France. They rejected some doctrines of the church, and they rebelled especially against its government by pope and priesthood — so that an old by-word, "I had rather be a Jew," became, for them, "I had rather be a priest"!

The church had made many vain attempts to reclaim these heretics by gentle persuasion, and finally, the great reforming pope, Innocent III, proclaimed a "holy war" against them, declaring them "more wicked than Saracens." The feudal nobles of northern France rallied gladly to this war. Aside from religious motives, they hated the democracy which was beginning to appear in the rising towns of the south, and they hungered greedily for the rich plunder of that more civilized region. A twenty years' struggle, marked by ferocious massacres, crushed the heretics, along with the prosperity — for a century — of what had been the richest province of France.

When *open* resistance ceased in desolated Languedoc, the pope set up a special court to hunt out and exterminate any *secret* heretics remaining there. Soon afterward, *this court*, enlarged and reorganized, *became a regular part of the government of the church for suppressing heresy.* In this final form it is commonly known as the *Spanish* Inquisition. It held sway also in Portugal and Italy, as well as in the wide-lying possessions of Spain; but England and the Scandinavian lands never admitted it, and France only in very slight degree.

The Spanish Inquisition and Protestantism

In the south of Europe, now, the Inquisition became one means of stifling the new Protestant heresies. Its methods were atrocious. Children were encouraged to betray their parents, and parents their children. Often upon secret accusation by spies, a victim disappeared, without warning, to underground dungeons. The trial that followed was usually a farce. The court seldom confronted the accused with his accuser, or allowed him witnesses of his choosing; and it extorted confession by cruel tortures, carried to a point where human courage could not endure. Acquittals were rare. The property of the convicted went to enrich the church, and the heretic himself was handed over to the government for death by fire.

Persecution of unbelievers was characteristic of the age. It disgraced every sect, Protestant as well as Catholic. But no Protestant land possessed a device so admirably calculated to accomplish its purpose as the Inquisition. In Spain, especially, it sifted out for destruction thousands upon thousands of the stoutest hearts and best brains, and played a great part in the intellectual blight that soon fell upon that people (p. 171).

FOR FURTHER READING. — Ward's *The Counter-Reformation* is the best brief account of its subject. Much interesting matter on Jesuit missionaries can be found in Parkman's histories, especially in *Pioneers of New France*, chs. v and vi, and *Jesuits in North America*, ch. ii.

CHAPTER II

ENGLAND AND THE PROTESTANT MOVEMENT

Henry VIII and his quarrel with the pope

In England, separation from Rome was at first the act of the monarchs, and the motives were personal and political. Henry VIII (the second Tudor [1]) had shown himself zealous against Luther, and had even written a book to controvert Luther's teaching, in return for which the pope had conferred upon him the title, "Defender of the Faith." A little later, however, Henry desired a divorce from his wife, the unfortunate Catherine of Aragon, aunt of Charles V (p. 126), with whom he had lived for nineteen years. Catherine's only child was a girl (Mary), and Henry was anxious for a son, in order to secure a peaceful succession at his death. More to the point, he wished sinfully to marry Anne Boleyn, a lady of the court. After long negotiation, the pope refused to grant the divorce. Thereupon Henry put himself in the place of the pope so far

[1] Cf. p. 113. The following table of Tudor rulers shows also the claim of the first ruler of the next royal family.

(1) Henry VII (1485–1509) (See p. 113).

Children of Henry VII:
- Margaret (m. James IV of Scotland)
  - James V of Scotland
    - Mary Queen of Scots
      - (6) James I of England (1603–1625) the first *Stuart* king
- (2) Henry VIII (1509–1547)
  - (4) Mary (1553–1558) (daughter of Catherine of Aragon)
  - (5) Elizabeth (1558–1603) (daughter of Anne Boleyn)
  - (3) Edward VI (1547–1553) (son of Jane Seymour)
- Mary (grandmother of Lady Jane Grey)

as his island was concerned, and secured the divorce from his own courts.

Three wives of Henry are named in the footnote on the preceding page. He had also three more, — marrying the third on the day after he beheaded Anne Boleyn for alleged immoral conduct. One other of the six was beheaded on a similar accusation; and one was divorced, after six months, because homely.

A Church of England

The secession of the English church was accomplished in the years 1532–1534 by two simple but far-reaching measures of Henry's servile Parliament. (1) The clergy and people were forbidden to make any further payments to "the Bishop of Rome"; and (2) the "Act of Supremacy" declared Henry the "only supreme head on earth of the Church of England." When Parliament passed these laws, Luther's movement was some twelve years old, and the Augsburg Confession had just been put into form. Zwingli had just been slain in Switzerland, and Calvin was about to take up his work.

So far, in England, there had been no attack on the religious doctrines of the old church; *and Henry wished none.* But his chief advisers, especially Cranmer, Archbishop of Canterbury, who had pronounced his divorce, had strong Protestant leanings; and so *some additional measures were secured.* The doctrine of purgatory was declared false; and the Bible, *in English,* was introduced into the church service, in place of the old Latin liturgy. The use of the English Bible was even permitted to private persons, *except* "husbandmen, artificers, journeymen, and women below the rank of gentlewoman" (a gentry title).

The "Pilgrimage of Grace"

Most of England accepted these changes calmly, and even the clergy made no serious resistance, as a class, to the overthrow of the pope's power. But the monasteries were centers of criticism, and the north of England, more conservative than the south, was restless. Finally Henry hung ten friars, who had spoken blunt words about his second marriage, and began to seize monastery property. Then *the northern counties rose,* to march upon London.

Economic causes, too, had a part in the rising. The peasants were full of discontent at new conditions that will be described later (p. 182), and at a general rise in the cost of living which marked that period almost as emphatically as a like rise has marked the first of the twentieth century. The banner of the rebels bore a *plow* alongside *the wounds of Christ.*

Henry's policy of "frightfulness"

Henry's generals broke up this "Pilgrimage of Grace" by promises of redressing grievances and of full pardon. But then Henry wrote: "You must cause such dreadful executions on a good number of the inhabitants, — hanging them on trees, quartering them, and setting their heads and quarters in every town, — as shall be a fearful warning." And to carry out this treacherous policy of "frightfulness," *seventy-four leaders of the rising* were executed, — among them, *all the abbots in the north of England.*

Dissolution of the monasteries

Then Henry determined to root out resistance, and to enrich himself, by the utter ruin of the monasteries. A commission, which had hastily pretended to investigate them, declared them grossly corrupt. The report was grossly unfair, but it had been determined upon in advance; and, at the king's wish, Parliament dissolved the seven hundred such institutions in England.

A little of the wealth of the monasteries was set aside to found schools and hospitals (in place of the work in such lines formerly done by the monasteries themselves), but Henry seized most of the monastic lands for the crown. Then he parceled out parts of them, shrewdly, to new nobles and the gentry. Thousands of influential families were enriched by such gifts, and became centers of hostility to any reconciliation with Rome that would ruin their private fortunes.

This dissolution of the monasteries was a deed of terrible cruelty. Many abbots who tried to resist the king's will were put to death; but the most cruel results were felt by those who lived. Eight thousand monks and nuns were driven, penniless, from their homes, and some eighty thousand other people lost their means of livelihood. But Henry had destroyed hostility to his "reform," and had planted it deep in the interests of the country gentry and nobles. It is true, too, that, when things finally adjusted themselves to the revolution,

TEWKSBURY ABBEY, one of the few buildings of this class to escape ruin.

the prosperity of England was increased by having the former property of the monasteries in lay hands.

Henry burns Protestants and hangs Catholics

These changes were as far as Henry would go. He had permitted little change in doctrine; and, to the close of his long reign, he beheaded "traitors" who recognized papal headship, and burned "heretics" who denied papal doctrines. In one day, in 1540, three "heretics" and three "traitors" suffered death. One Protestant martyr was Anne Askewe, a gentlewoman of good family, who was burned for insisting, "The bread of the communion cannot be God." The most famous among the many noted Catholic martyrs was Sir Thomas More, the greatest Englishman of the day (p. 134). More had been Henry's chief minister, for a time. He was willing to allow the king's power over the church, so far as all temporal matters were concerned; but he could not take an oath denying the pope's authority in spiritual matters. He was beheaded, and his head was impaled to wither on London Bridge.

Sir Thomas More. — After Rubens' copy of Holbein's portrait.

Every effort had been made to induce More to yield, and he had been plied with argument by subtle logicians. He was a broad-minded man and a statesman, — not disposed to die for a quibble. But conscience, not verbal quibble, was at stake. And when he had taken his stand, and the boat was bearing him down the Thames to prison, he was heard to exclaim, — "I thank the Lord, the field is won!" He had indeed won a supreme victory, not only for his own soul, but for the spiritual freedom of all the world.

Edward VI: persecution of Catholics

Henry was succeeded by his son Edward VI (1547–1553). The new king was a boy of nine, and during his short reign the government was held by a rapacious clique of Protestant lords. Partly to secure fresh plunder from the ruin of the church, this government tried to carry England into the full current of the Protestant movement. Priests were allowed to marry. The use of the old litany, and of incense, holy water, and the surplice, was forbidden. Commissioners to carry out these commands throughout England sometimes broke the stained glass windows of sacred buildings and tore from the pedestals the carved forms of saints. Rebellion broke out, this time in southwestern England, but was put down cruelly. Several Catholics were burned as heretics and conspirators, — among them Father Forest, who was roasted barbarously in a swinging iron cradle over a slow fire.

During this period, the *English Prayer Book* was put into its present form, under the direction of Cranmer (p. 154); and articles of faith for the church were adopted which inclined toward Calvinistic doctrine.

Queen Mary tries to restore Catholicism

Henry had had Parliament fix the order in which his children should be entitled to succeed him; and so when Edward died at fifteen, the throne passed to his elder half-sister, Mary (1553–1558). Mary was a daughter of Catherine of Aragon (p. 153). She was an earnest Catholic, and naturally she felt an intense personal repugnance for the Protestant movement which had begun in England by the disgrace of her mother. Mary's own crown, too, had been threatened by Protestantism. To prevent the accession of a Catholic, the Protestant lords had plotted to seat on the throne Lady Jane Grey, a distant relative of the royal family (footnote, page 153). The attempt failed, and Jane Grey, a girl of lovely character, was beheaded.

The nation was still overwhelmingly Catholic in feeling. The Protestants were active, organized, and influential; but they were few in numbers, and Mary had no difficulty in doing away with the Protestant innovations of her brother's time. But *Mary wanted* more than this. She wished to undo her father's work, and *to restore England to its allegiance to the pope.* Parliament readily voted the repeal of all anti-Catholic laws, but it refused stubbornly to restore the church lands. Finally the pope wisely waived this point. Then the nation was solemnly absolved, and received back into the Roman church.

Mary's persecutions

But Mary destroyed her work (1) *by marrying Philip of Spain*, son of the Emperor Charles V, and (2) *by a bloody persecution of Protestants.*

All English patriots dreaded, with much reason, lest little England be made a mere province of the world-wide Spanish rule; and even zealous Catholics shuddered at the thought of the Spanish Inquisition which their imagination pictured looming up behind the Queen's hated Spanish bridegroom.

This dread of the Inquisition made the people unusually sensitive to Mary's religious persecution. That persecution in itself was quite enough to rouse popular fear and hatred. *In a few months,* more than two hundred and seventy martyrs were burned, — nearly half the entire number that suffered death for conscience' sake in all English history. Catholics had died for their faith under both Henry and Edward; but *there had been no such piling up of executions;* and, moreover, most of those Catholic victims had been put to death, *nominally,* not for religious opinions, but as detected traitors; and the executions (with a very few exceptions) had taken place not by fire but by the more familiar headsman's ax. England had taken calmly the persecutions by these preceding sovereigns, but it was now deeply stirred.

The most famous martyrs of Mary's persecution were Archbishop Cranmer and Bishops Ridley and Latimer. Latimer had preached in approval of the torture of Father Forest (p. 158); but now he showed at least that he too knew how to die a hero. "Play the man, Master Ridley," he called out to his companion in martyrdom, as they approached the stake; "we shall this day, by God's grace, light such a candle in England as, I trust, shall never be put out."

Mary's unpopularity

Other causes, too, made Mary unpopular. To please her husband (Philip) she led England into a silly and disastrous war with France, and then managed it so blunderingly that England lost Calais, its last foothold on the continent. England had never seemed more contemptible to other nations or in greater perils. Apparently, it was doomed to become the prey of Spain or France.

Mary had come to the throne amid a burst of popular enthusiasm. She was a pure-minded but narrow woman, seeking earnestly to do her duty; but, after a reign of five years, she died more universally detested than any other English sovereign had ever been except the tyrant John. As Henry's parliaments had arranged, she was succeeded by her half-sister, Elizabeth, then twenty-five years old.

Queen Elizabeth

Elizabeth (1558–1603) was the daughter of Henry VIII and Anne Boleyn. From her father, she had a strong body, powerful intellect, an imperious will, and dauntless courage; and

KENILWORTH CASTLE. — From a fresco painting of 1620. Queen Elizabeth gave this castle to her favorite, the Earl of Leicester, who entertained the Queen there in a splended pageant described in Scott's *Kenilworth*. The walls enclosed seven acres.

from her mother, vanity and love of display. From both parents she took a sort of bold beauty and a certain strain of coarseness. She had grown up in Henry's court among the men of the New Learning (p. 133), and was probably the best educated woman of her century, — speaking several languages and reading both Latin and Greek. She has been called "a true child of the Renaissance," too, in her freedom from moral scruple (p. 132). To Elizabeth, says a great historian, "a lie was simply an intellectual means of avoiding a difficulty."

She was often vacillating in policy; but she was a keen judge of men, and had the good sense to keep about her a group of wise and patriotic counselors, chief of whom were Walsingham and Cecil (whom she made Lord Burghley).[1] Now and then, in fits of passion, she stormed at these men like a common virago, but she never let them go; and her shrewd common-sense made her the real ruler even among such statesmen. Above all, she had a deep love for her country. After more than forty years of rule, she said proudly, and, on the whole,

KENILWORTH CASTLE TO-DAY. — From a photograph.

truly, — "I do call God to witness, never thought was cherished in my heart that tended not to my subjects' good."

And England repaid her love with a passionate and romantic devotion to its "Virgin Queen." Except for her counselors, men knew little of Elizabeth's deceit and weaknesses. They saw only that her long reign had piloted England safely through a maze of foreign perils, and had built up its power and dignity abroad and its unity and prosperity at home,

[1] The Lords Salisbury, who have played so large a part in the England of the nineteenth and twentieth centuries, are Cecils, and direct descendants of Elizabeth's Cecil.

while her court was made glorious by splendid bands of statesmen, warriors, and poets. Amid the petty squabbles of succeeding reigns, England looked back with longing to "the spacious days of great Elizabeth."

The "Elizabethan Settlement"

When Elizabeth came to the throne, at least two thirds of England was still Catholic in doctrine. Elizabeth herself had no liking for Protestantism, while she did like the pomp and ceremonial of the old church. She wanted neither the system of her sister nor that of her brother, but would have preferred to go back to that of her father. But the extreme Catholic party did not recognize her mother's marriage as valid, and so denied Elizabeth's claim to the throne. This forced her to throw herself into the hands of the Protestants. She gave all chief offices in church and state to that active, intelligent, well-organized minority; and the "Elizabethan Settlement" established the English Episcopal church much as it still stands. At about the same time, *John Knox* brought Calvinism from Geneva to Scotland, and organized *the Scotch Presbyterian church.*

The Act of Uniformity

Early in Elizabeth's reign, an "Act of Uniformity" had ordered all people to attend the Protestant worship, under threat of extreme penalties; but for many years this act was not enforced strictly, and Catholics were permitted to have their own services, if they were cloaked by a pretense of privacy. But after Catholic plots against her throne began, Elizabeth adopted stronger measures. Many leading Catholics were fined and imprisoned for refusing to attend the English church. And, under a new law, Catholic priests, and others who made converts from Protestantism to Catholicism, were declared guilty of *treason.* Many martyrs suffered torture on the rack and death on the scaffold — nearly as many as had died in the persecution of "Bloody Mary"; but Elizabeth, like her brother, succeeded in making such executions *appear* punishment of traitors for political plots, instead of religious persecution.

Persecution of Catholic "traitors"

The Spanish Armada, 1588

England was constantly threatened by the two great powers of Europe, Catholic France and Spain. Neither, however, was willing to see the other gain England; and by skillfully playing off one against the other, Elizabeth kept peace for many years and gained time for England to grow strong. Gradually it became more and more clear that the real foe was Spain. Then Elizabeth secretly gave aid to the Dutch, who were in rebellion against Philip II of Spain (p. 167), and, for years, English adventurers like Francis Drake sailed away on their own account, half pirate fashion, to attack Spain in the New World.

ELIZABETH as she went to a Thanksgiving Service at St. Paul's after the defeat of the Armada.

Finally Philip turned savagely upon England. Drake ruined his first preparations for invasion by sailing daringly into the harbor of Cadiz and burning the Spanish fleet, — "singeing the beard of the Spanish king," as the bold sea-rover described it. But in 1588 the "Invincible Armada," blessed by the pope, at last set sail for England. English ships of all sorts — mostly little merchant vessels hastily transformed into a war navy — gathered in the Channel; and, to the amazement of the world, the small but swift and better handled English vessels completely outfought the great Spanish navy in a splendid nine days' sea fight. As the shattered Spaniards fled around the north of Scotland, a mighty storm completed their overthrow. Spain never recovered her supremacy on the sea, — *and the way was prepared for the English colonization of America.*

England becomes Protestant

To the chagrin of Spanish king and Roman pope, the mass of English Catholics had proved more English than papal, and had rallied gallantly to the Queen; and, for young Englishmen, *the splendid struggle made Protestantism and patriotism seem much the same thing.* The rising generation became largely Protestant; and before Elizabeth's death (1603) even the Puritan doctrines from Geneva and from Presbyterian Scotland had begun to spread widely among the people.

Ireland, the third part of the British Isles, remained Catholic. Henry II (p. 78) had tried to conquer Ireland; but, until the time of the Tudors, the English really held only a little strip of land ("the English Pale") near Dublin. The rest of Ireland remained in the hands of native chieftains. In the seventh and eighth centuries Irish schools had been the most famous in Europe; but now constant war had rooted out the old beginnings of Irish culture, and the Irish tribes were half barbarous.

Ireland remains Catholic

Henry VIII established English authority over most of the island and destroyed the monasteries, the chief remaining centers of industry and learning. Shortly before the Armada, Spain made attempts to use the island as a base from which to attack England. Alarmed to frenzy by this deadly peril at their back door, Elizabeth's generals then completed the military subjugation with atrocious cruelties. Tens of thousands of men, women, and children were killed, or perished of famine in the Irish bogs; and great districts of the country were given to English nobles and gentry. Incessant feuds continued between the peasantry and these absentee landlords, and the Irish nation looked on the attempt to introduce the Church of England as a part of the hated English tyranny. As English patriotism became identified with Protestantism, so, even more completely, Irish patriotism became identified with Catholicism.

The Elizabethan Renaissance

Elizabeth's reign was part of a period of important change in industry which will be treated later (pp. 181 ff.). The reign is best known, however, for (1) the religious changes we have been tracing, and (2) for the "*Elizabethan Renaissance.*"

Except for the "Oxford Reformers" (p. 134), England had lagged behind in the early Renaissance. But now it took a leading place. *Edmund Spenser* created a new form of English poetry in his *Faerie Queene*. And the splendor of the Elizabethan age found a climax in English drama, with *Shakspere* as the most resplendent star in a glorious galaxy that counted such other shining names as *Marlowe, Greene, Beaumont, Fletcher,* and *Ben Jonson*. Not less splendid, possibly even more important, was the scientific progress of *Harvey* and *Francis Bacon* (p. 179).

FOR FURTHER READING. — Green's *History of the English People* is the best general account for this period. Creighton's and Beesly's lives of *Elizabeth* are good short biographies.

CHAPTER III

A CENTURY OF RELIGIOUS WARS

SPAIN AND THE NETHERLANDS

Philip II of Spain

When Philip II succeeded his father (p. 145) as king of Spain and of the Sicilies, and master of the Netherlands, he was *the most powerful and most absolute monarch in Europe.* The Spanish infantry were the finest soldiery in the world. The Spanish navy was the unquestioned mistress of the ocean. Each year the great "gold fleet" filled Philip's coffers from the exhaustless wealth of the Americas. In 1580 the ruling family in Portugal died out, and that throne was seized by Philip — by virtue of a relationship to the extinct family.[1] Thus Portugal's East India empire fell to Spain, and the Spanish boast that the sun never set upon Spanish dominions became literal fact. Philip himself was a plodding, cautious toiler, who worked like a clerk day after day in a bare room with a table and two stiff chairs. He was despotic, cruel, unscrupulous, ambitious, and an ardent Catholic.

The Dutch Rebellion

Charles V had disregarded the old liberties of the Netherlands (p. 125), and had set up the Inquisition in that country with frightful consequences. Protestant writers used to claim that from fifty thousand to one hundred thousand men and women were burned, strangled, or buried alive within the Netherlands during Charles' reign. These numbers appear to be mere guesses; but the actual facts were horrible. Still the great majority of the people had been attached to Charles as their native sovereign, and had felt a warm loyalty to his government. Philip continued all his father's abuses, without possessing any of his redeeming qualities in Dutch eyes. He was a foreign

[1] Portugal reëstablished her independence, by revolt, in 1640.

master — not a Hollander by birth as Charles had been — and he ruled from a distance and through Spanish officers. Finally, Protestant and Catholic nobles joined in demands for reform and especially that they might be ruled by officers from their own people.

Alva's Council of Blood

Philip's reply was to send the stern Spanish general, *Alva*, with a veteran Spanish army, to enforce submission. Alva's council is known as the *Council of Blood*. It declared almost the whole population guilty of rebellion, and deserving of death with confiscation of goods. Alva proceeded to enforce this atrocious sentence by butchering great numbers — especially of the wealthy classes — and in 1568 a revolt began.

The struggle between the little disunited provinces and the huge world-empire lasted forty years. In the beginning the conflict was for political liberty, but it soon became also a religious struggle. It was waged with an exasperated and relentless fury that made it a byword for ferocity even in that brutal age. City after city was given up to indiscriminate rapine and massacre, with deeds of horror indescribable.

Over against this dark side stands the stubborn heroism of the Dutch people, hardly matched in history, — a heroism which saved not themselves only, but also the cause of Protestantism and of political liberty for the world, and made their little spot of sea-rescued land a true "holy land" to all who love freedom.

William of Orange

William, Prince of Orange, was the central hero of the conflict. Because he foiled his enemies so often by wisely keeping his plans to himself, he is known as *William the Silent;* and his persistency and statesmanship have fitly earned him the name "the Dutch Washington." Again and again, he seemed to be crushed; but from each defeat he snatched a new chance for victory.

The Relief of Leyden

The turning point of the war was the relief of Leyden (1574). For many months the city had been closely besieged. The people had devoured the cats and rats and were dying grimly of starvation. Once they murmured, but the heroic burgomaster (mayor) shamed them, declaring they might have his body to eat, but while he lived they should never surrender to the Spanish butchers. All attempts to relieve the perishing town had failed. But fifteen miles away, on the North Sea, rode a Dutch fleet with supplies. Then William the Silent cut the dikes and let in the ocean on the land. Over wide districts the prosperity of years was engulfed in ruin; but the waves swept also over the Spanish camp, and upon the invading sea the relieving ships rode to the city gates. Dutch liberty was saved.

In memory of its heroic resistance, William offered Leyden exemption from taxes or the establishment of a university. The citizens finely chose the latter; and the University of Leyden, ever since one of the most famous universities in Europe, arose to commemorate the city's deed.

Never again was Spain so near success, though the war lasted many years longer. In 1584, by a dastardly offer of immense reward, Philip II found an assassin to murder William the Silent; but another great antagonist was just ready to enter the conflict.

England aids Holland

Holland had been fighting England's battle as well as her own: only the Dutch war had kept Philip, from attacking England. Englishmen knew this; and, for years, hundreds of English volunteers had been flocking to join the Dutch army. Elizabeth herself had many times helped the Dutch by secret supplies of money, and now in 1585 she sent a small English army to their aid. This was the immediate signal for the Spanish Armada; and the overthrow of Spain's naval supremacy by the splendid English sea dogs (p. 163) added tremendously to Holland's chances. True, the ten southern provinces of the old Netherlands finally gave up the struggle, and returned to Spanish allegiance. They were largely French in race and Catholic in religion. Protestantism was now completely stamped out in them. After this time, they are known as the Spanish Netherlands, and finally as modern Belgium.

THE NETHERLANDS
at the Truce of 1609
SCALE OF MILES
0 10 20 30 40 50 60 70 80
The Seven United Provinces
The Provinces Retained by Spain
NORTH SEA
EAST FRIESLAND
Embden
Jemmingen
GRONINGEN
Groningen
Heiligerlee
WEST FRIESLAND
OVERYSSEL
Enkhuisen
Alkmaar
Zuyder Zee
Haarlem
Amsterdam
Naarden
Deventer
Leyden
HOLLAND
The Hague
Utrecht
Zutphen
Delft
R. Rhine
Doesburg
Brill
Rotterdam
R. Waal
Nimwegen
Dort
Grave
Mook
D. OF CLEVE
SCHOUWEN
Ziericksee
Gertruydenberg
I. OF WALCHEREN
Middleburg
Goes
Breda
Flushing
Venlo
Sluys
Scheldt
Hulst
Turnhout
Ostende
Bruges
Antwerp
Ghent
Neuss
Dendermonde
Mechlin
Dunkirk
Gravelines
Ingelmunster
Alost
Cologne
FLANDERS
Maastricht
Ypres
Brussels
St. Trond
Waterloo
Ramillies
Liege
LIMBURG
St. Omer
Lille
Gembloux
Namur
Orchies
Mons
NAMUR
ARTOIS
Valenciennes
Arras
Douai
HAINAULT
Cambray
Cateau Cambresis
PICARDY
LUXEMBURG
Luxemburg
R. Oise
R. Aisne
R. Meuse
CHAMPANGE
BISHOPRIC OF VERDUN
BISHOPRIC OF METZ
R. Marne
Paris
LORRAINE
ARCHBISHOPRIC OF TREVES
DUCHY OF JULICH
ARCHBISHOPRIC OF COLOGNE
WESTPHALIA
R. Ems
Rhine
Meuse
LIEGE
BRABANT

Dutch Independence

The seven northern provinces, — Dutch in blood and Protestant in religion, — maintained the conflict, and won their independence as The United Provinces, or the Dutch Republic — though that independence was not formally recognized by Catholic Europe for half a century more. The government consisted of a representative "States General" and a "Stadtholder" (President). The most important of the seven provinces was Holland, by whose name the union was often known.

Holland's splendid period

The most marvelous feature of the struggle between the little Dutch state and Spain was that Holland grew wealthy during the contest, although the stage of the desolating war. The Dutch drew their riches not from the wasted land, but from the sea; and during the war they plundered the possessions of Spain in the East Indies. The little republic built up a vast colonial empire; and, especially after Spain's naval supremacy had been engulfed with the Armada, the Dutch held almost a monopoly of the Asiatic trade for all Europe. One hundred thousand of their three million people lived constantly upon the sea.

Success in so heroic a war stimulated the people to a wonderful intellectual and industrial activity. Holland taught all Europe scientific agriculture and horticulture, as well as the science of navigation. In the seventeenth century the presses of Holland are said to have put forth more books than all the rest of Europe. Motley sums up this wonderful career, —

> "The splendid empire of Charles V was erected upon the grave of liberty. . . . But from the hand-breadth of territory called Holland rises a power which wages eighty years' warfare [1] with the most potent empire upon the earth, and which, during the struggle, becomes itself a mighty state, and, binding about its slender form a zone of the richest possessions of the earth, from pole to tropic, finally dictates its decrees to the empire of Charles."

Spain's decay

On the other hand, Spain sank rapidly into a second-rate power. The bigot, Philip III, drove into exile the Christianized Moors, the descendants of those Mohammedans left behind when the Moorish political power had been driven out. They

[1] Peace was not made, formally, until 1609.

numbered more than half a million, — perhaps a twentieth of the entire population, — and they were the foremost agriculturalists and almost the sole skilled artisans and manufacturers. Their pitiless expulsion inflicted a deadly blow upon the prosperity of Spain.

For a time the wealth she drew from America concealed her fall, and she continued to furnish money for the Catholic powers through the Thirty Years' War (p. 174). But after the Armada she never played a great part in Europe, and, *living on the plunder of the New World*, she failed to develop the industrial life which alone could furnish a true prosperity. Moreover, the Inquisition steadily "sifted out the most flexible minds and the stoutest hearts," until a once virile race sank into apathy and decay.

The Battle of Lepanto

One great service Spain had rendered Christendom just before England and Holland broke her power. For a generation, Turkish fleets, almost unchecked, had ravaged the Christian coasts of the Mediterranean, even burning villages far inland and sweeping off the peasants into captivity. Cyprus had fallen before their attack, and Malta had been saved only by the heroic resistance of the Knights of St. John.[1] Finally Spain, Venice, and the pope joined their naval strength, and in 1571 the combined Christian fleet *annihilated the great Turkish navy at Lepanto*, on the Greek coast. Lepanto was the greatest naval battle the world had seen for eighteen hundred years — since the ancient wars between Romans and Carthaginians. Over six hundred ships engaged. The Turks lost thirty thousand men, and twelve thousand Christian rowers were freed from horrible slavery at the oar. The Turks never recovered naval importance, and indeed, the turning point of their power is often dated from this defeat.

[1] Read Prescott's account of the siege of Malta in his *Philip II*, if available. When driven from Asia, about 1300, the Knights of St. John (p. 93) removed to Rhodes and remained for centuries an outpost of Christendom in constant warfare with the Turk. Not long before Lepanto they had been expelled from Rhodes and had then fortified themselves anew upon the rocks of Malta.

WARS OF THE FRENCH HUGUENOTS

The Huguenots

The French Protestants were Calvinists, and are known as Huguenots. By 1560, they counted one man out of twenty in the population; and (because Calvinism appealed by its logic mainly to intellectual people) their numbers were made up almost wholly from the nobles and the wealthy middle class of the towns. Francis I and his son, Henry II, persecuted the new faith, but not continuously enough to crush it.

Guises and Bourbons

Henry was followed by his three sons, — Francis II, Charles IX, and Henry III, — all weak in body and in mind. During their reigns (1559–1589), power was disputed between two groups of great lords. Each was closely related to the failing royal family, and each hoped to place a successor upon the throne. One of these groups was the *Catholic Guise* family; the other was the *Protestant Bourbons*, who counted as their leaders the King of Navarre and the Prince of Condé. In the background was the chief figure of all, the crafty and cruel Queen-mother, *Catherine of Medici*, who played off one party against the other in whatever way might best promote her own control over her feeble sons.

War between the two factions opened in 1562 and lasted, with brief truces, to 1598. Even more than the other struggles of the period, it was marked by assassinations and treacheries, which struck down almost every leader on either side. The most horrible event of this character was the *Massacre of St. Bartholomew* (August 24, 1572).

The Massacre of Bartholomew

An honest attempt had just been made to establish a lasting peace. A marriage had been arranged between the sister of King Charles IX and the young Henry, King of Navarre (a small border state on the south of France); and, too, the grandest Frenchman of the age, the Protestant *Coligny*, became one of Charles' chief counselors, and soon won remarkable influence over him. But Catherine of Medici had not expected to see her own power over her son so superseded, and now she joined the Guises in secret attacks upon Coligny.

An attempt to assassinate Coligny failed, and the king

threatened vengeance for the attack. Then the conspirators, to save themselves, played upon his religious bigotry with a plot to cleanse France from heresy at one blow; and his consent was finally won for a general massacre of the Huguenots. Large numbers of that sect were assembled in Paris to witness the marriage of their chief; and at the appointed moment, the mob of Paris bathed in Huguenot blood. Ten thousand victims fell in France.

Henry of Navarre

Henry of Navarre escaped from the massacre, and, on the death of the French king, in 1589, he was the heir to the throne. But he did not become king of France, as *Henry IV*, until after four years more of civil war with the Catholic League.

Philip II of Spain aided the League. He hoped to seat a puppet on the French throne and virtually add that country to the realms of Spain. But in Henry of Navarre he met the third of the three great leaders on whom his imperial schemes went to wreck. Henry drove the Spanish army in shameful rout from France in the dashing cavalry battle of *Ivry*. Then, to secure Paris, which he had long besieged, he accepted Catholicism, declaring lightly that "so fair a city" was "well worth a mass." His purpose, of course, was not only to secure the capital, but also to give peace to his distracted country.

Becomes Henry IV

Edicts of Nantes

In 1598 Henry's Edict of Nantes established toleration for the Huguenots. (1) They were granted full equality before the law. Before this, the forms of oaths required in law courts had been such as a Protestant could not take, and therefore a Huguenot could not sue to recover property. (2) They were to have perfect liberty of conscience *in private*, and to enjoy the privilege of *public* worship except in the cathedral cities. And (3) certain towns were handed over to them, to hold with their own garrisons, as a security for their rights. This last measure was no doubt needful, but it carried with it a political danger: it set up a state within a state, and hindered the unity of France.

Henry and Sully

Henry IV proved one of the greatest of French kings, and he was one of the most loved. With his sagacious minister, the *Duke of Sully*, he set himself to restore prosperity to desolated

France. One of his treasured sayings was, that if he lived, the poorest peasant should have a fowl in the pot on a Sunday. Roads and canals were built; new trades were fostered; and under the blessings of a firm government, the industry of the French people once more with marvelous rapidity removed the evil results of the long strife. In 1610 Henry was assassinated by a half-insane Catholic fanatic.

Cardinal Richelieu

Henry's son, Louis XIII, was a boy of nine years. Anarchy again raised its head; but France was saved by the commanding genius of *Cardinal Richelieu,* who became the chief minister of the young king. Richelieu was a sincere patriot, and, though an earnest Catholic, his statesmanship was guided by political, not by religious, motives. He crushed the great nobles and he waged war upon the Huguenots to deprive them of their garrisoned towns, which menaced the unity of France. But when he had captured their cities and held the Huguenots at his mercy, he kept toward them in full the other pledges of the Edict of Nantes. He aided the German Protestants against the Catholic emperor, in the religious war that was going on in Germany, and so secured a chance to seize territory from the Empire for France. To make the king supreme in France, he waged war *against* the Protestants within the nation: to make France supreme in Europe, he waged war *for* the Protestants of Germany.

THE THIRTY YEARS' WAR IN GERMANY (1618–1648)

Conditions in Germany after the Peace of Augsburg

Fortunately for German Protestants, the two immediate successors of Charles V on the imperial throne were liberal in temper, disinclined either to persecution or to religious war. So for sixty years after the Peace of Augsburg (p. 144), the new faith gained ground rapidly. It spread over much of South Germany and held almost complete possession of Bohemia, the home of the ancient Hussite reform. Strife was incessantly threatening, however. The Hapsburgs strove to restrict Protestantism in their dominions, while the Protestant princes systematically evaded the promise to restore church lands.

This period of uneasy peace in Germany is just the period of the religious wars in the Netherlands and in France. Then, in 1618, the last of the great religious wars came in Germany — a century after Luther posted his theses at Wittenberg. It is known as the *Thirty Years' War* (1618–1648), and it was the most destructive and terrible war in all history until the World War.

Bohemia rebels

The *signal* for the struggle was an attempt of Protestant Bohemia to make itself independent of the Catholic Hapsburg Empire. Bohemian independence lasted only a few weeks; but this was long enough to call all Germany into two armed camps. The Protestant German princes, however, showed themselves disunited, timid, and incapable; and, had the war been left to Germany, a Catholic victory would soon have been assured. But *all over Europe sincere and religious Protestants felt deeply and truly that the war against the Catholic Hapsburgs was their own war* — much as all free peoples have felt in the World War when liberty was imperiled by Hohenzollern autocracy. First Denmark (1625–1629) and then Sweden (1630) entered the field in behalf of the Protestant cause; and at last (1635–1648) Catholic France under Richelieu threw its weight also against the Hapsburgs who so long had ringed France about with hostile arms.

Wallenstein and Gustavus Adolphus

The war was marked by the careers of four great generals, — Tilly and Wallenstein on the imperial side, and Gustavus Adolphus, king of Sweden, "the Lion of the North," and Mansfeld, on the side of the Protestants. Gustavus was at once great and admirable; but he fell at the battle of Lützen (1632), in the moment of victory; and thereafter the struggle was as dreary as it was terrible. Mansfeld and Wallenstein from the first deliberately adopted the policy of *making the war pay, by supporting their armies everywhere upon the country;* but during the short career of Gustavus, his blond Swede giants were held in admirable discipline, with the nearest approach to a regular commissariat that had been known since Roman times.

Gustavus' success, too, was due largely to new tactics. Muskets, fired by a "match" and discharged from a "rest," had become an important portion of every army; but troops were still massed in the old fashion that had prevailed when pikemen were the chief infantry. Gustavus was the first general to adapt the arrangement of his troops to the new weapons.

Devastation of Germany

The calamities the war brought were monstrous. It was a blasting ruin, from which Germany had not fully recovered in the middle of the nineteenth century. Season by season, for a generation of human life, armies of ruthless freebooters harried the land with fire and sword. The peasant found that he toiled only to feed robbers and to draw them to outrage and torture his family; so he ceased to labor, and became himself robber or camp-follower. *Half the population and two thirds the movable property of Germany were swept away.* In many large districts, the facts were worse than this average. The Duchy of Wurtemberg had fifty thousand people left out of five hundred thousand. In Bohemia, thirty thousand happy villages had shrunk to six thousand miserable ones, and the rich promise of the great University of Prague was ruined. Everywhere populous cities shriveled into hamlets; and for miles upon miles, former hamlets were the lairs of wolf packs. Not until 1850 did some sections of Germany again contain as many homesteads and cattle as in 1618.

Even more destructive was the result upon industry and character. Whole trades, with their long-inherited skill, passed from the memory of men.[1] Land tilled for centuries became wilderness. And men became savages. The generation that survived the war came to manhood without schools or churches or law or orderly industry.

Peace of Westphalia

The war was closed by the Peace of Westphalia. This treaty was drawn up by a congress of ambassadors from nearly every European power. It contained three distinct classes of stipulations: provisions for religious peace in Germany; territorial

[1] An instance of this is the wonderful old German wood carving. A genuine old piece of German cabinetwork is easily placed before 1618, because the war simply wiped out the skill and the industry.

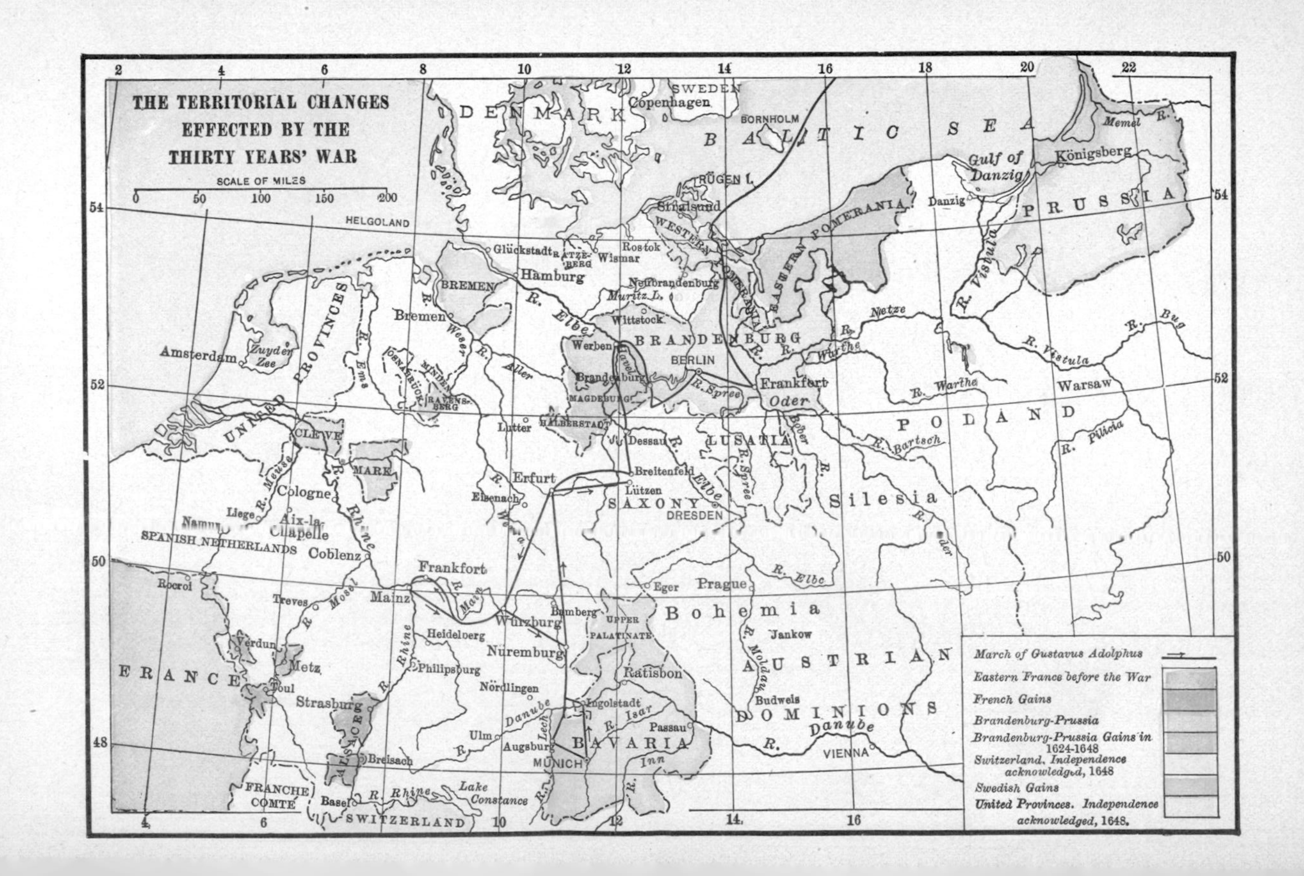
THE TERRITORIAL CHANGES
EFFECTED BY THE
THIRTY YEARS' WAR
SCALE OF MILES
0 50 100 150 200
March of Gustavus Adolphus
Eastern France before the War
French Gains
Brandenburg-Prussia
Brandenburg-Prussia Gains in 1624-1648
Switzerland. Independence acknowledged, 1648
Swedish Gains
United Provinces. Independence acknowledged, 1648.
DENMARK
SWEDEN
Copenhagen
BORNHOLM
BALTIC SEA
RÜGEN I.
Stralsund
WESTERN POMERANIA
EASTERN POMERANIA
Gulf of Danzig
Danzig
Königsberg
Memel R.
PRUSSIA
HELGOLAND
Glückstadt
RATZEBERG
Wismar
Rostok
Hamburg
Neubrandenburg
Muritz L.
Wittstock
BREMEN
Bremen
R. Weser
R. Elbe
R. Aller
Werben
BRANDENBURG
BERLIN
Brandenburg
MAGDEBURG
HALBERSTADT
Lutter
R. Spree
Frankfort
Oder
R. Warthe
Netze
R. Vistula
R. Bug
Warsaw
POLAND
R. Pilicia
R. Bartsch
Bober
LUSATIA
Dessau
Breitenfeld
Lützen
SAXONY
DRESDEN
Silesia
R. Oder
R. Elbe
Amsterdam
Zuyder Zee
UNITED PROVINCES
R. Ems
OSNABRÜCK
MINDEN
RAVENSBERG
CLEVE
MARK
R. Meuse
Cologne
Liege
Aix-la-Chapelle
SPANISH NETHERLANDS
Coblenz
R. Rhine
Erfurt
Eisenach
R. Werra
Frankfort
Mainz
R. Main
Würzburg
Bamberg
UPPER PALATINATE
Eger
Prague
Bohemia
Jankow
R. Moldau
Budweis
AUSTRIAN DOMINIONS
Danube
VIENNA
Rocroi
Treves
R. Mosel
Verdun
Metz
Toul
FRANCE
Strasburg
ALSACE
Breisach
Heidelberg
Philipsburg
Nuremburg
Nördlingen
Ratisbon
Ingolstadt
R. Isar
Passau
Danube
Ulm
Augsburg
Lech
BAVARIA
MUNICH
Inn
FRANCHE COMTE
Basel
R. Rhine
Lake Constance
SWITZERLAND

rewards for France and Sweden; and provisions to secure the independence of the German princes against the Empire.

1. *The principle of the Peace of Augsburg was reaffirmed and extended.* Each sovereign prince in Germany was to choose his religion; and his subjects were to have three years to conform to his choice or to withdraw from his realm.

Many of the South German Protestants were then driven into exile by their Catholic lords. This was the first cause of the coming to America of the "Pennsylvania Dutch." Most of the German immigration to America before the Revolution was connected with this expulsion or with the devastation of the Rhine provinces a little later by Louis XIV of France (p. 232).

2. *Sweden,* which was already a great Baltic power, extending around both the east and west shores of that sea (p. 55), *secured also much of the south coast:* Pomerania — with the mouths of the Oder, Elbe, and Weser — was the payment she received for her part in the war. This gave Sweden control over German commerce. *France annexed most of Alsace,* with some fortresses on the German bank of the Rhine. The Congress also expressly recognized *the independence of Switzerland and of the Dutch Provinces.*

3. The Empire lost more than mere territory. *Various political rearrangements within Germany* made clear its weakness. The separate states were given the right to form alliances with one another *or even with foreign powers.* The imperial Diet became *avowedly* a gathering of ambassadors for discussion, but not for government: no state was to be bound by decisions there without its own consent.

Conditions at the close of the Religious Wars

The religious wars filled a century — from the struggle between the German princes and Charles V (1546) to the Peace of Westphalia (1648). *They left the Romance*[1] *South Catholic, and the*

[1] *Romance* is a term applied to those European peoples and languages closely related to the old Roman rule — like the Italians, Spanish, and French.

Teutonic North Protestant. Politically, France emerged, under the Bourbon branch of the Capetians, stronger and more united than ever, quite equal in power to any two states of Europe. England and Sweden had both risen into "Great Powers." Two new federal republics had been added to the European family of nations, — Switzerland and the United Provinces; and the second of these was one of the leading "Powers." The danger of a universal Hapsburg empire was forever gone. Spain, the property of one Hapsburg branch, had sunk from the first place in Europe to a third-rate power. The Holy Roman Empire, the realm of the other branch, was an open sham. Far to the east loomed indistinctly a huge and growing Russian state.

Advances in physical science in the age of Religious Wars

This age of wars and persecution in religion, almost without notice at the time, was also an age of advance in science, which was to change the life of men and women more than the wars of Wallenstein and Gustavus. Indeed it was just at this time that what we call *the scientific method* of *investigation* and *experiment* was really born into the world.

Copernicus and the solar system

All men had believed the earth the center of the universe, with sun and stars revolving around it. But in 1543 a Polish astronomer, Copernicus, published a book proving that the earth was only one member of a solar system which had the sun for a center. This discovery did more than revolutionize astronomy: it revolutionized thought about man's place in the world, by opening up such immensities of worlds and such possibilities of other forms of life as had never before been dreamed of. Columbus, half a century before, had discovered a "New World": Copernicus revealed a new universe.

From fear of persecution, Copernicus had kept his discovery to himself for many years — until just before his death, when the "religious wars" were just beginning. Those wars themselves checked study and discovery in parts of Europe; and persecution, for a while, repressed scientific discoveries in Catholic countries. At the opening of the Renaissance (p. 118) the popes had been the foremost patrons of the new learning; but now the reaction against the Protestant revolt had thrown control into conservative hands, and the church used its tremendous powers to stifle new scientific discoveries.

Harvey and the circulation of the blood

Still much was done. In Elizabeth's day in England, the physician, William Harvey, rediscovered the circulation of the blood (p. 148) and so made possible modern medicine. And in Italy Galileo discovered the laws of falling bodies and of the pendulum (as they are now taught in our textbooks on physics), invented the thermometer, and, taking a hint from a Dutch plaything, constructed the first real telescope. With this, in 1610, he *demonstrated* the truth of Copernicus' teachings by showing the "phases" of the planet Venus in its revolution about the sun. True, Galileo was summoned to Rome by the pope, imprisoned, and forced publicly to recant his teaching that the earth moved around the sun; but, as he rose from his knees, he whispered to a friend — "None the less, it does move."

Galileo

The method of experiment

And more important than any specific discovery about sun or the human body was the discovery of a new way of finding out truth about the world. For centuries scholars had tried to learn only by reading ancient *authorities*, and perhaps by *reasoning* a little further, in their own minds, upon what these authorities taught. But the new discoveries had been made in another way; and now, Francis Bacon, in England, set forth eloquently the necessity of *experiment* to discover new facts. And before 1700, in Italy, France, and England, great *scientific societies* were founded, to encourage scientific investigation.

Still for more than a century, these new discoveries reached a very small part of even the most enlightened nations. The average Puritan, for instance, who settled Massachusetts, twenty years after Galileo, believed the earth a flat surface lighted by sun and stars that moved around it. Francis Bacon himself, almost a century after Copernicus, never knew that the earth revolved around the sun; and, Englishman though he was, he had never heard of Harvey's discoveries — and believed that an ape's heart, worn on a man's breast, would make him brave. A new truth, in those times, did not get the world's attention in a day.

FOR FURTHER READING. — England is covered by previous references. It is not worth while for the student to read on the Wars, except for some brilliant story like Willert's *Henry of Navarre*, and for Holland. For that country, see *The Student's Motley*, an admirable and brief condensation of Motley's great history of the Dutch Republic. Source material can be found in Robinson's *Readings*.

EXERCISES

1. *Dates* for rapid drill: 1520, 1588, 1648.
2. Review the Reformation as a whole in each country to the close of the religious wars.

PART II

ENGLAND IN THE SEVENTEENTH CENTURY

CHAPTER IV

ENGLISH INDUSTRY IN 1600

Changes in England, 1450–1600

The century and a half from 1450 to 1600 (filled in England by the Wars of the Roses and the Tudor reigns) was a period of tremendous change, intellectual, religious, political, and economic.

(1) The Renaissance created a new intellectual life, with the spontaneous energy and the abounding self-reliance that we associate with the names of Shakespere and Elizabeth and Raleigh.

(2) The reformation introduced new church organization and new religious feeling.

(3) On the ruins of the two chief political forces of earlier times, — feudalism and the church, — the sovereigns built up a "New Monarchy" (p. 113).

(4) Industry was revolutionized in town and country.

The first three changes have been treated. The industrial change was the most fundamental of all. It has been referred to several times and we will now look at it as a whole.

The change in English rural industry

The golden age for English peasants was the half century from 1450 to 1500, just after the disappearance of villeinage. The small farmer lived in rude abundance; and even the farm laborer had his cow, sheep, or geese on the common, his four-acre patch of garden about his cabin, and good wages for his labor on the landlord's fields. Sir John Fortescue (p. 112) boasts of this prosperity, as compared with that of the French peasantry: "They [English peasants] drink no water, unless at times by way of penance. They are fed in great abundance with all kinds of flesh and fish. They are clothed in good woolens. . . . Every one, according to his rank, hath all things needful to make life easy and happy."

The large landlords had been relatively less prosperous. Since the rise of their old laborers out of villeinage, they were "land-poor." They paid high wages while, under the wasteful common-field system, crops were small (p. 68).

The "inclosures" after 1500 A.D.

But by 1500 a change had begun which enriched the landlords and cruelly depressed the peasants. This change was the process of "inclosures" for sheep raising. There was a steady demand for wool at good prices to supply the Flemish markets (p. 124), and enterprising landlords began to raise sheep instead of grain. Large flocks could be cared for by a few hands, so that the high wages mattered less; and profits proved so enticing that soon there was a mad rush into the new industry.

But sheep-raising called for large tracts of land. It was possible only for the great landlords; and even these were obliged to hedge in their share of the common "fields." Therefore, as far as possible, they turned out small tenants whose holdings interfered with such "inclosures," and often they inclosed also the woodlands and meadows, in disregard of ancient rights of common pasture. Sir Thomas More, in his *Utopia* (p. 134), lamented these conditions bitterly:

"A careless and unsatiable cormorant may compass about and inclose many thousand acres within one pale, and the husbandmen be thrust out of their own; *or else by fraud, or violent oppression, or by wrongs and injuries, they be so worried that they be compelled to sell.* . . . They [the landlords] throw down houses; they pluck down towns [villages], and leave nothing standing but only the church, to be made a sheep-house."

Then More gives this piteous picture of the peasants who have been driven from their homes:

"By one means or another, either by hook or by crook, they must needs depart, poor wretched souls — men, women, husbands, wives, fatherless children, widows, woeful mothers with young babes. . . . All their household stuff . . . suddenly thrust out, they be constrained to sell it for a thing of nought. And when they have wandered till that be spent, what can they then else do but steal, and then justly, pardy, be hanged, or else go about begging? And yet then also they be cast into prison as vagabonds, because they go about and work not, — whom no man will set to work though they never so willingly proffer themselves thereto."

Passing of the free farmers

Other statesmen, too, bewailed that sheep should take the place of the yeomanry who had won Crécy and Poitiers, and who, Bacon said, were also "the backbone of the revenue"; and the government made many attempts to check inclosures. But law availed nothing. Nor did peasant risings and riots (p. 155) help. On the other hand, Henry VIII's transfer of monastery lands (a fifth of England) to greedy private landlords increased the inclosure movement tremendously; and it went on until the profits of sheep-raising and grain-raising found a natural level.

This came to pass before 1600. The wool market was supplied, and the growth of town populations raised the price of grain. These towns, as we shall explain (p. 184), became the basis for a new sort of prosperity for England, and the land changes created a wealthy landed gentry, to take a glittering part in society and politics.

But this new "prosperity" had a somber background. Half of the villages in England had lost heavily in population, and many had been wholly swept away. Great numbers of the peasants, driven from their homes, became "sturdy beggars" (tramps); *and all laborers were thrust down to a lower standard of life*, because the cost of food and clothing rose twice as fast as wages.

More than before even, rural England had become a landlord's country. One reason why wages stayed so low was that the gentleman "justices of the peace," *appointed* by the crown, were given power to fix wages for farm work. And when tramps spread terror through the rural districts, the justices hung them in batches. In fifty years, in the glorious day of Shakespere and Elizabeth, seventy thousand "beggars" were executed.

These conditions explain in part why so many Englishmen were eager to go to America. John Winthrop, the great Puritan leader of the Massachusetts colony (himself from the prosperous landlord class), declared "England grows weary of her inhabitants, so as man who is the most precious of God's creatures, is here more vile and base than the earth we tread upon and of less prize among us than a horse or an ox."

Growth of manufactures

Meantime, England was becoming a manufacturing country. From the time of the Yorkist kings, the sovereigns had made the towns their special care. Elizabeth welcomed gladly the skilled workmen driven from the Netherlands by the Spanish wars, and from France by the persecution of the Huguenots. Colonies of these foreign artisans were given their special quarter in many an English city, with many favors, and were encouraged to set up there their manufactures, of which England had previously known almost nothing. Soon, English wool was no longer sold abroad. It was worked up at home. These new manufactures gave employment to great numbers of workmen, and finally absorbed the classes driven from the land.

And of commerce

This manufacturing fostered commerce. By 1600, England was sending, not merely raw materials as formerly, but her finished products, to distant markets. "Merchants"[1] increased in wealth and in numbers, so as to form a new class in society. In 1350 a royal inquiry could find a list of only 169 important merchants in England. In 1601 more than twenty times that number were engaged in the Holland trade alone.

By purchase of land and by royal gifts from the confiscated church property, the members of this class rose into the new gentry, and their capital and energy helped to restore prosperity to the land.

[1] A "merchant" was a trader who sent goods to a foreign country. Companies were formed to trade with Russia, or India, or other distant parts of the world: and sometimes a single merchant owned a considerable fleet of ships for such trade (cf. Shakespere's Antonio, in *The Merchant of Venice*).

The "Domestic system"

The rapid growth of manufactures brought with it a change in the position of the workers. The old gild system broke down in England and was replaced by the so-called "domestic system" of manufacturing. The work was still carried on by hand, and mostly in the master's house; but the masters demanded and finally secured liberty from gild control. This greater freedom permitted the more rapid introduction of improved methods.

CHAPTER V

PURITAN ENGLAND — UNDER THE FIRST STUARTS

At every moment some one country, more than any other, represents the future and the welfare of mankind. — EMERSON.

The English Church in 1600

For two generations after 1600, *the burning questions in English politics and religion had to do with Puritanism.* Within the established Episcopal church the *dominant* party had strong "High-church" leanings. It wished to restore so far as possible the ceremonial of the old Catholic church, and it taught that the government of the church by bishops had been directly ordained by God. This party was ardently supported by the royal "head of the church" — Elizabeth, James, Charles, in turn; but it was engaged in constant struggle with a large, aggressive Puritan party.

Puritanism

Puritanism was much more than a religious sect. It was an ardent aspiration for reform in many lines. In *politics* it stood for an advance in popular rights; in *conduct,* for stricter and higher morality; in *theology,* for the stern doctrines of Calvin; in *church matters,* for an extension of the "reformation" that had cut off the English church from Rome.

"Low-church" non-conformists

Two groups of Puritans stood in sharp opposition to each other, — the influential "Low-church" element within the church, and the despised Separatists outside of it. The Low-churchmen had no wish to separate church and state. They wanted one national church — a Low-church church — to which everybody within England should be forced to conform. They desired also to make the church a more far-reaching moral power. To that end, they aimed to introduce more preaching into the service, to simplify ceremonies, and to abolish altogether certain customs which they called "Romish," — the use of the surplice, and of the ring in marriage, of the sign of the cross in baptism, and (some of them) of the prayer-book. Most of them did not care as yet to change radically the established *form of church government;* but they looked upon all church machinery not as divinely instituted, as the High-churchmen did, but as of human origin. Some of them had begun, indeed, to speak with scant respect of bishops, and there was *a subdivision among them inclined to the Presbyterian church government,* as it existed in Scotland. It is this large Low-church branch of Puritanism with which in the seventeenth century English history is mainly concerned.

The Separatists

The Independents (or "Puritans of the Separation") believed that there should be *no* national church, but that each local religious organization should be a little democratic society, wholly *separate* from the civil government, and even *independent* of other churches. These Independents were the Puritans of the Puritans. They were the germs of later Congregationalism. To all other sects they seemed mere anarchists in religion. Elizabeth persecuted them savagely, and her successor continued that policy. Some of the Independent churches fled to Holland; and one of them, from Scrooby in northern England, after staying several years at Leyden, founded Plymouth in America (the "Pilgrims" of 1620), — and so pointed the way for the larger Low-church emigration to Massachusetts Bay ten years later.

Political conditions in 1600

Political liberty in England had fallen low under the Tudors. True, no law could be made without consent of Parliament, and that body controlled all new grants of money. But the monarch (or his ministers) prepared nearly all measures that came before Parliament; he could veto any act of Parliament; and, after a law had been made, he sometimes nullified it by special proclamations. Moreover, the monarch had so many ways of injuring a private man that it was extremely hazardous for any one persistently to oppose him.

But, *after all, Henry VIII and Elizabeth had ruled absolutely, only because they made use of constitutional forms* (p. 113) and because they possessed a shrewd tact which taught them just where to stop. Moreover, toward the close of Elizabeth's reign, when foreign perils were past, *the tone of Parliament began to rise again.* Men spoke boldly of checks upon the royal power; and Parliament and the courts forced the great queen to give up her pet practice of granting trade monopolies to her favorites. It was plain to keen observers that only the reverence for Elizabeth's age and sex, and the gratitude due her for her great services to the kingdom, held off an open clash between sovereign and Parliament. Upon her death, the clash began, — to last eighty-five years.

The "divine-right" Stuart kings

Elizabeth was succeeded by *James I* (James Stuart), already king of Scotland (footnote, p. 153). James was learned and conceited, — "the wisest fool in Christendom," as Henry IV of France called him. He believed sincerely in the "divine right" of kings. That is, he believed that the king, as God's anointed, was the source of law and could not himself be controlled by law. He wrote a pompous and tiresome book to prove this. He and his son after him not only *practiced* absolutism, but they also *preached* it on every occasion. They were despots *on principle.*

And the English people

The nation had been growing restive under the cloaked, beneficent, elastic tyranny of the strong Tudors: naturally it rose in fierce opposition against the noisy, needless, and uncompromising tyranny of the weak Stuarts. *From 1603,* when the first James mounted the throne, *until 1688,* when his grandson, the second James, ignominiously ran away from it, *England was engaged in strife between this "divine right" of kings and the right of the people.*

England the world's hope

Through all that seventeenth century, too, this little patch of land was the last remaining battle ground for liberty. In all other important states, — in Spain, in France, in Austria, in the Scandinavian lands, in the petty principalities of Germany and Italy, — despotism was supreme. In England both sides recognized this fact. Said the second Stuart king, Charles I, in a crisis of his reign, "I am ashamed that my cousins of

France and Spain should have completed what I have scarce begun." And at the same time a patriot exclaimed in exhortation to his party, "England is the last country which retains her ancient liberties; let them not perish now."

> The student should note, *at this point*, that the doctrine and practice of "divine-right" autocracy, *which England never accepted*, remained dominant on the continent of Europe until less than a hundred years ago, and that it has disappeared from Germany only with the World War. Kaiser Wilhelm of Germany, about 1900, repeatedly stated the doctrine in words strangely like those of James in England three centuries before — *and Germany accepted them with applause.*

There were, as yet, no organized political parties. But there was a "court party," devoted to the royal power, consisting of most of the nobles and of the "High-church" clergy, and an opposition "country party," consisting of the mass of country gentry, some Puritan nobles, and the Puritan element generally.

Now the issue between the two was promptly stated. In the first few weeks of his new sovereignty, James gave several practical proofs of his disregard for law and of his arbitrary temper. On his royal entry from Scotland, he ordered a thief to be hanged *without trial;* and when he summoned his first parliament he commanded that contested elections should be settled, *not by Parliament* as formerly, but by his courts. And then, in a famous utterance, he summed up his theory: "As it is atheism and blasphemy in a creature to dispute what God can do, so it is presumption and high contempt in a subject to question what a king can do." This became the tone of the court party.

Struggle between James I and Parliament

When Parliament assembled, it took the first chance to answer these new claims. The king, as usual, opened Parliament with a "speech from the throne." As usual, the Speaker of the Commons replied; but, in place of the usual thanks to his majesty, he reminded James bluntly of his limited powers.

"New laws," said the Speaker, "cannot be instituted, nor imperfect laws reformed . . . by any other power than this high court of Parliament." The Commons backed up this speech by a long paper, setting forth popular rights in detail and asserting that the privileges of Englishmen were their inheritance "no less than their lands and goods.'

James seldom called Parliaments after this, and only when he had to have money. Whenever he did, *there was wrangling between Parliament and king.*

Fortunately, the regular royal revenues had never been much increased, while the rise in prices and the wider duties of government called for more money than in former times. *Both Elizabeth and James were poor.* Elizabeth, however, had been economical and thrifty. James was careless and wasteful, and could not get along without new taxes.

Thus Parliament was able to hold its own. It insisted stubbornly on its control of taxation, on freedom of speech, and on its right to impeach the king's ministers. In the Parliament of 1621, the Commons expressed dissatisfaction with a marriage that James had planned for his son Charles with a Spanish princess. James roughly forbade them to discuss such "high matters of state." "Let us resort to our prayers," said one of the members, "and then consider this great business." The outcome of the consideration was a resolution, "(1) that the liberties, privileges, and jurisdictions of Parliament are the ancient and undoubted birthright of the subjects of England; and (2) that the arduous and urgent affairs concerning the king, the state, the church, the defense of the realm, the making and maintenance of laws, and the redress of grievances, which happen daily within this realm, are proper subjects for debate in Parliament; and (3) that in the handling and proceeding of those businesses, *every member of the Commons . . . has freedom of speech* . . . to bring to conclusion the same."

James tore out this page of the records and dissolved Parliament. But Charles was personally insulted by the Spanish court, where he had gone to visit the princess; and in the last year of James' life the prince succeeded in forcing him into war with Spain — to the boundless joy of the nation.

The early Parliaments of Charles I

In March, 1625, in the midst of shame and disgrace because of mismanagement of the war, James died. In May, *Charles I* met his first Parliament. He quarreled with it at once, dissolved it, and turned to an eager prosecution of the war, trusting to win the nation to his side by glorious victory. Ignominious failure, instead, forced him to meet his second Parliament in 1626.

It is now that Sir John Eliot stands forth as leader of the patriots. Eliot is the "first great Commoner." In her earlier struggles with her kings, England had depended upon nobles for leaders. The Tudor monarchs had begun to use members from the rising gentry as ministers of the crown. Now one of this class was to *lead the opposition* to the crown.

The significance of this lay not merely in the greater liberality of thought among the gentry, as compared with the nobles, but even more in their greater *numbers*. In earlier struggles, when a popular leader fell, like Simon of Montfort, there was no one to take his place, and the cause fell. But in this seventeenth century, an Eliot, a Hampden, a Pym, each found, at need, a worthy successor, or group of successors, to take up the work.

Sir John Eliot

Eliot was a Cornish gentleman, thirty-three years of age, courtly in manner, ardent and poetic in temper. His mind was enriched by all the culture of the "New Learning," and afterward in weary years of imprisonment he found consolation in his Tacitus, Livy, Epictetus, and Seneca. He was an athlete and a courtier, and at the same time a deeply religious Puritan; but his mind was never tinged with the somber feeling of later Puritanism.

And the "responsibility" of the king's ministers

Eliot stood for the control of the king's ministers by Parliament. Everything else, he saw, was likely to prove worthless, if the executive could not be held responsible. The *king's person* could not be so held, except by revolution, but *his min-*

isters might be *impeached;* and, under fear of this, they might be held in control. So Eliot persuaded the Commons to impeach the Duke of Buckingham, the king's favorite and the instrument of much past tyranny under James. Charles stopped the proceedings by casting Eliot into prison — in plain defiance of parliamentary privileges — and dissolving Parliament.

The king tries "benevolences"

The king fell back upon "benevolences" to raise a revenue. This was a device that *originated* during the Wars of the Roses two centuries before. During those long struggles, Parliament could not meet regularly and taxes could not be collected. A king *had* to depend therefore, for long intervals, not upon parliamentary taxes, but upon "good-will" gifts (*benevolences*) from men of wealth in his party. The first king after the war, the Yorkist Edward IV, continued from choice to collect benevolences *as he met rich men* in his progresses through the kingdom; and the first Tudor, Henry VII, reduced the thing to a system. Through his minister, Morton, he *sent out written demands* to rich men over all England.[1]

England deeply resented this method of "supply," because thereby a king was *plainly* made independent of parliamentary control. And so the young Henry VIII at his accession, despot as he was, sought popularity by formally giving up the evil practice and even handing over Morton, the tool of his father's extortion, for execution.

Now, a century later, Charles revived the evil practice, and *had his sheriffs in the county courts ask benevolences from all* taxpayers. But county after county refused to give a penny, often with cheers for Parliament. Some sheriffs refused to *ask* for the "free gift." The County of Cornwall (Sir John

[1] To some Morton said that their luxurious living showed that they were easily able to supply their king's needs; to others, that their economy of life proved that they must have saved wherewith to aid their sovereign. Thus every man of consequence found himself impaled, the people said, on one prong or the other of "Morton's Fork." Perhaps the most important point of this story is that it reminds us of the recent introduction of forks (*two* pronged instruments) at table. Cf. p. 71

Eliot's county) answered "that if they had but two kine, they would sell one to supply his majesty, — *in a parliamentary way.*"

The "forced loan"

Then Charles tried a "forced loan." This was really a tax levied by the usual tax machinery, — a tax thinly disguised by the false royal promise to repay it. The king's party used both force and persuasion. Pulpits, manned now by the anti-Puritan party, rang with the cry that to resist the king was eternal damnation. As a patriot of the time put it, the "High-church" clergy "improved the highwayman's formula into 'Your money or your life *eternal*.'"

England resists

And Charles made use of more immediate penalties. Poor freeholders who refused to pay were "pressed" into the navy, or a turbulent soldiery was quartered in their defenseless homes; and two hundred English gentlemen were confined in disgraceful prisons, to subdue their obstinacy. One young squire, John Hampden, who had based his refusal to pay upon a clause in Magna Carta, was rewarded with so close an imprisonment that, his kinsman tells us, "he never did look the same man after." Equal heroism was shown by hundreds of unknown men. George Radcliffe wrote from his prison to his "right dear and loving wife" (who was eager to have him submit in time to have Christmas with her), "Shall it be thought I prejudice the public cause by *beginning* to conform, which none yet hath done of all that have been committed [imprisoned], save only two poor men, a butcher and another, — *and they, hooted at like owls among their neighbors!*"

Parliament of 1628

The forced loan raised little revenue; and with an armament poorly fitted out, Buckingham sailed against France, with which his blundering policy had brought England into war. For the third time in four years an English army was wasted to no purpose; and, sunk in debt and shame, Charles met his third Parliament in 1628. Before the elections, the imprisoned country gentlemen were released, and *some seventy of them* (all who appeared as candidates) *sat in the new Parliament*, in spite of the royal efforts to prevent their election.

And the "Petition of Right"

Charles asked for money. Instead of giving it, the Commons debated the recent infringements of English liberties and some way to provide security in future. The king offered to give his *word* that such things should not occur again, but was reminded that he had already given his *oath* at his coronation. Finally the House passed "the Petition of Right," a document that ranks with Magna Carta in the history of English liberty. This great law first recited the ancient statutes, from Magna Carta down, against arbitrary imprisonment, arbitrary taxation, quartering of soldiery upon the people in time of peace, and against forced loans and benevolences. Then it named the frequent violations of right in these respects in recent years. And finally it declared all such infringements illegal.

CHARLES I. — After a famous portrait by Van Dyck.

The Lords tried to save the king's dignity by adding an evasive clause to the effect that Parliament did not intend to interfere with "that sovereign power wherewith your majesty is intrusted." But the Commons rejected the amendment after a striking debate. "Sovereign power," said one, "would mean power above condition; they could not leave the king that, for he had never had it." "The king's *person* I will call sovereign," said another, "but not his power"; and a third added, "Magna Carta is such a fellow that he will have no sovereign." Finally, the Lords, too, passed the Petition, and Charles, after evasive delays, felt compelled to sign it.

In form, the document was a petition: *in fact*, when passed, and assented to by the king, *it became a revision of the constitution down to date*, so far as the personal rights of Englishmen were concerned. Almost at once, however, in recess of Parliament, Charles broke its provisions regarding taxes.

Eliot's Resolutions

Parliament reassembled in bitter humor. Heedless of the king's plea for money, it turned to punish the officers who had acted as his agents in the recent infringements of the Petition of Right. Then the Speaker stopped business by announcing that he had the king's command to adjourn the House.[1] Men knew that it would not be permitted to meet again, and there followed a striking scene. Two of the patriots (Holles and Valentine) bounded to the Speaker, thrust him back into his chair and held him there.[2] Sir Miles Hobart locked the doors against the king's messenger, putting the key in his pocket; and Eliot in a ringing speech moved a series of resolutions which were to form the platform of the liberal party in the dark years to come. Royalist members cried, Traitor! Traitor! Swords were drawn. Outside, an usher pounded at the door with a message of dissolution from the king. But the bulk of the members sternly voted the resolutions, declaring *traitors to England* (1) any one who should bring in innovations in religion without the consent of Parliament, (2) any minister who should advise the illegal levy of taxes, (3) any officer who should aid in their collection, and (4) every citizen who should voluntarily pay them.

Eliot's death

And in the moment's hush, when the great deed was done, Eliot's voice was heard once more, and for the last time, in that hall: "For myself, I further protest, as I am a gentleman, if my fortune be ever again to meet in this honorable assembly, where I now leave off, I will begin again." Then the doors swung open, and the angry crowd surged out. Eliot passed

[1] The king could *adjourn* the Parliament from time to time, or he could *dissolve* it altogether, so that no Parliament could meet until he had called for new elections.

[2] If the Speaker left the chair, business was at an end.

to the Tower, to die there a prisoner four years later. But Eliot's friends remembered his words; and, when another Parliament did meet, where he had left off, *they began again.*

Eliot could have had his liberty if he had bent to acknowledge himself wrong. His wife died; friends fell away; consumption attacked him, and his enemies knew that he must yield or die. His son petitioned for his release, on the ground that doctors had certified that without it he could not live. The king refused: "Though Sir John be brought low in body, yet is he as high and lofty in mind as ever." A month later, Eliot was dead. His son presented another petition, that he might have his father's body for burial. This request too was refused, and there was inscribed on the paper, — a mean act of a mean king, — "Let Sir John's body be buried in the church of that parish where he died." So Eliot's body rests in the Tower in some unmarked and unknown spot — which matters little, since free government in England and America is his monument.

The "No-Parliament" years

On the dissolution of the third Parliament of Charles, England entered a gloomy period. The king issued royal edicts in place of laws, and no Parliament met for eleven years (1629–1640). During this period, in many ways, the government sought the welfare of the nation, and it gave particular attention to the needs of the poor; but its methods were thoroughly despotic.

To avoid the necessity of calling Parliaments, Charles now began to practice rigid economy. He sought, too, ingeniously to find new ways to get money, and, among other devices, his lawyers invented "ship-money." In time of invasion, seaboard counties had now and then been called upon by the kings to furnish ships for the national navy. Charles stretched this custom into a precedent for collecting a "*ship-money* tax" from *all* England in *time of peace.*

John Hampden (p. 193) refused to pay the twenty shillings assessed upon his lands, and the famous *ship-money case* went to the courts (1637). James, in his time, had turned the courts

John Hampden and the "ship-money" tax

into servile tools by dismissing the only judge (Sir Edward Coke) who dared oppose his will. And now the slavish judges decided for the king — as had been expected. The king's friends were jubilant, seeing in the new tax "an everlasting supply on all occasions"; but Hampden had won the moral victory he sought. The twelve-day argument of the lawyers attracted wide attention, and the court in its decision was compelled to state the theory of despotism in its naked hideousness. It declared that there was *no power to check the king's authority* over his subjects, — their persons or their money, — "For," said the Chief Justice, "*no act of Parliament makes any difference.*" If England submitted now, she would deserve her slavery.

Laud and Wentworth

The chief servants of the crown during this period were Archbishop Laud and Thomas Wentworth. Wentworth had been one of the leaders in securing the Petition of Right, but soon afterward he passed over to the side of the king and became Earl of Strafford. His old associates looked upon him as a traitor to the cause of liberty.

Laud was an extreme High-churchman and a conscientious bigot. He reformed the discipline of the church and ennobled the ritual; but he persecuted the Puritan clergy cruelly, with imprisonment and even by the cutting off of ears.

As a result of this and of the political discouragement, that sect founded the colony of Massachusetts Bay. Practically all the immigration this colony received, before the American Revolution, came in the ten years 1630–1640, while Charles ruled without Parliament.

The Scottish Covenanters

In 1638 Laud tried to force Episcopacy on Presbyterian Scotland.[1] But when the clergyman of the great church at Edinburgh appeared first in surplice, prayerbook in hand,

[1] That Scotland had been becoming Presbyterian is noted above, on p. 162. Scotland had been joined to England when her King James had become king of England, but each country had its own Parliament, laws, and church. The union was "personal," and consisted in the fact that the two countries had the same king. This remained the theory until 1707 (p. 215).

Jenny Geddes, a servant girl, hurled her stool [1] at his head, crying, — "Out, priest! Dost say mass at my lug [ear]!" The service broke up in wild disorder, and there followed a strange scene in the churchyard where stern, grizzled men drew blood from their arms, wherewith to sign their names to a "Solemn Oath and Covenant" to defend their own form of religion with their lives. This Covenant spread swiftly over all Lowland Scotland, and the Covenanters rose in arms and crossed the border.

The Long Parliament

Charles' system of absolutism fell like a house of cards. He could get no help from England without a Parliament; and (November, 1640) he called *the Long Parliament.* The great leaders of that famous assembly were the Commoners *Pym, Hampden, Sir Harry Vane,*[2] and, somewhat later, *Cromwell.*

John Pym's leadership

Pym took the place of Eliot, and promptly indicated that the Commons were the real rulers of England. When the Lords tried to delay reform, he brought them to time by his veiled threat: he "should be sorry if the House of Commons had to save England *alone.*"

And Eliot's old program

The Scots remained encamped in England; so the king had to assent to Parliament's bills. Parliament first made itself safe by a law *that it could be dissolved only by its own vote.* Then it began where Eliot had left off, and sternly put into action the principles of his last resolutions. Laud, who had "brought in innovations in religion," and Wentworth, who had advised and helped carry out the king's policy, were condemned to death as traitors. The lawyers who had advised ship-money, and the judges who had declared it legal, were cast into prison or driven into banishment. And forty committees were appointed, one for each county, to secure the punishment of the lesser officers concerned in the illegal acts of the government. Then Parliament abolished the Court of the Star Chamber

[1] Churches had no pews. People who wished to sit during the sermon carried their own stools.

[2] Vane had spent some time in Massachusetts and had been governor there.

and the High Commission, — two rather new courts which worked without juries and which, therefore, Charles had been able to use as instruments of tyranny. Meanwhile, the many martyrs whom Laud had imprisoned were freed from their dungeons, and welcomed to London by a joyous multitude that strewed flowers beneath the feet of their horses. These measures filled the first year,[1] and so far the Commons had been united — in punishing and redressing past grievances.

Parliament hesitates

But now a split began. Moderate men, led by the broad-minded Hyde and the chivalrous Falkland, thought enough had been done. Parliament had taught the king a stern lesson: to do more would mean danger of revolution and anarchy, for which these men had no wish. So they drew nearer to the king.

On the other hand, more far-sighted leaders, like Pym and Hampden, saw the necessity of securing safeguards for the future, since to them it was plain that the king's promises were worthless. Moreover, a small Presbyterian and Independent party ("Root and Branch" men), under Vane and Cromwell, wanted to overthrow Episcopacy.

Pym's "Remonstrance"

Pym brought matters to a head by introducing a Grand Remonstrance, — a series of resolutions which appealed to the country for support in further measures against the king and the High-church party. In particular it proposed (1) that a synod of clergy should meet to reform the church; and (2) that the king's choice of ministers (his chancellor, and so on) should be subject to the approval of Parliament. After an all-day and almost all-night debate, marked by bitter speech and even by the drawing of swords, the Commons adopted the Remonstrance *by the narrow majority of eleven votes*, amid a scene of wild confusion (November 22, 1641). Said Cromwell, as the House broke up, "If it had failed, I should have sold all I possess tomorrow, and never seen England more."

Charles tried to reverse this small majority against him by destroying Pym, Hampden, and three other leaders, on a charge of treasonable correspondence with the invading Scots.

[1] The trial of Laud came later, but he was already a prisoner.

Charles' attempt to seize "the five members"

No doubt they had been technically guilty of treason. But such "treason" against Charles was the noblest loyalty to England. The Commons paid no attention to the king's charges; and *so Charles entered the House in person, followed to the door by a body of armed cavaliers, to seize "the five members."*

News of his coming had preceded him; and, at the order of the House, the five had withdrawn. Charles did not know this, and ordered the Speaker to point them out. The Speaker protested that he had "no eyes to see, nor tongue to speak," but as the House should direct him. "Well, well!" said the king; "my eyes are as good as another's"; and standing in the Speaker's place he looked over the room. "I see the birds are flown," he added, in a different tone, — and walked out baffled, followed by angry shouts of "Privilege! Privilege!"[1]

Charles' despotic attempt, and weak failure, consolidated the opposition. London rose in arms, and sent trainbands to guard Parliament. And Parliament now demanded that the king give it *control of the militia and of the education of the royal princes.* Charles withdrew to the conservative North, and unfurled the standard of civil war (1642).

For Further Reading. — Green's *English People* (or his *Short History*) is thrillingly interesting for this and the following periods.

[1] Referring to the privilege of members of Parliament to be free from arrest, except on the order of the House itself (p. 112).

CHAPTER VI

THE GREAT REBELLION AND THE COMMONWEALTH

The Civil War, 1642–1645

Many men who had gone with Parliament in its reforms, now chose the king's side rather than rebellion and the danger of anarchy. The majority of the gentry sided with the king, while in general the trading and manufacturing classes and the yeomanry fought for Parliament. At the same time, the struggle was a true "civil war," dividing families and old friends. The king's party took the name "Cavaliers" from the court nobles; while the parliamentarians were called "Round Heads," in derision, from the cropped hair of the London 'prentice lads.[1]

Cromwell's Ironsides

And at first Charles was successful. The shopboys of the city trainbands could not stand before the chivalry of the "Cavaliers." But *Oliver Cromwell,* a colonel in the parliamentary army, had raised a troop known as *Ironsides.* He saw that the only force Parliament could oppose to the habitual bravery of the English gentleman was the religious enthusiasm of the extreme Puritans. Accordingly, he drew his recruits from the Independents of the east of England, — mostly yeomen farmers. They were men of godly lives, free from the usual license of a camp. They fell on their knees for prayer before battle, and then charged with the old Hebrew battle psalms upon their lips. By this troop the great battle of Marston Moor was won. Then Cromwell was put in chief command. He reorganized the whole army upon this "*New Model*"; and soon after, the victory of *Naseby* virtually closed the war (1645).

[1] The portraits of Cromwell and Vane (pp. 202, 204) show that Puritan *gentlemen* did not crop their hair. Short hair was a "class" mark.

There is an instructive contrast between the civilized nature of this war and the character of the Thirty Years' War in Germany, which was going on at the same time. In England noncombatants were rarely molested, and there was little needless destruction of property. And says John Fiske: "If we consider merely its territorial area or the number of men slain, the war of the English Parliament against Charles I seems a trivial affair . . . but if we consider the moral and political issues involved, and the influence of the struggle on the future welfare of mankind, we soon come to see that there never was a conflict of more world-wide significance than that from which Oliver Cromwell came out victorious. . . . If ever there were men who laid down their lives in the cause of all mankind, it was those grim old Ironsides, whose watchwords were texts from Holy Writ, and whose battle cries were hymns of praise."

CROMWELL. — After Lely's portrait.

Quarrel between Independents and Presbyterians

When the war began, many Episcopalians in Parliament withdrew to join the king. This left the Presbyterians almost in control. Before long this party was strengthened still further by the need of buying the aid of Presbyterian Scotland. *Then Parliament made the English church Presbyterian.*

Soon, it began to *compel* all men to accept this form of worship. On this point, the Presbyterian Parliament and the Independent "New Model" quarreled. Charles, now a prisoner, tried to play off one against the other, — intending, with shameless duplicity, to keep promises to neither. "Be quite easy," he wrote his wife, "as to the concessions I may grant. When the time comes, I shall know very well how to treat these rogues; and, instead of a silken garter [the badge of an honorary order of knighthood] I will fit them with a hempen halter."

These dissensions and intrigues led to a "Second Civil War." But now the real government of England was in the army. A council of officers, with Cromwell for their head, prepared plans; and the whole army "sought the Lord" regarding them in monster prayer-meetings.

The army quickly stamped out the royalist and Presbyterian risings. Then, under order from the council of officers, Colonel Pride "purged" the House of Commons by expelling 143 Presbyterians. After "Pride's Purge" (December, 1648), Parliament rarely had an attendance of more than sixty (out of an original membership of some five hundred). The "Rump" were all Independents, and their leader was Vane. Pym and Hampden had died some time before.

The Commonwealth, 1648–1654

This remnant of Parliament, backed by the army, *abolished monarchy and the House of Lords*, and brought "Charles Stuart, that man of blood," to trial for treason to England. Charles was executed, January 20, 1649, dying with better grace than he had lived. Then the "Rump" Parliament abolished Presbyterianism as a state church, and *declared England a republic*, under the name of the Commonwealth. "*The people*," said a famous resolution, "*are, under God, the original of all just power;* and the Commons of England in Parliament assembled, being chosen by the people, have the supreme power in this nation."

Battle of Worcester

The Scots were not ready for such radical measures, and they were angry at the overthrow of Presbyterianism. So they crowned the son of the dead king as Charles II, and invaded England to place him on the throne. Cromwell crushed them at Worcester, and the young "King of Scots" escaped to the continent.

Cromwell and the Rump

The Rump continued to rule for four years more. But it was only a shadow of the Parliament elected thirteen years before. Cromwell and the army grew anxious to see the government put on a permanent basis, and they felt that this could be done only by a real Parliament. The Rump was unwilling to dissolve; but at last, under Cromwell's insistence, it agreed to do so.

HARRY VANE.

Cromwell learned, however, that it was hurrying through a bill which would make its members a part of the new Parliament *without reëlection,* and which, indeed, would give them power to reject elected members if they chose. Cromwell felt that he was being tricked. Hurrying to the House with a file of musketeers, he dispersed it (1653) with an unusual burst of passion. "Come," he said, "I will put an end to your prating. You are no Parliament! I say, you are no Parliament!" His old friend, Vane, reproached his violence loudly. Cromwell turned with savage contempt: "Harry Vane! Sir Harry Vane! The Lord deliver me from Sir Harry Vane!" And after his officers had led the Speaker from the chair, Cromwell added to the remaining members, — "It's you that have forced me to this. I have sought the Lord, night and day, that he would slay me rather than put me upon the doing of this work."

Cromwell's outburst of temper at the Rump was natural. He saw that it was going to be almost impossible for him to

The Protectorate, 1654–1660

preserve the form of parliamentary government, when the only representatives of the nation had failed him — poor representatives though they were. There was no power that could even claim the right to *call* a Parliament. Cromwell and the army, however, summoned a *national convention*, to make a new constitution, and he made two other sincere attempts at Parliaments. But all these bodies proved dilatory and factious; and Cromwell grew more and more hasty and arbitrary.

Finally he and the army officers impatiently took the construction of new machinery of government into their own hands. Cromwell assumed the title of *Lord Protector* (1654); and the following six years are the period of the Protectorate.

The real difficulty was that the Independents were only a small fraction of the nation. They had won mastery by war, and they kept it through the discipline of the army. Cromwell became practically a dictator, with greater power than Charles had ever had. His rule was stained by cruelties in Ireland; but in other respects it was wise and firm. He made England once more a Great Power, peaceful at home and respected abroad; and he gave freedom of worship to all *Protestant* sects, — a more liberal policy in religion than could be found anywhere else in that age except in Holland and in Roger Williams' little colony just founded in Rhode Island.

At the best, however, Cromwell's rule was the rule of force, not of law. The noble experiment of a republic had failed miserably in the hands of its friends; and, on Cromwell's death, the nation, with wild rejoicings, welcomed back Charles II in "*the Restoration*" *of 1660.*

Excursus upon religious freedom

This is a good point at which to note the slow growth of religious freedom. The Puritan Long Parliament, *in 1641* (while still led by broadminded men like Pym, Hampden, and Hyde), demanded from Charles I certain reforms in the church; but it protested that it did not favor religious toleration: "We do declare it to be far from our purpose to let loose the golden reins of discipline and government in the church, to leave private persons or particular congregations to take up what form of divine worship they please. *For we hold it requisite that there should be throughout the whole realm a conformity to that order which the laws enjoin.*"

No better statement was ever made of the almost universal opinion. Even people who no longer thought any one religion essential to salvation did think *one form essential* to good order in society.

True, in that same year, Lord Brooke (a Puritan nobleman with *Independent* convictions) wrote nobly in a treatise on religion: "*The individual should have liberty.* No power on earth should force his practice. One that doubts with reason and humility may not, for aught I see, be forced by violence. . . . Fire and water may be restrained; *but light cannot.* It will in at every cranny. Now to stint it, is [to-morrow] to resist an enlightened and inflamed multitude. *Can we not dissent in judgment, but we must also disagree in affection?*"

Only a few rare spirits anywhere in the world, however, reached this lofty view. Outside Holland and Roger Williams' baby colony of Rhode Island, few had advanced as far as Cromwell. The world was not ready for religious freedom.

FOR FURTHER READING. — Green's Histories as before (cf. p. 143 above). Carlyle's *Cromwell* (in his *Heroes and Hero-worship*) may well be read. George MacDonald's *St. George and St. Michael* and Scott's *Woodstock* are excellent fiction for the Civil War, and they present somewhat different views.

CHAPTER VII

THE RESTORATION AND THE REVOLUTION

The Restoration of 1660

With the Restoration, the great age of Puritanism closed. The court, and the young cavaliers all over the land, gave themselves up to shameful licentiousness. Of course, among the country gentry and the middle class of the towns, there continued to be large numbers of religious, God-fearing homes; and in places even the somber morality of the Puritans survived. But fashionable society followed largely the example of the court circle.

Court literature, too, was indescribably corrupt and indecent. But, in just this age of defeat, Puritanism found its highest expression in literature. *John Milton*, years before, had given noble poems to the world — like his *L'Allegro* — but for many years he had abandoned poetry to work in Cromwell's Council and to champion the Puritan cause in prose pamphlets. Now, a blind, disappointed old man, he composed *Paradise Lost*. And *John Bunyan*, a dissenting minister, lying in jail under the persecuting laws of the new government, wrote *Pilgrim's Progress*.

The Episcopal church restored

The established church became again Episcopalian, as it has since remained. In the reaction against Puritan rule, the new Parliament passed *many cruel acts of persecution*. Two thousand Puritan preachers were not only driven from their pulpits, but were forbidden to earn a living by teaching, or even to come within five miles of any city or borough in England. *All dissenters* — Catholic and Protestant — were excluded from the right to hold municipal office. And all religious worship except the Episcopalian was punished with severe penalties.

In spite of all this, the great political principles for which the early Puritan Parliaments of Charles I had contended were

Political liberty preserved

victorious. Even their old enemies adopted them. The Parliament that was elected in the fervor of welcome to the restored monarch was wildly enthusiastic for king and for church. Charles knew he could never get another so much to his mind; and so he shrewdly kept this "Cavalier Parliament" through most of his reign — till 1679. But even the Cavalier Parliament insisted strenuously, and successfully, on Parliament's sole right to impose taxes, regulate the church, and control foreign policy. And Charles' second Parliament adopted the great Habeas Corpus Act, which still secures Englishmen against arbitrary imprisonment — such as had been so common under Charles' father. The *principle* of this act was older than Magna Carta; but the law of Charles' time first provided *adequate machinery*, much as we have it in America to-day, *to enforce the principle.*

Charles II, 1660–1685

Charles II was careless, indolent, selfish, extravagant, witty. He is known as the "Merry Monarch." One of his courtiers described him in jesting rhyme as a king "who never said a foolish thing, and never did a wise one."

But though lazy, Charles had real ability. He said lightly that he "had no mind to go on his travels again," and at any cost he avoided a clash with Parliament. However, in return for secret grants of money from Louis XIV of France, he shamefully made England a mere satellite of that country in foreign affairs; and at home he cautiously built up a standing army. There is reason to think that beneath his merry exterior Charles was nursing plans for tyranny far more dangerous than his father's; but he died suddenly (1685) before he was ready to act.

Beginning of political parties

Real political parties first appeared toward the close of this reign. Charles had no legitimate son; and his brother and heir, James, was a Catholic of narrow, despotic temper. The more radical members of Parliament introduced a bill to exclude him from the throne; and their supporters throughout England sent up monster petitions to have the bill made law. The Catholics and the more conservative part of Parliament, especially those who believed that Parliament had no right to change the succession, sent up counter-petitions expressing horror at the proposal. These "Abhorrers" called the other petitioners *Whigs* (Whey-eaters), a name sometimes given to the extreme Scotch Calvinists with their sour faces. The Whigs called their opponents *Tories* (bog-trotters), a name for the ragged Irish rebels who had supported the Catholic and royal policy in the Civil War.

Whigs and Tories

The bill failed; but the rough division into parties remained. It was a long time before there was any regular organization or precise platform; but, in general, *the Whigs believed in the supremacy of Parliament,* and sought on every occasion to limit the royal authority; while *the Tories* sustained the royal authority and *wished to prevent any further extension of the powers of the people.*

James II, 1685–1688

James II lacked his brother's tact. He arbitrarily "suspended" the laws against Catholics, tried to intimidate the law courts, and rapidly increased the standing army. It was believed that he meant to make the established church Catholic; and this belief prepared England for revolution. The Whig leaders called for aid to *William of Orange,* the Stadtholder of Holland, who had married James' daughter Mary. William landed with a few troops. James found himself utterly deserted, even by his army, and fled to France.

The "Glorious Revolution"

The *story* of this Revolution of 1688 is not a noble one. Selfishness and deceit mark every step. William of Orange is the only fine character on either side. There is no longer a patriot Eliot or Pym or Hampden, or a royalist Hyde or Falkland. As Macaulay says, it was "an age of *great measures* and *little men*"; and the term "glorious," which English historians have applied to the Revolution, must be taken to belong to results rather than to methods.

The Bill of Rights

Those *results* were of mighty import. A Convention-Parliament declared the throne vacant, drew up the great Declaration of Rights, the "third great document in the Bible of English

Liberties," and elected William and Mary joint sovereigns *on condition of their assenting to the Declaration.* The supremacy of Parliament over the king was once more firmly established. *The new sovereigns,* like the old Lancastrians, *had only a parliamentary title* to the throne.

The next regular Parliament enacted this *Declaration* of Rights into a "Bill of Rights." *The Bill of Rights* stated once more the fundamental liberties of Englishmen, as Magna Carta and the Petition of Right had done. The final clause declared that no Roman Catholic should ever be eligible to ascend the throne It fixed the order of succession (1) in the children of William and Mary, if any; (2) in Mary's sister *Anne.*

To understand the results of the Revolution at the close of the seventeenth century, we must carry the political story in part into the eighteenth.

William III, 1688-1702

William III was a great-grandson of William the Silent. He ranks among England's greatest kings. But he was unpopular, as a foreigner. (He spoke only his native Dutch, not English.) His reign (1688–1702) was spent mainly in war against the overshadowing might of Louis XIV of France. While only Stadtholder of Holland, William had already become the most formidable opponent of Louis XIV's schemes; and now the French king undertook to restore James II to the English throne.

This began a series of wars between France and England — the "Second Hundred Years' War." With slight intervals of peace, the struggle lasted from 1689 to 1815. The story will be told in future chapters. Now it is enough to note that the long conflict turned the government's attention away from reform and progress at home. During the next century and a quarter, there were great changes in England, especially in farming and manufactures; but they were changes made *by the people,* without notice by the government. These changes will be studied in later chapters. Just in the first years, however, some remarkable reforms were made by Parliament, both in politics and in religion. These were properly part of the Revolution.

Act of Toleration

The religious reform was embodied in the *Act of Toleration of 1689.* The Revolution of 1688 was essentially the work of the English church. But the persecuted Protestant dissenters had rallied to its aid — against the Catholic James; and William insisted that Parliament should now grant them freedom of worship. This was done.

The law, however, did not apply to Catholics, Jews, or Unitarians. These three classes remained excluded not only from all right to worship in their own way — under severe penalties — but also from the right to hold office or attend the universities. Indeed the *Protestant* dissenters were not allowed to do either of these last things. Still, to permit by law the public exercise of more than one religion was a great step forward.

The chief gains in political liberty, connected with the Revolution, come under four heads:

Gains in political liberty

1. The Stuart kings had frequently interfered shamelessly with the independence of the courts. Now the judges were made removable only by Parliament, not by the king.

2. A triennial bill ordered that a new Parliament should be elected at least once in three years. This put an end to such abuse as the long life of the Cavalier Parliament In 1716 the term was changed to *seven years,* and in 1911, to five. A Parliament may dissolve itself sooner than this; but it cannot last longer.

3. Parliament hit upon a simple device which, indirectly, has put an end completely to the old way in which kings abused their power of dissolving Parliaments. After the Revolution, *Parliaments determined to pass "revenue bills"* (furnishing money for government expenses) only for a year at a time — instead of for the life of the sovereign, as had been customary — and *not to pass such bills at all until other business had been attended to.* In like fashion, the Mutiny Act, which gives officers authority over soldiers, was passed henceforth only for short periods.

That is, Parliament adopted the regular policy of *delegating power of purse and sword for only one year at a time.* Thenceforward, Parliaments have been assembled each year, and they have practically fixed their own adjournments.

4. The greatest problem of parliamentary government (as Sir John Eliot had seen) was to control the "king's ministers" and make them really the ministers of Parliament. Parliament could remove and punish the king's advisers; but such action could be secured only by a serious struggle, and against notorious offenders. Some way was wanted to secure ministers acceptable to Parliament *easily* and *at all times.*

Beginning of cabinet government

This desired "Cabinet Government" was secured *indirectly* through the next century and a half; but the first important steps were taken in the reign of William. At first William tried to unite the kingdom, and balance Whigs and Tories, by keeping the leaders of both parties among his ministers. But he was much annoyed by the jealousy and suspicion which Parliament felt toward his measures. Sometimes, too, there were dangerous deadlocks between king and Parliament at critical times.

Then a shrewd political schemer suggested to the king that he should choose *all* his advisers and assistants from the Whigs, who had a majority in the House of Commons. Such ministers would have the confidence of the Commons; and that body would support their proposals, instead of blocking all measures. William accepted this suggestion; and a little later, when the Tories for a time secured a majority, he carried out the principle by replacing his "cabinet" with leading Tories. This was the beginning of ministerial government, or cabinet government.

William, however, was a powerful ruler. He was not a tyrant in any way; but he believed in a king's authority, and *he succeeded for the most part in keeping the ministers the "king's ministers"* — to carry out his policy. Queen Anne (1702–1714) tried to maintain a similar control over her ministry. But, like William and Mary, she too died without living children;

and the crown passed by a new *Act of Settlement* to a great grandson of James II, the German George I, who was already Elector of Hanover.[1] (This law excluded nearer heirs of James, because they were Catholics, and it makes the title of every English sovereign since Anne.) Then cabinet government won.

Growth of cabinet government under the Georges

Neither George I nor his son George II spoke English; and so far as they cared for matters of government at all, they were interested in their German principality rather than in England. They did not even attend "cabinet" meetings.

[1] Hanover was given a vote in the electoral college of the Holy Roman Empire in 1691. The following table shows the relationship of the Hanoverians to the Stuarts:

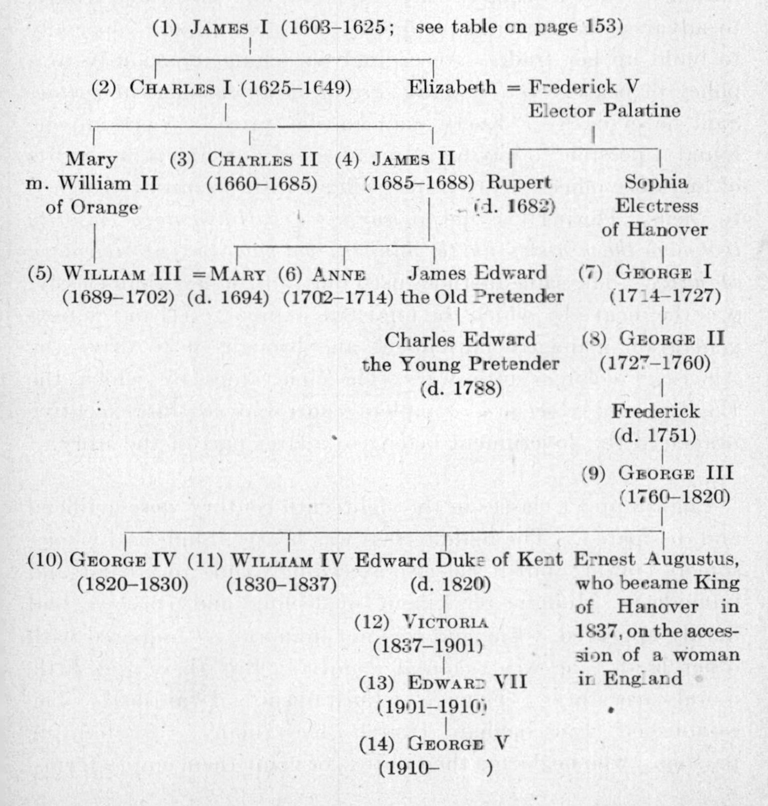

During their half-century (1714–1760), the government of England was left to the group of ministers, or "the cabinet." For nearly half the period (or from 1721 to 1742) the leading man in the cabinet was the Whig *Sir Robert Walpole.* Walpole selected the other ministers, and put before Parliament his own plans under the king's name. He is properly called "the first Prime Minister." Thus the reigns of these two stupid German Georges gave a great impetus to true cabinet government. *The "king's ministers" were fairly on the way to become the "ministers of Parliament."*

Sir Robert Walpole

Unhappily, Parliament itself did not yet really represent the nation. Walpole sought earnestly, and on the whole wisely, to advance the material prosperity of England, and especially to build up her trade. Accordingly he clung tenaciously to a policy of peace. *But he ruled largely by unblushing corruption.* Said he cynically, "Every man has his price." Certainly he found it possible to buy many members of Parliament with gifts of lucrative offices — oftentimes offices with no duties attached to them. During his rule, *it was not a parliamentary majority that made the ministry, but the ministry that made the parliamentary majority.* The same method, used only a little less shamelessly, was the means by which the ministers of George III in the next generation managed Parliament and brought it to drive the American colonies into war. The final steps by which the English people secured complete control over this executive branch of the government belong to a later part of the story.

English society in the eighteenth century

English upper classes in the eighteenth century were artificial and dissipated. The middle class was hearty, bluff, and wholesomely honest; but it was also exceedingly rude and coarse and immodest. Modern refinement of feeling and conduct had hardly appeared. England was not immoral. Compared with other lands, she was a moral country. But there was little moral earnestness. The age of Puritanism had vanished. The established Episcopalian church had many "fox-hunting parsons," who neglected their duties, or made them empty forms, while they sought the companionship of the neighboring squires in sports and in drinking bouts.

The Methodist revival

A protest against this lack of moral earnestness in the church and in society was the great Methodist movement. The founder was John Wesley, about 1738. While a student at Oxford, some years earlier, Wesley had established a religious society among his fellow students; and these young men were nicknamed Methodists, because of their regular habits. Wesley became a clergyman of the established church; but he soon came to place special emphasis on the idea of sudden and absolute "conversion" from sin. Aided by his brother Charles and by the powerful preacher Whitefield, he journeyed through England, holding great "revivals" in vast open-air meetings, preaching the love of Christ and its power to save from sin.

Wesley was a man of wonderful spirituality; but his fellow clergy for the most part were shocked at his method and refused to take him into their pulpits, and his converts came almost wholly from the lower classes. Much against the wish of the original leaders, the movement finally was organized as a dissenting "Methodist church." But Wesley's work went further than merely to found a new church, mighty as that church has become. The greatest result of the Methodist movement was found in the revivifying and spiritual quickening that followed within the established church and throughout all English life — somewhat as the Protestant revolt had reformed the Catholic church.

"Great Britain"

Meantime "England" was becoming "Great Britain." James I (1603) joined Scotland and England under one crown (p. 197). A century later (1707) this "personal union" was made a true consolidation by "the Act of Union," adopted by the parliaments of both countries. Scotland gave up her separate legislature, and became part of the "United Kingdom," with the right to send members to the English Parliament and to keep her own established Presbyterian church. Halfway between these two dates, Cromwell completed the conquest of Ireland. And that same seventeenth century had seen another and vaster expansion of England and of Europe, to which we now turn.

FOR FURTHER READING. — It is desirable for reading students to continue Green at least through the Revolution of 1688. Blackmore's *Lorna Doone* is a splendid story which touches some passages in the history of the closing seventeenth century.

EXERCISE. — The dates in English seventeenth-century history are important for an understanding of early American history: especially, 1603 (accession of James I) 1629–1640 (No-parliament period); 1648–1660 (Commonwealth); 1660 (Restoration); 1688 (Revolution).

CHAPTER VIII

EXPANSION INTO NEW WORLDS

Commercial conditions and the discovery of America

The sixteenth and seventeenth centuries — the age of the English Renaissance, of the Protestant Revolt, of the beginnings of scientific experiment, of the Puritan movement, and of the growth of political liberty in England — saw also the expansion of Europe into New Worlds east and west.

During the Crusades Europe had learned to depend on Asiatic spices, sugars, cottons, silks, and metal wares as necessities of daily life. For two hundred years a vast caravan trade brought these articles, in ever growing streams, from central Asia to the eastern shores of the Mediterranean for shipment to the West. But in 1453 the Turks captured Constantinople, the emporium of the northern route from Asia to Europe by the Black Sea; and year by year the same ruthless barbarians crept further south, endangering the remaining routes by caravan and by the Red Sea.

Europe, just awakening from the long torpor of the Middle Ages, and armed with the new "mariner's compass" (p. 221), eagerly sought new trade routes into Asia. Portugal found one, to the south, around Africa. Columbus, aided by the Spanish Isabella, tried a still bolder western route — and stumbled on America in his path.

Effect upon European thought

These discoveries worked revolutions in European life and thought. The size of the known earth had been more than doubled; and from the first the marvels of the new regions added vastly to the intellectual stir in Europe — as we may see, in part, in Shakspere's *Tempest*. More than this, the discoveries *proved* to all men that many old, long unquestioned ideas about the earth were false. True, the Ancients had held correct ideas about the size and shape and nature of the earth, and had *played* with the notion of sailing around it. Aristotle speaks of "persons" who held that it might be possible; and Strabo, a Roman geographer, suggested even that one or more continents might lie in the Atlantic between Europe and Asia.

But during the Middle Ages men had come to believe that the known habitable earth was bounded on all sides by an uninhabitable and untraversable world, — on the north by snow and ice, on the south by a fiery zone, on the west by watery wastes stretching down an inclined plane up which men might not return, and on the east by a dim land of fog and fen, the abode of strange and terrible monsters.[1] The Indian Ocean, too, was thought to be a *lake*, encompassed by the shores of Asia and Africa.

New geographical knowledge

These false views had been partly corrected by a better geographical knowledge of Asia, gained in the thirteenth and fourteenth centuries. About 1260, Louis IX of France (p. 85) sent Friar Rubruk as ambassador to the court of the Tartar Khan in central Asia; and the friar on his return reported that he had heard of a *navigable ocean east of Cathay* (China), with a marvelously wealthy island, Zipango (Japan).

This rumor of an ocean to the east made a leap in men's thought. In England, that remarkable man, Friar Bacon (p. 103), at once raised the question whether this ocean might not be the same as the one that washed Europe on the west and whether men might not reach Asia by sailing west into the Atlantic. Indeed, Bacon wrote a book to support these conjectures, adding many opinions of the Ancients; and extensive extracts from this volume were copied into a later book, which was to become a favorite of Columbus. Such speculation implies that *scholars* understood the sphericity of the earth. Saracenic schools had preserved the old Greek knowledge in this matter, and some European thinkers had been familiar with it, even in the "Dark Ages."

[1] For some of these ideas, see the curious and interesting *Travels* of Sir John Mandeville (thirteenth century).

Next the Mongols, who, for a time, ruled all northern and central Asia, opened China to western strangers to a degree altogether new for that land; and, while Mongol dominion lasted, many strangers and merchants visited the East. Among these were three Venetians, the *Polo* brothers, who on their return sailed from Peking through the straits into the Indian Ocean and up the Persian Gulf. *This proved true the rumor of Rubruk regarding an eastern ocean, and proved also that the Indian Ocean was not landlocked.*

ILLUSTRATION IN A THIRTEENTH CENTURY MANUSCRIPT, showing a Monk teaching the Globe.

And the new truth reached a large proportion of the very small part of Europe that read books. Travelers in that age did not often write descriptions of their travels. One of these Polos, however, being captured, soon after his return, in a sea fight between Venice and Genoa, remained a prisoner in Genoa for some years; and the stories that he told of his adventures were written down by one of his fellow captives. Thus was made "The Book of Ser Marco Polo," one of the most popular books of the Middle Ages.

From this time it was possible to think seriously of reaching India by sailing west. Soon afterward, as we have described, commercial conditions changed so as to impel men earnestly to try it.

The Portuguese voyages

The Portuguese, under Prince Henry the Navigator, had already been engaged in building up a Portuguese empire in Africa and in the islands of the Atlantic (Azores, Canary, and Verde [1]); and about 1470 they began to attempt to reach India

[1] The name "Cape Verde" indicates the surprise of the discoverers (1450) at verdure so far south.

by sailing around Africa. In 1486 a Portuguese captain, Bartholomew Diaz, while engaged in this attempt, was carried far to the south in a storm, and on his return to the coast he found it *on his left hand* as he moved toward the north. He followed it several hundred miles, well into the Indian Ocean. Then his sailors compelled him to turn back to Portugal. India was not actually reached until the expedition of Vasco da Gama in 1498, after more memorable voyages in another direction.

Columbus at the Council Table of Ferdinand and Isabella. — From the painting by Brozik in the Metropolitan Museum, New York.

Columbus, 1492

One of the sailors with Diaz in 1486, when in this way he rounded the Cape of "Good Hope," was a Bartholomew Columbus, whose brother Christopher also had sailed on several Portuguese voyages. Now, however, for some years, Christopher Columbus had devoted himself to the more daring theory that India could be reached by sailing west into the open Atlantic. Portugal, well content with her monopoly of African exploration, refused to assist him to try his plan. Henry VII of England also declined to furnish him ships. But finally the high-minded Isabella of Castile, while the siege of Granada was in progress, fitted out his small fleet, and in 1492 Columbus added America to the possessions of Spain.

The ships and other tools used by these early discoverers seem imperfect indeed to us. Happily they did have the one indispensable instrument for their work — and the curious story of its discovery is worth a place here. In 1258, Brunetto Latini, the tutor of Dante, visited Friar Bacon in England, and wrote to a friend in Italy as follows:

The mariner's compass

"Among other things he [Bacon] showed me a black, ugly stone called a magnet, which has the surprising quality of drawing iron to it; and if a needle be rubbed upon it and afterward fastened to a straw, so that it will swim upon water, it will instantly turn to the pole star. . . . Therefore, be the night never so dark, neither moon nor stars visible, yet shall the sailor by help of this needle be able to steer his vessel aright. This discovery so useful to all who travel by sea, must remain concealed until other times, because no master mariner dare use it, lest he fall under imputation of being a magician, nor would sailors put to sea with one who carried an instrument so evidently constructed by the devil. A time may come when these prejudices, such hindrances to researches into the secrets of nature, will be overcome; and then mankind will reap benefits from the labor of such men as Friar Bacon, who now meet only with obloquy and reproach."

These discoveries by Columbus and the Portuguese at the end of the fifteenth century, revolutionized also the distribution of wealth in Europe. The center of historical interest shifted westward once more. The Mediterranean, for two thousand years the one great highway between Europe and the Orient, gave way to the Atlantic and the "passage round the Cape." And with the decay of Mediterranean trade, the cities of Italy lost their leadership both in commerce and in art, while vast gain fell to the seaboard countries on the Atlantic.

Center of historical interest shifts westward

For a hundred years, it is true, the direct material gains were confined to the two countries which had begun the explorations. Portugal built up a great and rich empire in the Indian Ocean and in the Pacific, and an accident gave her Brazil. Otherwise, the sixteenth century in America belongs to Spain.

Spain in America

The story of her conquests is a tale of heroic endurance, marred by ferocious cruelty, — "all horrid transactions," as an old Spanish chronicler said. Not till twenty years after the discovery, did the Spaniards advance to the mainland of America for settlement; but, once begun, her handful of adventurers swooped north and south. By 1550, she held all South America (save Portugal's Brazil), all Central America, Mexico, the Californias far up the Pacific coast, and the Floridas. The gold from Mexico and Peru helped to give Spain her proud place as the mightiest country in Europe, and she guarded these American possessions jealously. The Gulf of Mexico and the Caribbean Sea were Spanish lakes, and the whole Pacific was a "closed sea." Frenchman or Englishman, caught upon those waters, found his grave beneath them.

Defeat of the Armada, 1588

Nor was Spain content with this huge empire on land and sea. She was planning grandly to occupy the Mississippi valley and the Appalachian slope in America and to seize Holland and England in Europe; but in 1588 she received her fatal check, at the hands of the English sea dogs, in the ruin of her Invincible Armada.

That victory was a turning point in *world* history. Spain never regained her old supremacy on the sea; and so the other seaboard countries of Western Europe were free to try their fortunes in America. But Holland, in her half-century of rebellion against Spain, turned her chief energies to seizing Portugal's old empire in the Orient, which had now become Spain's (p. 166). The Swedish colonies on the Delaware were never formidable to the claims of other nations, after the death of Gustavus Adolphus (p. 175). And so *North America was left to France and England.*

France in America

For a time, France seemed most likely to succeed Spain as mistress in *North* America. A quarter of a century, it is true, went to exploration and failure; but in 1608 Champlain founded the first permanent French colony at Quebec. Soon canoe-fleets of traders and missionaries were coasting the shores of the Great Lakes and establishing stations at various points still known by French names. Finally, in 1682, after years of gallant effort, La Salle followed the Mississippi to the Gulf, setting up French claim to the entire valley.

From that time New France consisted of a colony on the St. Lawrence, in the far north, and the semi-tropical colony of New Orleans, joined to each other by a thin chain of trading posts and military stations along the connecting waterways.

La Salle Taking Possession of the Mississippi Valley for France, at the mouth of the river. From an imaginative painting by Marchand, at the St. Louis Exposition in 1904.

French advantages

It is easy to point out certain French advantages in the race with England for North America. At home French statesmen worked steadily to build a French empire in the New World, while the English government for the most part ignored English colonies. The thought of such empire for their country, too, inspired French explorers in the wilderness — splendid patriots like Champlain, Ribault, and La Salle. France also sent forth the most zealous and heroic of missionaries to convert the savages. These two mighty motives, patriotism and missionary zeal, played a greater part in founding New France than in establishing either Spanish or English colonies. Moreover, the French could deal with the natives better than the stiffer, less sympathetic English could; and the French leaders were men of far-reaching views.

Weak points in French colonization

But though the French colonies were strong in the leaders, they were weak in some vital matters that depended on the mass of the colonists. They lacked homes, individual enterprise, and political life.

Lack of homes

1. New France was not a country of agriculture. Except for a few leaders and missionaries, the settlers were either unprogressive peasants or reckless adventurers. For the most part they did not bring families, and, if they married, they took Indian wives. Agriculture was the only basis for a permanent colony; but these colonists did not take to regular labor: instead they turned to trapping and the fur trade, and adopted Indian habits.

2. The French government sought, in vain, to remedy this by sending over cargoes of "king's girls," and by offering bonuses for early marriages and large families. The easiest remedy would have been to let the Huguenots come. They were skillful artisans and agriculturists, and, while they held towns for themselves (pp. 173, 174), they had shown some fitness for self-government. But Louis XIV of France, while he lavished money in sending undesirable immigrants, refused to let heretics found a new state. In large part, it was religious bigotry which lost France her chance.

Exclusion of the Huguenots

Paternalism in industry

3. Paternalism smothered private enterprise in industry. New France was taught to depend, not on herself, but on the aid and direction of a government three thousand miles away. Trade was shackled by silly restrictions, and hampered by silly encouragements. The rulers did everything. "Send us money to build storehouses" ran the begging letters of the colonial governors to the French king. "Send us a teacher to make sailors. We want a surgeon." And so, at various times, requests for brickmakers, iron-workers, pilots. New France got the help she asked; but she did not learn to walk alone.

Lack of political life

4. Political life, too, was lacking. France herself had become a centralized despotism; and, in New France, as a French writer (Tocqueville) says: "this deformity was seen as though magnified by a microscope." No public meetings could be held without special license from the governor; and, if licensed, they could do nothing worth while. The governor's ordinances (not the people) regulated pew rent, the order in which dignitaries should sit in church, the number of cattle a man might

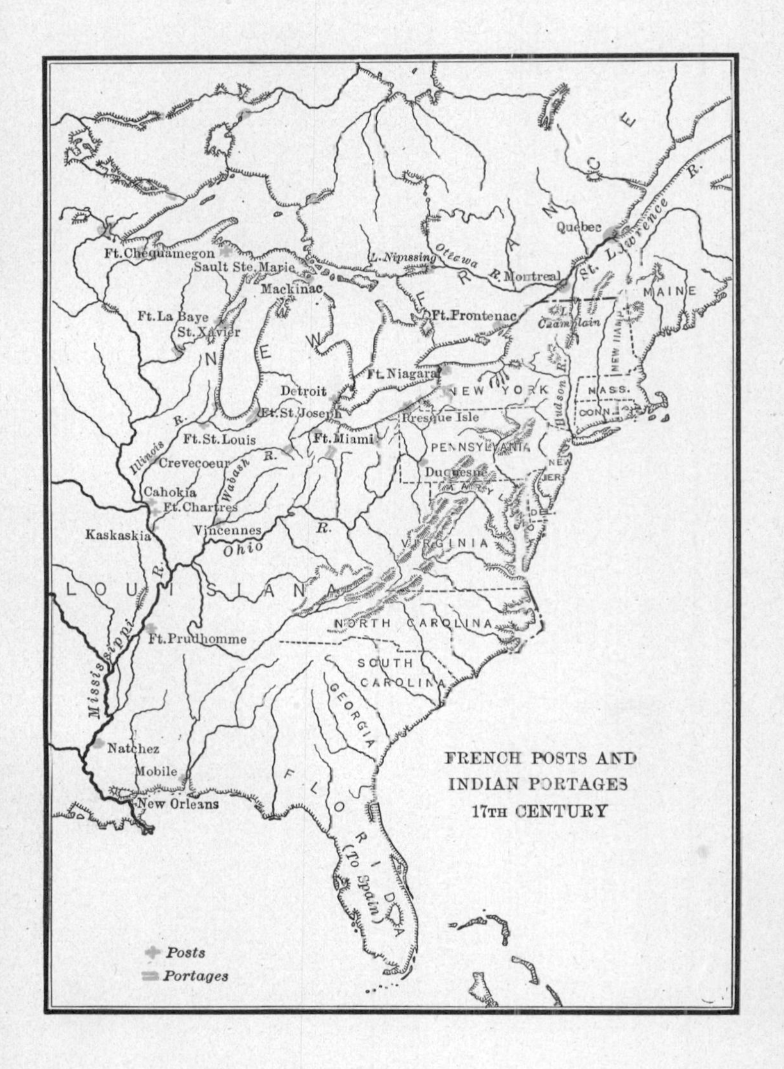
FRENCH POSTS AND
INDIAN PORTAGES
17TH CENTURY
NEW FRANCE
Quebec
St. Lawrence R.
Ottawa R.
L. Nipissing
Montreal
MAINE
L. Champlain
NEW HAMP.
MASS.
CONN.
Hudson R.
NEW YORK
Ft. Frontenac
Ft. Niagara
Ft. Chequamegon
Sault Ste. Marie
Mackinac
Ft. La Baye
St. Xavier
Detroit
Ft. St. Joseph
Presque Isle
PENNSYLVANIA
NEW JER.
Duquesne
MARYLAND
DEL.
Ft. Miami
Ft. St. Louis
Illinois R.
Crevecoeur
Wabash R.
Cahokia
Ft. Chartres
Kaskaskia
Vincennes
Ohio R.
VIRGINIA
LOUISIANA
Mississippi R.
Ft. Prudhomme
NORTH CAROLINA
SOUTH CAROLINA
GEORGIA
Natchez
Mobile
New Orleans
FLORIDA
(To Spain)
Posts
Portages

keep, the pay of chimney sweeps, the charges in inns, and so on. "It is of greatest importance," wrote one official, "that the people should not be at liberty to speak their minds."

Worse than that — the people had no minds to speak. In 1672, Frontenac, the greatest governor of New France, tried to introduce the elements of self-government. He provided a system of "estates" to advise with him, — a gathering of clergy, nobles, and commons (citizens and merchants); and he ordered that Quebec should have a sort of town meeting twice a year to elect aldermen and to discuss public business. The home government sternly disapproved these mild innovations, reminding Frontenac that at home the kings had done away with the old States General (p. 86), and directing him to remember that it was "proper that each should speak for himself, and no one for the whole." The plan fell to pieces; *the people cared so little for it that they made no effort to save it.*

England's rivalry with Spain in America

Very different was the fringe of English colonies that grew up on the Atlantic coast, never with a king's subsidies, often out of a king's persecution, and asking no favor but to be let alone.

During the last quarter of the sixteenth century, when Elizabeth's reign was half gone, England entered openly on a daring rivalry with the overshadowing might of Spain. Out of that rivalry, English America was born — by the work not of sovereigns, but of individual adventurous patriots. Reckless and picturesque freebooters, like Drake and Hawkins, sought profit and honor for themselves, and injury to the foe, by raiding the wide-flung realms of New Spain. More farsighted men, like Raleigh, saw that English colonies in America would be "a great bridle to the Indies of the Kinge of Spaine," and began attempts so to "put a byt in the anchent enemy's mouth."

Motives of English promoters at home

Sir Humphrey Gilbert and Raleigh, in Elizabeth's reign, made the first attempts. These came to nothing, because just then the energies of the nation were drained by the exhausting struggle with the might of Spain in Europe. Then

James became king, and sought Spanish friendship; and Englishmen began to fear lest their chance for empire was slipping through their fingers. Men said that a terrible mistake had been made when Henry VII refused to adopt the enterprise of Columbus, and all the more they insisted that England should not now abandon Virginia, — "this one enterprise left unto these days."

FRANCIS DRAKE KNIGHTED BY QUEEN ELIZABETH on the deck of his ship, the Golden Hind, at his return from raiding Spanish America in his voyage round the globe (1581). — From a contemporary drawing by Sir John Gilbert.

Motives of colonists

Moreover, population had doubled in the long internal peace since the Wars of the Roses, rising to some four million people. This was still only a tenth as many people as the island supports to-day; but, under the industrial system of that time, England needed an outlet for this "crowded" population (p. 184). The more enterprising of the hard-pressed yeomanry were glad to seek new homes; and this class furnished most of the manual labor in the early colonies.

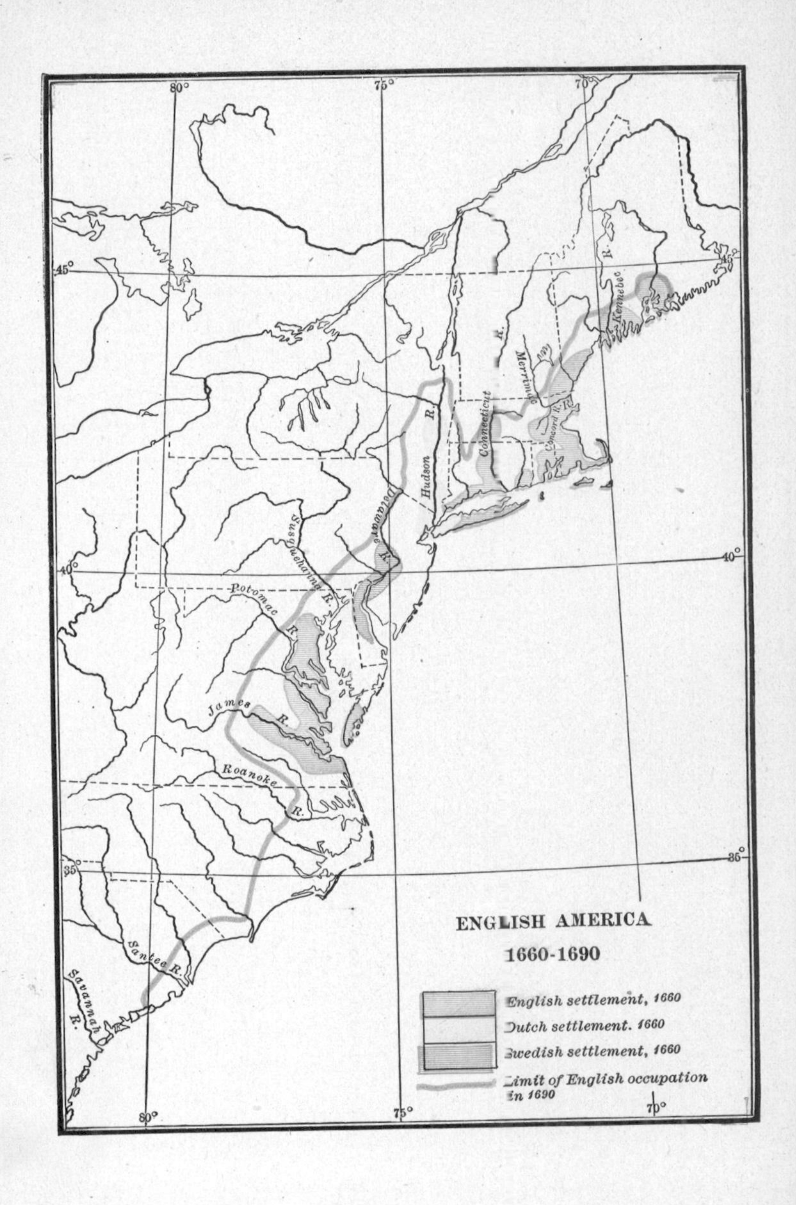

ENGLISH AMERICA
1660-1690
English settlement, 1660
Dutch settlement, 1660
Swedish settlement, 1660
Limit of English occupation in 1690
Hudson R.
Connecticut R.
Merrimac
Concord R.
Kennebec R.
Delaware R.
Susquehanna R.
Potomac R.
James R.
Roanoke R.
Santee R.
Savannah R.

But captains and capitalists, too, were needed; and a new condition in England just after the death of Elizabeth turned some of the best of the middle class toward American adventure. Until James made peace with Spain (1604), the high-spirited youth, and especially the younger sons of gentry families, fought in the Low Countries for Dutch independence (p. 168) or made the "gentlemen-adventurers" who under commanders like Drake paralyzed the vast domain of New Spain with fear. Now these men sought occupation and fortune in colonizing America, still attacking the old enemy, and in his weakest point. These young adventurers were not used to steady industry, and they were restless under discipline. But when they had learned somewhat of the needs of frontier life, their pluck and endurance made them splendid colonists.

Puritanism

Such were the forces in English life that established Virginia, early in the reign of James I. Toward the close of that same reign, *Puritanism was added to the colonizing forces*, and, before the Long Parliament met, there was a second patch of English colonies on the North Atlantic shore. After this, the *leading* motive for colonization was a desire to better one's worldly state — to win a better home or more wealth than the Old World offered — though, late in the century, religious persecution in England played its part again in founding the great liberal colony of Pennsylvania. And so, from one cause and another, at the time of the "Revolution of 1688," the *English settlements in America had expanded into a broad band of twelve great colonies, reaching from the Penobscot to the Savannah, with a total population of a quarter of a million.*

England's success

These colonies all enjoyed the English Common Law, with its guarantees for jury trial, freedom of speech, and other personal liberties (such as were known in no other people's colonies for two hundred years); and almost as soon as founded, they developed also a large degree of political liberty. They all possessed their own self-governing representative assemblies, modeled on the English Parliament.

Transfer of English freedom to America

Moreover, not all England, but only the more democratic

Democratic tendencies intensified

part of English life, was transferred to America. No hereditary nobles or monarch or bishop ever made part of colonial America. And that part of English society which did come was drawn toward still greater democracy by the presence here of unlimited free land. When the Puritan gentlemen, who at first made up the governing body in Massachusetts colony, tried to fix wages for carpenters by law, as the gentry did in England, the New England carpenters simply ceased to do carpenter work and became farmers. Thus wages rose, spite of aristocratic efforts to hold them down. Free land helped to maintain equality in industry, and so in politics; and the English colonies from the first began to diverge from the old home in the direction of even greater freedom.

At the same time, *the colonists were essentially English. Their free institutions were all English in origin;* and they themselves were Englishmen on a distant frontier. Free land did not make New France democratic and self-governing. *Frenchmen and Englishmen in the New World developed along lines of despotism or freedom upon which their old homes had started them.*

In the next chapter we shall see how the story of American colonization merged with the story of European wars. The conflict in Europe (p. 210) between William III of England and Louis XIV of France became a hundred years' conflict (1690–1815) for empire in America and Asia.

For Further Reading. — The student should study the expansion of Europe in Woodward's *Expansion of the British Empire*, I, 1–263; Seeley's *Expansion of England;* or Caldecott's *English Colonization.*

PART III

THE AGE OF LOUIS XIV AND FREDERICK II

1648–1789

CHAPTER IX

FRENCH LEADERSHIP

The period we study in the next three short chapters covers the century and a half from the close of the hundred years of religious wars to the beginning of the French Revolution (1648–1789). During these 141 years the map of Europe was incessantly shifting. The student should *read* the story, but the teacher may find it best to conduct recitations with open books and to fix only a few summaries.

The "Balance of Power"

The last part of the Thirty Years' War, we saw, was something besides a religious conflict. The Hapsburgs had long ringed France about with peril; and so Catholic France at last aided Protestant Germany and Holland to break the power of Catholic Austria and Spain. Such attempts to destroy a too powerful neighbor are characteristic of the next hundred years of war. The chief object of statesmen became to keep any one country from growing too strong for its neighbors' safety. This was called maintaining the Balance of Power. *For many years France was the country that threatened that balance,* and so league after league of other countries was organized against her. International morality was low and selfish, however, and commonly the nations were willing to let a strong Power rob a weaker neighbor, if they could find "compensation" (and

Threatened by France

maintain the "balance") by themselves robbing some other weak state.

Dynastic wars

Another curious fact is that these wars were *dynastic* wars (wars in the interests of ruling *families*) more than any others that Europe had ever seen. And the personal likings and hatreds of kings, as well as their family interests, interfered sometimes with their devotion to the "balance of power."

During most of the long period, the stage is held by one or another of three great rulers, Louis XIV of France (1643–1715), Peter the Great of Russia (1689–1725), and Frederick the Great of Prussia (1740–1786). The main influence of Peter was spent directly upon his own country; but Louis and Frederick belonged to all Europe, and the period is covered by *the Age of Louis XIV and the Age of Frederick II.*

Early years of Louis XIV

In the early years of Louis XIV it seemed that his reign was to rival that of Henry IV. With his great minister, *Colbert*, he introduced economy into the finances, encouraged new manufactures, built roads, introduced canals, and watched zealously over the growth of New France in America. But in 1667 he began a series of wars that filled most of the remaining forty years of his reign. During this half-century despotic France threatened freedom for the world, as Spain had done a century before, and much as Hohenzollern Germany has recently been threatening it.

First series of wars of Louis XIV

In the first twelve years of war, Louis sought to seize territory on his northeastern frontier. The Dutch Republic was his chief obstacle. Finally, Louis dropped all other plans, in order to crush that little state. In 1672, without warning, he seized the duchy of Lorraine — much as the Germans seized Luxemburg at the opening of the recent World War — and so won access to Holland's frontier, which he crossed with a splendid army of 100,000 men. The Dutch intrusted their government to William of Orange (who afterward became William III of England). William was not a supreme genius, like his great-grandfather, William the Silent; but he was faithful, persistent, and heroic. More than any other man he foiled the ambition of France.

Friends urged upon William that conflict with the mighty power of Louis was hopeless, and that he could only see his country lost. "There is a way never to see it lost," he replied quietly; "that way is to die on the last dike." With such grim determination, he finally cut the dikes, and the North Sea drove out the French armies. Meantime William toiled ceaselessly in building up against France an alliance of European powers, until Louis was compelled to accept peace with only slight gains of territory from the Spanish Netherlands.

The Edict of Nantes revoked

During ten years of truce that followed, Louis continued to seize bits of territory along the Rhine — including the "free city" of Strassburg. But the important event of this period was his treatment of the Huguenots. In 1685 he revoked the Edict of Nantes, and tried to compel the Huguenots to accept Catholicism. Dragoons were quartered in the Huguenot districts, and terrible persecutions fell upon those who refused to abandon their faith. Protestantism did finally disappear from France. But, though Louis tried to prevent any heretic from leaving France alive, tens of thousands (perhaps 300,000 in all) escaped to Holland, Prussia, England, and America.[1] The effect of this flight on France corresponded in a measure to the effect of the expulsion of the Moriscoes (p. 171) on Spain. It was a crushing blow to the prosperity of the country. The rest of Louis' reign was a period of failure.

Later wars of Louis XIV

The second series of wars began in 1689, when William of Orange had become king of England (p. 210). As before, the French armies seemed invincible in the field; but, as before, William checked Louis by building up a general European alliance against him. England had now taken Holland's place as the center of opposition to French despotism. Louis fought mainly to get more Rhine territory; *but this time he kept no gains.* This war is known in American history as "King William's

[1] In America the Huguenots went mainly to the Carolinas; but some old Virginia families trace their origin to this immigration. In New York John Jay and Alexander Hamilton were both of Huguenot descent. And in Massachusetts the Huguenot influence is suggested by the names of Paul Revere, Peter Faneuil, and Governor Bowdoin.

War." *The struggle had widened from a mere European war into a Titanic conflict between France and England for world-empire.*

The war-methods of France in this struggle were horrible. French armies deliberately depopulated large districts. A striking passage of Macaulay tells the fate of one Rhine province:

"The commander announced to near half a million human beings that he granted them *three days grace*. . . . Soon the roads and fields were black with innumerable men, women, and children, fleeing from their homes. . . . Flames went up from every market place, every parish church, every county seat."

This was the last time in Europe that such atrocious and barbarous warfare was seen — until Germany used even more ferocious methods in the World War. Germany's sin, in part, is that she has remained on a level that the rest of Europe outgrew more than two hundred years ago.

The "Spanish Succession"

Next, Louis sought extension on his other land frontier. Charles II, the last Spanish Hapsburg, was dying. The crown would go naturally either to the Austrian Hapsburgs or to the sons of Louis XIV, who were nephews of Charles. Louis finally agreed to a partition treaty, drawn up by William of Orange, for dividing the Spanish realms among the powers of Europe. But the proud Spanish people, who had not been consulted, had no mind for such an assassination of their empire. They preferred instead the accession of Louis' younger grandson as Philip V. When Louis became sure of this (1700), he decided to snatch the whole prize. He placed Philip on the Spanish throne, and said exultantly, "The Pyrenees no longer exist."

But Europe united against France and Spain in the "War of the Spanish Succession," known in American history as "Queen Anne's War." In this struggle, for the first time, success in the field lay with the Allies. The English *Marlborough* and the Hapsburg *Prince Eugene* were two of the greatest generals of history, and they won terrible victories over the hitherto invincible armies of France, at *Blenheim* in Bavaria, and at *Ramillies, Oudenarde,* and *Malplaquet* in Belgium, the suffering battleground of these struggles.

Peace of Utrecht

The Peace of Utrecht (1713) left Philip king of Spain, but he had to renounce for himself and his heirs all claim upon the French throne. *France gained no territory in Europe*, and in America *she lost Newfoundland and Nova Scotia to England. England also acquired command of the Mediterranean,* by securing from Spain the fortress of *Gibraltar* and the island of *Minorca. Spain lost all her European possessions outside her own peninsula,* ceding her *Netherland provinces, the kingdom of Sicily,* and *Naples,* and *the great Duchy of Milan* in North Italy, *to Austria.* This last was the beginning of an Austrian control in Italy which was to prove pernicious for two centuries.

Exhaustion of France

Louis XIV dazzled the men of his age, and won the title of the Great King (*Grand Monarque*); but we can now see that his aims were mistaken, even from a purely selfish view. His predecessors had fought for security against the hostile embrace of the Hapsburgs. After 1648, that danger had passed away Louis fought only to enlarge his borders.

In this aim he was partially successful; but his wars exhausted France and left the nation burdened with debt through the next century. At the close of his reign, the industry of France was declining under a crushing taxation, of which *more than half went merely to pay the interest on the debt he had created.* And in his unjust attacks upon petty properties of his neighbors in Europe, he had wasted strength that might have intrenched France as mistress in Asia and America.

French leadership in Europe

Intellectually, however, France was now the acknowledged leader of Europe. This continued to be true through the next century. The court of Louis XIV was the model on which every court in Europe, large or small, sought to form itself. French thought, French fashions, the French language, spread over Europe and became the common property of all polite society.

This admiration for France was due partly to an outburst of French poetry at this time. It was the first great age in French literature. The leading authors were the dramatists, Corneille, Racine, and Molière. A striking illustration of the influence of this French literature is that a great English school of writers modeled themselves upon it — the body of "correct poets," of whom *Pope* is the most famous member. At the same time, this literature was brilliant and sparkling, rather than great. "The work is not constructive, but imitative It is not free and strong, but careful and studied."

The age of despots

"*I am the state*" is a famous saying ascribed to Louis XIV. Whether he said it or not, he might have done so with perfect truth. So might almost any monarch of his day, outside of England. Monarchs were everything; the people, so far as government was concerned, were nothing. Louis called the English Parliament "an intolerable evil." If England and Holland had not withstood his ambitious dreams of empire, free government would then have perished from the earth.

CHAPTER X

THE RISE OF RUSSIA

The South-Slavs (Serbs and Bulgarians), we have noticed, were long kept down by Turkish conquest (p. 221). In like fashion, the Slavs of Russia for some centuries remained backward because of even more cruel conquest by savage and heathen Tartars.

Russia and the Tartar Conquest

Early Russian history is a blank or a mass of doubtful legends. We know only that before the year 900, there was a prince at Moscow ruling over the Russian Slavs from Novgorod to Kiev. Toward the close of the next century, Greek Christianity was introduced from Constantinople, and Greek civilization began slowly to make progress among the Russians. But Russia was exposed to danger from the east. Geographically it is merely a small part of the vast plain stretching across northern Asia, peopled in that day by savage nomad tribes of Tartars. About 1200, a great military leader appeared in Asia among these Tartars. Taking the title *Genghis Khan* (Lord of Lords) he organized the scattered nomad tribes into a terrible fighting machine, and set out to conquer the world. The ancient Scythian and Hunnish invasions were repeated upon a larger scale and with greater horrors. Genghis turned fertile countries into deserts and populous districts into tombs, marked by enormous pyramids of blackened corpses. He conquered China, northern India, and Persia, while his son invaded Europe. In 1223 the rising Christian state of Russia was crushed, and the Mongol empire reached from Peking and the Indus to Crimea and the Dnieper.

The death of the Great Khan (1227) recalled his son to Asia, but, ten years later, the assault on Europe was renewed. Moscow was burned, and northern Russia became a tributary province. Poland and Hungary were ravaged and conquered. Half of Europe became Tartar, and these new Huns even

CHURCH OF ST. BASIL, MOSCOW, built in the reign of Ivan the Terrible (1554–1557). The building was painted brilliantly in all the colors of the rainbow.

crossed the Danube. But again Western Europe was saved from a greater peril than Turkish conquest by the death of a Mongol emperor. Soon afterward the vast Tartar realm fell into fragments, and the pressing danger passed away. For three centuries, however, a Tartar state, *the Golden Horde*, maintained itself in southern Russia; and the whole later development of Russia has felt the baleful influence of Tartar dominion.

Ivan the Terrible

In 1480 a tributary Russian prince threw off the Tartar yoke, and one of his near successors, Ivan the Terrible, took the title *Tsar* (from *Caesar*, the old Roman title for an emperor). Under this Ivan, by 1550, when the religious wars were beginning in Western Europe, Russia reached from the inland Caspian northward and westward over much of the vast eastern plain of Europe, stretching even into Asiatic Siberia. But it had no seacoast except on the ice-locked Arctic, and no touch with Western Europe. Tartars and Turks still shut it off from the Black Sea; the Swedes shut it from the Baltic (p. 177); and the Poles prevented any contact with Germany. *Thus the Russians were really Asiatic* in geography. The tsars imitated the Tartar khans in their rule and court. The people were Asiatic in dress, manners, and thought. They belonged to the Greek church; but they had no other tie with European life.

Peter the Great

To make this Russia a *European* Power was the work of Peter the Great. Peter was a barbaric genius of tremendous energy, clear intellect, and ruthless will. He admired the material results of Western civilization, and he determined to Europeanize his people. As steps toward this, he meant to get the Baltic coast from Sweden, and the Black Sea from the Turks, so as to have "windows to look out upon Europe."

1689-1725

Early in his reign, the young Tsar decided to learn more about the Western world he had admired at a distance. In Holland, as a workman in the navy yards, he studied shipbuilding. He visited most of the countries of the West, impressing all who met him with his insatiable voracity for information. He inspected cutleries, museums, manufactories, arsenals, departments of government, military organizations. He collected instruments and models, and gathered naval and military stores. He engaged choice artists, goldbeaters, architects, workmen, officers, and engineers, to return with him to Russia, by promises, not well kept, of great pay.

Peter "Europeanizes" Russia

With these workmen Peter sought to introduce Western civilization into Russia. The manners of his people he reformed by edict. He himself cut off the Asiatic beards of his courtiers and clipped the bottoms of their long robes. Women were ordered to put aside their veils and come out of their Oriental seclusion. Peter "tried to Europeanize by Asiatic methods." He "civilized by the cudgel." *The upper classes did take on a European veneer. The masses remained Russian and Oriental.*

Expansion toward the open seas

Peter was more successful in starting Russia on her march toward the European seas. On the south, he himself made no permanent advance, despite a series of wars with Turkey; but he bequeathed his policy to his successors, and, from his day to the opening of the World War, Constantinople was a chief goal of Russian ambition.

The "Baltic window" Peter himself secured, by victory over Charles XII of Sweden, "the Glorious Madman of the North." Sweden was a thinly populated country with no great natural resources. For a century a line of great kings and the disciplined bravery of her soldiery had made her a leading power in Europe; but such leadership could hardly be permanent. She had grown at the expense of Russia, Poland, Denmark, and Brandenburg; and when Charles XII came to the Swedish throne (1697) as a mere boy of fifteen, these states leagued against him.

Charles was a military genius, and for a long time he was victorious against this overwhelming coalition. But he wore out his resources in winning victories that did not destroy his huge antagonists. Early in the struggle he defeated Peter the Great at *Narva*, with an army not more than an eighth as large as the Russian force; but while Charles was busied in Poland and Germany, Russia recovered herself, and in 1709 Peter crushed Charles at *Pultava*.

Peter reaches the Baltic

Peter had said that the Swedes would teach him how to beat them. Now this had come to pass. *Sweden never recovered her military supremacy.* Russia secured the Swedish provinces on the east coast of the Baltic *as far north as the Gulf of Finland.* These districts had been colonized, three centuries before, by German nobles (p. 87) and German civilization was strongly implanted there. Thus the acquisition not only gave Russia a door into Europe, but actually brought part of Europe inside Russia. It was in this new territory that Peter founded St. Petersburg, recently renamed *Petrograd.*

Later growth to 1800

The next important acquisition of territory was under the Empress Elizabeth, daughter of Peter, who seized part of Finland from Sweden. Toward the close of the century, under Catherine II, Russia made great progress on the south along the Black Sea and on the west at the expense of Poland (p. 249). This last change can be understood only in connection with the rise of Prussia.

CHAPTER XI

PRUSSIA IN EUROPE — ENGLAND IN NEW WORLDS

Frederick of Hohenzollern elector of Brandenburg

One of the German "marks" established in the tenth century as bulwarks against the Slavs (p. 87) was Brandenburg. Under a race of fighting margraves it grew from century to century, and about 1200 its ruler became one of the "Electors" of the Empire. In 1415, the first line of Brandenburg Electors ran out; and *Frederick of Hohenzollern*, a petty count in the Alps (like the Hapsburgs a century and a half before), *bought* Brandenburg from the *Emperor*. The new family was to play the same grasping part in North Germany that the Hapsburgs played in the South.

The Hohenzollerns gain Prussia

Shortly after 1600 came the next important acquisition of territory. By family inheritance, the Elector of Brandenburg fell heir to two considerable principalities, — the duchy of Cleves on the extreme west of Germany, and the *duchy of Prussia, outside the Empire* on the extreme east. Prussia was the name of a district which the Teutonic Knights[1] had conquered in the fourteenth century from the heathen Slavs, and which they held as vassals of the king of Poland (map after p. 98). It had been *partly* colonized by Germans, but its people remained for the most part a mass of Letts and Slavs.

Thereafter the Hohenzollern Electors ruled three widely separated provinces, — on the Rhine the Elbe, and the Vistula (map, p. 248). *The object of their politics was to unite these regions by securing the intermediate lands.*

[1] One of the Orders of fighting monks (p. 93) that grew up during the Crusades. The head of the Order became Duke of Prussia. One of these dukes, who died without direct heirs, in 1618, was a distant relative of the Elector of Brandenburg.

Toward the close of the Thirty Years' War, Frederick William, "the Great Elector," came to the throne of Brandenburg — a coarse, cruel, treacherous, shrewd ruler. The Protestants were getting the upper hand in the war. Frederick William joined them, and, as his reward, at the Peace of Westphalia he secured eastern Pomerania. *This brought Brandenburg to the sea.* The king of Poland, too, was forced to surrender his feudal suzerainty over Prussia. Thus the Elector became also, as *Duke of Prussia*, an *independent* sovereign.

The "Great Elector" and the Thirty Years' War

1618-1648

The "Great Elector" now crushed out all local assemblies of nobles in his provinces, and all local privileges, making his rule as absolute as that of Louis XIV of France. Then he built up an army among the largest and best in Europe, much more costly than his poor realms could well support. He was shrewd enough, however, to see the need of caring for the material welfare of his subjects, if they were to be able to support his selfish plans; and so *his long reign* (1640–1688) *marks the beginning of the boasted Hohenzollern policy of "good government."* He built roads and canals, drained marshes, encouraged better agriculture, and welcomed to his realms, with their manufactures, the Huguenot fugitives from France, after the revocation of the Edict of Nantes.

Paternal despotism

Frederick, son and successor of the Great Elector, was besought by Austria to join the alliance against Louis XIV (p. 231). In reward for his aid, he then secured the Emperor's consent to his changing the title "Elector of Brandenburg" for the more stately one of "King in Prussia" (1701). The second king of Prussia, Frederick William I, was a rude "drill sergeant," memorable only as the stupid father of Frederick the Great. He did, however, expend what intellect he had, and what money he could wring from his subjects, in enlarging the Prussian army; and he had a curious passion for collecting "*tall* soldiers" from all over Europe.

The kingly title

Frederick II ("the Great") ascended the Prussian throne in 1740. In the same year the Hapsburg Emperor, Charles VI, died without a male heir, and Frederick began his long reign

Frederick the Second's wars

by an unjust but profitable war. The Emperor Charles had secured solemn pledges from the powers of Europe, *including Prussia,* that his young daughter, Maria Theresa, should succeed to his Austrian possessions. But now, with his perfectly prepared army, *without having even declared war,* on a trumped-up claim, Frederick seized Silesia, an Austrian province.

This high-handed act was the signal for a general onslaught to divide the Austrian realms. Spain, France, Savoy, Bavaria, each hurried to snatch some morsel of the booty. But Maria Theresa displayed courage and ability. Her subjects, especially the gallant Hungarian nobles, rallied loyally to her support, and, a little later, England and Holland added their strength to the Austrian side. This "War of the Austrian Succession" closed in 1748. Frederick had shown himself greedy and unscrupulous, but also the greatest general of the age. He kept Silesia. Prussia now reached down into the heart of Germany and had become the great rival of Austria.

England and France rivals for world empire

Much more important, though less striking, *was the contest outside Europe.* In America a New England expedition captured the French fortress of Louisburg. In India the French leader, Dupleix, saw the chance to secure an Asiatic empire for his country, and captured the English stations in that country.

The treaty of peace restored matters to their former position, both in America and Asia, but *the war made England and France feel more clearly than ever before that they were rivals for vast realms outside Europe.* Whether Prussia or Austria were to possess Silesia, whether France or Austria were to hold the Netherlands, were questions wholly insignificant in comparison with the mightier question as to what race and what political ideas should hold the New Worlds.

The "Seven Years' War," 1756–1763

In 1756 Austria began a war of revenge. Maria Theresa had secured the alliance of Russia, Sweden, and even of her old enemy, France. Four great armies invaded Prussia from different directions, and Frederick's throne seemed to totter. His swift action and his supreme military genius saved his country, in the victories of *Rossbach* and *Leuthen*. And the next year England entered the struggle as his ally. England and France had remained practically at war in America and India through the brief interval between the two European wars;[1] and now that France had changed to Austria's side, England saw no choice but to support Prussia.

In America this "Seven Years' War" is known as the "French and Indian War." The struggle was literally world-wide. Red men scalped one another by the Great Lakes of North America, and Black men fought in Senegal in Africa; while Frenchmen and Englishmen grappled in India as well as in Germany, and their fleets engaged on every sea. The most tremendous and showy battles took place in Germany; and, though the real importance of the struggle lay outside Europe, still the European conflict in the main decided the wider results.

England wins America and India from France

William Pitt, the English minister, who was working to build up a great British empire, declared that in Germany he would conquer America from France. He did so. England furnished the funds and her navy swept the seas. Frederick and Prussia, supported by English subsidies, furnished the troops and the generalship for the European battles. The striking figures of the struggle are (1) Pitt, the great English imperialist, the directing genius of the war; (2) Frederick of Prussia, the military genius, who won Pitt's victories in Germany; (3) Wolfe, who won French America from the great Montcalm; and (4) Clive in India.

The story of the conquest of India calls for a brief outline. In that rich land of marvels, the struggle was not properly between the French and English governments, but between rival French and English trading companies — who, however, were more or less backed by their governments. India had a densely settled population and an ancient civilization. The chief ruler over most of the mighty peninsula was a Mohammedan prince at Delhi, in the north, known commonly as *the Great Mogul*. Under him were numerous *viceroys* (Nabobs),

[1] Braddock's campaign in America (1754) took place during this interval.

many of whom were really independent sovereigns in their huge districts. And, in the West and South, several Hindoo states kept their old independence under their native *Rajahs*.

After 1600 this tangle of Indian government was complicated further by settlements of European traders with grants of privileges and territory from the Great Mogul or from some Nabob. By 1700, the French Company held many important posts, while the English had established themselves at Bombay, Madras, and Calcutta — ports widely separated even by sea. These English settlements were governed much as Virginia was for a while about a century before, by a company of English merchants (the British *East India Company*) with its seat in London.

Dupleix (p. 242) had built up a powerful league of native states on the side of the French, and had almost driven the English out of India. But now he had been recalled by the short-sighted French government, and so the ground was cleared for a great English leader. *Clive* was an unknown English clerk at Madras. The native Nabob of Bengal treacherously seized the English post at Calcutta, induced the garrison to surrender on the promise of good treatment, and then suffocated them horribly by packing the one hundred and forty-six Europeans in a small, close dungeon, the famous Black Hole of Calcutta, through the hot tropical night. The young Clive was moved to vengeance. He organized a small expedition of a thousand Englishmen and two thousand faithful native troops, and at *Plassey* (1757) he overthrew the Nabob's Oriental army of sixty thousand men. Soon after, English supremacy was thoroughly established.

The Peace of 1763

The treaty of peace, in 1763, *left Europe without change*. But *in India*, the French retained only a few unfortified trading posts. *In America*, England received Florida from Spain, and Canada and the eastern half of the Mississippi Valley from France. France ceded to Spain the western half of the Mississippi Valley, in compensation for the losses Spain had incurred

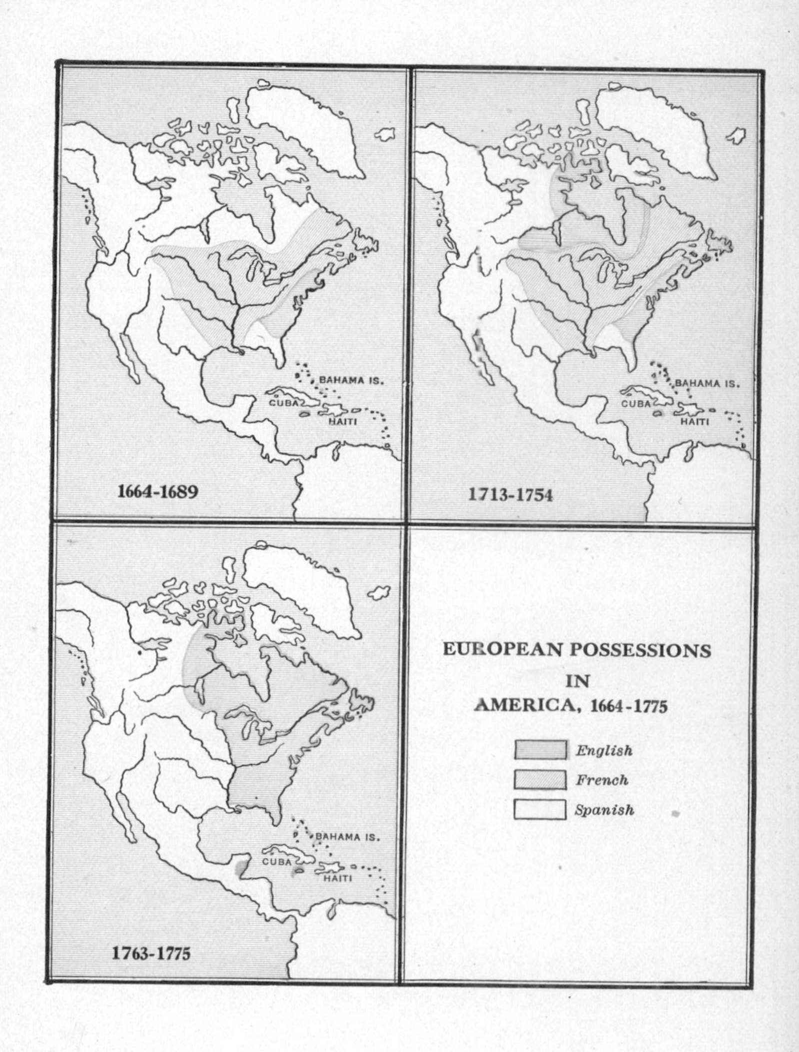
1664-1689
1713-1754
1763-1775
BAHAMA IS.
CUBA
HAITI
EUROPEAN POSSESSIONS
IN
AMERICA, 1664-1775
English
French
Spanish

as her ally; and, except for her West Indian islands, *she herself ceased to be an American power.* England had dispossessed her there as she had in India.

Spain still held South America and half North America; but her vast bulk was plainly decaying day by day. Holland's wide colonial empire, too, was in decline. *England stood forth as the leading world-power.*

Why England won America

The struggle in America had really been a war, not between Montcalm and Wolfe, but between two kinds of colonization. The better kind won. Man for man, the French settlers were more successful woodmen and Indian fighters than their English rivals; but *they could not build a state so well.* They got a good start first, and they had much the stronger position. But, after a century of such fostering care as we described on p. 224, *the French colonies did not grow.* When the final conflict began, in 1754, *France, with a home population four times that of England, had only one twentieth as many colonists in America as England had* — 60,000 to about 1,200,000.

Moreover, despite her heroic leaders, the mass of French colonists had too little political activity to care much what country they belonged to, so long as they were treated decently. French centralization did make it possible for a capable governor to wield effectively all the resources of New France;[1] while among the English there were interminable delays and disastrous jealousies. *But the English needed to win only once.* If Montcalm had conquered Wolfe, and had then been able to occupy Boston and New York, he could never have held them even as long as King George did a few years later. The colonists would have fought the French with vastly more determination than they did England in the Revolution. But Wolfe's one victory at Quebec settled the fate of the continent.

The lack of political vitality and of individual enterprise in industry was the fatal weakness of New France. The opposite

[1] The advantage was offset by a tendency to corruption which always threatens a despotic system. Says Parkman (*Montcalm and Wolfe*, II, 30), "Canada was the prey of official jackals." Of this his volumes give many illustrations.

qualities made England successful. Says John Fiske: "*It is to the self-government of England, and to no lesser cause, that we are to look for the secret of that boundless vitality which has given to men of English speech the uttermost parts of the earth for an inheritance.*"

The American Revolution

The American Revolution is the next chapter in this series of wars. That war began because the English government unwisely insisted upon managing American affairs after the Americans were quite able to take care of themselves. Its real importance, even to Europe, lay in the establishment of an independent American nation and in teaching England, after a while, to improve her system of colonial government.[1] But at the time, France and Spain saw in the American Revolution a chance to revenge themselves upon England by helping the best part of her empire to break away.

England did lose most of her empire in America; but she came out of the war with gains as well as losses, and with glory little tarnished. She had been fighting, not America alone, but France, Spain, Holland, *and* America. Theodore Roosevelt has put finely the result and character of this wider struggle (*Gouverneur Morris*, 116):

"England, hemmed in by the ring of her foes, fronted them with a grand courage. In her veins the Berserker blood was up, and she hailed each new enemy with grim delight, exerting to the full her warlike strength. Single-handed she kept them all at bay, and repaid with crippling blows the injuries they had done her. In America, alone, the tide ran too strong to be turned. But Holland was stripped of all her colonies; in the East, Sir Eyre Coote beat down Hyder Ali, and taught Moslem and Hindoo alike that they could not shake off the grasp of the iron hands that held India; Rodney won back for his country the supremacy

[1] The English colonial system in America had not been cruel or tyrannical nor *seriously* hampering in industry. Indeed, on both the industrial and political side, it was vastly more liberal than was the colonial policy of any other country in that age. But after Canada fell to England (p. 244), so that the colonists in the English colonies no longer feared French conquest, they began to resent even the slight interference of the English government. The freest people of the age, they were ready and anxious for more freedom. Cf. West's *American People*, pp. 185–191.

of the ocean in that great sea-fight where he shattered the splendid French navy; and the long siege of Gibraltar [p. 233] closed with the crushing overthrow of the assailants. So, with bloody honor, England ended the most disastrous war she had ever waged."

The secession of the American colonies did not injure England, as her friends and foes had expected it to do. The commerce of the United States continued to be carried on mainly through England, and, very soon, the new nation, with its growing wealth, was buying more English goods than the old colonies

CROSSED SWORDS of Colonel William Prescott and Captain John Linzee, who fought on opposite sides at Bunker Hill. A grandson of Prescott and a granddaughter of Linzee married, and the offspring of this marriage mounted the swords in this way "in token of international friendship and family alliance." From a photograph of the mounted swords, which are now in the room of the Massachusetts Historical Society.

had been able to pay for. For her territorial loss, England found compensation, too, to some degree, in the acquisition of Australia.

"Partition" of Poland

Just before the American Revolution began, Russia, Prussia, and Austria united to murder the old kingdom of Poland, so as to divide the carcass. The anarchy of Poland gave its neighbors excuse. The population consisted of about twelve million degraded serfs, and one hundred thousand selfish, oligarchic nobles. The latter constituted the government. They met in occasional Diets, and, when the throne became vacant, they elected the figurehead king. Unanimous consent was required for any vote in the Diet, — *each noble possessing the right of veto.*

Under such conditions, the other Powers of Europe had begun to play with Poland at will. Catherine II of Russia

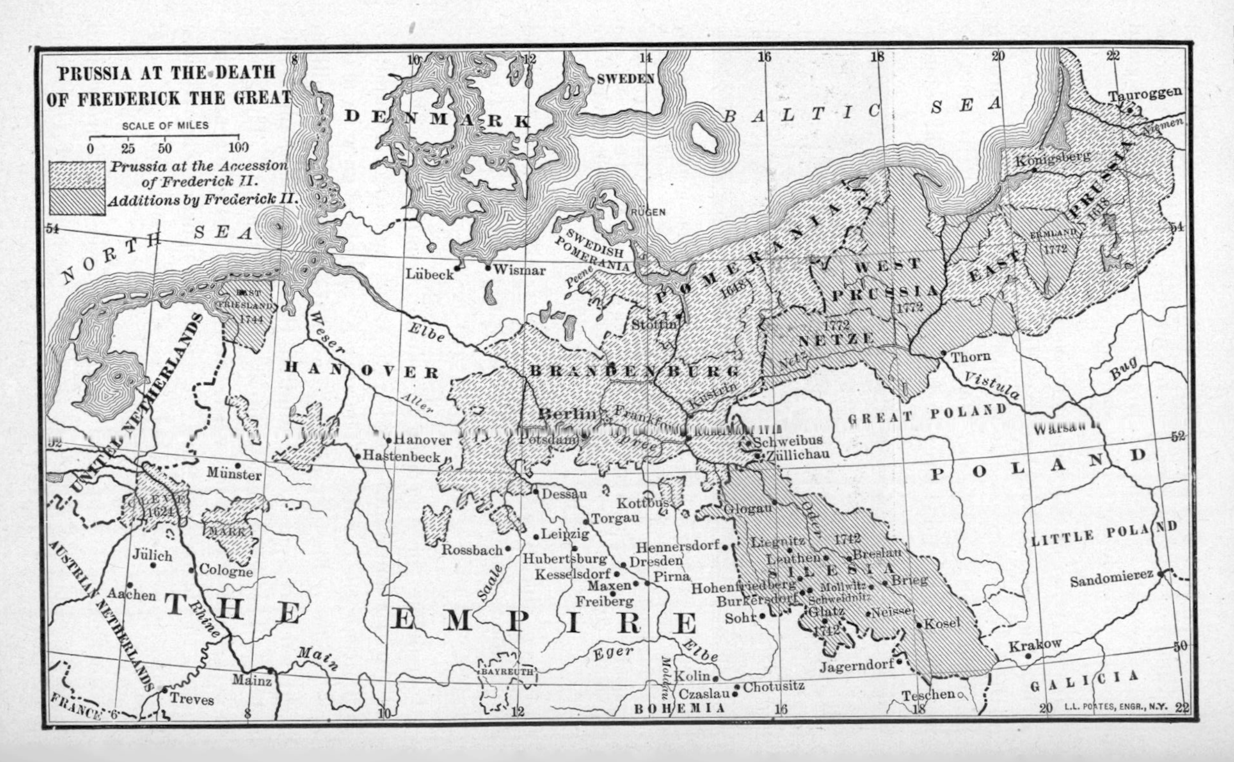
PRUSSIA AT THE DEATH
OF FREDERICK THE GREAT
SCALE OF MILES
0 25 50 100
Prussia at the Accession of Frederick II.
Additions by Frederick II.
NORTH SEA
BALTIC SEA
DENMARK
SWEDEN
RÜGEN
SWEDISH POMERANIA
POMERANIA
1648
WEST PRUSSIA
1772
EAST PRUSSIA
1618
ERMLAND 1772
NETZE
1772
BRANDENBURG
HANOVER
SILESIA
1742
POLAND
GREAT POLAND
LITTLE POLAND
GALICIA
BOHEMIA
THE EMPIRE
UNITED NETHERLANDS
AUSTRIAN NETHERLANDS
FRANCE
EAST FRIESLAND 1744
MARK
CLEVES 1624
BAYREUTH
Tauroggen
Königsberg
Thorn
Warsaw
Sandomierez
Krakow
Teschen
Jagerndorf
Kosel
Neisse
Brieg
Breslau
Mollwitz
Schweidnitz
Glatz
Liegnitz
Leuthen
Hohenfriedberg
Burkersdorf
Sohr
Glogau
Schweibus
Züllichau
Küstrin
Frankfort
Stettin
Berlin
Potsdam
Dessau
Kottbus
Torgau
Leipzig
Hubertsburg
Kesselsdorf
Dresden
Pirna
Maxen
Freiberg
Hennersdorf
Rossbach
Kolin
Czaslau
Chotusitz
Lübeck
Wismar
Hanover
Hastenbeck
Münster
Cologne
Jülich
Aachen
Mainz
Treves
Elbe
Weser
Aller
Oder
Netze
Peene
Vistula
Bug
Niemen
Spree
Saale
Eger
Moldau
Main
Rhine
L.L. POATES, ENGR., N.Y.

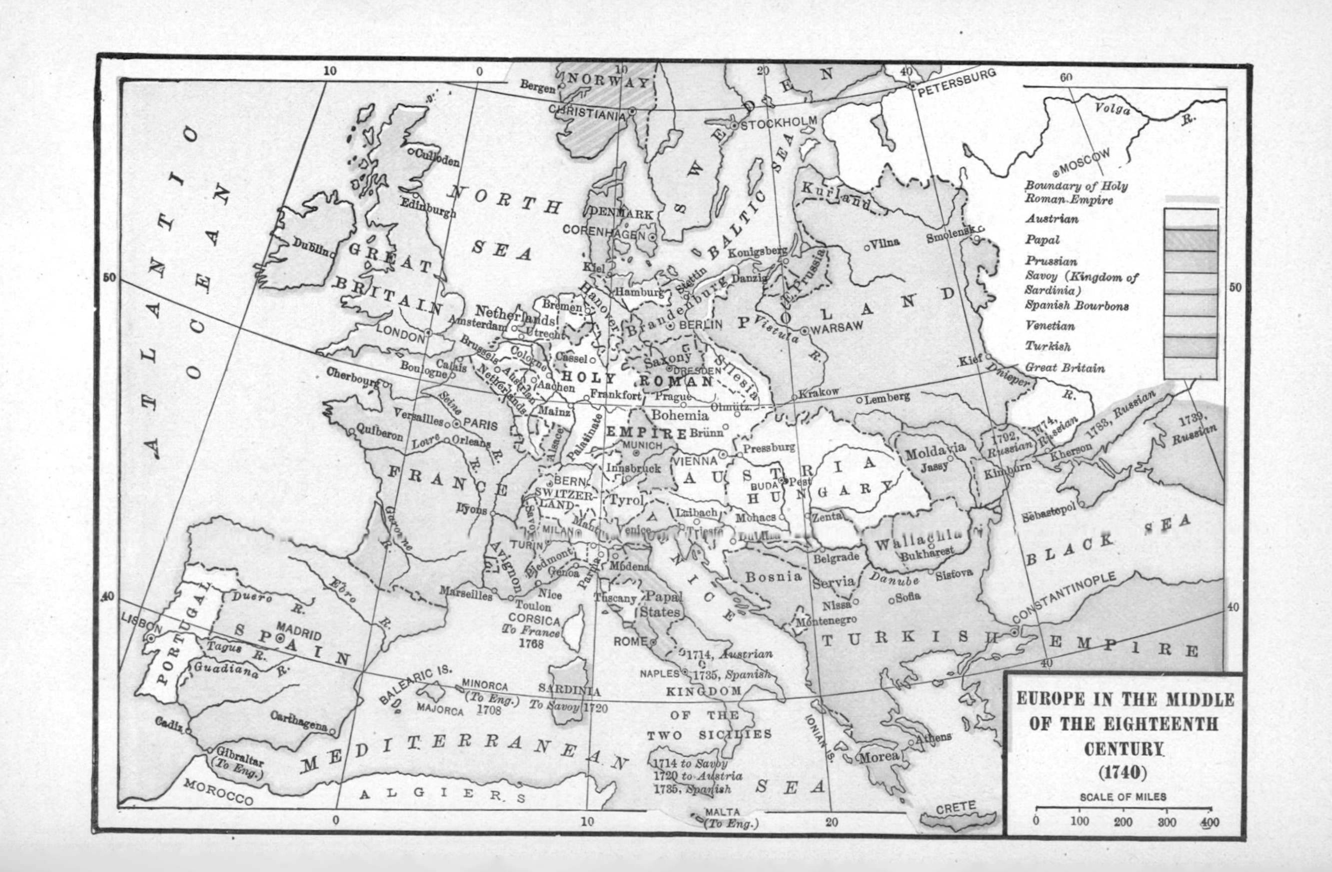
EUROPE IN THE MIDDLE OF THE EIGHTEENTH CENTURY (1740)
SCALE OF MILES
0 100 200 300 400
Boundary of Holy Roman Empire
Austrian
Papal
Prussian
Savoy (Kingdom of Sardinia)
Spanish Bourbons
Venetian
Turkish
Great Britain
ATLANTIC OCEAN
NORTH SEA
BALTIC SEA
BLACK SEA
MEDITERRANEAN SEA
NORWAY
SWEDEN
POLAND
GREAT BRITAIN
FRANCE
SPAIN
PORTUGAL
HOLY ROMAN EMPIRE
AUSTRIA
HUNGARY
TURKISH EMPIRE
KINGDOM OF THE TWO SICILIES
ALGIERS
MOROCCO
Bergen
CHRISTIANIA
STOCKHOLM
PETERSBURG
MOSCOW
Volga R.
Kurland
Vilna
Smolensk
Culloden
Edinburgh
Dublin
DENMARK
COPENHAGEN
Kiel
Hamburg
Stettin
Konigsberg
Danzig
Prussia
Hanover
Bremen
Brandenburg
BERLIN
Vistula R.
WARSAW
Netherlands
Amsterdam
Utrecht
LONDON
Brussels
Cologne
Cassel
Saxony
DRESDEN
Silesia
Calais
Boulogne
Austrian Netherlands
Aachen
Frankfort
Prague
Krakow
Lemberg
Kief
Dnieper R.
Cherbourg
Versailles
PARIS
Seine R.
Mainz
Alsace
Palatinate
Bohemia
Olmütz
Brünn
Quiberon
Loire
Orleans
MUNICH
Pressburg
VIENNA
Innsbruck
Tyrol
BERN
SWITZERLAND
BUDA
Pest
Moldavia
Jassy
1792, Russian
1774, Russian
1783, Russian
1739, Russian
Kinburn
Kherson
Lyons
Savoy
MILANO
Laibach
Mohacs
Zenta
Sebastopol
Garonne R.
TURIN
Venice
Trieste
Dalmatia
Wallachia
Bukharest
Avignon
Piedmont
Genoa
Parma
Modena
Belgrade
Bosnia
Servia
Danube
Sistova
Ebro R.
Duero R.
Marseilles
Nice
Toulon
Tuscany
Papal States
Nissa
Sofia
CONSTANTINOPLE
LISBON
MADRID
CORSICA
To France 1768
Montenegro
Tagus R.
Guadiana R.
ROME
1714, Austrian
1735, Spanish
NAPLES
BALEARIC IS.
MINORCA
(To Eng.) 1708
MAJORCA
SARDINIA
To Savoy 1720
Cadiz
Carthagena
Gibraltar (To Eng.)
IONIAN IS.
Athens
Morea
1714 to Savoy
1720 to Austria
1735, Spanish
MALTA
(To Eng.)
CRETE

determined to seize a large part of the country. Frederick II persuaded Austria to join him in compelling Catherine to share the booty.

The "First Partition," in 1772, pared off a rind about the heart. The Second and Third Partitions (1793, 1795), which completed the work and "assassinated the kingdom," had not even the pretext of misgovernment in Poland. The Poles had undertaken sweeping reforms, and the nation made an heroic defense under its hero-leader Kosciusko; but the great robbers wiped Poland off the map. *Russia gained far the greatest part of the territory, and she now bordered Germany on the east, as France did on the west.*

Plainly the true policy of the Germans, early and late, would have been the honest one of supporting the "buffer states" — Poland and Burgundy — against the greed of Russia and France. Failure to do so left Germany exposed to immediate attack by powerful enemies and compelled her to build up artificial frontiers of fortresses and bayonets.

Frederick "the Great" in peace

Frederick II had shown himself a greedy robber and a military genius. With brutal cynicism he avowed absolute freedom from moral principle where a question of Prussia's power was at stake. Success, he declared, justified any means. This faithlessness he practiced, as well as taught; and his success made this policy the creed of later Hohenzollerns.

But there was another side to Frederick's life, which, more properly than his war or his diplomacy, earns him his title of "the Great." Most of his forty-six years' reign was passed in peace, and he proved a father to his people. The beneficent work of the Great Elector was taken up and carried forward vigorously. Prussia was transformed. Wealth and comfort increased by leaps. The condition of the peasantry was improved, though, of course, they remained serfs; and the administration in all its branches was made economical and efficient. Unlike all the earlier Hohenzollerns, Frederick was also a patron of literature, though he admired only the artificial French style of the age, and he was himself an author.

The "benevolent despots"

Frederick is a type of the "crowned philosophers," or "benevolent despots," who sat upon the thrones of Europe in the latter half of the eighteenth century, just before the French Revolution. Under the influence of a new enlightened sentiment, created by a remarkable school of French writers (p. 260), government underwent a marvelous change. It was just as aristocratic as before, — no more *by* the people than before, — but despots did try to govern *for* the people, not for themselves. Sovereigns began to speak of themselves, not as privileged proprietors, but, in Frederick's phrase, as "the first servants of their states."

Catherine of Russia, Charles III of Spain, Leopold, Archduke of Tuscany, Ferdinand of Naples, Joseph II of Austria, all belonged to the class of philosophic, liberal-minded, "benevolent despots," of this period. In Sweden and Portugal two great ministers sought to impose a like policy upon the kings. All these rulers *planned* far-reaching reforms, — the abolition of serfdom, the building up of public education, and the reform of the church.

Frederick's genius and tireless energy accomplished something for a time; but *on the whole the monarchs made lamentable failures*. One man was powerless to lift the inert weight of a nation. The clergy and nobles, jealous for their privileges, opposed and thwarted the royal will. Except in England and France, there was no large middle class to supply friendly officials and sympathy. The kings, too, wished no participation by the people in the reforms: everything was to come from above. When the "benevolent despots" had to choose between benevolence and despotism they always chose despotism.

The most remarkable, and in some ways the greatest of these philosophic despots, was *Joseph II of Austria,* the son of Maria Theresa. His task was harder than that of any of his fellows because his realms were so heterogeneous, —

peopled by Germans, Hungarians, South-Slavs, Poles, Bohemians, Italians, Netherlanders. Joseph sought to abolish the ancient local distinctions in these varying districts, to introduce one orderly government, with one official language (German), and within his new state to foster education, abolish monasteries, establish freedom of religion, and even to do away with serfdom. All noble and clerical classes, however, resisted him fiercely; and Joseph died disheartened, dictating for himself the epitaph, "Here lies a king who designed many benefits for his people, but who was unable to accomplish any of them."

The kings had failed to bring about sufficient reform; *and now, in France, the people were to try for themselves.*

FURTHER READING upon the subject of the last three chapters may profitably be confined to a continuation of that proposed at the close of Chapter vii, on the Expansion of Europe into the New Worlds. George Burton Adams' essay, "Anglo-Saxon Expansion," in the *Atlantic Monthly* for April, 1897, is excellent reading. For the great struggle in America, the student should read Parkman's Works, especially his *Montcalm and Wolfe* and his *Half Century of Conflict.* The following biographies, too, are good: Wilson's *Clive,* Malleson's *Dupleix* and *Lord Clive,* Bradley's *Wolfe,* Bright's *Maria Theresa,* Bain's *Charles XII,* Lyall's *Warren Hastings,* Morley's *Walpole,* and Bury's *Catherine II.*

REVIEW EXERCISES

1. **Fact Drills.**
   a. Dates with their significance: 1520, 1618–1648, 1640–1649, 1660 1688, 1713, 1740, 1763, 1783.
   b. List ten important battles between 1500 and 1789.
2. Review by countries, with "catch-words," from 1500, or from convenient event of about that date, and review English history from Alfred the Great to the French Revolution.
3. Make a brief paragraph statement for the period 1648–1787, to include the changes in territory and in the relative power of the different European states.

PART IV

THE FRENCH REVOLUTION

You must teach that the French Revolution was an unmitigated crime against God and man. — KAISER WILHELM II of Germany, in an address to teachers of history.

The Revolution was a creating force, even more than a destroying one. It was an inexhaustible source of fertile influences. — FREDERIC HARRISON.

The student may well bear in mind these opposing views as he studies the following chapters.

CHAPTER XII

ON THE EVE

A true "revolution"

Italy had started for the world an intellectual revolution; Germany, a religious revolution; now France was to start the political and social revolution in Europe. More than any of the earlier "revolutions" in history, too, the French upheaval deserves the name *revolution.* The English Revolution of 1688 swept away a temporary interference with old lines of growth: it was a "*conservative* revolution," restoring the nation to an *old* groove. The American Revolution was merely a sudden step *forward* in a direction in which America had long been progressing: it did not change habits of life or of thought. But the French Revolution overturned and *destroyed a society* that had been growing up for centuries; it cut loose from the past; and it started France upon *new* lines of growth.

I. THE ABUSES

France had a population of 25 millions. *One out of each hundred was a "privileged" drone* — a noble or a clergyman. These

The privileged few

two orders, together, owned *half* the soil and *all* the fine buildings. They had many "special privileges" by law, and were exempt from the most burdensome taxes. Moreover, they received, in pensions and in sinecure[1] salaries, a large part of the crushing taxes paid by the nation, besides taking directly from the peasant a fourth of his income in church dues and feudal payments.

The nobles

The privileged nobles rendered no service to society. They had been useful in early times, but the kings now gave all political offices to men of the lower classes, and the nobles themselves abandoned their remaining duty, as captains of local industry, to become mere courtiers. Said Arthur Young, an English gentleman who traveled extensively in France just before the Revolution, — "Exile alone forces the French noble to do what an English noble does by preference: to reside upon his estate, to improve it."

The clergy

The higher clergy, bishops and abbots, were all from noble families, — younger sons who were provided for by office in the church. They received immense revenues for doing nothing, — paying paltry sums to subordinates who did their work, while they themselves lived at court in idle luxury or vice. *The village priests* lived on mere pittances. They were not "privileged." They numbered many devoted men, and the Revolution found them mostly on the side of the people.

The quarter million of privileged drones were supported by twenty-three millions of unprivileged, overburdened workers, — the peasants and the workmen in towns.

The peasants

Arthur Young (above) describes bitterly the hideous wretchedness of the peasantry. Among other piteous stories, he tells of a woman whom he talked with on the road and whom he supposed to be seventy years old, but who proved to be only twenty-seven. Toil, want, and hard fare robbed the workers of youth and life. Famine was chronic in the fertile land of France, as it has been in Russia in recent years. *Taxation and*

[1] A sinecure is an office to which no duties are attached ("without care").

feudal extortion discouraged farming. A fourth of the land lay waste. Of the rest, the tillage was poor, — little better than a thousand years before. The yield was a third less than in England. And if crops failed in one province, starvation followed, although neighboring provinces might possess abundance. Poor roads, and high tolls, and poverty, and the government's carelessness made it impossible for one district to draw relief from another.

At other times, when things were not so bad, great numbers lived on a coarse bread made of bran and bark and acorns — because of which, says an *official* report of the time, "the children very commonly die."

Conditions varied greatly, however, in different parts of France, and in some districts the peasants were fairly prosperous. As a whole they were far ahead of the peasants in Germany or Italy or Spain or Austria, though vastly below the English peasants. They played a part in the Revolution *because they had already progressed far enough to feel discontent and the possibility of further progress.*

Survivals of serfdom

A million and a half were still serfs, but these were nearly all in Alsace or Lorraine, — regions seized from Germany not long before (pp. 177, 230 ff.), where German serfdom still lingered. Elsewhere they had become free in person, and many of them owned little garden spots of land.

But even when the peasant owned land, *he owned it subject to many ancient feudal obligations.* He could leave it, if he liked (with no chance to do better); and he could not be turned off so long as he made the customary payments in labor and in produce. That is, he had advanced out of serfdom to a state of villeinage somewhat like that of the English villeins before the Peasant Rising of 1381. Like them, a French peasant was oppressed by a lot of annoying and costly restrictions, which varied somewhat from place to place. In general, he could not sell his land without buying his lord's consent, or sell any of his crop except in the lord's market, with tolls for the privilege. Commonly, he could still grind his grain only at the lord's mill, leaving one sixteenth the flour, and he could bake only in the lord's oven, leaving a loaf each time in pay.

Most grievous of all the feudal burdens were the nobles' rights to hunt. The peasant must not under any circumstances injure the rabbits or pigeons or deer that devoured his crop; but the nobles at will might ride over the crops to chase the game. On penalty of death, the peasant might not carry a gun, even to kill wolves. He could not enter his own field, to till it, when the pheasants were hatching or the rabbits were young. Year after year the crops were trampled by huntsmen or devoured by game.

Town workers

In the towns the laborers were little better off than those in the country. Writers of the time describe them as pallid, haggard, dwarfed, — "sullen masses of rags and misery," huddled in garrets and cellars. The gild system of the Middle Ages had lost its usefulness, but remained, except in England (p. 185), with all its old power to interfere with individuals. Commonly it forbade a master to keep more than one apprentice, or to sell any goods which he had not himself manufactured. A "cobbler" who mended shoes could not make new ones. A baker could make bread, but not cakes. A hatter in Paris who improved his hats (and took trade from other hatters) by mixing silk in his wool, had his whole stock burned, because gild regulations ordered "pure wool" for hats. The "masters" decided when to admit journeymen to their class; and if a journeyman ventured to manufacture by himself before being so admitted, the government sent him to prison or to the galleys, and seized his goods. In general, the gild regulations kept the poorer workmen from any chance to rise into the better paid trades, and hampered the prosperity even of the shopkeepers and small manufacturers.

The middle class

We have surveyed the narrow apex and the broad base of society. Between the two came an important middle class, composed of bankers, lawyers, physicians, men of letters, merchants, and shopkeepers (gild "masters"). This class was smaller than the "middle class" in England, but much larger than in any other European country. It was to furnish most of the leaders of the Revolution, and, indeed, to make a revolution possible.

National bankruptcy

The immediate occasion for the Revolution was the bankruptcy of the government. The monarchy felt no responsibility to the nation, and so it spent money extravagantly, wastefully, wickedly. Louis XIV, we have seen, left France burdened with a huge debt. The cynical, dissolute Louis XV wasted as much in vice as his predecessor had wasted in war. Much of the rest of the revenue was given away in pensions to unworthy favorites and needy nobles, or stolen by corrupt officials.

There was no "national" treasurer. All the receipts from taxation were subject to the king's order — as if they had been his private banking account. No report was made to the nation as to how taxes were spent; but some facts leaked out. On the eve of the Revolution, three maiden aunts of the king received $120,000 a year for their food — most of which, of course, went to enrich dishonest servants. Some $17,000,000 went each year in grants to members of the royal family and in pensions. This amounted to about $50,000,000 in our values to-day.

Shameful taxation

The treasury, emptied in these shameful ways, was filled in ways equally shameful. Taxes were frightful, but the privileged orders practically escaped them. *The clergy were exempt by law*, and *the nobles escaped by their influence*. The richest man in France, the Duke of Orleans, stated the case frankly. "I make arrangements with the tax officials," he said, "and pay only what I wish." *Large numbers of the wealthier men of the middle class escaped also*, often by purchasing exemption in the form of sinecure offices connected with the royal household.

Thus payment was made only by those least able to pay; and various clumsy devices made the collection needlessly burdensome even on them (p. 238). Two of the many direct taxes were especially offensive and oppressive.

1. The peasant was compelled to leave his own work, no matter how critical the harvest time, at the call of an official, to toil *without pay* on roads or other public works. This labor tax was called the *corvée.*

2. The chief tax had once been a land tax. This now was assessed only on peasant villages, and *it had become a wholly arbitrary tax,* fixed each year by the government. On one occasion, an official wrote: "The people of this village are stout, and there are chicken feathers before the doors. The taxes here should be greatly increased next year." So, too, if a villager lived in a better house than his neighbors, the officials made him pay a larger share of the common village tax. So the peasants concealed jealously what few comforts they had, and left their cottages in ruins.

It has been estimated that on the average a peasant paid half his income in *direct taxes to the government.* Feudal dues and church tithes raised these payments to over four fifths his income. From the remaining one fifth, he had not only to support his family but also to pay various *indirect* taxes.

The salt tax

The most famous indirect tax was that upon salt.[1] This was called the *gabelle.* It raised the price of salt many times its first value. No salt could be bought except from the government agents, and every family was compelled by law to purchase from these agents at least seven pounds a year for every member over seven years of age. This amount, too, was for the table only. If the peasant salted down a pig, he must buy an additional supply for that purpose. To make this absurd condition worse, the people in some districts in France had to pay twice, five times, or ten times as much by way of salt tax as did their neighbors in adjoining districts. Thousands of persons every year were hanged or sent to the galleys for trying to evade the tax.

This salt tax was "farmed" to collectors, who paid the govern-

[1] The man who *sold* the salt paid the tax to the government. The man who bought salt had of course to pay back the tax in a higher price. A tax collected in this way is called an *indirect* tax.

ment a certain amount down, and then secured what they could get above that amount for their own profit. *Only one fifth the amount collected reached the treasury.* Many other indirect taxes — on candles, fuel, grain, and flour — were farmed out in similar fashion.

Complex tariffs

Another class of vexatious indirect taxes were the tolls and tariffs on goods. These payments were required *not only at the frontier* of France, but again and again, at the border of each province and even at the gate of each town, as the goods traveled through the country. Workmen who crossed a river from their homes in one district to their day's work in another had to pay a tariff on the luncheon in their pockets; and fish, on their way to Paris from the coast, paid *thirteen times their first cost* in such tolls.

The government

The government was a *centralized* despotism (p. 19). Directly about the king was a *Council of State.* Subject to the king's approval, it fixed the taxes and the levy for the army, drew up edicts, and indeed ruled France. Its members were appointed by the king, and held office only at his pleasure.

France was made up of about thirty districts, which corresponded roughly to the old feudal provinces. At the head of each such province was a governor appointed by the king. Subject to the royal power, he was an unchecked despot, with tremendous power for good or evil.

In the parish the mayor or syndic was sometimes chosen by the people, sometimes appointed by the governor; but the governor could always remove him at will. The parish assembly could not meet without the governor's permission, and it could not take any action by itself. Had the wind damaged the parish steeple? The parish might *petition* for permission to repair it, — at their own expense, of course. The governor would send the petition, with his recommendation, to the Council of State at Paris, and a reply might be expected in a year or two. Tocqueville declares (*France before the Revolution*) that in the musty archives he found many cases of this kind where the original sum needed for the repairs would not have exceeded five dollars.

Arbitrary imprisonment

The government could send any man in France to prison without trial, merely by a "letter" with the royal seal. Such "*letters of the seal*" were not only used to remove political offenders, but they were also often given, *or sold*, to private men who wished to remove rivals. The government of Louis XV issued 150,000 such letters.

Usually the imprisonments were for a few months; but sometimes the wretch was virtually forgotten and left to die in prison, perhaps without ever learning the cause of his arrest. Arthur Young (p. 253) tells of an Englishman who had been kept in a French prison thirty years, although not even the government held a record of the reason. Very properly did Blackstone, the English law writer, class France with Turkey as countries where "personal liberty" was "wholly at the mercy of the ruler."

An inefficient despotism

This centralized machinery was clumsy. It was complicated by the fact that France was still a patchwork of territories which had been seized piece by piece by the kings. Each province had its own laws and customs, its own privileges and exemptions or partial exemptions, as with the salt tax. Voltaire complained that in a journey one changed laws as often as he changed horses. France was covered with shadows of old local governments, which had lost their power *for action*, but which remained powerful to *delay and obstruct* united action.

II. THE SPIRIT OF CHANGE

A revolution, it has been said, requires not only abuses but also ideas. The combustibles were ready; so were the men of ideas, to apply the match.

The revolution in ideas

Science had upset all old ideas about the world outside man. The telescope had proved that other planets like our earth revolved around the sun, and that myriads of other suns whirled through boundless space; and the English *Newton* had shown how this vast universe is bound together by the unvarying "laws" of unseen gravitation. The microscope had revealed an undreamed-of world of minute life in air and earth and water all around us; and air, earth, water (and fire) themselves had changed their nature. The Ancients had taught that they were the "original elements" out of which everything else was made up. But the French *Lavoisier*, founder of modern chemistry, had lately decomposed water and air into gases, and shown that fire was a union of one of these gases with earthy carbon.

Such a revolution, in the way of looking at the *material* world, prepared men to ask questions about the *world of men* and society. Tradition and authority had been proven silly in the first field: perhaps they were not always right in the other field. England, with its freedom of speech and of the press, had led in this revolt against the authority of the past. But English writers were relatively cautious. Their speculations were carried much farther by French writers who quickly spread their influence over all Europe. *About 1750 there began an age of dazzling brilliancy in French literature and scholarship.* Never before had any country seen so many and so famous men of letters at one time. Of the scores, we can mention only four foremost ones — Voltaire, Montesquieu, Diderot, and Rousseau.

Voltaire and his associates

Voltaire, in 1750, had already won his fame, and he ruled as the intellectual monarch of Europe for thirty years more. He came from the middle class. As a young man, the king had imprisoned him for libel by a "letter of the seal"; and a dissipated noble, angered by a witticism, had hired a band of ruffians to beat him nearly to death. Some years of exile he spent in England, where, he says, he "learned to think." Most of his writing was destructive; but the old in Europe needed to be swept away, before new growth could start. He had biting satire, mocking wit, keen reasoning, and incisive, vigorous style. So armed, he attacked daringly the absurdities in society and the superstitions and scandals of the church.

He railed at absentee bishops of licentious lives; he questioned the privileges of the nobles; and he pitilessly exposed the iniquity of the gabelle and of the "letters of the seal." The church seemed to him the chief foe to human progress;

and in his invective against its abuses he sometimes confused it with Christianity itself. So too did most of the other writers in this brilliant company. But "their glory lies not in their contempt for things holy, but in their scorn for things unjust." Voltaire's powerful plea for religious tolerance and his lifelong exposure of the folly and wrong of religious persecution had much to do with creating the free atmosphere in which we live to-day. We must remember that many of his books were burned by order of the church and the government, and that he ran grave personal risks. Our American Lowell says, "We owe half our liberty to that leering old mocker"; and Professor Jowett of Oxford, an English Churchman, declares that Voltaire "did more good than all the Fathers of the Church together." He is often incorrectly called an atheist. He was not a Christian, but he was a deist, — a firm believer in a God revealed in nature and in the human soul.

VOLTAIRE. — The bust by Houdon.

Montesquieu, in a famous book, *The Spirit of Laws*, contrasted French despotism with constitutional liberty in England.

In 1751 Diderot and a group of companions published the first volume of the great French *Encyclopedia*, a work which was completed twenty years later, in thirty-seven volumes. The purpose of "the Encyclopedists" was to gather up all the results of the new science and new thought, and to make them known to larger numbers. In particular, they criticized religious persecution and the salt tax and like abuses in government; and on every occasion they wrote of the benefits of industry and commerce. Says John Morley, "They were vehement for the glories of peace, and passionate against the brazen glories of war." The Encyclopedia has been called a "rising in battle array of all the men of the new era against all the powers of the past."

Rousseau and democracy

Voltaire and his fellows admired the constitutional monarchy of England; but they looked for reform rather from some enlightened, philosophic despot. One alone among them stood for democracy. This was *Rousseau*. He wrote much that was absurd about an ideal "state of nature" before men "invented governments" and created an "artificial civilization"; but he taught, more forcefully than any man before him, the sovereignty of the whole people. His most famous book (*The Social Contract*, 1762) opens with the words, "Man was born free, but he is now everywhere in chains"; and it argues passionately that it is man's right and duty to recover freedom. Rousseau's moral earnestness and enthusiasm made his doctrine almost a religion with his disciples. He was the prophet of the political side of the coming Revolution.

Some years before the French Revolution began, the ideas, and even some of the phrases, of Rousseau began to have a powerful influence in America. They did not create the American Revolution, but they helped that great movement to justify itself in words. Passages in the Declaration of Independence and in many of the original State constitutions about natural equality and freedom, are popularly supposed to be due to American admiration for Rousseau. Rousseau, however, drew these ideas to a great extent from John Locke and other English writers of the seventeenth century and we cannot always tell whether an American document is affected by Rousseau or directly by the older but less impressive English literature.

Fashionable liberalism

When the French writers *began* to attack hoary abuses, they ran extreme personal risks and played an heroic part. The same movement, however, that produced these men of letters was at work in all social circles. The writers intensified the movement, and, before long, criticism of existing arrangements became general. Liberalism, in words if not in acts, became fashionable.

Even the privileged orders began to talk about their own uselessness. When the great noble in a popular play was asked what he had done to deserve all his privileges, and when his lackey answered for him, "Your Excellency took the trouble to be born," the audience of nobles in the boxes laughed and applauded.

Upon the whole, however, the mass of the privileged classes remained selfish and scornful. *The chief influence of the new philosophy was in its effect upon the unprivileged masses.* The third estate became conscious of its wrongs and of its power. Said a famous pamphlet by *Siéyès* on the eve of the Revolution, "*What really is the third estate? Everything. What has it been so far in the state? Nothing. What does it ask? To be something.*" And at the time the privileged orders are often refered to merely as a "malign ulcer" which ought to be cut out of the social body.

III. THE GOVERNMENT ATTEMPTS REFORMS, 1774–1789

Louis XVI

In 1774 the dissolute but able Louis XV was succeeded by the well-disposed but irresolute *Louis XVI.* This prince had a vague notion of what was right and a general desire to do it, but he lacked moral courage and will power. His weakness was as harmful to France as his predecessor's wickedness. He abandoned the wisest policy and the best ministers, rather than face the sour looks of the courtiers and the pouts of the queen.

Marie Antoinette

The Queen was Marie Antoinette, daughter of the great Maria Theresa of Austria. She was young, high-spirited, and lovely, but ignorant, frivolous, and selfishly bent upon her own pleasures. The king was greatly influenced by her, and almost always for evil.

Reform began, and finally the Revolution began, because the royal treasury was bankrupt. When Louis XVI came to the throne, the national debt was some five hundred million dollars, a huge sum for that day, and it was increasing each year by ten million dollars more. This condition stirred Louis to spasmodic attempts at reform, and he called to his aid Turgot, a man of letters, a reformer, and an experienced administrator.

Turgot's reforms

Turgot had been a Provincial governor for many years, and had made remarkable improvements in his district. Now he set about conferring still greater benefits on all France. He abolished the forced labor on the roads, the internal tariffs on grain, and the outgrown gilds with their tyrannical restrictions. "The right to labor," said his public proclamation on this occasion, "is the most sacred of all possessions. Every law by which it is limited violates the 'Natural Rights' of man, and is null and void." He also cut down the frivolous expenses of the court, and curtailed the absurd pension list remorselessly.

He planned other vast and far-reaching reforms, — to recast the whole system of taxation, to equalize burdens, to abolish feudal dues, and to introduce a system of public education: "a whole *pacific* French Revolution in that head," says Carlyle. But the nobles grumbled sullenly at the prospect of having to bear their proper share of taxation; the courtiers looked black; the queen hated the reformer, who interfered with her pleasures; and so Louis grew cold, and, after only twenty months, dismissed the man who might perhaps have saved France from a revolution of violence.

Necker's Report

All Turgot's reforms were swiftly undone; but, in 1776, Necker, another reformer, was called to the helm. Necker was not a great statesman like Turgot, but he was a good business man with liberal views, and he might have accomplished something for the treasury if his difficulties had not been tremendously augmented in an unforeseen manner. In 1778 France joined America in her war against England (p. 246). The new "loans"[1] to support the expense of the war *increased* the

[1] When a nation sells bonds to raise money, the proceeding is called a loan.

national debt, and made it even more impossible to pay the annual interest.

Then Necker laid before the king a plan for sweeping reform, much along Turgot's lines; but the universal outcry of the privileged classes caused Louis to dismiss him from office (1781).

But Necker had let the nation know, for the first time, just how it was being plundered, and to what base ends. His "Plan" had been accompanied by a "report" on the finances. This paper set forth plainly just how much money was raised; by what taxes it was raised; and how it had been spent — mainly on the court and its unworthy pastimes. This report was printed, and was eagerly read over all France by the middle class.

Calonne and the Notables

Meantime, however, all the old abuses were restored for a time; and a new minister of finance, the courtly Calonne, adopted the policy of an unscrupulous bankrupt, and tried to create credit by lavish extravagance. For some years this was successful; but in 1786 the treasury was running behind to the amount of *forty million dollars* a year! Even adroit Calonne could borrow no more money to pay expenses or interest. Under these conditions, the minister persuaded Louis to call together the "Notables of France."

The Notables were composed of only such leading nobles and clergy as the king pleased to summon; but they came from all parts of France, and they at least represented France better than the little clique of courtiers did. To this amazed gathering, Calonne, the pet minister of the court, suggested the hated plan of Turgot and of Necker, — that the privileged orders give up their exemption from taxation. It was necessary to get more money, and that could be done only by taxing those who had something wherewith to pay. But now all cried out against the minister, — the few Liberals for what he had done in the past, the many Conservatives for what he now proposed to do, — and Calonne, too, had to go.

The Notables were still stubborn; so the king dismissed them, and tried to force the plan upon the nobles by royal edict —

The Parlement of Paris

as the only way to avoid bankruptcy. Before a royal edict was put in force, it had to be "registered" (put down upon a record) by a great law-court known as the Parlement of Paris — and afterward by like bodies in the provincial capitals — in order that the courts might know just what the law was. In a few cases in past centuries, the Parlement, instead of registering an edict, had sent it back to the king with a list of their objections, in hope of securing some modification. If the king was determined, however, he merely summoned the Parlement before him and *ordered* them to register — which always had ended the matter. But the Parlement, like the Notables, represented the privileged orders. It refused to register this edict even after the royal session, and cloaked its dislike to reform under the excuse that *the only power in France which could properly impose a new tax was the States General.* Louis banished the Parlement, *but it had given a rallying cry to the nation.*

Demand for States General

The States General (p. 86) had not met since 1614. Suggestions for assembling it had been made from time to time, ever since Louis XVI became king. At the session of the Notables, Lafayette had called for it. Now, after the action of the Parlement, *the demand became universal* and imperious. Finally, August, 1788, the king yielded. He recalled Necker and promised that the States General should be assembled.

A summary causes of the Revolution

The chief institutions of France were: —

(1) *a monarchy*, despotic and irresponsible, but in weak hands and anxious to keep the good opinion of the nobles;

(2) *an aristocracy*, wealthy, privileged, corrupt, skeptical;

(3) *an established church*, wealthy and often corrupt.

Below, spread *the masses*, a necessary but ugly substructure.

Like conditions existed *over the continent*. In France, as compared with the other large countries, the nobles had fewer duties, the peasantry had risen somewhat, and more of a middle class had grown up. That is, feudal society was more decayed, and the industrial state was more advanced, than in other continental countries. This explains why the Revolution came in France. Revolutions break through in the weakest spots.

First among the causes of the Revolution, we must put the unjust privileges of the small upper class and the crushing burdens borne by the great non-privileged mass. These evils were no greater than for centuries before, but the consciousness of them was greater. Not only was the system bad, but men knew that it was bad. The masses were beginning to demand reform, and the privileged classes and the government had begun to distrust their rights. Their power of resistance was weakened by such doubts. This new intellectual condition was due primarily to the new school of French men of letters.

The *bankruptcy of the national treasury* opened the way for other forces to act. It started the government itself upon the path of reform; and *the inefficiency and indecision of the government* led the people finally to seize upon the reform movement themselves, — a result greatly hastened by the political doctrines made popular just before by Rousseau.

The American Revolution helped *directly* to bring on the French Revolution by sinking the French monarchy more hopelessly into bankruptcy. In other *indirect* ways the American movement contributed to that in France. Lafayette and other young nobles who had served in America came home with liberal ideas strengthened; and the French regiments that had fought side by side with the American yeomanry had imbibed democratic ideas and were soon to declare themselves "the army of the nation," not of the king. Said Arthur Young in 1789, "The American Revolution has laid the foundation for another one in France."

Further, to run a centralized despotism with real success calls for a Caesar or a Napoleon. But hereditary monarchy in Europe in the eighteenth century had ceased to furnish great rulers. The American Jefferson, with some exaggeration, wrote from Paris in 1787 that not a king in Europe had ability needful to fit him for a Virginia vestryman. Louis XIV had been a tireless worker. But the selfish, indolent Louis XV said to his favorite, "Let the good machine run itself. It will last our time. After us, the deluge." On his deathbed, the same shameless king said, — "I should like very much to see how Berry will pull through." Under "Berry" (Louis XVI), the "machine" went to pieces and the "deluge" came.

FOR FURTHER READING. — *Source material* may be found in Robinson's *Readings*, including some extracts from French men of letters of this age.

Modern Accounts: Shailer Mathews' *French Revolution*, 1–110, is the best one account. Mrs. Gardiner's *French Revolution*, 1–32, is very good. The student should certainly read either one of these, or the somewhat longer account in Lowell's *Eve of the French Revolution.* If the student can read further still, there is nothing better or more interesting than John Morley's *Lives* of Voltaire, Rousseau, and Diderot, and his essays in his *Miscellanies* on "France in the Eighteenth Century" and on "Turgot." Say's *Turgot* is a good biography.

CHAPTER XIII

THE REVOLUTION IN TIME OF PEACE

MAY TO AUGUST, 1789: THE ASSEMBLY AT VERSAILLES

Election of the States General

In electing the States General, the country was divided into districts. The nobility and clergy of each district came together to choose delegates. The delegates of the third estate were elected *indirectly* by "electoral colleges." In choosing these colleges, all *taxpayers* had a voice.

But before the elections, two points had been widely and earnestly discussed in France. The ancient States General had been a meeting of three "orders" sitting in separate "houses," each with one vote. For the time to which France had now come, this was plainly absurd. Under such an arrangement the two privileged orders, representing only one hundredth of the nation, would have two thirds the vote, and would block all reform. Accordingly all Liberals, like Lafayette and Siéyès, had urged (1) that the third estate should have twice as many members as either nobles or clergy; and (2) that all three orders should sit together and vote "by head." The king had finally been induced to order the "double representation" for the third estate; but the second and vital point, the manner of voting, he had left unsettled.

When finally chosen, the States General consisted of about 600 members of the third estate, 300 nobles, and 300 clergy. Of this last order, two thirds were village priests. The delegates possessed no political experience; but the bulk of the third estate were lawyers, and, as a whole, the gathering was scholarly and cultured.

May 5, 1789, the king opened the States General at Versailles.[1]

[1] Read Carlyle's account of the procession. Louis XIV had built a splendid palace at Versailles, — twelve miles southwest of Paris, — and this place remained the favorite residence of the French kings.

One house or two

The royal address suggested some reforms; but it was plain that the king hoped mainly for more taxes, and enthusiastic Liberals were sadly disappointed. Even Necker's three-hour address, which followed the king's, dwelt only upon the need for prompt action to relieve the government's financial straits.

The nobles and the clergy then organized as *separate* chambers, after the ancient fashion. The third estate insisted *that all three orders should organize in a single chamber,* — where its membership (with some help from the liberal nobles and the priests) could outvote the other orders combined. There followed a deadlock for five weeks.

But delay was serious. The preceding harvest had been a failure, and famine stalked through the land. In Paris, every bakeshop had its "tail" of men and women, standing through the night for a chance to buy bread. Such conditions called for speedy action, especially as the ignorant masses had got it into their heads that the marvelous States General would in some way make food plenty.

The "National Assembly"

Finally (June 17), on motion of Siéyès (p. 263), an ex-priest, *the third estate declared that by itself* it represented *ninety-six per cent* of the nation, and that, with or without the other orders, *it organized as a National Assembly.*[1] *This was a revolution. It changed a gathering of feudal "Estates" into an assembly representing the nation as one whole. Nothing of this kind had ever been seen before on the continent of Europe.*

The Tennis Court Oath

Two days later, the National Assembly was joined by half the clergy (mainly parish priests) and by a few liberal nobles. But the next morning the Assembly found sentries at the doors of their hall, and carpenters within putting up staging, to prepare for a "royal session." Plainly the king was about to interfere. The gathering adjourned to a tennis court near by, and there with stern enthusiasm they unanimously took a memorable oath[2] *never to separate until they had established the constitution on a firm foundation* (June 20).

[1] See Anderson's *Constitutions and Documents*, No. 1, for the decree.

[2] See the text in Anderson's *Constitutions and Documents*, No. 2.

The idea of a written constitution had come from America. Six years earlier, Franklin, our minister to France, had published French translations of the constitutions adopted by the new American States. The pamphlet had been widely read, and much talked about. The instructions[1] of delegates to the Assembly had commonly called for a constitution. To make one became now the chief purpose of the Assembly. That body, indeed, soon became known as *the Constituent Assembly.*

Vacillation of the king

Now king and Assembly clashed. On June 23 Louis summoned the three estates to meet him, and told them that they were to organize as *separate bodies,* and to carry out certain *specified* reforms. If they failed to comply with the royal wishes, the king would himself "secure the happiness of his people." The people themselves were to have no real hand in the reform of their country. The weak king had decided at last to play the impossible part of a "benevolent despot."

When the king left, the nobles and higher clergy followed. *The new "National Assembly" kept their seats.* There was a moment of uncertainty. It was a serious matter for quiet citizens to brave the wrath of the ancient monarchy. Mirabeau, a noble who had abandoned his order, rose to remind the delegates of their great oath. The royal master of ceremonies, reentering, asked haughtily if they had not heard the king's command to disperse. "Yes," broke in Mirabeau's thunder; "but go tell your master that *we are here by the power of the people,* and that nothing but the power of bayonets shall drive us away." Then, on Mirabeau's motion, the Assembly decreed the inviolability of its members: "Infamous and guilty of capital crime is any person or court that shall dare pursue or arrest any of them, *on whose part soever the same be commanded.*"

[1] Nearly every gathering for choosing delegates to the Assembly had drawn up a statement of grievances and had suggested reforms, for the guidance of its representatives. These *cahiers* (kä-yā') are the most valuable source of our knowledge of France before the Revolution. See *Pennsylvania Reprints*, IV, No. 5, for examples, or, more briefly, in Robinson's *Readings*.

The king's weakness prevented conflict. Paris was rising, and the French Guards, the main body of troops in the capital, when ordered to fire on the mob, rang their musket butts sullenly on the pavement. The next day, forty-seven nobles joined the National Assembly. In less than a week, *the king ordered the rest to join.*

The dismissal of Necker

However, the court planned a counter-revolution, and again won over the weak king. A camp of several thousand veterans was collected near Paris, — largely German or Swiss mercenaries, who could be depended upon. Probably it was intended to imprison leading deputies. Certainly the Assembly was to be overawed. July 9, Mirabeau boldly declared to the Assembly that this was the royal policy; and, on his motion, the Assembly requested the king immediately to withdraw the troops. The king's answer was to banish Necker, the idol of the people, who had opposed the great policy.

This was on the evening of July 11. About noon the next day, the news was whispered on the streets. *Camille Desmoulins,* a young journalist, pistol in hand, leaped upon a table in one of the public gardens, exclaiming, "Necker is dismissed. It is a signal for a St. Bartholomew of patriots. To arms! To arms!" By night the streets bristled with barricades against the charge of the king's cavalry, and the crowds were sacking gunshops for arms. *Three regiments of the French Guards joined the rebels.* Some rude organization was introduced during the next day, and, on the day following, *the revolutionary forces attacked the Bastille.*

Fall of the Bastille, July 14

The Bastille was the great "state prison," like the Tower in England. In it had been confined political offenders and victims of "letters of the seal." It was a symbol of the "Old Régime," and an object of detestation to the liberals. It had been used as an arsenal, and the rebels went to it at first only to demand arms. Refused admission and fired upon, they made a frantic attack. The fortress was virtually impregnable; but after some hours of wild onslaught, it surrendered to an almost unarmed force, — "taken," as Carlyle says, "like

Jericho, by miraculous sound." Then the hangers-on of the attacking force massacred the garrison, and paraded their heads on pikes through the streets.

Out at Versailles, Louis, who had spent the day hunting and had retired early, was awakened to hear the news. "What! a riot, then?" said he. "No, Sire," replied the messenger; "a revolution." The anniversary of the destruction of the Bastille (July 14) is still celebrated in France as the birthday of political liberty, like our July 4.

FALL OF THE BASTILLE. — From an old print of a drawing by Prieur.

This rising of Paris had saved the Assembly. The most hated of the courtiers fled from France in terror. The king visited Paris, sanctioned all that had been done, sent away his troops, *accepted the tricolor* (red, white, and blue), the badge of the Revolution, *as the national colors,* and recalled Necker.

Local anarchy

The fall of the Bastille gave the signal for a brief mob-rule over all France. In towns the mobs demolished *local* "bastilles." In the country the lower peasantry and bands of vagabonds plundered and demolished castles, seeking especially to destroy the court rolls with the records of servile dues, and to slay the hated deer and pigeons.

Each district had its carnival of plunder and bloodshed. The king could not enforce the law: the machinery of the old royal government had collapsed. The Assembly did not dare interfere vigorously, because it might need the mob again for its own protection. Six days after the fall of the Bastille, the moderate Liberals proposed to issue a proclamation denouncing popular violence. From an obscure seat on the Extreme-Left, *Robespierre*, then an unknown deputy, protested vehemently: "Revolt? This revolt is liberty. To-morrow the shameful plots against us may be renewed, and who will then repulse them if we declare rebels the men who have rushed to our protection!"

The middle class reorganize society

But everywhere *the middle class did organize successfully* against anarchy — and so really saved the Revolution.[1] In Paris, during the disorder of July 13, the electoral college of the city (the men who chose the delegates of Paris to the States General) reassembled and assumed authority to act as a Municipal Council. In other towns the like was done, and in a few weeks, France was covered with new local governments composed of the middle class. This was the easier, because in many cases the electoral colleges, instead of breaking up after the election, had continued to hold occasional meetings during the two months since, in order to correspond with their delegates in the National Assembly.

The first act of the Paris Council had been to order that in each of the sixty "sections" (wards) of the city, two hundred men should patrol the streets, to maintain order. This, or something like this, was done in all the districts of France. This new militia became permanent. It took the name "National Guards," and in Paris Lafayette became the commander. Like the new municipal councils, the Guards were made up from the middle class, and before the middle of August, these new forces had restored order.

[1] Compare the failure of the middle class in Russia in the Revolution of 1917–18.

August 4: abolition of privilege

Meantime, on the evening of *August 4*, the discussions of the Assembly were interrupted by the report of a committee on the disorders throughout the country. The account stirred the Assembly deeply. A young noble, who had served in America with Lafayette, declared that these evils were all due to the continuance of feudal burdens and to the special privileges of his class; and, with impassioned oratory, he moved their instant abolition. One after another, in eager emulation, the liberal nobles followed, each proposing some sacrifice for his order, — game laws, dovecotes, tithes, exclusive right to military office, and a mass of sinecures and pensions.

Every proposal was ratified with applause. Our American minister, Gouverneur Morris, was disgusted with the haste, and even Mirabeau called the scene "an orgy of sacrifice." On the other hand, the French radical, *Marat*, in his newspaper, *The Friend of the People*, cried out against any feeling of gratitude. "Let us not be duped," he wrote. "When the lurid flames of burning castles have illuminated France, these people have kindly given up their old privilege of keeping in chains men who have already won their liberty by arms." But, on the whole, the work was necessary and noble, and it has never been undone. *The night of August 4 saw the end of feudalism and of legal inequalities in France.*[1] This was one reason why anarchy and riot was so easily suppressed in the provinces. Had the Russian nobles been equally wise and swift in 1917, the Russian Revolution might have been spared much extravagance and anarchy.

In three months — May 5 to August 5, France had been revolutionized. The third estate had asserted successfully its just claim to represent the nation. Its favorite motto was the famous phrase — *Liberty, Fraternity, and Equality*. "Equality" it had won: the odious privileges of the aristocracy, and all class distinctions before the law, had been forever swept away. Toward "Liberty," much progress had been made: the local

[1] Anderson, No. 4, and *Pennsylvania Reprints*, I, No. 5, give the decrees as finally put in order a few days later.

units of the country had set up new popular governments, and had organized new citizen armies to protect them. And the Assembly was at work upon a new constitution for the nation at large. "Fraternity" has not yet been achieved in any land.

TO SEPTEMBER, 1791: THE ASSEMBLY IN PARIS

The March of the Women, October 5

Even after the new harvest of 1789, food remained scarce and some riots continued. To maintain order, the king brought a regiment of soldiers to Versailles. The "patriots," as the liberal party called themselves, feared that he was again plotting to undo the Revolution. Extravagant loyal demonstrations at a military banquet emphasized the suspicion. It was reported that young officers, to win the favor of court ladies, had trampled upon the tricolor and had displayed instead the old white cockade of the Bourbon monarchy.

The men of Paris tried to go to Versailles to secure the person of the king, but the National Guards turned them back. Then (October 5) thousands of the women of the market place, crying that French soldiers would not fire upon women, set out in a wild, hungry, haggard rout to bring the king to Paris — away from the influence of the reactionary courtiers at Versailles. In their wake followed the riffraff of the city.

Lafayette permitted the movement to go on, until there came near being a terrible massacre at Versailles; but his tardy arrival, late at night, with twenty thousand National Guards, restored order. In the early morning, however, the mob broke into the palace, and the queen's life was saved only by the gallant self-sacrifice of some of her guards. The king yielded to the demands of the crowd and to the advice of Lafayette; and the same day a strange procession escorted the royal family to Paris, — the mob dancing in wild joy along the road before the royal carriage, carrying on pikes the heads of some slain soldiers, and shouting, "Now we shall have bread, for we are bringing the baker, the baker's wife, and the baker's little boy." The king's brothers and great numbers of the nobles fled from France, —

and many of these 150,000 "Emigrants" strove at foreign courts to stir up war against their country.

The Assembly in Paris was no longer in danger of interference from the king, but during the two years more that it spent in making a constitution, it was threatened often with violence from the mob. The sessions were all open to the public, and the galleries jeered and hissed and threatened speakers whom they disliked. Sometimes, too, the mob attacked conservative delegates on the street. Soon, nearly a fourth of the Assembly withdrew, declaring that it was no longer free.

Progress by the Assembly mob influence

Political clubs arose, too, and became a mighty power outside the Assembly. The most important of these clubs was the *Jacobins*, which took its name from the fact that it met in a building belonging to the Dominicans. In Paris that order was called Jacobins, because its first home in that city had been at the church of St. Jacques.

Political clubs

In this Jacobin club some of the radical deputies met to discuss measures about to come before the Assembly. Soon others besides deputies were admitted, and the club became the center of a radical democratic party.

Lafayette tried to organize a "Constitutionalist Club," with more moderate opinions; and various attempts were made at royalist clubs. But the clubs, like the galleries, were best fitted to add strength to the radicals.

Meantime the Assembly divided into definite political parties. On the Speaker's right, the place of honor, sat the extreme Conservatives, known from their position as the *Right*. They were reactionists, and stood for the restoration of the old order.

Political parties

Next to them sat the *Right-Center*. This party did not expect to restore the old conditions, but they did hope to prevent the Revolution from going any farther, and they wished to keep political power in the hands of the wealthy landowners.

The *Left-Center*, the largest body, wished neither to restrict power to the very wealthy, nor to extend it to the very poor, but to intrust it to the middle class. In this group sat Mirabeau,

Lafayette, and Siéyès. Both parties of the Center wished a constitutional monarchy.

The *Extreme-Left* comprised some thirty deputies who were disciples of Rousseau. They wished manhood suffrage. In this group sat Robespierre.

In the legislatures of *continental Europe* a like arrangement of parties is still customary. The Conservatives sit on the right, the Liberals on the left; and they are still known as the Right and the Left. *In England* the supporters of the ministry sit on the right, and the opposition on the left, and the two parties change place with a change of ministry; so in that country the "Left" and the "Right" are not party names.

Mirabeau

One man in the Assembly was really a party in himself. Mirabeau (p. 271) was a marvelous orator, a statesman of profound insight, and a man of dauntless courage. He never hesitated to oppose the mob if his convictions required it; and often he won them to his side. But he had lived a wild and dissolute life, and so could not gain influence over some of the best elements of the Assembly. His arrogance, too, aroused much jealousy. Both Necker and Lafayette hated him.

Mirabeau was resolutely opposed to anarchy, and he wanted a strong executive. After the "march of the women," he felt that the danger to the Revolution lay not so much in the king as in the mob. Thereafter, he sought to preserve the remaining royal power — and to direct it. He wished the king to accept the Revolution in good faith, and to surround himself with a liberal ministry chosen from the Assembly. As the mob grew more furious, he wished the king to leave Paris and appeal to the provinces of France against the capital, — only, he urged especially, the king must not go toward the east, lest the people think he meant to flee to Austria.

Flight of the king

The king hesitated, and Mirabeau died (April 2, 1791), broken down by the strain of his work and by dissolute living. Then Louis decided to flee, not to the French provinces, but *to Austria*, to raise war, not against the Paris mob, but against

France and the Revolution. The plot failed, because of the king's indecision and clumsiness. The royal family did get out of Paris (Louis in disguise as a valet), but they were recognized and brought back prisoners.

"Massacre of the Champs de Mars"

This attempt of the king led to another popular rising. This time the purpose was to force the Assembly to dethrone the king. A petition for such action, and *for the establishment of a republic,* was drawn up, and crowds flocked out to sign it at the Champs de Mars, — an open space near the city where a great celebration of the fall of the Bastille had just been held. Some disorder occurred. The municipal authorities seized the excuse to forbid the gathering, and finally Lafayette's National Guards dispersed the jeering mob with volleys of musketry. Many more people were killed — unarmed people, exercising merely the right of petition — than there were soldiers killed when the women and mob of Paris had marched upon Versailles two years before; but those soldiers, whose heroism histories have chanted ever since, were largely aristocratic officers; while this time the slain were merely workingmen *and their wives* — and history has had little to say about it.

Split between Bourgeoisie and the Working Class

This "Massacre of the Champs de Mars" (July 17) marks a sharp division between the working class and the middle class. For the time, the latter carried the day. In the next six weeks the victorious Assembly completed and revised its two years' work; and September 14, 1791, after solemnly swearing to uphold the constitution, Louis was restored to power.

THE CONSTITUTION OF 1791

The Declaration of the Rights of Man

First in the new constitution came a noble "Declaration of the Rights of Man" — after the example of the Bills of Rights in some of the American State constitutions. It proclaimed, —

(1) "Men are born equal in rights, and remain so."

(2) "Law is the expression of the will of all the people. Every citizen has a right to a share in making it; and it must be the same for all."

And so on, through a number of provisions. It made all Frenchmen equal before the law, and equally eligible to public office. It abolished hereditary titles and confirmed the abolition of all special privileges. It established jury trial, freedom of religion, and freedom of the press. The great Declaration has justified the boast of the Assembly — that it "shall serve as an everlasting war cry against oppressors."[1]

A constitutional monarchy under middle-class control

The Declaration of Rights cared for *personal* liberties. The arrangements concerning the government secured a very large amount of *political* liberty. There was established a *limited monarchy,* with a large degree of *local self-government,* under *middle-class control.*

The Central Government was made to consist of the king and a Legislative Assembly of *one* House — since an "upper" House would have been likely to be strongly aristocratic. The king could not dissolve the Assembly, and his veto could be overridden if three successive legislatures decided against him on any measure.[2] A new Assembly was to be chosen each second year.

Attempt to "decentralize"

Local government was made over wholly. The historic provinces, with their troublesome peculiar privileges and customs, were wiped from the map. France was divided into eighty-three "Departments" of nearly equal size. The Departments were subdivided into districts, and the district was made up of communes (villages or towns, with their adjacent territory). The map of France still keeps these divisions.

Each Department and district elected a "General Council" and an executive board, or "Directory." The forty thousand communes had each its elected Council and mayor. So much authority was left to the communes, that France under this constitution has been called "a loose alliance of forty thousand

[1] Read the "Declaration of the Rights of Man," in the *Pennsylvania Reprints,* I, No. 5, or in Anderson, No. 5.

[2] The new American States had just begun to try another way to limit the old absolute veto — permitting a two-thirds vote to override the President or governor. The French plan of a "suspensive' veto has been most popular in free countries in Europe.

little republics." France tried to go *too fast* toward "decentralization"; and, as we shall see, the plan never worked.

Graded qualifications for voting

The franchise was not given to all, despite the second statement quoted above from the Declaration of Rights. About one fourth of the men had no vote. A voter had to have enough property to pay taxes equal to three days' wages of an artisan.

Then these "active citizens," or voters, were graded further, according to their wealth, into three divisions. The first class could only vote. The second could hold offices in communes and districts, and be chosen to electoral colleges. Only the third, and wealthiest, class could be chosen to the higher offices.

Thus political supremacy was secured to the middle class by two devices, — (1) graded property qualifications, and (2) indirect elections. Both these devices to dodge democracy were used in the American States of that day. No American State then had manhood suffrage.

National control of the church

In the disorders of 1789 people ceased to pay the old and unjust taxes. It was some time before new ones could be arranged for. Meanwhile the Assembly secured funds by seizing and selling the church lands — more than a fifth of all France.

When the government took the revenue of the church, of course it also assumed the duty of paying the clergy and maintaining the churches. This led to national control of the church. The number of higher clergy was greatly reduced, and the clergy of all grades were made elective, in the same way as civil officers. Unfortunately they were required to take an oath of fidelity to the constitution in a form repulsive to many sincere adherents of the pope. Only four of the old bishops took the oath; and two thirds of the parish priests, including the most sincere and conscientious among them, were driven into opposition to the Revolution. The greatest error of the Assembly was in arraying religion against patriotism.

The peasants become landowners

On the other hand, vast good followed from the sale of the church lands. At first, sales were slow; and so, with these lands as security, the Assembly issued paper money (assignats), which was received again by the government in payment for the lands. This currency was issued in such vast amounts that it depreciated rapidly — as with our "Continental" currency a few years before. Serious hardships followed; but in the final outcome, the lands passed in small parcels into the hands of the peasantry and the middle class, and so laid the foundation for future prosperity. France became a land of small farmers, and the peasantry rose to a higher standard of comfort than such a class in Europe had ever known.

CHAPTER XIV

THE APPROACH OF WAR

SEPTEMBER, 1791, TO APRIL, 1792

The Legislative Assembly

France had been made over in two years, on the whole with little violence. The bulk of the nation accepted the result enthusiastically, except as to some portions of the new organization of the church. Most men believed that the Revolution was over. The moderate Liberals very largely withdrew from active politics, and did not even vote in the election of the new Legislative Assembly.

On the other hand, a small but vigorous minority of radical spirits was dissatisfied with the restrictions on the franchise and with the restoration of monarchy. This minority possessed undue weight, because of its organization in political clubs. The original Jacobin club had set up daughter societies in the chief towns all over France; and these daughters were strictly obedient to the suggestions of the mother-club in Paris. No other party had any political machinery whatever. Moreover, the Jacobins had the sympathy of the large class that had no votes; and in many cases these "passive" citizens proved an important factor in the election, terrorizing the more conservative elements by mob-violence.

The Constituent Assembly had made its members ineligible to seats in the Legislative Assembly, where their political experience would have been of the utmost value. The regulation was well meant — to prove unselfishness — but it was extremely unfortunate. The seven hundred and forty-five members of the Legislative Assembly were all without experience in politics. They were mostly young provincial lawyers and journalists; and there was not among them all one great proprietor or practical administrator.

Democratic gains

Parties had shifted toward democracy. There was no party in the new Assembly corresponding to the old Right and Right-Center of the Constituent Assembly. The new *Right* corresponded to the old *Left-Center*. Its members were known as *Constitutionalists,* because they wished to preserve the constitution as it was. *Outside* the House this party was represented by Lafayette, who, since the death of Mirabeau, was the most influential man in France. In the Assembly the party counted about one hundred regular adherents, but, for a time, the four hundred members of *the Center,* or "The Plain," voted with it on most questions. The Plain, however, was gradually won over to the more radical views of the Left.

Girondists and Jacobins

This *Left* consisted of about two hundred and forty delegates, many of them connected with the Jacobin clubs. The greater part were to become known as *Girondists,* from the Gironde, the name of a "Department" (p. 280) from which the leaders came. They wished a republic, but they were unwilling to use force to get one. They feared and hated the Paris mob, and they wished to intrust power to the provinces rather than to the capital. The leaders were hot-headed, eloquent young men, who spoke fine sentiments, but who were not fit for decisive action in a crisis.

The members of the Extreme-Left, known from their elevated seats as the Mountain, were the quintessence of Jacobinism. This party wished a democratic government by whatever means might offer, and it contained the men of action in the Assembly.

Foreign perils

The new inexperienced Assembly, with its tremendous problems at home to solve, was at once threatened also by foreign perils. The emigrant nobles, breathing threats of invasion and vengeance, were gathering in arms on the Rhine, under protection of German princes. They were drilling mercenary troops, and they had secret sympathizers within France. In the winter a treacherous plot to betray to them the great fortress of Strassburg all but succeeded. The danger was real. The Assembly sternly and properly condemned to death all Emigrants who should not return to France before a certain date; *but the king vetoed the decree.*

And back of the Emigrants loomed the danger of foreign intervention. The attempted flight of Louis in June had shown Europe that he was really a prisoner. His brother-in-law, the Emperor Leopold, then sent to the sovereigns of Europe a circular note, calling for common action against the Revolution, inasmuch as the cause of Louis was "*the cause of kings*"; and a few days later, Leopold and the King of Prussia joined in asserting their intention to arm, in order to aid their "brother."

The Revolution and European kings

War was almost inevitable. The Revolution stood for a new social order. It and the old order could not live together. Its success was a standing invitation to revolution in neighboring lands. If the cause of Louis was "the cause of kings," so was the cause of the Revolution "the cause of peoples." The kings felt that they must crush it before it spread.

The Assembly accepts war

The Legislative Assembly welcomed the prospect of war. It demanded of Leopold that he disperse the armies of the Emigrants and that he apologize for his statements. Leopold replied with a counter-demand for a change in the French government such as to secure Europe against the spread of revolution. Then in April, 1792, France declared war.

The insolent attempts of German princes to dictate the policy of the French people rightly aroused a tempest of scorn and wrath; but the light-heartedness with which the Legislative Assembly rushed into a war for which France was so ill prepared is at first a matter of wonder. The explanation, however, is not hard to find.

The Constitutionalists expected war to strengthen the executive (as it would have done if Louis had gone honestly with the nation), and they hoped also that it would increase their own power, since Lafayette was in command of the army.

On the other hand, the Girondists suspected Louis of being in secret league with Austria (suspicions only too well founded), and they knew that France was filled with spies and plotters in the interests of the Emigrants. The nervous strain of such a situation was tremendous, and the majority of the Assembly preferred open war to this terror of secret treason. Moreover, the Girondists hoped vaguely that the disorders of war might offer some good excuse to set up a republic.

Opposition by "the Mountain"

The only voices raised against the war were from the Mountain and its sympathizers in the Jacobin club. Constitutionalists and Girondists were to find their ruin in the war they recklessly invited; while the three men most active in opposing war — *Robespierre, Danton,* and *Marat* — were to be called by it to virtual dictatorship.

Marat

Marat was a physician of high scientific attainments. He was jealous and suspicious, and he seems to have become half-crazed under the strain of the Revolution. Early in the days of the Constituent Assembly, his paper, "The Friend of the People," began to preach the assassination of all aristocrats. But Marat was moved by sincere pity for the oppressed; and he opposed war, because, as he said, its suffering always fell finally upon the poor.

Robespierre

Robespierre before the Revolution had been a precise young lawyer in a provincial town. He had risen to a judgeship, — the highest position he could ever expect to attain; but he had resigned his office *because he had conscientious scruples against imposing a death penalty* upon a criminal. He was an enthusiastic disciple of Rousseau. He was narrow, dull, envious, pedantic; but logical, incorruptible, sincere. "That man is dangerous," Mirabeau had said of him; "he will go far; *he believes every word he says.*" In the last months of the Constituent Assembly, Robespierre had advanced rapidly in popularity and power; and now, although without a seat in the Assembly, he was the most influential member of the Jacobin Club. He opposed the war, because he feared — what the Constitutionalists hoped — a strengthening of the executive.

Danton

Danton was a Parisian lawyer. He had early become prominent in the radical clubs; and next to Mirabeau he was the strongest man of the early years of the Revolution. He was well named "the Mirabeau of the Market Place." He was a large, forceful, shaggy nature, and a born leader of men. Above all, he was a man of action. Not without a rude eloquence himself, he had no patience with the fine speechifying of the Girondists, when deeds, not words, were wanted. He opposed the war, because he saw how unprepared France was, and how unfit her leaders. When it came, he brushed aside these incompetent leaders and himself organized France.

FOR FURTHER READING. — The best one-volume history of the Revolution is that by Shailer Mathews. Next comes Mrs. Gardiner's, somewhat more conservative and decidedly less interesting. There are excellent brief treatments in H. Morse Stephens' *Revolutionary Europe, 1789-1815*, and in Rose's *Revolutionary and Napoleonic Era*. The best of the larger works in English is H. Morse Stephens' *History of the French Revolution*. Carlyle's *French Revolution* remains the most powerful and vivid presentation of the forces and of many of the episodes of the Revolution, but it can be used to best advantage after some preliminary study upon the age, and it is sometimes inaccurate. Among the biographies, the following are especially good: Belloc's *Danton*, Belloc's *Robespierre*, Willert's *Mirabeau*, Blind's *Madam Roland*, and Morley's "Robespierre" (in *Miscellanies*, I). For fiction, Dickens' *Tale of Two Cities* and Victor Hugo's *Ninety-Three* are notable. (The last half dozen titles pertain especially to the period treated in the next chapter.) Anderson's *Constitutions and Documents* and the *Pennsylvania Reprints*, I, No. 5, contain illustrative source material.

CHAPTER XV

THE REVOLUTION IN WAR

FALL OF THE MONARCHY: APRIL TO SEPTEMBER, 1792

The king's vetoes

At the declaration of war, the French levies at once invaded Belgium (then an Austrian province p. 233), but were rolled back in defeat. The German powers, however, were busy robbing Poland (p. 249), and a few weeks more for preparation were given France before the storm broke. During these weeks, the Assembly decreed the banishment of all non-juring priests (those who refused to take the oath to the constitution), many of whom were spies; and it provided for a camp of twenty thousand chosen patriots to guard the capital. *Louis vetoed both Acts,* and immediately afterward he dismissed his Liberal ministers (June 13, 1792).

> Despite the veto, a small camp was formed, under the pretense of celebrating the festival of the destruction of the Bastille. Among the forces so collected were six hundred Marseillaise, sent in response to the call of the deputy of Marseilles for "six hundred men who know how to die." These men entered Paris, singing a new battle hymn, which was afterward chanted on many a Revolutionary battle field and which was to become famous as *The Marseillaise.*

And the riot of June 20

The populace was convinced, and rightly, that the king was using his power treasonably, to prevent effective opposition to the enemies of France; and *on June 20* there occurred an armed rising like those of July and October, 1789. An immense throng presented to the Assembly a monster petition against the king's policy, and then broke into the Tuileries, the palace of the royal family, to compel the king to withdraw his vetoes. For hours a dense mob surged through the apartments. Louis was crowded into a window, and stood there patiently, not without courageous dignity. *A red*[1] *cap*, sign of the Revolution, was handed him, and he put it upon his head; but to all demands for a recall of his vetoes he made firm refusal. By nightfall the building was cleared. Little harm had been done, except to furniture; and indeed the mob had shown throughout a surprising good nature.

Lafayette and the court

There followed an outburst of loyalty from the Moderates. Lafayette, in command on the frontier, left his troops and hastened to Paris, to demand the punishment of the leaders of the mob and the closing of the Jacobin Club. The middle class was ready to rally about him; and, if the king had been willing to join himself to the Constitutionalists, Lafayette might have saved the government. But the royal family secretly preferred to trust to the advancing Austrians; and Lafayette was rebuffed and scorned. He returned to his army, and the management of affairs at Paris passed rapidly to the Jacobins.

France girdled with foes

France was girdled with foes. The Empire, Prussia, and Savoy[2] were in arms. Naples and Spain were soon to join. Sweden and Russia both offered to do so, if they were needed. In July a Prussian army, commanded by old officers of Frederick the Great, crossed the frontier; and two Austrian armies, one from the Netherlands and one from the upper Rhine, converged upon the same line of invasion. The French levies were outnumbered three to one.

Worse still, the army was utterly demoralized by the resignation of many officers *in the face of the enemy*, and by a justifiable suspicion that many of those remaining sympathized with the invaders. Within France, too, were royalist risings and plots for risings, and the king was in secret alliance with the enemy.

[1] This color had already supplanted the tricolor as the emblem of the working-class revolution.

[2] This state of North Italy included the island of Sardinia, and is often referred to by that name.

The queen — whom the Paris mob now began to hate, as "the Austrian Woman" — had even communicated the French plan of campaign to the Austrian invaders.

Brunswick's Proclamation: July 25

Brunswick, the Prussian commander, counted upon a holiday march to Paris. July 25 he issued to the French people a famous proclamation declaring (1) that the allies entered France to restore Louis to his place, (2) *that all men taken with arms in their hands should be hanged*, and (3) that, if Louis were injured, he would "inflict a memorable vengeance" by delivering up Paris to military execution.[1]

This insolent bluster, with its threat of Prussian "frightfulness," was fatal to the king. France rose in rage, to hurl back the boastful invader. But before the new troops marched to the front, *they insisted upon guarding against enemies in the rear*. The Jacobins had decided that Louis should not be left free to paralyze action again, at some critical moment, by his veto. They demanded his deposition. The Girondists were not ready for such extreme action; but the Jacobins carried their point by insurrection.

August 10: Louis deposed

Led by Danton, they forcibly displaced the middle-class municipal council of Paris with a new government; and this "Commune of Paris" prepared an attack upon the Tuileries for *August 10*. If Louis had possessed ability or decision, his Guards might have repulsed the mob; but, after confusing them with contradictory orders, the king and his family fled to the Assembly, leaving the faithful Swiss regiment to be massacred. Bloody from this slaughter, the rebels forced their way into the hall of the Assembly to demand the king's instant deposition. Two thirds of the deputies had fled, and the "rump" of Girondists and Jacobins decreed the deposition and imprisonment of Louis, and the immediate election, by *manhood suffrage*, of a Convention to frame a new government. Lafayette tried to lead his troops against Paris to restore the king. He found his army unwilling to follow him, — ready, instead, to arrest him, — and so he fled to the Austrians — by

[1] Anderson, No. 23, gives the Proclamation.

whom he was cast into prison, to remain there until freed by Napoleon's victories. The French nation at large had not desired the new revolution, but accepted it as inevitable. The nation was more concerned with repulsing foreign foes than with balancing nice questions as to praise or blame in Paris.

Surrender of Verdun

The rising of August 10 had been caused by the fear of foreign invasion and of treason at home. The same causes three weeks later led to one of the most terrible events in history. The "Commune of Paris," under Danton's leadership, had packed the prisons with three thousand "suspected" aristocrats, to prevent a royalist rising. Then, on August 29 and September 2, came the news of the shameful surrender of Longwy and Verdun, — two great frontier fortresses guarding the road to Paris.

And the September Massacres

Paris was thrown into a panic of fear, and the Paris volunteers hesitated to go to the front, lest the numerous prisoners recently arrested should break out and avenge themselves upon the city, stripped of its defenders. So, while Danton was pressing enlistments and hurrying recruits to meet Brunswick, the frenzied mob attacked the prisons, organized rude lynch courts, and on September 2, 3, and 4 massacred over a thousand of the prisoners with only the shadow of a trial.[1] These events are known as *the "September massacres."*

Whether the Jacobin leaders had a secret hand in *starting* the atrocious executions at the prisons will probably never be known. Certainly they did not try to stop them; but neither did the Assembly, nor the Gironde leaders, nor any other body of persons in Paris. Says Carlyle: "Very desirable indeed that Paris had interfered, yet not unnatural that it stood looking on in stupor. Paris is in death-panic . . . gibbets at its door. Whosoever in Paris hath heart to front death finds it more pressing to do so fighting the Prussians than fighting the slayers of aristocrats."

The Jacobins, however, did openly *accept* the massacres, when committed, as a useful means of terrifying the royalist

[1] The fairest account in English of these massacres is that by Stephens. II, 141–150.

Excused by the Jacobins

plotters. When the Assembly talked of punishment, Danton excused the deed, and urged action against the enemies of France instead. "It was necessary to make our enemies afraid," he cried. ". . . Blast my memory, but let France be free." The "frightfulness" which the Prussians *meant* to use against all Frenchmen fighting for freedom, the French Jacobins *did use* to crush treason at home.

France "at war with kings"

Freed from internal peril, France turned upon her foes splendidly. Danton became the leading member of the executive committee of the Assembly, and at once he infused new vigor into the government. "We must dare," his great voice rang out to the hesitating Assembly, "and dare again, and ever dare, — and France is saved!" In this spirit he toiled, night and day, to raise and arm and drill recruits. France responded with the finest outburst of patriotic enthusiasm the world had ever seen in a great civilized state. September 20 the advancing Prussians were checked at *Valmy;* and November 9 the victory of *Jemmapes,* the first real pitched battle of the war, opened the Austrian Netherlands to French conquest. Another French army had already entered Germany, and a third had occupied Nice and Savoy.

These successes of raw French volunteers over the veterans of Europe called forth an orgy of democratic enthusiasm. The new National Convention met September 21 (1792), and became at once, in Danton's phrase, "a general committee of insurrection for all nations." It ordered a manifesto *in all languages,* offering the alliance of the French nation to all peoples who wished to recover their liberties; and French generals, entering a foreign country, were ordered "*to abolish serfdom, nobility, and all monopolies and privileges, and to aid in setting up a new government upon principles of popular sovereignty.*"[1] One fiery orator flamed out, — "Despots march against us with fire and sword. We will bear against them Liberty!"

Starving and ragged, but *welcomed by the invaded peoples,* the

[1] The decrees are given by Anderson, No. 28.

The Revolutionary propaganda

French armies sowed over Europe the seed of civil and political liberty. *The Revolution was no longer merely French.* It took on the intense zeal of a proselyting religion, and its principles were spread by fire and sword.

The First French Republic

When the new Convention met, the Constitutionalist party had disappeared.[1] *The Girondist leaders* (the Left of the preceding assembly) now *sat upon the Right* and seemed to have the support of the whole Convention, *except for a small party of the Mountain,* where sat Robespierre, Danton, and Marat, with the rest of the deputies of Paris and the organizers of the Revolution of August 10.

On its first afternoon the Convention declared monarchy abolished, and enthusiastically established "The French Republic, One and Indivisible." [2]

Execution of the king

The radicals were bent also upon punishing Louis. They were satisfied of his treason, and they wished to make reconciliation with the old order of things impossible. Said Danton: "The allied kings march against us. Let us hurl at their feet, as the gage of battle, the head of a king." The Girondists wished to save Louis' life, but their majority was intimidated by the galleries; and "Louis Capet" was condemned to death for "treason to the nation," and duly executed. This was the bloody answer of the Republicans to the silly Divine-Right doctrine of the European sovereigns that peoples were the property of their kings.

Constitution of the Year I

Early in 1793 the Convention proposed a new written constitution for the Republic. This document was extremely democratic. It swept away all the checks of indirect elections and property qualifications, and made all citizens "equally

[1] Note the progress of the Revolution: the old Royalists who made the Right of the First Assembly had no place in the Second; while the Constitutionalists, who had made the Left in the First Assembly, and the Right in the Second, had vanished from the Third.

[2] The student should keep distinct the three great assemblies: First, the *Constituent Assembly* (or the National Assembly) which made the first constitution; Second, the *Legislative Assembly*, which declared war and called for the election of its successor by manhood suffrage; and, Third, the *Convention*, which deposed Louis, declared a Republic, and made war on kings.

sovereign." Further, it made all acts of the legislature subject to a "referendum." This *Constitution of the Year I* [1] was itself submitted to such a referendum, and *was adopted by the nation.*

No country had ever had so democratic a constitution. *Nor had any great nation ever before adopted its government by direct vote.* Four years earlier, the much less democratic constitution of the United States was ratified *indirectly,* — by State conventions; and only two of the State constitutions had been submitted to the people.

The constitution, however, never went into operation. The Convention suspended it, declaring that France was in danger, and that the government must be left free from constitutional checks until war was over. This was one of the first demonstrations in history of the fundamental truth that war is a despot's game, and that democracies can play it successfully only by ceasing, for the time, at least, to be democracies.

Treason and dissension

France was indeed in danger. The execution of the king was one factor in deciding England, Spain, Holland, Naples, and Portugal to join the war against France, and it offended many French patriots. Dumouriez, an able but unscrupulous general, who had succeeded Lafayette as the chief military leader, tried to play traitor, in the spring of 1793, by surrendering Belgian fortresses to the Austrians and by leading his army to Paris to restore the monarchy. *His troops refused to follow him,* and he fled to the enemy; but Belgium was lost for a time, and once more the frontier was open to attack.

[1] The Convention adopted a new Calendar. September 22, the first day of the Republic, was made "*the first day of the Year One* of a new era." There followed twelve months of thirty days each, and then five great holidays dedicated to liberty. Each month was divided into three *decades*, and each tenth day was a holiday (in place of the Seventh day of rest and worship). The months took their names from the seasons, — Vintage month, Fog month, Frost month, for autumn; Snow, Rain, Wind months, for winter; Budding, Flower, and Meadow months, for spring and early summer; and Harvest, Heat, and Fruit months, to close the year. Holidays were no longer dedicated to saints, but to the plow, the cow, the grape, and so on. This is an interesting illustration of the way in which the Convention cut loose from the past.

Ever since the Convention met, dissension had threatened between the Gironde majority and the Mountain. The Mountain was supported by the masses of Paris. Outside the capital, the Girondists were much the stronger. They wished to remove the Convention from Paris; and the Mountain *accused* them of desiring to break up the "Indivisible Republic" into a federation of provinces.

The Girondists give way to the Jacobins

The Girondists took the moment of foreign danger, in the spring of 1793, to press the quarrel to a head. They accused Marat of stirring up the September massacres, and persuaded the Convention to bring him to trial. Then they were mad enough to charge Danton with *royalist* conspiracy.

Danton, who was straining his mighty strength to send reinforcements to the armies of France, pleaded at first for peace and union; but, when this proved vain, he turned savagely upon his assailants. "You were right," he cried to his friends on the Mountain, who had pressed before for action against the Girondists, "and I was wrong. There is no peace possible with these men. Let it be war, then. They will not save the Republic with us. It shall be saved without them, saved in spite of them."

While the Girondists debated, the Mountain acted. It was weak in the Convention, but it was supreme in the galleries and in the streets and above all in the Commune of Paris. The Commune, which had carried the Revolution of August 10 against the Legislative Assembly, now marched its forces against the Convention, June 2, 1793, and held it prisoner until it passed a decree imprisoning thirty of the leading Girondists. Others of that party fled, and *the Jacobin Mountain was left in power*.

The fate of the Girondists has aroused much sympathy; but the Jacobin victory was the only means to save the Revolution with its priceless gain for humanity. Says John Morley (*Essay on Robespierre*), "The deliverance of a people beset by strong and implacable foes could not wait on mere good manners and fastidious sentiments, when those comely things were in company with the most stupendous want of foresight ever shown by a political party."

JUNE, 1793, TO MARCH, 1794; JACOBIN RULE

Gironde rebellion and foreign invasion

Fugitive Girondists aroused the provinces against the Jacobin capital. They gathered armies at Marseilles, Bordeaux, Caën, and Lyons. Lyons, the second city in France, even raised the white flag of the monarchy, and invited in the Austrians, — whereupon the Girondists in the city threw down their arms, gallantly choosing death rather than alliance with the enemies of France. Elsewhere, too, royalist revolt reared its head. In the remote province of Vendée (in ancient Brittany), the simple, half-savage peasants were still slavishly devoted to king, priest, and hereditary lord, and they rose now in wild rebellion against the Republic. The great port of Toulon even admitted an English fleet and army. The Convention, with Paris and a score of the central Departments, faced the other three fourths of France as well as the rest of Europe.

And the Committee of Public Safety

So far, the Revolutionists had been afraid of a real executive, as a danger to freedom; but these new perils forced the Convention to intrust power to a great "Committee of Public Safety." Said one member, the Convention "established the despotism of liberty, in order to crush the despotism of tyrants." The Committee consisted of twelve members, — all from the Mountain. The Convention made all other national committees and officers the servants of this great Committee, and ordered even the municipal officials to give it implicit obedience.

The Committee were not trained administrators, but they were men of practical business sagacity and of tremendous energy, — such men as a revolution must finally toss to the top. In the war office, *Carnot* "organized victory"; beside him, in the treasury, labored *Cambon* with his stern motto, "War to the manorhouse, peace to the hut"; while a group of such men as *Robespierre* and *St. Just* sought to direct the

Revolution so as to refashion France according to new ideals of democracy and of welfare for the common man.[1]

Nearly a hundred "Deputies on Mission"[2] were sent out to all parts of France to enforce obedience to the Committee. They reported every ten days to the Committee; but, subject to its approval, they exercised despotic power, — replacing civil authorities at will, seizing money or supplies for the national use, imprisoning and condemning to death by their own courts. Moreover, to secure energy in the management of the war, and to prevent further treachery like that of Lafayette and Dumouriez, two Deputies on Mission accompanied each of the fourteen armies of the Republic, with authority to arrest a general at the head of his troops.

Order, union, and victory

Never has a despotism been more efficient than that of the great Committee and its agents. In October Lyons was captured. On the proposal of the Committee the Convention ordered that the rebel city should be *razed to the ground*. Toulon was taken, despite English aid, and punished sternly. Other centers of revolt, paralyzed with fear, yielded. Order and union were restored, and Carnot could send another million of men to join the armies of France. Before the year closed, French soil was free from danger of invasion, and French armies had taken the offensive on all the frontiers. Peril from without was past.

"All France and whatsoever it contains of men and resources is put under requisition," said the Committee, in a stirring proclamation to the nation (August 23, 1793).[3] "The Republic is one vast besieged city. . . . The young men shall go to battle; it is their task to conquer; the married men shall forge arms, transport baggage and artillery, provide subsistence; the women shall work at soldiers clothes, make tents, serve in the hospitals; children shall scrape old linen into surgeon's lint; the old men shall have themselves carried into public places,

[1] Stephens' *French Revolution*, II, 285 (and also his *Revolutionary Europe*, 133) has an admirable account of the men of the Committee. A dramatic account of their meetings is given by John Morley in his *Robespierre*.

[2] They were "deputies" in the Convention, sent out by the great Committee on special "missions."

[3] The decree is given in full by Anderson.

and there, by their words, excite the courage of the young and preach hatred to kings and unity for the Republic."

"In this humor, then, since no other will serve," adds Carlyle, "will France rush against its enemies; headlong, reckoning no cost, heeding no law but the supreme law, Salvation of the People. The weapons are all the iron there is in France; the strength is that of all the men and women there are in France. . . . From all hamlets towards their departmental town, from all departmental towns toward the appointed camp, the Sons of Freedom shall march. Their banner is to bear 'The French People risen against Tyrants.' . . .

"These soldiers have shoes of wood and pasteboard, or go booted in hay-ropes, in dead of winter. . . . What then? 'With steel and bread,' says the Convention Representative, 'one may get to China.' The generals go fast to the guillotine, justly or unjustly. . . . Ill-success is death; in victory alone is life. . . . All Girondism, Halfness, Compromise, is swept away. . . . Forward, ye soldiers of the Republic, captain and man! Dash with your Gallic impetuosity on Austria, England, Prussia, Spain, Sardinia, Pitt, Coburg, York, and the Devil and the World!

"See accordingly on all frontiers, how the 'Sons of Night' astonished, after short triumph, do recoil; the Sons of the Republic flying after them, with temper of cat-o-mountain or demon incarnate, which no Son of Night can withstand. . . . Spain which came bursting through the Pyrenees, rustling with Bourbon banners, and went conquering here and there for a season, falters at such welcome, draws itself in again, — too happy now were the Pyrenees impassable. Dugomier invades Spain by the eastern Pyrenees. General Mueller shall invade it by the western. '*Shall*,' that is the word. Committee of Public Safety has said it; Representative Cavaignac, on mission there, must see it done. 'Impossible,' cries Mueller; 'Infallible,' answers Cavaignac. 'The Committee is deaf on that side of its head,' answers Cavaignac. 'How many want'st thou of men, of horses, of cannon? Thou shalt have them. Conquerors, conquered, or hanged, Forward we must.' *Which things also, even as the Representative spake them, were done.*"

The "Long Terror"

The Committee had not hesitated to use the most terrible means to secure union and obedience. Early in September of 1793 it adopted "Terror" as a deliberate policy. This "Long Terror" was a very different thing from the "Short Terror" of the mob, a year before. The Paris prisons were crowded again with "Suspects"; and *each day* the Revolutionary tribunal, after farcical trials, sent batches of them to the guillotine.

Among the victims were the queen, many aristocrats, and also many Constitutionalists and Girondists — heroes of 1791 and 1792. In some of the revolted districts, too, submission was followed by horrible executions; and at Nantes the cruelty of *Carrier*, the Deputy on Mission, half-crazed with blood, inflicted upon the Revolution an indelible stain.

Over much of France, however, the Terror was only a name. The rule of most of the great Deputies on Mission was bloodless and was ardently supported by the popular will. In all, some fifteen thousand executions took place during the year of the Terror, — nearly three thousand of them in Paris.

This terrible policy proved effectual. After two months of the Terror, Paris was tranquil and resumed its usual life. There were no more riots and almost no crime, even of the ordinary kind. France was again a mighty nation, united and orderly at home and victorious abroad. Says Carlyle, —

"Overhead of all of this, there is the customary brewing and baking. Labor hammers and grinds. Frilled promenaders saunter under the trees, white-muslin promenadresses, with green parasols, leaning on your arm. . . . In this Paris, are twenty-three theaters nightly [and] sixty places of dancing."

The Terror was a sure weapon, ready to hand in a moment of death peril to liberty. The Convention did not shrink from using it. That much may be said in explanation. Still the "Reign of Terror" remains a terrible blot on human history.

At the same time it does not stand all by itself. John Morley, a cultivated English scholar, calls it "*almost* as horrible" as the scenes the English enacted six years later in Ireland (p. 462) without such mighty reason. And it was far less terrible than the *needless* vengeance inflicted by the conservative middle-class government of Paris in 1871 upon twenty thousand victims from the working class (p. 489), — over which the world shudders very little.

A study of the Revolution must notice this bloodshed, but ought not to put much emphasis on it. It is not in any way the significant thing about the Revolution. Indeed, it was not

Violence only an incident due to foreign peril

the product of the Revolution itself, but of foreign war. The significant thing about the Revolution is the national awakening which swept away an absurd, tyrannical society, founded on ancient violence and warped by time, to replace it with a simpler society based on equal rights. Literature has been filled with hysterics about the violence. It is well for us to shudder — but there is no danger that we shall not, for those who suffered were *the few* who "knew how to shriek," and so arouse sympathy for their woe. The danger is that we forget the relief to the *dumb multitudes* who had endured worse tortures for centuries, but whose inarticulate moanings hardly attract attention in history. As Carlyle justly says, not for a thousand years had any equal period in France seen so little suffering as just those months of revolution and "terror."

Positive Reform

If the Convention destroyed much, it built up vastly more. It made the Revolution a great and fruitful reform. The grim, silent, tense-browed men of the Committee worked eighteen hours out of every twenty-four. Daily, they carried their lives in their hands; and so they worked swiftly, disregarding some niceties of detail, and cutting knots that did not easily loosen. While Carnot, "Organizer of Victory," was creating the splendid army that saved liberty from despots, his associates were laying the foundations for a new and better society. They were "organizing" civilization.

Mainly on their proposals, the Convention made satisfactory provision for the public debt that had crushed the old monarchy. It adopted *the beginning* of a simple and just code of laws. It abolished imprisonment for debt and gave property rights to women, forty years ahead of England or America. It accepted the metric system of weights and measures, abolished slavery in French colonies, instituted the first Normal School, the Polytechnic School of France, the Conservatory of France, the famous Institute of France, and the National Library, and *planned* also a comprehensive system of public instruction, the improvement of the hospitals and of the prisons, and the reform of youthful criminals. Said Danton, "Next to bread, education is the first need of the people." As Shailer Mathews says, "No government ever worked harder for the good of *the masses*"; and says H. Morse Stephens:

"It is probable that as the centuries pass, the political strife . . . may be forgotten, while the projects of Cambacérès and Merlin toward codification, the plans of Condorcet and Lakanal for a system of national education, and Argobast's report on the new weights and measures, will be regarded as making great and important steps in the progress of the race. . . . The Convention laid the foundations upon which Napoleon afterward built. In educational as in legal reform, the most important work was done during the Reign of Terror."

For Further Reading. — One of the histories named at the close of the last chapter ought to be used for library work as far as the close of this chapter. Carlyle also should surely be read.

Exercise. — Instructive parallels and contrasts between the course of the French Revolution, as to violence and class divisions, with the course of the Russian Revolution of 1917–1918.

RUIN OF THE JACOBINS, MARCH, 1794, TO MARCH, 1795

The Jacobins break up into factions

The Jacobins had established their supremacy over all other parties by the "Terror"; but after some months they themselves broke up into factions. The Committee of Public Safety continued to uphold the inner circle of its members (led by Robespierre) who had charge of carrying on the Terror; but, outside the Committee, that policy was attacked violently from both sides.

1. The Paris Commune, led now by the coarse *Hébert,* clamored for *more* blood. This group wished to level rich and poor by wholesale confiscation, and to execute all who might be feared as opponents of such measures. In Paris they carried another part of their program to success for a time. They closed all Christian worship, and substituted for the worship of God a "worship of Reason," with ribald blasphemy.

This atheism aroused Robespierre to denounce the Hébertists in the Convention as dangerous to the Revolution. Twice the Commune had reversed the control of a National Assembly by insurrection. Now it tried a third time, but failed; and Robespierre sent Hébert and his leading friends to the guillotine (March, 1794).

2. On the other hand, Danton was weary of bloodshed. He was the only man in France whose popularity and influence rivaled that of Robespierre. For months he had been urging in the Convention that "Terror" was no longer needed, now that France was victorious without and tranquil within. And Danton's friend, Camille Desmoulins (p. 272), started a witty newspaper to criticize the policy of the great Committee, suggesting in its place a "Committee of Mercy," to bind up the wounds of France. In April Robespierre accused both men of "conspiracy," and sent them to the guillotine.[1]

Danton's danger had been plain, and his friends had urged him to strike first. "Better to be guillotined than to do more guillotining," he answered. As he mounted the scaffold, he faltered a moment at the thought of his wife, whom he loved tenderly. But rallying, he said grimly to the executioner, — "Show my head to the people. It is worth while. They do not see the like every day."

The rule of Robespierre

Robespierre, for the next three months, seemed sole master[2] of France. He reopened the churches, and offset Hébert's Festival of Reason by making the Convention solemnly celebrate a "Festival to the Supreme Being."[3] He aimed to create a new France, with simple and austere virtues, like those Rousseau pictured in his ideal "state of nature." This he believed could be done by education. He secured from the Convention a decree for a system of universal public educa-

[1] Just before the Revolution began, a humane Dr. Guillotin had invented a device (consisting of a heavy knife sliding down swiftly between two upright supports) to behead criminals. This "guillotine" was much more merciful and certain in its operation than the older custom of beheading by an axe in the hands of a man.

[2] Marat had been murdered by Charlotte Corday. The story may be presented as a special report.

[3] Robespierre was not a Christian; he was a deist, like Voltaire.

tion. The opening sentences of the decree read: "The rise of an oppressed nation to democracy is like the effort by which nature rose out of nothingness to existence. We must entirely refashion a people whom we wish to make free, — destroy its prejudices, alter its habits, limit its necessities, root up its vices, purify its desires. The state must therefore lay hold on every human being at his birth and direct his education with powerful hand." The most enthusiastic follower of Robespierre was St. Just; and the fragments of St. Just's *Institutes* express the ardent hopes of these Terrorists.

Boys of seven were to be handed over to the "school of the nation," to be trained "to endure hardship and to speak little." Neither servants nor gold or silver vessels were to be permitted. The nation was to possess "the happiness of virtue, of moderation, of comfort, — the happiness that springs from the enjoyment of the necessary without the superfluous. The luxury of a cabin and of a field fertilized by your own hands, a cart, a thatched roof, — such is happiness." St. Just declared that he would blow his brains out if he did not believe it *possible to remodel* the French people along such lines.

During his three-months' rule, Robespierre coupled the proclamation of these fine theories with a terrible increase in the policy of the "Terror" — to clear the field. The number of executions rose to two hundred a week. The Convention trembled for its own safety, and at last it turned savagely on Robespierre. On July 27, when he began to speak, he was interrupted by shouts of "Down with the tyrant!" Astounded, he stammered confusedly; and a delegate cried, — "See, the blood of Danton chokes him." Quickly he was tried and executed, with a hundred close adherents.

Fall of Robespierre

The "Terror" now came to an end, and some extreme laws were repealed. In December, 1794, encouraged by the reaction against the radicals, the fugitive members of the Right once more appeared in the Assembly; and in March, 1795, even the survivors of the expelled Girondists were admitted. The Jacobins roused the populace of Paris in a desperate attempt to undo the reaction; but the middle class had rallied, and the mob was dispersed by troops and by organized bands of "gilded youth." The populace was disarmed, the National Guards were reorganized, and there followed over France a "White Terror," wherein the conservative classes executed or assassinated many hundreds of the Jacobin party — whereof, since this was not a "Red" Terror, history makes little mention.

1795–1799: THE DIRECTORY

The Directory

A new "Constitution of the Year III" (1795) replaced the constitution of the Year I and confirmed middle-class rule in the Republic. The government established by this document is called "The Directory." This was the name of the *executive*, which consisted of *a committee of five*, chosen by the legislature. The legislature consisted of *two* Houses. Property qualifications for voting were restored.

Royalist rising swept away

The constitution was submitted to a popular vote; but, before the vote was taken, at the last moment, the expiring Convention decreed that two thirds of its members should hold over as members of the new Assembly.[1] This arrangement was submitted to the people, along with the constitution, and was practically made a condition to the latter. It was carried by a small majority, while the constitution was ratified by an overwhelming vote. In Paris the secret Royalists took advantage of the dissatisfaction among the people at this arrangement to stir up a revolt. They were joined by twenty thousand National Guards. The Directory was in terror. But it had four thousand regular troops, and it happened to hit upon a brilliant young officer to command them. That officer posted cannon about the approaches to the Convention hall, and mowed down the attacking columns with "a whiff of grapeshot" (October 5, 1795).

The Directory remained in power four years more; but the chief interest for this period centers in the rise of the officer who had saved it, and whose name was Napoleon Bonaparte.

[1] Cf. the story of the Rump Parliament, p. 204.

CHAPTER XVI

THE RISE OF NAPOLEON

Expansion before Bonaparte

In 1795, when the government of the Convention was merged in the Directory, France had already made great gains of territory. On the northeast, *Belgium had been annexed, with the vote of its people. Nice* and *Savoy*, on the southeast, had been added, in like manner. *The eastern frontier had been moved to the Rhine*, by the seizure of all the territory of the Empire on the west side of the river. *Holland* had been converted into a dependent ally, as the "Batavian Republic," with a constitution molded on that of France. Prussia, Spain, and most of the small states had withdrawn from the war. Only England, Austria, and Sardinia kept the field.

Bonaparte in Italy

The Directory then determined to attack Austria vigorously, both in Germany and in her Italian provinces (p. 233). Two splendid armies were sent into Germany; and a small, ill-supplied force in Italy was put under the command of Bonaparte. The wonderful genius of the young general (then twenty-seven years old) made the Italian campaign the decisive factor in the war. By rapid movements, he separated the Austrian and Sardinian forces, beat the latter in five battles in eleven days, and forced Sardinia to conclude peace. Turning upon the brave but deliberate Austrians, he won battle after battle, and by July he was master of Italy. Austria, however, clung stubbornly to her Italian provinces; and during the following year, four fresh armies, each larger than Napoleon's, were sent in succession from the Rhine to the Po, only to meet destruction. In October, 1797, Austria agreed to accept Venice from Bonaparte, in exchange for Lombardy and Belgium, which she had lost, and war on the continent closed with the "Peace of Campo Formio."

To the Italians, Bonaparte posed at first as a deliverer, and his large promises awoke the peninsula to the hope of a new national life. Something was accomplished. Oligarchic Genoa became "the Ligurian Republic," and the Po valley was made into "the Cisalpine Republic." Bonaparte swept away feudalism and serfdom and the forms of the old Austrian despotism, and introduced civil equality and some political liberty. At the same time, however, with amazing perfidy, he tricked the ancient state of Venice into war, seized it with a French army, and afterward coolly bartered it away to Austria.

BONAPARTE AT ARCOLA. The French troops were breaking at a critical point, when the young general forced his way to the front, caught a falling standard, and by his presence, restored the fortune of the day. — After the painting by Gros.

Upon even the states friendly to him, Bonaparte levied enormous contributions, to enrich his soldiers and officers, to fill the coffers of France, and to bribe the Directory. His proclamation upon taking command of the Army of Italy had been significant of much to come: "Soldiers, you are starving and in rags. The government owes you much, but can do nothing for you. I will lead you into the most fruitful plains of the world. Teeming provinces, flourishing cities, will be in your power. There you may reap honor and glory and wealth."

Works of art, too, and choice manuscripts Bonaparte ravished from Italian libraries and galleries, and sent to Paris, to gratify French vanity; and when the Italians rose against this spoliation, he stamped out the revolts with deliberate cruelty.

Character of Napoleon Bonaparte

The Italian campaigns first showed Napoleon Bonaparte to the world. He was born in Corsica in 1769. His parents were Italians, poor, but of noble descent. In the year of his birth, Corsica became a possession of France. The boy passed through a French military school, and when the Revolution began he was a junior lieutenant of artillery. The war gave him opportunity. He had distinguished himself at the capture of Toulon (p. 297); and, chancing to be in Paris at the time of the rising against the Directory, in 1795, he had been called upon to defend the government. In reward he was given, the next year, the command of the "Army of Italy."

Napoleon was one of the three or four supreme military geniuses of history. He was also one of the greatest of civil rulers. He had profound insight, a marvelous memory, and tireless energy. He was a "terrible worker," and his success was largely due to his wonderful grasp of masses of details, — so that he could recall the smallest features of geography where a campaign was to take place, or could name the man best suited for office in any one of a multitude of obscure towns. He was not insensible to generous feeling; but, like Frederick II of Prussia (p. 249), he was utterly unscrupulous and deliberately rejected all claims of morality. "Morality," said he, "has nothing to do with such a man as I am." Perfidy and cruelty, when they suited his ends, he used as calmly as appeals to honor and patriotism.

His generalship lay largely in unprecedented rapidity of movement, and in massing his troops against some one weak point of an enemy. "Our general," said his soldiers, "wins his victories with our legs." Moreover, the French army was superior to any army in Europe. Elsewhere military office came by birth or by purchase. In the Revolutionary armies of France, it came by merit and genius. All of Napoleon's great lieutenants had risen from the ranks. One of his most dashing generals (Jourdan) had been a tailor; another (Murat) a waiter. Napoleon always cherished this democratic character of the army. "Every soldier," said he, "carries a marshal's baton in his knapsack."

In early life Bonaparte may have been a sincere Republican; but he hated anarchy and disorder, and, before his campaign in Italy was over, he had begun to plan to make himself ruler of France. He worked systematically to transform the army's earlier ardor for liberty into a passion for military glory and plunder. He became the idol of the soldiery, and then used the military power to overthrow the civil authority.

> Before Campo Formio he had said to a friend, "Do you suppose I conquer for the lawyers of the Directory? . . . Do you think I mean to found a Republic? What an idea! . . . *The nation wants a head,* a chief illustrious for great exploits; it does not care for theories of government. . . . The French want glory. As for liberty, of that they have no conception. . . . I am everything to the army. Let the Directory try to take my command from me, and they will see who is master."

Bonaparte in Egypt

England alone continued the war against France; and the next year (1798) Bonaparte persuaded the Directory to let him attack Egypt, as a step toward attacking England's power in India. He won a series of brilliant battles in Egypt; but suddenly his fleet was annihilated by the English under *Nelson,* in the *Battle of the Nile,* and his gorgeous dreams of Oriental empire faded away.

Escape to France

Then Bonaparte deserted his doomed army, and escaped to France, where he saw new opportunities. War on the continent had been renewed. In 1798 the Directory had brought about a change in the government of Switzerland and had organized that country as "the Helvetic Republic." They had also driven the pope from Rome and dispossessed other Italian rulers, to make way for new republican states. The Great Powers of Europe were alarmed at these measures. England succeeded in drawing Russia and Austria into another coalition; and so far, in the new war, the campaigns had gone against France. Bonaparte's failure in distant Egypt was not comprehended, and the French people welcomed him as a savior.

Overthrow of the Directory: Bonaparte, First Consul

The Directory had proven disgracefully corrupt. Each of three years in succession — 1797, 1798, 1799 — the elections had gone against it; but it had kept itself in power by a series of *coups d'état*,[1] or arbitrary interferences with the result of the voting. Now Bonaparte used a *coup d'état* against it. His troops purged the legislature of members hostile to his plan; and a Rump, made up of Bonaparte's adherents, abolished the Directory and elected Bonaparte and two others as *Consuls*, intrusting to them the preparation of a new constitution. "Now," said the peasantry, "we shall have peace, thanks to God and to Bonaparte"; and by a vote of some three million to fifteen hundred, the French people accepted the constitution that virtually made Bonaparte dictator. France was not really ready for the freedom that Paris had won for her so unexpectedly by revolution. If Bonaparte had not seized power, some other military chief surely would soon have done so.

FOR FURTHER READING. — High school students will hardly get time to read upon the Directory period, apart from Napoleon's story. For that, see references on pages 325–326.

[1] Literally, a "stroke of state." This is the name given in France to infractions of the constitution by some part of the government through the use of force. Happily the thing itself has been so unknown to English history that the English language has to borrow the French name. The attempt of Charles I to seize the five members (p. 200) was something of the sort. The coming century was to see many a *coup d'état* in France; and like phenomena have been common in other European countries.

CHAPTER XVII

THE CONSULATE, 1799–1804

Peace of Amiens, 1802

Bonaparte's first work as consul was to crush foreign foes. In 1800 he won the great battle of *Marengo* over the Austrians in Italy, and General Moreau crushed another Austrian army in Bavaria at *Hohenlinden.* Austria and Russia then made peace with France; and two years later *the Peace of Amiens* (1802) closed the strife between France and England. For a brief period, the world was free from war. Napoleon appeared both a conqueror with dazzling victories and also the restorer of the long-desired peace.

Constitution of the Consulate

The Consulate was confirmed by the Constitution of the Year VIII (1800). The government was to *rest on manhood suffrage,* but that suffrage was to be "*refined by successive filtrations.*" The adult males, some five million in all, were to choose one tenth their number; the five hundred thousand "Communal Notables," so chosen, were in turn to choose one tenth *their* number; these fifty thousand "Departmental Notables" were to choose five thousand "National Notables."

But all this voting was only to settle *eligibility. The executive was to appoint* communal officers at will out of the Communal Notables, departmental officers out of the Departmental Notables, and members of the legislature and other chief officers out of the National Notables.

The legislature was to be broken up into four parts: a *Council of State* to prepare bills; a *Tribunate* to discuss them, without right to vote; a *Legislative Chamber* to vote upon them, without right to discuss; and a *Senate,* with power to veto.

Siéyès, who planned this constitution, had intended to break up the executive in like manner into one consul for war, an-

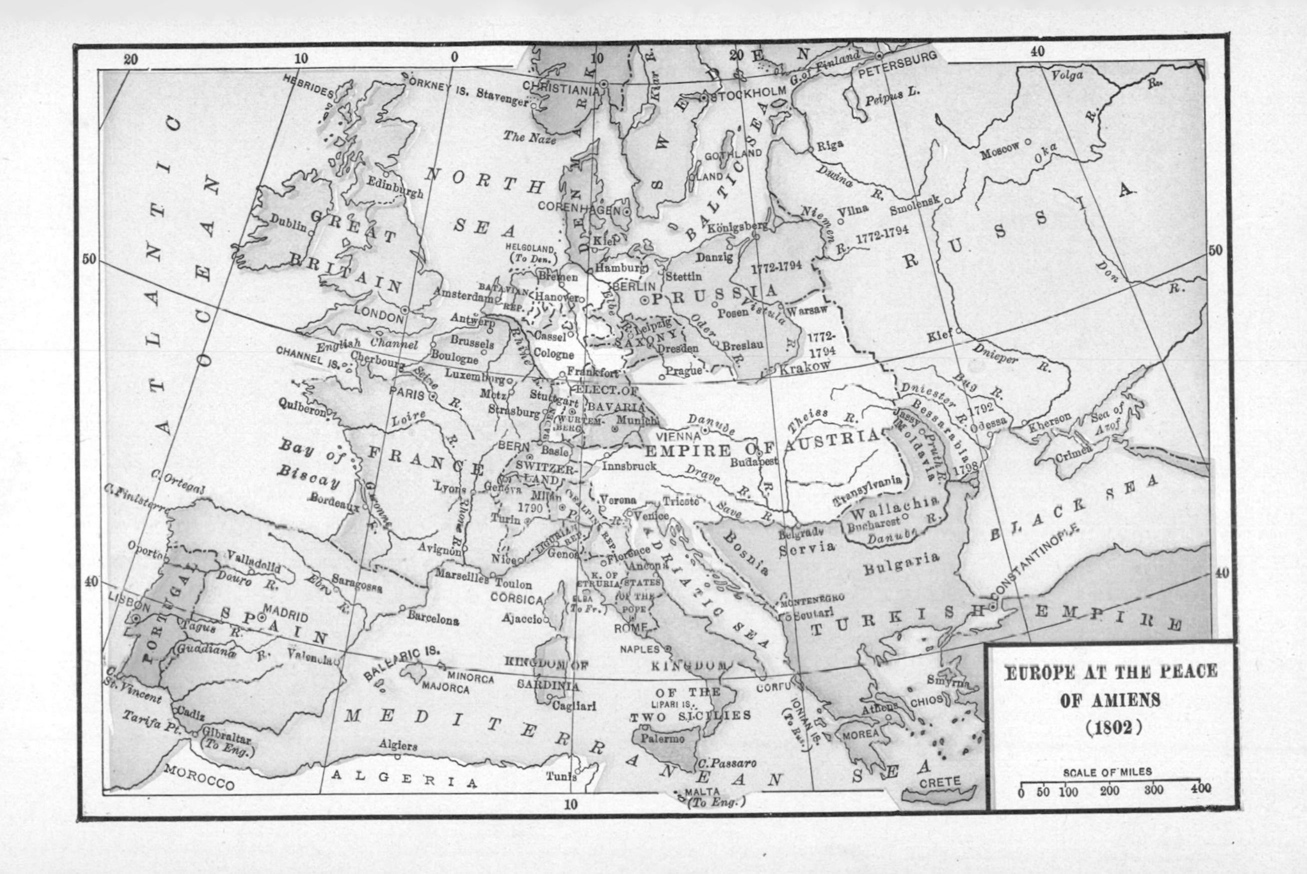
EUROPE AT THE PEACE
OF AMIENS
(1802)
SCALE OF MILES
0 50 100 200 300 400
ATLANTIC OCEAN
NORTH SEA
BALTIC SEA
MEDITERRANEAN SEA
BLACK SEA
ADRIATIC SEA
GREAT BRITAIN
FRANCE
SPAIN
PORTUGAL
PRUSSIA
RUSSIA
SWEDEN
DENMARK
EMPIRE OF AUSTRIA
TURKISH EMPIRE
KINGDOM OF SARDINIA
KINGDOM OF THE TWO SICILIES
SWITZERLAND
BAVARIA
SAXONY
ALGERIA
MOROCCO
LONDON
PARIS
MADRID
LISBON
BERLIN
VIENNA
ROME
NAPLES
STOCKHOLM
CHRISTIANIA
COPENHAGEN
PETERSBURG
CONSTANTINOPLE
Moscow
Bay of Biscay
English Channel
CHANNEL IS.
HEBRIDES
ORKNEY IS.
HELGOLAND (To Den.)
BATAVIAN REP.
CISALPINE REP.
LIGURIAN REP.
K. OF ETRURIA
STATES OF THE POPE
ELBA (To Fr.)
CORSICA
BALEARIC IS.
MINORCA
MAJORCA
MALTA (To Eng.)
Gibraltar (To Eng.)
IONIAN IS. (To Rus.)
CRETE
MOREA
CHIOS
1772-1794
1772-1794
1790
1792
1793

other for peace, and a "Grand Elector" who should appoint the consuls and other great officials, but should then have no part in the government. Here Napoleon intervened. He was willing to accept a system of elections that never elected anybody, and a legislature that could not legislate; but he changed the shadowy "Grand Elector" into a *First Consul*, with all other parts of the constitution subject to his will.

Bonaparte became First Consul. His colleagues, as he put it, were "merely counselors whom I am expected to consult, but whose advice I need not accept." Directly or indirectly, he himself filled all offices, and no law could even be proposed without his sanction.

Centralization intensified

Local administration was highly centralized, without even those checks upon the central power that had existed before the Revolution (p. 259). For each Department Napoleon appointed a Prefect, and for each subdistrict a Subprefect. Even the forty thousand mayors of towns and villages were appointed by the First Consul or by his agents, and held office at his will; "nor did there exist anywhere independent of him the authority to light or repair the streets of the meanest village in France."

This new administration was vigorous and fearless; and under Napoleon's energy and genius, it conferred upon France great and rapid benefits. But, in the long run, *the result was to be unspeakably disastrous*. The chance for Frenchmen to train themselves at their own gates in the duties and responsibilities of freemen, by sharing in the local government, was lost; and the willingness to depend upon an all-directing central power was fixed even more firmly than before in their minds. (Cf. p. 19.)

Restoration of order

Within France Bonaparte used his vast authority to restore order and heal strife. Royalist and Jacobin were welcomed to public employment and to favor; and a hundred and fifty thousand exiles, of the best blood and brain of France, returned, to reinforce the citizen body. An agreement with the pope ("the Concordat") reconciled the Catholic church to the state.

The last of the benevolent despots

All bishops were replaced by new ones *appointed* by Napoleon and consecrated by the pope. The church became Roman again, but it was supported and controlled by the state.

Reforms

The reform work of the great Convention of '93 had been dropped by the Directory. Some parts of it were now taken up again. Public education was organized; corruption and extravagance in the government gave way to order and efficiency; law was simplified and justice was made cheaper and easier to secure.

The "Code Napoleon"

This last work was the most enduring and beneficent of all. The Convention had begun to reform the outgrown absurdities of the confused mass of French laws. The First Consul now completed the task. A commission of great lawyers, working under his direction and inspiration, swiftly reduced the vast chaos of old laws to a marvelously compact, simple, symmetrical code.

This body of law included the new principles of equality born of the Revolution. It soon became the basis of law for practically all Europe, except England, Russia, and Turkey. From Spain it spread to all Spanish America, and it lies at the foundation of the law of the State of Louisiana. Napoleon himself declared, after his overthrow, "Waterloo will wipe out the memory of my forty victories; but that which nothing can wipe away is my Civil Code. That will live forever." [1]

Material prosperity

The material side of society was not neglected. The depreciated paper money (p. 281) was restored to a sound basis, and industry of all kinds was encouraged. Paris was made the most beautiful city of Europe, and it was given an excellent water supply. Parks and public gardens were provided, while, here and there, rose triumphal arches and columns. Roads, canals, and harbors were built, and old ones were improved. And, chief of all, the economic gain of the peasants in the Revolution (p. 282) was preserved. The peasantry were landowners, free from their old burdens; and workmen secured

[1] Special reports: the Legion of Honor; Napoleon's encouragement of science.

two or three times the wages they had received ten years before. Under such conditions the people displayed new energies, and, with the establishment of quiet and order, they quickly built up a vast material prosperity.

In short, Bonaparte destroyed political liberty; but he preserved equality before the law, along with the economic gains to the working classes from the Revolution. The burden of taxation was made to rest with fair justice upon all classes. The peasant paid not four fifths his income in taxes, as before the Revolution, but about one fifth; and he got much more in return than before.

The last of the benevolent despots

In all this reconstruction the controlling mind was that of the First Consul. Functionaries worked as they had worked for no other master. Bonaparte knew how to set every man the right task; and his own matchless activity (he sometimes worked twenty hours a day) made it possible for him to oversee countless designs. His penetrating intelligence seized the essential point of every problem, and his indomitable will drove through all obstacles to a quick and effective solution. His ardor, his ambition for France and for glory, his passion for good work, his contempt for difficulties, inspired every official, until, as one of them said, "the gigantic entered into our habit of thought."

But the benefits that Bonaparte conferred upon France were the work of a beneficent despotism, not of a free government. He worked as a Joseph II (p. 250) of greater ability might have done. Bonaparte was the last and greatest of the benevolent despots, and it was soon plain that he meant to seize the outer trappings of royalty as well as its power.

CHAPTER XVIII

THE FRENCH EMPIRE, 1804–1814

"Emperor Napoleon the First"

In 1802 Bonaparte had himself elected "Consul for Life." He set up a court, with all the forms of monarchy, and began to sign papers by his first name only — Napoleon — as kings sign. Then, in 1804, he obtained another vote of the nation declaring him "Emperor of the French," and he solemnly crowned himself at Paris, with the presence and sanction of the pope, as the successor of Charlemagne.

Plebiscites

Napoleon always claimed that he ruled by the "will of the French people"; and each assumption of power was given a show of ratification by a popular vote, or *plebiscite*. But the plebiscite was merely the nation's Yes or No to a question *framed by the master*. The result of a No could never be foreseen; and it was not hard so to shape questions that men would rather say Yes than risk the indefinite consequences of saying No. *The nation had no share at any stage in shaping the questions upon which it was to vote;* and even the vote was controlled largely by skillful coercion. A plebiscite was a thin veil for military despotism; but it was at least a standing denial of the old doctrine of "divine right." At the same time, it must be acknowledged that the French people tamely surrendered to a despotic master who flattered their vanity and fed their material prosperity.

System of spies

Personal liberty was no longer safe. Napoleon maintained a vast network of *secret police and spies*, and in ten years he sent thirty-six hundred men to prison or into exile by his mere order. *The press* was subjected to stern and searching censorship. *No book* could be published if it contained opinions offensive to the emperor, even in matters only slightly related to politics. Thus Madame de Staël was not allowed to say that the drama of

Iphigenia by the German Goethe was a greater play than the work of the French Racine upon the same plot. *Newspapers* were forbidden to print anything "contrary to the duties of subjects." They were required to omit all news "disadvantageous or disagreeable to France," and in political matters they were allowed to publish only such items as were furnished them by the government. Thus the *Moniteur*, the leading official paper, made no mention of the destruction of the French fleet by Nelson at Trafalgar (p. 317) in 1805.

Free speech suppressed

Moreover, they were required to praise the administration. "Tell them," said Napoleon, "I shall judge them not only by the evil they say, but by the good they do not say." Even *the schools* were made to preach despotism, and were commanded to "take as the basis of their instruction fidelity to the Emperor." *Religion*, too, was pressed into service. Every village priest depended, directly or indirectly, upon Napoleon's will, and was expected to uphold his power. An *Imperial Catechism* was devised, and used in all schools, expressly to teach the duty of all good Christians to obey the emperor.[1]

The "Napoleonic Wars"

In 1802 Napoleon told his Council of State that he should welcome war and that he expected it. *Europe*, he declared, *needed a single head*, an emperor, to distribute the various kingdoms among lieutenants.[2] He felt, too, that victories and military glory were needful to prevent the French nation from murmuring against his despotism.

Naturally, other nations felt that there could be no lasting peace with Napoleon except on terms of absolute submission. Under such conditions as these, war soon broke out afresh. England and France came to blows again in 1803, and there was to be no more truce between them until Napoleon's fall. During the next eleven years, Napoleon fought also three wars with Austria, two with Prussia, two with Russia, a long war with Spain, and various minor conflicts.

[1] Extracts are given in Anderson's *Documents*, No. 65.

[2] This is the way in which the German Hohenzollerns have recently been planning to secure European "peace." Cf. p. 612.

The European wars from 1792 to 1802 belong to the period of the French Revolution proper. Those from 1803 to 1815 are "Napoleonic wars," due primarily to the ambition of one great military genius. In the first series, Austria was the chief opponent of the Revolution: in the second series, England was the relentless foe of Napoleon.

THE VENDÔME COLUMN — made from Russian and Austrian cannon captured in the Austerlitz campaign. The figures on the spirals represent scenes in that campaign, and upon the summit, 142 feet high, stood a statue of Napoleon. The name Vendôme comes from the name of the public square. Students of ancient history will naturally compare this column with similar Roman military monuments. Napoleon, like the later Hohenzollerns, was fond of imitating the works of the Roman world-empire.

On the breaking out of war with England, Napoleon prepared a mighty flotilla and a magnificent army at Boulogne. England was threatened with overwhelming invasion if she should lose command of the Channel even for a few hours. So sure did Napoleon feel of his prey that he even prepared a medal to be struck in London, upon his expected entry there, to commemorate his victory; but all his attempts to get together a fleet to compete with England's failed.

In 1805 Austria and Russia joined England in the war. With immediate decision, Napoleon transferred his forces from the Channel to the Danube, annihilated two great armies, at *Ulm* and *Austerlitz* (October and December), and, entering Vienna as a conqueror, forced Austria to a humiliating peace. That country gave up her remaining territory in Italy, and her Illyrian provinces, and surrendered also many of her possessions in Germany.

Prussia had maintained her neutrality for eleven years; but now, with his hands free, Napoleon goaded her into war, crushed her absolutely at *Jena* (October, 1806), occupied Berlin, and soon afterward dictated a peace that reduced Prussia one half in size and bound her to France as a vassal state.

Peace of Tilsit

Less decisive conflicts with Russia were followed by the Peace of Tilsit (July, 1807). The Russian and French emperors met in a long interview, and Tsar Alexander was so impressed by Napoleon's genius, that, from an enemy, he became a friend and ally. France, it was understood, was to rule Western Europe; Russia might aggrandize herself in the Eastern half at the expense of Sweden, Turkey, and Asia; and the two Powers were to unite in ruining England by shutting out her commerce from the continent.

Trafalgar

England had proved as supreme on the seas as Napoleon on land. *In 1805*, at *Trafalgar*, off the coast of Spain, Nelson destroyed the last great fleet that Napoleon collected. Soon afterward a secret article in the Treaty of Tilsit agreed that Denmark (then a considerable naval power) should be made to add her fleet to the French; but the English government struck first. It demanded the surrender of the Danish fleet into English hands until war should close, and finally it compelled the delivery by bombarding Copenhagen.

Napoleon's "Continental System"

After this, Napoleon could not strike at England with his armies, and he fell back upon an attempt to ruin her by crushing her commerce. All the ports of the continent were to be closed to her goods. Napoleon stirred French scientists into desperate efforts to invent substitutes for the goods shut out of the continent. One valuable result followed. The English cruisers prevented the importation into France of West-India cane sugar; but it was discovered that sugar could be made from the beet, and the raising of the sugar-beet became a leading industry of France.

This Continental System did inflict damage upon England,

but it carried greater harm to the continent, which simply could not do without the manufactures of England, then the workshop of Europe. At times, even the French armies had to be clothed in smuggled English goods, and they marched into Russia in 1812 (p. 324) in English shoes.

"War of 1812" in America

England's retort to the Continental System was an attempt to blockade the coast of France and her dependencies to all neutral vessels. In these war measures, both France and England ignored the rights of neutral states. One result was the War of 1812 in America. In this struggle, unhappily, we let ourselves be tricked into fighting upon the side of the European despot, against the only champion of freedom, and upon the whole, into fighting that power which we had least reason to fight.[1] Happily, in that day, America's part could not be decisive, and the contest did not much affect the European result.

On the other hand, Napoleon's attempts to enforce his System led him from one high-handed measure to another, until Portugal and Russia rose against him, and so gave Central Europe another chance to win freedom (pp. 324–325).

Napoleon and the Spanish people

Portugal refused to obey Napoleon's order to confiscate the English vessels in her ports. Thereupon Napoleon's armies occupied the kingdom. From this act, Napoleon passed to the seizure of Spain, placing his brother Joseph upon the throne. But the proud and patriotic Spanish people rose in a "War for Liberation," and it was soon plain that a new force had appeared. Hitherto, Napoleon had warred against governments, and had dictated peace when the rulers were in his power: now, first, he had to fight with a *people* in arms. Brilliant victories merely transferred the outbreaks from one quarter to another and called for more and more of his energies. England seized her opportunity, too, and sent an army under Wellesley (afterward Duke of Wellington) to support the Peninsular revolt. To the end, this struggle continued to drain

[1] As if, in 1914–1918, we had let Germany draw us to her side, as she hoped, because the English blockade of Germany hurt our commerce.

Napoleon's resources. Long after, at St. Helena, he declared that it was really the Spanish war that ruined him.

Napoleon after Wagram

In 1809, encouraged by the Spanish rising, Austria once more entered the lists, but a defeat at *Wagram* forced her again to submission. Napoleon now married a princess of Austria. He was anxious for an heir, and so divorced his former wife, Josephine, who had borne him no children, to make way for marriage with a grandniece of Marie Antoinette. This union of the Revolutionary emperor with the proud Hapsburg house marks in some respects the summit of his power.

Napoleon's new map of Europe

At the moment, the Spanish campaigns seemed trivial; and after Wagram, Napoleon was supreme in Central Europe. This period was marked by sweeping changes in territory. The most important may be grouped under four heads.

The Batavian Republic (p. 305) was converted into the Kingdom of Holland, with Napoleon's brother Louis for its sovereign. Later, when Louis refused to ruin his people by enforcing the Continental System rigidly, Napoleon deposed him, and *annexed Holland to France,* along with the whole north coast of Germany as far as Denmark.

In Italy the new republics and the old petty states were disposed of, one after another. Even the pope was deprived of his principality. When these changes were complete, Italy lay in three fairly equal divisions. *In the south* Napoleon's brother, Joseph, ruled as King of Naples; and when Joseph was promoted in 1809 to the throne of Spain, he was succeeded in Naples by Murat, one of Napoleon's generals. *In the northeast* was the "Kingdom of Italy," with Napoleon himself as king — as Charlemagne and Otto and their successors had been "kings of Italy"! *The rest of the peninsula was made a part of France,* and was organized as a French Department.

The Illyrian provinces on the eastern coast of the Adriatic were annexed directly to France.

Most important of all were the changes in *Germany.* To comprehend the significance of Napoleon's work there, one must first grasp the bewildering conditions *before* his interference.

Germany before Napoleon

Before Napoleon there was no true political Germany. The Holy Roman Empire was made up of:

Two "great states," Austria and Prussia, each of them half Slavonic in blood;

Some thirty states of the "second rank," like Bavaria and Wurtemberg;

About two hundred and fifty *petty* states of the "third order" (many of them under bishops or archbishops), ranging in size from a small duchy to a large farm, but averaging a few thousand inhabitants;

Some fifteen hundred "knights of the empire," who in England would have been country squires (pp. 84–85), but who in Germany were really independent monarchs, with an average territory of three square miles, and some three hundred subjects apiece, over whom they held power of life and death;

About fifty-six "free cities," all in misrule, governed by narrow aristocracies (p. 99).

Each of the two hundred and fifty states of the "third rank," like the larger ones, was *an absolute monarchy*, with its own laws, its own mimic court and army, its own coinage, and its crowd of pedantic officials. The "Sovereign Count" of Leimburg-Styrum-Wilhelmsdorf kept a standing army of one colonel, nine lower officers and two privates! Each of the fifteen hundred "knights" had his own system of tariffs and taxes.

One more factor must be taken into account in order to get an idea of the indescribable confusion. *Rarely did one of these petty principalities have its territory compact.* Many a state of the second or third order *consisted of several fragments* [1] (obtained by accidents of marriage or war), *sometimes widely scattered*, — some of them perhaps wholly inside a larger state to which politically they had no relation. No map can do justice to the quaint confusion of this region, about the size of Texas, thus broken

[1] As indicated by such compound names as the one above.

into eighteen hundred governments varying from an empire to a small estate, and scattered in fragments within fragments.[1] It is little wonder that the philosopher Lessing, the greatest German between Luther and Goethe, should have said: "Patriotism I do not understand; at best it seems an amiable weakness which I am glad to be free from."

Napoleon's beginnings of consolidation

Napoleon had begun his rearrangement of Germany at Campo Formio (p. 305). By that treaty (and by subsequent arrangements), princes of the Empire were allowed to recompense themselves for the territories they had lost to France by absorbing the ecclesiastical states and most of the "free cities."

After Austerlitz and Jena, more radical changes followed. Austria and Prussia were weakened. The first became an inland state. The second was halved and pushed altogether beyond the Elbe, while its recent Polish acquisitions were turned into the Duchy of Warsaw. Besides so depressing the two great states, Napoleon proceeded to form a further check upon them by augmenting the states of the second rank. Bavaria, Saxony, and Wurtemberg were made kingdoms, with territories enlarged at the expense of Austria and of smaller neighboring states; while out of old Prussian territory and of the electorate of Hanover was formed a new "Kingdom of Westphalia," for Napoleon's brother Jerome.

At the same time, the large states were encouraged or compelled to absorb the territories of the knights and of the petty principalities within or adjoining their borders. Thus the "political crazy quilt" of eighteen hundred states was simplified to thirty-eight states. This tremendous consolidation, surviving the rearrangements after Napoleon's fall, paved the way for later German unity.

End of the Holy Roman Empire

Nearly all these German states, except Austria and Prussia, were leagued in the "Confederation of the Rhine," under Napoleon as "Protector." This amounted to a dissolution of the Holy Roman Empire, and in 1806 Francis II laid down that venerable title. Napoleon himself posed as the successor of

[1] These conditions are dimly suggested by the map after p. 118.

the Roman emperors. Francis was allowed to console himself with the title "Emperor of Austria," for his *hereditary* realms, instead of his previous title, "Arch-Duke of Austria."

How far does Napoleon deserve gratitude for so sweeping away old and obstructive features in the map of Germany? He had not much personally to gain by his action in this matter. Seemingly the explanation, in large part at least, is that he was a born administrator to whom disorder and confusion was hateful; and, when he could, he cleaned it up — much as a good housewife sometimes aches to clean up her neighbor's neglected and dusty parlor.

Social reform in Germany

And Napoleon's influence, too, began great social reforms in Germany. In the Confederacy of the Rhine and in the many kingdoms of Napoleon's brothers and generals, serfdom and feudalism were abolished, and civil equality and the "Code Napoleon" were introduced. Everywhere, too, the administration of justice was made cheap and simple, and the old clumsy and corrupt methods of government gave way to order and efficiency.

Stein in Prussia

Most striking of all was the reform in Prussia. Elsewhere the new methods were introduced by French agents or under French influence. In Prussia, reform came from a Prussian minister, and was adopted in order to make Prussia strong enough to cast off the French yoke.

Jena had proved that the old Prussian system was utterly rotten. The guiding spirit in a new Prussian ministry was *Stein*, who labored to fit Prussia for leadership in freeing and regenerating Germany.[1] The serfs were changed into free peasant-landowners. The caste distinctions in society were broken down. The old law had recognized distinct classes, — peasants, burgesses, and nobility, — and had practically forbidden an individual to pass from one class into another. Even the land had been bound by the caste system: no noble

[1] Curiously enough, this almost solitary progressive among Prussian statesmen was Prussian not by birth but by adoption.

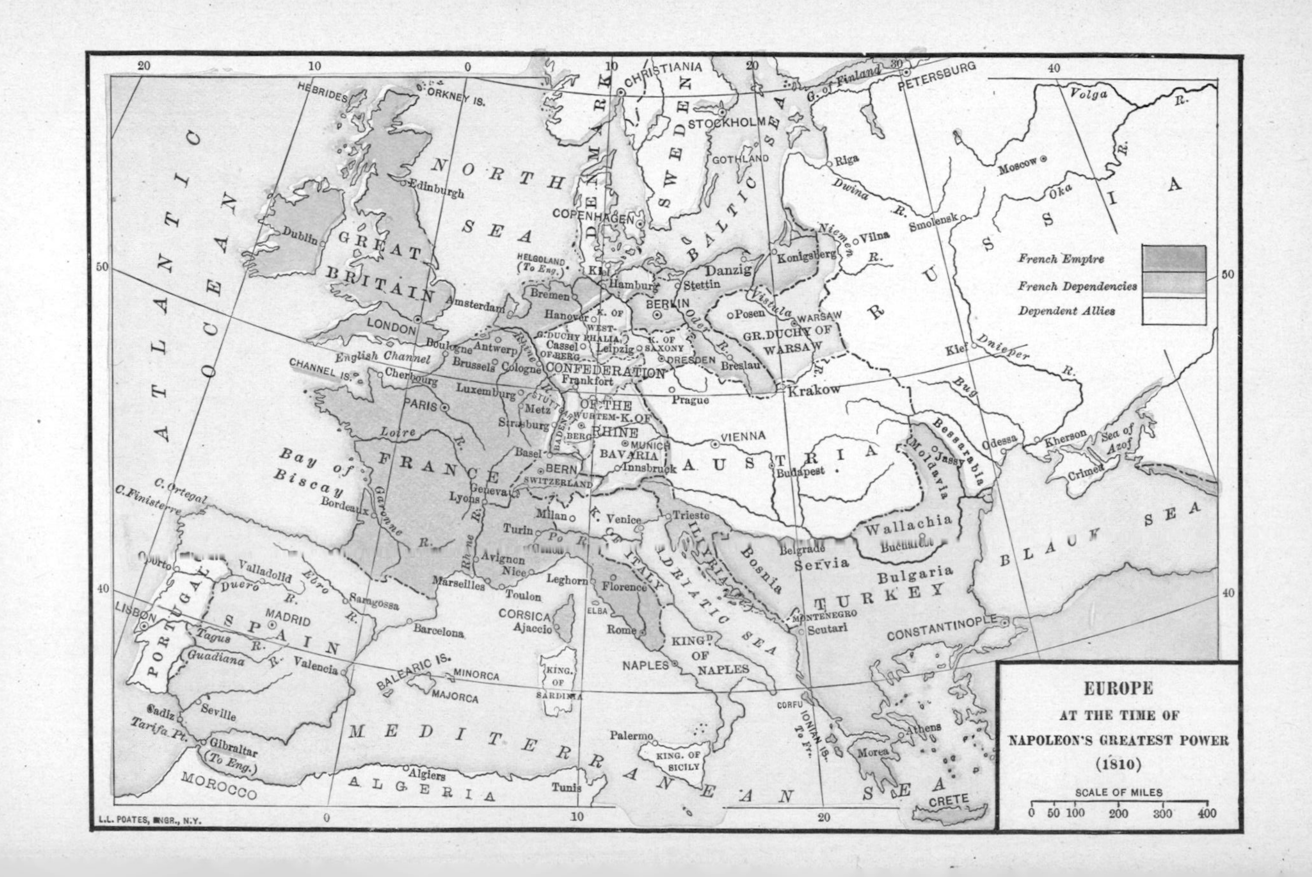
EUROPE
AT THE TIME OF
NAPOLEON'S GREATEST POWER
(1810)
SCALE OF MILES
0 50 100 200 300 400
French Empire
French Dependencies
Dependent Allies
ATLANTIC OCEAN
NORTH SEA
BALTIC SEA
MEDITERRANEAN SEA
ADRIATIC SEA
Bay of Biscay
English Channel
GREAT BRITAIN
FRANCE
SPAIN
PORTUGAL
RUSSIA
AUSTRIA
TURKEY
SWEDEN
DENMARK
CONFEDERATION OF THE RHINE
GR. DUCHY OF WARSAW
ILLYRIA
ITALY
KING. OF NAPLES
KING. OF SICILY
KING. OF SARDINIA
SWITZERLAND
BAVARIA
Bosnia
Servia
Bulgaria
Wallachia
Moldavia
Bessarabia
MOROCCO
ALGERIA
LONDON
PARIS
MADRID
LISBON
BERLIN
VIENNA
PETERSBURG
CONSTANTINOPLE
STOCKHOLM
COPENHAGEN
CHRISTIANIA
L.L. POATES, ENGR., N.Y.

could sell land to the citizen of a town; nor could noble or townsman sell to a peasant. All this was now done away. Some self-government was granted to the towns. And many of the best principles of the French reforms were adopted. Napoleon's insolence and the domination of the French armies at last had forced part of Germany into the beginning of a new national patriotism; and that patriotism began to arm itself by borrowing weapons from the arsenal of the French Revolution.

NAPOLEON TOWARD THE CLOSE OF HIS REIGN.

Greatest extent of Napoleon's sway

In 1810 Napoleon's power had reached its widest limits. The huge bulk of France filled the space from the Ocean to the Rhine, including not only the France which we know, but also Belgium, half of Switzerland, and large strips of German territory, — while from this central body two outward-curving arms reached toward the east, one along the North Sea to the Danish Peninsula, and the other down the coast of Italy past Rome.

This vast territory was *all organized in French Departments.* The rest of Italy and half the rest of Germany were under Napoleon's "protection," and were ruled by his appointees. Denmark and Switzerland, too, were his dependent allies; and Prussia and Austria were unwilling ones. Only the extremities of the continent kept their independence, and even there, Sweden and Russia were his friends.

But Russia was growing hostile. Alexander was offended by the partial restoration of Poland (as the Duchy of Warsaw).

The Continental System, too, was growing more and more burdensome. Russia needed English markets, and in 1811 the Tsar refused longer to enforce the "System."

The "Retreat from Moscow"

Napoleon at once declared war. In 1812 he invaded Russia and penetrated to Moscow. The Russians set fire to the city, so that it should not afford him winter quarters; but, with rare indecision, he stayed there five weeks, hoping in vain that the Tsar would offer to submit. Then, too late, in the middle of October, when the Russian winter was already upon them, the

NAPOLEON LEAVING MOSCOW. — From an imaginative painting.

French began the terrible "Retreat from Moscow," fighting desperately each foot of the way against cold, starvation, and clouds of Cossack cavalry. Nine weeks later, twenty thousand miserable scarecrows recrossed the Niemen. The "Grand Army," a half million strong, had left its bones among Russian snows.

Battle of Leipzig

The Russians kept up the pursuit into Germany, and the enthusiasm of the Prussian people forced the government to declare against Napoleon. University professors enlisted at the head of companies of their students in a "war of liberation." Women gave their jewels and even their hair, to buy arms and supplies. The next summer, Austria also took up arms. By tremendous efforts, Napoleon raised a new army of boys and old men from exhausted France, and for a time he kept the field victoriously in Germany; but in October, 1813, he met crushing defeat at *Leipzig*, in the "Battle of the Nations."

Fall of Napoleon

Napoleon retreated across the Rhine. His vassal kings fled from their thrones, and most of the small states now joined his enemies. England, Russia, Austria, and Prussia, acting in close concert, took to themselves the name "The Allies," and maintained a perfect understanding. After Leipzig, they proposed peace, offering to leave Napoleon his crown, with the Rhine for the boundary of France. Like a desperate gamester, bound to win or lose all, Napoleon rejected these terms. The Allies then advanced to the Rhine, and offered peace with the French boundaries of 1792. Napoleon again refused. The Allies invaded France at several points, with overwhelming numbers; and, in spite of Napoleon's superb defense, they entered Paris victoriously in March, 1814, and dictated peace.

The Allies made Napoleon a large allowance, and granted him the island of Elba, in the Mediterranean, as an independent principality. The Bourbon heir to the French throne, one of the Emigrant brothers of Louis XVI, appeared, *promised a constitution* to France, and was quietly recognized by the French Senate as Louis XVIII.[1] The Allies avoided the appearance of imposing this king upon France, but they liked the arrangement. To make it popular, they granted liberal terms of peace. France kept her territory as it was before the Revolution. The Allies withdrew their armies without imposing any war indemnity, such as France had exacted repeatedly from other countries; nor did they even take back the works of art that French armies had plundered from so many famous galleries in Europe.

For Further Reading. — The best brief accounts of the Napoleonic era are given in Stephens' *Revolutionary Europe, 1789–1815* and in Rose's

[1] The son of Louis XVI had died in prison at Paris in 1795. According to the theory that he began to reign upon his father's death in 1793, he is known as Louis XVII.

Revolutionary and Napoleonic Era. The many histories of Napoleon are most of them defaced by extreme partisanship on one side or the other, or are too long for general use. Probably the best treatment is also the most recent, — Rose's *Napoleon the First.* Anderson's *Constitutions and Documents* gives an admirable selection of documents. Kennan's *Folktales about Napoleon* is a curious and interesting volume.

PART V

A PERIOD OF REACTION, 1815–1848

CHAPTER XIX

THE CONGRESS OF VIENNA: RESTORATION

Political chaos in Europe

Napoleon had wiped away the old map of Europe, and now *his* map fell to pieces. All the districts which had been annexed to France since 1792, and all the states which had been created by Napoleon, were left without governments. The *old* rulers of these states were clamoring for restoration. Other rulers wanted new acquisitions to pay for their exertions against Napoleon There was also a fear pervading Europe that from France either new and dangerous "Revolutionary" ideas or a new military conqueror might overrun the world. To settle these problems — to arrange for "restoration," "reparation," and "guarantees" — the four "Allies" invited all the sovereigns of Europe to a "Peace Congress."

The Congress of Vienna

The *Congress of Vienna* assembled in November, 1814. The crowd of smaller monarchs and princes were entertained by their Austrian host in a constant round of masques and revels, while the four great Allies (Russia, Austria, Prussia, England) did the work in private committee. From time to time, as they reached agreements, they announced results to the Congress for public ratification.

The territorial rearrangements fall under three heads.

Territorial rearrangements: "restorations"

1. *Italy was left in twelve states, and Germany, in thirty-eight.* These were all *restored* to their old ruling families. (The other phases of the "restoration" can be treated most conveniently in the next chapter.)

Guarantee against French attack

2. *The states along the French frontier were strengthened,* as one "*guarantee*" against future aggression by France. (1) Holland was made into the Kingdom of the Netherlands, under the House of Orange, and Belgium was added to it, although the Belgians wished to be independent and objected very strongly to being made Dutch. (2) Nice and Savoy were given back to the Kingdom of Sardinia, to which was added also the old Republic of Genoa. (3) German territory west of the Rhine, now taken back from France, was divided between the powerful kingdoms of Prussia and Bavaria. (4) The Congress guaranteed the "neutrality" of Switzerland, promising that all would join in punishing any country which in future wars should march troops through that state. Thus the entire European frontier next France, from the North Sea to the Mediterranean, was powerfully fortified.

3. *The remaining rearrangements had to do,* directly or indirectly, *with "compensating" the Allies* for their exertions and losses. Under cover of high-sounding phrases about founding "a durable peace based upon a just division of power," the Congress became "a Congress for loot" and began a disgraceful scramble for spoils.

Plunder for the Allies

(1) *England* had stood out alone for years against the whole power of Napoleon, and she had incurred an enormous national debt by acting as paymaster of the various coalitions. In repayment, she now kept Malta, the Ionian Islands, Cape Colony, Ceylon, and a few other colonial acquisitions, mainly from the old Dutch empire, which she had occupied during the war.

The "Second Hundred Years' War" can now be seen as a whole, in relation to world-empire. *The first period* (1689–1763) is covered in pp. 231–233, 242–245: it is known in America as the period of Intercolonial Wars. It ended with the exclusion of France from North America and India, to England's gain. *The second period* (1775–1783) is the period of the American Revolution. England lost the richest part of her American empire, but she made gains elsewhere at the expense of France, Spain, and Holland, and acquired Australia. *The third period,* the wars of the French Revolution and Napoleon (1792–1815), left England the one great colonial power. Spain[1] and Holland still had some possessions outside Europe; but their holdings were insignificant beside England's.

(2) *Austria* received back all her lost territory, except distant Belgium in place of which she accepted Venetia and Lombardy, much to the distaste of the inhabitants of those districts.

(3) Alexander, Tsar of Russia, secured Finland from Sweden; and he demanded also further reward in Poland. The Duchy of Warsaw (p. 321), he insisted, should be made into a kingdom of Poland, and he should be the king. *But this plan conflicted with Prussian ambition.*

(4) *Prussia* gained Pomerania from Sweden; but the Prussian king insisted also upon regaining the Polish provinces that Napoleon had taken from him for the Duchy of Warsaw. Alexander promised to aid Prussia to get Saxony instead. The king of Saxony had been a zealous ally of Napoleon to the last; and so, Alexander urged, it would be proper to make an exception in his case to the careful respect shown by the conquerors to all other "legitimate rulers."

The Allies nearly fall out

Prussia was ready to accept this; but Austria feared such extension of Prussia toward the heart of Germany, and vehemently opposed the plan. England took her side. Thus the four Allies were divided, — Russia and Prussia against Austria and England, — and came to the verge of war with one another. Perhaps the most interesting result of this was the way in which *France wormed her way back into the European circle.* The Allies had meant to give that "outlaw nation" no voice whatever at the peace table. But Talleyrand, the shrewd French diplomat, was present at Vienna as a looker-on; and now, by offering French aid to Austria and England at a critical

[1] For Spain's loss of colonial empire, cf. p. 340.

moment, he won a place for his country in the Congress, and, as he said, exultingly but rather prematurely, "broke up forever the alliance against her."

Finally a compromise was made — the more readily that Napoleon had broken loose (see below). In addition to her gain of Pomerania, Prussia took *half* of Saxony and considerable German territory, recovered from France, *west* of the Rhine (see above).

It should be noted that *Sweden, which in the time of Peter the Great had surrounded the Baltic, had now retired wholly into the northern peninsula.* There, however, she found some compensation. *Denmark* (which had been the ally of Napoleon) *now had to surrender Norway, and this land the Congress of Vienna turned over to Sweden* in return for Finland and Pomerania. How, out of this arrangement, the Norwegians won independence in a ninety years' struggle is told in a later chapter, — one of the finest stories of the nineteenth century.

Napoleon's brief return: "The Hundred Days"

During the dissensions regarding Saxony, the Congress was startled by the news that Napoleon had left Elba. A few months of Bourbon rule had filled France with unrest. The Tricolor, under which Frenchmen had marched in triumph into nearly every capital in Europe, had been replaced by the Bourbon White flag, and many Napoleonic officers had been dismissed from the army to make way for returned Emigrants, who for twenty years had fought against France. Thus the army was restless. The extreme Royalists were talking, too, of restoring the land of the church and of the Emigrants, though it had passed for a generation into other hands. In consequence, the peasants and the middle class were uneasy.

Napoleon, learning how matters stood, landed in France, almost unattended. The forces sent to capture him *joined his standard;* and in a few days, he entered Paris in triumph, without firing a shot, as he had foretold he would do. The king and the old Emigrants emigrated again. Napoleon offered

EUROPE AFTER THE CONGRESS OF VIENNA (1815)
German Confederacy
SCALE OF MILES
0 50 100 200 300 400
ATLANTIC OCEAN
NORTH SEA
BALTIC SEA
MEDITERRANEAN SEA
ADRIATIC SEA
BLACK SEA
Bay of Biscay
English Channel
SWEDEN AND NORWAY
DENMARK
GREAT BRITAIN
FRANCE
SPAIN
PORTUGAL
RUSSIA
KINGDOM OF Warsaw POLAND
Prussia
GERMAN CONFEDERATION
EMPIRE OF AUSTRIA
SWITZERLAND
TURKISH EMPIRE
KINGDOM OF THE NETHERLANDS
KINGDOM OF SARDINIA
KINGDOM OF THE TWO SICILIES
STATES OF THE POPE
Kingdom of Bavaria
Kg. of Saxony
Lombardo-Venetia
Bessarabia
Moldavia
Wallachia
Transylvania
Bulgaria
Servia
Bosnia
MONTENEGRO
ALGERIA
MOROCCO
CORSICA
CRETE
HEBRIDES
ORKNEY IS.
CHANNEL IS.
BALEARIC IS.
MINORCA
MAJORCA
HELGOLAND (To Eng.)
MALTA (To Eng.)
IONIAN IS. (To Eng.)
Gibraltar (To Eng.)
CHRISTIANIA
STOCKHOLM
G. of Finland
ST. PETERSBURG
Peipus L.
Riga
Moscow
Smolensk
Vilna
Kief
Odessa
Kherson
Sea of Azof
Crimea
CONSTANTINOPLE
Smyrna
Athens
CORFU
Scutari
Belgrade
Bucharest
Budapest
VIENNA
Krakow
Breslau
Prague
DRESDEN
Leipzig
BERLIN
Posen
Stettin
Danzig
Königsberg
W. Prussia
E. Prussia
Hamburg
Bremen
Hanover
Kiel
COPENHAGEN
Edinburgh
Dublin
LONDON
Amsterdam
Antwerp
Brussels
Cassel
Cologne
Frankfort
Luxemburg
Metz
Strasburg
Stuttgart
Baden
Würtemberg
MUNICH
Innsbruck
Trieste
Venice
Verona
MILAN
K. OF SARDINIA
Turin
Genoa
Nice
Monaco
Leghorn
G. D. OF TUSCANY
ELBA
Florence
Ancona
ROME
NAPLES
Palermo
Tunis
Algiers
PARIS
Nantes
Bordeaux
Lyons
Avignon
Marseilles
Toulon
Ajaccio
Andorra
Geneva
BERN
Barcelona
Saragossa
Valencia
MADRID
Valladolid
Seville
Cadiz
LISBON
Oporto
C. Ortegal
C. Finisterre
C. St. Vincent
Tarifa Pt.
Volga R.
Oka
Don R.
Dnieper R.
Bug R.
Dniester R.
Pruth R.
Niemen R.
Vistula R.
Oder R.
Elbe R.
Rhine R.
Danube R.
Theiss R.
Drave R.
Save R.
Po R.
Rhone R.
Seine R.
Loire R.
Garonne R.
Ebro R.
Douro R.
Tagus R.
Guadiana R.
Guadalquivir R.
20
10
0
10
20
40
50
40

a liberal constitution, and France accepted it by an overwhelming plebiscite.

The Allies, however, refused even to treat with Napoleon. They declared unrelenting war upon him as "the disturber of the peace of Europe," and promptly moved powerful armies to the French frontier. No time was given Napoleon for preparation, and the odds were overwhelming. After a brief rule, known as the Hundred Days, he was crushed at *Waterloo* by the English under Wellington and the Prussians under Blücher (June 18, 1815), and sent this time to hopeless exile, under guard, on the distant volcanic rock of St. Helena in the South Atlantic.

The Duke of Wellington.

Mild terms for France

The Allies reëntered Paris, "bringing Louis XVIII in their baggage," as the French wits put it, and *dictated to France a new treaty*, much more severe than that of 1814. Prussia, indeed, urged that France should be dismembered, as she herself had been after Jena. Some Prussian papers talked of killing off the whole French people "like mad dogs," and moderate statesmen wished to take Alsace and Lorraine (as Bismarck did do fifty years later) and other territory that had been seized from Germany by Louis XIV. But Alexander and England insisted on milder punishment, in order that the people might not utterly reject the Bourbon rule; and France was required only (1) to give up some small strips of land containing about a half-million people, (2) to pay a small war indemnity ($140,000,000), and (3) to restore the works of art which Napoleon's armies had plundered from European galleries.

Some rivers "internationalized"

During the Hundred Days, the Congress finished its work. Some of its later measures were highly praiseworthy. England persuaded the Powers to join in a declaration against the slave trade;[1] and the navigation of rivers flowing through or between different countries was declared free to the commerce of all countries ("internationalized"). A country in possession of the mouth of a river had been in the habit of closing it against the trade of other nations. Thus Spain, while she held both banks of the mouth of the Mississippi (1783–1801), had tried to follow this policy—to the wrath of American settlers up the river and on the Ohio. The principle established at Vienna was a step forward for civilization. Moreover, it was worth much for Europe to recognize that it had common interests, and that it could arrange them in a peaceful Congress. This was an advance from eighteenth century politics toward the Hague Congress, the Peace Congress of 1919, and the League of Nations.

A peace of kings, not of peoples

The Congress of Vienna, to be sure, had no thought of this great movement. *That "assemblage of princes and lackeys" stood for reaction.* As an English historian says, — "It complacently set to work to turn back the hands of time to the historic hour at which they stood before the Bastille fell." *It represented kings, not peoples.* All the republics which had appeared since the French Revolution and also the *old* republics — the United Provinces, Venice, and Genoa — were given to monarchs. "Republics," said the Austrian Metternich (p. 335), "seem to have gone out of fashion." Switzerland was the only republic left in Europe, — and it was given an inefficient, loose union, far less effective than it had enjoyed under Napoleon's supremacy. *Peoples were never consulted.* The Congress transferred Belgians, Norwegians, Poles, Venetians, from freedom to a master, or from one master to another, — in every case *against their fierce resentment.*

The next hundred years were to be busied very largely in

[1] Thereafter, England kept ships of war on the African coast to capture pirate slaving vessels. But, unhappily, the United States was unwilling to grant the necessary "right of search"; and so, until 1861, the horrible African slave trade continued to be carried on mainly by ships under the protection of the Stars and Stripes, — although the foreign slave trade had been *illegal* in the United States since 1808.

undoing the work of this first Peace Congress, until not one stone of its building was left upon another. Thus, when the next great Peace Congress met, in 1919, it had only to turn back to the Congress of Vienna for a perfect example of "How not to do it."

EXERCISES. — Add to the list of dates the following: 1776, 1789, 1815. The teacher will note that some phases of the work of the Congress are best seen after the study of the "alliances" to enforce peace and to preserve order (p. 568).

CHAPTER XX

CENTRAL EUROPE TO 1820

The history of the nineteenth century is the history of the influences which the French Revolution left. — FREDERIC HARRISON.

No land touched by the French Revolution was ever again quite the same. — FREDERICK A. OGG.

Absurdities of the reaction after 1815

The *immediate* result of the Congress of Vienna was a victory for reaction and despotism. In many states, especially in the pettier ones, the restoration of the old rulers was accompanied by ludicrous absurdities. The princes who had scampered away before the French eagles, came back to show that they had "learned nothing and forgotten nothing." They set out to ignore the past twenty years. In France a school history spoke of Austerlitz as "a victory gained by General Bonaparte, a lieutenant of the king"! The Elector of Hesse censured his military Commandant for "omitting quarterly reports during the preceding ten years" — during which the Elector had been a fugitive in England. The king of Sardinia restored serfdom. The Papal States and Spain again set up the Inquisition. In some places French plants were uprooted from the botanical gardens, and street lamps and vaccination were abolished because they were "French improvements."

The statesmen of the Great Powers must have smiled to themselves at some of these absurd extremes; but they, too, almost universally strove to suppress progress. Five states — Russia, Austria, Prussia, France, and England — really determined the policy of Europe. The first four were "divine right" monarchies. Louis XVIII *gave* France a limited Charter, but it carefully preserved the theory of divine right. That theory, of course, could have no place in England, where the monarchy rested on the Revolution of 1688; but even in England the Whigs were discredited, because they had sympathized at first with the French Revolution. For some years the government there was in the hands of the Tory party, which was bitterly opposed to progress.

Metternich, the evil genius of the reaction

"The rule of Napoleon was succeeded by the rule of Metternich." Metternich was the chief servant of the Emperor of Austria, and the real director of Austrian policy. He was subtle, adroit, industrious, witty, unscrupulous. Napoleon said of him that he "mistook intrigue for statesmanship"; and Stein (p. 322) complained that he was "overfond of complications" and did not know how to do business "in the great and simple way."

Far more than any other one man, Metternich had guided proceedings in the Congress of Vienna, and he continued to be the evil genius of Europe from 1814 to 1848. He summed up his political creed thus: "Sovereigns alone are entitled to guide the destinies of their peoples, and they are responsible to none but God. . . . Government is no more a subject for debate than religion is." The "new ideas" of democracy and equality and nationality[1] ought never to have been allowed to get into Europe, he said; but, since they were *in*, the business of governments must be to keep them *down*. He was too shrewd to expect to bring back altogether the days before the French Revolution; but he did hope to arrest all change at the lines drawn by the Congress of Vienna. In his more sanguine moments, indeed, he spoke of the democratic impulses resulting from the Revolution as "a gangrene, to be burned out of Europe with red-hot iron."

The political reaction was the more galling to the friends of liberty because the "Wars of Liberation" in 1812–1814 had

[1] The sentiment of nationality is the feeling among all the people of one race, speech, and country that they should make one political state, or become a "nation." This feeling tended to draw all Germans into one German state, and all Italians into one Italian state. In any conglomerate state, like Austria in that day, the feeling of nationality was likely to be a disrupting force.

Disappointment of European Liberals

been essentially *popular* uprisings. The Prussian king had made repeated appeals to national patriotism, and had twice *promised* a constitution. Austria and England had held out hopes of union and freedom to the Italians. And the Spanish rebels had adopted a free constitution for their country.

Thus the Liberals of Europe had greeted Napoleon's overthrow with joyous acclaim; but soon it seemed that Waterloo had done little toward freeing Europe. It simply "replaced one insolent giant by a swarm of swaggering pygmies." The allied despots had used the peoples to overthrow a rival despot, and then they betrayed the peoples and recalled their promises only as a jest. A few months after Waterloo, the English poet Byron lamented that "the chain of banded nations has been broke in vain by the accord of raised-up millions"; and, "standing on an Empire's dust" at the scene of the great battle, and noting "how that red rain has made the *harvest* grow," he mused: —

> "*Gaul* may champ the bit and foam in fetters,
> But is *Earth* more free?
> Did nations combat to make *one* submit,
> Or league to teach *all* kings true sovereignty? . . .
> Then o'er *one* fallen despot boast no more."

The Germanic Confederation

Metternich's *chief* victory at the Congress of Vienna lay in *the new organization of Germany*. No one thought of restoring the discredited Holy Roman Empire. Liberal Germany, represented by Stein (p. 322), had hoped for a *real* union, either in a consolidated German Empire or in a new federal state. But Metternich saw that in a true *German* empire, Austria (with her Slav, Hungarian, and Italian interests) could not long keep the lead against Prussia. He preferred to leave the various states practically independent, so that Austria, the largest of all, might play them off against one another. The small rulers, too, were hostile to a real union, because it would limit their sovereignties. Metternich allied himself, in the Congress, with these princes of the small states, and won. The thirty-eight German states were organized into a "Germanic

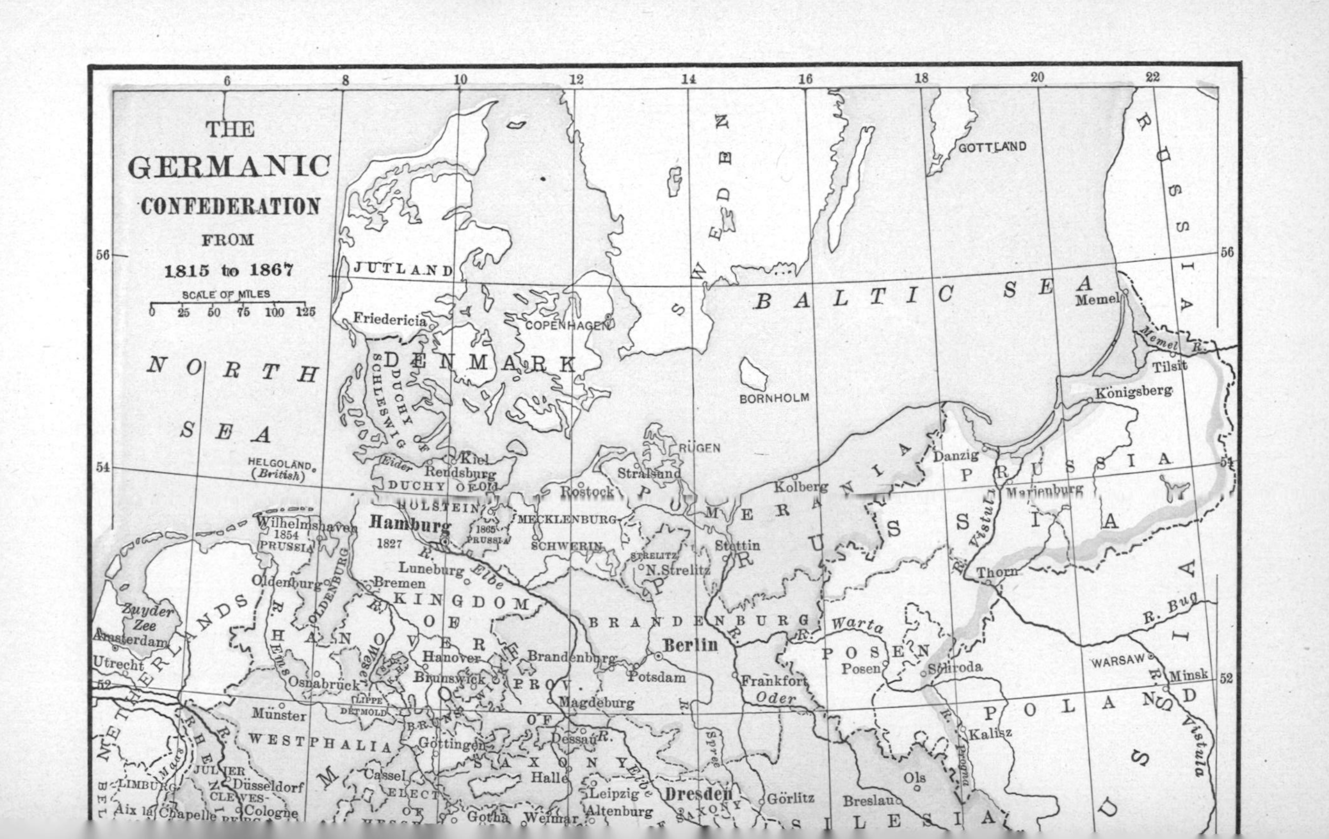
THE GERMANIC CONFEDERATION FROM 1815 to 1867
SCALE OF MILES
0 25 50 75 100 125
NORTH SEA
HELGOLAND (British)
JUTLAND
Friedericia
DENMARK
COPENHAGEN
DUCHY SCHLESWIG
Eider
Kiel
Rendsburg
DUCHY OF HOLSTEIN
Hamburg
1827
1865 PRUSSIA
Wilhelmshaven
1854 PRUSSIA
OLDENBURG
Oldenburg
Bremen
Luneburg
Elbe
KINGDOM OF HANOVER
Hanover
Brunswick
LIPPE
DETMOLD
Osnabrück
Ems
Weser
Münster
WESTPHALIA
Göttingen
Cassel
ELECT
Gotha
Weimar
Halle
Leipzig
Altenburg
Dresden
SAXONY
PROV. OF SAXONY
Magdeburg
Dessau
Brandenburg
Potsdam
Berlin
BRANDENBURG
Spree
Frankfort
Oder
Görlitz
Breslau
SILESIA
Ols
MECKLENBURG-SCHWERIN
STRELITZ
N.Strelitz
Rostock
Stralsund
RÜGEN
POMERANIA
Stettin
Kolberg
BORNHOLM
BALTIC SEA
SWEDEN
GOTTLAND
Danzig
Marienburg
Vistula
Thorn
PRUSSIA
Königsberg
Tilsit
Memel
Memel R.
RUSSIA
POSEN
Posen
Warta
Kalisz
Prosna
POLAND
WARSAW
Minsk
R. Bug
Vistula
NETHERLANDS
Zuyder Zee
Amsterdam
Utrecht
RHENISH PR.
JULIER
CLEVES-
LIMBURG
Maas
Düsseldorf
Cologne
Aix la Chapelle
56
54
52
6
8
10
12
14
16
18
20
22

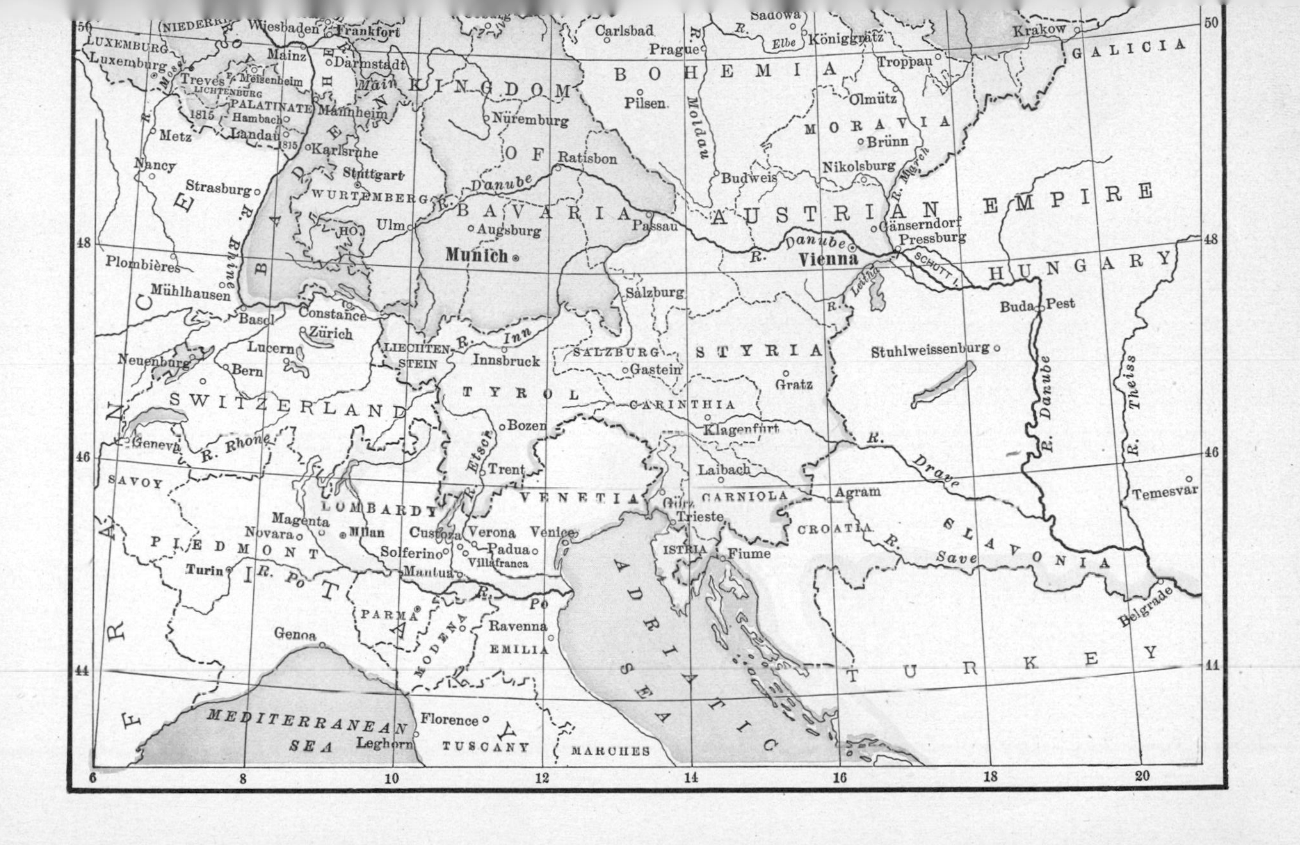

KINGDOM OF BAVARIA
AUSTRIAN EMPIRE
BOHEMIA
MORAVIA
GALICIA
HUNGARY
FRANCE
BADEN
WURTEMBERG
HO.
PALATINATE
LICHTENBURG
LUXEMBURG
SWITZERLAND
LIECHTENSTEIN
TYROL
SALZBURG
STYRIA
CARINTHIA
CARNIOLA
CROATIA
SLAVONIA
ISTRIA
VENETIA
LOMBARDY
PIEDMONT
SAVOY
ITALY
PARMA
MODENA
EMILIA
TUSCANY
MARCHES
TURKEY
ADRIATIC SEA
MEDITERRANEAN SEA
Luxemburg
Treves
Metz
Nancy
Strasburg
Plombières
Mühlhausen
Wiesbaden
Frankfort
Mainz
Darmstadt
Mannheim
Hambach
Landau
Karlsruhe
Stuttgart
Ulm
Augsburg
Munich
Nüremburg
Ratisbon
Passau
Carlsbad
Prague
Pilsen
Sadowa
Königgrätz
Budweis
Troppau
Olmütz
Brünn
Nikolsburg
Gänserndorf
Pressburg
Vienna
Krakow
Buda
Pest
Stuhlweissenburg
Temesvar
Belgrade
Salzburg
Gastein
Gratz
Klagenfurt
Laibach
Agram
Görz
Trieste
Fiume
Innsbruck
Bozen
Trent
Verona
Venice
Padua
Villafranca
Custozza
Solferino
Mantua
Milan
Magenta
Novara
Turin
Genoa
Ravenna
Florence
Leghorn
Basel
Constance
Zürich
Lucern
Bern
Neuenburg
Geneva
R. Rhine
R. Main
R. Moselle
R. Danube
R. Inn
R. Elbe
R. Moldau
R. March
R. Leitha
R. Drave
R. Save
R. Theiss
R. Etsch
R. Po
R. Rhone
SCHUTT I.
1815
6
8
10
12
14
16
18
20
44
46
48
50

Confederation," *a loose league of sovereigns.* (Thirty-four of the members were sovereign princes; the other four were the governments of the surviving "free cities," — Hamburg, Bremen, Lübeck, and Frankfort.) Each state controlled its own government, its own army, its own tariffs, and its own foreign diplomacy. They even kept the right to form alliances with foreign powers, — although they did promise not to make war upon one another.

The Confederacy had no distinct executive, judicial, and legislative departments. Its *one* organ was a Federal Diet at Frankfort. This was merely *a standing conference of ambassadors* appointed by the sovereigns: no important action could be taken without the consent of *every* state. Before many years the Diet was the laughingstock of Europe. "It was not a government at all: it was a polite and ceremonious way of doing nothing."

A few constitutions

But though the chance for making one German nation had been lost, *the Liberals still hoped,* for a time, for free political institutions in *the separate states.* Within the next four years, constitutions *were* granted by the liberal Grand Duke of Weimar and by the rulers of Nassau and of the four South German states, Wurtemberg, Bavaria, Baden, and Hesse-Darmstadt. (Germany south of the river Main is known as South Germany.) The people in these southern districts had been greatly influenced by the French Revolution, and their rulers made these grants largely in order to secure popular support against possible encroachments of Austria or Prussia upon their territory. The constitutions left the princes still the real rulers of their states; but they provided for *equality of all classes before the law,* for *freedom of the press,* and for *representative assemblies with control over new taxes.* (Most taxes continued from year to year, without new enactment.)

King Frederick William III of Prussia, also, appointed a committee to draw up the constitution he had promised (p. 336). But he was a weak, vacillating man, and greatly influenced by the nobles, who railed bitterly at the idea of free institutions.

The committee dawdled along for four years, and finally the king repudiated his pledge.

Disappointment and radical agitation

Outside the Rhine districts the Liberals were not numerous, but the group was influential, — made up of writers, journalists, students, professors, and most of the rest of the small educated middle class. By 1817, they had become indignant at the delays and evasions by which promised constitutions were withheld. In October, the three-hundredth anniversary of Luther's defiance of the pope and the fourth anniversary of the Battle of Leipzig were celebrated together at the Wartburg castle in the Duchy of Weimar. The Jena University students turned the celebration into a demonstration of liberal feeling. They sang patriotic and religious songs, made a few ardent speeches, and, in the evening, threw some old textbooks into a bonfire, — having first labeled them with the names of reactionary works especially hated by the Liberal party.

This boyish ebullition threw sober statesmen into spasms of fear, and seemed to them to prelude a revolutionary "Reign of Terror." Metternich took shrewd advantage of the opportunity to wean the king of Prussia from his earlier liberalism. Unhappily, Metternich's hand was strengthened by the foolish crimes of some Liberal enthusiasts. A small section of radical agitators preached that even assassination in the cause of liberty was right; and, in 1819, a fanatical student murdered Kotzebue, a Russian representative in Germany, who was supposed to be drawing the Tsar away from his earlier liberal sympathies.

The Karlsbad Decrees

Metternich was prompt to seize the chance. He at once called the leading sovereigns of Germany to a conference at Karlsbad. There he secured their approval for a series of resolutions, which he afterward forced through the Diet at Frankfort. These Karlsbad Decrees of 1819 were especially directed against *free speech* in the press and in the universities. They forbade secret societies among students; they appointed a government official in every university to discharge any professor who should preach doctrines "hostile to the public order"; they set up a rigid censorship of all printed matter; and they created a standing committee to hunt down conspiracies.

For thirty years the Karlsbad Decrees remained the fundamental law of the Germanic Confederacy; and under them thousands of enthusiastic youths were sent into exile or to prison for long terms, for singing forbidden patriotic songs, or for wearing the colors black, red, and orange, — the colors of the old Empire, now adopted as the symbol of German unity. "Turnvater Jahn," the organizer of the patriotic Turner societies in the time of Napoleon, and the poet Arndt whose songs had done much to arouse the people against French rule, were both persecuted. Learned professors who would not consent to be completely muzzled were driven from the universities. Men ceased to talk politics, and left matters of government to princes. Germany was started upon the incline down which she was to slide to a fatal abyss.

For Further Reading. — The most desirable general treatment of the nineteenth century for high schools is Hazen's *Europe Since 1815*. Duplicate copies of this work will be better than a multiplicity of references; but students should have access also to Andrews' *Modern Europe* and Seignobos' *Europe Since 1814*. Carlton Hayes' *Modern Europe*, II, deals with the period 1815–1915 in an exceedingly interesting way, but from a more "radical" view-point than the other works mentioned here.

CHAPTER XXI

THE SOUTH OF EUROPE — REVOLUTIONS OF 1820

The Spanish "Constitution of 1812"

The first attacks upon Metternich's system came from the South of Europe. To understand them we must turn back a moment to notice conditions in Spain. The Spanish patriots who rose in 1808 against Napoleon (p. 318) found themselves without a government. Their king was in the hands of the French The insurgent leaders came largely from the small, educated middle class, who had been converted to the ideals of the early French Revolution. These leaders set up a representative assembly (the Cortes), and, in 1812, they adopted a liberal constitution. This "Constitution of 1812" was modeled largely upon the French Constitution of 1791, and it was the standard about which the Liberals of southern Europe were to rally for a generation.

Independence of Spanish America

Meantime, when Napoleon seized Spain, the Spanish American states refused to recognize his authority, and so became virtually independent under governments of their own. At first, most of these new governments were in name loyal to the Spanish crown. During the next few years, however, the Spanish Americans experienced the benefits of freedom and of free trade with the world, and began to follow the example of the United States, which had so recently been merely a group of European colonies. By 1820, all the Spanish states on the continent of America had become virtually independent nations[1] — in which movement they had been directly encouraged by England and the United States.

Restoration of Ferdinand

After the fall of Napoleon, the Spanish king, Ferdinand, returned to his throne. He had promised to maintain the new

[1] Special report: the story of the heroic Bolivar.

constitution; but he soon broke his pledges, restored all the old iniquities, and cruelly persecuted the Liberal heroes of the "war of liberation."

The Spanish Revolution of 1820

In 1820 he collected troops to subdue the revolted American colonies; but the service was unpopular, and one of the regiments, instead of embarking, raised the standard of revolt and proclaimed the Constitution of 1812. Tumult followed in Madrid. The king, cowardly as he was treacherous, yielded, called the Cortes, and restored the constitution.

Revolution spreads through the South of Europe

This Spanish Revolution of 1820 became the signal for like attempts in other states. Before the year closed, *Portugal* and *Naples* both forced their kings to grant constitutions modeled upon that of Spain. Early in the next year, the people and army of Piedmont [1] rebelled, to secure a constitution for the Kingdom of Sardinia. Lombardy and Venetia stirred restlessly in the overpowering grasp of Austria. And the Greeks began a long and heroic struggle for independence against Turkey.

This wide-spread unanimity of action was due in part to secret revolutionary societies, already in existence. The most important of these was the *Carbonari* ("charcoal burners"). It had been formed in Italy in the time of Napoleon, to drive out the French, and was continued there to drive out Austrian rule and to unite Italy.

We have seen how Metternich used the Germanic Confederacy, designed for protection against foreign attack, to stifle liberalism in Germany. We are now to observe how he adroitly twisted an alliance of monarchs from its original purpose in order to crush these revolutions in Southern Europe.

Intervention by "the Holy Alliance"

After Waterloo, while the four "Allies" were still in Paris (November 20, 1815), they agreed to preserve their union and to hold meetings from time to time. The purpose was to guard against any future aggression by France. But when the

[1] Piedmont ("Foot of the Mount") was the district between the Alps and the plains of Lombardy. It was the most important part of the Kingdom of Sardinia.

revolutions of 1820 began, Metternich assembled the *absolute* sovereigns of Austria, Russia, and Prussia in a "Congress" at Troppau, where they signed gladly a declaration that they would *intervene* to put down revolution against any established government. This principle of "*intervention*" was a proclamation that the "divine right" monarchs would support one another against the nations. It was directed against the right of a people to make its government for itself.

England protests

England protested against this doctrine, both before and after the meeting, and formulated in opposition to it the principle of "non-intervention." This was the doctrine that each nation should manage its internal affairs as it chose. On this issue, England now withdrew from the alliance of 1815. Undaunted by England's protests, however, a decision to enforce the Troppau program was adopted by the united eastern despots, known popularly from this time as *the Holy Alliance*.

This name belongs strictly not to this outgrowth of the political alliance of November, 1815, but to a wholly different league organized two months earlier by the Tsar, under the influence of strong religious emotion. In September, 1815, Alexander had presented to the monarchs a brief agreement whereby the signers would promise to govern their respective peoples as "branches of one Christian nation" in accordance with "the precepts of justice, charity, and *peace*." (*Pennsylvania Reprints*, I, No. 3.) No one took very seriously this "pious verbiage," as Metternich called it, except the Tsar himself and his friend Frederick William of Prussia; but, from motives of courtesy, it was signed by every Christian ruler on the continent, except the pope. This League called itself the "Holy Alliance," but it never had existence except on paper. *Its name came to be applied to the Troppau league*, — so different in composition and purpose. The confusion was helped by the fact that the three despotic sovereigns who signed the Troppau agreement were also the *first three signers* of the "Holy Alliance."

But Italian constitutions are crushed

The first success of the despot league came in divided and helpless Italy. A few months after Troppau, the three allied monarchs met again at Laibach. With them now was Ferdinand of Naples, another treacherous Bourbon king. He had sworn solemnly to uphold the new Neapolitan constitution

(p. 341), and had invoked the vengeance of Heaven upon his head if he should prove unfaithful. But at the moment of these protestations he was in secret correspondence with Metternich, and now he came to Laibach for help to regain his absolutism. The Laibach meeting sent an Austrian army to Naples. The Neapolitans were defeated; and Ferdinand returned, surrounded by Austrian bayonets, to glut his vengeance upon the Liberals, with dungeon and scaffold.

Three days after the Neapolitan defeat came a revolt in Piedmont (March 10, 1821). The "Congress of Laibach" promptly marched eighty thousand Austrians into North Italy, while one hundred thousand Russians were held ready to support them; and the Piedmontese were easily crushed.

Spanish constitutionalism crushed

Flushed with success, the "Holy Alliance" determined next to overthrow also the Spanish constitution, from which the "contagion of liberty" had spread. In 1822 the despotic Powers were summoned to a Congress at Verona, and now they were joined by France. England again protested vigorously. The French representative tried to reconcile England by pleading that a constitution might be all very well in Spain, but that it should be a constitution *granted by the king*, not one *forced upon him* by rebels against his authority. Wellington, the English representative, Tory though he was, fitly answered this "divine right" plea: "Do you not know, sir, that it is not kings who make constitutions, but constitutions that make kings?"

But, against this "Holy Alliance" of despots, England could do no more than protest, so far as war upon the continent was concerned; and, with the sanction of the "crowned conspirators of Verona" (as Sydney Smith called them in England), a French army restored the old absolutism in Spain. Then the Bourbon Ferdinand in Spain, like his namesake in Naples, busied himself for many months in a *reactionary* "Reign of Terror" — infinitely more despicable, more senseless, more cruel, and more harmful, than any that "revolutionists" in Europe have ever perpetrated. (Cf. pp. 110, 143.) Meantime Metternich was congratulating himself with "pious" blasphemy, "God seems willing to use me as his instrument to restore order to Europe."

The next wish of the "Holy Alliance" was to restore monarchic control in the revolted Spanish colonies. But here they failed. On the sea England was supreme. The Allies could not reach America without her consent, and she made it known that she would oppose the intended expedition with all her great might. Once more, as in Napoleon's day and in Philip II's, and now again in the Hohenzollerns', the English sea power saved liberty.

Spanish America saved by England and the Monroe Doctrine

America shares in the credit of checking the despots. Canning, the English minister, urged the United States to join England in an alliance to protect Spanish America. The United States chose to act without formal alliance,[1] but it did act along the same lines. President Monroe's message to Congress in 1823 announced to the world that this country would oppose any attempt of the despotic Powers to extend their "political system" to America.[2] Probably the decided position of *either* England or the United States would have caused the Powers to abandon their project. Acting together, the two nations were certainly irresistible in America; and the "Holy Alliance" quietly dropped its plan.

When reproached afterward, in Parliament, for not having done more to preserve constitutionalism in Spain, Canning replied with the proud boast, "I called the New World into existence to redress the balance of the Old." It is possible to argue that both America and England acted from selfish motives, rather than from love of liberty. England wanted to keep her commerce with the free Spanish states; and the United States objected to the neighborhood of a strong Power that might interfere with her leadership or with her safety. There is no doubt, however, that, along with these proper though selfish motives, both countries were actuated also by principle and by sympathy with freedom.

[1] See West's *American People*, p. 425 ff.

[2] This is one part of the famous Monroe Doctrine.

The accusation against Canning and the tone of his reply show what the real feeling of the English people was.

Almost at once Metternich met another check, in the affairs of Greece. The rising there had been accompanied by terrible massacres of all Turks dwelling in the country, and the exasperated Turkish government was now putting down the rebellion by a war of extermination. For a time Metternich hoped to bring about intervention by the allied Powers to restore Turkish authority; but he failed from two causes.

Greek independence secured

1. *The educated classes of Western Europe had been nourished mainly on the ancient Greek literature* (p. 132), and now their imagination was fired by the thought that this struggle against the Turks was a contest akin to that ancient war against the Persians which Herodotus, Xenophon, Plutarch, and Æschylus had made glorious to them. The man who did most to widen this sympathy was Byron, the English poet. He closed a career of mingled genius and generosity and wrongdoing by a noble self-devotion, giving fortune and life to the Greek cause; and his poems, invoking the magic of the old names of Marathon and Salamis, stirred Europe to passionate enthusiasm. No schoolboy to-day can read the stirring lyric, "The Isles of Greece," without quicker pulse-beat; but the European youth of Byron's time were moved more deeply than the present generation can easily understand by the allusions in such passages as these:

> "Standing on the Persian's grave,
> I could not deem myself a slave";
>
> . . . .
>
> "Ye have the letters Cadmus gave;
> Think ye he meant them for a slave!"

Numbers of volunteers followed Byron to fight for Greek liberty, and before any government had taken action, the Turks complained that they had to fight all Europe.

2. *The Russian people, untouched by this Western passion, still felt a deep sympathy for the Greeks as their co-religionists,* and a

deeper hatred for the Turks as their hereditary foes; and so Metternich lost his chief ally. For though the Tsar at first discountenanced the Greek rising, and even punished Russian officers who had encouraged it, still he was too much influenced by the feeling of his people to join in open intervention against the revolution.

Battle of Navarino

Finally, indeed, intervention came, but *for* the Greeks, not against them. The English, French, and Russian fleets had proceeded to Greece to enforce a truce, so as to permit negotiation. The three fleets were acting together under the lead of the English admiral, who happened to be the senior officer. Almost by chance, and chiefly through the excited feelings of the common sailors, the fleets came into conflict with the Turkish fleet, and annihilated it in the battle of *Navarino* (October, 1827). The English commander had gone beyond his instructions, but excited public feeling gave the government no chance to disown him. So the three Powers forced Turkey to grant independence to the Greeks.

Elsewhere, however, Metternich was triumphant. Distant Greece did not affect his system in Western Europe — and the success of the Greeks did not come anyway for many years. For ten years after the overthrow of the gallant Spanish Revolution, the reactionists had things their own way from England to Greece.

The next attack on Metternich's system came from France in 1830. That story demands that we survey the story of France from Waterloo.

CHAPTER XXII

FRANCE AND THE REVOLUTIONS OF 1830

When Louis XVIII became king (p. 325), he saw that France must have some guarantee of the personal rights which the Revolution had won. He refused indeed to accept a constitution which the old Senate of Napoleon tried to force upon him, but he himself *gave* to the nation the "*Charter of 1815.*" In this way he saved the theory of "divine right." The preamble expressly declared the king the source of all authority. But the provisions of the document, otherwise, closely resembled the rejected constitution, and *gave the people of France more liberty than any other large country on the continent then had.*

The Bourbon "divine right" monarchy

The legislature had two Houses, — the *Peers*, appointed for life by the king, and the *Deputies*. These last were elected; but a very high property qualification let only one man in seventy vote. To be eligible for *election*, a man had to be still more wealthy, — so much so that in some districts it was hard to find any one to send to the legislature. The king kept an *absolute veto* and *the sole right to propose laws.*

The "Charter of 1815"

Purchasers of the *church lands* (confiscated and sold during the Revolution) were guaranteed in title. Religious liberty, equality before the law, free speech, and freedom of the press were confirmed. In local government, the centralized system of Napoleon was retained.

In 1824 Louis was succeeded by his brother, Charles X, who was an extreme reactionary. He wanted to restore lands to the church, to give it control of all education and to punish all old Revolutionists. By force and fraud, aided by the limitations on voting, the government secured a reactionary legislature. Then the king and legislature curtailed the free-

Charles X attempts further reaction

dom of the press, closed the historical lectures of the famous Guizot (a very moderate Liberal), joined the other crowned conspirators of Verona in overthrowing liberty in Spain (p. 343), plundered $200,000,000 from the national treasury for returned Emigrants, and strengthened still further the influence of the oligarchy by giving the largest landlords a double vote.

Even this legislature, however, annoyed Charles because of the vigorous protests of the few Liberals; and in 1827 he dissolved it, expecting under the new law to secure a still more submissive body.

The issue was drawn clearly. Thiers, a brilliant young journalist, preached the constitutional theory in the words "The king *reigns*, but does not *govern*," and he made repeated and significant references in his paper to the English Revolution of 1688. On the other hand, Charles announced frankly that he regarded the legislature only as an *advisory* council.

The elections showed that even the narrow body of voters was earnestly opposed to the king's doctrine. The intellect of France and the influential part of the press were with the Liberal party; and, despite all court influence, the Liberals received a decisive majority.

When Charles still tried to rule through a ministry of Ultras, the Assembly issued a bold address (March 2, 1830), calling for the dismissal of the ministry, that "menace to public safety." The address was carried by a vote of 221 to 182. Charles at once dissolved the Chamber. Public interest was intense, and the aged Lafayette journeyed through France to organize the Liberals for the contest at the polls. The new elections in June destroyed the Ultra party. Every deputy who had voted against the ministry was reëlected, and the Liberals gained also fifty of the remaining seats.

The "July Ordinances" of 1830

Twice defeated by the votes of even the oligarchic landlords, but no whit daunted, the stubborn monarch tried a *coup d'état*. He suspended the Charter by a series of edicts, known as the July Ordinances. These Ordinances (1) forbade the publication of newspapers without royal approval, (2) dissolved the new legislature (which had not yet met), (3) promulgated a new law for elections so as to put control even more into the hands of reactionaries, and (4) ordered the election of another legislature.

Metternich had foreseen this deed, and its probable result. He lamented the free press and the representative system in France; but he warned the French ambassador that an attempt now to do away with these "plague spots" would ruin the dynasty: "The men of lead," said he, "are on the side of the Constitution; Charles X should remember 1789."

The Ordinances were published July 26, 1830. Forty-one journalists of Paris at once printed a protest, declaring the ordinances illegal and calling upon France to resist them. The journalists had in mind only *legal* resistance, not violence; but there were in Paris a few old Revolutionists who were ready to go further, and they were powerful in a crisis because of their organization in secret societies.

The same evening these radicals decided upon revolt, and appointed "Committees of Insurrection" for the various districts of the city. The next morning angry crowds thronged the streets, and threw up barricades out of paving stones. That night Lafayette reached Paris, to take charge of the revolt, and on the following morning the fighting began.

The "July Days"

The 28th, 29th, and 30th are the "Three Days of July." On the 28th the crowd cried, "Down with the ministry!" but, as their blood became heated with fighting, they began to shout, "Down with the Bourbons!" The regular troops lacked good leadership, and they hated to fire on the rebel flag, — *the old tricolor*. About four thousand men were slain in the three days. At his palace at St. Cloud, in the suburbs, the king hunted as usual; and, on each evening, messengers from the sorely beset troops were kept waiting overnight, so as not to disturb the royal game of whist, while the scepter was slipping forever from the old line of "divine-right" French kings. Suddenly Charles opened his eyes to his danger, and fled to England. *Outside Paris, there was no fighting, but the nation gladly accepted this "Second French Revolution."*

The end of divine-right in France

A limited monarchy

The "Divine-Right monarchy" in France was replaced by a constitutional kingship. The legislature, which Charles had tried to dissolve, restored the tricolor as the flag of France, made the Charter into a more liberal constitution, and then offered the crown to Louis Philippe (a distant cousin of Charles), *on condition that he accept this amended Charter.* The old Charter had declared that the king ruled "by the grace of God." The new document added the words, "*and by the will of the nation.*" In actual fact, Louis XVIII had ruled *by hereditary title,* and *had given* a charter to France. Louis Philippe, "King of the Barricades," ruled *by election,* and *a constitution was imposed upon him.*

The Charter amended

In this vital respect, the Second French Revolution corresponded to the English Revolution of 1688. In other ways it did not go so far. It did (1) give to the legislature the right to introduce bills, and (2) double the number of voters, extending the franchise to all who paid forty dollars in direct taxes, and lowering the age qualifications from forty years to thirty years. *This still left twenty-nine men out of thirty without votes,* making a voting body of less than 200,000 in a total population of some 30,000,000.

As a youth Louis Philippe had taken the side of the First Revolution in 1789, and had fought gallantly in the French Revolutionary armies, until the extremists drove him into exile. Then, instead of joining the royalist emigrants in their attacks on France, he had fled to England and America, — where he earned his living by teaching French.

Spread of revolution

This "Second French Revolution" was followed by revolts over all Europe. For a moment, Metternich's system tottered. Belgium broke away from the king of Holland, to whom the Congress of Vienna had given it. Poland rose against the Tsar, to whom the Congress had given it. The *states of Italy* rose against Austria and the Austrian satellites, to whom the Congress had given them. And in Germany there were uprisings in all absolutist states, to demand the constitutions which the Congress had *not* given.

The final gains, however, were not so vast as at first they

Gains and losses in 1830

seemed. Belgium did become an independent monarchy, with the most liberal constitution on the continent. To that country as well as to France the Revolution brought permanent profit. Indeed France joined England in protecting Belgium against "intervention" — so that Metternich called London and Paris "the two mad-houses of Europe." A chief gain of the 1830 revolutions was that constitutional France was definitely lost to the divine-right Holy Alliance.

But Tsar Nicholas crushed the Poles, took away the constitution that Alexander had given them during his rule, and made Alexander's "Kingdom of Poland" into a mere Russian province. Austria crushed the Italian revolts. And though four small German states secured constitutions, still the general despotic character of the Germanic Confederacy was not modified. While Austria was busied in Italy, it is true, there had seemed some hope of progress for Germany; but Metternich soon had his hands free, and at once he set about restoring "order."

Still, reaction had lost much of its vigor and confidence, and it was being slowly undermined by a quiet but growing public opinion. Metternich's genius sufficed to keep his system standing, as long as it was not disturbed from without; but when the next year of Revolutions came, that system fell forever in Western Europe.

That successful "Revolution of 1848" began in France, but it was to be the work of a new class of workingmen, — factory workers, — who themselves were the product of a new industrial system that had grown up first in England. We must go back for that story (see Part VI below).

PART VI

ENGLAND AND THE INDUSTRIAL REVOLUTION

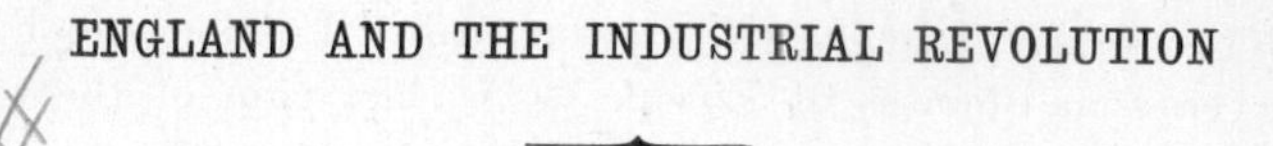

CHAPTER XXIII

THE REVOLUTION IN METHODS OF WORK

While France was giving the world her first great social and political revolution, with noise and blood, toward the close of the eighteenth century, England had been working out quietly an even greater revolution which was to change the work and daily life of the masses of men and women and children over all the world. This "revolution" was at first a change in the ways in which certain kinds of work were done; so we call it "the Industrial Revolution."

The "Industrial Revolution"

Not all the legislation of the great French Convention of '93, nor Napoleon's "forty victories," nor even his code that would "live forever," nor the assembled statesmen at Vienna, — nor all these together, — had so much to do in deciding how you and I should live to-day as did this Industrial Revolution which we are now to study. It was not wrought by kings, or diplomats, or generals, or even by dazzling intellectual geniuses, but by humble workers busied in homely toil, puzzling day after day over wheels and belts and rollers and levers, seeking some way to save time.

Little change in industry for 1000 years before 1750

Our life and labor differs far more widely from that of our great-great-grandfathers in the time of the American Revolution, than their life and labor differed from that of men in the time of Charlemagne a thousand years before. In the days of Voltaire and George Washington, men raised grain, and wove cloth, and carried their spare products to market, in almost precisely the same way in which these things had been done for four thousand or six thousand years. The discovery of America had added corn (maize) and he potato to the world's food plants, and had enormously increased the production of sugar (in the West Indies) and so made its use more general. But in Europe itself a farmer rarely had as great a variety of vegetables in his garden as the ancient Egyptian or Roman farmer had. The English or American or French farmer with strenuous toil scratched the soil with a clumsy wooden plow not unlike those shown on Egyptian monuments six thousand years old. He had no other machine for horses to draw, except a rude harrow and a cart, almost as ancient in style. He sowed his grain by hand, cut it with the sickle of ancient times, and threshed it out with the prehistoric flail, if he did not tread it out on his barn floor by cattle, as the old Egyptians did.

Carpenters' tools, too, did not differ much, either in number or style, from a set, four thousand years old, found recently in Crete. Blacksmiths and masons used tools as ancient in origin. The seventeenth century had seen the invention of sawmills driven by water power (like the earlier grist mills); but these only cut the logs into rough boards. All planing and other dressing of lumber was still done by hand, as was also all the work now done by machines in furniture factories and joiners' shops. Merchandise was still carried from place to place on pack horses or mules, or sometimes in clumsy carts sinking to the axles in muddy roads; and travel was mainly on horseback, though slow coaches toiled along on a few main roads, six horses to each vehicle.

Household lights were still dim, ill-smelling candles or smoky and flaring torches. If a householder carelessly let the fire in his fireplace go out, he borrowed live coals from a neighbor, or struck sparks into tinder with flint and steel. If man or child had to have an arm amputated, the pain had to be borne without the merciful aid of anesthetics. The few cities were still medieval. London and Vienna boasted of lamp posts, but the dim light was supplied by a poorly burning oil. In Paris, on the main streets, the mud lay a foot deep in rainy weather.

Arthur Young, in 1787, wrote of Paris, — "Walking, which in London is so pleasant and clean *that ladies do it every day* (!), is here a toil and a fatigue to a man, and an impossibility to a well-dressed woman."

The revolution in English agriculture

The first improvements came in England — in agriculture. Early in the eighteenth century, landlords had introduced *a better system of "crop-rotation,"* raising roots like beets and

FARM TOOLS IN 1800: all shown here except the wagon.

turnips on the field formerly left fallow (p. 67). This proved just as good for the ground, and the added root crops made it possible *to feed more cattle.* Besides the direct profits, the additional cattle furnished more manure, which *enriched the soil* and increased all crops. English gentlemen, accordingly, felt encouraged *to breed better cattle and sheep,* and so to produce more beef and wool.

Mechanical invention in agriculture came a little later. In 1785 the *first threshing machine* was invented, and enterprising "gentlemen farmers" soon began to use it; but it was exceedingly crude. The *cast-iron plow* appeared about 1800. This was soon to work a marvelous revolution in farming — permitting deeper plowing and more rapid work; but for some time, even in America, farmers were generally prejudiced against it, asserting that the iron "poisoned" the ground. The *cradle scythe* — a hand tool, but a vast improvement on the old sickle for harvesting grain — was patented *in America*

Modern Plowing — since 1900. The *tractor*, steam or gasoline, is an American invention. Note the width of the swath, and remember that the movement forward is much more rapid than any horse can plow. Note, too, the comfort in which the men work.

in 1803. Drills, seeders, mowers, reapers, binders, were still in the future; but in 1800 the era of farm machinery was just at hand.

The revolution in transportation

When these changes in agricultural *production* were just beginning, there came also a change in transportation. England began to improve her main roads about 1750, building "turnpikes," with frequent barriers where tolls were collected from travelers to keep up repairs. A Scotch engineer, MacAdam, gave his name to "macadamized roads." Before the American Revolution began, Englishmen were boasting of the "astounding change" in rapidity of travel and transport of goods.

A SPINNING WHEEL still in use in Switzerland. Its use is common also in rural parts of the Balkans and of Scandinavia.

In a few years they had even better reason for such boasts. The ancient Egyptians and Babylonians had dug canals and used them to carry goods. Louis XIV and Frederick the

Great had constructed a few in France and Prussia. But now England gave canals a wholly new importance in commerce. The first one with a system of locks, to permit a boat to pass from one level to another, was built in 1761, to bring coal to Manchester from a mine seven miles away. And before 1800, England was better supplied with canals than she had been with roads in 1700. The boats were "towed"

Courtesy of the Great Falls Mfg. Company, Somersworth, N. H.

MODERN SPINNING MACHINERY.

by horses driven along a tow path. One horse could draw many times the weight he could draw on land over even the best roads, and most bulky merchandise was soon carried by the new water roads.

The revolution in spinning

The change that was really to revolutionize the working society, however, came not in farming nor in transportation, but in manufacturing, — and first in spinning. In Queen Elizabeth's time the fiber of flax or wool was drawn into thread by the distaff and spindle, as among the Stone Age "Lake Dwellers," four or five millenniums before. But in the seventeenth century in England, the distaff was replaced by the *spinning wheel,* — run first by one hand, but afterward by the foot of the spinner. Even the wheel, however (such as may now and then still be found tucked away in an old attic), drew out only *one thread at a time.* To spin thread enough to weave into the cloth for a family's clothing was a serious task. A weaver with his clumsy hand loom could weave all the thread that eight spinners could supply. Weavers didn't get thread fast enough, and soon after 1750 they began to think about swifter ways to secure it. In 1761 the English Royal Society for the Encouragement of Manufactures offered a prize for an invention for swifter spinning. Three years later, in 1764 (the last year of Louis XIV in France), an English weaver, *James Hargreaves,* noticed that his wife's spinning wheel, tipped over on the floor, kept whirling away for a surprising time. Taking a hint from this new position, he invented a machine where one wheel turned eight spindles, and spun *eight threads,* instead of one. Hargreaves called the new machine the "Jenny," from his wife's name. Soon it was improved so as to spin sixteen threads at a time.

Water power for hand power

The thread was not satisfactory, however, for all parts of cloth manufacture; but in 1775 *Richard Arkwright,* a barber and peddler, devised a new sort of spinner without spindles. He ran his wool or cotton through a series of rollers revolving at different rates, to draw out the thread; and he drove these rollers *by water power,* not by hand, and so called his machine a "*Water Frame.*" Four years later (1779), *Samuel Crompton,* an English weaver, ingeniously combined the best features of the "Jenny" and the "Water Frame" into a new machine which he called "*the mule*" — in honor of this mixed parentage. With "the mule," one spinner could spin *two hundred threads at a time.*

Crompton received $300 from the manufacturers, who piled up wealth from his invention! He was a shy man, who spent his life in poverty, making his "mule" and improving it. When he was sixty years old, Parliament gave him $25,000 (in 1820), as a recognition of his services to England; but he spent this in attempting new inventions, and died extremely poor, in 1827.

Two hundred threads seem few enough to us, acquainted with machinery such that a man, with one or two boys, winds

Copyright by Underwood and Underwood.

A PRIMITIVE LOOM IN JAPAN TO-DAY

twelve thousand spools at once; but in the latter part of the eighteenth century, "the mule" was a revolution, and it produced other revolutions. Now *the weavers had too much thread;* they could not keep up with the spinners, and *it was necessary to improve their processes.*

The revolution in weaving

The weavers still used the hand loom, older than any of the records of history. Threads were first drawn out lengthwise on a frame: this made the warp. Then the weaver drove his shuttle by hand back and forth between those threads with the woof (cross threads). *Edmund Cartwright*, a clergyman of the church of England, gave his energies to discovering a better process, and in 1784 (the year after England surrendered America) he patented a "*power loom*," in which the shuttle *threw itself back*

Courtesy of the Draper Company, Hopedale, Massachusetts.

A MODERN LOOM.

and forth automatically. Then the weavers could keep up easily; and by later improvements, before 1800, it became possible for one man to weave more cloth than two hundred could in 1770.

The cotton gin and the supply of cotton

The next need was more cotton ready to spin. Eli Whitney, in America, met this by inventing his *Cotton Gin*, wherewith one slave could clean as much fiber from the seed as three hundred had been able to clean before. This was in 1793. In that year the United States exported 200,000 pounds of cotton. In 1800 the amount was 20,000,000 pounds, and in 1803, 40,000,000 pounds. All this went to feed the new manufactures in England.

Two minor inventions accompanied these greater ones. Instead of bleaching cloth white slowly by air and sunshine, a

Courtesy of the Library of Congress.

AN EARLY COTTON GIN.

way was found to do it swiftly by using a chemical (chlorine). And instead of printing patterns on cotton cloth (calico) with little blocks, — first a block of one color, and then one of another, — the patterns were soon graven on rollers which printed all the colors at one time as the cloth passed over them.

The steam engine

The next need was a better power to drive the new machines. Water had largely replaced hand power; but water sometimes failed, and it was not present at all in many places where it would have been welcome. This need was supplied by *James Watt's* improvements on the *steam engine*.

The remarkable English friar, Roger Bacon (p. 103), before 1300, had speculated on the expansive power of steam as a motive power for the future, and a nobleman of Charles I's time is believed to have constructed a steam engine that pumped water; but, if he did, the invention and inventor both perished in the civil war between king and Parliament.[1] At all events, in the second half of the eighteenth century, steam engines had been invented that could pump water, and they were used to draw water out of flooded mines. These engines, however, had only an up-and-down movement; they were clumsy and slow; and they wasted steam and fuel. James Watt, an instrument-maker, was called upon to repair a model for such an engine, and became interested in removing these defects. By 1785, he had constructed engines that worked much more swiftly, economically, and powerfully, and *which could transmit their power to wheels* (and so drive machinery) by an arrangement of shafts and cranks.

In 1785 steam was first used to drive spinning machinery. Fifteen years later, there were more steam engines in England than water wheels, and four had found their way to America.

Improvements in working iron

One more series of inventions completed this wonderful circle of the eighteenth century, where one discovery had so led on to another. Engines and power machines could be built in a satisfactory manner only from iron; but in 1790 the manufacture of iron was still slow and costly, and the product was poor stuff. In that year, however, steam began to be used to furnish a new blowing apparatus which gave a *steady blast* of air, in place of the old bellows and like arrangements. This made possible more rapid and more perfect work in iron. Soon, too, new and better ways were found to change the brittle "castings" into malleable "wrought" iron.

Thus, by 1800, the "age of steam and iron" had begun in England, and to some degree in America. The continent of Europe

[1] George McDonald's *St. George and St. Michael* tells the story.

remained closed against it for some years longer, by Napoleon's Continental System; but on his fall it began to win its way there also.

Since prehistoric man found ways to make fire and bake pots and spin and weave (with spindle and loom) and extract iron from ore, there had been no change in man's work that compared in any degree with this tremendous revolution in the

Courtesy of the Colorado Fuel and Iron Company.

A PART OF THE STEEL WORKS IN PUEBLO, COLORADO, TO-DAY.

latter half of the eighteenth century. The American Revolution and even the greater French Revolution were dwarfed by the gigantic Industrial Revolution.

America and new inventions

Before we leave this age of invention, we must note two applications of the steam engine, and also a few separate inventions, in all of which America had a large share.

Some of Watt's engines, we said, found their way to America before 1800. Here, in that day, the chief need was locomotion.

And, since there was no time at first to build roads over our vast territory, we wanted first locomotion *by water*. Rivers were used to carry goods easily *down* the current; but some means to force a boat *upstream* was needed. Therefore, in America, ingenious mechanics at once sought to apply the new steam engine to navigation, — and produced the steamboat.

The steamboat

As early as 1789, *John Fitch*, a poor, unschooled carpenter with wonderful inventive genius, built a ferryboat with paddles driven by a steam engine of his own make. He even ran this boat up the river at Philadelphia, as well as down, and showed it there for some months. But men with money in America

THE CLERMONT. From the model in the National Museum at Washington.

were still old-fashioned; and Fitch could not raise money to extend the use of his invention. He next tried his fortune in the new West, where such motive power was sadly needed, but with no better success; and finally, in bitter disappointment and despair, he killed himself in a Kentucky tavern.

During those same years Philadelphia had another neglected genius, *Oliver Evans*, who also built a steam engine suited for locomotion; but, like Fitch, he failed to secure money to carry his invention to practical success. Soon after, however, *Robert Fulton* was more fortunate. He, too, met with one rebuff. He offered his steamboat to Napoleon as a means whereby that baffled conqueror might transport his waiting army from Boulogne to England, in spite of English sailing vessels (p. 316).

Happily for freedom, Napoleon repulsed him disdainfully and stupidly as a faker — and so lost the chance to become undisputed master of the world. And some three years later Fulton secured money from Chancellor Livingstone of New York. In 1807, amid jeers of the lookers-on, he launched *The Clermont*, furnished with an engine from England, and made a trial trip *up* the Hudson, from New York to Albany, at about five miles an hour. The next year a regular line of steamboats plied between the two cities, and men were eagerly waiting for them elsewhere.

In 1811 *The Orleans* was launched on the Ohio at Pittsburg, to voyage to the distant city for which it was named. The

First Steam Passenger Train in America (November 12, 1831). The engine was modeled upon Stephenson's "Rocket," which, some months before, had drawn a train from Manchester to Liverpool.

War of 1812 interrupted steamboat building, but in 1820 sixty such vessels plied the waters of the Ohio and Mississippi, and some of them were finding their way up the muddy Missouri, between herds of astonished buffalo.

The steam railway

If steam could drive boats, why not coaches on land? Experiments began at once for steam locomotives.

The horse "tramways" had been in use in England, especially at the mines, for many years — merely a short line of rails on which loaded carts could be drawn more easily than on the bare ground. Soon after 1800, a Cornishman, *Richard Trevethick*, used a steam engine to furnish the power for a short tramway; but this was merely a *stationary* engine of the ordinary type. The problem was to get a *traveling* engine. In 1811 John Stevens, in America, began twenty years of vain effort to interest moneyed men in his plan for such a "locomotive"; but success was won first in England by *George Stephenson,* who had spent his poor, unschooled boyhood in helping his father tend a stationary pumping engine in a coal mine.

In 1814, Stephenson completed a locomotive which was used to haul carts of coal on tramways from mines to a near-by canal.

HARVESTING IN 1831. McCormick's first successful horse-reaper. The "self-binder" was a later feature. Here the three women and one man are tying the grain into bundles. This photograph, based upon a "reconstruction," and the following one, are furnished by the International Harvester Company.

Then, in 1825, a *passenger* line, *twelve miles long,* was opened in England; and in 1828, in America, the aged Charles Carroll, one of the signers of the Declaration of Independence, drove the gold spike that marked the beginning of the great Baltimore and Ohio Railroad. *In 1833* a steam railway carried passengers from London to Liverpool in ten hours (a four-hour trip now), whereas the old stage-coach had taken sixty. The railway age had begun.

The tremendous importance of the railroad, however, did not show fully until some twenty years later. The early rails were of wood, protected from wear by a covering of iron "straps" — which had an awkward way of curling up at a loosened end. The cars were at first merely lines of "coaches," almost precisely the old stage-coaches. The *name* coach still remains in

HARVESTING TO-DAY. A Mogul Kerosene Tractor pulling two McCormick reapers and binders with mechanical shockers. The tractor is managed by the man on the front reaper. Two men take the place of six human beings in the previous cut and do many times as much work.

England, and the *form* was kept there, and elsewhere in Europe, until very recently; but in America a more convenient form was soon introduced. Fifteen miles an hour on early roads was thought quite amazing.

In many other ways, mechanical inventions began to affect human life soon after 1800. The rapidity with which they appeared may be judged partly from the records of the American

Other leading industrial inventions — to 1850

patent office. From 1790 to 1812 that office registered less than eighty new inventions a year. From 1812 to 1820 the number rose to about 200 a year, and in 1830 there were 544 new patents issued. Twenty years later the thousand mark was passed, and in 1860 there were five thousand.

These inventions mostly *saved time* or *helped to make life more comfortable or more attractive.* A few cases only can be mentioned from the bewildering mass. The *McCormick reaper* (to be drawn by horses) appeared in 1831, and multiplied the farmer's efficiency in the harvest field by twenty. (This released many men from food-production, and made more possible the growth of cities and of manufactures.) *Planing mills* created a new industry in woodworking. "*Colt's revolver*" (1835) replaced the one-shot "pistol." *Iron stoves* began to rival the ancient fireplace, especially for cooking. *Friction matches,* invented in England in 1827, were the first improvement on prehistoric methods of making fire. Illuminating gas, for lighting city streets, made better order possible at night, and helped improve public morals In 1838 the English *Great Western* (with *screw propeller* instead of side paddles, and with coal to heat its boilers) *established steam navigation between Europe and America.* The same year saw the first successful use of huge *steam hammers,* and of anthracite coal for smelting iron. In 1839 a Frenchman, Daguerre, began photography with his "daguerrotype." Still earlier, a French chemist had invented the canning of foods. In 1841 two Americans, Dr. Morton and Dr. Jackson, independently discovered the value of *ether as an anesthetic,* — an incomparable boon to suffering men and women. The *magnetic telegraph,* invented in 1835, was made effective in 1844. The Howe *sewing machine* was patented in 1846; and the next year saw the first *rotary printing press.*

This book does not plan to treat American history at large, because that subject receives better attention in separate volumes. But this topic of *invention* cannot be discussed without entering the American field. In 1820 a famous English writer, influenced partly by the ugly feeling awakened by the War of 1812, had exclaimed, — "Who in the four quarters of the globe reads an American book, . . . or drinks out of American glasses, . . . or sleeps in American blankets?" But in 1841 in Parliament a member of the English cabinet confessed that the great majority of helpful inventions came from America.

For Further Reading. — Cheyney, *Industrial and Social History of England*, 203–223; Hobson, *Evolution of Modern Capitalism*; Thurston, *Growth of the Steam Engine*.

CHAPTER XXIV

THE REVOLUTION IN THE WORKERS' LIVES

Rapid increase of wealth

The introduction of machinery and of steam power produced at once (by 1800) tremendous changes in the lives of all men, but especially of workingmen. With the new machinery, labor produced much more wealth. Robert Owen, a cloth manufacturer at New Lanark in Scotland, said in 1815 that his two thousand operatives produced more than all the workmen in Scotland forty years before.[1]

This change ought to have been purely good. It should have meant a gain for all the world. Especially it should have meant more comfort and more leisure for the workers. In practice, it meant something very different. Too large a share of the new wealth went to a new class of capitalists. This was not the fault of Hargreaves, Crompton, Watt, and their fellows: the fault lay in human society.

Gains and losses to the workers

Part of the increased wealth did go at last, and indirectly, to the common gain in lower prices. Every one, the workmen included, can buy cloth or hardware cheaper than before the Industrial Revolution began. This is a vast gain. It is the thing about the Revolution which justifies a vast deal of the suffering that it has caused. It makes possible more life and some better life.

But the revolution also resulted *directly* in much lower life for just those who, we should have supposed, would be the first benefited. This was particularly true in the beginning. To understand this we must look once more at the condition of workmen *before* the invention of machinery.

[1] Note that *wealth* is not money. It is any desirable thing produced or obtained by labor.

Workmen under the old "Domestic System"

Under the "domestic system" (p. 185) all manufactures had been handmade (as the word "manufacture" signifies). Hours of labor were long and profits were small, because there was little surplus wealth to divide. But workmen worked in their own homes, under reasonably wholesome conditions. Their labor was varied. They owned their own tools. They had considerable command over their hours of toil. Their condition resembled that of the farmer of to-day more than that of the modern factory worker.

Thus, in England and America especially, the artisan drew part of his support from the plot of ground about his cottage. Even the iron workers of Sheffield (famous for its cutlery since 1400) lived in little homes surrounded each by its garden where the workman could spend a dull season profitably. Defoe, the author of *Robinson Crusoe*, describes a like condition which he saw among the weavers in Yorkshire, about 1725:

> "The land was divided into small inclosures of from two acres to six or seven acres each, seldom more, every three or four pieces having a house belonging to them; hardly a house standing out of speaking distance from another. . . . At every considerable house there was a manufactory. Every clothier keeps one horse at least to carry his manufactures to market, and every one generally keeps a cow or two, or more, for his family. . . . The houses are full of lusty fellows, some at their dye vat, some at their looms, others dressing the cloth; the women and children carding or spinning, all being employed from the youngest to the eldest."

The tragedy of sudden change

But hand workmen could not match tireless iron machines driven by steam. They could not produce enough cloth — at the lower prices at which it was sold after 1800 — to support themselves even with the aid of their garden spots. The Industrial Revolution came swiftly — upturning the whole system of manufacturing before a hale man turned into an old one. The hand weavers were people slow to accept change. Many of them could not understand the drift of the times. They had gained, in generation after generation, a skill of which they were proud and which had made them envied by other workmen. They did not see how a new contrivance of wood and iron could make that painfully gained skill of hand a worthless thing and cast them down into the position of wholly unskilled workers. Great numbers of the old weavers kept up the losing fight, for their lifetime, under harsher and harsher conditions;[1] and, from time to time, such laborers rose in ignorant but natural riots to smash machinery and burn factories.

This sort of tragedy has been repeated time after time with millions of workers, as the Industrial Revolution (which is still in progress) has replaced one process by a quicker one. It happened not long ago, when the linotype replaced hand typesetting. Masses of workers have paid for every gain to the world by terrible personal loss that destroyed families and ruined lives. Society, which profits so splendidly, has not yet learned how to insure its workers against this unfair loss. But, in 1800, the thing was new. There was no accident insurance or old-age insurance or pension system, such as many countries are now coming to have; and the class of workmen who were ruined made a larger part of the total population than have ever again been so affected at one time.

Still the most serious evils in 1800 fell not upon the workmen who kept up this hopeless fight against steam and machinery, but upon the hundreds of thousands of workmen who accepted the change and tried to work under it.

The new Factory system

The new machinery was costly. Workmen could not own it as they had owned their old tools. Nor did they know how to combine to own it in groups. It all passed into the hands of wealthy men, who hired workers ("operatives") to "operate" it. This marks the beginning of a new organization of labor. The old slave system gave way to serfdom in agriculture and to a gild organization in manufactures. Gilds gave way to the domestic system. And now the domestic system gave way to the present Capitalist system, or Wage system, or Factory system.

The new "capitalist"

The capitalist manufacturer was a new figure in European life (cf. pp. 94, 100), appearing first in England. There, by 1800, the capitalists ranked alongside the country gentlemen

[1] George Eliot's *Silas Marner* is the story of such a weaver.

and the merchant princes as the "upper" middle class, just below the titled nobility in social standing and often superior to them in wealth. The appearance of this new figure was in many ways a gain to society; but there was also a bad side.

The capitalist manufacturer was not himself a workman, like the old "master" in the gilds or in the domestic system. He was only an "employer." He erected great buildings called factories, filled them with costly machines, bought the necessary "raw material" (cotton, wool, or iron, as the case might be), and paid wages.

The new "proletariat"

And if the capitalist was a new figure in middle-class society, *the capitalless and landless worker* was a much more significant new figure in the "lower classes." Unlike the capitalist, he was a helpless one. He now furnished nothing but his hands. Great numbers of men wanted work; and, moreover, much of the work on the new machinery could be done by women and children — especially in all cloth manufactures, where the work consisted largely in turning a lever, or tying broken threads, or cleaning machinery. Until the operatives learned how to combine, so as to bargain collectively, the capitalist could fix wages and hours and conditions as he pleased.

Cleavage between classes

Thus the new manufacturing society was made up of two distinct and hostile classes. Under the gild and domestic systems, apprentices and journeymen had expected to rise, sooner or later, to be "masters"; and at all times they lived on terms of constant intercourse with their masters, who worked side by side with them, shared their hardships, and had a sort of fatherly guardianship over them. Under the new system, a particularly enterprising and fortunate workman might now and then rise into the capitalist class (as a villein had now and then become a noble in old days); but on the whole, the line was drawn as distinctly, in Europe,[1] between soft-handed capitalist and hard-handed workman in 1800, as between armored noble and stooped peasant in 1200.

[1] In America, the relative scarcity of labor, and the presence of free land, made this cleavage less complete for many years more.

Moreover, the capitalist had no personal contact with his workmen. He employed not three or four, living in his own family, but hundreds or thousands. He never saw them, to know them, outside the factory, and he did not even know their names except on the payroll. There was no chance for real sympathy or understanding between him and his "hands."

Change in the homes of the workers

These changes, so far noted, are more or less permanent results of the capitalist system. We still have them in our society. But in 1800, in England, there was another result more immediately disastrous to the worker. He was compelled to change his whole manner of life for the worse. He must reach the factory within a few minutes after the first whistle blew, about sunrise, and stay there until sunset or dusk. So the capitalist built long blocks of ugly tenements near his factory, to rent; and the workmen moved from their rural village homes, with garden spots and fresh air and varied industry, into these crowded city quarters.

The rise of cities

The factory system produced cities with marvelous rapidity. In 1750 England was still a rural country, with only four or five towns that had more than 5000 people. In 1801 cities had leaped into life everywhere. More than 100 towns counted 5000 people. And in 1891, the number of such towns was 622. In 1700 the entire population of England and Wales (not including Scotland or Ireland) was somewhere between four and five millions. In 1801, when the first accurate census was taken, it was 8,893,000. Most of the increase had come in the last half of the century, and practically all of it had come in cities. During the next half-century, population doubled again, rising to 17,928,000 in 1851; and in the second half of the same century it very nearly doubled once more (32,526,000 in 1901).

The factory system has helped to produce rapid growth of population and of cities in all civilized lands; but *nowhere else* (except in the United States, where immigration has added millions) *has the growth been so enormous as in England; and in no other country did rapid growth begin until England had faced and begun to solve the new problems.*

For the growth of cities, together with the factory system, did give rise to wholly new problems. For a time no one saw them clearly. The employers, most directly responsible, felt no responsibility, and were engaged in an exciting race for wealth. The new cities grew up without water supply, or drainage, or garbage-collection. Science had not learned how to care for these needs properly, and law had not begun to wrestle with them. The masses of factory workers and their families dwelt in den-like garrets and cellars — a family stuffed indecently into a squalid unwholesome room or two — bordering on pestilential alleys, in perpetual filth and disease and misery and vice. In 1837 one tenth of the people of the great city of Manchester lived in cellars. The employment of women in the factory destroyed the home for a large part of the nation.[1]

And their new problems

Carpenters and masons commonly worked *from sunrise to sunset* — or even from dawn to dark — just as farm laborers often do still. Such long hours for toil were terribly hard: but they could be endured when spent in fresh air, amid outdoor scenes, in interesting and varied activity. But this long labor day was now carried into the factory. There it was unendurable and ruinous, because of foul air, poor light, nerve-racking noise of machinery, the more monotonous character of factory labor — the workman spending his day in repeating over and over one simple set of motions, — and because there it crushed women and children.

Long hours and monotonous labor

This was true even in America, when factories grew up here after 1815. Many years ago, Professor Ely of Wisconsin University wrote (*Labor Movement in America*, 49): — "The length of actual labor [in 1832] in the Eagle Mill at Griswold [Connecticut] was fifteen hours and ten minutes. The regulations at Paterson, New Jersey, required women and children to be at work at half-past four in the morning. . . . Operatives were taxed by the manufacturers for the support of churches. . . . Women and children were urged on by the use

Illustrations from America in 1830

[1] Women had done most of the spinning under the old domestic system; but they had done it then at odd spells, as part of the household work.

of the rawhide." Hope Factory (Rhode Island) rang its first bell ten minutes before the "break of day" (sunrise); the second bell, ten minutes later; and in five minutes more the gates were locked upon tardy comers Labor lasted in summer till eight at night; and a committee of laborers claimed that by keeping the factory clock always slow, the employer lengthened this horrible labor-day by twenty or twenty-five minutes more.

	Bell rings for work to commence	Bell rings for breakfast	Bell rings for return to work	Bell rings for dinner	Bell rings for return to work	Work ceases
Jan. & Feb.	Sunrise	—	—	12.30	1.10	7.
March 1st to 20th	Sunrise	7.30	8.10	12.30	1.10	7.
March 20th to Apr. 30th	Sunrise	7.	7.40	12.	12.40	Sunset
May, June, and July	4.55	6.30	7.10	12.	12.55	6.45
Aug. 1st to 15th.	Sunrise.	6.30	7.10	12.	12.55	6.45
Aug. 15th to Sept. 20th	Sunrise	7.	7.40	12.	12.55	Sunset
Sept. 20th to Oct. 30th	Sunrise	7.30	8.10	12.30	1.10	7.
Nov. and Dec.	Sunrise	—	—	12.30	1.10	7.

Breakfast before commencing work in Nov. Dec. Jan. & Feb.

FACSIMILE OF TIME CARD OF MACHINE SHOP IN PROVIDENCE, R. I., FOR 1848. From Tarbell's "Golden Rule in Business" in the *American Magazine* for April, 1915.

The only respite from work during the day was twenty-five minutes for breakfast and as much more for dinner — both meals eaten inside the walls from cold lunches brought by the workers.

These factories were not exceptions: they were typical. A Convention of New England Mechanics at Boston in 1832 declared that two fifths of all persons employed in American factories were children, whose day of toil averaged fourteen hours, and who had no chance whatever for schooling.

Child slavery in England

In England, conditions were at first worse than this. Parish authorities had power to take children from pauper families and apprentice them to employers; and dissolute parents sometimes sold their children into service by written contracts. In the years just before 1800, gangs of helpless little ones from six and seven years upwards, secured in this way by greedy contractors, were *auctioned off*, thousands at a time, to great factories, where their life was a ghastly slavery. They received no wages. They were clothed in rags. They had too little food, and only of the coarsest sort. Often they ate standing at their work, while the machinery was in motion. They were driven to toil sometimes sixteen hours a day, in some places by inhuman tortures. They had no holiday except Sunday; and their few hours for sleep were spent in dirty beds from which other relays of little workers had just been turned out. Schooling or play there was none; and the poor waifs grew up — girls as well as boys — if they lived at all, amid shocking and brutal immorality. When one batch of such labor had been used up, another was ready at little cost; and employers showed a disregard for the physical well-being of these "white slaves," such as no prudent negro-driver could ever afford toward his more costly black chattels.

The beginnings of reform

In 1800 a terrible epidemic among children in factory districts aroused public attention; and Parliament "reduced" the hours of labor for children-apprentices to *twelve* a day. The apprentice system, however, was abolished soon after, and the new law did not apply to the remaining child-operatives who were supposed to be looked after by their parents. In 1819 and in 1831 laws were passed to shorten hours for these children also, but they were not enforced; and the old conditions continued with little gain until after *political* reforms which we are soon to study.

Lord Ashley (Earl of Shaftesbury), whose championship helped finally to remedy these evils, spoke with great emotion forty years later (1873) of how he used to stand at the factory gates and watch the children come out, — "sad, dejected, cadaverous creatures," among whom "the crippled and distorted forms might be counted by hundreds." The poet

Southey in 1833 declared of the factory system that the "slave trade is mercy compared with it." And the piteous story called forth a passionate protest from the heart of England's woman poet against this hideous phase of English civilization (Mrs Browning's *Cry of the Children*): —

"'For oh,' say the children, 'we are weary,
And we can not run or leap.
If we cared for any meadows, it were merely
To drop down in them and sleep. . . .'
"'How long,' they say, 'how long, O cruel nation,
Will you stand to move the world on a child's heart —
Stifle down with a mailed heel its palpitation,
And tread onward to your throne amid the mart!
Our blood splashes upward, O gold-heaper,
And our purple shows your path.
But the child's sob in the silence curses deeper
Than the strong man in his wrath.'"

"Inclosures" in rural England

Another unhappy change during this same period destroyed the yeomen of rural England. In America one reason why factory workers were so at the mercy of employers was that in 1800 they could no longer find "free land," as workers could do in colonial times. Good farming land near the Eastern cities was all taken up; and the remote land in the West had not yet been opened by the government to settlement in small lots so that poor men could get hold of it.

But in England things were worse. There it was not a matter of the absence of just land-laws, but the presence of unjust laws. The new profits in farming (p. 354) made landlords eager for more land. They controlled Parliament; and that body passed law after law, after 1760, *inclosing the "commons"* for the benefit, not of the *common* good, but *of their class*.

These new inclosures were outwardly more decent than those of the seventeenth century. Pains were taken to "compensate" every villager for the share he lost in the village commons. But, whatever the intention of the law, the compensation proved ridiculously inadequate. Usually it was in the form of a little cash, which the peasant spent without any lasting improvement in his condition. A rhyme of the day expresses the feeling of the poor at this renewal of the ancient inclosure movement: —

> "The law locks up the man or woman
> Who steals the goose from off the common;
> But leaves the greater villain loose
> Who steals the common from the goose."

And Goldsmith's pathetic "Deserted Village" pictures the result and gives its stern warning:

> "Ill fares the land, to hastening woes a prey,
> Where wealth accumulates, and men decay."

The peasant farmers, having lost their old pasture land by these inclosures, could no longer maintain themselves against the competition of the privileged landlord, who also alone had money to buy the new machinery coming into use. *Small farmers were compelled to sell out;* while the merchants and new manufacturing capitalists were eager to buy, both because of the new profits in agriculture and because social position and political power in England in that day rested on ownership of land.

A landlord country

In 1700, in spite of the older inclosure movement of the sixteenth century, England had still some 400,000 peasant farmers. These with their families made nearly half the total population. But by 1800, though population had doubled (p. 374), this class of independent small farmers had disappeared and rural England was merely a country of great landlords. The dispossessed yeomanry drifted to the new factory towns to swell the unhappy class there already described, and to make its condition worse by increasing the competition for work. Or they remained to till the landlord's land, living on his estate as "cottagers," subject to removal at his order.

Since this change, until very recently, the classes connected with the land in England have been three, — landlords, *tenant-farmers*, and laborers. The first class comprised a few thousand gentry and nobles. Each such proprietor divided his estate into "farms," of from a hundred to three hundred acres, and leased them out to men with a little capital, who are known as "farmers." This second class worked the land directly, with the aid of the third class, who had no land of their own but who labored for day-wages.

The landlords as a rule prided themselves upon keeping up their estates. They introduced costly machinery and improved methods of agriculture, more rapidly than small proprietors could, and they furnished some of the money necessary to put farms and buildings into good condition. Their own stately homes, too, encompassed by rare old parks, gave a beauty to rural England such as no other country knew. (During the World War, these glorious oaks have been cut to furnish lumber for England; and much of this beauty has been lost.) The farmers, compared with the farm-laborers, were an aristocratic and prosperous class; but, of course, they had always been largely influenced by their landlords. And they did not *own* their land. Peasants became free in England some centuries sooner than in France or Germany; but in no other European country have the peasants so completely ceased to be owners of the soil as in modern England. In 1876 a parliamentary inquiry found only a quarter of a million (262,886) landowners with more than an acre apiece. France, with about the same population, had more than twenty times as many landowners.

EXERCISE. — Note the transitions in rural labor in England: (1) serf and villein labor to about 1350, and then a decay of that system until it disappears, about 1450; (2) inclosures (for sheep farming), driving a large part of the peasantry from the soil, 1450–1600; then, after a prosperous period, (3) the new period of inclosures for large grain farming, 1760–1830. (Recent attempts to restore the peasantry to the soil will be noted on pp. 476–477.)

Note also the transitions in manufacturing: the gild system to about 1600; the domestic system, 1600–1760; the factory system of to-day.

The "*Industrial* Revolution" applies especially to the change in *Manufacturing*, due to the use of machinery and steam, in the period from 1760 to 1820. The *Agricultural* Revolution helped on the Industrial Revolution by furnishing workmen for the new factories.

CHAPTER XXV

THE REVOLUTION IN IDEAS ABOUT GOVERNMENT

The "Let-alone" idea of government

A group of scholars and writers soon put into form the new ideas about carrying on industry and producing wealth. They called their new science *Political Economy*. It was founded by Adam Smith, about the beginning of the American Revolution. Its fundamental principle then was that *government must keep hands off*, unless called in as a policeman to keep order. "Laws" of "supply and demand," it taught, were "natural laws" among men (as gravitation was in the physical universe) and could not be meddled with, except to do harm. Supply and demand must be left absolute to determine prices, quality of goods, wages, and other conditions of employment. Only so could the "greatest happiness of the greatest number" be secured.

This became known as the "*Manchester doctrine*," because it was so universal among manufacturers in that leading center of manufactures. It is also called by a French name, — *Laissez faire* ("let alone," or "let it go"). English merchants accepted it no less readily than manufacturers, in their hatred of the old tariffs which hampered their trade; and it soon became almost a religion to the *town* middle class. The prosperous capitalist class resented all thought of interference in their business by government. Such interference *in past times*, they easily proved, had been foolish and harmful, even when best intended, and usually it had been intended to benefit a specially privileged *few*, at the cost of the many.

The Socialist idea

It is easy now to see that this new doctrine suited the strong, but that it was totally unchristian in its disregard of the weak. Quite as much as any feudal system, it produced happiness for a few and misery for the greatest number. The horrible conditions of the factory towns (p. 375) were its first fruits. Many tender-hearted men, like John Stuart Mill in England, were so imbued with the teaching that they continued long to proclaim it. But other men called this political economy a "dismal science," and soon many thinkers, in search of a cure for social ills, swung over to some form of what is now called Socialism.

Early Socialists

The first "Socialists" were very unscientific in their ideas, but they were moved by a deep love for suffering humanity. They believed that men by laws or by mutual arrangements could set up a society of common goods and brotherly love, — such as Sir Thomas More had pictured in *Utopia.* Three names among these early Socialists deserve mention.

Saint-Simon was a French noble who had aided America in the Revolution. Afterward, in a lifetime of study, he taught that government ought to manage all industry and secure to each worker a reward suitable to his service. He called his great book *The New Christianity.*

Fourier also was a Frenchman. He thought government unable to manage industry on such a scale as Saint-Simon advocated. Instead, he urged that *groups of workmen* (and their families) should organize in little "phalanxes" of two thousand members each, — each phalanx to own its own capital and to divide products in nearly equal parts between the *capital, labor,* and *management.* Horace Greeley, in America, was deeply interested in this plan; and a number of New Englanders (Emerson and Hawthorne among them) tried such an experiment at Brook Farm in 1841.

Robert Owen (p. 370) was a wealthy English manufacturer. His ideas for reform were much like Fourier's; and he used his wealth to establish a number of such coöperative colonies in England and in America — as at New Harmony, Indiana. His colonies all failed finally; but meantime he had given an impulse to coöperative societies for buying and selling goods, which ever since have accomplished great good; and his influence did much to spread faith in human brotherhood and to arouse the men who were to lead in social reforms in the next generation.

Modern Socialism

Modern Socialists look back on all these early attempts as well-meant efforts of dreamers, and trace their present doctrine to Karl Marx. Marx was born in 1818 in Germany. He attended the University of Berlin, and was intended by his family for a University professor; but his radical ideas kept him from obtaining such a position. He began to publish his works on Socialism about 1847. Germany and then France drove him away, as a dangerous disturber of order; and he spent the last forty years of his life (died 1883) in England, where, perhaps even more than in America, men of all creeds and opinions have found full freedom of speech.

Marx threw aside the idea that benevolent persons could introduce a new era of coöperation by agreement. He believed, however, that a new coöperative organization of society was going to succeed the present individualistic organization, as inevitably as that had followed the gild and slave organization, — not by humanitarian legislation, but through tendencies in human development that could not be controlled. All history, he said, had been the story of class struggles. Ancient society was a contest between master and slave; medieval society, between lord and serf; present society, between capitalist and workers. The workers, he was sure, will win, when they learn to unite, by transferring ownership of all machinery (all "means of production") to the nation as a whole, instead of leaving it and its profits in the hands of a few. He foretold the recent concentration of wealth and industry in great combines, and said that such combination would be a step toward the coöperative state, since it would make it easier for the masses to seize the "means of production."

In the name of "democracy and human welfare," Marx called to the working class of all lands to unite. "You have nothing to lose but your chains," he said. "Unite, and make the world your own," so as to inaugurate a golden future, "when all shall work, but none have to work too long or too hard. Then no one will grow rich at the expense of others, but each may receive honorable reward for any service that he renders society. Then degrading poverty and insolent wealth will both vanish; and emancipated humankind will move forward grandly to unforeseen conquests over nature, and live as one vast family, in brotherly love."

Labor, the Socialist teaches, is the source of all wealth, — food, clothing, houses, machinery, books, pictures, railroads. Labor, he insists, produced the capital which now controls further production and so controls labor. He would have labor instead own all capital — that is, all wealth employed in producing more wealth. This does not mean that the Socialists wish to divide property, or to keep individuals afterward from owning houses, libraries, carriages, jewels, clothing, of their own. They do not wish to abolish private ownership of those things which we use for ourselves, but only of those things which we use to produce more wealth.

Nor do Socialists usually wish to pay all men alike for their work. They would have the nation own the property now owned mainly by great trusts and corporations, and then pay salaries and wages, as corporations now do — except that as the nation would not try to keep most of the profits, there would be more for wages. And as all would work, no one would have to work so long.

Students who pay any attention to Socialism admit that its ideals are noble and attractive, and that the evils in present society are real and cruel. But the great majority do not believe that the Socialist program would work as its advocates teach; and they hope to lessen the ills of society without surrendering private enterprise and industrial initiative to any such degree as the Socialists think necessary.

For Further Reading. — Kirkup, *History of Socialism*, 1–167; or Spargo, *Socialism*, 1–181. (John Spargo is an American Socialist whom the organization "read out of the party" in 1917, because he supported the war against Germany.)

PART VII

CONTINENTAL EUROPE, 1848-1871

CHAPTER XXVI

THE REVOLUTION OF 1848

I. IN FRANCE

The middle-class monarchy

In France the divine-right Bourbon monarchy, we have seen, gave way in 1830 to *a constitutional Orleans monarchy*. Louis Philippe (p. 350) liked to be called "the Citizen King." He walked the streets in the dress of a prosperous shopkeeper, a green cotton umbrella under his arm, chatting cordially with passers-by, and he sent his children to the public schools. This was perfectly sincere conduct. *He had little understanding*, however, of the needs of France, or *of the feelings of the masses below the shop-keeping class.* For eighteen years (1830–1848) the favor of the middle class upheld his throne. Only the richest citizens had any share in political power (p. 350); but the whole middle class held military power, since it was organized in the armed and trained National Guards — to which no workingmen were admitted.

In the legislature there were two main parties. Thiers (p. 348) led the more liberal one, which wished the monarchy to be a figurehead, as in England; Guizot (p. 348), the conservative leader, wanted to leave the king the real executive, and to resist all further liberalizing of the government. Both Guizot and Thiers were famous historians.

Guizot's policy of stagnation, 1840–1848

From 1840 to 1848, Guizot was in control as the chief minister. France was undergoing rapid industrial growth, and needed tranquillity and reforms. Guizot gave it tranquillity. His ministry was the most stable that France had known since the days of Napoleon. But, in his desire for tranquillity, he ignored the other great need, and opposed all reform. Proposals to reduce the enormous salt tax, to extend education, to reform the outgrown postal system, to improve the prisons, to care for youthful criminals, were alike suppressed. He kept France not so much tranquil as stagnant.

Thus, after a time, the bright, brainy public men were nearly all driven into opposition; and even the interests of the middle class suffered. In 1842 Lamartine, another brilliant historian-statesman, attacked Guizot with a bitter speech in the legislature, declaring him so "inert" and "immovable," that "a post would answer as well all purposes of government."

"Placemen": organized corruption

But Guizot could not be overthrown by lawful means. The franchise was too narrow; and he had organized the vast patronage of the government for public corruption too skillfully. In America the constitution forbids the President to appoint Congressmen to paid offices, such as postmasters or customhouse collectors. But in France it was the regular practice to make members of the legislature "placemen" of this sort, as in England a century earlier (p. 214). This evil was the greater, since in France the government appointed not only *national* officials as with us, but also all *local* officers, like our county and State officials and city mayors and chiefs of police.

Narrow electorate

Less than 200,000 men could vote (p. 350), and the government had 300,000 offices to buy voters with. Then when an election was over, Guizot strengthened his majority in the legislature by appointing members to profitable offices, or by giving them lucrative business contracts from the government. At one time, half the legislature held considerable revenues at Guizot's will, and gave their votes at his nod. Personally, Guizot was incorruptible and rather austere; but he ruled by organizing corruption.

In the matter of *political* reform Thiers' party asked only (1) to forbid the appointment of members of the legislature to salaried offices, and (2) to widen the franchise so that *one man out of twenty* could vote. Guizot smothered both proposals. France already had too many voters, he declared; 'not more than 100,000 men in the country were capable of voting with good judgment.'

The Liberals try to appeal to public opinion

Finally the Liberals began to appeal to that vast part of the nation that had no vote. They planned a series of mass meetings and public demonstrations, to bring public opinion to bear on the legislature. According to American or English ideas, the proceeding was perfectly proper. But the French government forbade it — and brought on a revolution.

This "Revolution of 1848" was the work of the class of factory workers that had been growing up, almost unnoticed by political leaders of either party. Until 1825, when the Industrial Revolution was fairly complete in England, it had not begun in France. Cloth manufactures there were still carried on under the "Domestic system." *But in the next ten years*, 5000 power-looms were installed in factories; and in ten years more, the number had grown to 30,000. In 1815 there was only one steam engine in the country, aside from a dozen or so used to pump water; but in 1830 there were 625, and in 1850 there were more than 5000. The first French railway of importance was opened in 1843.

The new "Socialists" among the workmen of Paris

Late as all this was, the Industrial Revolution came in France sooner than in any other country of the continent. And it came soon enough so that, by 1848, a large factory-population had grown up in cities like Bordeaux, Lyons, Toulouse, and Paris. Moreover, more than the working class then in any other land, the alert, intellectually nimble French workingmen of the towns were influenced by the new teachings of Socialism. Their chief spokesman was *Louis Blanc*, an ardent young editor, who preached especially "*the right to work.*" Every man, he urged, had a right to employment. To insure that right, he wished the nation to establish workshops in different trades and give employment in them to all who wished it and who could not get it elsewhere. In the end, according to his plan, the workers would manage the workshops.

Blanc was an unselfish, high-minded man, moved by deep pity for the suffering masses; and his proposals were urged with moderation of word and style. But among his followers there were a few crack-brained enthusiasts, some criminally selfish adventurers, and many ignorant men easily incited to violence. Large numbers of the workingmen of Paris, in particular, had adopted phrases, not only about the "right to work," but also about "the crime of private property," as a sort of religious creed. This class was first revealed as a political power in the revolution that followed.

The "February Days"

In 1848 the Liberals appointed a monster political demonstration in Paris for February 22 — choosing that day in honor of the American celebration. At the last moment the government forbade the meeting. The leaders obeyed and stayed away; but the streets were filled all day with angry, disappointed crowds, shouting "Down with Guizot!" The National Guards, when called out to disperse the mob, themselves took up the cry. The next day Guizot resigned.

The last of the Capetians

Peace seemed restored; but that night a collision occurred between some troops and the mob; and the Socialists and Radicals seized the chance to rouse the masses against the monarchy. The bodies of a few slain men were paraded through the poorer quarters of the city in carts, while fervid orators called the people to rise against a monarchy that massacred French citizens. By the morning of the 24th, the streets bristled with barricades and the mob was marching on the Tuileries. Louis Philippe fled to England, disguised as a "Mr. Smith." His government had lost the support of the middle classes, and it collapsed. "The February Days" saw the end of the Capetian monarchy in France.

The Provisional Government of 1848

The Chamber of Deputies was about to proclaim the infant grandson of Louis Philippe as king, when the room was invaded by a howling mob, flourishing muskets and butcher-knives and calling for a republic. In the midst of this tumult the few deputies who kept their seats hastily appointed a "Provisional Government."

This body was at once escorted by the mob to the Hotel de Ville (a sort of town hall), where it found another provisional government already set up by the Radicals and Socialists. By a compromise, some of this latter body were incorporated in the first. The Provisional Government was now made up of three elements: *Lamartine*, the poet-historian, represented the Moderate Republicans; *Ledru-Rollin* was the representative of the Radical Republicans ("the Reds"), who wished to return to the "Terror" of 1793; and *Louis Blanc* represented the Socialists. On the whole, Lamartine proved to be the guiding force.

The difficulties before the government were tremendous. For sixty hours it was in the presence of an infuriated and drunken mob. A crowd of 100,000 armed men was packed into the streets about the Hotel de Ville, and delegations from it repeatedly forced their way into the building to make wild demands upon the "government." That government must at once disperse this seething multitude, avert plunder and massacre, clear away barricades, bury the dead and care for the wounded, and supply food for the great city wherein all ordinary business had ceased. All this, too, had to be accomplished without any police assistance.

Lamartine

Time after time, during the sixty hours' session, was Lamartine called from the room to check invasions by new bands of revolutionists. Said the spokesman of one of the bands: "We demand the extermination of property and of capitalists, the instant establishment of community of goods, the proscription of the rich, the merchants, those of every condition above that of wage-earners, . . . and finally the acceptance of the red flag, to signify to society its defeat, to the people its victory, to all foreign governments invasion."

Lamartine grew faint with exhaustion and want of food. His face was scratched by a bayonet thrust. But his fine courage and wit and persuasive eloquence won victory over every danger. To help appease the mob, however, the Government hastily adopted a number of radical decrees, writing them hurriedly upon scraps of paper and throwing them from a window to the crowd. One declared France a Republic. Another abolished the House of Peers. Still others established manhood suffrage, shortened the 11-hour working day to 10 hours, and *affirmed the duty of the state to give every man a chance to work.*[1]

The "workshop" army

A few days later, the decree recognizing the "right to work" was given more specific meaning by the establishment of "national workshops" (on paper) for the unemployed. In the business panic that followed the Revolution, great numbers of men had been thrown out of work. The government now organized these men in Paris, as they applied, into a "workshop army," in brigades, companies, and squads, — paying full wages to all it could employ and a three-fourths wage to those obliged to remain idle.

Over one hundred thousand men, many of them from other cities, were soon enrolled in this way; but, except for a little work on the streets, *the government had no employment ready for such a number.* The majority of the government, too, succeeded in placing the management in the hands of a personal enemy of Blanc's, and it seems to have been their intention that the experiment should fail, so as to discredit Blanc with the populace. The experiment was not in any sense a fair trial of the socialistic idea. It was a police provision and a temporary poor-law. It preserved order and distributed alms, but it also gave a formidable organization to a terrible force with which the new Republic would soon have to reckon.

The new Assembly

A new "Constituent Assembly," elected by manhood suffrage, met May 4. The Revolution, like that of 1830, had been confined to Paris. The rest of France had not cared to interfere in behalf of Louis Philippe, but it felt no enthusiasm for a republic and it abhorred the "Reds" and the Socialists. This, too, was the temper of the Assembly. It accepted the revolution, but it was bent upon putting down the Radicals.

[1] A number of these decrees are given in Anderson's *Documents.*

As soon as this became evident, the mob rose once more (May 15), and burst into the legislative hall, holding possession for three turbulent hours. At last, however, some middle-class battalions of the National Guard arrived, under Lamartine, to save the Assembly.

The Paris workmen crushed

The rescued Assembly promptly followed up its victory. After making military preparations, it suddenly abolished the workshop army — without any provision for the absorption of the men into other employments. A conservative French statesman has styled this "a brutal, unjust, blundering end to a foolish experiment." The men of the workshop army rose. They comprised the great body of the workingmen of Paris, and they were aided by their semi-military organization. The conflict raged for four days, — the most terrible struggle that even turbulent Paris had ever witnessed. Twenty thousand men perished; but in the outcome, the superior discipline and equipment of the Assembly's troops crushed the Socialists for another generation. Then eleven thousand prisoners were slaughtered in cold blood, or transported for life. This is another of those cruel and senseless "White Terrors" which arouse very little indignation in society, although society is amazed that the class punished in such fashion should develop bitter class hatreds.

The Constitution of "the Second Republic"

The Assembly now turned to its work of making a constitution. The document[1] was made public in November. It was not submitted to a popular vote. It provided for a legislature of one house, and for a four-year president, both to be chosen by manhood suffrage. A month later (December 10) *Louis Napoleon*, a nephew of Napoleon Bonaparte, was elected the first president of this "Second French Republic" by an overwhelming majority.

"The Napoleonic Legend"

Napoleon's political capital was his name. A group of brilliant writers, of whom, strangely enough, Thiers was chief, had created a "Napoleonic legend," representing the rule of the First Napoleon as a period of glory and prosperity for

[1] The document is given in Anderson's *Constitutions and Documents*.

France, broken only by wars forced upon Napoleon by the jealousy of other rulers. These ideas had become a blind faith for great masses in France. Louis Napoleon had long believed that he was destined to revive the rule of his family. Twice in the early years of Louis Philippe's reign he had tried to stir up a Napoleonic revolution, only to become a laughing-stock to Europe. But now to the peasantry and the middle class, alarmed by the specter of Socialism, Napoleon's name seemed the symbol of order and peace. He received over five and a half million votes, to about one and a half million for the next highest candidate.

FOR FURTHER READING. — Hazen (see page 339 of this volume), 114–194. (Andrews' *Modern Europe* and Seignobos' *Europe since 1814* remain good.) On early French Socialists, Robinson and Beard's *Readings*, II. 78–80. On the national workshops of 1848, *ib.*, 80–84.

II. CENTRAL EUROPE IN '48

The "March Days" in Central Europe

The year 1848 was "the year of revolutions." In central Europe Metternich's system had lasted until that time. For long, however, the forces of revolution had been gathering strength for a general upheaval. Metternich, now an old man, saw this. In January he wrote to a friend, "The world is very sick. The one thing certain is that tremendous changes are coming." A month later, the *February* rising in Paris gave the signal for *March* risings in other lands. Metternich fled from Vienna in a laundry cart; and all over Europe thrones tottered — except in stable free England on the west, and in stable despotic Russia and Turkey on the east.

Within a few days, in Holland, Spain, Denmark, and Sweden, to save their crowns, the kings granted new constitutions and many liberties. In every one of the German states, large or small, the rulers did the like. So, too, in Italy in the leading states, — Sardinia, Tuscany, Rome, and Naples. In all these countries the administration passed for a time to the hands of liberal ministries pledged to reform. *Everywhere, too, the remains of feudal privilege were finally abolished.*

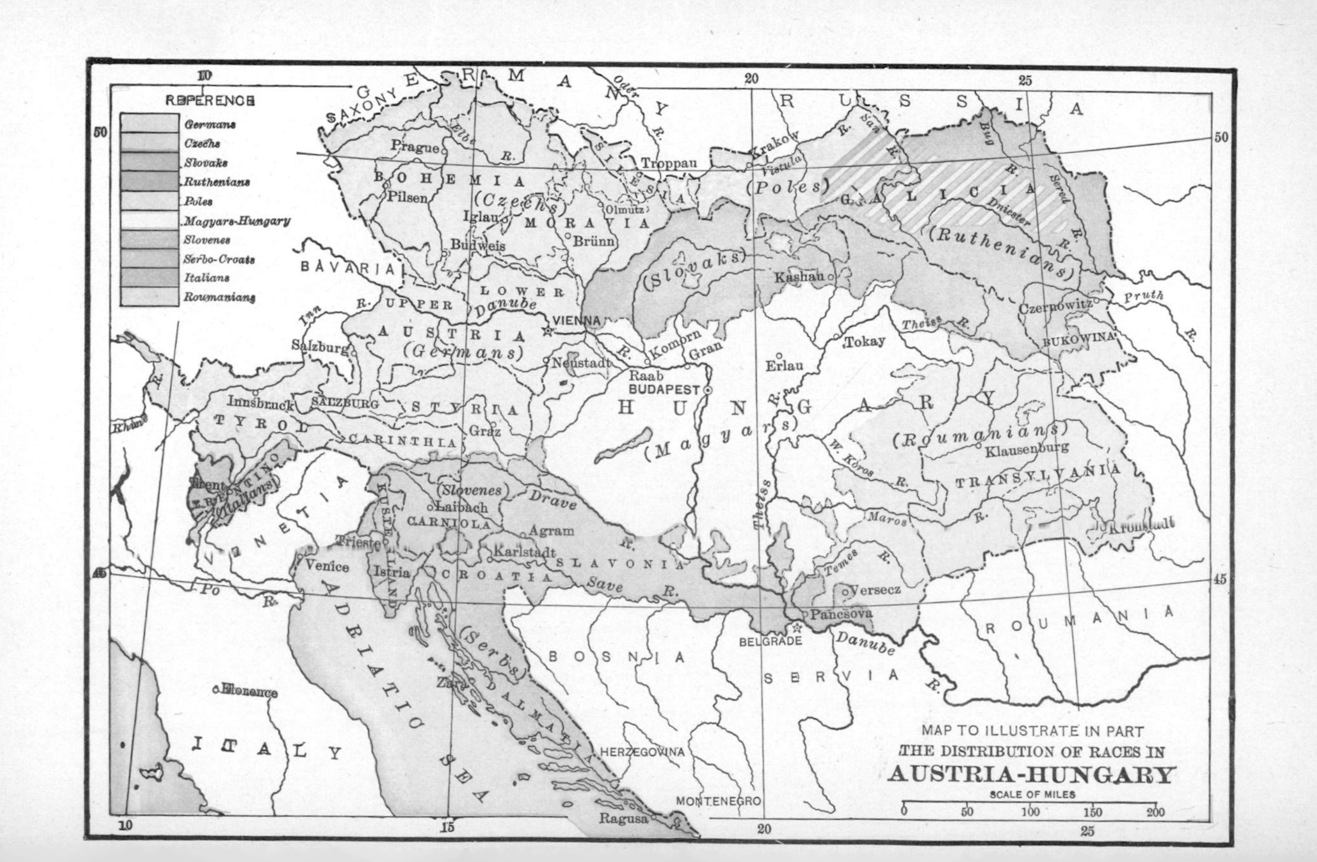
REFERENCE
Germans
Czechs
Slovaks
Ruthenians
Poles
Magyars-Hungary
Slovenes
Serbo-Croats
Italians
Roumanians
GERMANY
SAXONY
BAVARIA
RUSSIA
BOHEMIA
(Czechs)
MORAVIA
SILESIA
GALICIA
(Poles)
(Ruthenians)
(Slovaks)
BUKOWINA
UPPER
LOWER
AUSTRIA
(Germans)
SALZBURG
STYRIA
CARINTHIA
TYROL
TRENTINO
(Italians)
VENETIA
CARNIOLA
(Slovenes)
KUSTENLAND
CROATIA
SLAVONIA
HUNGARY
(Magyars)
TRANSYLVANIA
(Roumanians)
ROUMANIA
BOSNIA
SERVIA
HERZEGOVINA
MONTENEGRO
DALMATIA
(Serbs)
ITALY
ADRIATIC SEA
Prague
Pilsen
Iglau
Budweis
Brünn
Olmutz
Troppau
Krakow
Kashau
Czernowitz
Tokay
Erlau
Klausenburg
Kronstadt
Versecz
Pancsova
BELGRADE
VIENNA
Neustadt
Komorn
Gran
Raab
BUDAPEST
Salzburg
Innsbruck
Graz
Laibach
Agram
Karlstadt
Trieste
Istria
Venice
Trent
Zara
Ragusa
Florence
Elbe R.
Oder R.
Vistula
San R.
Bug R.
Dniester R.
Sered R.
Pruth R.
Theiss R.
Theiss
W. Koros R.
Maros R.
Temes R.
Danube
Drave R.
Save R.
Inn R.
Rhine
Po R.
10
15
20
25
45
50
MAP TO ILLUSTRATE IN PART
THE DISTRIBUTION OF RACES IN
AUSTRIA-HUNGARY
SCALE OF MILES
0 50 100 150 200

Outside France the chief interest centers (1) in the Austrian Empire, the storm-center; (2) in Germany, which Austria had so long dominated; and (3) in Italy, much of which was subject to Austria.

A. The Revolution in the Austrian Empire

The Revolution in the Austrian realms

March 13, two weeks after the French rising, the students of the University of Vienna and the populace of the city rose in street riots, to the cry, "Down with Metternich." After his escape, the crowds about the Emperor's palace began to call for a constitution, with freedom of speech and with an elected legislature. The Emperor promised these and other reforms, and appointed a liberal ministry to put them in operation.

But the Austrian Empire was a vast conglomerate. It included many peoples and several distinct states. Two subject states in particular now demanded self-government. These were Bohemia and Hungary. The Austrians proper were Germans. They made the bulk of the inhabitants in the old duchy of Austria, and they were the ruling class elsewhere in the Empire, comprising, too, a portion of the population everywhere. Still they made up less than one fourth of all the inhabitants. In Bohemia *the bulk* of the inhabitants were the *native Slavs* (Czechs); and in the Hungarian half of the Empire, the Hungarians (p. 87) were the dominant people. *Hungary itself, however, was also a conglomerate state.* In many of its *border* districts (map opposite), the *Slav* peoples (Croats, Serbs, Slavonians) made the larger part of the population.

In Bohemia and Hungary the March risings were not merely for *liberalism,* as in German Austria. They were also for Bohemian and Hungarian home rule. These peoples, however, did not yet demand complete independence. So the Emperor skillfully conciliated both states by granting constitutional governments with a large measure of home-rule and the official use of their own languages (instead of German). Then he used the time so gained to crush similar national movements in Italy (below).

Race jealousies aid autocracy

In all this, the government had yielded only to a momentary necessity. The Emperor had no intention of keeping his solemn promises, but was bent on restoring old conditions. In this despotic purpose, he had an ally in *race jealousy*. The German Liberals dreaded Slav rule, especially in Bohemia, where many Germans lived. Soon, disturbances there between the two races gave the Emperor excuse to interfere. The army was now ready, — as it was not in March, — and, in July, the Emperor replaced the constitution he had just given to Bohemia by military rule. Alarmed at this sign of reaction, the Radicals rose again in Vienna, and got possession of the city (October); but the triumphant army, recalled now from Bohemia, captured the capital after a savage bombardment.

The old Emperor (Ferdinand) was embarrassed somewhat by his recent solemn promises to the Liberals and to the subject peoples. But now he abdicated in favor of his nephew, the shrewd *Francis Joseph*. This new ruler pleaded that he had never consented to any weakening of his absolute powers, and at once restored absolutism both in Bohemia and in the central government of the Empire. (This is the ruler who continued to guide Austria almost to her final overthrow in the World War.)

The Hungarian Republic falls

Hungary remained to be dealt with. Here, too, race jealousies played into the hands of despotism. The Slavs wanted independence from the Hungarians; and if they had to be subject at all, they preferred German rule from distant Vienna rather than Hungarian rule from Budapest. The Hungarians had just crushed a rising of the Croats for independence. When the new Emperor came to the throne, the Croats rose again, *this time with imperial aid.* Accordingly, the Hungarians refused to acknowledge Francis Joseph as emperor. Instead they declared Hungary a republic, chose the hero *Kossuth* president, and waged a gallant war for full independence. For a time they seemed successful; but the Tsar, in accordance with the compact between the monarchs of the Holy Alliance, sent a Russian army of 150,000 men to aid Austria, and Hungary was crushed (April–August, 1849).

It remained only for Austria to reëstablish her authority in Germany, which had been left for a time to Prussia and the German Liberals (*B*, below).

B. In Germany

The March Revolution in Prussia

Even Prussia in '48 had its scenes of blood and slaughter. In Berlin, from March 13 to March 18, excited middle-class crowds thronged the streets. They made no attempt at serious violence against the government, however, until, in some way, never clearly understood, a sharp conflict took place with the troops on the 18th. The army inflicted terrible slaughter on the unorganized citizens; but Frederick William IV was neither resolute enough nor cold-hearted enough to follow up his victory. To pacify the people, he sent into temporary exile his brother William, who had commanded the troops; and he took part in a procession in honor of the slain, wearing the red, gold, and black colors of the German patriots. Then he called a Prussian parliament to draw up a constitution. He tried also to put himself at the head of the movement for German national union. "From this time," he declared, "Prussian interests will be absorbed in those of Germany."

The Frankfort Assembly

Meantime, a "people's movement" for German unity had got under way. Early in March, prominent German Liberals gathered at Heidelberg and called a German National Assembly, to be chosen by manhood suffrage, — arranging the number of representatives from each German state. *May 18, 1848,* the National Assembly met *at Frankfort.* This was the first representative assembly of the German people.

The Assembly had two fatal weaknesses.

1. *It did not really represent the whole German people,* much as it wished to do so, *but only a small middle class of "intellectuals." The nobility* — with a few rare exceptions — held wholly aloof and hostile. *The peasantry* were too slavish to have any

sympathy with the movement. Bismarck, a reactionary young Prussian noble, tells us, later, that it would have been easy to rally the Prussian peasantry for a march upon Berlin to rescue the king from the revolutionary influences there. And even *the merchants* of the middle class cared for union only or chiefly in order to get rid of vexatious tariffs between the various states — and cared for freedom not at all.

2. *The Assembly was led by talkers and scholars*, not by statesmen or men of action. The members could not understand the necessity of compromise or of prompt action. They spent precious months in wordy orations and in laying down comprehensive theories of government.

During May and June, the Assembly did organize an ineffective "provisional government"; but meanwhile *Austria had crushed Bohemia* (p. 394). The next four months at Frankfort went to debating a bill of rights, while all chance of securing any rights was being lost. During this time, *Austria restored "order" finally in Italy* (p. 400) *and recovered Vienna from the Radicals*. Over all Germany, too, the commercial class was becoming bitterly hostile to the revolution because of the long-continued business panic; and the new Prussian parliament at Berlin, which was to have drawn up a liberal constitution, had provoked Frederick William into dissolving it. To be sure, the king himself then gave a constitution to Prussia; but it was of a very conservative character. In other German states, too, the rulers were overthrowing liberal ministries which had been set up after the March Days.

Austria interferes

These were the conditions in October when the Frankfort Assembly at last took up the making of a constitution. Two questions then divided the Assembly: (1) should the new government be monarchic or republican; and (2) should the new nation include despotic Austria with her vast non-German population. The republicans had no chance whatever to succeed, but they helped to delay action on the more practical question. The wrangling went on through the winter of 1849, until Austria finally got her hands free elsewhere and announced that she would permit no German union into which she did not enter *with all her provinces.*

Then the Radicals gave up the impossible republic, and the Assembly took the step it should have taken months before. It decided for a consolidated union *without Austria* under the name of the German Empire; and it offered the imperial crown to Frederick William of Prussia. But it was six months too late. The first enthusiasm among even the middle class was gone. And Frederick William was timid: he was influenced by a sense of "honor among kings," so that he hesitated to take advantage of the Austrian Emperor's embarrassments with revolted subjects; and he felt a growing aversion to the movement which, a few months before, he had called "the glorious German revolution." After some hesitation, he declined the crown "bespattered with the blood and mire of revolution." In despair the Radicals resorted to arms to set up a republic. They were promptly crushed. The National Assembly vanished in the spring of 1849, and many German Liberals, like Carl Schurz, fled, for their lives, to America. The "people's" attempt to make a German nation had failed — because the German "people" as a whole were not fit for union or freedom.

The people's movement fails

Next *the princes* tried — with no better success. In the summer of 1849, despite the protests of Austria and Bavaria, *twenty-eight* rulers of North German states organized a league under the lead of the Prussian king.

The attempt of princes for German unity

Several of the princes, however, were half-hearted, joining only through fear of popular risings. Austria, with Hungary now at her feet, organized the South German states into a counter-league, and demanded the restoration of the old Confederation. The Austrian government announced bluntly that it meant to humiliate Prussia. Austrian and Prussian troops met on the borders of Bavaria. Shots were exchanged; but the Prussian army was not ready. The Russian Tsar showed himself ready to aid Austria in Germany as he had done in Hungary. Finally Frederick William made ignominious submission to the Austrian demands in a conference at Olmütz

The "Humiliation of Olmütz"

(November, 1850); and *Austria restored the old Germanic Confederation of 1815.*

C. The Revolution of '48 in Italy

Italy betrayed both by Napoleon and the Allies

Italy had been in fragments since the days of the Roman Empire. Her people, however, had not forgotten that once she had ruled the world. Through the Middle Ages, enthusiastic Italians had dreamed of national unity, and some of the great popes had hoped for a union of the peninsula under papal leadership. About 1800, the proclamations of Bonaparte in his Italian campaigns, promising independence, again awoke hope in Italian hearts; and, under his control, some advance was made toward union (pp. 306, 319).

Then, when the European coalition was struggling with Napoleon, in 1813 and 1814, the generals of the Allies appealed to the Italian populations with glowing promises. An English force landed at Genoa, with its flag inscribed "Italian Liberty and Independence"; and Austrian proclamations announced: "We come to you as liberators. Long have you groaned beneath oppression. You shall be an independent nation."

Italy and the Congress of Vienna

The Congress of Vienna ignored these promises and hopes. Even the Napoleonic improvements were undone, and medieval conditions were restored. Lombardy and Venetia became Austrian provinces (p. 329), and most of the rest of the peninsula was handed over to Austrian influence. Bourbon rule was restored in the south over the Kingdom of the Two Sicilies, where the king pledged himself to allow no institutions more liberal than those permitted by Austria in her districts. Dukes, dependent upon Austria, were set up in Tuscany, Modena, and Parma. Between these duchies and Naples lay the restored Papal States, with the government in close sympathy with Austria. The northwest was given back to the Kingdom of Sardinia [1] under a native line of monarchs, to whom the people

[1] During the Napoleonic wars, an English fleet kept Sardinia safe from French conquest when the other dominions of her rulers were taken from them.

were loyally attached. This was the one Italian state (besides the pope's territories) where the ruler was not strictly dependent on Austrian protection. But even in Sardinia until 1848 the government was a military despotism. "Italy," said Metternich complacently, "is a mere geographical expression."

This remained true from 1815 to 1848. The story of the Italian revolutions of 1820 and the Holy Alliance has been told. In 1830, after the July Revolution in Paris, new revolutions broke out in the Papal States and the small duchies, but these movements also were soon put down by Austria.

"Young Italy"

The ten years from 1830 to 1840, however, did see the organization of "Young Italy" by Mazzini. Mazzini was a lawyer of Genoa and a revolutionary enthusiast who was to play, in freeing Italy, a part somewhat like that of Garrison and Phillips in preparing for our American Civil War. His mission was to create a great moral enthusiasm. His words and writings worked wonderfully upon the younger Italians of the educated classes, and his Society of Young Italy replaced the older Carbonari (p. 341). Young Italy had for its program a *united Italian Republic.* The dea of a free and united Italy grew steadily, until even some of the rulers became imbued with it. Especially did the Liberals hope much from Pius IX, a liberal Italian, who was chosen pope in 1846, in opposition to the wishes of Austria.

Thus when the revolutions of 1848 broke out, Italy was ready to strike for national union and independence. In 1820–1821, the extremities of the peninsula had been shaken; in 1830, the middle states; in 1848, there was no foot of Italian soil not convulsed, and this time the revolutionists sought *union* as ardently as *freedom.*

Italian Revolutions in '48

On the news of Metternich's flight, Milan and Venice drove out their Austrian garrisons. Then Charles Albert, king of Sardinia, gave his people a constitution and put himself at the head of a movement to expel Austria from the peninsula. The pope and the rulers of Tuscany and Naples promised loyal aid. Venice and other small states in the north voted enthusiastically for incorporation into Sardinia.

Defeats at Custozza and Novara

But the king of Naples was dishonest in his promises; and even the liberal and patriotic pope was not ready to break fully with Austria. Except for a few thousand volunteer soldiers, Charles Albert got no help from Italy south of Lombardy; and, July 15, 1848, he was defeated at *Custozza*. Then the movement passed into the hands of the Radicals. Venice and Florence each set up a republic; and in February, 1849, the citizens of Rome, led by Mazzini, drove away the pope and proclaimed the "Roman Republic."

JOSEPH MAZZINI

These republican movements succeeded, for the hour, only because Austria was busied in Bohemia and Hungary. But soon a strong Austrian army was sent to Italy. Charles Albert took the field once more, but was defeated decisively at *Novara* (March, 1849); and Venice was captured in August after gallant resistance. Louis Napoleon restored the pope to his Roman principality, and left a French garrison there for his protection during the next twenty years, to 1870.

The failure of the Italians, however, was not shameful, like that of the Germans. They had come near to success; and they failed, not because of their own faults, but because of crushing foreign interference. The splendid attempt had at least revealed the fact that "United Italy," once a dream of scattered enthusiasts only, had grown into a passionate faith for the whole people.

Mazzini's challenge to victorious reaction

This well-grounded faith, not merely for a free Italy but for a free Europe, was finely spoken to the world by Mazzini, with splendid courage, in the very hour of discouraging defeat. Mazzini had barely escaped with his life; but in 1849, from his refuge in England, while less fortunate associates were dying in Italy on scaffolds and under tortures in dungeons, he uttered to the exultant forces of reaction this clear-sounding challenge:

> "Our victory is certain; I declare it with the profoundest conviction, here in exile, and precisely when monarchical reaction appears most insolently secure. What matters the triumph of an hour? What matters it that by concentrating all your means of action, availing yourselves of every artifice, turning to your account those prejudices and jealousies of race which yet for a while endure, and spreading distrust, egotism, and corruption, you have repulsed our forces and restored the former order of things? *Can you restore men's faith in it,* or do you think you can long maintain it by brute force alone, now that all faith in it is extinct? . . . Threatened and undermined on every side, *can you hold all Europe forever in a state of siege?*"

FOR FURTHER READING ON 1848. — Hazen's *Europe Since 1815*, 152–186. Andrews and Seignobos have good accounts also; and Phillips' *European History, 1815–1899*, is especially excellent for 1848.

CHAPTER XXVII

WESTERN EUROPE FROM 1848 TO 1871

(From the Year of Revolutions through the Franco-Prussian War)

Except to the few men of faith, like Mazzini, the risings of '48 seemed to have been in vain. True, feudalism was at last gone forever, even from Austria, and the Holy Alliance was finally disrupted by the rivalry between Prussia and Austria. But in government, the restoration of despotism appeared complete. The Revolution had closed in Italy with the defeat of Novara (March, 1849), in the Austrian realms with the fall of the Hungarian Republic (July, 1849), and in Germany with the "humiliation of Olmütz" (December, 1850). In France it was swiftly going, and was to disappear in 1851 with Napoleon's *coup d'état* (below).

For the next generation of human life, interest on the continent centered in three lands, — France, Italy, Germany. And of these only Italy during that period was to make true and lasting progress.

I. FRANCE: THE SECOND EMPIRE, 1852–1870

The shame of France: "Napoleon the Little"

In 1830 and in 1848, France had led liberal Europe; but for the next twenty years, after she had crushed so bloodily the workingmen of Paris, her story is one of shame. Fearing the "class-hatred" which they themselves had done so much to provoke, the middle class threw themselves into the arms of a despot for security — while this despot was posing to the working class as their champion against this same middle class.

Louis Napoleon, President of the Republic (p. 391), was constantly at loggerheads with the Assembly. From the first, he plotted secretly to overthrow the republican constitution — to which he had repeatedly sworn fidelity — and to make himself master of France.

The Assembly played into his hand. In 1849 it passed a reactionary law which disfranchised a large part of the workingmen of the cities. *After the law had been passed,* Napoleon criticized it vehemently, so as to appear to the workingmen as their champion. At the same time, the discontent of the artisans made the middle class fear a revolution; and that class turned to Napoleon as the sole hope for order. Thus the chief elements in the state dreaded the approaching close of Napoleon's presidency.

The *coup d'état*

The constitution forbade a reëlection; and an attempt to amend this clause was defeated by the Assembly. Thus that body had now seriously offended both the artisan class and the middle class; and Napoleon could overthrow it with impunity.

In semi-royal progresses through France, Napoleon had been preparing the nation for his blow. He found fault with the Assembly freely, and his speeches were filled with references to the "glory" of the former French Empire, and to the benefits conferred upon France by "my great uncle." All important offices in the army and in the government were put into the hands of his tools and his trusted friends; and on *December 2, 1851,* he carried out the most striking *coup d'état* in all French history.

During the preceding night, some eighty men whose opposition was especially feared — journalists, generals, and leaders in the Assembly — were privately arrested and imprisoned; and all the printing offices in the city were seized by Napoleon's troops. In the morning the amazed people found the city posted with startling placards. These announced the dissolution of the Assembly, proposed a new government with Napoleon at its head, and promised an appeal to the nation for ratification.

The Assembly tried to meet but was dispersed by soldiers, and most of the members were imprisoned. During the next few days a few Radicals began to raise barricades here and there in the streets; but these were carried by the soldiers with pitiless slaughter, and the conflict was made an excuse for a "reign of terror," in accordance with a policy of "frightfulness." Batches of prisoners, taken at the barricades, were shot down after surrender. The Radical districts of France were put under martial law. And thousands of men were transported to penal settlements, virtually without trial.

Ratified by France

Under these conditions, a few days later, the country was invited to vote Yes or No upon a new constitution making Napoleon President for Ten Years with dictatorial power. France "ratified" this proposal by a vote of seven and a half million out of eight million. In November of the next year, *a nearly unanimous vote made the daring adventurer Emperor of the French,* under the title *Napoleon III.* (The Bonapartists counted the son of Napoleon I as Napoleon II, though he never reigned.)

The unanimity in the vote was due partly to shameless interference at the polls. The army was voted first, for an example; and in many places the rural population was marched to the polls, under military authority. Such measures, however, were not necessary to secure a large majority. Except for a small body of Liberals and Socialists, France fell willingly into Napoleon's arms.

"Elections" under the Empire

The "Second Empire" was modeled closely upon that of Napoleon I. During its early years, *political life* was suspended. The people, it is true, elected a Legislative Chamber (a greater popular power than existed under the First Empire); but the Emperor *appointed* a Senate and a Council of State; while for some years the Chamber could consider no bill that had not been put before it by the Emperor and his Council. The legislature was not even a *free* debating society; its function was to register edicts.

At the election of a "legislature," the government presented for every elective position an "official candidate," for whom the way was made easy. Opposing candidates could not hold public meetings, nor hire the distribution of circulars. They were seriously hampered even in the use of the mails, and their placards were torn down by the police, or industriously covered by the official bill-poster for the government candidate. The ballot boxes, too, were supervised by the police, and, no doubt, were sometimes "stuffed." Moreover Napoleon subsidized a large number of newspapers, and suppressed all that were unfavorable to him.

No personal liberty

Personal liberty, also, was wholly at the mercy of the government. The servants of prominent men were likely to be the paid spies of the police. Under the "Law of Public Security" (1858), Napoleon could *legally* send "suspects," *without trial*, to linger through a slow death in tropical penal colonies (as he had been doing *illegally* before). Many thousands are said to have perished in this way. Upon the passage of this law, an order was sent to each prefect to arrest a fixed number of men in his department, *using his own choice in selecting them*. The total arrests under this order exceeded two thousand. The purpose was merely to intimidate the nation — another use of a despot's policy of "frightfulness."

"FRANCE IS TRANQUIL" (a favorite phrase with Napoleon III). A cartoon from *Harper's Magazine*.

Napoleon accepted by France

Napoleon's methods had been those of a dastardly conspirator, and his rule was a despotism. But he seems honestly to have deceived himself into the belief that he was "a democratic chief." His government, he insisted, rested upon manhood suffrage in elections and plebiscites. The Restoration (1815–1830), he said, was the government of the great landowners; the Orleans Monarchy was the government of the middle class; the Empire was the government of the people.

Because of "prosperity"

In partial recompense for loss of liberty, too, he gave to France great material and economic progress. Industry was encouraged. Leading cities were rebuilt upon a more magnificent scale; and Paris, with its widened streets, shaded boulevards, and new, glorious public buildings, was made the most beautiful capital in the world. Asylums and hospitals were founded; schools were encouraged, and school libraries were established. And a system of vast public works throughout the Empire afforded employment to the working classes. France secured her full share of the increase of wealth and comfort that came to the world so rapidly during those years. The shame is that France was bribed to accept the despicable despotism of Napoleon by this prosperity — and by the tinsel sham of "glory" in war.

And military glory

In 1852 Napoleon had declared "The Empire is Peace"; but he found himself irresistibly impelled to war, in order to keep the favor of the army and of the populace by reviving the glories of the First Empire. His foreign policy soon became aggressive; and the first years of his reign (1854–1859) saw a series of victories that dazzled France. For forty years, — ever since the fall of Napoleon I, — Europe had been free from great wars. Napoleon III reintroduced them. The two most important wars of this period were the *Crimean* (1854–1856) and the *Italian* (1859).

The Crimean War

1. France had a trivial quarrel with Russia over the guardianship of Christian pilgrims at Jerusalem. England was hostile to Russia, fearing lest that Power should force itself to the Mediterranean and endanger England's route to India; and, it is fair to add, English Liberals feared Russian autocracy (the main support then of the despotic Holy Alliance) much as Liberals in recent years have feared German autocracy. Russia and Turkey were at war in the Black Sea. Through Napoleon's intrigues, France and England joined Turkey. The struggle was waged mainly in the Crimea, and took its name from that peninsula. Russia was defeated, but no permanent results of importance were achieved. At the close of the contest, however, Napoleon gathered representatives of all the leading Powers at the Congress of Paris, to make peace, and France seemed again to have become the arbiter in European politics.

2. In 1859 Napoleon joined the Kingdom of Sardinia in a war against Austria to free Italy. He won striking victories at Magenta and Solferino, near the scene of the early triumphs of the First Napoleon over the same foe; and then he made unexpected peace, to the dismay and wrath of the half-freed Italians. For his pay, Napoleon forced Italy to cede him the provinces of Nice and Savoy (pp. 305, 328).

The Italian War of 1859

But the second half of Napoleon's rule was a series of humiliations and blunders.

Napoleon favored the Southern Confederacy in the American Civil War, and repeatedly urged England, in vain, to unite with him in acknowledging it as an independent state. Thus he incurred the hostility of the United States.

Blunders in Napoleon's later foreign policy

Then in 1863 he entered upon a disastrous scheme in Mexico. That country had repudiated its debts. Several European governments had sent fleets to its ports to compel payment to their citizens; but soon it became plain that Napoleon meant much more than the mere collection of debts. Thereupon, the other governments withdrew from the enterprise. Napoleon then sent a large army to overthrow the Mexican Republic and to set up as "Emperor of Mexico" his protégé, Maximilian, an Austrian prince, brother of Emperor Franz Joseph.

Napoleon expected (1) to secure a larger share of the Mexican trade for France; (2) to increase the prestige of France as arbiter in the destinies of nations; and (3) to forward a union of the Latin peoples of Europe and America, under French leadership. His act was a defiance of the Monroe Doctrine of the United States, but his purpose seemed triumphant until the close of the American Civil War. Then the government of the United States demanded the withdrawal of the French troops from Mexico. Napoleon was obliged to comply. Soon afterwards Maximilian was overthrown by the Mexicans, and captured and shot.

More serious still were a number of checks in Napoleon's attempts on the Rhine frontier. These brought about his

And some restoration of political liberty

fall in 1870. That story will be told after we have studied the rise of Germany. Here we need only note that as Napoleon lost favor with the French populace, through these humiliations in foreign relations, he felt compelled to yield to France a larger share in the government. In particular, during the latter years of his rule, the Legislative Chamber became almost a real legislature, with perfect freedom of debate. France had begun to "come back."

FOR FURTHER READING. — See comment on pp. 339, 401, as to books. Hazen, 194–300, gives the best one story. On the Coup d'État, Robinson and Beard's *Readings*, II, 88–94.

II. THE MAKING OF ITALY, 1849–1861

Piedmont the hope of Italy

Meantime Italy had been made. "Forty-nine" had shown that the Kingdom of Sardinia was the only state from whose *government* real help could be hoped for in a struggle for Italian unity. There the ruling house had proved itself ready to dare greatly and sacrifice much for the cause. At home, too, the king had given a liberal constitution to his people. Thenceforward, the hopes of Italian liberals turned to that state. The making of Italy is the history of Piedmont from 1849 to 1861.

Victor Emmanuel II

The night after the defeat of Novara (p. 400), Charles Albert abdicated the crown, and his son, *Victor Emmanuel II*, became king of Sardinia. The young prince was an intense patriot. A popular story told how, as he rallied his shattered regiment at the close of the fatal day of Novara, and withdrew sullenly from the bloody field, covering the retreat, he shook his clenched fist at the victorious Austrian ranks with the solemn vow, — "By the Almighty, my Italy shall yet be!"

The new king was put at once to a sharp test. Austria demanded that he abolish the new constitution, hateful to Austria's divine-right despotism. If he would do so, Austria offered easy terms of peace, with promise of military support against any revolt. At the same time the inexperienced and obstinate Sardinian parliament was embarrassing the king by foolish opposition and criticism. But Victor Emmanuel nobly refused the Austrian bribe. Said he, "I would rather lose my crown." In consequence, he had to submit to severe terms from Austria and a heavy indemnity. But a frank appeal to his people for support gave him a new loyal parliament, which ratified the peace, and his conduct won him the title of "the Honest King."

Cavour

Austria, which Sardinia wished to expel from Italy, had 37,000,000 people. Sardinia was poor and had only 5,000,000 people. The king and his great minister, Cavour, bent all energies to strengthening Sardinia for another struggle and to securing allies outside Italy. Victor Emmanuel was essentially a soldier. Cavour was the statesman whose brain was to guide the making of Italy. The king's part was loyally and steadily to support him. Exiles and fugitive Liberals from other Italian states were welcomed at the Sardinian court and were often given high office there, *so that the government seemed to belong to the whole peninsula.* Cavour carried through the parliament many economic, military, and social reforms. And, in 1854, he sent a small but excellent Sardinian army to assist the allies against Russia in the Crimean War (p. 406). Mazzini called this action a monstrous moral degradation, and many other Liberals condemned it bitterly as immoral; but it is well to see Cavour's two reasons for it.

And the Crimean War

1. The Crimean War, unnecessary as it was, was, after all, in a way a defiance of despotic Russia. Italy had special reason to join in this feeling toward Russia: the Tsar had been strongly opposed to the liberal movements of 1848; he had helped crush Hungary, virtually an ally of Sardinia in the war of that period; and he had declined to recognize the accession of Victor Emmanuel.

2. Cavour wished to show that Sardinia was a military power, and to secure for her a place in the councils of Europe, so as to obtain intervention for Italy against Austria. This second reason, of course, was the deeper motive. Said an Italian officer to his soldiers digging in the trenches before Sebastopol, "Of this mud our Italy is to be made."

Cavour at the Congress of Paris

At the Congress of Paris in 1856 (p. 406) Cavour's policy bore fruit. Cavour sat there on full equality with the representatives of the Great Powers; and, despite Austria's protests, he secured attention for a convincing statement of the needs of Italy. Upon all minds he impressed forcefully *that Italian unrest could never cease, nor European peace be secure, so long as Austria remained in the peninsula.*

The French alliance

Three years later this patient diplomatic game was won. As a young man, in exile from France, Louis Napoleon had been involved in the plots of the Carbonari for Italian freedom (p. 341). Cavour now drew him into a secret alliance. In return for a pledge of Nice and Savoy, which had once been French for a short time, Napoleon promised to come to the aid of Sardinia *if Cavour could provoke Austria into beginning a war.*

Sardinia absorbs Lombardy

Austria played into Cavour's hand by demanding, as a war ultimatum, that Italy reduce her army. Napoleon at once entered Italy, declaring his purpose to free it "from the Alps to the Adriatic." His victories of Magenta and Solferino (p. 407) drove Austria forever out of Lombardy, which was promptly incorporated into Sardinia. *This was the first step in the expansion of Sardinia into Italy.* The population of the growing state had risen at a stroke from five millions to eight.

Venetia remained in Austria's hands, but Napoleon suddenly made peace. The Italians felt that they had been betrayed by "the infamous treaty"; [1] and probably they were right. Napoleon had no wish that Italy should be one strong, consolidated nation; and he began to see that a *free* Italy would be a *united* Italy.

Sardinia absorbs the duchies

But more had already been accomplished than the mere freeing of Lombardy. At the beginning of the war, the peoples of the duchies (Parma, Modena, and Tuscany) had driven out their dukes (dependents of Austria) and had set up provisional governments. At the peace, Napoleon had promised Austria that the dukes should be restored. He had stipulated, how-

[1] Read James Russell Lowell's *Villafranca*, to get an idea of the wrath of freedom-loving men at Napoleon's betrayal.

ever, that Austria should not use force against the duchies; and the people now insisted upon incorporation with Sardinia.

For eight months this situation continued, while Cavour played a second delicate diplomatic game with Napoleon. Only a foreign army could again place the dukes upon their thrones, and Cavour finally persuaded Napoleon to leave the matter to a plebiscite, his own favorite device in France. In March, 1860, the three duchies by almost unanimous votes[1] declared again for annexation. *This was the second step in expansion* — and the first example in Europe of "self-determination," as we now use the phrase. Sardinia was enlarged once more by one third. It had now become a state of eleven million people, comprising all Italy north of the papal districts, except Venetia.

GARIBALDI'S MONUMENT IN TURIN. Garibaldi was the soldier of Italian freedom, as Mazzini was its prophet, and Cavour its statesman.

Garibaldi adds South Italy

The next advance was due in its beginning to Garibaldi (a gallant republican soldier in the Revolution of 1848), who had now given his allegiance loyally to Victor Emmanuel. In May, 1860, Garibaldi sailed from Genoa with a thousand red-shirted fellow-adventurers, to arouse rebellion in Sicily. Cavour thought it needful to make a show of trying to stop the expedition. When it was safely under way, he expressed his "regret" in a note to the Powers of Europe. And he had

[1] In Tuscany the vote stood 366,571 to 14,925; and this was the largest adverse vote.

sent a message to the Sardinian admiral, — "Try to place your fleet between Garibaldi and the Neapolitan cruisers. *I hope you understand me.*" The admiral "understood" very well that he was to protect, not hinder, the expedition. Garibaldi landed safely in Sicily and won the island almost without bloodshed. Crossing to the mainland he easily occupied Naples also, while the Bourbon king fled. Obeying a popular demand, *Garibaldi proclaimed Victor Emmanuel "King of Italy."*

CAVOUR. From Desmaisons' lithograph.

With the assent of the people

Garibaldi then *planned* to seize Rome from its French garrison. Such a move would have brought on intervention from both Austria and France, and would have put at hazard all that had been gained. Cavour made prompt decision. Victor Emmanuel with the Sardinian army moved south to take up the war in the Kingdom of Naples, and to check Garibaldi's mad march. Rome and the surrounding territory was left to the pope; but the Marches and Umbria (the eastern part of the Papal States) were allowed, with the Kingdom of Naples, to vote on the question of annexation to Sardinia. The vote was even more nearly unanimous than that in the duchies had been.

A new "Kingdom of Italy"

These additions made the third step in the expansion of "Sardinia" into "Italy." The new state now comprised all the peninsula except Rome and Venetia; and it reached from the Alps to Sicily. This time the population was raised from eleven to twenty-two millions. In February, 1861, the first "Italian parliament" met at Turin and enthusiastically confirmed the establishment of the "Kingdom of Italy." Cavour's statesmanship was triumphant. In this first parliament of the new nation an opposition party to the great minister hardly raised its head. Five months later, Cavour was dead, broken down by the terrible strain of his work. His last words were, "Italy is made — all is safe." His achievements rank among the most marvelous in all modern statesmanship.

The acquisition of the two remaining provinces, Venetia and Rome (1867 and 1870), was intertwined with the making of Germany (below).

For Further Reading. — Bolton King's *Italian Unity* is the best single work. Good accounts will be found in Probyn's *Italy*, Bolton King's *Mazzini*, Dicey's *Victor Emmanuel*, or Cesaresco's *Cavour*. Hazen, Andrews, Seignobos, and Phillips, all contain brief treatments. Good material will be found in Robinson and Beard's *Readings*, II.

Exercise. — Trace the expansion of Sardinia into Italy on the map, p. 623.

Special Report. — Garibaldi's life and adventures.

III. THE MAKING OF GERMANY, 1861–1871

William I of Prussia

Napoleon III ruled France for some twenty years. During the first half of this period, Cavour made the Kingdom of Italy. Those years had been barren in Germany; but during the next ten years Bismarck, by far less justifiable methods, was to make a German Empire.

"Forty-nine" had shown Prussia as the only nucleus in that day for a German nation; and even from Prussia nothing could be expected as long as Frederick William IV reigned. But in 1861 that king was succeeded by his brother, *William I*. This was the prince who had been banished for a time in 1848 to satisfy the Liberals (p. 395). That party had nicknamed him "Prince Cartridge." He was a conservative of the old school, and he had bitterly opposed the mild constitutional concessions of his brother. But he was also a patriot to the core. He had tingled with indignation at the humiliation of Olmütz. He hoped, too, with all his heart, for German unity; and he believed

The Prussian army system

that this unity could be made only after expelling Austria from Germany. To expel Austria would be the work of the Prussian army.

The Prussian army differed from all others in Europe. Elsewhere the armies were of the old class, — standing bodies of mercenaries and professional soldiers, reinforced at need by raw levies from the population. The Napoleonic wars had resulted in a different system for Prussia. In 1807, after Jena, Napoleon had required Prussia to reduce her army to forty-two thousand men. The Prussian government, however, had evaded Napoleon's purpose to keep her weak, by passing fresh bodies of Prussians through the regiments at short intervals. Each soldier was given only two years' service. Part of each regiment was dismissed each year and its place filled with new levies. These in turn took on regular military discipline, while those who had passed out were held as a reserve.

Neglected, 1815–1861

After the Napoleonic wars were over, Prussia kept up this system. The plan was to make the entire male population a trained army; but it had not been fully followed up. Since 1815, population had doubled, but the army had been left upon the basis of that period. No arrangements had been made for organizing new regiments; and so many thousand men each year reached military age without being summoned into the ranks. Indeed, not half were called.

King William's first efforts were directed to increasing the number of regiments so as to accommodate 60,000 new recruits each year. To do this required a large increase in taxes. But the Prussian parliament (Landtag) was jealous of military power in the hands of a sovereign hostile to constitutional liberty, and it resolutely refused money. Then William found a minister to carry out his will, parliament or no.

Otto von Bismarck

This man, who was to be the German Cavour, was Otto von Bismarck. Thirteen years earlier, Count Bismarck had been known as a grim and violent leader of the "Junkers," the extreme conservative party made up of young landed aristocrats (p. 396). He held to the doctrine of the divine right of kings;

and when he was announced as the head of a new ministry, the Liberals ominously prophesied a *coup d'état*.

Something *like* a *coup d'état* did take place. The Prussian constitution declared that the ministers must be "responsible" to the Landtag, or parliament. But this did not mean responsible in the Modern English sense: that is, it did not mean that they must resign if outvoted; but only that they might be held to account for their actions. William stood steadfastly by his minister; and for four years Bismarck ruled and collected taxes unconstitutionally.

The army reorganized

Over and over again, the Landtag demanded Bismarck's dismissal, and many violent scenes took place. The Liberals threatened to hang him, — as very probably they would have done if power had fallen to them by another revolution. Unable to do that, they challenged him repeatedly to duels. Bismarck in turn denounced any prospect of alliance between the government and democracy as "shameful"; railed at the Liberals contemptuously as "mere pedants," and told them bluntly that the making of Germany was to be "a matter not of speechifying and parliamentary majorities, but of blood and iron." And for years he grimly went on, muzzling the press, bullying or dissolving parliaments, and overriding the national will roughshod.

Meantime, the army was greatly augmented, so that practically every able-bodied Prussian became a soldier with *three* years training in camp. First of any large army, too, this new Prussian army was supplied with the new invention of breech-loading repeating rifles, instead of the old-fashioned muzzle-loaders; and *Von Moltke*, the Prussian "chief of staff," made it the most perfectly organized military machine in Europe.

Bismarck's "trilogy" of wars

From the first, Bismarck intended that this reconstructed army should expel Austria from Germany and force the princes of the rest of Germany into a true national union. It had not been possible for him to *avow* his purpose; but time was growing precious, and he began to look anxiously for a chance to use his new tool. By a series of master-strokes of unscrupulous and daring diplomacy, he brought on three wars in the next seven years, — the Danish War (1864), the Six Weeks' War with Austria (1866), and the Franco-Prussian War (1870–1871). Out of these war clouds emerged a new Germany.

Sleswig-Holstein and the Danish War

For a long period the two duchies, *Sleswig* and *Holstein*, at the base of the Danish peninsula, had been loosely connected with the kingdom of Denmark. The union was one of those "personal" unions that have often confused the map of Europe. That is, the Danish king was also the duke of these two provinces. They were not subject to Danish law, but had assemblies of their own. The people of Sleswig were, in the main, Danes by blood; but in the southern province the population was German.

In 1863, the King of Denmark abolished the Sleswig assembly and incorporated that duchy in the Kingdom of Denmark. Something of this kind had been talked for fifteen years. Many people in Germany resented the prospect that Holstein might meet a like fate, and wished instead that the duchies, under an independent ruler of their own, should become a member of the Germanic Confederation. This situation caused a revival of many conflicting and complicated claims by various German princes, who, each in his own behalf, disputed the claim of the Danish king in the duchies. At any time, it was long felt, this Sleswig-Holstein question might plunge Europe into war.

In all this obscure and confused mess, one thing is absolutely clear: Prussia had no claim whatever to any part of the duchies, but Bismarck had determined that Prussia should get them. He felt no moral hesitation, and he had skillfully guarded against interference by the Powers. Russia he had conciliated by aiding her a few months before to put down a Polish rebellion, so that the grateful Tsar was willing to give him a free hand. Napoleon III, as Bismarck afterward explained, "had been allowed to deceive himself" into thinking that France would be permitted to annex Rhine territory to "indemnify" her for Prussia's proposed gain; England would not fight unsupported. Austria might have been expected surely to try to keep Denmark strong, as a check upon Prussia; but *Austria, the natural ally of Denmark, Bismarck made his accomplice* in the robbery by appealing to her greed. This was perhaps the greatest triumph in all Bismarck's crooked and wicked diplomacy. All the rest of his plan rested upon it. In 1864 the Prussian and Austrian armies seized the duchies, despite the gallant resistance of the Danes.

The "Six Weeks' War" with Austria

Then Bismarck forced Austria into war over the division of the spoils. He claimed both duchies for Prussia; and, though at Austria's indignant protest a system of joint protection was temporarily arranged, it soon became plain that the Prussian minister meant to secure all the booty.

King William, however, had scruples. He wanted to fight Austria, but he wanted a just cause. Bismarck had drawn Italy into an alliance by which that country promised to join in an attack upon Austria; but to satisfy his king, he must provoke Austria into some offensive act. So he was driven to desperate wiles. He continued to make absurd demands regarding the duchies, such as he knew could not be granted. At last, the German Diet summoned Prussia to refer the whole matter to its decision (perfectly in accord with the rules of the Confederation). Bismarck agreed to do this, *if the Diet would first exclude Austria from the Germanic Confederation.* Under Austria's lead the Diet then declared war on Prussia, "the wanton disturber of the national peace" (June 14, 1866). Bismarck was as jubilant as Cavour had been when *he* had drawn Austria into war in 1859.

Practically all Germany held to Austria. But Bismarck and Von Moltke were certain of success. In three days the Prussian army seized Hanover, Hesse, and Saxony, — the important hostile states in North Germany; and in less than three weeks from the declaration of war, Austria was completely crushed at *Sadowa* (Königgratz) in Bohemia. The war is known as "the Six Weeks' War."

The peace gave Venetia to Italy (p. 413). The other still more important provisions come under two heads. The first set augmented Prussian territory. The second set reorganized Germany.

1. *Prussia annexed* Hesse, Hanover, Nassau, and the "free city" of Frankfort. These acquisitions *consolidated her formerly scattered lands*. She also kept Sleswig-Holstein, with the magnificent harbor of Kiel. Her territory was enlarged one half; and her population rose to thirty millions. No other German state approached this — now that Austria was no longer to be a German state.

> Frederick II at his accession ruled over two and a half million subjects. This number was doubled during his reign, with some new territory. By 1815, it had doubled again, to ten millions. In the next half-century (1815–1866), the population had doubled, without additions of territory. The Six Weeks' War raised it from twenty to thirty millions. (Compare the map opposite with that on page 248.)

The North German Confederation

2. Austria definitely withdrew from German affairs, and the Confederation of 1815 was replaced by two federations. The first was known as *The North German Federation*. This union was placed under Prussian presidency. It was not a loose league like the old Confederacy, but *a true federal state* with much the same constitution as the later German Empire. The second federation included the four South German states, — Bavaria, Wurtemberg, Hesse-Darmstadt, and Baden. This union was intended to be similar to the old Confederacy of 1815, of which, indeed, it was a survival.

Liberals won over to autocracy and militarism

A third and indirect result of the war concerns the character of the Prussian government. After Sadowa, Bismarck was the idol of the Prussian people. As soon as his purpose to fight Austria became plain, the Liberal opposition in Prussia had been hushed. The Landtag passed enthusiastically the act of indemnity he requested for his previous illegal acts, and gave him a hearty support that made it easier for him to complete his

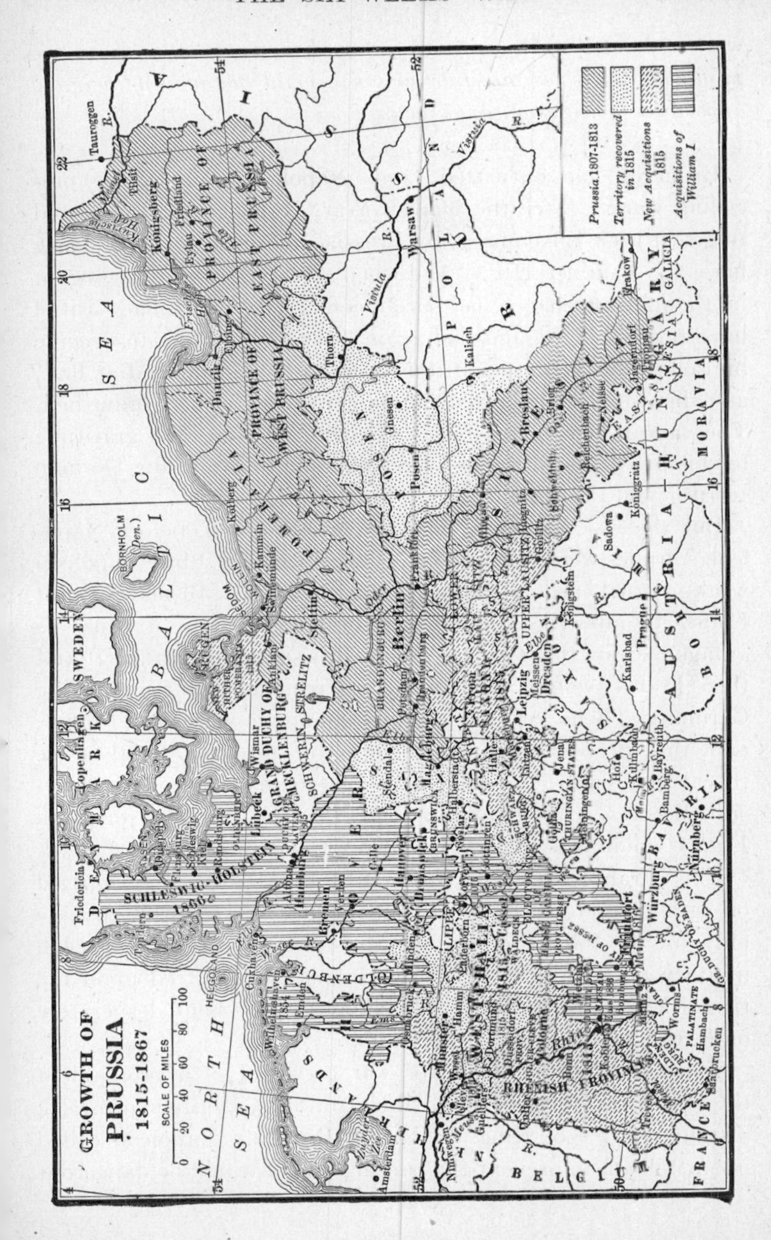
GROWTH OF
PRUSSIA
1815-1867
SCALE OF MILES
0 20 40 60 80 100
Prussia 1807-1813
Territory recovered in 1815
New Acquisitions 1815
Acquisitions of William I
BALTIC SEA
NORTH SEA
SWEDEN
DENMARK
POLAND
BELGIUM
FRANCE
AUSTRIA-HUNGARY
BOHEMIA
MORAVIA
GALICIA
BAVARIA
SAXONY
SILESIA
POSEN
POMERANIA
BRANDENBURG
HANOVER
WESTPHALIA
RHENISH PROVINCE
SCHLESWIG-HOLSTEIN
PROVINCE OF EAST PRUSSIA
PROVINCE OF WEST PRUSSIA
GRAND DUCHY OF MECKLENBURG SCHWERIN
STRELITZ
OLDENBURG
Berlin
Warsaw
Konigsberg
Danzig
Stettin
Breslau
Dresden
Leipzig
Prague
Posen
Hamburg
Bremen
Frankfort
Cologne
Sadowa
Koniggratz
Vistula
Oder
Elbe
Rhine

work. *Now that the military policy had apparently proven so profitable, the Prussian Liberals in general abandoned their old opposition to Prussian autocracy.*

Bismarck and Napoleon III

Bismarck had outwitted Louis Napoleon in both the preceding wars. After the Danish War, Napoleon had expected to get at least Luxemburg, by Prussia's aid, in return for giving her a free hand (p. 416). And when the Six Weeks' War began, he thought his chance had surely come. Bismarck had visited him shortly before, and had again "permitted" him to deceive himself. Napoleon meant, however, to remain neutral at first, and then step in at the critical moment to save the vanquished. The vanquished, he was sure, would be Prussia. In gratitude for his protection, Prussia would sanction his annexing German territory on the Rhine.

But the war was over, *and over the other way,* before Napoleon's armies were ready. The chance was past: but Napoleon weakly tried negotiation. He suggested to Bismarck that France be allowed to annex part of Bavaria (one of Prussia's antagonists in the war), to offset Prussia's annexations; and then France would give Prussia a free hand in reorganizing Germany. Bismarck was already planning war with France, and this proposal delivered Napoleon into his hands. He revealed it privately to the South German states. *This terrified them into a secret alliance with Prussia.* Now a war with France would fuse the two German Confederations into one.

This Franco-Prussian War (1870–1871) Bismarck hurried on with characteristic craft. But his success was made possible only by the folly and envy of the rulers of France. French military authorities looked with jealousy and hatred upon the rise of a German nation; and Napoleon was bent desperately on retrieving his tottering reputation.

The immediate occasion for war grew out of a proposal of the Spaniards to place upon their throne a German prince, a distant relative of King William of Prussia. Napoleon called upon William to prevent this, urging that it would be dangerous to the peace of Europe. It would have left France between two Hohenzollerns, as in the seventeenth century she had been between the two Hapsburgs. William did induce his relative to decline the offered crown. Napoleon, however, was bent upon humiliating William. So the French ambassador insisted that William should give a definite pledge that the offer, if renewed, would not be accepted. King William very properly declined to do this; but his refusal, though firm, was so courteous that there was no cause for offense.

Bismarck tricks France into the Franco-Prussian War

This interview took place at Ems. William at once telegraphed an account of the meeting to Bismarck at Berlin; and Bismarck himself tells us how his own dishonest cunning brought war out of this situation after all. Bismarck was at dinner with Moltke, speculating hopefully upon the chances for the war they wanted. The king's telegram arrived. "As I read it to him," says Bismarck, "Moltke's whole bearing suddenly changed. He looked old and sick. . . . I asked him if [in case of war] we might surely count upon victory. On his affirmative reply, I said 'Wait a minute,' and, seating myself at a small table, I boiled down those two hundred words [of the king's message] to about twenty, but without otherwise altering or adding anything. *It was the same telegram, yet something different* — shorter, more determined, less dubious. I handed it [to Moltke], and asked, 'Well, how does *that* do?' 'Yes,' said Moltke, 'it will do *in that form*.' And he immediately became quite young and fresh again. *He had got his war, his trade.*" [1]

The Ems telegram

As Bismarck had "edited" the telegram, it made King William seem to insult the French envoy. Bismarck at once gave out the message in this deceitful and irritating form to the press; and, as he hoped, France took fire and declared war (July 19, 1870).

A few French statesmen had kept their heads, Thiers among them, and had opposed the declaration, on the ground that

[1] Anderson's *Constitutions and Documents* gives in parallel columns the "Ems Dispatch" and Bismarck's version.

The arrogance and inefficiency of Napoleon's government

France was not properly prepared. But Napoleon's war-minister answered such objections by the boast, "We are thrice ready, down to the last soldier's shoestring"; and France, which for centuries had never been beaten by *one* foe, shouted light-heartedly, "On to Berlin." The first attempts to move troops, however, showed that the French government was honeycombed with corruption and inefficiency. Regiments lacked men. There was no discipline. Arsenals were empty. Transportation was not ready where it was needed, and supplies of all sorts were of poor quality. The French fought gallantly; but they were outnumbered and outgeneraled at every point.

"German efficiency" surprises the world

Marked, indeed, was the contrast between this French inefficiency and the "German efficiency," now revealed to Europe. The news that France had declared war reached Berlin late at night. Von Moltke was awakened by an aide, for directions. The story goes that the great general merely turned over, saying, "You will find all instructions in the upper right hand drawer in my desk. Telegraph the orders as filed there."

At all events, twelve days after the declaration of war (August 1), Germany had put one and a quarter million of trained troops into the field and had massed most of them on the Rhine. The world had never seen such marvelous perfection of military preparation Carlyle wrote "It took away the breath of Europe." August 2, William took command at Mainz. The Prussians won victory after victory. One of the two main French armies — 173,000 men — was securely shut up in *Metz*. And, September 2, the other, of 130,000 men, was captured at *Sedan*, with Napoleon in person. Napoleon remained a prisoner of war for a few months, and soon afterward died in England. Meantime the Prussians pressed on to the siege of Paris.

The German Empire

Out of the war clouds emerged a new German Empire. The South-German peoples went wild with enthusiasm for Prussia. By a series of swift treaties, while this feeling was at its height, Bismarck brought them all into the North German Confederation. Then he arranged that the King of

Bavaria and other leading German rulers should ask King William to take the title of *German Emperor*. And on January 18, 1871, while the siege of Paris was still going on, in the ancient palace of French kings at Versailles, William solemnly assumed that title. This act was soon ratified by a parliament of all Germany.

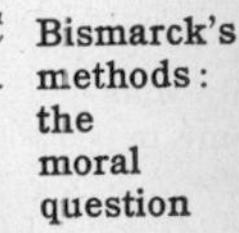
Bismarck's methods: the moral question

Germany had been made not merely by "blood and iron," but also by fraud and falsehood. One can hardly tell the story

PROCLAMATION OF THE GERMAN EMPIRE. From the painting by von Werner. Compare with the humiliation of the German envoys in the same place forty years later, when that Empire, born of war, had been destroyed by another war of its making; see p. 686.

of such gigantic audacity and successful trickery without seeming to glorify it. Of course, Bismarck did not work for low or personal ends. He was inspired by a real and broad patriotism. The national union which he made had to come before the German people could reach the best elements of modern life.

But he sought his end by base means. Bismarck's *methods* were distinctly lower than Cavour's; and his success tended to lower the tone of morality among nations. "Treaties," he said, "are scraps of paper"; and again, "when Prussia's power is in question I know no law." His policy of fraud and violence, too, while successful at the moment, left Germany troubled with burning questions, and burdened with the crushing weight of militarism and with the rule of the police and the drill sergeant in private life (pp. 507–513). In his Prussian hate for democracy and in his Prussian contempt for international morality, he started the new Empire upon the road which, forty years later, plunged it into the abyss.

Italy wins Rome in 1870

One good thing came from Bismarck's victory over Napoleon. At the outbreak of war in 1870, Napoleon was obliged at once to withdraw his garrison from Rome (p. 400). Then Victor Emmanuel's troops at last marched into Italy's ancient capital, and the Roman citizens ratified this consummation of the union of Italy by an almost unanimous vote. (Cf. map on p. 623.)

The later story of France and Germany can be best understood after studying the growth of constitutional government in England.

For Further Reading. — Hazen, *Europe Since 1815*, 240–306. Headlam's *Bismarck*, and his *Germany from 1815 to 1889*, are excellent.

Exercise. — 1. Review the story of Germany from the Congress of Vienna to the establishment of the Empire. 2. The story of Italy from 1814 to the final union of the peninsula in 1870. Note that from 1850 to 1870 continental European history in concerned with (1) the shame of the Second Empire in France for the entire period; (2) the glorious making of Italy in the first half; and (3) the making of Germany by fraud and violence in the second half.

PART VIII

ENGLAND 1815–1914: REFORM WITHOUT REVOLUTION

England in the nineteenth century served as a political model for Europe. The English developed constitutional monarchy, parliamentary government, and safeguards for personal liberty. Other nations have only imitated them. — SEIGNOBOS.

CHAPTER XXVIII

THE "FIRST REFORM BILL," 1832

Political retrogression of the eighteenth century

In the eighteenth century, we have seen, England acquired a world-empire and gave the world the Industrial Revolution. But, in political matters, that century was singularly uninteresting. In the preceding century England had led the world in political progress; and she was to do so again in the nineteenth century. But in the eighteenth, except for *accidental* progress in the matter of ministerial government (p. 212 ff.), England actually went backward in freedom. *Parliament* had never been democratic in make-up, and, after 1688, it *shriveled up into the selfish organ of a small class of landlords.*

"Virtual representation"

This came about largely by accident. The House of Commons contained 658 members. Ireland sent 100, and Scotland 45. Each of the 40 English counties, large or small, sent two. The rest came from "parliamentary boroughs" in England and Wales. The old kings had summoned representatives from whatever boroughs they pleased; but a borough which had once sent representatives had the right, by custom, to send them always afterward. At first the power to "summon" new boroughs was used wisely to recognize new towns as they grew up. But the Tudor monarchs, in order better to manage parliaments, had summoned representatives from little hamlets which had no just claim to representation. These were "pocket boroughs" — owned or controlled by some lord of the court party.

Unrepresented cities

This bad condition was made worse by natural causes. In early times the south of England, with its fertile soil and its ports on the Channel, had been the most populous part; but in the eighteenth century, with the growth of manufactures, population shifted to the coal and iron regions of the north and west. In Elizabeth's day that part of the island had only insignificant towns. Before 1800, great cities grew up there, like Birmingham, Bradford, Leeds, Liverpool, Manchester, Sheffield, some of them with more than 100,000 people (p. 374). But these new towns could get no representation in Parliament, because after the "Restoration" of 1660 the kings had lost the right to create new boroughs, just when that power might have been used to public advantage.

And represented ruins

Conditions had become unspeakably unfair and corrupt. *Dunwich* was under the waves of the North Sea, which had gradually encroached upon the land. But a descendant of an ancient owner of the soil possessed the right to row out with the sheriff on election day and choose himself as representative to Parliament for the submerged town. *Old Sarum* was once a cathedral city on the summit of a lofty hill; but new Sarum, or Salisbury, a few miles away on the plain, drew the population and the cathedral to itself until not a vestige of the old town remained. Then the grandfather of William Pitt bought the soil where Old Sarum had stood, and it was for this "pocket borough" that the great Pitt entered Parliament. It was wittily said at the time, that the Pitt family had "an hereditary seat in the House of Commons." So, *Gatton* was a park, and *Corfe Castle* a picturesque ruin, — each with a representative in Parliament.

Then there were a great number of petty villages or little towns, with six or a dozen or fifty voters. Bosseney in Cornwall had three cottages. It had, however, nine voters, eight of them in one family. And these voters elected two members to Parliament. Even in large towns, the rules which determined the right to vote were often fantastic, and sometimes they shut out all but a fraction of the inhabitants. Portsmouth, with 46,000 people, had only 103 voters; and in Weymouth in 1826, the right to vote went with the right to share in the rents of certain ancient village property, — and so twenty persons, some of them paupers, voted because of their title each to one twentieth of a sixpence.

"Pocket boroughs"

Many of these places also, with few voters, were "pocket boroughs," — the voters being dependent upon a neighboring landlord and always electing his nominee. Large places had sometimes a like character. In 1828, at Newark, the Duke of Newcastle drove out 587 tenants who had ventured to vote against his candidate. Complaint was made in Parliament; but the Duke answered calmly, "Have I not a right to do what I like with my own?" So the Duke of Norfolk filled eleven seats; and fully two thirds of the whole House of Commons were really the appointees of great landlords.

"Rotten boroughs"

When not pocket boroughs, such places commonly were "rotten boroughs." That is, the few voters sold the seats in Parliament as a regular part of their private revenue. In 1766 Sudbury advertised in the public press that its parliamentary seat was for sale to the highest bidder. Moreover, all voting was viva-voce, and the polls were held open for two weeks — so that there was every chance to sell and buy votes.

The House of Commons had become hardly more representative than the House of Lords. As the English historian Macaulay said, the "boasted representative system" of England had decayed into "a monstrous system of *represented ruins* and *unrepresented cities*."

Reform checked by foreign war, 1689–1815

Progressive men had long seen that Parliament no longer represented the nation. *The reason why no reform had been secured was that from 1689 to 1815 all energies went to the long French wars.* In the twelve years (1763–1775), between the "Seven Years' War" (p. 243) and the American Revolution, the Whig leaders did attempt wise changes. In 1766 William Pitt declared that Parliament must reform itself from within, or it would soon be reformed "with a vengeance" from without; and during the next few years many mass meetings urged Parliament to take action.

George III opposes reform

But George III was determined to prevent reform. The war with America was connected closely with this determination. George felt that his two indolent and gross predecessors had allowed kingly power to slip from their hands (p. 214). He meant to get it back, and to "be a king" in fact as well as in name, as his mother had urged him. To do this, he must be able to control Parliament. It would be easier to control it as it was then — made up so largely of representatives of pocket boroughs — than to control a Parliament that really represented the nation.

Relation to the American Revolution

Therefore, when just at this time the Americans began to cry, "No taxation without representation," King George felt it needful to put them down. If their claim was allowed, so must be the demand of Manchester and other new towns in England for representation in Parliament. But if the American demand could be made to seem a treasonable one, on the part of a distant group of rebels, then the king could check the movement in England also. This explains why King George took so active a part against America.

The American victory seemed at first to have won an immediate victory for English freedom also. King George was forced to say that he was "pleased to appoint" among the leading ministers his chief enemy, Charles Fox, the special friend of America. And William Pitt the Younger at once took up the work of reform. Even before peace was declared, Pitt asserted vehemently: Parliament "is not representative of the people of Great Britain. It is representative of nominal boroughs, and exterminated towns, of noble families, of wealthy individuals." This condition, he declared, alone had made it possible for the government to wage against America "this unjust, cruel, wicked, and diabolical war."

Reform checked by hatred for the French Revolution

In the years that immediately followed, Pitt introduced three different bills for reform; but, before anything was accomplished, came the French Revolution. This shelved all prospect of success. In 1790 on a proposal for reform, the keynote of the opposition was struck by a Tory speaker who exclaimed that no wise man would select a hurricane season to repair his roof, however dilapidated. Soon the violence of the Revolutionists in France turned the whole English middle class definitely against change — and projects for reform slumbered for forty years more (1790–1830).

This unhappy check came just when the evils of the Industrial Revolution were becoming serious. But *the Tory party, which carried England stubbornly to victory through the tremendous wars against Napoleon, was totally unfitted to cope with internal questions.* Its leaders looked on every time-sanctioned abuse as sacred. Even after the fall of Napoleon, they refused to listen to proposals for change.

Tory reaction *after* the Napoleonic wars

The peace of 1815 was followed by a general business depression, — the first modern "panic." Large parts of the working classes had no work and no food. This resulted in labor riots and in political agitation. The Tory government met such movements by stern laws, forbidding public meetings (without consent of magistrates) under penalty of death; suspending habeas corpus (for the last time in England until the World War); and suppressing debating societies.

This repressive policy, with the denial of free speech, had begun, properly enough, during the Napoleonic war, to guard against treason (as in the American Espionage Act during the recent World War); but it was carried to absurd and tyrannical extremes and was kept up after all need was gone. In 1812 two editors were condemned to a year's imprisonment for saying that a rival paper had been guilty of exaggeration in calling the Prince of Wales an Adonis (a Greek of great beauty). Between 1808 and 1821, ninety-four other journalists were punished for libelous or seditious utterances, and twelve of them were condemned to transportation to penal colonies. Several of these condemnations came *after* the war. The government even prosecuted men for sedition who merely signed petitions for the reform of Parliament.

Says Dr. Cross (*History of England*, 869), "The hide-bound Tories in the Ministry lumped the Radicals, violent and peaceful, frenzied and sensible, without discrimination, as revolutionists." As in like action by reactionaries at all times in all lands, this was partly from honest ignorance, partly from cruel and unscrupulous partisanship. A parliamentary committee solemnly charged the Radicals with intending to destroy or distribute private property. And the infamous "Oliver the Spy," a government agent, "manufactured" false evidence, and stirred up risings among the poor, so as to have something to "reveal" to his credulous and unscrupulous employers. Juries usually refused to condemn men accused by the government on such evidence; but there were three executions and several transportations. The *only* measure adopted by the government to *remedy* the causes of disorder was a grant of £1,000,000, *to build new churches*, on the ground that the social disquiet was "due to inadequate religious instruction" (instead of to inadequate food).

Some early reform movements

The year 1821 marks the beginning of slow gains for reform. In 1825 parliament recognized the right of workingmen to unite in labor unions — which had always before been treated as *conspiracies*. In 1828 political rights were restored to Protestant dissenters (p. 211; — Baptists, Presbyterians, Methodists); and the next year the same justice was secured for Catholics. The atrocious laws regarding capital punishment, too, were partially modified. The English penal code of the eighteenth century has been fitly called a "sanguinary chaos." Its worst faults, like the abuses of the rotten borough era in politics, were due to the English dislike for change. Whenever in the course of centuries a crime had become especially troublesome, some Parliament had fixed a death penalty for it, and no later Parliament had ever revised the code. In 1660 the number of "capital crimes" was fifty (three and a half times as many as there were in New England at the same time under the much slandered "blue laws"), and by 1800 the number had risen to over two hundred. To steal a sheep, to snatch a handkerchief out of a woman's hand, to cut down trees in an orchard, were all punishable by death. The reformer *Romilly* had long agitated for the repeal of these absurd and cruel laws; and in 1823 Parliament struck the death penalty from 100 offenses.

Struggle for parliamentary reform begins in 1830

The year 1830 really begins the new era. George IV was succeeded by his brother William IV, a more liberal-minded king; and the French Revolution of the same year, by its *moderation* and by its success, strengthened the reform party in England. A new Parliament was at once chosen; and the Whigs promptly introduced a motion to reform the representation. The prime minister was the Tory *Wellington,* the hero of Waterloo. He scorned the proposal, declaring that he did not believe the existing representation "could be improved"! This speech cost him his popularity, both in and out of Parliament. He was compelled to resign; and the Whigs came into power with *Earl Grey* as prime minister. Grey was a stately English lord, whose eloquence at the trial of Warren Hastings forty years before had been celebrated by Macaulay. In the House of Commons the chief member of the ministry was Lord John Russell. He was the son of a duke, and his title of Lord at this time was only a "courtesy title."

Fall of Wellington

The Whig leaders

Lord Russell drew the bill for the reform of Parliament. In introducing the measure in the Commons, he pictured the amazement of a stranger who had gone to England to study the free representative government of which Englishmen boasted. The stranger would be shown, said Lord Russell, a ruined mound [p. 426], and be told that that mound sent two representatives to Parliament. He would be taken to a stone wall with three niches in it, and be told that those niches sent two representatives to Parliament. He would see a green park, with no sign of human habitation, and be told that that park sent two representatives to Parliament. And then he might chance to see populous towns, full of human enterprise and industry, but he would be told that most of those towns sent *no* representatives to Parliament.

A moderate reform

The Bill was a very moderate one: It aimed only (1) *to distribute representation* somewhat more fairly, and (2) *to extend the franchise* to a somewhat larger class of voters. The *manner of voting* was not affected, because Earl Grey objected to the ballot system.

Representation was to be taken away from 56 "rotten" or "pocket" boroughs, and one member was to be taken from 30 more small places under 4000 people each. The seats gained in this way were given to new boroughs that needed representation. The suffrage was extended to all householders in the towns who owned or rented houses worth $50 a year, and to the whole "farmer" class in the country (p. 380). *Farm laborers and the artisan class in towns* (who lived in tenements or as lodgers) *were still left out.*

The king *forced* to yield to his ministers

To the Tories this mild measure seemed to threaten the foundations of society. Fierce debates lasted month after month. In March of 1831 the ministry carried the "second reading" by a majority of *one* vote. It was plain that the Whig majority was not large enough to save the bill from hostile amendment. (A bill has to pass three "readings," and amendments are usually considered after the second.) The ministry decided to dissolve, and "appeal to the country" for better support. The king was bitterly opposed to this plan. A passionate scene took place between him and his ministers, but he was forced to give way — and so, incidentally, it was settled that the ministry, not the king, dissolves Parliament. *This means that Parliament really dissolves itself.*

Lords and Commons

The dissolution proved that the ministry meant to stand or fall on the bill. People showed their joy everywhere by illuminating windows; and a mob smashed the windows of Wellington's castle because they were not lighted. The Whigs went into the campaign with the cry, "The Bill, the whole Bill, and nothing but the Bill." Despite the unrepresentative nature of Parliament, they won an overwhelming majority. In June Lord Russell introduced the bill again. In September it passed the Commons, 345 to 239. Then the Lords again calmly voted it down.

One session of the second Parliament was wasted. The nation cried out passionately against the House of Lords. There was much violence, and England seemed on the verge of revolution.

In December the same Parliament met for a new session. Lord Russell introduced the same bill for the third time. It passed the Commons by an increased majority. This time the Lords did not venture altogether to throw it out, but they tacked on hostile amendments.

The "Eleven Days"

The king had always had power to make new peers at will. Lord Grey now demanded from the king authority to create enough new peers to save the bill. William refused. Grey resigned. For eleven days England had no government. The Tories tried to form a ministry, but could get no majority. Angry mobs stormed about the king's carriage in the streets. It was feared that William and Wellington might try to overthrow the Whigs by a *coup d'état;* and the Whig leaders went so far as secretly to prepare for civil war. Finally the king recalled the Whig ministry.

The Lords become an *inferior* House

William was still unwilling to create new peers, but he offered to use his personal influence to get the upper House to pass the bill. Happily, Earl Grey was firm to show where real sovereignty lay; and finally the king was compelled to sign the paper (still exhibited in the British Museum) on which the Earl had written, "The King grants permission to Earl Grey . . . to create such a number of new peers as will insure the passage of the Reform Bill." This ended the struggle. It was not needful actually to make new peers. The Tory lords withdrew from the sessions, and the bill passed, June 4, 1832.

Incidentally the long contest had settled two points in the constitution:

It had shown how the Commons could control the Lords.

The "King's ministers" became the nation's executive

It had shown that the ministers are not the king's ministry, except in name, but that they are really the ministry, or servants, of the House of Commons. This principle has never since been threatened. The king acts only through the ministers. Even the speech he reads at the opening of Parliament is written for him, and without consulting him; and he cannot change a phrase in it.

Excursus on ministerial government

The way in which a change in ministry is brought about should be clearly understood. If the ministry is outvoted on any matter of importance, it must resign. If it does not do so, and claims to be in doubt whether it has really lost its majority, its opponents will test the matter by moving a vote of "lack of confidence." If this carries, the ministry takes it as a mandate to resign.

There is only one alternative: If the ministry believes that the nation will support it, it may dissolve Parliament, and "appeal to the country." If the new Parliament gives it a majority, it may go on. If not, it must at once give way to a new ministry.

In form, the new ministry is chosen by the king; but in reality, he simply names those whom the will of the majority in the Commons has plainly pointed out. Indeed, he names only one man, whom he asks to "form a government." This man becomes *prime minister*, and selects the other ministers. In a parliamentary election, Englishmen really vote also for the next prime minister, just as truly, *and about as directly*, as we in this country vote for our President. If the king asks any one else to form a ministry but the man whom the Commons have accepted as their leader, probably the man asked will respectfully decline. If he tries to act, he will fail to get other strong men to join him, and his ministry will at once fail. If there is any real uncertainty as to which one of several men is leader, the matter is settled by conference among the leaders, and the new ministry, of course, includes all of them.

A curious feature to an American student is that all this complex procedure *rests only on custom* — nowhere on a written constitution. Each member of the Cabinet is the head of some great department — Foreign Affairs, Treasury, War, and so on. The leading assistants in all these departments — some forty people now — are included in the ministry. About twenty of the forty, — holding the chief positions, — make the inner circle which is called the Cabinet.

The Cabinet is really "the Government," and is often referred to by that title. It *is the real executive; and it is also the "steering committee" of the legislature.* In their private meetings the members of the Cabinet decide upon general policy. In Parliament they introduce bills and advocate them. As ministers, they carry out the plans agreed upon The prime minister corresponds in a way to a combination of the President and the Congressional Speaker in America. The Cabinet is what our cabinet would be if the President were merely its head, and if its members had seats in Congress with control over the order of business in that body, and with power to dissolve it and appeal to the people if Congress differed with it.

The English referendum

The English dissolution, it should be seen clearly, is a sort of referendum. It gives the English people a better chance to express their will *directly* on *particular* important questions than we in America get — except in very rare instances. That is one reason why many Englishmen claim that their government — in spite of the "figurehead royalty" — is really more democratic than ours. The English government does respond *more quickly* to the will of the nation than ours does.

Responsibility for legislation clearly fixed

Moreover, *the union of executive and legislature fixes responsibility.* In America, Congress passes a multitude of bills and appropriations, often by log-rolling processes, for which no party and no leading member will confess responsibility. In England, the ministry is responsible for every bill that is passed. Either the ministry introduces the bill to begin with, or at least permits or adopts it. If not willing to do that, it either defeats the bill, or is itself defeated. It cannot dodge responsibility to the nation. Quite as much, too, it is responsible if it fails to introduce and pass bills desired by the nation.

The king's veto has disappeared in these changes. The last veto was one by Queen Anne in 1707. Now the only veto is a dissolution of Parliament by the ministry; and if the country is in favor of the "vetoed" measure, the next Parliament is certain to make it into law.

The English "Speaker"

The Speaker of the House of Commons, it should be understood, holds a very different position from the Speaker in America. Here he is the party leader of the majority party. Until 1911, he appointed committees so as to give complete control of Congress to his own party, and he still has great influence in such matters; and in debates, he recognizes members in such order as he and the leaders of his party have decided upon — not simply as they claim the floor. In England, the Speaker is absolutely non-partisan, — a true presiding "moderator," bound to treat all members and parties impartially.

No authority in England can set aside a law of Parliament, as our Supreme Court sometimes does with laws of Congress. There is no possibility of a deadlock between legislature and executive; nor, since the "mending" of the House of Lords in 1914 (p. 480), can there be any long-continued deadlock between the two Houses of the Legislature. An election is followed by the immediate meeting of the new Parliament, while in the United States a new Congress does not meet, commonly, until thirteen months after its election. The English election, too, is very often to decide some particular important question. The English people can express their will in such an election, and feel sure that it will be made promptly into law.

Progress in England and America in the thirties contrasted

This is the place to note certain *relations between American and English Democracy*. The First Reform Bill in England was one episode in a general period of democratic advance. The Second French Revolution and its results for Europe have been mentioned. In America, too, much progress was made at about the same time. All the original States had shut out large classes from voting (more than half all the men on an average) and still larger classes from holding office, by graded property qualifications. But in 1821, fifteen of the twenty-four States had manhood suffrage, and the number was steadily growing. Public officials, too, and the "gentleman" class, were just ceasing to wear powdered hair, knee breeches, and silk stockings, to mark themselves off from the common people.

Moreover, the wider franchise of the American States was being used more directly than at first. In 1800 only six of the sixteen commonwealths of that day chose presidential electors by the voters directly; but, after 1832, South Carolina was the only State that continued to choose them by the legislature. The electors, too, were no longer supposed to be a select coterie who were to "refine" the popular judgment by their own higher intelligence. They had become — what they have since remained — "mere letter carriers," to register the will of the people.

In England the nation politely shelved the old hereditary, monarchic executive by taking over its powers through a committee of the elected Parliament. In America the people captured the old indirectly elective, aristocratic executive, by making it directly responsive to the popular will. The victory of Jackson, in the election of 1828, marks this change. He was called the "chosen Tribune of the people." Since that time, the President has been more truly representative of the people's will than Congress has. One result of the contrast between English and American democracy is that, while the royal veto has utterly vanished, the Presidential veto has steadily grown in importance.

Thus we have two types of democratic government in the world, both developed by English-speaking peoples. They differ from each other mainly in regard to the executive. In the United States, the executive is a president, or governor, independent of the legislature. The other republics upon this continent have adopted this American type. In England, the executive has become practically a steering committee of the legislature. This type is the one adopted by most of the free governments of the world outside America.

EXERCISE. — With the last pages, review pp. 209–214, on the Revolution of 1688 and the *beginning* of cabinet government.

FOR FURTHER READING. — The most brilliant story is Justin McCarthy's *Epoch of Reform*, 25–83. Rose's *Rise of Democracy*, 9–52, is excellent. See also one or more of the following: Hazen's *Europe Since 1815*, 409–415, 428–438; Beard's *English Historians*, 538–548, 549–565, and 594–607 (extract from Bagehot's *English Constitution*); Robinson and Beard's *Readings*, II, 239–245; Cheyney's *Readings*, 679–690. Weyman's *Chipping Borough* (fiction) shows forcefully the mob influence in 1832 and reflects faithfully the snobbishness of the middle-class Liberals of the time.

CHAPTER XXIX

POLITICAL REFORM IN THE VICTORIAN AGE

The "Victorian age"

The First Reform Bill introduced a new era, which we call *the Victorian age.* In 1837 William IV was succeeded by his niece, Victoria, whose reign filled the next *sixty-four years.* Victoria came to the throne a modest, high-minded girl of eighteen years. She was not brilliant, or particularly intellectual; but she grew into a worthy, sensible, good woman, of splendid moral influence, deeply loved by her people and admired by all the world. In 1840 she married Albert, the ruler of a small German principality; and their happy, pure, and lovely family life, blessed with nine children, was an example new to European courts for generations.

Victoria kept willingly the position of a "constitutional" sovereign; but, on some critical occasions, she did induce her ministers to moderate their intended policy. The most notable instance of this sort was in 1861, when her suggestion and influence softened a communication from the English government to the United States which otherwise might have driven the two countries into war — the Mason and Slidell incident at the opening of our Civil War.

World conditions at its opening

The Victorian age was a period of peace, prosperity, refinement of morals, intellectual glory, democratic advance, and of tremendous expansion of civilization in space. To appreciate this progress of the last two thirds of the nineteenth century, it is needful to grasp conditions when the Victorian era began. The world was still a small, despotic world, far more remote from the great progressive world of 1900 than from the world of 1600. Civilization held only two patches on the globe, — western Europe and eastern North America. In the latter, the real frontier of the United States reached less than one third the way across the continent, and politics and society were dominated by the slave power. Europe knew "Germany" only as a pious aspiration of revolutionaries, and "Italy" as a "geographical expression." Metternich stood guard over central Europe. On the east hung Russia, an inert mass, in the chains of her millions of serfs. Under the contemptible Orleans monarchy, France was taking breath between spasmodic revolutions. England herself had only in part thrown off the long oligarchic rule of her landlord class. The rest of the globe hardly counted: a fringe of Australia held a convict camp; eastern Canada was a group of jealous petty provinces, learning to agitate in a disorderly fashion for self-government; Spanish America, prostrate in anarchy, gave as yet little hope of its coming renaissance; Japan was to sleep a generation longer; while the two largest continents were undisturbed in their native barbarism, except for England's grasp upon the hem of India and South Africa.

VICTORIA TAKING THE CORONATION OATH. After the painting by Landseer at Windsor Palace.

England's world-leadership

Throughout the century England remained the most powerful and the richest country in the world, — leading especially in manufacturing, in commerce, in sea-power, and in literature.

In this last respect, English leadership is marked by a long list of famous names. True, *Burns*, *Byron*, and *Scott* belong to the age of the Georges; *Wordsworth* and *Macaulay*, too, had begun their activity before the accession of Victoria. But *Browning*, *Tennyson*, *Dickens*, "*George Eliot*," and *Thackeray* are only a part of the dazzling Victorian galaxy in poetry and fiction, while such names as *Darwin*, *Tyndal*, and *Huxley* suggest some of the services of Victorian scientists to the world. During the same period, the literary charm of *Carlyle*, *Ruskin*, and *William Morris* enabled them to preach effectively to all English-speaking peoples their new views of life and of art.

After 1832, England a middle-class aristocracy

In Parliament, *reform crowded upon reform*. The First Reform Bill gave votes to 650,000 people — or to *one out of six grown men*. This was five times as liberal as the French franchise after the Revolution of 1830. *Political power* in England *had passed from a narrow, selfish landlord oligarchy to a broad enlightened middle-class aristocracy*. For more than forty years (1790–1830), Parliament had openly been contemptuous of public opinion. Thenceforward it has always been promptly responsive to that force.

Liberals and Conservatives

The great political parties soon took new names. The name *Conservative* now began to replace Tory, and *Liberal* replaced Whig. During the next forty-two years (1832–1874), the Tories, or Conservatives, were in power less than one sixth of the time. After those forty years, they, too, adopted a liberal policy toward the working classes, and secured longer leases of power.[1]

[1] Reference Table of Administrations:

	Liberals	*Conservatives*		*Liberals*	*Conservatives*
1830–34	Grey		1859–66	(1) Palmerston (2) Russell	
1834–35		Peel	1866–68		Derby
1835–41	Melbourne		1868–74	Gladstone	
1841–46		Peel	1874–80		Disraeli
1846–52	Russell		1880–85	Gladstone	
1852		Derby	1885–86		Salisbury
1852–58	(1) Aberdeen (2) Palmerston		1886	Gladstone	
1858–59		Derby	1886–92		Salisbury

Disraeli and Gladstone

The man who did most to educate the Conservatives into this new attitude toward social reform was *Disraeli*, the real leader of the party through the third quarter of the nineteenth century. By birth Disraeli was a Jew. He was an author, and a man of brilliant genius. Some critics called him "a Conservative with Radical opinions," while others insisted that he had no principles in politics. Carlyle expressed the general amazement at Disraeli's attitude and at his success in drawing his party with him, — "a superlative Hebrew conjurer, spell-binding all the great lords, great parties, great interests, and leading them by the nose, like helpless, mesmerized, somnambulant cattle."

GLADSTONE in old age. — From a photograph.

An even more important figure was Disraeli's great adversary, *William E. Gladstone*. Gladstone entered Parliament in 1833, at the first election after the Reform Bill, and soon proved himself a powerful orator and a master of debate. He was

REFERENCE TABLE OF ADMINISTRATION: — *Cont.*

	Liberals	*Conservatives*		*Liberals*	*Conservatives*
1892–95	(1) Gladstone (2) Rosebery		[1915–1918	A coalition war-ministry, led by Lloyd George]	
1895–1906		(1) Salisbury (2) Balfour	1919–	A coalition ministry, mainly Conservatives, led by Lloyd George.	
1906	Campbell-Bannerman Asquith (to 1915)				

then an extreme Tory. By degrees he grew Liberal, and thirty years later he succeeded Lord Russell as the unchallenged leader of that party. For thirty years more he held that place, — four times prime minister, — and at the close of his long career he had become an advanced Radical. His early friends accused Gladstone bitterly as inconsistent or treacherous; but the world at large accepted his own simple explanation of his changes, — "I was brought up to distrust liberty; I learned to believe in it." For the last quarter-century of his life he was widely revered as England's "Grand Old Man."

After this general survey, we turn to some of the details of England's progress in the Victorian age.

Working-class discontent after 1832

The Tories at once accepted the result of 1832, as the Conservative party in England always does when a new reform has once been forced upon them. *But they planted themselves upon it as a finality.* Even the Whigs, who were by no means democrats, agreed in this "finality" view. In the Parliament of 1837 a Radical moved a resolution in favor of a further extension of the franchise; but Lord Russell, speaking for the ministry, condemned it savagely, and only twenty-two votes supported it. A few eager Radicals for a time kept up a cry for a more liberal franchise, but soon they gave up the contest, to take part in the great social legislation of the period.

The trade-union movement

But outside Parliament, and outside the sovereign middle class, lay the *masses of workingmen*, who knew that the victory of 1832 had been won largely by their sympathy and public demonstrations, and who felt that they had been cheated of the fruits.[1] This class continued restless; but they lacked leadership, and, in ordinary times, their claims secured little attention. At first, disappointed in politics the workingmen turned to trade-unions, and sought to get better wages and shorter hours by strikes. As in America at the same time, an attempt was made at a nation-wide organization, — which in 1834 enrolled nearly a million members. But employers

[1] There is an admirable treatment in Rose's *Rise of Democracy*, ch. ii.

united, dismissed all union workmen, and, aided by the conservative courts, stamped out the movement. A strike by a union the courts held a "conspiracy." Under medieval common-law practice they transported six labor leaders to the Australian penal settlements, and for many years the labor movement lay crushed.

The Chartist agitation

Then the Radicals turned again to politics. There were two marked periods of agitation at intervals of nearly twenty years, — just before 1848 and again before 1867. The earlier is the famous *Chartist movement.* Even before the First Reform Bill, there had been an extensive agitation for a more radical change, and the extremists had fixed upon six points to struggle for: (1) manhood suffrage, (2) equal electoral districts, (3) abolition of all property qualification for membership in Parliament, (4) payment of members, (5) the ballot, and (6) annual elections. In 1837 the Radicals renewed their agitation, and these "Six Points" were embodied in the *Charter* they demanded. Excitement grew for years,[1] and in the forties, many *Chartists* looked forward to rebellion. Men drilled and armed; and the government was terrified into taking stringent precautions.

Five of the six points have since become law, and the unimportant sixth point is no longer asked for. But to the prosperous English Liberal of 1840 these Chartist demands seemed to promise revolution and anarchy. One reverend writer opposed the demands by such arguments as these: "What would you gain by *universal suffrage?* . . . All workmen would become politicians . . . [and] spend their time . . . in what would only increase their poverty. *Vote by ballot* would be nothing but a law for rogues and knaves, nothing but a cloak for . . . hypocrisy. . . . The Chartist doctrine of equality is diametrically opposed to nature and to the word of God." (For equally absurd opposition in America to manhood suffrage, twenty years earlier, see West's *American People*, pp. 376–377, 477.)

[1] Charles Kingsley's *Alton Locke* is a powerful story of this period.

"Forty-eight" was the critical year. The reform was set back by the English revulsion against the violent revolution going on upon the continent. The Chartists adopted a resolution, "All labor shall cease till the people's Charter becomes the law of the land." This was the first attempt at a national strike for political purposes. But the plan for monster demonstrations, with great petitions and processions, fizzled out, and the "year of revolutions" saw no disturbance in England that called for more than a few extra policemen.

The Second Reform Bill, 1867: England a democracy

The next agitation took its rise from the suffering of the unemployed while the American Civil War cut off the supply of cotton for English factories, and it was strengthened by the hard-won victory of the democratic North in that war over the aristocratic South. This time no one dreamed of force. The agitators could count safely on winning, through the rivalry of the two political parties. The Liberals, under Russell, introduced a reform measure, but lost power because they did not go far enough. Then, said Disraeli, cynically, "If the country is bound to have reform, *we* might as well give it to them" — and stay in office; and *the "Second Reform Bill"* was finally passed *in 1867* by a Conservative ministry.

Lord Derby was prime minister; but, as he sat in the Lords, it was necessary to intrust some Commoner with special leadership in the lower House. This task fell upon Disraeli, who became (as is usually the case under such conditions) the real genius of the administration.

All householders (owners or renters) and *all lodgers who paid ten pounds a year for their rooms,* became voters. Thus this bill gave the franchise to *the artisan class*, raising the number of voters to over *three million,* or to something over half the adult male population. John Stuart Mill aroused no little amusement by proposing votes for women.

The *unskilled laborers* in town and country, and the male house-servants, still had no votes; but England had taken a tremendous step toward democracy. This victory of 1867, like that of 1832, was followed by a period of sweeping legislation for social reforms, — mainly in Gladstone's Liberal ministry, 1868–1874 (p. 456). Then, after a Conservative ministry, led by Disraeli and chiefly concerned with foreign matters (p. 458), Gladstone took office again, and the "Third Reform Bill" (1884) in large measure enfranchised the unskilled laborer and the servant class.

The Third Reform Bill, 1884

This raised the electorate to *over six millions*, and (except for unmarried sons, without property, living in the father's family, and for laborers living in very cheap houses) it gave votes to practically all self-supporting men. The next year, Parliament did away with the chief remaining inequalities in representation by dividing England into parliamentary districts, like our congressional districts.

It is well to fix clearly the nature of these three Reform Bills. The First (1832) enfranchised the middle class (merchants, shopkeepers, professional men, etc., besides the gentry, freeholders, and members of borough corporations, who had the franchise before). The Second (1867) enfranchised the artisans in the towns. The Third (1884) enfranchised unskilled laborers, leaving less than one seventh the adult males without a vote.

Four other reforms in this period made English politics clean and honest.

Other reforms in politics

In 1870 the secret ballot was introduced. The form adopted was the excellent one known as the Australian ballot, from its use in Victoria. Most of the States of our Union have since then adopted the same model.

Between 1855 and 1870, the civil service was thoroughly reformed. In earlier years, public offices had been given to reward political partisans, in as disgraceful a degree as ever marked American politics. But since 1870, appointments have always been made after competitive examinations, and there has been no removal of appointed officials for party reasons. England had completed this great reform before the United States began it.

In 1868 Parliament turned over to the courts the trial of contested elections. In Stuart times, when the kings sometimes attempted to control the composition of Parliament, it was needful for the Commons themselves to have the right to decide between two men who claimed the same seat. That need had passed away; and the decision of contested elections in Parliament, as in our legislatures still, was often made by a strict "party vote," without regard to the merits of the opposing claims. In transferring these cases to the courts, England led the way in a reform which other free countries will in time adopt.

Bribery in elections, direct and also indirect, was effectively checked by the "Corrupt Practices Prevention Act" of 1883, drawn along lines more recently adopted in the United States.

Local government reform

The extension of the franchise in the three great "Reform" bills applied only to *parliamentary* elections. But local government also called for reform. It had been highly aristocratic. It was not *centralized,* as in France; but each local unit was in the hands of the *local* aristocracy.

The need

The two rural units, the *counties* and the *parishes,* were altogether controlled by the country gentry, without even the form of an election. (1) The crown appointed a Board of *Justices of the Peace,* for life, from the most important gentlemen of each county, and this Board managed all matters of *county government,* acting both as judges and as county commissioners. (2) *Each parish* was ruled by a *vestry* of twelve gentlemen who formed a *close corporation, holding office for life, and themselves filling vacancies.*

In the towns, the government was usually vested in a mayor and a council, who were virtually self-elected for life. This town rule had long been indescribably corrupt. The "corporation," as the government was called, never represented any large part of the inhabitants. The members spent public funds as they pleased, — largely in salaries to themselves, and in entertainments and state dinners, — and they rented public property to one another at nominal prices, while all the pressing needs of the great and growing city populations were ignored.

Reform in town government begins in 1835

The corrupt town government was the first part of local government to be reformed. Earl Grey's ministry in 1833 appointed "a commission of inquiry"; and, after the report of the commission in 1835, Lord Russell introduced a Municipal Reform Bill. The measure provided that 183 boroughs (indicated by name) should each have a municipal council *elected by all who paid local taxes*. The Lords went wild with dismay at this "gigantic innovation," and by votes of 6 to 1, they amended nearly every clause in the bill so as to make it worthless. At this time, O'Connell, the Irish agitator, started a movement to abolish the House of Lords. "It is impossible," said he, "that it should last, — that such a set of stupid, ignorant, half-mad fops and coxcombs should continue so to lord it." The Commons refused the amendments; and after a four months' struggle the Lords yielded. From time to time, through the century, new towns were added to the list, as need arose, and finally, in 1882, it was provided that any town might adopt this form of government for itself.

The municipal reform of 1835 was immediate and successful. English town government ever since has been honest, efficient, and enlightened, — a model to all other democratic countries, and a full half-century ahead of America. The best citizens serve in the town councils. The appointed officials, like the city engineer, city health officer and so on, are men of high professional standing, who serve virtually for life and are never appointed or removed for political purposes. The government costs less and gives more than in American cities, and the scandals that disgrace our city governments are unknown. The form of government is that known as the "Council plan": the mayor is hardly more than a presiding officer. He is elected by the council, and he has no veto. The cities own their own water and lighting and street car systems to a much greater degree than in America.

County Councils

In the rural units, reform did not come until 1888 and 1894. In the counties and parishes, the gentry rule was honest, but it broke down in the nineteenth century, under the burden of new duties. Finally, in 1888, the Conservative ministry of Lord Salisbury passed the County Council Bill, providing for the election of a Council for each county by all local taxpayers. A new interest in local affairs followed, and the elected Councils began to change the face of England by their energetic government. Six years later, the last ministry of Gladstone extended this movement by the still more important Parish Councils Bill.

Parish and District councils

These two laws have made local government in the rural units thoroughly democratic. The elements are four. (1) The parish has a primary assembly (*parish meeting*). (2) Parishes with more than three hundred people have also an elective *Parish Council.* (3) Larger subdivisions of the county, known as Districts, have elective *District Councils.* And (4) at the top is the elective *County Council.* The powers of all these local bodies are very great. From the beginning of these reforms, women have had the right to vote for local Councils and to sit in them, on the same terms as men.

The London County Council

London had not been included in the previous municipal reform acts, but in 1888 it was made an "administrative county." Since 1888 the representative County Council of London, ruling six million people, has been one of the most interesting governing bodies in the world.

The sixteenth century in England had seen a *new absolutism* rise upon the ruins of the old feudalism and the old church. The struggle of the seventeenth century had resulted in replacing this absolutism with *representative government highly aristocratic* in character Then, by natural decay, this had hardened into the *narrow oligarchy* of the eighteenth century. The nineteenth century saw the victory of *democracy* — and by peaceful *evolution*, without bloody revolution.

For Further Reading. — On the Second and Third Bills, interesting treatments are to be found in Hazen, Rose, McCarthy's *History of Our Own Times*, and in the younger McCarthy's *England under Gladstone.* Beard's *English Historians*, 566–581 and 582–593, is admirable. On the Chartists, Rose, 84–146; Hazen, 446–450.

CHAPTER XXX

SOCIAL REFORM IN THE VICTORIAN AGE

Social reforms just after the First Reform Bill

The thirties were a period of humanitarian agitation, as well as of democratic advance. In England, *Charles Dickens* wrote his moving stories of the abuses in the courts, the schools, the factories, the shops. *Carlyle* thundered against injustice, in *Chartism* and in *Past and Present; Mrs. Browning* pleaded for the abused children in touching poems (p. 378). Public men, like *Wilberforce, Romilly,* and *Shaftesbury,* urged reform in Parliament.

> So in America, the thirties saw the beginning of the "woman's rights" movement, including demands for coeducation, equal property rights with men, and the right to vote. Massachusetts founded the first *public* hospital for the insane. Special schools soon appeared for the blind and the deaf. The temperance movement and the abolition movement got fairly under way.

After carrying the Reform Bill of 1832, Earl Grey dissolved Parliament. The new Parliament, chosen by the enlarged citizen-body, contained a huge majority for the Liberals. Earl Grey's ministry remained in office for three years more, — years packed with social reforms. It freed the Negro slaves in the West India colonies, *paying the colonists for their loss.*[1] It began to free the hardly less miserable "white slaves" of the English factory towns, by a new era of factory legislation (p. 451). It freed the Irish peasants from the obligation of paying tithes to support the Episcopalian clergy, whom they hated.

[1] SPECIAL REPORT: Wilberforce, and his work for emancipation.

It swept away some more excesses of the absurd and bloody criminal code (p. 430). It abolished the pillory and the whipping post, and began to reform the foul and inhuman conditions in the prisons. It began the reform of local government (p. 447); and it made a first step toward public education, by a national grant of £20,000 a year to church schools.

In 1839, after strenuous struggles, this grant was increased to £30,000. A member of the Ministry, in arguing for that pitiful increase, reminded Parliament that it had just voted £70,000, without a murmur, to build new stables of the Queen.

The Factory Act of 1833

The most important legislation of the century was the *labor and factory legislation.* Gradually Englishmen awakened to the ugly fact that the new factory system was ruining, not only the souls, but also the *bodies* of hundreds of thousands of women and children, so as to threaten national degeneracy. In 1833, among the first acts of the "Reformed parliament," Lord Ashley (p. 377) secured a factory law limiting the work of children (under thirteen years) to forty-eight hours a week, and that of "young people" (from thirteen to eighteen years) to sixty-nine hours a week (or twelve hours on five days and nine hours on Saturdays). Some provision was made also for educating children and for a few holidays; and the *employment of children under nine* (*!*) was strictly forbidden.

The bill was fought bitterly by most of the manufacturers, who urged (1) that it would oblige them to reduce wages and raise prices; (2) the hypocritical plea that it took from the workingman his "freedom of contract," or right to sell his labor as he chose; and (3) that it would cost England her industrial leadership among nations, and drive capital away to countries where there was no such mischievous legislation. But public opinion had at last been aroused, and the bill became law. Fortunately, it provided for salaried "factory inspectors"; and these officers, after many prosecutions, compelled the employers to obey it.

The Factory Act of 1847

In 1847 a still greater factory law limited the labor of women and "young persons" (between 14 and 16) to *ten hours a day*, with only half-time for "children" (between 9 and 14) and with provision for schooling in the vacant half of the day. Indirectly, this law fixed a limit upon the hours of men also, because, after the women and children had all left a factory, it was not profitable to keep the machinery going. *Thus ten hours became the factory working-day* many years before this goal was reached generally in America.

Woman and child labor in mines

The legislation of 1833 applied only to factories for weaving goods. But in 1840, a parliamentary commission made public the horrible condition of women and children in the coal mines, — stunted, crippled, misshapen wretches, living in brutal indecency. Children began work underground at five or six years of age, and rarely saw daylight. Girls and women worked almost naked among the men. The working hours were from twelve to fourteen a day; and in the wet underground passages, two or three feet high, women were compelled to crawl back and forth on hands and knees, hauling great carts of coal by chains fastened to their waists. A law at once forbade underground labor by women and children.

Later factory acts

The principles of factory legislation were soon extended to other lines of manufactures. Of the long series of later acts, the most important are *Asquith's Factory Act of 1895* (which, along with other wholesome provisions, prohibits *the employment of any child under eleven years of age*),[1] and the great *Act of 1901*, which revised and advanced the factory legislation of the preceding century. Since 1901, no child under 12 can be employed at all in any sort of factory or workshop; and for employees between 12 and 16, a physician must certify that there is no danger of physical injury from the employment. *Night work* for women and children is strictly forbidden.

[1] FOR FURTHER READING. — Gibbin's *Industrial History of England*, 175–176, and Cheyney's *Industrial and Social History*, 224–262. Vivid statements are given also in Justin McCarthy's *Epoch of Reform*, *History of Our Own Times*, and *England in the Nineteenth Century*, and in Lecky's *History of England*, VI, 219–225.

These acts have been accompanied by many provisions to secure good lighting and ventilation in factories and workshops, and to prevent accidents from machinery, by compelling the employer to fence it in with every possible care. In 1880 an *Employers' Liability Act* made it easy for a workman to secure compensation for any injury for which he was not himself to blame; and in 1897 a still more generous *Workman's Compensation Act* secured such compensation for the workmen by a simple process without lawsuits. These acts have been copied in the last few years by progressive States in our Union.

Workman's Compensation Act

Lord Grey retired in 1834; but his Liberal successors began the modern liberal policy toward the English colonies by a new "Government Act" for Canada in 1839 (p. 470), and introduced penny postage in 1840. Previous to this, the charge on letters had been very high, sometimes several shillings, and had varied according to distance and to the size and shape of the letter. It had involved cumbrous calculations for each letter, and the amount had been collected in cash by the carriers. When the change was suggested, the postal authorities protested earnestly and sincerely — as conservative officials still protest against every new reform — declaring that under the proposed plan the carriers would never be able to handle the letters, or that it would cost ruinous sums to do so. Rarely indeed has a simple change done more for the well-being of the poorer classes.

Other reforms before 1840

THE FIRST ADHESIVE POSTAGE STAMP, 1840. The design was used, unchanged, to 1870.

The Conservative ministry of Peel (1841–1846) was marked by the abolition of the Corn Laws. Those laws had put an excessively high tariff on imported grain. Their aim was to encourage the raising of foodstuffs in England, so as to make sure of a home supply; and during the Napoleonic war this policy perhaps had been justifiable. The money profits, however, had always gone mainly to the landlords, who enacted the laws in Parliament and who raised rents high enough to

The old "Corn Laws"

confiscate the benefits which the high prices might otherwise have brought to the farmer. After the rapid growth in population had made it impossible for England to produce enough food for her people anyway, the landlords' monopoly of breadstuffs had become an intolerable burden upon the starving multitudes.

The needless misery among this class finally aroused great moral indignation. In 1838 the Anti-Corn-Law League was organized by *Richard Cobden* and *John Bright,* and for years it carried on a wonderful campaign of education through the press and by means of great public meetings. The manufacturing capitalists were made to see that the Corn Laws taxed them, indirectly, for the benefit of the landlords — since to enable their workmen to live, they had to pay higher wages than would otherwise have been necessary. And so the selfish interests of this influential manufacturing class were thrown to the side of this particular reform.

The Irish Famine forces free trade in food

Finally, in 1846, a huge calamity was added to the same side of the scales. This was *the Irish Famine.* The population of Ireland had been increasing rapidly, until it amounted to over eight millions. The greater part were poor peasants, living in misery, with the potato for almost their sole food. Suddenly, in 1846, in a night, came a blight that ruined the crop for the year; and, despite generous gifts of food from all the world, two million people died of starvation.[1]

The government in England had already been considering a reform of the Corn Laws, and this terrible event in Ireland forced it to act. As John Bright afterward said for the reformers, "Famine itself, against whom we fought, took up arms in our behalf." Peel decided to sweep away the tax and to let food in free; and, despite bitter opposition from the landlords of his own party, the reform was adopted.

One interesting result of the bitter feeling of the Tory landlords was the passing of the factory act of 1847 (p. 452).

[1] A million more emigrated to America in the next four years (1847–1850). This was the first large immigration of Catholic Irish to this country.

That much needed reform was vehemently opposed by *manufacturing* Liberals, like John Bright, who believed it would ruin English industry. But the landlord Tories, who had just been beaten by Bright on the Corn Laws, grimly took their revenge by forcing this other reform upon the manufacturing capitalists. The whole story shows that neither division of the capitalist class could see any needs of the working class that conflicted with their own unjust profits.

THE PARLIAMENT BUILDINGS at Westminster, London; completed in 1852, after the "Old Parliament Buildings" had been destroyed by fire, in 1834. Westminster Abbey is visible in the distance.

Free trade adopted as a policy

Peel was soon overthrown by a party revolt, but the Liberals took up the work and carried it farther. They abolished one protective tariff after another, until, *by 1852, England had become a "free trade" country.*

This policy was never afterward seriously questioned in England (whose manufactures and commerce have prospered so marvelously under it) *until 1903*. For some years preceding that date, to be sure, some of the Conservative party talked of a policy of "fair trade," or a system of retaliatory tariffs against countries whose tariffs shut out British manufactures; and finally, in 1903, Joseph Chamberlain, a member of the Conservative cabinet, declared that the time had come for England to adopt a policy of that kind and at the same time to secure closer trade relations with her colonies. In 1909 and 1910 the Conservative party made their campaigns on this issue — in opposition to the radical internal tax reform of Lloyd George (p. 478); but so far (1919), they have not won the nation.

The first international exhibition

In 1851, mainly through the influence of Prince Albert, came the great *Crystal Palace Exhibition*. This was the first of many international exhibits of industries and arts, with the idea of bringing the peoples of the world to understand one another better and to profit by one another's progress in art and industry. It was hailed by Queen Victoria, too hopefully, as a guarantee of lasting peace. Six million visitors attended the exhibit; and conservative Englishmen deplored the flooding of England with foreign immorality!

For some twenty years after the Corn-Law reform, England saw little legal reform aside from the extensions of free trade and of the factory legislation already mentioned.

Gladstone's reform administration, 1868–1874

Then, after the enfranchisement of the artisan class by the Reform Bill of 1867, came Gladstone's great reform administration (1868–1874), which rivals in importance that of Earl Grey in the thirties. In 1870 it established alongside the old private and parochial schools a new system of public schools, or, as the English call them, Board Schools.[1] It abolished purchase of office in the army, and completed the civil service reform (p. 446). It introduced the ballot (p. 446). It opened English universities to others than the members of the Church

[1] So called because they are managed by elected Boards. The term "public school" in England had been appropriated by the great secondary schools, like Rugby and Eton, though there is, of course, no public control over them.

These Board Schools have revolutionized the English working-class. About the middle of the nineteenth century, more than a third of the newly married couples had to sign their names in the marriage registers with their "marks." In 1903 only two per cent were unable to write their names. This fact is full of promise for those European lands which are still struggling with gross illiteracy.

of England. It passed further factory laws. It definitely repealed the old conspiracy laws, under which labor-unions had been persecuted, and it gave legal rights to such unions, permitting them to incorporate and secure the rights at law of an individual. It also arranged honorably the Alabama Arbitration Treaty with the United States. It "disendowed" and "disestablished" the English Church in Ireland, and carried through important land reforms for Ireland (p. 463).

Since the days of Henry VIII and Elizabeth, the Episcopal Church had held the ancient property of the Catholic Church in Ireland. The Celtic Irish population, however, clung with amazing fidelity to the old faith, so that in 1835 a parliamentary inquiry failed to find one Protestant (except the Episcopalian clergyman) in any one of 150 parishes.

After Gladstone's "disestablishment," the Episcopal Church in Ireland was separated from political power, and was upon an equal footing legally with any other church; but the "disendowment" was only partial. The church lost all income from taxes (tithes), and much of its property was taken from it to create funds for the Catholics and Presbyterians in the island; but it kept its buildings and enough other property to leave it still very rich. All this, which to one party seemed only a partial remedying of a huge ancient injustice toward a whole people, seemed to another party a new and unpardonable injustice; and many good churchmen never forgave Gladstone for his "act of robbery."

The labor unions desert Gladstone

But Gladstone at this time would not go far enough to satisfy the Irish; and, despite the trade-union law, he offended the labor party by a new law regarding strikes. This law recognized the right of a union to strike, but made criminal any show of intimidation. It forbade strikers to revile those who remained at work; and it is reported that under the law seven women were sent to prison for crying "Bah!" at a workman who had deserted the strikers. The ministry lost more and more of its support, and finally Gladstone "dissolved." In the election, the labor unions voted for the Conservatives; and that party secured a large majority, for the first time since 1832.

Disraeli's imperialistic administration, 1874–1880

Then followed *Disraeli's administration (1874–1880) with its "dazzling foreign policy."* The only reform at home was the repeal of the law against strikes. Gladstone's ministry had been exceedingly peaceful and honorable in dealing with foreign nations. Disraeli, leader of the new ministry, characterized this attitude as weak, and said that it had "compromised the honor" of England. He adopted an aggressive foreign policy, and tried to excite English patriotism by "jingo"[1] utterances and conduct. By act of Parliament, Queen Victoria was declared "Empress of India"; the Boers of the Transvaal were incited to war, so that England might seize their lands; and in 1878, when Russia conquered Turkey (p. 593) and seemed about to exclude the Turks from Europe, Disraeli interfered. He got together a Congress of the Powers at Berlin, and saved enough of European Turkey to shut Russia off from the Mediterranean. This was England's greatest sin in her foreign relations during the century; and though quickly repented of by the people (below), it bore bitter fruit forty years later — furnishing, as it did, in part, the chance for the opening of the World War.

Gladstone's second ministry, 1880–1885

Gladstone came forth from retirement to carry on a great campaign against this policy of supporting the Turk in his mastery over the Christian populations of southeastern Europe. His appeal to the moral sense of the English people was successful; and in the election of 1880 the Liberals secured an overwhelming majority. The evil work of the Congress of Berlin could not now be undone; but Gladstone's new ministry passed the Third Reform Bill and it also completed the purification of English politics, by adopting the law against "Corrupt

[1] This word comes from a popular music hall song of 1878:
"We don't want to fight; but, by jingo, if we do
We've got the men, we've got the ships,
We've got the money, too."

Practices" (p. 447). Soon, however, this Liberal ministry found itself occupied with Irish questions, about which English politics were to revolve for the next fifteen years. Some explanation of Irish affairs must precede further survey of English matters.

FOR FURTHER READING. — Details on particular topics can be found in McCarthy's *Epoch of Reform* (for the years 1830 to 1850), *History of Our Own Times* (1837–1880), and in the younger McCarthy's *England under Gladstone*. Briefer accounts for the whole period are given in Hazen's *Europe Since 1815*, in McCarthy's *England in the Nineteenth Century*, and in Rose's *Rise of Democracy*. See also Carlton Hayes' *Modern Europe*, II.

CHAPTER XXXI

ENGLAND AND THE IRISH QUESTION

In the history of Ireland . . . we may trace with singular clearness the perverting and degrading influences of great legislative injustices. — LECKY.

Ireland to 1700

The English people proper are Saxon-Norman mixed with Celtic blood; the Welsh, Highland Scots, and Irish are Celts. In the larger of the British Isles, the English, Welsh, and Scots live at peace; but for centuries the Irish in the smaller island have been restless under English rule.

Ireland has been an unfortunate and misgoverned land. In the seventh and eighth centuries, she had begun to show brilliant promise (p. 99); but this early civilization vanished in the wars of the Danish invasions, which for three hundred years inflicted upon Ireland all the woes suffered by England for the generation before Alfred the Great.

Thus Henry II of England found the island sunk in misery and barbarism and torn by incessant tribal strife. Unhappily for both English and Irish, Henry's conquest (p. 164) was left incomplete; and war, anarchy, and misgovernment filled three centuries more, down to the time of Henry VIII. Sir John Davis, a poet-historian and statesman of Elizabeth's time, wrote, "If it had been practised in Hell as it has been in Ireland, it had long since destroyed the very kingdom of Beëlzebub."

The religious difficulty

Henry VIII and Elizabeth completed the subjugation of the island; but now the English and Irish civilizations had grown far apart, and the two people could not easily mingle. Moreover, the English had become Protestant, and the difference in religion added a tremendous difficulty. There was real danger that Catholic Ireland might join Spain against Protestant England (p. 164); and so the mutual hate and fear between Irish and English grew more and more intense. About 1600, the government began to try to make Ireland English by crushing out the native language and customs and religion, and by reducing the native population to mere tillers of the soil for their conquerors. On trumped-up charges, with every imaginable form of force and fraud, the lands of even the loyal Irish gentry were confiscated to furnish estates for English adventurers; and a war of extermination was waged against all who remained in arms.

Cromwell and William III

Just before the Civil War in England, the goaded Irish rose in fierce rebellion. A little later the merciless hand of Cromwell restored order with a cruelty which makes his name a by-word in Ireland to-day. Toward the close of the century, the Irish sided with James II against William III, but were defeated at the *Battle of the Boyne* (1690). The Treaty of Limerick (1691), however, promised them the enjoyment of their own religion and certain other privileges; but these promises were treacherously broken by the English settlers, who controlled the parliament of the island, so that Limerick is known as "the City of the Broken Treaty."

Ireland in the eighteenth century

During the eighteenth century the fate of Ireland was wretched beyond description. In Ulster, the northern province, the population was mainly English. Elsewhere *six sevenths of the land* belonged to English landlords, most of whom lived in England and spent their rents there. Those who stayed in Ireland made up the ruling class of the island. Six sevenths *of the people* were Catholic Irish. A few of these, especially in the west, were country gentlemen; a considerable number more were tenant farmers; but the great bulk were a starving peasantry, working the land for Saxon landlords and living in mud hovels, — each with an acre or two of ground about it.

"Rack rent"

Farmers and laborers alike were "tenants at will." That is, they could be evicted at the landlord's word. Population was so crowded that there was always sharp competition to get farms and cottages, and so the landlord could make his own terms. If the tenant improved the buildings or drained the land, he commonly found at once that he had to pay more rent, so that he himself got no profit from his extra labor. This system of "rack rent" made the peasantry reckless and lazy; and the fact that the law of their masters was used only to oppress them, trained them to hate and break the law.

In 1798 the Irish rebelled. They were promised aid by the French Directory; but the help did not come in time, and the rising was put down with horrible cruelty.

The Rebellion and the "Union"

A change in the government followed. For several centuries, there had been a separate parliament for Ireland, controlled by the English settlers; but after 1798 *England consolidated the government of the two islands.* The *Act of Union* (1800) abolished the Irish legislature, and gave Ireland one hundred representatives in the English Parliament. Ireland became subject directly to English rule and English officials.

These were the conditions at the opening of the nineteenth century. In 1803 a brilliant young Irishman, *Robert Emmet,* tried to organize a rebellion for Irish independence; but the effort failed miserably, and Emmet died on the scaffold.

Young Ireland

The struggle for the repeal of the Union began in 1830, in the first English Parliament in which Catholics were allowed to sit (p. 430). Forty of the Irish delegation were pledged to work for repeal, and they were led by the dauntless and powerful *Daniel O'Connell;* but the Irish famine of 1846 checked the agitation, and just afterward O'Connell died. Then a band of hot-headed young men tried conspiracy, and the fruitless and rather farcical rebellion of Young Ireland marked the year 1848.

And the Fenians

The next twenty years saw no progress. In 1866 came another rebellion, — *the Fenian Conspiracy,* organized by Irish officers who had served in the American Civil War. The danger did not become serious, but it convinced many liberal Englishmen that something must be done for Ireland, and Gladstone's reform ministry of 1868–1874 took up the task.

Then there opened a new period in Irish history. *The Episcopalian church in Ireland* (p. 457) *was disestablished,* and this was followed in 1870 by the first of a long series of important *reforms of the land laws.* Two things were attempted: (1) in case of eviction, it was ordered that the landlord must pay for any improvements the tenant had made; and (2) the government arranged to loan money on long time, and at low interest, to the tenants, so that they might buy their little patches of land. In 1881 and 1885 Gladstone's ministries extended and improved these laws until the peasants began to be true landowners, with a chance to develop new habits of thrift and industry.

Gladstone and Ireland, 1868–1885

Meantime, in 1870, a group of Irish members of Parliament had begun a new agitation for "Home Rule," and soon afterward the same leaders organized the "Land League," to try to fix rents, as labor unions sometimes try to fix wages. For the time, the Liberal ministries frowned on both these movements, and prosecuted the Land League sternly on the ground that it encouraged crime against landlords. At the same time, indeed, that the government was passing beneficent land laws, it was also passing "Coercion Acts" to establish martial law in Ireland. The Coercion Acts were resisted by the Irish members with a violence never before seen in an English Parliament, and Irish conspirators outside made various attempts to wreck the English government buildings with dynamite and to assassinate English officials.

Reform and coercion

But suddenly Gladstone made a change of front. In the new Parliament of 1884, eighty-six of Ireland's hundred and five members were "Home Rulers." They began to block *all* legislation; and Gladstone could go on only by securing their alliance. Moreover, *he had become convinced that the only way to govern Ireland was to govern it in coöperation with the Irish, not in opposition to them.* So in 1886 he adopted the "Home-Rule" plan and introduced a bill to restore a separate legislature to Ireland.

Gladstone converted to Home Rule

The Conservatives declared that this policy meant disunion and ruin to the Empire, and in this belief they were joined by many of the old Liberals, who took the name of *Liberal Unionists.* The Home Rule Bill was defeated; but it made the issue

Gladstone's retirement

in the next election a few years later, and in 1893 Gladstone tried to carry another such measure. This time, the Commons passed the bill, but the Lords threw it out. The bill differed in important particulars from the one before considered. Moreover, the majority for it in Parliament was narrow and plainly due only to the Irish vote. Thus Gladstone felt that the nation would not support him in any attempt to pass the bill by swamping the Lords with new peers. At this moment his age compelled him to retire from parliamentary life, and the Liberals, left for a time without a fit leader, went out of power.

Further land reform

The Conservatives and Unionists then tried to conciliate Ireland by extending the policy of government loans to the peasantry to an almost unlimited extent, though formerly they had railed at such acts as robbery and socialism; and they granted a kind of *local* "home rule," by establishing elective County Councils like those in England. The Irish members kept up agitation in Parliament, but for a long time even the Liberals seemed to have lost interest in Irish Home Rule; and indeed it was plain that nothing could be done until after "the mending or ending" of the House of Lords. This matter was soon forced to the front in connection with English questions (pp. 478 ff.).

FOR FURTHER READING. — Hazen's *Europe Since 1815*, 471–594; Johnston and Spencer's *Ireland's Story*.

CHAPTER XXXII

ENGLISH COLONIES AND DEPENDENCIES

After many years of wandering I have come to the conclusion that the mightiest factor in the civilization of the world is the imperial policy of England. — ADMIRAL GEORGE DEWEY (1899).

The English navy is presumably the most potent instrumentality for peace in the world. — THEODORE ROOSEVELT (December, 1918).

The British Empire

Of all peoples the English have been the most successful in colonizing new lands and in ruling semi-barbarous races. England began her colonial expansion on the North Atlantic coast of America and in the West Indies, in the seventeenth century. In 1776 she lost her most important colonies on the continent of North America; but the hundred years of war with France (1689–1815) gave her a new and vaster empire (pp. 328–329). In the nineteenth century this empire was tremendously expanded again, — mainly by peaceful settlement and daring exploration. In 1914 the British Empire covered nearly fourteen million square miles, or four times the area of the United States and nearly a fourth the land area of the globe; and its population numbered four hundred millions, or about one fourth of the whole human race. Forty millions of this number dwelt in the British Isles, and about fifteen million more of English descent lived in self-governing colonies, — mainly in Canada, Australia, and South Africa. The other seven eighths of the vast population of the Empire are of non-European blood, and for the most part they are subject peoples.

The outlying possessions are of two kinds: (1) those of continental importance in themselves, such as Canada, India, Egypt, Australia, New Zealand, South Africa, and the West Indian and South American colonies; and (2) coaling stations and naval posts commanding the routes to these possessions, such as Gibraltar, Malta, Cyprus, Ceylon, St. Helena, Trinidad, and scores more.

The self-governing colonies

Some colonies are completely self-governing, with no dependence upon England except in form. This is true of Canada, Australia, New Zealand, and South Africa. These colonies are said to have "*responsible governments.*" The English ministry appoints a *Governor General,* whose powers resemble those of the figurehead monarch in England. *But the people of the colony elect the local legislature; and the real executive is the local ministry, "responsible" to the legislature,* as the ministry in England is to Parliament.

Crown colonies

In another group of colonies, the governors and officials, sent out from England, really control the whole government. This class of "*crown colonies*" comprises most of the naval posts, like Gibraltar, and also those colonies lying in the torrid zone, where the population is mainly non-European.

India

India is a huge crown colony. Until 1857 it remained under the control of the East India Company (p. 244), but in that year came the *Sepoy mutiny,* — a rising of native soldiers, — and when order had been restored, India was annexed to the British crown. The English ministry appoints a Viceroy and a Council, and these authorities name the subordinate officials for the subdivisions of the vast country. In the smaller districts the English officials are assisted by native officers, and to some extent by elected councils of natives. Outside the territory ruled directly by England there are also nearly a thousand native principalities, large and small, where the governments are really directed by resident English "agents."

The English are making a notable attempt to introduce self-government and to get the natives to care for it. Towns are invited to elect municipal councils and to take charge of their streets and drainage and other matters of local welfare. The officers of the old East India Company were sometimes rapacious robbers, oppressing the natives to fill their own and the Company's coffers; but since India became a crown colony, English rule, for the most part, has been wise, firm, and just, and has aimed unselfishly at the good of the natives. India pays no taxes into the English treasury; indeed, she is a drain on that treasury. Her trade is a chief source of British wealth, but,

RAILWAY STATION AT BOMBAY. The purpose of the building, of course, is due to English civilization, but the architecture is native Indian.

as with all England's possessions,[1] that trade is open to the merchants of all countries on terms of full equality with English merchants. The petty, constant wars, which formerly were

[1] Some of the self-governing colonies, against English advice, have enacted tariff laws giving an advantage to the trade of the Empire ("preferential tariffs").

always wasting the land, have been wholly done away with, and the terrible famines, which from time immemorial have desolated it at intervals, have become fewer, and on the whole, less serious. As a result, population has increased rapidly, — over fifty per cent in a century, — and to-day more than three hundred million people dwell in India.[1] England has built railroads, and developed cotton industries. Cotton mills give a Western appearance to parts of that ancient Oriental land. India has 800 newspapers (printed in twenty different languages); and 6,000,000 students are being educated in schools of many grades.

Early in the World War the Germans tried to stir up native rebellion in India, mainly through Hindoos living in the United States. The flat failure of such plots, and the enthusiastic aid voluntarily given to England, indicate more attachment to English rule than had been supposed to exist. Still it remains true that the Hindoos cannot understand Western civilization, and they do not like it. Moreover, in the great war, England failed to throw herself generously upon Indian loyalty: she refused commissions to Hindoos, and lost a great chance to bind that people to her more closely.

Egypt

Egypt in name was one of the tributary states of Turkey until 1914. In fact, however, it had been independent for most of the nineteenth century, until, in 1881, a new master stepped in. The government had borrowed recklessly and spent wastefully, and the land was misgoverned and oppressed by crushing taxation. Then, in 1879, England and France jointly intervened to secure payment of debts due from the Egyptian Khedive to English and French capitalists. In 1881 came a native Egyptian rising against this foreign control. France withdrew. England stayed, restored order, and "occupied" the country.

England had a special motive for staying. The Suez Canal was opened in 1869. In 1875 the English government (Disraeli's administration) bought from the Egyptian

[1] Read Kipling's *William the Conqueror*.

government its share of the Canal stock, and the English intervention in Egypt was largely to protect this property.

After that time, Egypt was really an English protectorate. The Khedive and all the machinery of the old government remained unchanged; but an English agent was always present at the court "to offer advice," and the Khedive understood that this advice must be followed. Many Englishmen entered the service of the Egyptian government, too, and all such officers looked to the English agent as their real head.

When England put down anarchy in 1881, the ministry declared that the occupancy would be only temporary. This statement of Gladstone's ministry was made in good faith, and was in keeping with other parts of Gladstone's modest foreign policy. None the less, it has long been certain that no English government will willingly give up Egypt; and in 1914, during the great European war, England announced a full protectorate. The possession of that country, together with the mastery of the Suez Canal, insures the route to India; and Egypt has been made a base of operation, also, from which English rule has been extended into the Soudan (map facing p. 553) far toward Central Africa.

To Egypt itself, English rule has been an unmixed good. The system of taxation has been reformed, so that it is less burdensome and more productive. The irrigation works have been revived and improved, so that Egypt is richer, more populous, and with a more prosperous peasantry, than ever before. At the same time there has grown up a respectable party among the Egyptian people who believe that their country is now quite fit to stand alone — and that it has a right to try. This element made an earnest but vain attempt to get a hearing before the Peace Congress of 1919.

One of the most important features of the nineteenth century was the development of self-government in the *Anglo-Saxon* colonies of England. The loss of the American colonies had taught a lesson, and the next colony to show violent dissatisfaction had all its wishes granted.

The winning of self-government in Canada

This event took place in Canada in 1837. There were then only two "provinces" there. These thinly settled districts lay along the St. Lawrence, and were known as Upper and Lower Canada. They had been governed for many years much as Massachusetts or Virginia was governed before 1776. There had been a growing dissatisfaction because the legislatures did not have a more complete control over the finances and over the executive; and the accession of the girl-queen in England in 1837 was the signal for a rising. The rebellion was stamped out quickly; but an English commissioner, sent over to investigate, *recommended that the demands of the conquered rebels should be granted.* Parliament adopted this recommendation. In 1839 the two provinces were united and were granted "*responsible*" *ministries.* England, in name, retains a veto upon Canadian legislation; but it has never been used. In 1850 a like plan for self-government was granted to the Australian colonies, in 1852 to New Zealand, and in 1872 to Cape Colony in Africa.

Australia begins as a convict camp

The growth of the Australian colonies is a romantic story, worthy of a book to itself. England's original claim rested on landings by Captain Cook in his second voyage to the Pacific in 1769; but no settlement was attempted for almost a century. English colonization went instead altogether to the nearer American possessions. From the beginning of the American colonization, England had transported many convicts thither. The American Revolution put a stop to that practice. And so in 1787 England sent a shipload of convicts to the coast of "New South Wales." Sydney, so established, was the first English colony in Australia. For fifty years New South Wales remained a penal settlement (p. 444); but, after their terms of punishment, many ex-convicts became steady farmers, and the English government began to induce other settlers to "go out" by free grants of land and of farming implements. By 1821 the colony had a population of 40,000, and soon it became the main sheep-raising region in the world.

English expansion in Australia

By natural expansion, familiar to students of American history, this colony of New South Wales sent out offshoots in five other colonies, which, with the mother colony, covered the continental island: West Australia (1829), South Australia (1834), Tasmania (1835), Victoria (1851), and Queensland (1859). The black side of this splendid story was the cruel extinction of the native race, — a people of a much lower grade than the North American Indian.

Democratic progress in Australia

The Australian commonwealths have been pioneers in democratic progress. Before 1900, every man and every woman in each state had the right to vote. The government in each state owned the railroads. The "Australian ballot" and the Torrens system of land transfer came from these colonies; and a powerful Labor party in each has secured other radical reforms — which are seen better still perhaps in New Zealand.

New Zealand experiments in industrial democracy

"New Zealand" comprises a group of islands 1200 miles east of Australia. Settled and governed for a time from New South Wales, it became a separate colony in 1840. In 1911 it contained more than a million English-speaking inhabitants. For many years it has been perhaps the most democratic state in the world. Women secured the right to vote in 1893. Large estates have been broken up into small holdings by heavy taxation. A state "Farmers' Loan Bank" set the example followed in part by the United States in 1913. The most advanced factory laws and "social insurance" laws in the world have been found in New Zealand since 1893 and 1898; and there have been tried, since 1895, exceedingly interesting experiments in compulsory arbitration of labor disputes, with Boards of "Conciliation" to settle such differences if possible in their early stages.

South Africa: the Boers

South Africa was long an unsatisfactory part of the Empire for Englishmen to contemplate. England seized Cape Colony from the Dutch during the Napoleonic wars (p. 328). English settlers came in rapidly, but in 1834 a portion of the old Dutch colonists "trekked" (moved with families, ox-wagons, herds, and flocks) north into the wilderness, and set up an independent government in Natal. A few years later the British annexed Natal, and the Dutch again trekked into what is known as the Orange Free State, and, in 1848, once more into the country beyond the Vaal River. These "Transvaal" Dutch became involved in serious difficulties with the native Blacks, whom they enslaved and treated brutally, and a native rising threatened to exterminate all Europeans in South Africa. Under Disraeli (p. 458) England interposed, put down the Zulus, and extended her authority once more over the Boer states.

In 1880 the Boers rebelled, and with their magnificent marksmanship destroyed a British force at the *Battle of Majuba Hill.* Gladstone adopted the view that the Boers had been wrongfully deprived of their independence, and, without attempting to avenge Majuba Hill, he magnanimously withdrew the British claims and left to the Boers of the Transvaal a virtual independence, under British "protection." The exact relations between the two countries, however, were not well defined, and much ground was left for future disputes.

The Boer War

Soon afterward, gold was discovered in the Transvaal, and English and other foreigners rushed in, so as to outnumber the Boer citizens. The Boers, who were simple farmers, unable themselves to develop the country, had at first invited immigrants, but soon became jealous of their growing numbers and refused them all political rights. England attempted to secure better treatment for her citizens among these new settlers, and, under Salisbury's Conservative and Imperialistic ministry, was bent upon reasserting her authority in general. The Boers saw that England had determined to force them to a policy which would put the government of the little land into the hands of these foreign immigrants ("Outlanders"), and they declared war (1899). The Orange Free State joined the Transvaal, and the little republics carried on a marvelous and heroic struggle. They were finally beaten, of course; and England adopted a generous policy toward the conquered, making large gifts of money to restock their ruined farms, and granting liberal self-government, without any discrimination against her recent foes. When England became involved in the general European war of 1914, some of the Boers rose once more; but on the whole that people seem now content with the new and liberal English rule.

During the last half-century the English-speaking colonies have made one more great advance in free government. At

THE CANADIAN PARLIAMENT BUILDING AT OTTAWA

English colonies organized in great federal common-wealths

the time of the American Revolution, "Canada" meant merely the St. Lawrence settlements. In the nineteenth century these expanded westward, forming a splendid band of states[1] spanning the continent. Then, in 1867, the separate colonies of this British North America organized themselves into *the Dominion of Canada*. This is a *federal state*, similar to the United States, composed now of eight members, with a number of other "Territories." The union has a two-house legislature, with a re-

[1] Read Mrs. Humphry Ward's *Lady Merton, Colonist*, to get the spirit of the Canada of the West.

sponsible ministry; and each of the eight states has its own local legislature and ministry.

A similar union of the six Australian colonies into one federal state was agitated for many years; and, after two federal conventions and a popular vote, it *was finally established on the first day of the twentieth century.* Finally, *in 1909,* the four South African states were combined into a similar federation, with the name, "*The Union of South Africa.*" Thus three new English nations were formed, — each at its birth large enough to command respect among the nations of the world (each one double the size of the United States when its independence was achieved). Together, these three republics to-day (1919) contain an English-speaking population of some fifteen million souls, and their rapid growth contains vast promise for the future.

Ties between England and her colonies

The Boer War and the great European struggle of 1914 showed that there was a strong tie between England and her self-governing colonies. Australia, New Zealand, and Canada all made liberal gifts of troops and money to assist the mother country against the Boers; and in the World War they fought and sacrificed as splendidly as they could have done if they had been *directly* attacked by Germany.

The bond which holds together the Anglo-Saxon parts of the Empire is, however, almost wholly one of feeling. Certainly, if either Canada or Australia wished to set up as an independent nation, England would not dream of trying to hold it. Indeed from about 1850 to nearly 1900 the English Liberals were usually inclined to a "Little England" policy, ready to welcome any attempt of a colony to set up for itself. About 1880, however, an *imperial* patriotism began to show itself in English politics — born, perhaps, of closer communication by steam and electricity. This was fostered by such writers as Kipling; and, after 1900, the growing rivalry with Germany, and the consciousness of a common danger, drew mother state and daughter colonies into closer relations. The English statesman to-day who should invite Canada to drop out of the Empire, or who should provoke her into doing so, would be universally in England regarded as a traitor to his race.

There is no present danger of separation. The colonists have had no recent cause to complain, except in one respect: namely, they have had no voice in deciding the policy of the Empire toward foreign nations. This evil was largely offset by the fact that the English navy afforded protection to the Canadian and Australian trade, so that these great and wealthy countries were practically freed from all burden of military and naval defense. Still, the situation was not altogether satisfactory. A Canadian may properly wish a voice in the policy of the Empire; that is, he may wish to be a citizen in as full a degree as if he lived in England: and England may properly think that Canada ought to contribute something to imperial defense. It has been proposed to meet both these wants by some form of *Imperial Federation.*

This means that the different parts of the Empire would be left their present parliaments for local matters, but that the management of matters that concern the Empire as a whole would be turned over to a new parliament made up of representatives in fit proportion from England and her colonies. If such a federation can be carried out successfully, it will be the greatest triumph ever yet achieved by federal government and a new boon to civilization, equal perhaps to any political device yet developed by the English-speaking race. Meantime, so far as the old grievance of the colonies is concerned, the evil has been fully removed by the recognition of their delegates in the Peace Congress of 1919 and in the League of Nations.

FOR FURTHER READING. — Hazen, 523–545. A good longer account may be found in Woodward's *Expansion of the British Empire.* On recent developments, see Year Books and Almanacs.

CHAPTER XXXIII

RECENT REFORM IN ENGLAND: "WAR UPON POVERTY"

I hope that great advance will be made during this generation toward the time when poverty, with its wretchedness and squalor, will be as remote from the people of this country as are the wolves which once infested its forests. — LLOYD GEORGE, in 1909.

The Liberal program of 1892

Before the election of 1892, the Liberals had adopted a platform calling for Irish Home Rule (p. 463), for the disestablishment of the Episcopal church in Wales (where nine tenths of the people are dissenters), for a greater degree of local self-government, for sweeping reform in taxation, for old-age pensions, and — as a necessary step toward these things — for the "mending or ending" of the House of Lords. Twenty years carried this program to fulfillment.

How the Lords thwarted Gladstone's ministry of '92–'95 on the Home Rule matter has been told (p. 464). That ministry did pass the great Parish Councils act (p. 449), making England a complete democracy in local government. Gladstone's last speech in Parliament (sixty-one years after his first speech in that body) was in defense of that bill against attempted interference by the Lords. Said he, in solemn prophecy, — "The issue which is raised between an assembly, elected by more than 6,000,000 voters, and a small hereditary body, is a controversy which, once raised, must go forward to an issue." If health had let the "Grand Old Man" continue his leadership, the Lords would have had to meet then an attack upon their veto.

Land Reform in England

The Parish Councils Act helped along another vital reform. For many years the Liberal party had declared for making the peasantry once more the owners of farm lands, and the Conservatives had finally come to favor the measure. In 1890,

1200 men (out of a population of 32,000,000) owned a fourth of the soil of England, *and only one twenty-fourth of the population owned any land at all.* A series of Allotment acts (1883, 1887, 1892) had tried to remedy this great evil, but with little success. After 1894, however, the democratic Parish Councils began to buy land (and even to condemn it and take it at a forced sale), and then turn it over in small holdings to farm laborers, either on long leases or for purchase on easy terms. Slowly but surely *the English people began again to become the owners of England,* and the movement has been tremendously increased by the War of 1914–1918.

The Conservative rule, 1896–1905

After Gladstone's retirement, the Conservatives held power for ten years (1896–1905). They carried forward some social reforms which they had once bitterly opposed — such as factory reform and Irish-land reform — but they also placed the English Board schools under the control of the established church. These schools are attended mainly by the children of the working people. These are almost wholly dissenters. When the Liberals returned to power they gave their first efforts to repeal this law.

Return of the Liberals to power

And by 1905 the Liberals had found a group of new leaders, who still (1919) remain great figures in English public life, — *Mr. Asquith,* prime minister from 1908 to 1915; *Mr. Lloyd George,* his leading finance minister and a radical reformer in taxation, and afterward England's great war dictator; and *Mr. Winston Churchill.* The ministry which contained these men was supported by the largest parliamentary majority which had been seen since the First Reform Bill in 1832. *The same election sent fifty Labor representatives to parliament,* several of them avowed Socialists.

Fifty Labor members in 1900

The new ministry completed earlier legislation by a comprehensive Workingman's Compensation act (p. 453); but the first attempt to take the schools from the control of the church was successful only in part — owing to the veto of the Lords. That House, too, ventured to challenge conflict by vetoing a bill that tried to take away the "plural votes" of rich men.

The English law permitted a man to vote in as many counties as he held landed property. One clause in the Liberal platform of 1892 had been, "One man, one vote"; and, in like manner, the defense of this ancient privilege of property had become a matter of intense feeling with the English Conservatives. Since elections were held all on one day, however, the actual number of plural votes was not very large; but they remained a hateful class distinction.

The ministry wisely refused the challenge of the Lords to dissolve and appeal to the country on any *one* of these issues. Instead, they let the hereditary House pile up the account against it, until Englishmen should be ready to strike decisively. The final clash came over the budget

Lloyd George's budget of 1909

Each year the ministry presents a statement of the expenses it intends to incur, and of the taxes it proposes to lay wherewith to meet those expenses. This statement is the budget. In April of 1909 Lloyd George presented a budget which honestly horrified Conservatives, and which was the most socialistic step ever taken up to that time by a great government. Leading provisions were as follows: —

A *graduated* income tax took a large part of all incomes over $25,000, and *bore more heavily on unearned incomes than on those that are earned.*

A graduated inheritance tax took larger proportions than formerly of inheritances, — fifteen per cent of bequests over £1,000,000.

A much higher tax was placed on land that paid rents and royalties to landlords than on land worked by its owners.

Finally, and most important of all, there was a provision that when any man sold land for more than it had cost, he must pay one fifth the gain into the national treasury. This is known as a tax on the "unearned increment," and is a move toward the doctrine of the Single-taxers, who wish the community to take *all* such unearned increment.

The Conservatives attacked this budget violently as revolutionary. Especially they denounced the distinction regarding unearned incomes as an "invidious assault on the rights of property." Moreover, they claimed that the treasury did not need such vast income as was proposed. As to this last point, Lloyd George had declared that he was proposing a "war budget," — for "waging implacable war against poverty." (See also the theme sentence at the head of this chapter.) The other accusations were answered forcibly and directly by Mr. Winston Churchill, who frankly declared a man's right to property dependent upon the way in which he obtained it: "Formerly," said he, "the only question by the tax-gatherer was 'How much have you got?' . . . To-day . . . we ask also, '*How did you get it?* Did you earn it, or has it been left you by others? Was it gained by processes which are beneficial to the community, or by processes which have done no good to any one, but only harm? . . . Was it derived by active reproductive processes, or merely by squatting on a piece of land till enterprise and labor had to buy you out? . . . How did you get it?' That is the new question which is vibrating through the land."

LLOYD GEORGE in 1909. — From a photograph.

The Lords challenge conflict

The budget passed the Commons, but the Lords threw it out by a vote of five to one. For many centuries the upper House had not dared to interfere with a "money bill" (p. 111).

Now was the time for the reformers to strike. In the Commons Mr. Asquith promptly moved a resolution "That the action of the Lords is a breach of the Constitution and a usurpation of the rights of the Commons." *This resolution passed by a vote of three to one.*

The ministry supported by the nation

Then the ministry dissolved, and appealed to the country for support in restricting the power of the Lords. The election (January, 1910) gave the Liberals again a good working majority. The ministry announced at once that the budget would be again presented, and, after it, some proposal for change of the House of Lords. If the Lords stopped either measure, the ministry would again dissolve, and appeal to the nation.

The Lords now allowed the revolutionary budget to become law. The Liberals, however, pressed their attack on the veto power of the Lords. The death of King Edward (May, 1910) caused some delay; but in November the matter came again to a head. The Lords threw out the Commons' bill against them. As they had promised, the ministry dissolved. The new election (the second referendum within twelve months) gave them slight gains; and the new House of Commons enthusiastically passed a second bill to take away the Lords' veto. When the bill was sent to the other House, Mr. Asquith announced that five hundred new peers, if necessary, would be created to secure its passage.

The Lords lose the veto

Then the helpless Lords passed the law which reduced their House to a nonentity. Under this new law (August, 1911) any money bill passed by the Commons becomes law within a month, whether the Lords pass it or not; and the Speaker of the Commons decides whether a bill is or is not a money bill. Any other bill passed by the Commons *at three successive sessions* becomes law, in spite of a veto by the Lords. That is, the Lords' former veto is taken away *wholly* for a large and important class of bills, and is made *only a suspensive veto*, good for two years, for all other legislation. At last, *the hereditary part of parliament is made strictly subordinate to the representative branch.*

Even this is not satisfactory to the Radicals. There is plainly little use for an "upper House" at all, if it has so little power. Accordingly many proposals are being made to do away with hereditary Lords altogether in favor of some new "second House."

Social insurance, 1911

The Liberals then hastened to push through *their program of social reform.* (1) In 1908 they had already passed an Old-age Pensions act giving $1.25 a week to every person over seventy years old with a yearly income of less than £160. And on the first day of the next year, when the law took effect, more than half a million elderly men and women drew, from the nearest post offices, their first weekly pensions — not as a dole of charity but as due reward in payment for a long life of useful service to the commonweal. (2) An even more important move in the "war against poverty" was now made, in the National Insurance act of 1911. This act compelled every worker with a yearly income of less than $800 to insure against sickness, and offered tempting inducements for such insurance to workers with higher incomes. The benefits include weekly payments during sickness, *free medical care in health,* and free treatment in state hospitals when sick. (3) More radical still was a provision insuring workers in certain trades *against unemployment.* A workman out of work, without fault of his own, was promised a weekly sum for a term of fifteen weeks, and free transportation to a place where the free labor-bureaus may find him new work. Half the cost of all this insurance (but not of the old-age pensions) was taken from the wages of the workers; the other half was divided between the employers and the national treasury.

Thus England's social legislation included comprehensive factory acts, workingmen's compensation for injuries received in their work, insurance against sickness and against loss of time, and old-age pensions. By a radical system of taxation, the money to wage this war against poverty was taken especially from the wealthy, *and particularly from that class of wealthy men who received their incomes without rendering service to society in return.* Nearly all civilized countries are moving along these same lines; but no other had then gone quite so far.

Other reform before the War

Political reform, too, was pushed forward. In 1911 the maximum duration of Parliaments was limited to five years, instead of seven, and salaries ($2000 a year) were provided for members of Parliament.

This makes it more possible for poor men to sit in Parliament. For some years, labor unions had been in the practice of paying salaries to Labor representatives in the Commons; but the English courts had just declared that the unions had no right to use money for that purpose. The new law destroyed the force of this Tory judicial decision, and established one more of the "points" of the old Chartists. Moreover, the same Parliament finally passed "*Welsh disestablishment*" and *Irish Home Rule.* The Lords vetoed both measures in 1912 and in 1913, but in 1914 they became law over the veto (p. 480). In Protestant Ulster, however, the Conservative "Unionists" threatened rebellion to prevent Home Rule going into effect. When, a few weeks later, the World War began, the leaders in this program of violence gave it up; but in return the ministry secured an act from Parliament postponing the date when Home Rule and Welsh disestablishment should go into operation.

This delay, natural and probably necessary, was still one of the most unhappy results of the great war. The old hatreds seemed about to be wiped out. Previous reforms by the English Parliaments had abolished the English church in Ireland and had tried honestly to undo the injustice of centuries of English landlordism there by making the Irish peasants again the owners of their own land. A final act of justice seemed about to be performed, which would have left further Irish reform in Irish hands.

The delay produced a resentment as bitter as it was unreasonable. The Irish, in spite of vast numbers of noble exceptions, failed shamefully to do their full part in the war for democracy, spending their energies instead (sometimes in plots with German autocracy) to set up an independent Irish nation. And this, although plainly the attempt would have meant at that critical moment civil war between Ulster and the rest of Ireland — a war in which England *must* have intervened. On the other hand, England, fighting Germany for her life, used unwise severity in putting down one of these plots, where treason was clear, by the execution of the leaders. A righteous settlement has been made terribly hard.

"Votes for Women": the suffragettes

In 1912 the ministry introduced the "Fourth Parliamentary Reform Bill," extending the suffrage to *all* grown men and establishing the principle "one man, one vote." This bill was withdrawn, later, because of complications with the "equal suffrage" movement, which demands some mention here.

Until 1870, women in England (and in most European lands) had fewer rights than in America. To the law, a married woman was a minor. Her husband was her guardian, — almost her master. He might even beat her if she disobeyed him. Before 1900, property rights had gradually been granted women, though not so fully as in progressive American States. In 1870, when the English "Board schools" (p. 456) were created, women were given the right to vote for the Boards, and to serve upon them. In 1888 and 1894 they were given the franchise for the County Councils and Parish Councils (p. 449), subject to the same tax-paying restrictions that applied to men.

Then in 1893 the colony of New Zealand gave women full political rights, and in 1894 South Australia did so. In 1901 the new federal Australian Commonwealth granted women the franchise for the federal parliament. This was quickly followed by like action in the remaining states of the federation.

The action of these progressive English-speaking colonies[1] reacted upon Old England; and there the question was taking on a new character. In 1905 numbers of English women ex-

[1] And also the progress of equal suffrage in the United States, and in other European countries. See pp. 540, 544; also West's *American People*, pp. 689–690.

changed peaceful agitation for violence, in the campaign for the ballot. They made noisy and threatening demonstrations before the homes of members of the ministry; they broke windows; they invaded the House of Commons in its sittings; and at last they began even to destroy mail boxes and burn empty buildings.

The leaders in this movement were Mrs. Sylvia Pankhurst and her daughter Christobel. The purpose was to center attention on the demand "Votes for women," since, the leaders believed, the demand was sure to be granted if only people could be kept thinking about it. When members of this party of violence were sent to jail, they resorted to a "starvation strike," until the government felt compelled to release them — after trying for a time "forceful feeding."

Lloyd George was an open advocate of equal suffrage; but the ministry as a whole was unwilling to put its other reform program in peril by making woman suffrage "a government measure." When (1912) Mr. Asquith introduced the proposed parliamentary reform (p. 483), he promised that the ministry would *accept* an amendment for woman suffrage if the House should pass one. This did not content the women agitators. Violence increased; and the sympathies of the Liberals were so divided that the government finally withdrew the bill altogether, as it did another in 1914. When the great war began, in the fall of that year, Mrs. Pankhurst called upon her followers to drop all violence while the country was in peril; *and the devoted services of women to the country throughout the war removed the last opposition to equal suffrage.* In 1918 the "Fourth Reform Bill" became law, giving one vote to each man above twenty-one, and to each woman thirty years of age. This advanced age requirement was adopted as a temporary measure, while England's manhood power was so terribly reduced, so that the new Parliament should not be controlled too overwhelmingly by women's votes.

FOR FURTHER READING. — Ogg, *Social Progress in Contemporary Europe*, 265–279; Cross, *History of England*, ch. lvii; Larson, *Short History of England*, 617–639.

PART IX

WESTERN EUROPE FROM THE FRANCO-PRUSSIAN TO THE WORLD WAR, 1871–1914

CHAPTER XXXIV

FRANCE: CLOSE OF THE FRANCO-PRUSSIAN WAR

The Government of National Defense

The news of Sedan (p. 422) reached Paris, September 3, 1870. The city had been kept in ignorance of the previous disasters to French arms. Now it went mad with dismay and terror. The next day a mob invaded the hall where the legislature was already debating the deposition of Napoleon. So strengthened, a few Radical deputies tumultuously proclaimed the "Third Republic," and set up a provisional *Government of National Defense*.

This government tried at first to secure an honorable peace with Germany, protesting, truly, that the French *people* had not willed the war. But when Prussia made it plain that she intended to punish France by taking large slices of her territory, the conflict entered upon a new stage and became a heroic struggle for defense.

Second stage of the War

For this second stage of the Franco-Prussian War, there are two main features: the gallant resistance of Paris through a four months' siege, and a magnificent, patriotic uprising in the provinces. *Gambetta,* a leading member of the Government of Defense, escaped from Paris, in a balloon,[1] to organize the movement in the provinces. For a time success seemed possible. Exhausted France raised army after army, and amazed the world by her tremendous exertions. But unhappily Gambetta, instead of abandoning Paris to its fate and prolonging resistance by retiring slowly before the German advance, wear-

[1] This was long before the day of aëroplanes.

ing out the enemy in a hostile country, thought it necessary to hurl his half-trained forces upon the German lines, in the vain effort to relieve Paris. In the end it became apparent that the iron grasp of the German armies, with their perfect organization, could not be broken. The great population of Paris began to suffer the horrors of famine; the dogs and rats had been eaten; and on January 28 the city surrendered.

The National Assembly of 1871

There was no government in France with any real authority to make peace; and so an armistice was arranged, to permit the election of a *National Assembly* by manhood suffrage. Even the autocratic Bismarck had insisted upon this, since he meant that the whole French nation should give its consent to the terms he meant to impose. The Assembly met toward the close of February, 1871, and created a provisional government by electing *Thiers* "Head of the Executive Power of the French Republic."

Bismarck dictates harsh terms

The terms of peace were hard. The Prussians demanded Alsace and a part of Lorraine, with the great fortresses of Belfort, Metz, and Strassburg, and a huge war indemnity of one and a fifth billion dollars (some four times the cost of the war to Germany). Day after day the aged Thiers wrestled in pleading argument with Bismarck, the grim German Chancellor, to secure better terms. He did finally secure a reduction of the indemnity to one billion, and the retention of Belfort — much against the will of the Prussian war lords. In return for these concessions, however, the Prussians humiliated Paris by marching German troops in triumphal progress into the capital.

> Stern and ruthless as Bismarck was, he was too far-seeing to like these extreme measures. He knew they must arouse a deathless hostility in France. But the victorious military party was now too strong for him, he tells us, and he felt obliged to yield to its demands.

The "Commune of Paris," 1871

The National Assembly had hardly arranged peace with the foreign foe, before it had to meet a terrible rebellion at home. During the siege *all* the adult males of Paris had been armed as National Guards. When the siege was over, every one who could get away from the distressed city did temporarily remove, including one hundred and fifty thousand of the *wealthier* National Guards. Paris was left in control of the radical element. This element, too, kept its arms and its military organization; and it now set up a government of its own by choosing a large "Central Committee."

The National Assembly had established itself, not at Paris, but at Versailles. The radical Republicans of Paris suspected it of wishing to restore the monarchy. In fact, a large majority of the members *were* Monarchists, as events were soon to prove (p. 490). The Assembly, too, had put in command of the army a man who had assisted in Napoleon's *coup d'état*. Paris suspected him of preparing another such move in favor of some of the royalist pretenders. Moreover, the Assembly had aggrieved the poorer classes of Paris: it had insisted upon the immediate payment of rents and other debts incurred during the siege; and it did away in large measure with the pay of the National Guard, which, since the surrender, had been a kind of poor-relief. In addition to all this, the Reds and Socialists still remembered bitterly the cruel middle-class vengeance of '48 (p. 391).

For two weeks Paris and Versailles faced each other like hostile camps. The National Guards collected a large number of cannon in one of the forts of Paris. March 18 the Assembly sent a detachment of troops to secure these guns. A mob gathered to resist them. The Assembly's troops refused to fire, and looked on while two of their officers were seized and shot by the rebels.

For a time, there was still hope that a conflict might be averted. Paris decided to hold an election for a "General Council," and it was possible that the moderate element might win. Two hundred thousand votes were cast. The Radicals and Revolutionists elected sixty-four members, to about twenty Moderates. Then the Radical Council, acting with the "Central Committee," *set up the Commune, and adopted the red flag.*

In 1848 the Paris Radicals had learned that the *country* districts of France were overwhelmingly opposed to Socialism and to "Red Republicanism." So this new Paris Commune advocated extreme local self-government for all France. As Hanotaux, a prominent French historian, puts it, "The men of the Commune wished to make a Switzerland of France." If each city and village could become an almost independent state, then the Radicals hoped to carry out their socialistic policy in at least Paris and other large cities.

The supporters of this program wished the central government of France to be merely a loose federation of independent "communes"; and so they called themselves "Federals." They are properly described also as "Communards"; but the name "Communist," which is often applied to them, is likely to give a false impression. That latter name is generally used only for those who oppose private property. Many of the Communards were also Communists, but probably the majority of them were not.

The supporters of the Commune included the greater part of the citizens remaining in Paris. But France, though still bleeding from invasion, refused to be dismembered by internal revolt. The excited middle class felt, moreover, that the institution of property itself was at stake, and they confounded all Communards together as criminals seeking to overthrow society. Little chance was given to show what the Commune would have done, if left to itself. There is an interesting parallel between their program and that of the Russian Bolshevists in 1918. Like attempts to set up Communes took place at Marseilles, Toulouse, Narbonne, and Lyons; but they came to little, and the civil war was confined to Paris.

Civil War

April 2 the Versailles Assembly attacked Paris with the regular troops that had now returned from captivity in Germany. The struggle lasted two months and was utterly ferocious. The Assembly refused to treat the Communards as regular combatants, and shot down all prisoners. In retaliation, the Commune seized several hundred hostages from the better classes left in Paris, declaring that it would execute three of them for each of its soldiers shot after surrender. In fact, however, it did not carry out this threat; and the hostages were not harmed until the Commune had been overthrown. Then, in the final disorder, an unauthorized mob did put sixty-three of them to death, — the venerable Archbishop of Paris among them.

The bombardment of Paris by the Versailles government was far more destructive than that by the Germans had been. Finally the troops forced their way into the city, which was already in flames in many sections. For eight days more, desperate fighting went on in the streets, before the rebellion was put down.

The Commune had arranged mines in the sewers to blow up certain portions of the streets where the invaders were expected to enter; and, during its brief rule, it had cast down the triumphal column of Napoleon I (p. 316), on the ground that such glorification of wars of conquest was unworthy a civilized people. These facts, together with some destruction by the mob after the Commune had ceased to control the city, gave rise to the report that the Commune tried to destroy Paris when it could no longer retain possession. No such intention is needed to explain an enormous destruction under the conditions of the war. The world has never ceased to lament the loss to the art collections of the city.

Another "White" Terror

Court-martial executions of large batches of prisoners continued for many months, and some thirteen thousand survivors were condemned to transportation, before the rage of the victorious middle class was sated. There are few darker stains on the page of history than the cruelty and brutality of this middle-class vengeance.

For Further Reading. — Hazen's *Europe Since 1815*, 330–336, or Andrews' *Modern Europe*, II, 343–349. Also Robinson and Beard's *Readings*, II, 211–212.

CHAPTER XXXV

ESTABLISHMENT OF THE THIRD FRENCH REPUBLIC, 1871–1879

The Assembly monarchic in feeling

The Assembly had been elected simply with a view to making peace. In choosing it, men had thought of nothing else. *It was limited by no constitution, and it had no definite term of office.* Certainly, it had not been commissioned to make a constitution or to continue to rule indefinitely; but it did both these things.

Monarchic factions fail to unite

At the election, people had chosen conservative candidates, because they wanted men who could be counted upon not to renew the war rashly. The majority of the members proved to be Monarchists; and they failed to set up a king, only because they were divided into three rival groups, — Imperialists (Bonapartists), Orleanists (supporters of the Count of Paris, grandson of Louis Philippe), and Legitimists (adherents of the Count of Chambord, grandson of Charles X). These three factions agreed in believing that a new election would increase the strength of the Republicans; and so for five years they resisted all demands of the Republican members for dissolution.

Thiers President, 1871–1873

Now that peace had been made, and the rebellion crushed, the Assembly felt compelled to replace the "provisional government" by *some* more regular form. Accordingly it made Thiers "President of the Republic."

In truth, however, the government remained "provisional." The majority of the Assembly hoped to change to a monarchy at some favorable moment, and *they gave Thiers no fixed term of office.* Still, this presidency lasted more than two years longer (1871–1873), — the most glorious years of the old statesman's life, — and it was marked by three important features.

1. *France took up gallantly the huge work of reorganization.* Schools, army, and church were reconstructed (p. 495 ff.).

2. *France was freed from foreign occupation,* and Thiers won the proud title of "Liberator of the Territory." It had been intended that the vast war indemnity should be paid in installments through three years; and German garrisons were to remain in France until payment was complete. Germany had expected the indemnity to keep France weak for a long period. But France astonished all beholders by her rapid recovery. In eighteen months the indemnity was paid in coin, and the last German soldier had left French soil. The government loans (p. 500) were taken up enthusiastically by all classes of Frenchmen, — in great measure by the industrious and prosperous peasantry.

THIERS. — After the portrait by Bonnat in 1876.

3. *Republicanism was strengthened.* Thiers was an old Orleanist; but he saw that to set up a king was to risk civil war. Accordingly, he allied himself with the Moderate Republicans in the Assembly, and baffled triumphantly the efforts of the Monarchists. Meantime Republicanism grew stronger daily in the country.

Last chance of the Monarchists: MacMahon's presidency

In 1873 a momentary coalition of Monarchists and Radicals in the Assembly forced Thiers to resign. In his place the Monarchists elected *Marshal MacMahon,* an ardent Orleanist. *For some months a monarchic restoration seemed almost certain.*

Legitimists and Orleanists had at last united in support of the Count of Chambord, who agreed to adopt the Count of Paris as his heir. The Monarchists had the machinery of the government in their hands, and were just ready to declare the Bourbon heir the King of France, when the two factions split once more on the question of a symbol. The Orleanists wished to keep the tricolor, the flag of the 1830 Monarchy. But the Count of Chambord denounced the tricolor as the "symbol of revolution," and declared that he would not give up the white lilies of the old Bourbon monarchy, the symbol of divine right. On this scruple the chance of the Monarchists came to shipwreck.

The Constitution of the Third Republic

Then, in 1875, despairing of an immediate restoration, the Assembly adopted a constitution. Modified slightly by later amendments, this is the present constitution of the French Republic. It has never been submitted to the people.

The Constitution is very brief, because the Monarchist majority preferred to leave the details to be settled by later legislation, hoping to adapt them to a kingly government. The word "republic" did not appear in the original draft, but it was introduced, *indirectly,* by amendment. The first draft spoke of a "Chief Executive." An amendment changed this title to "President of the Republic"; but the change was adopted by a majority of only *one* in a vote of 705. *In 1884* a new amendment declared the republican form of government "*not subject to repeal.*"

The legislature consists of two Houses. The Senate contains three hundred members, holding office for nine years, one third going out each third year. (At first, seventy-five of the members were to hold office for life, but in 1884 an amendment declared that no more life members should be chosen.) The Deputies (lower House) are chosen by manhood suffrage for a term of four years.

When the Senate and the House of Deputies agree that it is desirable to amend the constitution, or when it is necessary to choose a president, *the two Houses meet together, at Versailles,* away from possible disturbances in Paris. In this joint form, they take the name *National Assembly*. A *majority vote* of this National Assembly suffices to change the constitution.

The executive consists of a *president*, elected for seven years by the National Assembly, and of *the ministry* he appoints. The president has much less power than the president of the United States. He is little more than a figurehead. He can act only through his ministers (cf. pp. 437, 438).

The ministers, as in England, are the real executive. They wield enormous power, directing all legislation, appointing a vast multitude of officers, and carrying on the government. Nominally, the president appoints the ministers; but, in practice, he must always name those who will be acceptable to the Deputies, and the ministry is obliged to resign when it ceases to have a majority to support its measures.

The Deputies maintain a control over the ministers by the right of *interpellation*. That is, any Deputy may address to the ministers a formal question, calling upon them to explain their action in any matter. Such a question must be answered fully; and it affords a chance to overthrow the ministry, by a vote of "lack of confidence."

The Republic securely established

Even after the adoption of the constitution, the Assembly did not give way at once to a new legislature. But almost every "by-election" (to fill a vacancy, upon death or resignation) resulted in a victory for the Republicans; and *by 1876* that party had gained a majority of the seats. It at once dissolved the Assembly, and *the new elections created a House of Deputies two thirds Republican.*

The Senate, with its seventy-five life-members, was still monarchic; and, with its support, MacMahon tried to keep a Monarchist ministry. During this contest the President and Senate dissolved the House of Deputies (as the constitution gives them power to do when they act together), and the ministry changed prefects and local officers all over France in order to control the election. But the Republicans rallied under the leadership of the fiery Gambetta (p. 485), and the new House of Deputies was even more strongly Republican than the preceding one. *This body then withheld all votes of supply*, until MacMahon appointed a ministry acceptable to it.

In 1879 the renewal of one third the Senate gave the Republicans a majority in that House also, and, soon after, MacMahon resigned. Then the National Assembly elected to the presidency *Grévy*, an ardent Republican; *and all branches of the government had at last come under Republican control.*

Stability of the Republic

For nearly a century, France had passed from revolution to revolution, until the world came to doubt whether any French government could be stable — much as the same forgetful world had felt about England in the seventeenth century. The present constitution of France is the eleventh since 1789. But in 1879, for the first time in the history of France, republican government was established by the *calm will of the nation.* Four times between 1792 and 1871 had the Republicans seized Paris; three times they had set up a republic; but never before had they truly represented the deliberate determination of the whole people. In 1879 they came into power, not by violence, but by an eight years' constitutional struggle against the political tricks of an accidental Monarchist majority. *This time it was the Republicans whom the conservative, peace-loving peasantry supported.* Even the World War did not bring any thought of a change in government.

CHAPTER XXXVI

FRANCE UNDER THE THIRD REPUBLIC

Church and State

The chief peril to the Republic has been its conflict with the clergy of the Catholic church. Seventy-eight per cent of the people of France are members of the Catholic church. Other religions make up about two per cent. Twenty per cent have no religious connection.

During the dubious period from 1871 to 1879, the Republican leaders felt that the bulk of the Catholic clergy were aiding the Monarchists with their tremendous influence. Cried Gambetta, in one of his fiery orations, — "Clericalism! That is our foe." Accordingly, when the Republicans came into power, they hastened to weaken the church by taking from it its ancient control over the family. Marriage was made a civil contract (to be performed by a magistrate) instead of a sacrament; divorce was legalized, despite the teachings of the Catholic church against it; and all religious orders were forbidden to teach in either public or private schools.

The mass of the Catholic nation supported this anti-clerical policy; but *extreme* Catholics were driven into fierce opposition to the government. The wise and gentle Pope Leo XIII, however, moderated the bitterness of the political warfare by recommending that French Catholics "rally" to the Republic, and try to get the privileges they needed by influencing legislation, not by trying to change the form of government (1893). On its side, the government then for a time let most of the anti-clerical laws rest quietly unenforced.

But about the year 1900, the Republicans and Radicals became alarmed again at the evidence of Monarchic sympathies still existing among the aristocracy, and even among army officers, and convinced themselves that these sympathies were due to the remaining clerical influence in the schools. In the years 1901–1903, thousands of church schools were closed by the police, sometimes amid riots and bloodshed. Pope Pius X protested, and deposed two French bishops who had acquiesced in the government's policy. The government recalled its ambassador from the papal court, and prepared a plan which it called "Separation of Church and State," but which zealous Catholics denounced as anti-religious robbery.

According to this new plan, a law of 1905 declared the nation the owner of all church property in France. Each religious congregation, however, was invited to reorganize as a "cultural association," and was promised permanent use of its old property if it did so. Protestant churches complied; but such organization was forbidden to Catholics by the pope as incompatible with the principles of the church. In the elections of 1906, however, the nation gave an overwhelming indorsement to the whole anti-clerical policy; and then the government evicted great numbers of Catholic clergy from their homes (for refusing to obey the law of 1905) and banished multitudes of them from the country. In 1914, when the great European war began, two thousand of these banished priests returned to France to fight in the ranks against the invaders of their country. The "kulturkampf" (struggle between church and state to control education) is not yet fully ended in France; but the splendid patriotism of the clergy in this great war will certainly result in some spirit of compromise for the future (1919).

Local government

For local government, France has been divided into 88 "Departments." Each Department has an executive officer, called a prefect, and a General Council. The prefect is *appointed* by the Minister of the Interior, and he may be removed by the same authority. He appoints police, postmen, and other local officers. The General Council is elected by universal suffrage. It exercises control over local taxation and expenditures, especially for roads, asylums, and, to some degree, for schools; but *its decisions are subject to the supervision of the central govern-*

ment. Indeed, the central government may dissolve a Departmental council at any time, and order a new election.

The communes of France, since the recovery of Alsace-Lorraine, number about forty thousand. They vary in size from great cities, like Marseilles,[1] to rural villages with only two or three hundred people. For all of them there is one system of government. Each has a mayor and a council. Until 1884, *the mayor* was appointed by the Minister of the Interior; since 1884, he has been elected by the municipal council. He is still regarded, however, as the officer of the central government, which may revise his acts or even remove him from office. *The municipal council* is elected by manhood suffrage. All its acts are subject to the approval of the prefect or the central government, and the latter may dissolve the council.

Such conditions do not seem very encouraging at first to an American student; but the situation, as compared with the past in France, is full of promise. Political interest is steadily growing in the communes, and *Frenchmen are learning more and more to use the field of self-government open to them.*

No bill of rights

The French system of law seems to an American or an Englishman to be wanting in safeguards for personal liberty. Unlike the previous French constitutions, the present constitution has *no "bill of rights."* That is, there are no provisions in the fundamental law regarding jury trial, habeas corpus privileges, or the right of free speech. Even if there were, the courts could not protect the individual from arbitrary acts of the government by appealing to such provisions, because, in case of conflict between a citizen and the government, the suit is tried, not in the ordinary courts, but in *administrative courts,*[2] made up of government officials. This does not mean that, in ordinary times, an accused man is likely to suffer injustice. As a rule, the administrative courts mete out fair treatment.

Administrative courts

[1] Paris and Lyons are each organized as a department, with even less self-government than the other departments of the country.

[2] Lowell, *Governments and Parties*, I, 50–55, or *Greater European Governments*, index.

But in case of any supposed danger to the government, they *may* become its champions — at the expense of the rights of a citizen. This fact was forced upon the world's attention some years ago in the infamous *Dreyfus trials*. This case is a good topic for special report by a strong student. It is only too true, however, that in times of excited feeling other democracies have shown quite as serious a disregard of personal liberty.

The zeal of the early Revolutionists for education (p. 300) has been noted. Said Danton, "Next to bread, education is the first need of a people." But, for want of time and money, their plans came to little; and for a long time after the Restoration, nothing was done. In 1827 over a third of the communes of France had no primary school whatever, and nearly a third of the population could neither read nor write.

Education

The real growth of popular education dates from the Third Republic. Almost as soon as the Franco-Prussian war was over, France adopted in large measure the German plan for schools — with certain improvements. To-day, in every commune there is a primary school or group of schools. Education is free and compulsory and strictly regulated by the state. That is, the central government appoints teachers and regulates the courses of study. Each department has an excellent system of secondary schools, called *lycées*, and the higher institutions are among the most famous in the world. From about 1890 they began to be sought by great numbers of advanced American students, who were more and more repelled by the undemocratic atmosphere of German universities. When its recent birth is considered, the educational system of France is marvelously efficient. France has taken once more a first place in Europe in literature, art, and science.

Increase of wealth

The advance of industry under the Third Republic has been enormous. In the forty years 1871–1911, the yearly production of wealth tripled (rising from one billion to three billions of dollars in value), though population grew less than one twentieth. In 1870, thirteen million tons of coal were mined; in 1911, forty-two millions. In 1870, less than 3000 patents were granted to inventors; in 1911, the number was nearly 15,000.

All this is the more remarkable when we remember that in losing Alsace-Lorraine to Germany, France had lost its richest iron districts — an almost indispensable source of wealth in modern times.

In the World War, at the very opening, Germany seized upon most of the remaining mineral districts of France, including all her coal fields, and held them to the close. Despite that fact, France actually increased her output of steel and iron manufactures during the war — finding a new source of energy in the water power of the slopes of the Pyrenees.

The French peasantry

But France is preëminently an agricultural country. The peculiar thing about French society, down to the War, has been the large number of small landowners and the prosperity of this landed peasantry. In 1900, more than half the entire population lived on the soil, and three fourths the soil was under crops. The great mass of cultivators owned little farms of from five to fifty acres; 3,000,000 proprietors had less than twenty-five acres each. The cultivation was scientific in a high degree. France supplied her population with foodstuffs, and exported a large surplus. The subdivision of the soil was carried so far that it was difficult to introduce the best machinery (though neighborhood associations were being founded to own machinery in common); but the peasant was intelligent, industrious, thrifty, prosperous, happy, and conservative.

Population stationary

The peasant wished to educate his son, and he had a high standard of living, compared with other European peasantry. With five or six children, a farmer owning five or ten acres found it almost impossible to keep up this high standard, and to leave his children as well off as he himself had been. Therefore the peasantry have not wished large families, *and for a long time population has been almost stationary.* By the census of 1911 it was a little under forty millions. The recovery of

Alsace-Lorraine, with its two millions of people, somewhat more than balances in numbers the losses in the War.

A nation of "little capitalists"

This population was a "nation of little savers," and consequently a nation of money lenders. Through the nineteenth century, England was the world's banker. In 1900, France was beginning to hold that place. When a government wished to "float" a huge loan, or when capitalists wished to finance some vast industrial enterprise, France commonly furnished the cash. She furnished England cash for the Boer war, and Russia cash for the war with Japan (p. 557), and American bankers and capitalists the sums needful to tide over the "crisis" of 1907–1908.

England still had more wealth than France; but it was largely "fixed" in long-time investments, while French wealth was growing rapidly and was held by a great number of people of small means, all seeking constantly for investments. The French national debt was not held, like the American or the English, in 1911, by men of great wealth, in large amounts, but by some 3,000,000 French people, — shopkeepers, clerks, artisans, day-laborers, small farmers, — in small amounts. The French government under the Third Republic had encouraged this tendency of the workingman and the peasant to save and to "invest," by issuing its bonds in small denominations — as low even as one franc (20 cents). An American who wished to invest in United States bonds had to have at least $100 at a time, — and then he often found it hard to get a bond. Under the Third Republic a Frenchman with 20 cents (1 franc) has no difficulty in buying a national certificate in any village. France was the first country to adopt this admirable plan of encouraging all citizens to become "bondholders" — and "stockholders in the national prosperity." The plan was followed by the United States, with the War Savings Stamps, during the World War.

German invasion in the War of 1914–1918 has made much of the fairest part of France a hideous desert, and has drained the rest of workers and of wealth. But the heroic people who for five terrible years of war showed a devotion to their country unsurpassed in history may be trusted now quickly to re-create her material prosperity by their skill and industry.

French politics: shifting ministries

Politics in France have been, much of the time, upon a lower level than business life. The best minds of France have not been present in the Assembly. That body has been broken into many parties (nine in the election of 1914); and the ministries have been kaleidoscopic in their changes. The 40 years from 1875 to 1915 saw 50 ministries. This meant woeful confusion and inefficiency; and the government has suffered from red tape and from a widespread taint of corruption in politics. As in America in the seventies and eighties of the last century, the government has been unworthy of the people, and, down to the World War, it had been a mighty factor in bringing disrepute upon the nation.

One promising feature was the growth of the Socialists into a true political party, working by regular constitutional means, not any longer by revolution. After 1900 the Socialists gained power rapidly; and, in the election of 1914, they became the largest of the nine elements in the Assembly. All recent ministries had contained leading Socialists, but the war called back to power more conservative statesmen — in the war ministry of Clemenceau, "the Tiger."

Loss of the old Colonies

About 1750 France bade fair to be the great colonial power of the world. The century-long duel with England was then half over. "New France" was written on the map across the valley of the St. Lawrence and the Mississippi, and the richest lands of the Orient seemed within the French grasp. Thirteen years later saw France stripped of all possessions outside Europe, except a few unimportant islands in the Indian Ocean and in the Antilles and some small ports in India (pp. 244–245).

A new colonial empire since 1830

In the nineteenth century France became again a colonial power. In 1830 the government of Charles X took advantage of an insult by the Dey of Algiers to a French consul to seize

French Algeria

territory in North Africa. In the middle of the century this foothold had grown, through savage and bloody wars, into complete military occupancy of Algeria; and in the early years of the Third Republic civil rule was introduced. Since 1880, Algeria has been not so much a foreign possession, or a colony, as a part of France separated from the rest by a strip of sea. The French make only a small part of the population, it is true, but the country is orderly and civilized. The settled portion, near the coast, is divided into three Departments, which are ruled essentially like the Departments in European France; and it has representatives in the French legislature. The inland parts of Algeria are still barbarous and disorderly, but to this long-desolate Barbary *coast,* French rule has restored the fertility and bloom that belonged to it as the garden of the ancient Roman world.

Nearly all the rest of the vast French colonial empire has been secured since the Franco-Prussian War. Algeria was of course only one of five great states on the Mediterranean coast of Africa, — Morocco, Algeria, Tunis, Tripoli, Egypt. All five had long been virtually independent Mohammedan kingdoms, though in name they had remained part of the decaying Turkish Empire. And all five, until Europeans stepped in, were in a vicious state of misrule, disorder, and tyranny. We have seen how in 1881 Egypt fell under England's "protection" (p. 469).

And Tunis

France quickly regretted that she had so easily given up her claim to share in that rich land; and so in the same year she seized gladly upon disorders in Tunis as an excuse for extending her authority, from Algeria eastward, over that country, making it a "protectorate." That is, France announced that she would control all the relations of Tunis with the outside world, but would leave unvexed its government over its own subjects at home — except that Frenchmen were to enjoy certain special trading privileges there. Before the World War, this "protectorate" had been changed fully into a colonial possession — a change quite inevitable under such conditions because of the incompetence and misrule of the native sovereigns.

Then, in 1904, France began in like fashion to extend her sway in North Africa toward the west; establishing a protectorate over part of Morocco. Spain had long controlled one part of that district; and, in 1905 at a European conference, it was agreed that France and Spain should oversee the country in partnership — spite of a violent attempt by the German Kaiser to secure an equal footing there.

And Morocco

Before seizing upon Tunis in 1881, — an act sure to arouse violent resentment in Italy, which looked upon Tunis as her own prey — the French government thought it necessary to lay its plans before Bismarck. That astute statesman at that time had not begun to have any colonial ambition for Germany, and he encouraged the French project, welcoming the chance to arouse hostility between France and Italy. (Indeed, with characteristic crookedness, he at the same moment encouraged Italy to hope for Tunis.) Soon afterward, however (p. 520), Germany herself entered the race for colonial empire; and in 1911 an extension of French rule in Morocco almost plunged Europe into war. William II of Germany sent a warship to Agadir, a harbor of Morocco, and "rattled the saber in the scabbard." But England supported France; and Germany was finally appeased by European consent to her seizing territory in the Kamerun (West Africa) and by the cession to her of part of the French Congo territory.

German rivalry

France has possessions in other parts of Africa. From the time of her ancient colonial empire she has always kept a hold upon Senegal; and since 1884 she has acquired huge possessions on both the east and west coasts, besides the great island of Madagascar (map facing p. 553).

Other French colonies in Africa

In America she holds Guiana (Cayenne), with a few ports in the Antilles. In Oceanica, between 1884 and 1887 she obtained New Caledonia and several smaller islands. Her most important colonies, outside Africa, are in the peninsula of Indo-China in southeastern Asia. Napoleon III seized Cambodia

And in Asia

(1862) and Cochin China (1863); and the Third Republic, with little more scruple, seized Tonking in 1884, Anam in 1886, and Siam to the Mekong in a savage war in 1893–1896. For many years, moreover, the "imperialistic" forces in France ("jingo" politicians and some large business interests) have sought an indirect control in Syria much like that which Germany was trying to establish in Asia Minor.

French colonial administration

The methods, then, by which France has secured most of her colonial empire have been about the same as those common with "civilized" states in dealings with barbarous and weak peoples. But *French rule has always been gentle, kindly, and, on the whole, wise.*

At the same time, France is not herself a colonizing nation — any more than in the seventeenth century (p. 245). Large parts of her empire in Africa are almost unpeopled, or are inhabited by savage tribes and are under military government. The total population of French colonies (not counting the "protectorates") is about 41 millions. But even in the settled portions the European population is small. The total area of the colonial possessions is about four million square miles, of which about three and a half million are in Africa. All the settled and orderly regions have a share in self-government, and most of them have representatives in the legislature at Paris.

FOR FURTHER READING. — The works mentioned on page 401 continue to be valuable for France well into the Third Republic. The important constitutional documents are given in Anderson's *Constitutions and Documents*.

For recent history of all European countries, every high school should have one or more good Reviews accessible or in the reading rooms, besides an *International Year Book* or *The Statesman's Year Book*, at least for every second or third year, and *The World Almanac* or *The Daily News Almanac*.

CHAPTER XXXVII

THE GERMAN EMPIRE, 1871–1918

The national industry of Prussia is war. — MIRABEAU, in 1790.

The Germanic Confederation of 1814–1867 was a loose confederacy of sovereign states. *The German Empire of 1871–1918 was a federal state* (p. 418). The central government was strengthened by the change, somewhat as was ours in America when we exchanged our Articles of Confederation for our present Constitution.

A despotic federal state

But this German "federated" Empire was *not a "free" government.* Federations are usually made up of republics: this one was made up mainly of monarchic states (4 kingdoms, 18 duchies, 3 "free cities"). The controlling body in the Empire was the Federal Council, or Bundesrath, consisting during most of its history of 56 delegates, *appointed* by the rulers of the different states and *directed* from day to day by those princes. Prussia had seventeen of these delegates, — and *fourteen* could negative any change in the constitution. The Bundesrath *prepared* measures for the legislature, and had a veto upon all laws.

The Federal Council

The Reichstag

The imperial legislature was the Reichstag — a one-House assembly elected by manhood suffrage. Of the 397 delegates, Prussia had 236. Practically, the power of this assembly was limited to accepting or rejecting proposals from the Bundesrath. Even its control over taxation was incomplete. Most revenue measures were not *annual* appropriations, but *standing* laws. That is, once passed, they could not be changed without the consent of the Bundesrath. The imperial ministry, appointed by the Emperor, was called "responsible"; but this was not in the English sense. The ministry was not obliged to resign if outvoted in the Reichstag. The Reichstag was little more than a debating society — but a debating society had value in a land where otherwise there was no free speech.

During most of the history of the Empire, Alsace was a "territory"; but in 1909 it was given statehood. At that time the number of delegates in the Reichstag was somewhat increased, but there was only a slight approach to a true reapportionment. The constitution had promised "periodic" reapportionment of representatives, to suit changes in population; but during the life of the Empire none took place, though population shifted greatly. In the American Congress, during that period, we had four reapportionments.

The Emperor an autocrat

In theory, the Emperor was only the life president of the federation. But this life presidency was hereditary in the kings of Prussia — somewhat as if the governor of New York were ex-officio President of the United States. Moreover, there was no provision for impeaching the Emperor; and, through his control over the ministry and over so large a part of the Bundesrath (he appointed the large Prussian delegation), he *controlled all foreign relations* and virtually held a veto upon all domestic legislation.

The Prussian constitution, 1848-1918

The Emperor held still mightier authority in the Empire from his position as despotic ruler of Prussia. Prussia had three fifths of the population of the Empire, and more than that part of the power. Her own divine-right "constitution" was the one "granted" by the king in '48 (p. 396). The upper House of the Prussian legislature was an hereditary body composed of bigoted Prussian "Junker" nobility. The lower House was elected; and all male citizens were supposed to have a voice in choosing it. But *the people voted in three classes*, according to wealth, in such a way as to give *two thirds* the representation to the richest *one sixth* of the voters. In Berlin in the election of 1902 a rich man's vote counted for that of fifty poor men.[1]

[1] For illustrations, see Davis' *Roots of the War*.

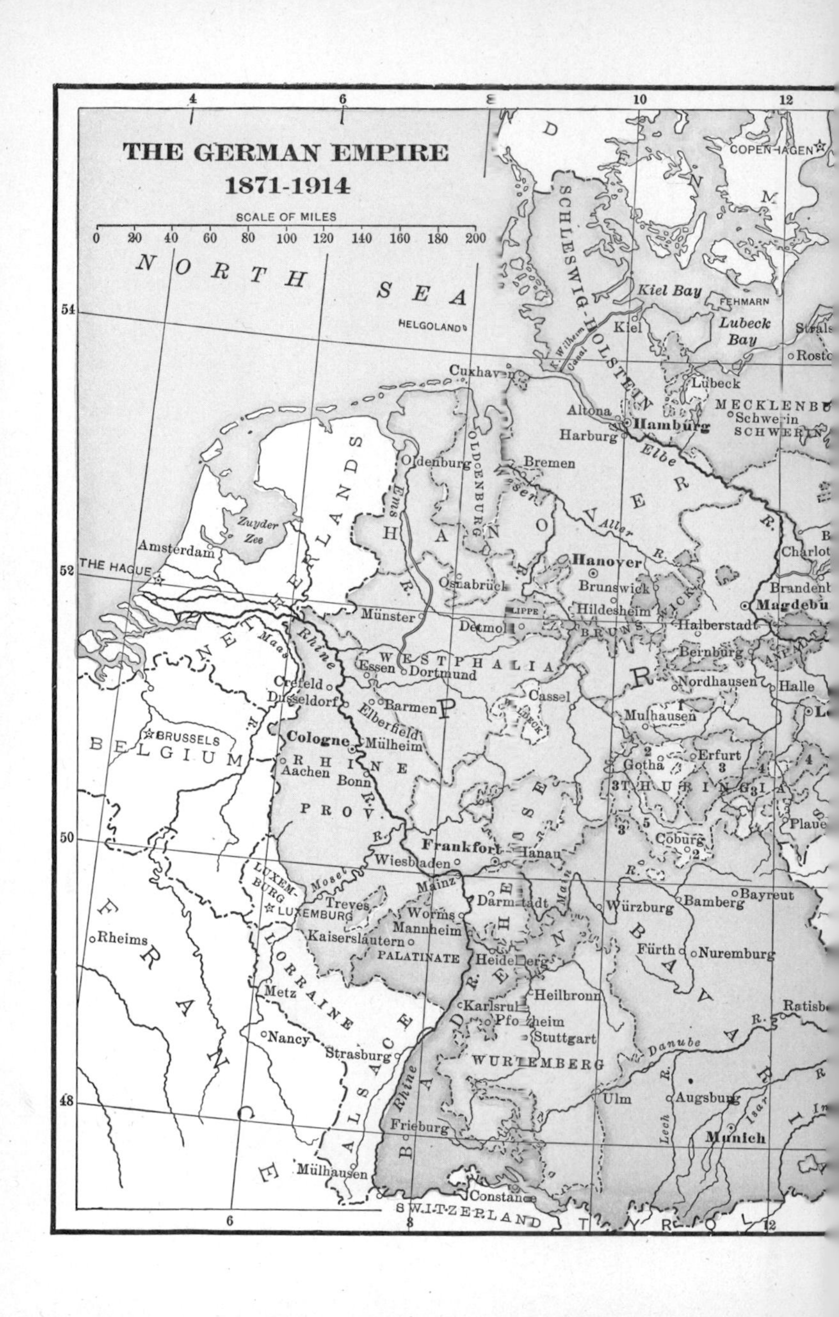

THE GERMAN EMPIRE
1871-1914
SCALE OF MILES
0 20 40 60 80 100 120 140 160 180 200
NORTH SEA
HELGOLAND
SCHLESWIG-HOLSTEIN
Kiel Bay
Kiel
FEHMARN
Lubeck Bay
COPENHAGEN
Cuxhaven
Lubeck
Altona
Hamburg
Harburg
MECKLENBURG
Schwerin
SCHWERIN
Bremen
Oldenburg
OLDENBURG
Elbe
Weser
Ems R.
Aller R.
NETHERLANDS
Zuyder Zee
Amsterdam
THE HAGUE
HANOVER
Hanover
Brunswick
Hildesheim
BRUNSWICK
Osnabrück
LIPPE
Münster
Detmold
Halberstadt
Magdeburg
Charlottenburg
Brandenburg
WESTPHALIA
Essen
Dortmund
Bernburg
ANHALT
Halle
Nordhausen
Crefeld
Düsseldorf
Barmen
Elberfield
Cassel
WALDECK
Mulhausen
BRUSSELS
BELGIUM
Cologne
Mülheim
RHINE PROV.
Aachen
Bonn
Rhine
Maas
Gotha
Erfurt
THURINGIA
Coburg
Plauen
Frankfort
Hanau
Wiesbaden
Mainz
HESSE
Darmstadt
Main R.
Würzburg
Bamberg
Bayreut
LUXEMBURG
Mosel
Treves
Worms
Mannheim
Kaiserslautern
PALATINATE
Heidelberg
Fürth
Nuremburg
BAVARIA
Rheims
FRANCE
LORRAINE
Metz
Nancy
Strasburg
ALSACE
Heilbronn
Karlsruhe
Pforzheim
Stuttgart
WURTEMBERG
Danube
Ratisbon
Ulm
Augsburg
Lech R.
Isar R.
Munich
BADEN
Frieburg
Mülhausen
Constance
SWITZERLAND
TYROL

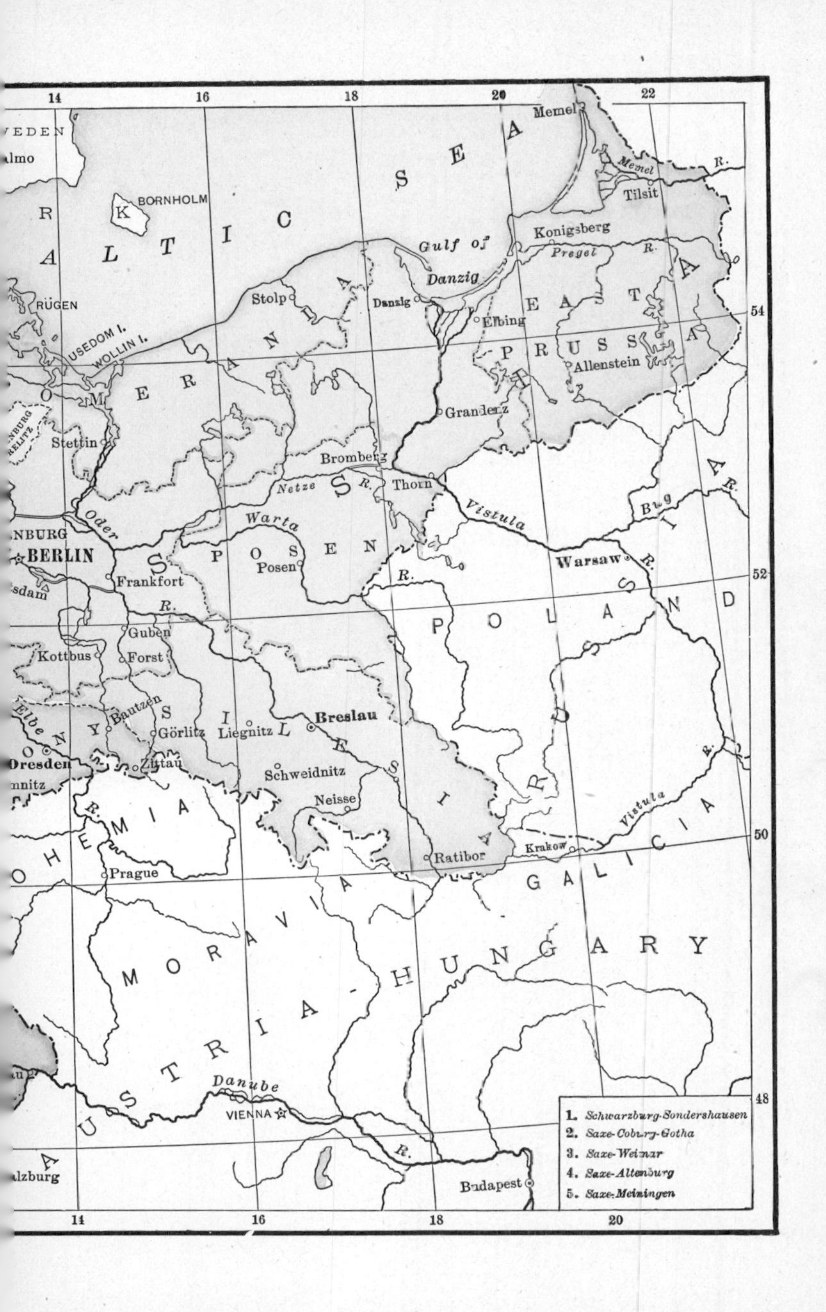
BALTIC SEA
BORNHOLM
RÜGEN
USEDOM I.
WOLLIN I.
Memel
Memel R.
Tilsit
Konigsberg
Pregel R.
Gulf of Danzig
Danzig
Elbing
Stolp
EAST PRUSSIA
Allenstein
POMERANIA
Graudenz
Stettin
Bromberg
Netze R.
Thorn
Vistula
Bug
Oder
Warta
POSEN
Posen
BERLIN
Frankfort
Warsaw
RUSSIA
POLAND
Guben
Kottbus
Forst
Bautzen
Görlitz
Liegnitz
Breslau
SILESIA
SAXONY
Dresden
Zittau
Schweidnitz
Neisse
Ratibor
Krakow
Vistula
GALICIA
BOHEMIA
Prague
MORAVIA
AUSTRIA-HUNGARY
Danube
VIENNA
Budapest
1. Schwarzburg-Sondershausen
2. Saxe-Coburg-Gotha
3. Saxe-Weimar
4. Saxe-Altenburg
5. Saxe-Meiningen
14
16
18
20
22
54
52
50
48

Then the legislature had little authority anyway. The king could adjourn or dissolve it, and could veto its acts *absolutely.* His ministers, too, were beyond its control.

Prussia and South Germany

The other states of the Empire were less despotic. All had representative legislatures; but few of them gave these legislatures real control over the administration. In general, South Germany was less military and more democratic than Prussia.

The Empire a paternal despotism

The imperial government was frugal and was supposed to be exceedingly honest and efficient, until at the close of the World War we learned that it had allowed privileged wealth to fatten upon the misery of the poor. It claimed to be paternal in the extreme. It made justice in the courts easy to secure; it guarded against food adulteration long before the rest of the world did; and in other ways it zealously protected the public health.

Militarism

But, alongside this watchful paternalism, there were grievous faults. Germany had been made by violence, and the result showed in *the spirit of militarism and in the predominance of the methods of the drill sergeant and the policeman.* A policeman's evidence in a court was equal to that of five independent witnesses, and his rule was all-pervading. Said a keen foreign observer (1896): — "The policeman strolls into your house or garden when he likes, much as a master enters the classroom to see that all is going on properly. If you go for a bath, he will forbid you to get out of your depth, swim you never so strongly. . . . To live in Germany always seems to me like a return to the nursery."

Even worse was the contemptuous and oftentimes brutal treatment of civilians by army officers. For years the newspapers contained reports of gross and unprovoked insults, and sometimes of violent assaults, by officers upon unoffending citizens, for which it was difficult to obtain redress in the courts. The most famous of these perhaps is the "Zabern incident."

Zabern, a little city in Alsace, contained a small garrison. Among the officers was a young Baron von Forstner, typical

The "Zabern incident"

Prussian junker. This young "hero" had already given occasion for one military trial because of trouble with citizens, and in November of 1913 he quarreled on the street with a lame shoemaker, who, he thought, failed to show him due deference. Feeling his "honor" injured, the noble baron drew his saber and hacked down the cripple — *whom two soldiers were holding for the purpose.* For this a court-martial sentenced the officer to one year in custody; but a higher court-martial at once reversed this judgment, and acquitted the baron as having acted only "in self-defense." Socialists in the Reichstag took up the case, and carried an overwhelming "vote of censure" upon the ministry — which had arrogantly defended the rowdy. This meant nothing. In any other parliament, the ministry would have resigned. But this German ministry smiled insolently and went on with their "order of the day."

No security for personal liberty

Nor was there any security for personal rights against even the non-military government. True, the constitution contained a *bill of rights,* but the courts had no power to declare void an unconstitutional law. The administration, too, could appeal cases in which it was interested to *administrative courts without juries.*[1] As a result, trial by jury, freedom of the press, freedom of public meetings, and free speech existed only in a limited degree. To criticize the Emperor in the press, ever so lightly, was likely to land the offender in jail for a considerable term. In January, 1898, it was reported on good authority that seventy German editors were in prison for that offense. The following anecdote illustrates how limited is the right of public meeting. In 1897 a landed proprietor gave a harvest festival for his workmen. Some fifty in all, they marched to a wood and had a picnic. A few days later the proprietor and several of the men were arrested on the charge of having held a public meeting without notifying the police. No other fault was alleged, but the offenders were sentenced to fines or short terms in jail.

[1] Russell's *Social Democracy,* 48-50, gives an interesting account of a famous trial of the Socialist Lassalle (p. 515).

This autocracy was upheld most of all by the landed squires, or junkers. Says Dr. Davis (*Roots of the War*, 188), — "A typical junker was the owner of a large landed property with a picturesque and uncomfortable ancient schloss (castle) dominating a village or town, where peasant children scrambled with pigs and chickens in the great dungheaps before the houses. He might come to enjoy city life. . . . He might reform his agricultural methods. . . . None the less he remained heart and soul a country aristocrat . . . accustomed to curse his inferiors, to cane his servants, and to despise all who lived by trade."

The junkers

This class furnished the officers of the army. For most of them, indeed, the army was the only possible career. Pay was pitifully small, and the nobles were poor. But the officer's social standing made it easy for him to find a wife among the daughters of wealthy merchants. No officer, however, could make such a marriage until a committee of higher officers had approved the bride — and the dower which was to atone for her ignoble blood.

German "Big Business"

The autocracy had one other pillar — a new element in German life. The junkers were largely Prussian and rural. But after 1870 Germany began to grow into a city Germany. The "industrial revolution," with the factory system, which had grown up in England before 1800 and in France by 1825, did not begin to make headway in Germany until nearly 1870. Then, indeed, manufactures and trade grew by leaps — aided by the coal and iron of Alsace-Lorraine and by subsidies from the huge war indemnity just then robbed of France. Science became the servant of manufactures as it had not before been in any other country. Especially was chemistry applied successfully to industries like the manufacture of dyes — which became practically a German monopoly. The whole artisan class, too, were trained to "efficiency" in trade schools, — which were distinctly class schools, suited on this German plan to an undemocratic land only, in which the son of an artisan must look for no "higher" station than his father.

All this meant a tremendous growth of cities. Hamburg grew from 350,000 people in 1870 to 1,000,000 in 1910; Berlin from 820,000 to 2,000,000; Essen from 50,000 to 300,000; while many wholly new centers of trade appeared where had been only farming hamlets. The population of the Empire doubled in these forty years; and all this increase was a city increase — which meant that the old city population was multiplied fourfold. Along with this change, there appeared a new figure in German life, the princely manufacturing capitalist. After 1880, the thousands of this class took their place — alongside the junker nobility — as a chief support of German autocracy with a vivid expectation of favors to be received in form of special privileges.

The war revealed this class as gross exploiters, fattening on their country's need. In no other land did war-profiteering prosper on so large a scale as in Germany, where the general misery was so terrible. This growth of huge war-fortunes was shown plainly by the government's income-tax reports in 1918, as published in German papers.

The Prussian army system

The junker and the capitalist made public opinion, but the autocracy had also its physical arm. After 1866, the Prussian army system was extended over all Germany. The fundamental principle was the universal obligation of all males to serve. The army was the armed nation. At twenty each man was supposed to enter the ranks for two years' active service. For five years more he was a member of the "active reserves," with two months in camp each year. These reserves were to be called out for regular service in case of war. For twelve years more he was listed in the territorial reserve — liable for garrison duty in time of war, and even for front rank service in special need. Exemption from training was usually allowed to the only son of a dependent widow, to students of theology, and to those unfit because of physical defects.

The Prussian victories of 1866 and 1870 convinced all Europe of the superiority of this system over the old professional armies, and nearly every state in Europe soon adopted it, with slight variations as to age and exemptions. Europe became a group of armed camps. Along with this went ever increasing attention to improved rifles, larger cannon, and other costly armament. The burden was enormous, and the direct cost was far less than the indirect cost involved in withdrawing so large a part of each man's best years from productive work. England, trusting to her navy, and the United States, trusting to her position, were the only large countries that dared refuse the crushing burden — and for England the cost of her navy was almost as serious. Certain good results, no doubt, as well as many evil ones, came from the military discipline; but on the whole that army system was the most woeful waste of human energy the world ever saw.

Europe adopts the German army system

Worse still, this militarism was a constant temptation to war; and, in Germany, the worst result was the way in which it helped to make the masses servile in private life under the rule of king, junker, and policeman. Flogging and other brutal punishment for slight offenses was the rule in the Prussian army; and there are reliably reported numerous cases of suicide by soldiers who were so mistreated by officers that they could no longer live in decent self-respect. Those who submitted to such "discipline" became slaves.

Militarism

Militarism was one phase of the Prussian danger to the world, as autocracy was the other phase. Militarism is not the same thing as having a large army, though it is likely to grow out of having one. *Militarism is a state of mind* regarding the army: a habit of thinking that the army is the most important matter, of exalting it above the civil powers at home, and of trusting to force in relations with other nations rather than to justice and good will and reason. In the long run, too, militarism leads to a servile attitude on the part of the people toward army officers, wholly incompatible with democracy.[1]

[1] War Encyclopedia, under "Militarism" and "Prussianism"; and C. Altschul's *German Militarism and Its German Critics*, esp. pp. 20–21.

Divine Right Emperors

The Emperor, head of the government and of the army, claimed obedience as of divine right. At his coronation, *William I* took the crown from the communion table, declaring, "The crown comes only from God, and I have received it from His hands." And in an election manifesto of 1882, he reminded all officials that "*the duty which you have sworn to perform* [in the oath of office] *extends to supporting the policy of the government at the elections.*"

In 1888 William was succeeded by his son, *Frederick III*. Frederick was an admirer of parliamentary government upon the English pattern. His wife Victoria was a daughter of the great English queen; and he had long been hostile to Bismarck. But Frederick was suffering from a fatal disease at the time of his accession, and his three months reign brought no change in the government.

Kaiser Wilhelm II

William II, the son of Frederick, returned to the principles of his grandfather. As a youth, he had been a great admirer of Bismarck; but it soon became plain that the two men were each too masterful to work together, and in 1890 the Emperor curtly dismissed the Chancellor from office. Thereafter, William II himself directed the policy of the Empire, and he was a greater force in European politics than any other sovereign in Europe. He believed thoroughly in the "divine right" theory, and he repeatedly stated it in as striking a form as ever did James I of England or Louis XIV of France, two or three centuries ago.

In the Visitors' Book in the Town Hall of Munich, he wrote, "The will of the king is the supreme law." In an address to his army, he said: "On me, as German Emperor, the spirit of God has descended. I am His sword and His vice-regent." In 1891, in an address to a body of military recruits, he said: "You are now my soldiers. You have given yourselves to me, body and soul. There is now but one enemy for you, and that is *my* enemy. In these times of socialistic intrigue, it may happen that I shall order you to fire upon your brothers or fathers. In such case you are bound to obey me without a murmur!" In 1897, in a prepared address, he set forth at length his office as a "vice-regent of God"; and the same year, his brother Henry, when about to set sail for China, in command of a German expedition, used the following words in a public address to the Emperor: "Of one thing I can assure Your Majesty. Neither fame nor laurels have charm for me. One thing is the aim that draws me on: it is to declare in foreign lands the *evangel of Your Majesty's hallowed person.*" "All-Highest" was a recognized form of address for the Emperor. And the phrase ironically attributed to him — "Me und Gott" — is no great exaggeration of the patronizing way in which he often referred to the Almighty as a partner in his enterprises — as in the famous address at Berlin in 1901: "We shall conquer even though we be surrounded by enemies; for there lives a powerful ally, the old, good God in heaven, who ever since the time of the Great Elector has always been on our side."

Germany and England

Some survey like the foregoing is needful to guard us against the "tyranny of names." England and Germany in 1914 were both "constitutional monarchies"; but that does not mean that they were in any way alike, even in government. They stood at the two poles of government. England had a democratic government, in which the monarchic and aristocratic survivals were practically powerless — mere matters of form; the German Empire was one of the most absolute autocracies in the world. England's ideals were based upon industry and world-peace: Germany's ideals were based upon militarism and conquest. Englishmen thought of the "state" as a condition for the full development of the individual man: Germans thought of individual men as existing primarily for the sake of the absolutist state. German capitalism was perhaps in itself no more grasping and greedy than like forces in other countries. But in England, America, or France, those forces must cease to work evil whenever the majority of the people are wise enough and good enough to will it so — and vote so: in Germany that capitalistic greed was backed by an irresistible military despotism against which the masses were powerless, either by ballots or bullets.

Bismarck's rule

For nearly twenty years after the Empire was established, Bismarck directed its course. The "Iron Chancellor" was a ruler of tremendous power of will; but he carried his policy of "blood and iron" into civil affairs — and failed. Three contests fill the period: the kulturkampf; the attempt to suppress the Socialists; the attempt to Germanize the border provinces.

The struggle with the Catholic church

1. The Empire had brought Catholic and Protestant Germany under one government. This resulted at once in a serious conflict between church and state. The immediate outbreak came in connection with a famous decree of the Vatican Council of 1870, affirming the pope to be infallible (incapable of error) in matters of faith and morals. The German bishops at the Council, true to the old traditions of Germany, refused to assent to this new statement, and withdrew in a body. Within a year they had for the most part fallen into line; but some of them maintained their position and took the name of *Old Catholics.* This sect was soon attacked vigorously by the orthodox bishops. Instructors in the clerical schools who did not teach the dogma of infallibility were suspended from their offices and excommunicated; teachers in the primary schools were dismissed; and the orthodox clergy refused to perform the marriage ceremony for followers of the Old Catholics.

Then Bismarck stepped in for the defense of the Old Catholics; and apparently he was not sorry for so good an occasion to assert the supremacy of the state over the church. Under his influence, the legislature took marriage and all education, private and public, from the control of the church. The Jesuits were expelled from Germany; the state assumed control over the education of priests; and the church was forbidden to exclude its own members except with government permission

The bishops and orthodox clergy formally refused to obey these laws, and Bismarck fell back upon a series of violent measures. Priests were deprived of office, and were even punished by long terms of imprisonment or by exile. The pope protested, and in 1875 he declared that the anti-clerical laws ought not to be obeyed. The Empire had already withdrawn its ambassador from the papal court, and Bismarck now confiscated ecclesiastical salaries and took into the government's hands all the property and revenues of the church, at the same time expelling all Catholic religious orders.

These measures have been described as having a military character, — "designed to cut off the enemy from his commissariat and to deprive him of his most active troops." From 1875 to 1879, the government held its position. One fifth the parishes in Prussia had no clergy; schools and seminaries were closed; chairs of theology in the German universities were vacant; houses of the clergy were raided by the police; and numbers of men of devoted Christian lives and broad scholarship languished in prison or in exile.

This persecution, however, was ineffective against the heroic resistance of the clergy, and it steadily lost favor among the people. A strong and growing "Catholic" party in the Reichstag, "*the Center*," hampered all Bismarck's projects; and finally he was forced to make terms with it, in order to secure the legislation he desired against the Socialists and for tariffs. In 1880 the government began its retreat; and *it abandoned step by step every position it had assumed in the quarrel.* The chief result of the contest was the large, watchful Conservative party, "the Center," during the rest of the life of the Empire. Bismarck had failed utterly.

Bismarck and the Socialists

2. Socialism did not become prominent in Germany until after 1848. German Socialism was founded by Karl Marx (p. 383), but its teachings were thrown among the masses by Lassalle, a brilliant writer and orator. When manhood suffrage was introduced in the election of the Reichstag of the North German Confederation, the Socialists got their first chance. They held eight seats in the Reichstag of 1867. Faithful to their doctrine of human brotherhood, these men in 1870 earnestly opposed the war with France, especially after

it became a war for conquest, and they criticized the seizure of Alsace-Lorraine against the will of the inhabitants.

This "unpatriotic" attitude resulted in a check. The leaders were tried for treason and condemned to years of imprisonment; and in the first Imperial Reichstag (1871) the party had only two representatives. But in 1874 the number had risen to nine, and in 1877, to twelve.

Bismarck then began to feel it needful to put down Socialism. His first effort to secure repressive laws from the Reichstag failed, but it called out two attempts by Socialist fanatics to assassinate the Emperor (1877, 1878). The criminals had no sanction from the Social Democratic party; but they played into Bismarck's hands. Taking swift advantage of popular alarm, he dissolved the Reichstag; and the new election gave a legislature ready to go all lengths against the "Red Specter." New laws gave the government authority to dissolve associations, break up meetings, confiscate publications, suspend habeas corpus privileges and jury trial, and banish suspects by decree, without any trial at all. Not content with these extraordinary powers, Bismarck made them retroactive, and at once banished from Berlin sixty or seventy men who had *formerly* been connected with the Socialists.

The Socialists met this ruthless severity with as much fortitude and heroism [1] as the Catholic clergy had shown in their conflict. Socialism for a time became an underground current. In 1881, just after the beginning of the repressive legislation, the Socialist vote fell off somewhat; but in the election of 1884 it had risen to over half a million — much more than ever before — and in 1887 it was over three fourths of a million. Then the repressive laws were allowed to expire; and in 1890 the vote was doubled. Again the Iron Chancellor had failed.

During the latter part of the struggle, it is true, Bismarck used also a wiser policy of cutting the ground from under the feet of the Socialist agitators by improving the condition of the working classes, along lines pointed out by the Socialists

[1] For an account, see Russell, *Social Democracy*, 103–114.

themselves. In 1884, he said, — "Give the workingman *the right to work* while he is well, and assure him care when he is sick, and maintenance when he is old, and the Social Democrats will get no hold upon him."

Bismarck tries state socialism

In accordance with these principles, Bismarck favored the introduction of great public works to afford employment, and he created a state fund to help insure the injured and the aged. (1) The state compelled the laborers to insure against sickness. (2) It insured them against accident, taking the premium from the employer. And (3) it paid old-age pensions to men over seventy years of age, out of a fund created partly by payments from the insured, partly by payments from the employers, and partly by a payment from the state treasury.

In this "Social insurance," Germany was a pioneer — though England and France have since passed by her. The condition of the laborers, however, remained miserable. The legislation was only a sop. It did not weaken Social Democracy. Indeed the Socialists railed at it as fear-inspired, poor-law legislation. To Bismarck, and to William II, it was the duty of the divine-right government to care for the laborer. To the Social Democrats, it is the right of the laborers themselves to control the government and to care for themselves through it.

Growth of the Socialist party

It is convenient here to carry the topic of Socialism down to the Great War. After 1898 the Socialists were much the largest political party, gaining heavily in every election. In 1912 the total vote, 12,188,000, was split among fifteen parties, but the Socialists cast 4,239,000 of those votes — or more than twice as many as any other party. This was largely, no doubt, because the Socialist conventions had put first in their platforms a number of practical *political and economic measures* which the average American or Englishman would not regard as dangerous, — such as universal suffrage (including "votes for women"); the initiative and referendum; equal electoral districts; payment of members of the Reichstag; responsibility of the government to the Reichstag; popular local government; securities for free speech; a militia system in place of the army system; an eight-hour labor day, with prohibition of employment of children under fourteen; freedom to organize labor unions; and progressive income taxes.

Socialist criticism of the government

In the Reichstag, speech was fairly free — as it was not elsewhere in Germany — and the Socialist deputies opposed bitterly the huge army and naval bills, with all the government's long preparation for war. Sometimes this opposition became personal and vehement. In 1894 the Socialist deputies unanimously kept their seats, when, at the opening of the Reichstag, cheers for the Emperor were called for; and in 1909 Philip Scheidemann exclaimed in debate that lying ("word-breaking") was "the most characteristic tradition" of the Hohenzollerns.

William II and the Socialists

William II, for a time, seemed disposed to use gentler methods than those that Bismarck had followed; but he, too, soon became alarmed at the growth of the Socialist vote, and in 1894–1895 he tried vehemently to secure another "exceptional law," even more sweeping than Bismarck's legislation. The proposed bill provided two years imprisonment for "publicly attacking religion, the monarchy, marriage, the family, or property, by insulting utterances." Under such a law, to suggest a change in the government to a republican form, or, indeed, to urge much milder changes, might constitute a crime; and so all Liberals joined with the Socialists in voting down the proposal. The Catholics did not dare to vote for it, lest their opposition to civil marriage should be treated as a crime.

Bismarck and the frontier peoples

3. Equally violent, and more long-continued, was Bismarck's effort to Germanize the Poles of Posen, the Danes of Slesvig, and the French of Alsace. To each of these subject peoples, Germany forbade all use of its own language. The Slesvig Danes were not allowed to teach any history in their schools prior to the time when they were seized by Prussia. The Poles were tempted by the government to sell their lands to German immigrants; and, when instead they sold cheap to

their own race, the lands were seized by the government (with compensation). But even then the Germans whom the government induced to settle in Posen rapidly became Poles in feeling, as those induced to settle in Alsace often became French. To the end, the delegates in the Reichstag from these three districts were always "in opposition" to the government. Again "blood and iron" failed,[1] though continued relentlessly for more than twenty years after Bismarck's rule. When the World War began, a German statesman said truly, "In Alsace, we are in an enemy's country." The Prussian system, begotten of force, had confidence only in force — and so proved itself unfit for the problems of modern life.

> There should be no trouble in distinguishing between this policy of *forceful* Germanization of *un*willing, conquered subjects, and our Americanization, by inducement, of those foreigners who of their own will have sought homes in our midst.

Growth of German commerce

In another matter, Bismarck's failure was less blamable, but equally clear. The old Germany of his youth had been an agricultural country. Foreign trade had been of little consequence. The new capitalist and commercial Germany that grew up after 1870 he never felt any real sympathy for. He saw its force, in part, but he did not understand it, or like it. After a short resistance, in 1878, he yielded to its demands for high protective tariffs, and, finally, to demands for subsidies wherewith to build up lines of merchant marine, like the Hamburg-American and North German Lloyd. *But the manufacturing interest began early to call also for a colonial empire,* outside Europe, for a safe and "sole" market. This demand Bismarck resisted for years. He was intensely proud of the Germany he had made, and wished only to preserve it.

The demand for a colonial empire

[1] A dramatic narrative of the failure, with much picturesque incident, is given in Davis' *Roots of the War*. 226–248. There is admirable material there for a "special report" by a student to the class.

But the manufacturers' demand for colonies was supported also by a people's demand. After 1880 the label "Made in Germany" began to be seen on all sorts of articles in all parts of the world, and before 1900 Germany had passed all countries except England and the United States in manufactures and trade. Still the nation was not content. Population was growing rapidly. In 1815 the states that made up the Germany of 1914 counted only 25 million people. Now those lands had come to count 67 millions — besides many million more who had sought homes in other lands. This growth had resulted in an immense emigration, mainly to the United States and to Argentina, Brazil, and other South American countries. And so, partly to meet the commercial demands of the capitalists, and partly to keep future German emigrants under the German flag, *Bismarck reluctantly adopted the policy of acquiring colonies.*

BISMARCK, after dismissal from office. From a photograph.

Growth of the colonial empire

Bismarck announced this plan *in 1884.* At that time Germany had no possessions outside Europe, and no war navy. But, though late in entering the scramble for foreign possessions, she made rapid progress, in part because England no longer felt any wish to secure new realms. Then, in 1890, the young William II dismissed Bismarck from office. This act was due to the natural conflict of wills between two stubborn men, but also partly to the fact that the new Emperor felt that the old Chancellor was "out of date." William stood, not for Bismarck's policy of *preserving* the great existing Germany of

And the fall of Bismarck

that day, but for a new "Pan-German" policy of making Germany greater — by means even more unscrupulous than those Bismarck had used — until she should be world-mistress. To this end, he sought to get colonies more eagerly than Bismarck had done.

Thereafter the colonial empire mounted by leaps. At the opening of the World War, Germany had vast possessions in Africa (map facing p. 553), a million square miles in all, mainly on the Guinea coast and in South Africa on both east and west coasts. The English self-governing colonies in South Africa, dreading the neighborhood of German militarism, had warned the government in England of the German plans for seizing this last territory and had vainly implored England to act first. But England felt that she had lands enough, and she had no wish to arouse German envy needlessly.

Germany in Australasia and in Asia Minor

In like manner, spite of warnings and protests from Australia, England permitted Germany to occupy much of the rich island of New Guinea. In the western Pacific also Germany secured many valuable groups of islands, and shortly after 1890 she began to obtain "concessions" in Asia Minor from the Turkish government. She did not get absolute title to territory there, but she secured, by treaties, many valuable rights of trade and of railroad building in those rich regions; and she expected some time to convert these claims into full ownership.

Germany seeks Turkish friendship

As a means to this end, the German government began to cultivate the favor of the Sultan of Turkey on all occasions, some of them shameful. The growing moral sense in international matters in England made it no longer possible for that country after 1880 to bolster up the dastard rule of the Turk over subject Christian peoples; but Germany stepped gladly into England's old place as champion of the Turk. This change appeared plainly during the horrible "Armenian Massacres" of 1894–1895. To check a probable move for Armenian independence, the Turkish government turned loose upon that unhappy province — for the first of several times to come —

hordes of savage soldiery to carry out a policy of frightfulness by licensed murder, pillage, and ravishment of a peaceful population. At least ten thousand Armenians were murdered. In England in 1895 monster mass meetings called upon the English government to intervene by arms. But Russia, fearful lest *her* Armenians might be encouraged to rebel, supported Turkey; France, just then hostile to England in colonial matters and bound to Russia as an ally, took the same side; and the German Emperor sent his photograph and that of his wife to the Assassin-in-chief of Turkey, to show his friendly adhesion. The English government felt powerless. From his retirement (p. 464) the aged Gladstone once more lifted his voice, urging that even under these hopeless conditions, England should alone challenge the world and take up the work of mercy; and the Tory prime minister, Lord Salisbury, confessed regretfully that in 1878 and 1854 "we put our money on the wrong horse." But he saw no chance to act. Two years later, however, when Turkey, backed by Germany, began similar outrages in the island of Crete, England succeeded in bringing Russia and France into a movement to compel Turkey to cede Crete to Greece.

Germany in China

In 1897 another field for German colonization opened, even more attractive. Two missionaries of German birth were murdered in China, and the Kaiser made that event an excuse to seize a valuable Chinese port, Kiau Chau, with a large adjacent territory. From this center, Germany acquired a "sphere of influence" in Shantung in which German capitalists developed mines and built railroads, as Russians were doing to the north, and Englishmen and Frenchmen to the south. Germany was rapidly converting a rich section of China into a German dependency; and a satirical German Socialist newspaper in a cartoon represented the Kaiser saying, — "If only my missionaries hold out, I may become master of all Asia."

But *as a colonizing nation, Germany did not prove a success.* Capitalists went in small numbers to Asia Minor and to China, but they did not go to Africa; and the mass of emigrants still sailed to America, giving up German citizenship. German colonies contained a population of some 14 million people in 1911, but only 20,000 of these were whites. The government was believed anxious to obtain possessions in South or Central America, where German emigrants might make their homes; and but for the Monroe Doctrine of the United States, some attempts in these lines would probably have been made. This was one reason for the deep hostility felt by the German government for the United States in the years just before the World War.

However, the matter of non-European homes for German emigrants became really of little consequence after 1900, because the number of emigrants became smaller. In the nineties the numbers were from 200,000 to 300,000 a year. But from 1909 to 1914 it was only from 20,000 to 30,000. The vast development of industry in Germany itself, along with the government's discouragement of emigration, decided intending emigrants to stay at home.

And Germany proved herself absolutely unfit to rule subject races in the tropics. In South Africa she turned the natives virtually into slaves to secure the ivory and rubber of the interior; and in 1907–1909, when the cruelly oppressed peoples rose in revolt, she put down the risings with medieval cruelty, practically exterminating the Herreros, one of the most promising of African races.

William II and his navy

In one particular Kaiser William took up a policy wholly unlike Bismarck's. He determined to make Germany a great naval power, as well as a great military power. He constructed the Kiel Canal, so that the navy might have perfect protection, and so that it might instantly concentrate in either the North Sea or the Baltic; and year by year, against violent Socialist resistance, he forced vast appropriations through the Reichstag to construct more and huger superdreadnoughts.

The excuse given for this was the need to protect the new trade and the new colonies; but the real motive, absolutely plain and often confessed by Germans, was to destroy England and weaken America at the first chance. Indeed the Kaiser and his advisers said openly that had their fleet been ready they would have attacked the United States at the time of the Spanish American War, and destroyed the Monroe Doctrine, with its check upon German plans in South America. In 1902 Germany had a difficulty with Venezuela, and showed a plain intention of at least seizing a port there as a naval base. Theodore Roosevelt, then President sent the American fleet, under Dewey, to the neighborhood, and gave Germany forty-eight hours in which to withdraw from Venezuela. This rather peremptory proceeding was successful. Germany withdrew; but from that time, we are told, her naval officers were deeply interested in finding the best plan for attacking New York.[1]

For Further Reading. — Dawson's *Bismarck and State Socialism* and Russell's *German Social Democracy* are good treatments of their subjects. Davis' *Roots of the War* is especially good upon this old Germany, pp. 24–38, 162–248.

Review Exercise. — Make a "brief," or outline, for the history of Germany from the French Revolution to the World War. Do the like for France and for England.

[1] Davis, *Roots of the War*, p. 360.

CHAPTER XXXVIII

ITALY SINCE 1870

The constitution of Italy is essentially that given to Sardinia in 1848. It provides for a limited monarchy of a liberal kind. By custom, as in France and England, the ministries are "responsible." That is, they resign when they no longer have a parliamentary majority. Local government and the courts are patterned upon the French model.

The government

Until 1882, a high property qualification was required for voters, — so that only one grown man in seven had the franchise. At that date, after two years' agitation, the franchise was given to all who could read and write, or who paid certain rents, or four dollars in direct taxes. This still shut out more than half the adult males. With the progress of education, however, the proportion of voters slowly increased; and in 1913 a new law established virtual manhood suffrage.

Education

In 1861 Italy had no schools except those taught by religious orders. In the next twenty years a fair system of public education was built up. Primary education is gratuitous, compulsory, and regulated by the state, but attendance is not well enforced. In 1861 seventy-four per cent of the population over six years of age could not read or write. In 1881 this percentage of illiterates had fallen to sixty-two, and in 1901 to fifty-six. The higher educational institutions are excellent, and Italian scholars hold a foremost place in science and history.

The crushing army system

The kingdom of Italy at its birth was far behind the other great states of Europe. Its proper tasks were to provide for public education, to repress brigandage, to build railroads, to foster useful industries, to drain malarial swamps and reclaim abandoned lands. In all this, much progress has been made;

but the government has been hampered by its poverty and by its tremendous expenditures for military purposes.

Italy was freed by force of arms, in 1859–1861. The new-born state, for many years more, feared that the work might be undone by France or Austria; and to the present time (1919) she has maintained *the usual European military system*, with longer terms of active service than were required in Germany or France, though she has been much less able to endure this burden than were those richer countries.

Taxation

Taxation is crushing; and yet, much of the time, the government can hardly meet expenses. For many years before the World War, a fourth of the revenue went to pay the interest on the national debt, and a large part of the rest was for military purposes, leaving only a small part for the usual and helpful purposes of government. To make ends meet, the government has been driven to desperate expedients. Salt and tobacco are government monopolies; the state runs a lottery; and taxation upon houses, land, and incomes is so exorbitant as seriously to hamper industry. Thus, canning fruit should be a highly profitable employment; but the government tax on sugar makes that industry impossible. The financial and military problem is the great question before Italy.

Agitation and politics

Economic distress led to political and socialistic agitation. The government at first met this by stern repressive legislation. Socialists and Republicans were imprisoned by hundreds, often on the charge of being anarchists; and for years at a time large parts of Italy were in "state of siege," or under martial law. The Radicals and Socialists, however, gained slowly in the parliament; and after 1900 violent repression was given up. Then at once it appeared, as in France, that the Socialists were a true political party; and of late years they have been strong even in the ministries.

A large emigration leaves Italy each year, mainly for Brazil and the Argentine Republic. Partly in hope to retain these emigrants as Italian citizens, the government took up a policy of securing *colonies*. Indeed the new-born kingdom of Italy almost at once began to dream of renewing ancient Italian control in the Mediterranean. Just across from Sicily lay Tunis, one of the rich but anarchic provinces of the decaying Turkish Empire. To be ready to seize this plum when ripe, Italy began to build a navy, and, at crushing cost, she finally made hers among the most powerful in the world. But before she was quite ready to act, France seized control in Tunis (1881). Bitterly chagrined,[1] Italy then used her military and naval force to secure valuable territory on the coast of Abyssinia (1885). From 1889 to 1896, indeed, she held a protectorate over all Abyssinia. In the latter year an Italian army was destroyed in the interior, and Italian control was reduced to the coast district. But in 1912–1913 this loss was much more than made good by the seizure of Tripoli from Turkey.

Army, navy, and the colonial empire

Another difficulty about territory long troubled Italy. When Austria gave back "Venetia" to Italy in 1867, it was not by any means the ancient Venetia in extent. Old Venetia had reached down the east coast of the Adriatic, through Dalmatia; and the modern seaport, Trieste, was still largely Italian in blood — though the country district about it was mainly Slav. Italy wanted the Dalmatian coast, with complete control of both sides of the Adriatic.

Italia Irredenta

In this matter, right and wrong were intermingled, and an absolutely just solution of the problem would not have been easy, even if all parties had wanted one. But another part of the same trouble was simpler as to right and wrong. "Lombardy," redeemed in 1859, certainly should have included the Trentine district on the south slope of the Alps, with its purely Italian population. This district Austria held unjustly — through the favor of Napoleon III; and this "Italia Irredenta" ("Unredeemed"), along with the unredeemed Trieste, was a constant source of danger to European peace.

Italy has also a serious problem in the relations of state and church. Almost all Italians are Roman Catholics; but the

State and church

[1] Note on the map how Italian control of Tunis would have made the Mediterranean two lakes ruled by Italy, and see p. 593.

government and the pope have been hostile to each other ever since the Kingdom of Italy was established. The clergy, of course, in the main adhere to the pope, while the great mass of the people earnestly support the government.

In 1870, when Italy took forceful possession of Rome, Pope Pius IX protested against the act as a deed of brigandage — though the citizens of Rome had ratified the union with Italy by a vote of ninety to one. The government has left the papacy every power it thinks consistent with the territorial unity of Italy. The pope is not an Italian subject, but, in all matters of form, is an independent sovereign, though his territory has been reduced to a single palace (the Vatican) and some small estates. Within this domain he keeps his own court, maintains his own diplomatic service, and carries on the machinery of a state. A generous annual income is also set aside for him by the government of Italy. The clergy and church throughout Italy are left by the government to manage their own affairs as completely as in the United States, except that the state pays the salaries, in compensation for the church lands it has seized.

In common with many zealous Catholics, however, Pope Pius IX felt that to exercise his proper influence as head of the church, he must be also an independent temporal prince. He refused to recognize the Italian state or to have anything to do with it, never left his palace grounds, and he styled himself the "Prisoner of the Vatican." His successors (1919) have followed this policy. For some time, no doubt, it was possible that in case of a general European war, Austria might restore the papacy as a temporal principality. The hope of some such result may have been back of the pope's failure to speak out against the crimes of Germany and Austria in the World War. Certainly the position of the papacy was not strengthened by its attitude in that struggle. Nor did the Italian priesthood show a patriotism in any way like that of the persecuted French priests.

CHAPTER XXXIX

THE SMALL STATES OF CENTRAL EUROPE

This long chapter is necessary for the understanding of Europe to-day. But it is suggested by the author that the class read it and talk it over with the teacher, without being held strictly responsible for its contents. Then, when necessary, the student can turn to it for reference.

I. AUSTRIA-HUNGARY, TO 1914

A "tangle of races"

Down to the World War, Austria remained "a tangle of races and a Babel of tongues." The peoples spoke eleven distinct languages, besides numerous dialects. A fourth of them were German (11 millions); a fifth Magyar, or Hungarian (9 millions); the rest were Italians, Jews, Illyrians, or Slavs. These Slavs made half the population, but they were broken up into many sub-races (p. 393 and map).

German supremacy to 1866

We have seen how the counter-revolution of 1849 restored absolute despotism to the central government, and crushed out all self-government in Bohemia and Hungary. In these non-German districts, for years, only the German language was allowed in the schools, the press, or the courts. For a Bohemian to publish a paper in his native language was a crime.

Austria wins a parliament in 1859

Naturally Bohemia and Hungary hailed with delight the defeat of Austria in 1859 by France and Italy. The Emperor Francis Joseph felt compelled to introduce liberal reforms, and so Austria was given a parliament. But the subject peoples remained unsatisfied; and after the next overthrow of Austria (by Prussia, in 1866) it was plain that something had to be done. The German element was not strong enough to rule alone. Accordingly the strongest *two* elements in the Empire joined hands to help each other keep control over all the other elements. The Emperor and the Hungarian leaders arranged a selfish bargain — which remained the constitution of Austria-Hungary down to 1918.

The "dual-monarchy," 1867–1918

Austria-Hungary became a dual monarchy, a federation of two states. Each half of the Empire had its own constitution and its own parliament. The two halves had the same monarch and a curious kind of a common legislature. These arrangements of 1867 sacrificed the Slavs. The Germans remained dominant in the Austrian half of the Empire, and the Magyars in the Hungarian half. The union of the two was not due to any internal ties between them, but wholly to selfish fears. Without Hungarian troops the Austrian Germans and their Emperor could not any longer hold Bohemia in subjection; and without Austria to support her, Hungary would lose her border Slav districts and perhaps be herself absorbed in Slav Europe.

Aspirations of subject-peoples

But of course such a union was one of unstable equilibrium. Bohemia ceased not to demand, if not independence, at least that she be admitted into the imperial federation as an equal third state. The Poles of Austria and of Hungary hoped for a revival of an independent Poland. The Italians longed to be annexed to Italy. The Roumanians of eastern Hungary wished to be joined to free Roumania. The Croats and Slovaks desired independence or union with Serbia. With the progress of humanity and education, toward the twentieth century, it became less possible for the two dominant races to use the old cruel methods to keep down the subject peoples. For many years, historians had ventured to prophesy that a general European war, if one came, would probably end this ill-sorted conglomerate state.

Some progress before 1914

In domestic matters, before the World War, the Austrian part of the empire had taken two great steps forward. (1) In 1868–1869 the German Liberals in the parliament secured laws for complete religious liberty for all men. These laws also took from the church its old control over marriage and the schools. The population is almost wholly Catholic; but it has supported this anti-clerical legislation, against even the severe condemnation of the pope. (2) In 1906, after many years of agitation, full and equal manhood suffrage was secured for local elections and for the lower House of the national parliament.

The parliament, however, contained twenty-eight distinct parties, largely on a basis of race jealousies. The election of 1913 made the Christian Socialists far the largest of any one party, giving them 96 members out of a total of 516. But the war, following almost at once, showed the parliament to be absolutely powerless for all purposes of real government. It was not in anyway consulted when the Emperor and his advisors brought on the war; and it was at once dissolved, and no new parliament allowed to meet for more than a year.

II. SPAIN

Constitution of 1812

Before 1800 the ideas of the French Revolutionists began to filter into Spain, but their welcome was confined to the small educated class. Napoleon's attack broke down the old monarchy and gave these Liberals a chance. They took the lead in the War for Independence (1809–1813); and, in the midst of that struggle, the Cortes drew up the famous Constitution of 1812 (p. 340).

Despotism from 1815 to 1833

Then followed the restoration of the cruel and suspicious Ferdinand VII, his treacherous overthrow of the constitution, its restoration by the revolution of 1820, and the armed intervention of the despotic Holy Alliance in 1823 (pp. 340, 343). For the next ten years the Liberals were persecuted vigorously. To own a foreign book was a crime. In 1831 a young man was hanged in Madrid for shouting "Hurrah for Liberty!" and a woman met the same fate for embroidering on a flag the words, "Law, Liberty, Equality."

"Government by revolution," 1833–1873

Ferdinand died in 1833; but, for forty years more, Spain passed from revolution to revolution, — none for liberty, each for some ruler or military chieftain. During the middle half of the century Spain had many "paper constitutions" but no constitutionalism. The government was "government by revolt." Every change was brought about by a coup d'état. The many successive military revolutions, however, were marked by surprisingly little bloodshed. It has been wittily said that during this period "revolution in Spain became a fine art." When an administration had grown sufficiently unpopular, some officer with docile battalions and a grievance would issue a "pronunciamento" declaring the existing government dissolved and naming the members of a new one. If the adventurer had counted his strength advisedly, the old government would vanish; if it stayed, the revolt usually disappeared. It was part of the political game to know, without fighting, when one was beaten. Some one has said that Spaniards developed a delicate tact in working revolutions, as English-speaking people work elections, with the least possible disturbance to the affairs of everyday life.

To be sure, after each of the meaningless commotions of these forty years, the victorious faction would "appeal to the nation" for sanction. But it used all the machinery of the government, including the police, to carry its candidates; and members of an opposing party, if active, were liable to be mobbed by the government party (the "party of the club"), or, if they resisted, to be locked up "to prevent a disturbance."

Meantime wasteful taxation and miserable misgovernment made the nation seethe with discontent; and in 1868 a Liberal uprising expelled the ruling Bourbon line, and set up a Provisional Government. For the next few years, this government begged prince after prince in Europe to accept the Spanish crown (cf. p. 420).

A republic, 1873–1874

These efforts failing, in 1873 the Liberals set up a republic, with *Castelar* as president. The constitution, said to have been drawn up in twenty-four hours, was never more than a form. The leaders made absurd promises which could not be kept: to reduce taxes, though the treasury was bankrupt; to do away with conscription, though the army was demoralized and revolt flourished; to abolish capital punishment, though crime was rampant.

But Castelar could learn; and six months of anarchy changed his views. Bourbon risings were making rapid progress in the northern provinces; the seaboard cities of the south had declared themselves independent communes, after the plan of Paris two years before; taxes ceased to come in; the remnants of the army were in mutiny; the towns were at the mercy of ruffians, and the country districts in the hands of bandits. Then, in a fortunate recess of the Cortes, Castelar turned his vague legal authority into a beneficent dictatorship. The choice, he saw, lay between bayonet rule in the hands of disciplined troops controlled by good men, and pike rule in the hands of a vicious rabble led by escaped galley slaves. He candidly abandoned his old theories, broke his foolish pledges, and with wise energy brought order out of chaos. He crushed the communes with an army recruited by a strict conscription, and checked crime and anarchy by military executions after swift drumhead courtmartials.

It was natural that he should be assailed as a tyrant. When the Cortes reassembled, his old friends passed a vote of lack of confidence. The commander of the troops asked for permission to disperse the Cortes; but, by resigning promptly, Castelar showed that he had no wish to prolong his personal authority. To-day no one doubts his good faith or good judgment, and the name of this republican statesman-author-dictator stands out as the chief glory of Spain in the nineteenth century.[1]

Constitutional monarchy, 1876

Castelar's resignation was followed by brief anarchy; but two more revolutions brought the nation to the restoration of the old Bourbon line, at the close of 1874, in the person of the young *Alphonso XII*. The new government proved vigorous and prudent; and in 1876 the present constitution introduced Spain to a somewhat more hopeful period.

The government

The government in theory rests mainly in the Cortes. This body consists of a Senate and a Congress. Half the senators

[1] Castelar had been professor of philosophy in the University of Madrid before he entered politics, and he ranks among the great orators of modern times. Hannay's *Castelar* is a brief and interesting biography.

are *elected*, while the rest are *appointed for life*. The congressmen are elected by *manhood suffrage* (since 1890).

The ministry is expected to resign if outvoted in the Cortes, but, in practice, *parliamentary majorities do not yet really make ministries.* Instead, ministries make parliamentary majorities, as in England a century and a half ago (p. 214). A ministry is formed by coalition between factions, and then it supplies itself with a good working majority by a new election. The ministry controls the elections pretty thoroughly; but such things are managed more decorously than formerly. Since 1876 no party has "called in the infantry."

Ten years of reform, 1881–1890

Until 1881 the energies of the government went mainly to restoring order. Then, for ten years, reform crowded upon reform. Jury trial was introduced; civil marriage was permitted; popular education was encouraged; the franchise was extended; the slaves in the colonies were freed; honest but vain attempts were made to improve the government of the colonies; and, above all, so far as Spain's welfare is concerned, the system of taxation was reformed.

In 1876 taxes were still levied in the wasteful, demoralizing way characteristic of France before the First Revolution, and both foreign trade and home industries were strangled by them. Conditions are still far from ideal, but the heaviest shackles have been struck off. As a result, trade has mounted by bounds; manufactures have developed; railroads and telegraphs have been tripled. Population has doubled in the last century, rising from ten millions to twenty, and the growth has been especially rapid in the last decades. Above all, the number of peasant landowners is rapidly increasing.

To be sure, the mass of the people are shiftless, excitable, bigoted. Still Spain is far from being a dying nation, as she is sometimes called. She is a reviving nation: and the increase in population and in wealth is a chief reason for the political stability of the last forty years. Under the new conditions, *constant revolution would be too costly.*

Until 1898, the surviving colonial empire (Cuba, the Philippines, and so on) was a drag upon progress. After 1876 a series of efforts was made to give good government and some measure of self-control to Cuba, which had been in incessant and wasting rebellion. But the problem was too difficult to be worked out by a country so backward at home. Corrupt officials oftentimes ruined the designs of the government; and in any case, the colonies were already so alienated by long misgovernment as to make the task hopeless.

Loss of Cuba

In 1894 Cuba rose again for independence. Spain made tremendous efforts to hold her, and for some years, at an immense cost, maintained an army of 200,000 men at a distance of 2000 miles from home. The warfare, however, was reducing Cuba to a desert; and finally, in 1898, the United States interfered. The Spanish-American War resulted in the surrender of all the Spanish colonies, except a few neighboring islands and some districts in northwest Africa.

Poverty and taxation

It may be hoped that this loss will prove a gain. The poverty of the government has been serious. The interest charge on the huge national debt is a crushing burden, and until 1900 the debt itself was constantly growing. Now that Spain no longer has the task of holding distant colonial possessions, she may conclude to reduce her absurd army system and to use the money for the development of the intellect of the people and of the resources of the land. She still has ambitions, however, to extend her colonial possessions in Africa; and she long kept a vague hope that, in case of a general European war, she might regain Gibraltar. This last consideration went far to make her somewhat pro-German in the World War.

Religion and education

Catholicism is the state religion. Though the constitution promises "freedom of worship," no other religious services are permitted *in public*. In this respect Spain is the most backward of European lands. She is also the most backward in education. There is a compulsory education law, but it is a paper edict. In 1909 a government investigation found 30,000 towns and villages with no public school whatever, while in 10,000 other places the schools were in hired premises — many of them grossly unfit for the purpose, — connected with slaughter-houses, cemeteries, or stables. The teachers were poor and poorly paid; and attendance was still poorer. The only schools in most of the country, outside these public schools, were "nuns' schools," teaching only the catechism and needle-work. Only one fourth the population could read and write.

Spanish Liberals have wished to change all this radically, (1) by *separating church and state*, and (2) by *excluding clerical control from the schools*. But the introduction of man-hood suffrage in 1900 proved disastrous to such reforms. It strengthened the Clericals and Conservatives in the Cortes, because of the absolute obedience paid at elections by the peasants to their priests, and for many years progress in education and in politics has almost ceased.

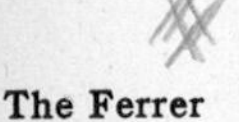

The Ferrer schools

About 1900 the horrible condition of the schools roused the wrath of a great teacher, Francesco Ferrer. This upright and courageous thinker founded a "modern school" to start a reform in Spanish education. His experiment was arousing great interest; but the Clerical party, fearing his influence, had him murdered judicially. The hold of the priests upon the working classes is so strong that in Spain, alone in European countries, Socialism appears only in a few large cities — and as a conspiracy rather than as a constitutional party. In 1910 there was a Socialist revolt in Barcelona. The Clericals charged that Ferrer had instigated this revolt. They had him tried *in secret* before a military tribunal, convicted him by the aid of *forged* papers, and killed him. "Ferrer schools" have been established in many lands.

III. THE REPUBLIC OF PORTUGAL

Establishment of the Republic

In 1821, as one of the results of the Spanish revolution of 1820 (cf. p. 341 ff.), the king of Portugal accepted a constitution drawn up by a group of Radicals upon the model of the Spanish constitution of 1812. For many years, however, the country was distracted by revolutions, and by wars between claimants for the crown; but about the middle of the nineteenth century, Portugal began to make some progress in constitutional government. Then, in 1910, a sudden uprising set up a republic, which so far (1919) seems stable. English influence controls foreign relations, so that Portugal is, in practice, almost an English protectorate.

Religion and education

Until 1910 Catholicism was the state religion. Indeed there were only a few hundred people of other faiths in the country. But the Republican government at once established *complete religious freedom*, confiscated the church property, and adopted a plan for the "separation of church and state" like that set up in France in 1906. Education, by law, is universal and gratuitous; but in practice the children of the poor do not attend school. The schools, too, are very poor. Portugal is more illiterate even than Spain. The chief peril to the Republic is ignorance.

Colonies are still extensive (in the Verde islands, in Africa, and in India), but they do not pay expenses, and it is doubtful whether so poor a country can afford to keep them. Their administration, too, is very bad.

Present problems

National finances are in a deplorable condition. In 1893 Portugal suspended payment of two thirds of the interest on her national debt. In 1894 France withdrew her ambassador, because of dissatisfaction at this treatment of French creditors. Such action gave rise to talk of possible intervention by European governments in Portuguese affairs. For some years the government has had an annual deficit. It would seem that the country must give up her costly army system and sell her colonies. One reason for maintaining her army has been fear of Spain.

Recent years have seen much distress from lack of employment or low wages, and many strikes accompanied by riots.

IV. BELGIUM

The Constitution of Belgium is still that of 1831, with a few amendments. It has an admirable bill of rights. The king acts only through "responsible" ministers.

A democratic franchise

In 1831 the franchise rested upon the payment of a considerable tax. When the revolutions of 1848 were upsetting so many governments, Belgium made a slight reduction in this qualification for voting. For nearly fifty years there was no further change; but meanwhile great city populations were growing up, with masses of artisans who had no votes. In the eighties only one man in ten could vote; and agitation began for further extension of the franchise.

The proposal secured little support in parliament, however, and bill after bill was voted down. In the early nineties the discontent of the Radicals became violent. In 1893 the Labor party declared a general strike, in order to exert political pressure, and the crowds of unemployed men in Brussels about the parliament house threatened serious riots. The militia was called out, but it showed a dangerous disposition to side with the rioters.

The members of parliament, looking on from their windows, changed their minds, and quickly passed a new franchise law, providing for *manhood suffrage with plural votes for wealth and education.* Each man was given *one* vote; *two* votes were given to each man over thirty-five years of age, if he possessed certain wealth, or if he were the head of a family with children; and *three* votes were given to men of high educational qualification and to those who had held important public office.

The new franchise produced unexpected results. From 1850 to 1884 the leading question in politics had been whether state or church should control education. The Liberals were in power the greater part of the time, and, by one bill after another, they had taken the schools wholly away from clerical influence.

The church and education

This resulted, however, in the growth of a large Clerical party. Then, the election of 1894 returned 104 Clericals, 15 Liberals, and 33 Socialists. Of the two million votes cast, *over a third were "plural votes," and these very largely reinforced the Clericals.* A new education bill (1895) placed the public schools under the supervision of the church, and provided state support for church schools. Education continued to make progress. In 1890, 16 per cent of the army recruits could not read or write; in 1910 the number was only 9 per cent. The Clerical party in Belgium is enlightened and progressive.

Belgium has ranked for many years among the leading industrial nations. In 1910 the population was seven and a half million — more than double that in 1815. The people were happy, contented, and prosperous. Then for more than four years (1914–1918) this little land was made the battle ground of the terrible World War; and its splendid heroism and unparalleled sufferings have excited the admiration and the sympathy of the civilized world (cf. pp. 614 ff.). At this writing (1919) the only political change due to the war is the recent introduction of simple manhood suffrage with the abolition of all plural votes. This promises a new era of democratic reform.

V. HOLLAND

Government

The royal family of Holland belongs to the great House of Orange, and the people are loyally devoted to it. The present sovereign is Queen Wilhelmina, who came to the throne in 1890 at ten years of age. The upper House of the States General (the parliament keeps that ancient name) is chosen by the local legislatures of the various provinces for nine years, one third going out each third year. This plan of partial renewals of a branch of the legislature has been adopted in many countries, as in the Senate of the United States, but it seems to have originated in Holland some centuries ago.

The House of Representatives (lower House of the States General) is elected directly by the people. Since 1896 about three fourths of the adult men have votes, — nearly all except paupers, vagabonds, and unmarried sons in poor families. The monarchy has been of the Prussian rather than the English type, until recently; but during the long minority of the girl-queen *the ministries began to be truly "responsible"* to the Representatives.

Wealth and prosperity

The country is rich and prosperous. The population (six millions in 1910) has grown in the last century even faster than that of Belgium. *The colonial empire,* despite great losses in the Napoleonic wars, is still vast and productive.

VI. DENMARK

To the Constitution of 1866

In the later Middle Ages, Denmark was an elective monarchy distracted by feudal anarchy. In 1660, after a shameful defeat by Sweden, it became an hereditary and absolute monarchy. In 1848 the king felt obliged to grant a paper constitution; but not until after the defeat[1] of 1864 did Denmark begin to have real constitutional development. A Democratic party ("Friends of the Peasants") then began to demand reform, and, after two years of clamor, a constitution was established.

Government

This constitution of 1866 promises freedom of speech and of the press, and creates a Diet (Rigsdag) of two Houses. The Landthing, or upper House, is composed partly of members appointed by the king, partly of members elected on a very high property basis. The Folkthing, or lower House, is elected. In 1901 the vote was given to all self-supporting men, thirty years of age, and in 1915 it was extended to all men and most women. In 1901, after a thirty years' contest, ministries were made responsible to the Representatives.

Coöperation and the high schools

Denmark is the special home of coöperation among farmers. The land is not naturally fertile. The people, until after the middle of the nineteenth century, were poor and ignorant. Agriculture was backward. The defeat by Prussia and Austria in 1864 left the little state disrupted and impoverished. Its people were forced to seek some escape from their condition.

A new system of schools pointed the way. Denmark contains 15,000 square miles with two and three quarter millions of people. That is, it has more people than Indiana, in less than half the territory. More than a third of these people are farmers. For them, ninety-eight high schools give instruction in agriculture and domestic economy, — twenty of the ninety-eight being special schools in agriculture. Most of

[1] Compare with the case of Austria after 1866, and France after 1870.

these schools, too, give special "short courses" in the winter, and these are largely attended by adult farmers and their wives. The schools are not merely industrial; even the short courses emphasize music and literature. They aim to teach not merely how to get a living, but also how to live nobly. And they have taught the Danish farmers the methods of successful coöperation. To-day Denmark is one of the most progressive and prosperous farming countries in the world.

Local coöperative societies are found in almost every distinct line of farm industry, — in dairying, in the hog industry, in marketing of eggs, in breeding cattle, in producing improved seed, in securing farm machinery, in loaning one another money (farm credits), and so on. The local societies are federated into national organizations. The central society that markets eggs and dairy products has an office in London as well as in Copenhagen, and owns its own swift steamers to ply daily between the two capitals. Little Denmark supplies England's forty millions with a large part of their eggs, bacon, and butter, — $10,000,000 worth, $32,000,000 worth, and $50,000,000 worth, respectively, in 1911.

Thanks to intelligent methods of farming, and of handling produce, these Danish articles command the top price in the London market; and, thanks to the coöperative system, the profits go to the producers, not to middlemen. Best of all, the Danish peasant, on eight or ten acres of land, is an educated man, cultured because of his intelligent, scientific mastery of his work. In 1891 an enlightened Old-Age pension system was adopted.

The coöperative movement in agriculture is found also, in only a slightly smaller degree, in Belgium, Holland, Norway, and Sweden, — all the other small states of Northern Europe. The movement is making much progress, too, in France.

VII. NORWAY AND SWEDEN

The Congress of Vienna, in 1814, took Norway from Denmark and gave it to Sweden (p. 330), to reward that country

The "union" of 1814

for services against Napoleon. But the Norwegian people declined to be bartered from one ruler to another without their own consent. A Diet assembled at *Eidvold,* declared Norway a sovereign state, adopted a liberal constitution, and elected a king (*May 17, 1814*). Sweden, backed by the Powers, made ready to enforce its claims, but finally a compromise was

A NORWEGIAN FJORD, — SOGUDAL.

arranged. The king abdicated, and the Diet elected the Swedish king as king of Norway, *on condition that he should recognize the new Norwegian constitution.*

Thus Norway and Sweden became a dual monarchy. The union was looser, however, than that of Austria-Hungary. The two countries had the same king, but they had no common ministry and nothing to correspond to the Austrian-Hungarian imperial parliament. Each kingdom kept its own constitution and its own legislature.

Norway's struggle for self-government

The arrangement lasted almost a century. But there was a growing chasm between the two lands. Sweden had a strong aristocracy and a considerable city population. Norway even then had only a weak aristocracy, and was a land of independ-

Storthing and royal vetoes

ent peasants and sturdy fisherfolk. The national legislature (Storthing) assembles as one house, but divides itself for most purposes into two chambers. The king of the dual state could not dissolve it, and, according to the constitution, *a bill became law in spite of his veto, if passed in three successive annual sessions.* In the early part of the century the Storthing succeeded in abolishing nobility in Norway, after two vetoes by the king, and in 1884 it established manhood suffrage against his will.

The chief interest in Norwegian politics in the nineteenth century lay in the agitation for a greater amount of self-government. Except for one period of about thirty years in the middle of the century, the contest was incessant, and after 1872 it grew bitter.

In 1872–1874 the Storthing passed a bill three times, requiring the ministries to resign if outvoted. King Oscar II declared truly that this was an amendment to the constitution, and therefore a change in the compact between the two countries. In such a case, he urged, the rule limiting his veto could not apply, and he declined to recognize the law. The Storthing impeached the ministers. Civil war seemed at hand; but a new election in 1884 showed that the Norwegians were almost unanimous in the demand, and the king yielded.

Oscar II came to the Swedish throne in 1872, just before the Norwegian national movement became violent; and his moderation and fairness had much to do with preventing an armed conflict, which impetuous men on either side were ready to precipitate. He was one of the greatest men who sat upon European thrones in the last century. Foreign nations paid a deserved tribute to his ability and fairness, by requesting him frequently to act as arbitrator in international disputes. The United States was interested in some of these arbitrations.

After this victory of 1884, the real executive, for all *internal* affairs in Norway, became Norwegian, not Swede. The Storthing passed at once to a demand for power to appoint Norwegian consuls, separate from the Swedish service. This demand also seemed to the king to involve a change in the constitution, — which put the regulation of *foreign* affairs into his hands, — and the Swedish party exclaimed that the proposed arrangement would ruin the slight union that remained between the two countries.

The struggle waxed vehement. In the course of the contest the Norwegians removed the symbol of union from their flag (1886–1888), after passing the bill to that effect each year for three sessions, and both countries at times made preparations for war. Indeed, Norway erected a costly line of fortifications on the frontier toward Sweden.

Norwegian independence

In May, 1905, when once more a long negotiation for separate consular service had failed, the Storthing, *by unanimous vote*, provided by its own act for Norwegian consuls. This was virtual secession, and the king refused to recognize it. The Storthing then declared the union dissolved. The aristocratic element in Sweden called for war; but King Oscar was nobly resolute that his two peoples should not imbrue their hands in each other's blood. The Swedish labor-unions, too, threatened a universal strike, to prevent violent coercion of their Norwegian brethren. In July the Norwegians declared in favor of independence in a great national referendum, by a vote of 368,000 to 184. Sweden bowed to the decision. *In September, 1905, to the eternal honor of both peoples, a peaceful separation was arranged upon friendly terms.*

Thus Norway became an independent nation. A small party wished the new nation to become a republic; but, in a second referendum, a large majority declared for a monarchy and chose a Danish prince (Haakon VII) for king.

Norway leads in Woman suffrage

In 1901 the Storthing gave the franchise in all municipal matters to women who paid (or whose husbands paid) a small tax. *In 1907* the parliamentary franchise was given to the same class of women. Thus, Norway was the first *sovereign nation* to give the full franchise to women. Women, too, sit in the Storthing. There is a strong demand for the extension of the franchise to *all* women on the same terms as men, — a demand certain to be granted in the near future.

Norway has two and a half millions of people; Sweden, more than twice as many. Sweden is also the richer country. The Norwegians, however, have the larger merchant navy, — more than four times as large as Sweden's, and the fourth in size in all Europe. This was one reason why, during the "Union," Norway felt it had a special interest in controlling the consular service. Norwegian authors, like the novelist-statesman Björnson and the poet Ibsen, stand in the front ranks of European literature, and such facts, no doubt, helped to make Norwegians discontented with their recent political inferiority.

Swedish reform since 1866

Until late in the nineteenth century Sweden was backward in politics. The diet was made up, medieval fashion, of *four* estates — nobles, clergy, burgesses, and peasants — and the king could always play off one class against another. In 1866 this arrangement was replaced by a modern parliament of two Houses, but for nearly half a century more the franchise excluded a large part of the adult males. Agitation for reform began vehemently in 1895. Seventeen years later, the right to vote for members of the lower House of the parliament was given to all adult men, but with many "plural" votes for wealth. At the same time women secured the franchise for all matters of local government. Then in 1919, with the surging rise of Democracy throughout the world, sweeping reforms abolished plural voting and established simple universal suffrage for men and women in both national and local affairs.

CHAPTER XL

THE SWISS REPUBLIC

Condition in 1830

Switzerland deserves a chapter to itself. The Congress of Vienna left the Swiss cantons in a loose confederacy (p. 332), not unlike that of the United States before 1789. The original "Forest Cantons" were pure democracies. They governed themselves (as some do still) by folkmoots, — primary assemblies of all the people. In Bern, Luzern, and some other of the rich "City Cantons," a few families had complete possession of the government, so that the rule was an hereditary oligarchy. But in 1830, after the success of the French revolution, popular risings established liberal local constitutions there also.

The Sonderbund War

The next change grew out of religious strife. The reorganized cantons of 1830 were Protestant, and now they became radical in politics. The old democratic cantons were Catholic, and were coming to be controlled by a new Clerical party. The confederacy seemed ready to split in twain. Some individual cantons, too, were torn by civil strife. Switzerland was organized in two camps.

The final struggle began in Aargau. In this canton, in the election of 1840, the Radicals won. The Clericals rose in revolt. To punish them, after suppressing the rising, the Radicals dissolved the eight monasteries of the canton. This act was contrary to the constitution of the Union; and the seven Catholic cantons in alarm formed a separate league, — the Sonderbund, — and declared that they would protect the Clericals in their rights in any canton where they might be attacked.

For the Sonderbund to exist at all was practically to dissolve the union. In 1847 the Federal Diet, now controlled by the

Radicals, ordered the Sonderbund to dissolve. The Sonderbund withdrew its deputies from the Diet, and "The Sonderbund War" was begun (1847) — seven cantons against fifteen. The despotic Powers of the Holy Alliance were preparing to interfere in behalf of the Sonderbund, and did furnish it with arms and money; but the Unionists (warned and encouraged by the English government) acted with remarkable celerity and crushed the Secessionists in a three weeks' campaign, before foreign intervention could begin. Metternich still intended to interfere, but the revolutions of 1848 rendered him harmless. Then the Radicals remodeled the constitutions of the conquered cantons, so as to put power into the hands of the Radicals there, and adopted a new national constitution.

There are many interesting points of likeness between the civil war in Switzerland and that a little later in the United States. In both countries there was a conflict between a national and a states' sovereignty party. In both, as a result of war, the more progressive part of the nation forced a stronger union upon the more backward portion. In both, too, the states which tried to secede did so in behalf of rights guaranteed them in the old constitution, which they believed to be endangered by their opponents.

The Constitution

By the new constitution of 1848, which with slight amendments is that of to-day, *the union became a true Federal Republic. The Federal Assembly* (national legislature) has two Houses, — *the Council of the States* and *the National Council.* The first consists of two delegates from each canton. The delegates are chosen by the cantonal legislatures, by whom also their term of office is fixed and their salaries are paid. This Council *represents the states' rights principle,* and in form it is a survival of the old Diet.

The other parts of the constitution, however, are new, and tend toward nationalism. The second House of the legislature, the National Council, *represents the people of the union.* The members are elected in single districts, like our Representatives, for a term of three years. The franchise is given to all adult males, and elections take place on Sundays, so that all may vote.

The Federal Executive is not a single president, but a committee of seven (*the Federal Council*), whose members are chosen by the Federal Assembly. One of the seven, especially named for the purpose, is the "President of the Council"; but

INTERLAKEN, a typical Swiss town.

he possesses little more authority than the other members. The Federal Council acts much as an English ministry, but it cannot dissolve the legislature, and it need not resign if its measures are rejected.

There is also *a Federal Judiciary*, chosen by the Federal Assembly; but it lacks the power of our American Supreme Court to declare laws void: it is bound to accept as valid all acts of the legislature.

Each canton, like each of our States, has its own constitution and government. In a few cantons the old folkmoot, or primary Assembly, is still preserved; in the others the legislature consists of one chamber, chosen by manhood suffrage. In each there is an executive council.

Direct legislation

As a rule, even in modern democratic countries, the people govern themselves only indirectly. They choose representatives (legislatures and governors), and these few delegated individuals attend directly to all matters of government. Democratic thinkers, however, demand that some way be found for the people themselves to take a direct part in lawmaking; and Switzerland was the first country to show how "direct democracy" can work under modern conditions. The two Swiss devices for this end are known as *the referendum* and *the popular initiative.*

The Referendum

The referendum is the older. It consists merely in referring laws that have been passed by the legislature to a popular vote. This practice really originated in America. The State of Massachusetts submitted its first constitution to a popular vote in 1778 and in 1780, and there were a few other applications of the principle in America at about the same time. A little later, the French Revolutionists adopted the practice for their constitutions; and the plebiscites of the Napoleons extended the principle to some other questions besides constitutions. The French Constitution of the Year I provided for a referendum on ordinary laws; but this constitution never went into effect. In America, after 1820, nearly all our States used the referendum on the adoption of new constitutions and of constitutional amendments; and sometimes other important measures were submitted to popular decision, both in State and city governments.

But Switzerland taught the world how to go farther than this. By the Constitution of 1848, all constitutional amendments, cantonal or national, must be submitted to popular vote, and in some cantons *this compulsory referendum is extended to all laws;* while, by an amendment of 1874, a certain number of voters *by petition may require the submission of any national law.* This last provision is known as the *optional referendum,* and it has been in use in the separate cantons for most of the nineteenth century.

The Initiative

The popular initiative is a purely Swiss development. It consists in the right of a certain number of voters, by petition, to frame a new bill and to compel its submission to the people. A little before 1848, this device began to be regarded as the natural complement of the referendum. Four cantons had already made some use of it, and the new Constitution of 1848 required all cantons to permit it on constitutional amendments, if a majority of voters so petitioned.

The cantons themselves rapidly adopted more generous measures than this; and, by 1870, in nearly all of them a small number of voters could introduce any law they desired. In 1891, by amendment, this liberal principle was adopted for the national government: *a petition of fifty thousand voters may frame a law, which must then be submitted to a national vote.*

Thus the people can act directly, without the intervention of the legislature. They can frame bills by the initiative, and pass on them by the referendum.[1] These devices for direct legislation are the most important advances made in late years by democracy. Recently, many of the more progressive States of the American Union have carried them (with the further device of the *recall*) to a higher degree of perfection even than in their Swiss home.

Place in history

Switzerland fills a far larger place in history and in human interest than her territory fills on the map. Since 1848 the Swiss have been one nation. The defeated party quickly accepted the result of the Sonderbund War in good faith, and now all Swiss look upon one another as fellow-countrymen. In the last half-century Switzerland has made amazing advances, and to-day it is one of the most progressive countries in the world. The schools are among the best in Europe: no other country has so little illiteracy. Comfort is well diffused. No

[1] A good account of the referendum and initiative in Switzerland is given in Seignobos, *Europe Since 1814*, 271–279 and 283–284.

other country to-day gives such complete equality of opportunity in industry and in politics. The population increases rapidly, and in 1896 it numbered three and a third millions. The army system is a universal militia service, lighter than has been known anywhere else in continental Europe during the last forty years.

Two thirds of the people are German; but French and Italian, as well as German, are "official" languages, and the debates in the Federal Assembly are carried on in all three tongues. *Race feeling,* which is so disintegrating a force in Austria, *works no harm in Switzerland.* The universal patriotism of the people is a high testimonial to the strength of free institutions, and of the flexible federal principle, in binding together diverse elements. Says President Lowell, of Harvard, "The Swiss Confederation, on the whole, is the most successful democracy in the world."

FOR FURTHER READING. — Seignobos' *Europe Since 1814*, 255–284, or Hazen's *Europe Since 1815*. Fuller accounts, of interest and great value, may be found in Lloyd's *A Sovereign People* and Crawford's *Switzerland of To-day* (1911).

CHAPTER XLI

THE EXPANSION OF EUROPE INTO AFRICA AND ASIA

Toward the year 1900, European politics were suddenly merged in world politics. The possession of petty counties on the Rhine or the Danube ceased to interest peoples who had fixed their eyes on vast continents.

New world-problems

Australia was already English. North America was held by the United States or England. South and Central America were protected beneath the shield of the Monroe Doctrine. *Africa,* however, was largely unappropriated, and in *Asia* the stationary and apparently helpless empires of China, Turkey, and Persia invited attack.

Partition of Africa

The division of the vast African continent was swift and peaceful. In 1880 only a few patches here and there on the coast were European; in 1891 the continent was mapped out between European claimants.[1]

For half a century, France had been extending her sway over Algeria on the north. For nearly double that time England had held Cape Colony on the south; and the events of 1881 (p. 468) put the Nile valley under English control. A generation earlier the explorations of Livingstone, an English missionary, and of Stanley, an American newspaper correspondent, had awakened interest in the heart of the "Dark Continent." In the early seventies Stanley proved that the upper Congo extended far into the interior, and that the immense region in the center of Africa was a rich and accessible country. In 1876, at the suggestion of King Leopold of Belgium, the *Congo International Association* was organized to explore Central Africa

[1] Caldecott's *English Colonization,* 112, has a good map illustrating the transformation of this decade of years. Note also the dates on the map in this volume, facing page 553.

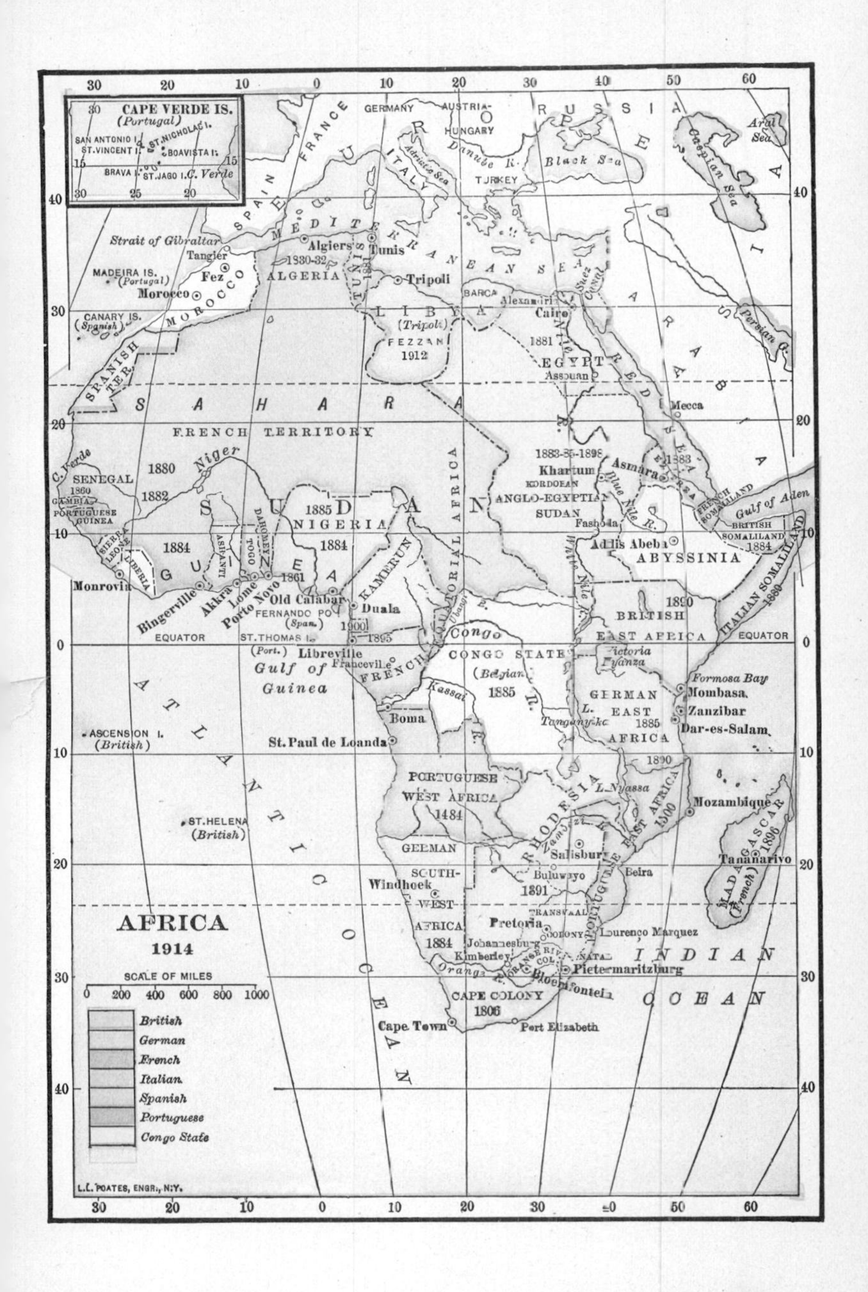

AFRICA
1914
SCALE OF MILES
0 200 400 600 800 1000
British
German
French
Italian
Spanish
Portuguese
Congo State
CAPE VERDE IS.
(Portugal)
ATLANTIC OCEAN
INDIAN OCEAN
MEDITERRANEAN SEA
SAHARA
FRENCH TERRITORY
SUDAN
GUINEA
Gulf of Guinea
EQUATOR
Strait of Gibraltar
Algiers
Tunis
Tripoli
Cairo
Alexandria
Mecca
Khartum
Addis Abeba
Monrovia
Libreville
Boma
St. Paul de Loanda
Mombasa
Zanzibar
Dar-es-Salam
Mozambique
Tananarivo
Windhoek
Pretoria
Johannesburg
Kimberley
Bloemfontein
Pietermaritzburg
Cape Town
Port Elizabeth
MOROCCO
ALGERIA
LIBYA
EGYPT
NIGERIA
KAMERUN
ABYSSINIA
BRITISH EAST AFRICA
CONGO STATE
GERMAN EAST AFRICA
PORTUGUESE WEST AFRICA
GERMAN SOUTH-WEST AFRICA
RHODESIA
CAPE COLONY
MADAGASCAR
L.L. POATES, ENGR., N.Y.

and to stop the horrible slave trade carried on by the Arabs; and in 1879 Stanley, in the service of Leopold and the Association, returned to the upper Congo and made the beginnings of a European state there.

In 1884 Bismarck called an international Congress at Berlin to consider conditions in Africa. As a result, the "Congo Free State" was formed, with a territory of 1,000,000 square miles, and with some thirty million native inhabitants. It was placed under the administration of Belgium: but it was pledged to neutrality and to free trade with all nations.

The establishment of the Congo State, and the Berlin Conference, were followed by the raising of the German flag in Africa (p. 520); and then began a wild scramble for territory, which quickly left all the continent European, except Abyssinia and Liberia. In 1900 the three leading European Powers in Africa were *England, France, and Germany.* Of these England was far in the lead. Aside from small territories at other parts on the coast, her sway extended over the whole Nile valley (the richest part of the continent) and over extensive territories in the south. Her ambition was to unite her possessions north and south; but the Congo State and German East Africa were thrust between. However, an English railway was got under way to join Cairo and Cape Town.

France would have liked to join her realms on the east and on the west of the continent; but she found English territory thrust in between. German ambition was thwarted in like manner. The three Powers seemed to have checkmated one another's efforts to dominate Africa.

Europe in Asia

The occupation of Asia by European states proceeded more slowly than that of Africa, but with increasing rapidity. Central and Northern Asia is Russian. The great, densely populated peninsula of Hindostan, with adjoining Burma, is English. The southeastern peninsula, since 1896, is mainly French. The only independent states left in this greatest of the continents in 1900 were Asia Minor (Turkey), Persia, Afghanistan, Siam, and China.

Of these, Afghanistan and Siam were mere remnants of "buffer states," separating England from Russia on one side and from France on the other. Persia, too, was virtually a dependency either of England or Russia, according to the varying fortune of those countries; and in the closing years of the nineteenth century it seemed that even the ancient Chinese Empire had begun to go to pieces. In those same years two new actors appeared upon the stage of world politics. A war between Japan and China, and the Spanish-American War, added the United States and Japan to the group of World Powers interested in China.

The United States and the Orient

Until the year 1900 the United States found scope for its energies in peopling its great territories and in developing resources at home. Content with leadership on the American continents, it resolutely kept out of European complications. But the Spanish-American War left it in possession of the Philippines; and during the war it annexed Hawaii. Thus it held the mastery of the Pacific and was brought to the door of Asia. In particular, the United States then became desirous to secure a fair show for its trade in China, one of its important customers.

The similarity of English and American views regarding China, and the likeness of the English and Americans in politics and culture, inclined the two peoples to act together in the East, in opposition to Russia and Germany. Both those countries had always treated their dependencies as estates to be managed for the benefit of the peoples possessing them. This low standard had long since been rejected by the English-speaking nations. Thus a broad human interest was given to the question as to which group of powers should impose its civilization upon the industrious but passive millions of China.

In 1899, President McKinley's Secretary of State, John Hay, sent a note to all the Powers interested in China urging them to agree that no one of them should shut out citizens of other lands from its "sphere of influence" there. This "open door" policy, forcefully supported by America and

England — and by all the small commercial countries — had much to do just then with preventing the complete dismemberment of China. Of course the main incentive of American policy was the wish to keep rich Oriental provinces open to American trade. But this policy — perfectly proper in itself — fell in happily with the interests of humanity. The main hostility to the American policy, in ways both open and secret, came from Kaiser William of Germany — so that in a moment of extreme irritation, Hay exclaimed "I had almost rather be the dupe of China than the chum of the Kaiser."

Japan

The victory of Japan over Russia (below) introduced still another factor into the problem. Until the middle of the nineteenth century, Japan had kept herself sealed to the outer world. For more than two centuries, indeed, to hold communication with foreigners had been a capital crime. But in 1853, Commodore Perry, under orders from the United States Government, by a show of force secured the admission of American trade to certain Japanese ports; and Japan began swiftly to exchange her Oriental civilization for Western culture. Before the close of the century army and navy, schools and industry, took on modern character; and in 1889 a liberal Mikado (emperor) proclaimed a constitution which created, in form, a limited monarchy, with a parliament of two houses and a responsible ministry.

In 1894–1895 Japan and China engaged in war over Korea. With amazing rapidity little Japan overcame her huge antagonist on land and sea. China agreed to cede the island of Formosa, Port Arthur, and the kingdom of Korea. The Russian Tsar, however, was already longing for these districts, and, backed by France, he forced Japan to renounce her gains upon the mainland. Japan was unprepared for war with these powers, and was wise enough to yield, but she began at once to make ready, patiently and skillfully, for the struggle with Russia which was to come ten years later (p. 557).

European Powers and China

In return for her interference against Japan, Russia secured from China the right to extend her Trans-Siberian railroad through Manchuria (p. 576). Then in 1898 she secured Port Arthur, the strongest naval fortress that China possessed. Roused by this advance of her rival, England at once demanded and obtained Wai-hei-wai, on the opposite shore of the Gulf, to enable her to check Russian movements. Somewhat earlier (p. 522), on a curious pretext, Germany had seized Kiau Chau, with the surrounding district; and now France seized the port of Kwang-Chau-Wau. Still earlier, France had begun to occupy the far southeast, and England had held the island of Hong Kong ever since 1842; but the recent seizures commanded Peking itself, and it began to look as if China were doomed to partition.

The Boxer risings

In 1900 the Chinese resentment at this prospect culminated in popular patriotic and fanatical uprisings which sought to exterminate the "Western barbarians." The movement was organized by a secret society known as the *Boxers*. Missionaries and scattered Europeans were massacred and the foreign embassies themselves were besieged at Pekin. The Powers (the United States and Japan included) sent joint forces to relieve their beleaguered representatives. After horrible and almost incredible barbarities by some of the invading armies, especially by the Russians (and by the Germans when they arrived late), Pekin was taken and sacked and the European residents were rescued.

The Russ-Jap War, 1904

Largely through the insistence of the United States, the indemnities from China were taken in money — in moderate amounts — instead of in territory. During the campaign, however, Russia had occupied Manchuria. She claimed that such action was necessary to protect her railroad there, and promised to withdraw at the return of peace. In 1902 this pledge was solemnly repeated; but, before 1904, it was clear that such promises had been made only to be broken, and that Russia was determined not to loosen her grasp upon the coveted province. Moreover, she began to encroach upon Korea. To Japan this Russian approach seemed to imperil not only her commercial prosperity (in Korea), but her independence as a nation. After months of futile negotiations, and a pressing ultimatum for Russian withdrawal, *Japan resorted to war*.

Diplomacy had assured Japan that she would have only Russia to fight. England and Japan, in 1902, in a treaty designed to preserve the integrity of China, had agreed to aid each other in war if either were attacked by more than one Power. Still the case for Japan looked dark. To most of the world, Russian advance in Asia seemed irresistible, and the little island-state seemed doomed to defeat.

But Russia fought at long range. She had to transport troops and supplies across Asia by a *single-track* railroad. Her railway service was of a low order (like all her forms of engineering), and her rolling stock was inferior and insufficient. Congestion of traffic and long delays at critical moments were the inevitable results. To be sure, it was supposed that immense supplies had already been accumulated at Port Arthur and in Manchuria, in expectation of war; but it proved that high officials of the autocracy had made way with the larger part of the money and that neither army nor navy was properly equipped. Inefficiency, corruption, lack of organization, were matched only by boastful overconfidence and silly contempt for the foe. These drawbacks could not be counterbalanced by Russia's immense but unavailable resources nor by the desperate bravery and heroic endurance of her poorly led soldiery.

Japan, on the other hand, had the most perfectly organized army, hospital service, and commissariat the world had ever seen. Her leaders were patriotic, honest, faithful, and always equal to the occasion; and the whole nation was animated by a spirit of ardent self-sacrifice. By her admirable organization, Japan was able, at all critical moments, to confront the Russians with equal or superior numbers, even after a year of war, when she had rolled back the battle line several hundred miles toward the Russian base.

At the outset, Japan could hope for success only by securing naval control of Asiatic waters. Russia had gathered at

Port Arthur a fleet supposedly much stronger than Japan's whole navy; but (*February 8, 1904*) Japan struck the first blow, torpedoing several mighty battleships and cruisers. The rest of the Russian fleet was blockaded in the harbor; and, to the end of the war, Japan transported troops and supplies by water almost without interference.

Yalu, Port Arthur, and Mukden

Korea was swiftly overrun. The Russians were driven back from the *Yalu* in a great battle, and again defeated at *Liaou Yang;* and after a seven months' siege, marked by terrible suffering and reckless sacrifice on both sides, the Japanese captured the "invulnerable" *Port Arthur* (January, 1905).

The severe northern winter interrupted the campaign; but in March, 1905, the Japanese resumed their advance. The *Battle of Mukden* was the most tremendous military struggle the world had seen. It lasted fifteen days. The battle front extended a hundred miles, and a million men were engaged, with all the terrible, destructive agencies of modern science at their command. The Russians were completely routed. They lost more than a hundred thousand men, and were driven back on Harbin in disorder.

Togo's naval victory

Russia's only chance was to regain command of the sea. During the winter of 1905, after a year of delays, a huge fleet, far exceeding the Japanese navy in number and in size, but poorly equipped and miserably officered, had set out on the long voyage from the Baltic. By a breach of neutrality on the part of France, it was allowed to rest and refit at Madagascar, and again at the French stations near Southern China; and in May it reached the Sea of Japan. There it was annihilated by the splendidly handled Japanese fleet, under Admiral Togo, in the greatest of the world's naval battles.

Treaty of Portsmouth

Theodore Roosevelt, President of the United States, now "offered his good offices" to secure peace; and a meeting of envoys was arranged (August, 1905, at Portsmouth, N. H.), at which the *Treaty of Portsmouth* was signed. Japan's demands were exceedingly moderate, and she yielded even a part of these at President Roosevelt's urgent appeal for peace. Russia

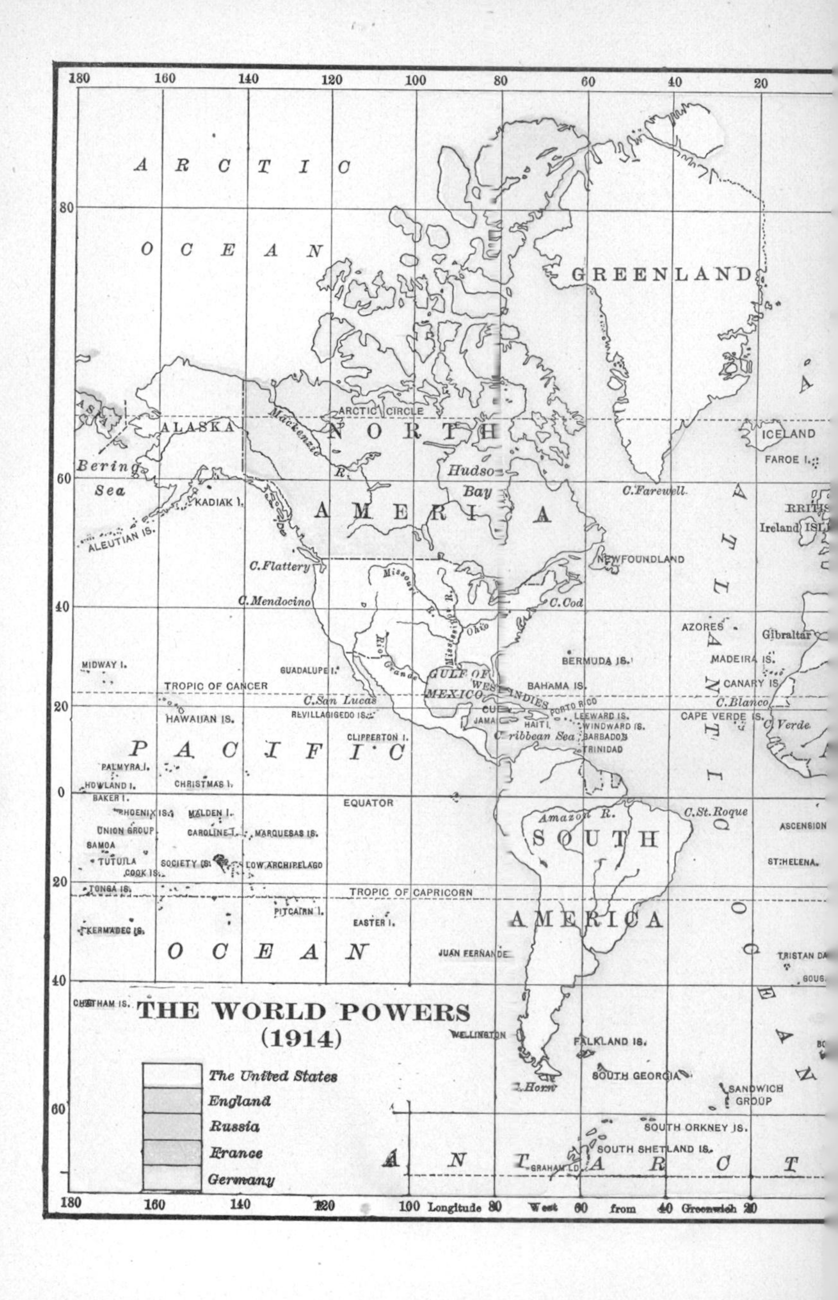
THE WORLD POWERS
(1914)
The United States
England
Russia
France
Germany
ARCTIC OCEAN
GREENLAND
NORTH AMERICA
SOUTH AMERICA
PACIFIC OCEAN
ATLANTIC OCEAN
ALASKA
Bering Sea
KADIAK I.
ALEUTIAN IS.
ARCTIC CIRCLE
Mackenzie R.
Hudson Bay
C. Farewell
ICELAND
FAROE I.
Ireland
NEWFOUNDLAND
C. Flattery
C. Mendocino
Missouri R.
Mississippi R.
Ohio
C. Cod
Rio Grande
GULF OF MEXICO
WEST INDIES
AZORES
Gibraltar
MADEIRA IS.
CANARY IS.
C. Blanco
CAPE VERDE IS.
C. Verde
BERMUDA IS.
BAHAMA IS.
PORTO RICO
HAITI
LEEWARD IS.
WINDWARD IS.
BARBADOS
TRINIDAD
Caribbean Sea
MIDWAY I.
TROPIC OF CANCER
HAWAIIAN IS.
GUADALUPE I.
C. San Lucas
REVILLAGIGEDO IS.
CLIPPERTON I.
PALMYRA I.
HOWLAND I.
BAKER I.
CHRISTMAS I.
EQUATOR
PHOENIX IS.
MALDEN I.
UNION GROUP
CAROLINE I.
MARQUESAS IS.
SAMOA
TUTUILA
COOK IS.
SOCIETY IS.
LOW ARCHIPELAGO
TONGA IS.
TROPIC OF CAPRICORN
PITCAIRN I.
EASTER I.
KERMADEC IS.
JUAN FERNANDEZ
Amazon R.
C. St. Roque
ASCENSION
ST. HELENA
TRISTAN DA
CHATHAM IS.
WELLINGTON
FALKLAND IS.
SOUTH GEORGIA
C. Horn
SANDWICH GROUP
SOUTH ORKNEY IS.
SOUTH SHETLAND IS.
GRAHAM LD.
ANTARCT
Longitude West from Greenwich
180
160
140
120
100
80
60
40
20

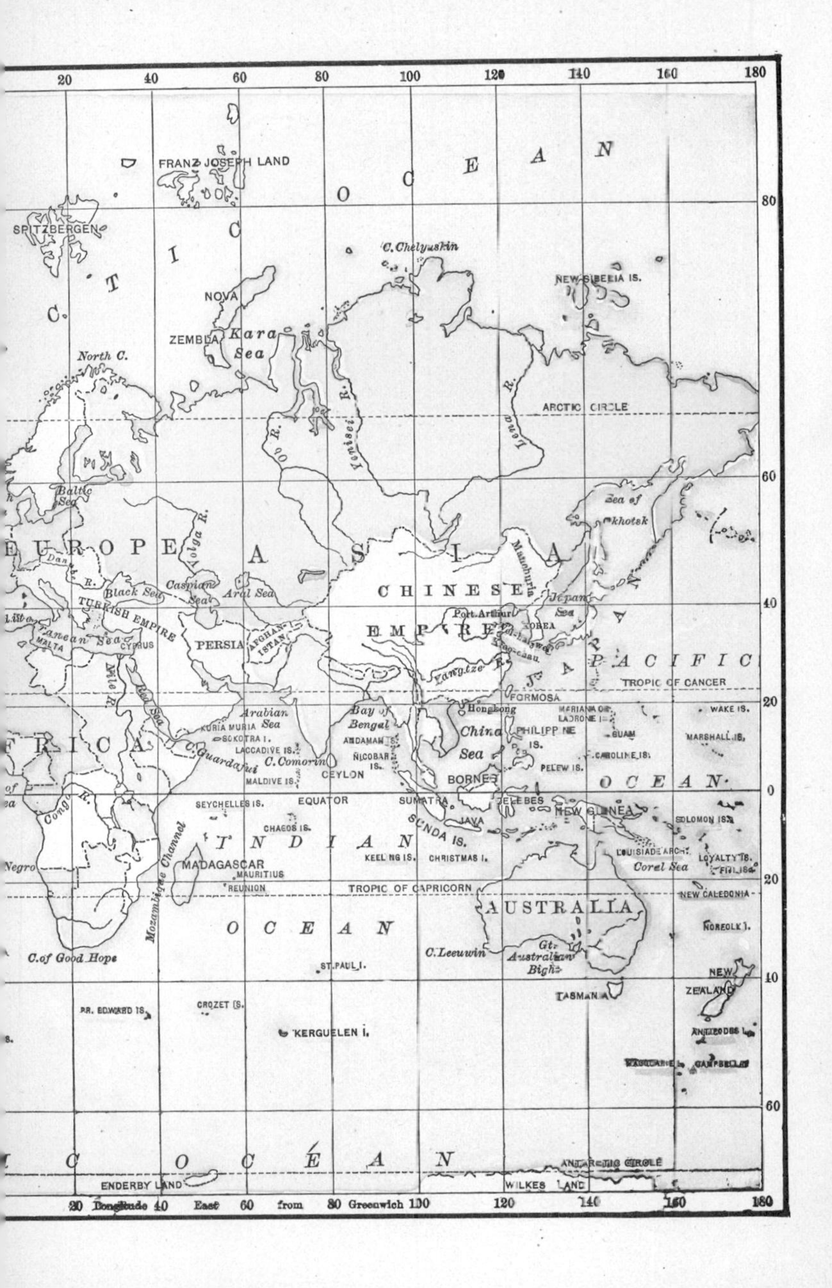
FRANZ JOSEPH LAND
SPITZBERGEN
NOVA
ZEMBLA
Kara Sea
North C.
C. Chelyuskin
NEW SIBERIA IS.
ARCTIC CIRCLE
Ob R.
Yenisei R.
Lena R.
Baltic Sea
Volga R.
EUROPE
ASIA
Black Sea
Caspian Sea
Aral Sea
TURKISH EMPIRE
MALTA
CYPRUS
PERSIA
AFGHANISTAN
CHINESE EMPIRE
Manchuria
Port Arthur
KOREA
Japan Sea
Sea of Okhotsk
Yangtze R.
TROPIC OF CANCER
FORMOSA
Hongkong
Arabian Sea
Bay of Bengal
China Sea
PHILIPPINE IS.
KURIA MURIA
SOKOTRA I.
LACCADIVE IS.
ANDAMAN IS.
NICOBAR IS.
C. Comorin
CEYLON
MALDIVE IS.
C. Guardafui
Red Sea
Nile R.
Congo R.
MARIANA OR LADRONE IS.
GUAM
WAKE IS.
MARSHALL IS.
CAROLINE IS.
PELEW IS.
BORNEO
CELEBES
SUMATRA
JAVA
NEW GUINEA
SOLOMON IS.
EQUATOR
SEYCHELLES IS.
CHAGOS IS.
SUNDA IS.
INDIAN OCEAN
PACIFIC OCEAN
KEELING IS.
CHRISTMAS I.
LOUISIADE ARCH.
LOYALTY IS.
FIJI IS.
Coral Sea
MADAGASCAR
Mozambique Channel
MAURITIUS
REUNION
TROPIC OF CAPRICORN
NEW CALEDONIA
AUSTRALIA
NORFOLK I.
C. of Good Hope
C. Leeuwin
Gt. Australian Bight
ST. PAUL I.
NEW ZEALAND
TASMANIA
PR. EDWARD IS.
CROZET IS.
KERGUELEN I.
ANTIPODES IS.
CAMPBELL IS.
ANTARCTIC CIRCLE
ENDERBY LAND
WILKES LAND
20 Longitude 40 East 60 from 80 Greenwich 100 120 140 160 180

agreed (1) to withdraw from Chinese Manchuria, (2) to cede the Port Arthur branch of her railroad to China, (3) to recognize a Japanese protectorate in Korea, and (4) to cede to Japan the southern half of Sakhalin, — an island formerly belonging to Japan but occupied by Russia in 1875.

The most important results of the war were indirect results. Russia was checked in her career of aggression in Europe and toward India, as well as in the Far East, and the collapse of her despotic government gave opportunity for the beginning of a great revolution in society and politics (p. 584). The appearance of Japan, on the other hand, as one of the foremost "World Powers," went far to check European greed for Asiatic territory.

CHAPTER XLII

THE PROMISE OF A NEW AGE BEFORE 1914

The twentieth century opened with glowing promise of a new era — despite such gloomy shadows as we have noticed in remote and ill-known regions like the Balkans. The *rate* of human progress had been accelerating tremendously. The nineteenth century had seen more change than the thousand years before. Theodore Roosevelt's day was farther removed from Napoleon's than Napoleon's was from Charlemagne's. In this mighty transformation of the world, the three main agents had been *democracy, scientific invention,* and *humane sentiment.*

I. DESPOTISM VANISHING

Growth of constitutionalism

As late as 1830, we have seen, England, Switzerland, and Norway were the only Old-World countries which were not absolute despotisms; and these countries were far from being the democracies they are now. During the remaining two thirds of the nineteenth century, constitutional government spread eastward from England through Europe, and west, from the United States to Japan. In 1900 Russia and little Montenegro (with the possessions of Turkey) were the only European states still unaffected by the movement. The remaining independent states of Asia — Turkey, Persia, China, and Siam — were still despotic. But in 1913 Siam was the only sovereign state on this earth without a representative assembly and some degree of constitutional government. The early revolution in Russia has been treated. In the other lands of the East the change had come even more peacefully — but perhaps even less perfectly.

A "Young Turk" party appeared in the more civilized parts of the Turkish Empire soon after 1900, agitating for a parliament. Early in 1908 its leaders organized an executive committee with headquarters at Saloniki. In July the Saloniki committee published a constitution and demanded that the Sultan accept it.

In Turkey

The army officers were largely "Young Turks," and the Sultan felt constrained to yield. In December of the same year the first Turkish parliament met, with magnificent ceremony. Foreign countries, however, embarrassed the movement seriously. Bulgaria seized this moment to turn her nominal dependence into absolute independence, and Austria formally annexed Bosnia and Herzegovina (p. 595). Conservative Turks accused the Young Turks of carelessly permitting this dismemberment of the empire, and a reactionary revolution broke out; but the army remained loyal to the constitution, and suppressed the revolt with little bloodshed. Constitutionalism, however, took no real hold upon the people.

In Persia, in 1906, the enlightened portion of the people were demanding a parliament so loudly that the monarch (Shah) called one, and issued a constitution. On his death, however, in 1907, his son bombarded the parliament house and arrested the liberal leaders. The provinces broke into revolt; and, in May of 1909, the Shah felt compelled to restore the constitution. The revolutionists then proceeded to depose him, seating on the throne his son, a boy of thirteen. The country has so far remained distracted by revolts and disorder.

In Persia

More amazing still is the revolution which swiftly changed vast "changeless China" into a republic. In the closing years of the nineteenth century, Western ideas began to spread among a small educated class in the empire; but the ruling dynasty (the Manchus) and the mass of the people were still hostile to reform. The dynasty, however, became hated as a result of national humiliations in the war with Japan and the Boxer war and in the seizure of territory by European nations; and then the marvelous victory of Westernized Japan

In China

over Russia reinforced the advocates of Western civilization for China. In 1909 the regent (Empress Dowager, whose Emperor-son was still a babe) promised a constitution "in the near future." The agitation of the Liberals forced her to fix the date first for 1915, and then for 1913. But this was not soon enough. In 1911 Central China rose in revolution, to make the many provinces of the empire into a Federal Republic.

The movement spread with marvelous rapidity, and in a few weeks the Republicans were in possession of the richest and most populous parts of the empire. They soon set up a provisional republican government, at Nanking, under the presidency of an enlightened patriot, *Dr. Sun Yat Sen.* In an attempt to save the monarchy, the Empress then issued a constitution, and called to power a moderate reformer, *Yuan Shih Kai* (yoo-an she ki). When it quickly appeared that this was not enough, the Manchus abdicated. Yuan Shih Kai established a provisional republican government at Peking, and opened negotiations with the Nanking government. To remove all hindrance to union, the noble Sun Yat Sen resigned. Then the two provisional governments elected Yuan Shih Kai president of the "Republic of China."

China a Republic

In April, 1913, the first Chinese parliament assembled, representing 400,000,000 people, or a fourth of the human race. The president, however, proved self-seeking and reactionary. Leading Liberals in the army and in politics were assassinated, supposedly by his orders, and it is even yet not sure that the country has gained more than a military dictatorship. A vast population like that of China cannot leap into civilization and true freedom in a day. Moreover, one of the saddest results of the Japanese encroachments still progressing (1919) is the impetus they give to a growing militarism, for self-defense, in China.

II. SCIENTIFIC AND MORAL PROGRESS

Three eras of invention after 1750

Still more marvelous than political advance was the scientific advance — and the way in which it changed its character. Ancient science was the plaything of philosophers: modern science now became the servant of mankind. The close of the eighteenth century saw those inventions in England that created the age of iron, substituted steam and machinery for hand power in production, and so created the "Industrial Revolution" (pp. 356 ff.). Toward the middle of the 19th century came a second remarkable burst of scientific invention,

Courtesy of the Carnegie Steel Company.

FORGING A RAILWAY CAR AXLE TO-DAY, at the Howard Axle Works, Homestead, Pa. The drop-hammer, about to strike the white-hot axle, weighs three and one-half tons. Fourteen such hammers are used in these works.

in which America led, again revolutionizing daily life and in particular applying machinery to *farm* production (pp. 366–369). Then, toward the close of that same century came the third group, replacing the age of steam by the age of electricity, and transforming once more the face of the world, and the daily habits of vast populations, before the eyes of men still under middle age. Gasoline engines and electric engines furnished new power for locomotion, for factory, and for field. Man explored the sea bottom in submarines and conquered the air. The electric street railway, the automobile, and auto trucks made for cleaner city streets, better country roads, and a vast saving of time and labor. Electric lights helped to banish crime along with darkness. Telephone, phonograph, wireless telegraphy gave men new power to do and to enjoy. And along with this went such a transformation of all earlier machinery and

Courtesy of the Carnegie Steel Company.

SHEARING OFF STEEL SLABS IN MODERN INDUSTRY.

processes as made those of 1850 merely quaint curiosities for museums.

Progress in medicine

It remains to mention, for this last period, *the new relation of science to medicine.* In the 80's the French biologist, Pasteur, broke the way, proving the germ theory of disease, and inventing methods of inoculation against some of the most dreaded forms, like hydrophobia. Devoted disciples followed in his footsteps. During the American occupation of Cuba after the

Spanish-American war, Major Walter Reed showed that ordinary malaria and the deadly yellow fever alike were spread by the bite of mosquitoes. In like manner it has been proved that certain fleas, carried by rats, spread the bubonic plague. In 1903 Dr. Charles W. Stiles proved that the inefficiency and low vitality of the "poor Whites" in the southern United States were due to the parasitic hookworm. The special causes of typhoid and tuberculosis have become well known; and as this passage is being written, the germ that causes the dreaded

ELECTRIC ENGINE. — The 20th Century Limited of the New York Central.

infantile paralysis has been discovered. Each such discovery has enabled men to fight disease more successfully. It is not improbable that in the not distant future all deadly contagious diseases may be practically banished from the earth, — as, according to medical journals, yellow fever is just now banished. Between 1850 and 1900 the average human life in civilized lands was lengthened by a fourth, and population was trebled.

III. SOCIAL UPLIFT

This larger and better life of the twentieth century, too, is bound together, for good and for ill, in a new human solidarity.

A new human solidarity

Our big world is more compact than the small world of 1800 was. Ox-cart and pack-horse have been replaced as carriers by long lines of cars moving thousands of tons of all kinds of freight swiftly across continents, while now the more precious articles and mails begin to be moved as by magic in airships, as Tennyson dreamed when in his youth he —

> "Saw the heavens fill with commerce — argosies of magic sails,
> Pilots of the purple twilight, dropping down with costly bales."

New methods of banking make it possible to transfer credit in an instant, by wire or wireless, between the most distant portions of the earth; and lines of communication are so organized that it costs no more to send a letter or parcel around the earth than around the nearest street corner. The Minnesota farmer's market is not Minneapolis, but the world. The Australian sheep-raiser, the Kansas farmer, the South African miner, the New York merchant, the London banker, are parts of one industrial organism.

All this solidarity means *one more revolution in industry.* The age of small individual enterprise has given way to an era of vast consolidation of capital and management — department stores, mighty corporations, huge trusts, flouring centers like Minneapolis, meat-packing centers like Chicago, money centers like Wall Street. And this consolidation has brought incalculable saving of wealth in economy of management and in utilization of old wastes into by-products. The new unity of society, too, has its *moral* side. Any happening of consequence is known within the hour in London, Petrograd, Pekin, New York, San Francisco, and, within a day, in almost every hamlet where civilized men live. A world opinion shapes itself, in ordinary times, as promptly as village opinion could be brought to bear upon an individual citizen a century ago.

A dark side

But even before the horrible catastrophe of the World War, it was plain enough that *all this modern progress had a darker side.* True, there was more life, and better life; and there was more wealth to support life. The workers, too, though they got too little of that wealth, got vastly more than they got in 1800. An industrious, healthy artisan of to-day usually has a more enjoyable life than a great noble a century ago. Still the industrial organization which produced wealth with gratifying rapidity failed to distribute it *equitably*. The world had become rich; but multitudes of workers remained ominously poor. Even in the most democratic countries, about nine tenths of the increased wealth was held by one tenth the population, while at least two tenths of the people were reduced to a stage of poverty that imperiled both health and decency. The apex of the social pyramid contained real captains of industry, but it contained also pirates and parasites. Service to society had less to do with its revenue than plunder and privilege had. The broad base of the pyramid contained multitudes whose poverty resulted from physical or mental or moral lack; but it contained other multitudes of willing, hard-working, sober men and women denied a chance at comfortable and happy life. And this modern poverty is harder to bear than that of earlier times because it is less necessary. Then there was little wealth to divide. Now the poor man is jostled insultingly by ostentatious affluence and vicious waste.

Failure as yet to distribute wealth

Throughout the civilized world earnest men and women, as never before in history, had begun to band themselves into many kinds of "social uplift" organizations to relieve or remove this misery. Until toward the close of the nineteenth century such movements were mainly charitable in their character. Then they began to work, not merely to cure the social disease, but to remove its cause. They ceased to call for charity, and began to work for social justice — for such an organization of industry as should secure to the worker a larger share of the product of his labor and so insure him against the need of charity. Enlightened thinkers and statesmen entered upon a new and more promising "War against Poverty," recognizing also that such a course was necessary, not merely for the welfare of the poor, but also for the salvation of all society. Said Lloyd George in the English House of Commons in 1913:

The demand for "social justice"

"You have hundreds of thousands of men working unceasingly for wages that bring them barely enough bread to keep them and their families from starvation. Generation after generation they see their children wither, from lack of air, light, and space — denied them by other men who have square miles of space to spare. *You forget that divine justice never passed by a great wrong.* You can hear *now,* north, south, east, west, an ominous rumbling. The chariots of retribution are drawing nigh."

IV. MAKING "ALLIANCES" FOR PEACE

By 1910, Europe had fallen into two hostile camps, the *Triple Alliance* and the *Triple Entente.*

The Triple Alliance

1. Before Bismarck fell from power, he had built the Triple Alliance. After 1871 he sought to isolate France, so as to keep her from finding any ally in a possible "war of revenge." To this end he cultivated friendship with all other European Powers, but especially with Russia and Austria. Austria he had beaten in war only a few years earlier (1866); but he had treated her with marked gentleness in the peace treaty, and the ruling German element in Austria was quite ready now to find backing in the powerful and successful German Empire.

Bismarck prefers Austria to Russia

Soon, however, Bismarck found that he must choose between Austria and Russia. These two were bitter rivals for control in the Balkans. The Slav peoples there, recently freed from the Turks, looked naturally to Russia, who had won their freedom for them, as the "Big Brother" of all Slavs and all Greek religionists. But Austria, shut out now from control in Central Europe, was bent upon aggrandizement to the south. In particular her statesmen meant to win a strip of territory through to Saloniki, on the Aegean, so that, with a railroad thither, they might control the rich Aegean trade. If Serbia were able to fulfill her dream of a South Slav state reaching to the Adriatic, she would interpose an inseparable Slav barrier to this plan, right across the path of Austria's ambition. Accordingly Austria sought always to keep Serbia weak and small;

while Russia, hating Austria even more than she loved the Balkan Slavs, backed Serbia.

This rivalry between Austria and Russia became so acute by 1879 that there was always danger of war; and in that year Bismarck chose to side with Austria as the surer ally. Accordingly he formed a definite written alliance with Austria to the effect that Germany would help Austria in case she had a war with Russia, and Austria would help Germany in case she were attacked by France and any other Power.

Italy drawn into Bismarck's league

Three years later, Bismarck drew Italy into the league, making it the Triple Alliance. Italy was so bitterly enraged at the French seizure of Tunis in that year (p. 503), in flat disregard of Italian imperialistic ambitions there, that she laid aside her ancient differences with Austria for a time and agreed to aid the Central Empires in any war in which they should be attacked by two or more Powers — in return for backing in her colonial ambitions.

The Dual Alliance of 1884

2. Then Russia and France, each isolated in Europe, drew together for mutual protection into a "Dual Alliance" (1884). But Bismarck hoped to draw England into his "triple" league; and his hope was not unreasonable. In the eighties and nineties, England and France were bitter rivals in Africa, and England and Russia, in Asia. England, however, clung to a proud policy of "splendid isolation." Then, after Bismarck's fall, she began to see in the German Emperor's colonial ambitions a more threatening rival than France; and Russia's defeat by Japan made Russia less dangerous. German militarism was deeply hateful to English democracy, and Germany's new commercial activity threatened England's trade, while the new navy that the Kaiser was building could be meant only to work England's destruction. Moreover, England and France were daily coming to a better understanding, and in 1903 a sweeping arbitration treaty put any war between them almost out of question. Soon afterward, England and Russia succeeded in agreeing upon a line in Persia which should separate the "influence" of one Power in that country from the

England's "splendid isolation"

"influence" of the other, so removing all immediate prospect of trouble between the two (1910).

The Triple Entente

From this time the Dual Alliance became the Triple Entente — England, France, and Russia. England was not bound by definite treaty to give either country aid in war; but it was plain that France and Russia were her friends, and that she could not look on quietly and see her friends crushed by Germany — which was showing marked hostility to her.

The alliances and peace

Each of the two huge armed leagues always protested that its aim was peace. No doubt many men in both — and nearly all in one — did shrink from precipitating a conflict between such enormous forces under the new conditions of army organization, quick transportation, and deadly explosives. For half a century (1871–1914), except for the minor struggles in the half-savage Balkans, Europe rested in an "armed peace."

A costly peace

But this "peace" was based upon fear, and it was costly. Year by year, each alliance strove to make its armies and navies mightier than the other's. Huge and huger cannon were invented, only to be cast into the scrap heap for still huger ones. A dreadnaught costing millions was scrapped in a few months by some costlier design. The burden upon the workers and the evil moral influences of such armaments were only less than the burden and evil of war. In every land voices began to cry out that it was all needless: that the world was too Christian and too wise ever again to let itself be desolated by a great war. And then came some interesting efforts to find new machinery by which to guard against war — in standing arbitration treaties, permanent international tribunals like the Hague Court, and occasional World Congresses.

V. INTERNATIONAL ARBITRATION

Efforts to avoid war

In earlier times an impending war was sometimes averted by diplomacy or by the mediation of a powerful neighbor. But arbitration, in the modern sense, means neither diplomatic negotiation nor mediation. It means adjudication of disputed points by an impartial body of experts resembling a law court, following the forms of a court of justice, hearing evidence and argument in public, and basing its decision on the merits of the case.

The first modern "arbitration"

The first arbitration of this kind in modern times was arranged by one clause[1] of the Jay Treaty of 1794 between England and the United States. For nearly a hundred years this sensible device continued to be used mainly by the two English-speaking nations; but before the close of the nineteenth century it began to spread rapidly to other lands. During that century several hundred disputes between nations were settled honorably, peacefully, and justly, by this process, — many of them critical disputes, which, except for arbitration, might easily have led to war. The student of American history will recall the arbitrations with England regarding the Alabama damages, the Bering Sea Seal Fisheries, the Venezuela territory, the Alaskan boundary, and several disputes concerning our northern boundary at the eastern and western extremities.

But all these cases of arbitration concerned some individual dispute, and in each case a special treaty had to be negotiated before arbitration could begin — with every chance for war before such an arrangement could be made. This left much to be desired; and the closing years of the nineteenth century saw agitation for "general arbitration treaties" by which nations might agree *in advance* to submit disputes to a certain court of arbitrators. In 1897 a treaty of this kind between England and the United States failed of adoption because of opposition in the United States Senate, though it had been recommended vigorously first by President Cleveland and afterward by President McKinley. Then leadership in this great movement passed for the time away from the English-speaking peoples.

The Hague Congress of 1899

On August 24, 1898, by order of Tsar Nicholas (a sentimental lover of peace), the Russian Minister of Foreign Affairs handed to the representatives of the different nations in St. Petersburg a written suggestion for a world conference to consider some

[1] Regarding the disputed boundary between Maine and Nova Scotia. See West's *American History and Government*, § 232, or *American People*, § 406.

means for arresting the danger of war and for lessening the burden of the armed peace. Out of this suggestion there grew the *Hague Peace Conference* of 1899.

Germany defeats proposals for disarming

Twenty-six nations were represented, including Mexico, Siam, Japan, China, and Persia, — practically all the independent states of the world except the South American republics. Never before had any gathering so nearly approached a "parliament of man," and never had an international congress accomplished so great a work. It was not possible to put any limit upon armament, because the German representatives refused to consider that matter; but agreements were reached to regulate the methods of war in the interests of greater humanity, and, in spite of German opposition, the Congress provided a permanent International Tribunal for arbitration between nations.

No nation was compelled to submit its quarrels to this Hague Tribunal, but machinery was ready so that nations could escape war, without loss of dignity, if they desired; and in the following years many important cases were so settled.

Chili and Argentina

The next step was for groups of nations to pledge themselves to make use of this machinery, or of similar machinery. This pledge is the essence of a "general arbitration treaty." The first such treaty was adopted in South America.

While the Hague Conference was sitting, Chili and Argentina (which had not been invited to the Conference) were on the verge of war over a boundary dispute in the Andes. For the next two years both governments made vigorous preparations, — piling up war taxes, increasing armaments, building and buying ships of war. But at the last moment a popular movement, led by bishops of the Catholic Church in the two countries, brought about arbitration; and soon after, the boundary was adjusted rationally by a commission of geographers and legal experts. So well pleased were the two nations with this individual case of arbitration that they proceeded to adopt a "general treaty" by which they bound themselves, for a period of five years, to submit *all* disputes which might arise between them to a specific tribunal.

This was the first "general arbitration treaty" ever actually adopted (June, 1903). But others were already in preparation in Europe; and, four months later (October, 1903), France and England adopted one, agreeing to submit future disputes to the Hague Tribunal. Others followed swiftly, until most civilized states were joined with one or more other states in such agreements, usually, however, with important reservations which often destroyed the force of the agreement.

THE CHRIST OF THE ANDES.

A monument of good-will standing at an elevation of 12,000 feet on the boundary line between Chile and Argentina, erected by the two countries to commemorate their arbitration of boundary dispute.

Hague Congress of 1907

In 1907 a Second Hague Conference met, at the suggestion of the United States. This time the South American republics were represented. The Conference extended somewhat the work of the first meeting. But again England's proposals to limit navies and armies failed *because of opposition from Germany and Austria.* It was growing more and more plain that all these noble efforts for peace were vain unless supplemented by radical measures of disarmament; and Germany's implacable opposition had made it plain that this was unattainable except by a better organized world.

Army increases in Europe in 1913

The year 1913, after local wars in the Balkans, saw a new outburst of militarism. Germany adopted a new army bill planning an increase of the army in peace from 650,000 to

870,000, with an immense money appropriation.[1] Three weeks later (July 20), France, in terror, raised her term of active service from two years to three, adding fifty per cent to her forces under arms. Austria and Russia adopted plans for similar reorganization of their armies. Even little Belgium, alarmed at the building of German railways to her border — at vast expense and with no apparent purpose except for invasion — adopted universal military service. Each country of course found excuse and incitement to further efforts in the like efforts by its rivals. In particular, German and Austrian papers published frenzied articles on the danger with which their countries were threatened by the proposed enormous increase of Russia's army and by new Russian railways that apparently looked to an invasion of Germany, just as German roads looked to an invasion of Belgium and France. The "balance" of power was a matter of unstable equilibrium. A touch would tip it into universal war.

Such was Western Europe when German autocracy and militarism seized a moment to try to conquer the world. For five terrible years, all energies went to that mighty struggle. To understand the huge calamity of 1914–1919 we must turn back once more, to look at the Slav part of Europe, which until just now had hardly touched our Western life.

[1] The Socialists in the Reichstag voted against the army bill, but immediately afterward most of them voted for the appropriation. This inconsistency has a partial explanation. The new taxes bore heavily upon large incomes and upon the landlords. The Socialists had long advocated this sort of taxation in vain.

PART X

SLAV EUROPE—TO THE WORLD WAR

CHAPTER XLIII

RUSSIA

Growth of territory

Russia's destruction of Napoleon's Grand Army, in 1813, changed the fate of Europe and revealed her own tremendous power. It became plain that the growth of this vast, aggressive, semi-Oriental state upon the edge of Western Europe had created new problems for all "Western" peoples.

In the fifteenth century (p. 237), the Russians held only a part of what is now South Central Russia, nowhere touching a navigable sea. Expansion, since then, has come partly by colonization, partly by war.

Until the time of Peter the Great, the advance was made almost wholly by the ceaseless movement of pioneers into the savage wilderness north and east. Like swarming hives, Russian villages along the frontier sent forward bands of people, each band to advance a little way and form a new village, driving out or absorbing the Tartar barbarians. On the east much of the advance was made by another kind of frontiersmen, called Cossacks. The Cossacks lived partly by agriculture, partly by grazing, and often they waged war on their own account against Turks and Tartars, somewhat as our early American frontiersmen won Kentucky from the Indians and Texas from Mexico. As early as the time of Ivan the Terrible (p. 237), a Cossack horde seized part of Siberia, and the movement to the Pacific was completed in 1707 by the seizure of Kamchatka.

The Siberian ports on the Pacific, however, were closed by ice almost as continuously as Archangel on the north. Naturally

The struggle for ice-free ports

Russia sought outlets to the seas other than these frozen oceans. From Sweden and Poland, we have seen, she won the eastern Baltic coast. Peter the Great seized the southern districts there, up to the Gulf of Finland, and the rest fell to Alexander I in return for his aid to the Allies against Napoleon (p. 329). But the Baltic is not a true door: in time of war, its narrow outlets are easily closed by a hostile Power. Hence the rulers of Russia looked covetously toward the *Atlantic* ports of Sweden and Norway.

Peter also began a struggle for the Black Sea, though the first real success there came to Catherine II (p. 239). A century of war against the Turks (1772–1878) made Russia mistress of the whole north and west coast, from Azof to the Danube; but Turkish Constantinople still closed the exit to the outer world, and Russian ambition long aimed at that key position — and the ancient capital of the Greek faith.

In Asia, Russian advance after 1800 was steady and terrifying. She aimed at ice-free Pacific ports on the east, and at the Persian Gulf and the Indian seas on the south, besides the rich realms of Central Asia and India. Shortly after 1850 she came into conflict with China on the northwest. In 1858 she reached the Amur, seizing northern Manchuria. Two years later she secured Vladivostock — ice free for most of the year.

The Trans-Siberian Railway

In 1895 the Trans-Siberian Railway was begun, and in 1902 that vast undertaking was completed to Vladivostock. This road is more than 5000 miles long, — nearly double the length of the great American transcontinental roads. Eventually it must prove one of the great steps in the advance of civilization; and it has been fitly compared in importance to the finding of the passage around the Cape of Good Hope or the building of the Suez or Panama canals. Meanwhile Russia had compelled China to cede the magnificent harbor of Port Arthur (p. 556) and the right to extend the Trans-Siberian Railroad through Chinese Manchuria to that port (1898).

The danger to India

On the south, just after the opening of the nineteenth century, Russia secured the passes of the Caucasus. By the middle of the century she had advanced into Turkestan. From that lofty vantage ground she planned a further advance toward India. In swift succession, heedless of England's threats, she secured Bokhara (1868), Khiva (1873), and Merv (1884), despite explicit pledges to England three years before. These Trans-Caspian districts are in the main rich and fertile, with valuable mines, and with a teeming, industrious population. In 1893 Russia reached the "roof of the world," the vast Pamir plateau, and soon extended a great Trans-Caspian railway to within seventy-five miles of Herat, the "key to India." Great Britain seemed ready to resist further advance by war; but a clash in Central Asia was postponed by Japan's victory in the extreme East.

Checked by Japan

In the last years of the nineteenth century Russia was busied with vast internal improvements, — not only the great railroads mentioned above, from Moscow to the Pacific and to the frontiers of India, but also a stupendous system of canals to connect her internal waterways. She was still in a primitive stage industrially, and these useful projects were carried on largely by foreign workmen and foreign capital. Under such conditions at home, Russia had every reason to desire peace abroad; but in 1904 the arrogant folly of her military classes plunged her into the war with Japan, as unjust as it proved ruinous. To the amazement of the world, Russia's huge power collapsed utterly on land and sea, and she was thrust back from Port Arthur and Manchuria (pp. 557–559).

Extent in 1910

In 1910 Russia covered eight and a half million square miles (between two and three times the area of the United States), or about one seventh the area of the habitable earth; and she had a population of one hundred and sixty millions, of which all but about thirty millions lived in Europe. (This was just about equal in number to the whole group of English-speaking peoples in the United States and the British Empire.) The population was made up of some seventy different nationalities, but the great central core, comprising over two thirds the whole, was composed of Russian Slavs.

The subject races

The subject races formed only a fringe about the center, and were rapidly being Russianized (p. 583). The largest of the subject nationalities were the Poles (twelve millions) and the Finns (something over three and a half millions). There were also about five million Jews dispersed throughout the larger cities of the empire, especially at the seaports, and more than thirteen million Tartars; but both these peoples were widely scattered and have never formed governments of their own as the Finns and Poles each have done.

The autocracy

Down almost to the world war, the government of Russia was an absolute despotism, — and highly centralized. In the middle of the nineteenth century no village could build a church or a school until the plan had been approved by a dilatory Board at St. Petersburg, and even a private house with five windows had to have a royal permit. But during all the century, too, a ferment of revolution was spreading through the land.

And the revolutionary movements

At the end of the Napoleonic wars, many young Russian officers came back to their homes full of the ideals of the French revolution. The Tsar himself (Alexander I, 1801–1825) had been educated by a liberal French tutor; and for a time, in a weak, sentimental, indecisive way, he favored a liberal policy, and introduced a few reforms. Metternich won him from these tendencies; and then many educated and liberal Russians began to be conspirators against Tsarism.

The serfs

The cause of the conspirators was long hopeless, because it had no interest for the masses. Nowhere else in the world was the gap so complete between upper and lower classes. Four fifths the population of European Russia were serfs, hardly touched by civilization. They were filthy, ignorant, degraded, and they lived in a world wholly apart from that of the small class of educated Russians.

And society

Besides the serfs, the rural population comprised a numerous nobility, who were landed proprietors; and in the cities there were small professional and mercantile classes. For two hundred years (since Peter the Great) these upper classes had

had at least a veneer of Western civilization. At the opening of the nineteenth century their conversation was carried on, not in Russian, but in French; and their books, fashions, and largely their ideas, were imported from Paris.

Reaction under Nicholas

The revolutionary conspirators from these upper classes were romantic dreamers. Alexander was succeeded by his brother Nicholas I (1825–1855), an intense reactionary, who at once abandoned Alexander's mild reforms and avowed a policy of despotic autocracy. In December of 1825, the revolutionists attempted a rising. They met with no popular support, and Nicholas exterminated almost the entire group with brutal executions, often under the knout. This cruelty, however, made "the Decembrists" martyrs to the next generation of generous-minded Russian youth; and their ideas lived on in the great Russian writers of the middle of the century, like Gogol and Turgeniev.

Beginning of the Slavophil movement

The reign of Nicholas I was marked also by the beginning of the Slavophil movement. This was a revolt among the educated classes to establish a native Russian culture, in contrast to the imported Western veneer. The Russians had begun to believe in themselves as the future leaders of a new civilization. They looked forward to a vast Pan-Slav empire (to include Bohemia and the Slav states of the Balkans) which should surpass Western Europe both in power and in the character of its culture. Nicholas gave his support heartily to the Slavophils, in large part because he despised the Western ideas as to liberty and constitutional government. The attempt to develop a native civilization was altogether wholesome; but unhappily in Russia *it was seized upon as an ally by despotism.*

Reforms of Alexander II

In the closing years of Nicholas, however, the humiliation of the Crimean War (p. 406) revealed the despotic bureaucratic system as weak, when pitted against Western Europe; and this helped the Russian liberals to win to their side the new Tsar, Alexander II (1855–1881). Alexander struck the shackles from the press and the universities, sought to secure just treatment for the Jews, introduced jury trial, established a system of graded representative assemblies in the provinces (the zemstvos), and, in 1861, against the almost unanimous opposition of the nobles, emancipated the fifty million serfs.

Emancipation of the serfs

Liberal Russia now looked for the millennium. Not only were the serfs freed from the jurisdiction of the nobles and from obligation to serve them: they were also given land. This of course was necessary if the peasants were to live at all. They had always dwelt in little village communities: in 1861 each village (mir) was left to manage its own local matters, and was given land for its support.

And the land problem

The land, like the serf, was taken from the noble; but not by confiscation, and not enough of it. Each mir was to pay for its land. The Tsar paid the noble landlord down; and the mir was to pay the Tsar in small installments spread over forty-nine years. Alexander and his liberal friends intended each village to receive at least as much land as the villagers had had for their support while serfs. But the noble officials, who carried out the details, managed to cut down the amount of land and to make the price unduly high. The peasants found themselves at once forced to eke out their scanty income by tilling the land of the neighboring landlord — on his terms. The annual "redemption payments" to the government, too, were excessive. More than half the peasant's labor went to satisfy the tax-collector. By 1890, one third the peasant body had pledged their labor one or more years in advance to the noble landlords — and so had been forced back into a new serfdom. Down to the Revolution of 1917 the land question remained the burning question in Russia.

The peasants re-enslaved

Moreover, until 1907, the government held each mir responsible *as a unit* for taxes and land payments. This helped to hold the peasants to the old medieval system of farming in common, with the wasteful three-field cultivation (p. 67). Labor brought small return. The peasants remained ignorant and wretched, with a death-rate double that of Western Europe. As late as 1900, half their children died under the age of five; and every now and then large districts were devastated by famine — while vast tracts of fertile land lay uncultivated.

Alexander's vacillating policy

Alexander "the Emancipator" after all was almost as vacillating in his liberalism as his father Alexander I had been. The peasants refused to believe that the Tsar meant them to pay for their land, or to give them such small allotments; and in countless places they rose in bloody riots against the nobility and the Tsar's officers. The reactionary parts of society urged upon Alexander that such risings were the product of the progressive writers and newspapers he had encouraged. As early as 1862 the Tsar was won to this view. He began at once to suppress the liberal press. Writers who had thought themselves within the circle of his friendship were imprisoned in secret dungeons or sent to hard labor in Siberian mines, — without trial, merely by decree, — and the brutal police sought to crush out all liberalism by barbarous cruelty.

Persecution of liberals

The Nihilists

The liberals, in the sixties, had come to include the great body of university students. These youths, — men and women of good family, — ardent for the regeneration of their country, now organized societies to spread information about the peasants' misery among the upper classes, and socialistic ideas among the peasants. These active Intelligentsia were cruelly persecuted, and in the later seventies one branch of the radicals decided to meet violence with violence — the only alternative to submission. Their secret organization was popularly known as the Nihilist society. They deliberately resolved to sacrifice their own lives to the cause of liberty, and by assassination after assassination they sought to avenge the barbarous persecution of their friends and to terrify the Tsar into granting representative government.

Alexander at last decided to grant part of their demands. He prepared a draft of a constitution which was to set up a National Assembly. But the day before this plan was to be announced, the Nihilists succeeded in killing him with a dynamite bomb.

Alexander III (1881–1894) returned without qualification to the policy of his grandfather Nicholas. What remained of Alexander II's reforms was undone — except that serfdom

Reaction intensified under Alexander III and Nicholas II

could not well be restored in law. The press was subjected to a sterner censorship. University teachers were muzzled, being forbidden to touch upon matters of government in their lectures. Books like Green's *English People* and Bryce's *American Commonwealth* were added to the long list of standard works whose circulation was forbidden. The royal police were given despotic authority to interfere in the affairs of the mirs. And a new emphasis was given to the Slavophil movement — which now became a ruthless organized effort to hammer into one mold all the varied populations of the Empire. All this reactionary policy was continued by the next — and the last — of the Tsars, the incompetent *Nicholas II* (1894–1917).

Religious persecution

In the Slavophil movement, Autocracy and Greek Orthodoxy were twin oppressors. The Finnish and German Lutherans of the Baltic regions, the Polish Romanists, the Armenian dissenters, the Georgians, and the Jews were all cruelly persecuted. Children were taken from parents to be educated in the Greek faith; native languages were forbidden in schools, churches, newspapers, legal proceedings, or on sign boards; and against the Jews (who had already been cruelly crowded into "the Jewish Pale") bloody "pogroms" were organized *by police officers* with every form of outrage, plunder, torture, and massacre.

And the Jews

When this persecution began, more than half all the Jewish race dwelt in Russia — whither they had fled in the Middle Ages from Western persecution. They now became the special objects of this new persecution. The peasants and poorer townsmen hated them because of their financial ability — for in modern Russia as in medieval England the Jews were the chief money lenders; and the official classes hated them because a large part of the Intelligentsia and of the more radical revolutionary leaders came from the Jewish race. One brutal minister of the Tsar loudly proclaimed that he would stifle the revolutionary agitation in Jewish blood. One third the Jews, he said, would be forced into the Greek Church; one third driven into exile; and the rest would perish of hunger and misery. It was this persecution that drove great numbers of Russian Jews to America.

Russian Church aids despotism

And, in return for the Tsar's aid against heresy, the Russian priests became spies for the autocracy in its political persecution, and betrayed to the police the secrets of the confessional.

Russianization of the Baltic region

In one respect the Baltic districts had more cause for complaint even than the Jews. Finland, the old German provinces (Livonia, Esthonia, Courland), and Poland all excelled Russia proper in civilization, and each of them, at its acquisition by Russia, had been solemnly promised the perpetual enjoyment of its own language, religion, and laws. Russianization may sometimes have been a not unmixed evil to barbarous regions on the east; but it was bitterly hard upon these progressive western districts.

Finland

Finland, in particular, was connected with Russia only through a "personal union": the Tsar was also grand-duke of Finland, but the duchy had its own constitution, its own representative Diet, and its free institutions, all guaranteed in the most solemn manner by each grand-duke at his accession. The Finns were industrious, peaceful, and prosperous, and gave no handle for interference. Still, the Slavophils finally got their way. In 1900 the process of making Finland a mere province of despotic and Slav Russia began; and, in spite of royal pledges and of the sympathies of the Western world for Finland, it was carried on rapidly, until the last vestiges of the ancient liberties of this little northern land were for a time swept away.

Underground Russia

In 1890, the police seemed to have crushed all reform agitation and all *open* criticism of the government. But there was an "Underground Russia" where modern ideas were working silently. Many liberals were growing up among the increasing class of lawyers, physicians, professors, and merchants, and, sometimes, among the nobles.

More important still was the fact that about 1890 Russia began to be touched by the industrial revolution which had

The Industrial Revolution

transformed England a hundred years, and Germany seventy years, before. Moscow had been a "sacred city" of churches, marked by spires and minarets. In 1890, it was becoming an industrial center, with huge factories and furnaces, marked by smoke-hung chimneys.

And Socialism

In such cities Socialism made converts rapidly among the new working class. There were two distinct bodies of these Russian Socialists. The larger body looked forward only to peaceful reform, like the Social Democratic party in other lands. The other was made up of Socialist-Revolutionists. This was a secret society, perfectly organized, which had absorbed the old Nihilists. It held that violence was necessary and right in the struggle to free Russia from the despotism which choked all attempts at peaceful reform. In this day of perfectly disciplined standing armies, with modern guns, open revolution is doomed to almost certain extinction in blood. So the Revolutionists worked by the dagger and the dynamite bomb, to slay the chief ministers of despotism. The society selected its intended victims with careful deliberation; and, when one had been killed, secretly posted placards proclaiming to the world the list of "crimes" for which he had been "executed." Spite of every precaution, the Revolutionists, with complete disregard of their own lives, managed to strike down minister after minister among the most hated of the Tsar's tools.

The liberal movement of 1906 = "the First Russian Revolution"

The opportunity of the reform forces seemed to have come in 1905. The failure of Russia in the Japanese war showed that the despotic government had been both inefficient and corrupt. High officials had stolen money which should have gone for rifles and powder and food and clothing for the armies. During the disasters of the war itself, other officials stole the Red Cross funds intended to relieve the suffering of the wounded. The intelligent classes were exasperated by these shames and by the humiliating defeat of their country, and began to make their murmurs heard. The peasantry were woefully oppressed by war-taxes. The labor classes in the towns were thrown out of employment, or lost wages in the general stagnation of industry. While the Japanese war was still running its disastrous course, Russia was convulsed, as never before, by strikes, peasant risings, and mutiny in army and navy.

For a while longer the government thought to stifle such popular manifestations in blood. One instance, famous because so near the royal palace and the homes of foreign ambassadors, sent a thrill of horror through the civilized world. A great number of loyal citizens in St. Petersburg (Petrograd) had sent a petition to the Tsar, asking him to hear them in person when, on the following Sunday, they should march to the palace to present their grievances — since they had lost faith in his officers. Then, Sunday morning, January 22, 1905, dense masses of men, women, and children, wholly unarmed, filled the streets leading to the royal palace. The Cossack cavalry charged these helpless throngs, and the palace troops mowed them down with machine guns.[1] This was "Red Sunday."

"Red Sunday"

Now, for once, the educated classes spoke out forcefully. The day after Red Sunday, leading citizens of the capital joined in a public declaration that "the government has declared war on the Russian people" and in an appeal to all good citizens to support the cause of reform. For a time the Tsar and his advisers felt compelled to yield. In March a representative assembly was promised, and, soon after, the Tsar issued a decree guaranteeing complete freedom of speech.

The Tsar calls the Duma

Nicholas stated, however, that the Duma (assembly) should have power only to *advise* him, and he excluded workingmen and professional classes from the right of voting in the election. Then followed a general strike. In October the railways were idle. In the cities, stores were closed. Power houses shut down, and electric lights went out. This finally brought the government to yield. New rules were issued for the election, and a royal decree established the "unshakable rule" —

[1] Robinson and Beard's Readings, II. 373 ff., gives a contemporary account.

"That no law can become binding without the consent of the Imperial Duma, and that the representatives of the People shall have a real participation in the control of the authorities appointed by us."

Class divisions among the Liberals

As after the Emancipation Edict forty-five years before, the Russian people went wild with joy and hope; and again bitter disappointment followed. All Russia had seemed united against autocracy in demands for *political* reform; but nevertheless Russia was divided within itself by a bitter class conflict. The city proletariat was struggling for radical economic change as well as for political reform; especially for shorter hours and higher wages, for which many long-continued strikes were then in progress. The middle-class liberals, and especially the employing capitalist class, hoped that representative government — with only the grant of more land to the peasants — would remedy Russia's ills. Immediately after issuing the October decree for the Duma, the Tsar threw himself once more into the arms of the reactionary official party, and sought to take advantage of this class division among the liberals. The prisons were emptied of criminals, who were then organized by the police as "patriots" — better known in history as the Black Hundreds; and within three weeks, in a hundred different places, some 4000 radicals and labor leaders were assassinated. In Odessa alone, in a four-days official massacre, a thousand persons were killed.

Reaction at court

The origin of soviets

This brutal violence of the government's friends gave increased standing among the people to the radical Socialist movement. In all great cities there had been organized a Council of Workmen's Deputies to guide the strikes. These Councils now began to be mighty political forces. The peasants, too, organized Councils of Deputies in many districts, and, in some places, revolutionarily inclined regiments made common cause with peasants and workingmen, and elected Councils of Soldiers Deputies. This was the birth of the later famous *soviets* — a desperate attempt to meet the Tsar's duplicity and brutality by a new working-class government.

But these soviet organizations at once began to antagonize the liberal capitalists by ill-timed demands as to hours and wages, enforced by general strikes. *Accordingly the middle classes held aloof,* while the Tsar's government used all its remaining strength in the early winter to crush the new soviets with an indescribably horrible vengeance.

Crushed for the time by the Tsar

In April of 1906, midst gloom and anarchy, with 75,000 of Russia's finest men and women suffering torment in dungeons as political prisoners, the Duma was at last brought together — the first representative assembly of the Russian nation. The Tsar had arranged the elections so as to leave most weight in the hands of the wealthy and noble classes, and the police interfered actively against radical candidates; but the revolutionary movement had swept everything before it. The largest party among the members were middle-class liberals, who called themselves *Constitutional Democrats*. The chief leader of this group was Miliukof, and it contained many other men of wise and moderate statesmanship. Next in numbers came the *Peasants,* with a program of moderate Socialism. The extreme Socialists of the towns had taken the name *Social Democrats,* and, under the lead of *Nicholai Lenin,* had in great measure refused to take part in the elections. Still they counted 25 members. Of the total of 400, only 28 were avowed supporters of autocracy. The Tsar's repudiation by the nation was complete.

The Duma of 1906

The world was amazed at the political ability of this first, inexperienced Russian Assembly. By practically unanimous vote it asked for four great political reforms, — universal suffrage, a "responsible" ministry, the abolition of martial law, and amnesty for all political offenders then in prison or in exile, — and for a long program of social reform, including the turning over of state lands to the suffering peasantry. All these requests were refused with insult by the Tsar, who had now surrounded himself with an intensely reactionary ministry. After proper persistence, the Duma wisely withdrew all but the agrarian demand. The Tsar announced that he

Dissolution of the Duma

was "sadly disappointed" that the Duma insisted upon meddling with matters that did not pertain to it; and July 21 he dissolved it, declaring that he himself would care for the needed reforms. *In vain now did the Constitutional Democrats appeal for support to the masses* — whose soviet organizations they had refused to help to save.

In October, 1906, an imperial edict decreed some land reforms (abolishing the "redemption payments" but leaving the peasants insufficient land), and called another Duma for March, 1907. Months of anarchy followed. The government fell back upon stern repression and intimidation, *to suppress not only disorder, but also political agitation.* To meet this tyranny, the extreme Revolutionists resorted to a new campaign of systematic political assassination. The unhappy land was again distracted also by peasant risings and by strikes, — which were put down brutally by Cossack "punitive expeditions" in which thousands of *unoffending* people perished. A new famine, too, was desolating many provinces.

Anarchy and violence

Fifty officials were assassinated in one week in August, just after the dissolution of the Duma, the victims ranging from ministers of state to petty police officers. Many others were wounded. During the following four months, 169 riots occurred and 244 bombs were thrown at officials. On the other hand, more than a thousand political offenders were executed, and fifty thousand were sent to Siberia or to prison, while the Revolutionists counted up 24,239 others slain by the soldiery in putting down or punishing riots. Prisoners were tortured mercilessly, and in many cases were flogged to death.

The extremists who engaged in the desperate policy of assassinating government agents expected death on the scaffold or by torture in prison. But the government virtually proscribed also the whole Constitutional Democratic party, to prevent its further political activity, murdering its leaders (learned and gentle scholars among them), or driving them into exile, or immuring them hopelessly in prison. During

End of the "First Revolution"

the year 1906, seven hundred of the small number of Russian editors were prosecuted for "sedition."

The Duma of 1907

The First Russian Revolution had been stifled. True, a second Duma met March 5, 1907. The liberal members of the former assembly, so far as they were not already in exile or in the grave, had been made ineligible for election. But this time the Social Democrats went into the campaign in earnest and elected nearly one third the members in spite of desperate efforts of the police to close their meetings and imprison their leaders. With the remnants of the Constitutional Democrats and the Peasants, there was a large majority opposed to the government. In June the Tsar ordered the Duma to expel some sixty Socialist members on the ground of treason. The Duma appointed a committee to investigate the charge. The Tsar at once dissolved it for this delay, and the police seized the accused delegates.

Later submissive Dumas

Then, contrary to plain promises in 1906, the Tsar changed once more the plan of elections, so as to give power very largely to the great landowners. The third Duma, elected on this new basis, met in November, 1907, and proved submissive to the Tsar's will. On the expiration of its term (in 1912), like methods secured a fourth Duma equally satisfactory to despotism. So did Russia enter the World War.

Finland in 1906–1907

One movement of some promise is yet to be mentioned: The Finns had seized the opportunity of the disorders of 1905–6 and forced the Tsar to restore for a time their ancient privileges. A Diet elected by manhood suffrage adopted a new constitution for Finland, which received the Tsar's approval in September, 1906. This constitution provided a single-house legislature elected by *universal* suffrage. Nineteen women sat in the Diet of 1907.

FOR FURTHER READING. — Hazen, 645–718, or Seignobos, 578–608 (does not cover recent years). Somewhat longer treatments are given in Skrine's *Expansion of Russia* and Nevison's *The Dawn in Russia*. Recent history — since 1904 — is covered in Spargo's *Bolshevism*, Arthur Ransom's *Russia in 1919*, and William Hard's *Raymond Robins' Story of Russia*.

CHAPTER XLIV

THE BALKANS: THE SEED PLOT FOR WAR

The Balkan races

A century ago, all Southeast Europe, beyond Austria and Russia, was part of Turkey. But the Turks were mere invaders. They were the rulers; but they were not numerous in Europe except near Constantinople, and they had no part in European civilization.

In no other part of the earth of so small extent was there such a mingling of distinct peoples — even apart from the Turkish conquest. The land is puckered and crumpled into a quaint network of interlacing mountains and valleys; and the inhabitants themselves were almost as much intermixed.

The Greeks

Besides the ruling Turk there were five distinct subject races. In the old Hellenic peninsula dwelt the Greeks, with the memories of their ancient greatness. North of the Danube lay the Roumanians, proud of their legendary descent from Roman colonists in Dacia. Their language to-day is closer to the old

Roumanians

Latin than is any other living European language, although in blood the people are no doubt now mainly Slav. Only half their race lived in "Roumania." One fourth dwelt in Bessarabia, which Russia had seized from the Turks in 1812; and another fourth were in Transylvania, which Hungary had held ever since she conquered it from the Turks in the eighteenth century.

Albanians

Between these Greek and "Roman" peoples lay the Bulgarians, the Serbs, and, along the Adriatic just north of Greece, the Albanians. These last were wild herdsmen, descendants of the ancient Illyrians. For the most part they had adopted Mohammedanism and they willingly supplied excellent troops for the Turkish army; but in other respects their poverty and their mountains made it possible for them to keep a rude sort of self-rule, without much interference from Constantinople. Serbs and Bulgars need a longer explanation.

The Serbs and their divisions

The Serbs were the leading survivors of the conquering South Slavs who settled in the Balkan regions in the sixth century. They have long been imbued with a natural ambition to restore their ancient empire as it stood when the Turk overthrew it in the fatal battle of Kossova, in 1389 (map after p. 120). But even more than the Roumanians, the South Slavs had been broken up by accidents of war. The northwestern part, the Bosnians, had remained independent longer than Serbia proper: and then, when they were conquered, their nobles became Mohammedans, to secure Turkish favor, though the peasants remained Greek Christians — like most of the subject peoples outside Albania. Other northern parts of Serbia, lands of the Croats and Slovenes, were reconquered from Turkey by Hungary in the eighteenth century, and so were no longer part of the home land, to which by race and language they belonged.

Montenegrins

Moreover, in the fastnesses of Montenegro ("Black Mountain") dwelt some 200,000 half-savage Serbs who had never yielded to the Turks, but had kept their freedom at the cost of "five hundred years of ferocious heroism." In Serbia itself, the Turks had for the most part killed off the nobles. The village life was left, however, much as it had been of old. The people managed their local matters in small democracies, and earned their living as farmers and herdsmen of droves of pigs. As in all Christian lands ruled by the Turk, oppression and cruelty dwarfed their civilization.

The Bulgarians

East of Serbia, beyond a dividing mountain range, lay the Bulgarians. The "Bulgars" came into the peninsula as conquerors from central Asia some two centuries later than the Slav Serbs. Originally they were baggy-trousered Asiatic nomads, akin to Tartars and Turks, and to-day they have intense pride in their ancient history as a race of conquerors. But in blood they have been so absorbed by the Slavs among whom they settled that there is little real difference in race between them and Roumanian on the one side or Serb on the other.

Race hatreds and rivalries

Still a long history of rivalry, warfare, and mutual cruelty has left an intense "race" hatred between Bulgars, Serbs, and Greeks; and this hatred has been made hotter by the fact that each one of the three has hoped to win for itself the northern Aegean coast from the decaying Turkish power. Turkish misrule has still further confused this perplexing picture. During her centuries of control, to keep Bulgarians and Serbs, either one, from rising unitedly against her, Turkey has transplanted whole groups of Bulgarian villages into Serbia, quite in the fashion of ancient Oriental despotisms, replacing them with villages of transplanted Serbs — so that each subject race should always have enemies in its midst.

The four great Slav branches

This is a proper place to survey the distinctive marks of the four great divisions of European Slavs: (1) *the Russians,* influenced by long Tartar domination in the Middle Ages, by admixture with various border peoples, and by the Greek Church; (2) *the Poles,* set off from the Russians by the adoption of Latin Christianity and by German instead of Tartar influence; (3) *the Bohemians* and neighboring Slavic peoples, now known as Czecho-Slovaks, resembling the Poles in their history but dominated in recent centuries by Austrian Germans; and (4) *these "South Slavs"* of the Balkans, with a promising Greek influence in the early Middle Ages, followed by a long and crushing subjection to the Turk which has lasted in part to our day.

The subject races win freedom

It is unnecessary to review here the agony of the century-long struggle by which the subject Balkan peoples finally threw off the Turkish yoke, but some parts of the story must be touched upon. The first successful revolt was the Greek rising in 1821–1828. The intervention of England, Russia, and France compelled Turkey to grant Greek independence (p. 346); and at the same time Roumania and Serbia advanced to the position of merely tributary states, dependent upon Turkey but ruled

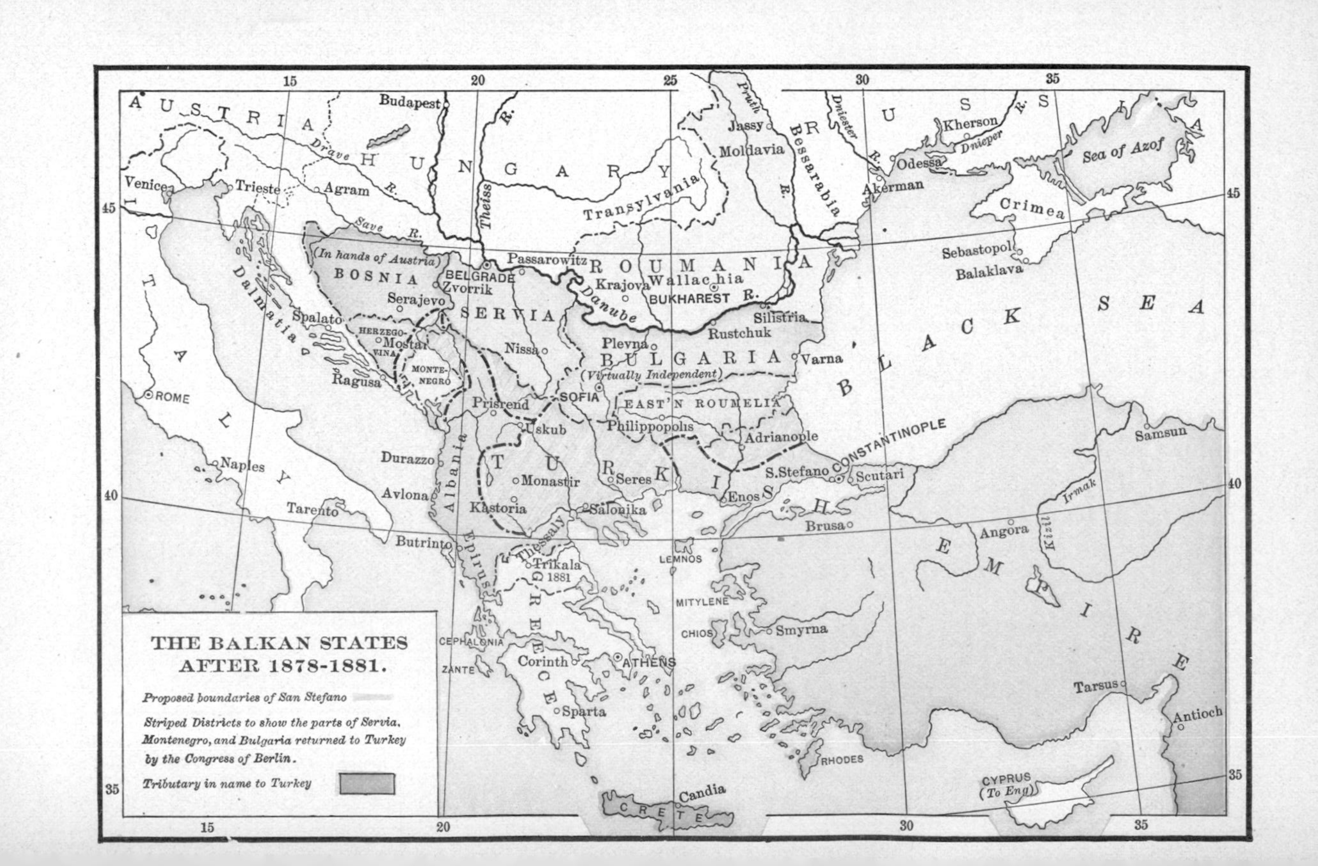
THE BALKAN STATES AFTER 1878-1881.
Proposed boundaries of San Stefano
Striped Districts to show the parts of Servia, Montenegro, and Bulgaria returned to Turkey by the Congress of Berlin.
Tributary in name to Turkey
AUSTRIA
HUNGARY
RUSSIA
ITALY
ROUMANIA
SERVIA
BULGARIA
(Virtually Independent)
EAST'N ROUMELIA
BOSNIA
(In hands of Austria)
HERZEGO-VINA
MONTE-NEGRO
TURKISH EMPIRE
GREECE
BLACK SEA
Sea of Azof
Crimea
Bessarabia
Moldavia
Wallachia
Transylvania
Dalmatia
Albania
Epirus
Thessaly
Budapest
Venice
Trieste
Agram
Drave R.
Save R.
Theiss R.
Danube R.
Pruth R.
Dniester R.
Dnieper
Kherson
Odessa
Akerman
Jassy
Sebastopol
Balaklava
Passarowitz
BELGRADE
Zvorrik
Serajevo
Spalato
Mostar
Ragusa
Krajova
BUKHAREST
Silistria
Rustchuk
Plevna
Nissa
Varna
SOFIA
Prisrend
Uskub
Philippopolis
Adrianople
CONSTANTINOPLE
S. Stefano
Scutari
Enos
Brusa
Samsun
Irmak
Kizil
Angora
Monastir
Seres
Salonika
Kastoria
Durazzo
Avlona
Butrinto
Trikala
1881
ROME
Naples
Tarento
LEMNOS
MITYLENE
CHIOS
Smyrna
CEPHALONIA
ZANTE
Corinth
ATHENS
Sparta
RHODES
Tarsus
Antioch
CYPRUS
(To Eng.)
CRETE
Candia
15
20
25
30
35
40
45

by their own princes. The Crimean War (1856) bolstered up the tottering Ottoman Empire for a time (p. 406), but a great collapse came twenty years later. At Berlin the Sultan had promised many reforms for his Christian subjects, but these promises bore no fruit; and in 1875–1876, the Serbs in Bosnia and the Bulgarians rose for independence. There followed the horrible events long known as the "Bulgarian Atrocities." Turkish soldiers destroyed a hundred Bulgarian villages with every form of devilish torture imaginable, and massacred 30,000 people, carrying off also thousands of Christian girls into terrible slavery.

"Bulgarian Atrocities" of 1876

Then Serbia sprang to arms; and Tsar Alexander II of Russia declared war on Turkey (1877) — in full accord with the demand of his people. The universal horror in Western Europe at the crimes of the Turk prevented for a time any interference; and in ten months the Russian armies held the Turks at their mercy. The Peace of San Stefano (1878) arranged for a group of free Slav states in the peninsula and for the exclusion of Turkey from Europe except for the city of Constantinople.

Russia's attempt to free the Balkans

Alexander would probably have kept on to secure Constantinople, had he not seen a growing danger of European interference. And even now Europe did intervene. Austria wanted a share of Balkan plunder; England feared the advance of Russia toward her communications with India; and so the Peace of San Stefano was torn up. The Congress of Berlin (p. 457), in 1878, dominated by Disraeli, the English Conservative, restored half the freed Christian populations to their old slavery under the Turk, handed over Bosnia to Austria to "administer" for Turkey, with a solemn provision that Austria should never annex the territory to her own realms; and left the whole Balkan district for the next third of a century in its old anarchy, with only slight gains for Serbia and Bulgaria. In fixing responsibility for the World War of 1914, this crime of 1878 cannot be wholly overlooked.

Interference by the Congress of Berlin, 1878

We have seen (p. 458) that while the English government under Disraeli was chiefly responsible for that crime, the English

Germany succeeds to England's place as the friend of the Turk

people promptly repudiated it at the polls. Gladstone came forth from retirement to stump England against the "shameful alliance with Abdul the Assassin"; and at the next elections (1880) Disraeli was overthrown by Gladstone with huge majorities. The wrong to the Balkans could not then be undone, but from this time England drew away from her old policy of courting Turkish friendship — wherein her place was quickly taken by Germany.

In order to win control in Asia Minor

No part of Germany's non-European empire (pp. 519–524) interested German ambition so deeply as her advance into Asia Minor. This began in earnest about 1900. Germany did not acquire actual title to territory there; but she did secure from Turkey various rich "concessions," guaranteeing her for long periods the sole right to build and operate great railroads and to develop valuable mining and oil properties. This "economic penetration" she expected confidently to turn into political sovereignty.

To secure such concessions, Germany had sought the Turk's favor in shameful ways. She loaned to the Sultan German officers to reorganize and drill the Turkish armies, and supplied him with the most modern arms to keep down the rising Christian natives under his yoke — as in the Turkish war with Greece for Crete in 1897. And in 1895, when new Armenian massacres had roused England so that great public meetings were calling for war upon Turkey, Kaiser Wilhelm sent to the Sultan his photograph and that of his wife, to show German friendship and support. Germany knew that if she could keep this position of defender of the tottering Ottoman Empire, she could before long make that Empire into a vassal state.

Germany joins in Austria's policy against a "Greater Serbia"

The prospect of German dominance in Asia Minor brought Germany and Austria into closer sympathy in their Balkan policies. Austria's interference in those regions had been purely bad. She aimed to keep the little Balkan states weak and mutually hostile to one another, and especially to prevent the growth of a "Greater Serbia," which might attract to itself

Austria's dissatisfied Slav subjects. Now (1898, 1899), Germany obtained concessions from Turkey for a railway from "Berlin to Bagdad," to open up the fabulously rich Oriental trade. A powerful Serbia, through which that line must pass, might have checked that project. Thenceforward, therefore, Germany was ready to back Austria unreservedly in Balkan aggression, or to use her as a cat's-paw there. And in return for support in the Balkans, Austria permitted herself to sink virtually into a vassal state of Germany, following blindly her lead in all other foreign relations.

The "Mittel-Europa" dream

Such was the origin of the German dream of a "Mittel-Europa" empire, reaching across Europe from the North Sea to the Aegean and the Black Seas, and on through Asia Minor to the Euphrates. This meant German leadership over Austria and Turkey and some sort of control, through them, over the Balkans. If this dream could be established upon a solid basis — and it very nearly was done — there would be created a supreme world power, before which states like France would sink into utter insignificance.

Austria annexes Bosnia

In 1908 came a step toward fulfilling the plan. Taking advantage of internal dissensions in Turkey, Austria formally annexed Bosnia, in flat contradiction to her solemn pledges (p. 593). This was not only a brutal stroke at the sanctity of treaties, but also it seemed a fatal blow to any hope for a reunion of that Slav district with Serbia. Serbia protested earnestly, and was supported by Russia. But the Kaiser "took his stand in shining armor by the side of his ally," as he himself put it; and Russia, still weak from her defeat by Japan and from her revolution of 1906, had to back down. Serbia was then forced by Austria's rough threats to make humiliating apologies — while at the same time an Austrian embargo against Serbian pork closed to the chief Serbian industry its only outlet to world markets, robbing it of all value. It is not strange that secret societies at once grew up in Serbia, pledged to hostility to the "odious and greedy northern neighbor who holds millions of Serb brothers in chains."

Then came two events less favorable to the Teutonic designs.

1. The first came from Italy. That state was eager to use the army and navy it had been maintaining at crushing cost, and it had long seen its ambitions for colonial empire balked.

The Italian war with Turkey, 1911

In 1911, seeking excuse in the ill treatment of some Italian traders in Tripoli, Italy declared war on Turkey and wrested from her that African province along with various Aegean islands. This act followed so closely the precedents by which France and Germany had been building up colonial empires that "Europe" was constrained to permit the deed with only mild protests. (Greece protested in vain that the Aegean islands were wholly Greek.) Italy's easy success inflamed her imperialists into putting forward programs for further expansion in the Aegean, in Asia Minor, and especially in Albania just across the Adriatic; and all of these designs were exceedingly distasteful to her two allies in the Triple Alliance.

The Balkan War of 1912

2. And Italy's victory encouraged another attack upon Turkey. United action by the mutually hostile Balkan states had seemed impossible. But in 1912, Bulgaria, Serbia, Montenegro, and Greece suddenly joined in a war to drive the Turk out of Europe — and to divide his possessions there among themselves. Serbia was to have northern Albania, with its seaports; Montenegro, the port of Scutari; Greece, southern Albania and a small strip of Macedonian coast; and Bulgaria, the bulk of Macedonia.

The allies won swift victories and in a few months were almost at the gates of Constantinople. Then "Europe" intervened to arrange the peace terms. Italy, like Austria, was hostile to a Greater Serbia; and at the insistence of these powers backed by Germany, a new Kingdom of Albania was created, shutting off Serbia once more from the sea she had reached, while Montenegro was forced, by threat of war, to give up to Albania Scutari, which she had conquered. Turkey was to surrender, mostly to Bulgaria, her remaining territory in Europe except for Constantinople. Germany had carried her points in this settlement; but her ally, Turkey, had collapsed, and events were at once to show that in siding with Bulgaria she had "put her money on the wrong horse."

The Second Balkan War, 1913

The treaty left Bulgaria almost the only gainer. The cheated allies demanded that she now share her gains with them. She refused; and at once (June, 1913) followed "the Second Balkan War." Greece, Serbia, Montenegro, and Roumania attacked Bulgaria. The Turks seized the chance to reoccupy Adrianople,

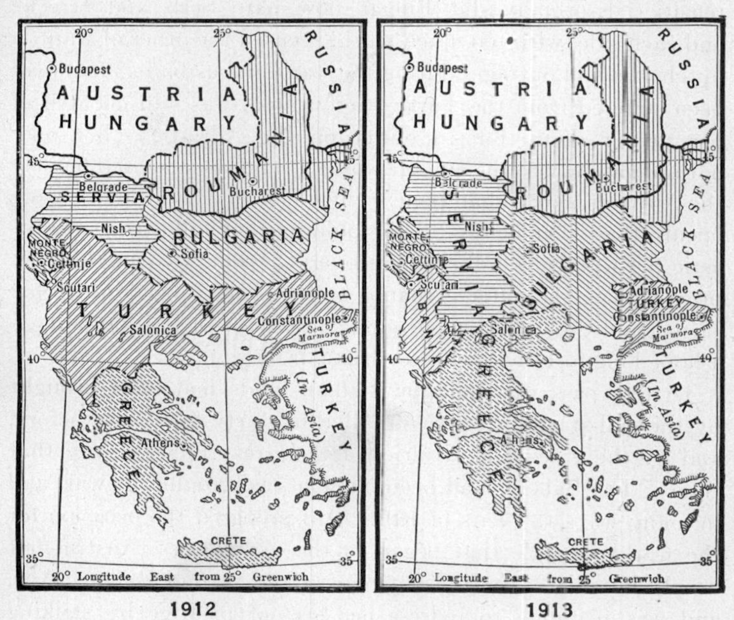

THE BALKAN STATES.

and were permitted to keep it. In a month Bulgaria was crushed, and a new division of booty was arranged. Greece won the richest prize, including the city of Saloniki; but each of the other allies secured gains in this "July War."

The Balkans in 1913

This contest left Roumania the largest Balkan state, with about seven and a half million people. Then came Serbia, Greece, and Bulgaria, each with about four and a half million. Montenegro had risen to nearly a half million. Albania counted

800,000; and remaining "Turkey in Europe," nearly two million. All these nations have a frightful amount of illiteracy, and none has much wealth. All had a legislature elected by manhood suffrage, but the monarchs were almost absolute.

The Balkan nations came out of the two wars not only terribly exhausted, but hating one another with ferocious intensity. Especially did Bulgar now hate Serb and Greek; and each side, with too much truth, accused the other of wanton butcheries and outrages during the war quite as bad as had ever been suffered from the Turk. Serbia, too, was still cheated of her proper desire for an outlet on the Adriatic — her only natural gateway to the outside world — and she resented fiercely the Austrian and Italian policy which had so balked her. More openly than ever before, in the months that followed, enthusiastic Serb patriots talked of recovering from Austria the Slav provinces of Dalmatia, Croatia, and Bosnia, for a South Slav state; and this talk was encouraged by hope of Russian aid, — a hope long fostered by secret Russian intrigue.

To this pass the unhappy Balkan lands had been brought by the evil-starred Congress of Berlin, thirty-five years before, and by the greed and rivalries of the Great Powers since that time. The Balkans had been made a seed-ground for war, and in many ways the wars of 1912–1913 prepared the occasion for the world struggle that began in the next year. Austria felt deeply humiliated by the outcome of the Second Balkan War, and was planning to redress her loss of prestige by striking Serbia savagely on the first occasion. Prince Lichnowsky, then German ambassador at London, tells us now that only England's honest desire for peace, and her coaxing Montenegro and Serbia into submission in 1913 at the close of the First Balkan War, prevented a world war then. A year later, England's efforts to a like end failed.

PART XI

THE WAR AND THE NEW AGE

CHAPTER XLV

GERMANY WILLS THE WAR

German war propaganda at home

The *occasion* for the World War, we have just said, was found in the Balkan situation; but for the *cause* we must turn back to Germany. For nearly half a century that country had been ruled by a Prussian despotism resting upon a bigoted, arrogant oligarchy of birth, and a greedy, scheming oligarchy of money. That rule had conferred on Germany many benefits. It had cared for the people as zealously as the herdsman cares for the flocks he expects to shear. But, in doing so, it had amazingly transformed the old peace-loving, gentle German people.

It had taught that docile race (1) to bow to Authority, rather than to Right;[1] (2) to believe Germany stronger, wiser, better than "decaying" England, "decadent and licentious" France, "uncouth and anarchic" Russia, or "money-serving" America; (3) to be ready to accept a program, at the word of command, for imposing German *Kultur* upon the rest of the world *by force;* (4) to regard war, even aggressive war, not as horrible and sinful, but as beautiful, noble, desirable, and right, — the final measure of a nation's worth, and the divinely appointed means for saving the world by German conquest; and finally (5) to disregard ordinary morality, national or individual, whenever it might interfere with the victory of the "Fatherland."

Insensibly to most of the rest of the world, this rabid and diseased patriotism of the Germans had become a menace to

[1] Observers have often confounded this trait "with respect for law,"— its precise opposite.

freedom and civilization. It was the strangest doctrine of national pride the world had ever heard. There were not wanting German writers to claim that Joan of Arc, Dante, and Jesus himself owed their merits to German blood — along with like astounding assumptions of German descent to explain Voltaire, Alexander the Great, and Julius Caesar. Napoleon even, it was urged by some enthusiastic German patriots, must have been descended from the German Vandals.

The viciousness of these German teachings about war must be shown briefly "out of their own mouths":

"Out of their own mouths"

"**War is the noblest and holiest expression of human activity.** For us, too, the glad, great hour of battle will strike. Still and deep in the German heart must live the joy of battle and the longing for it. Let us ridicule to the utmost the old women in breeches who fear war and deplore it as cruel and revolting. No; war is beautiful. Its august sublimity elevates the human heart beyond the earthly and the common. In the cloud palace above sit the heroes Frederick the Great and Blücher; and all the men of action — the great Emperor, Moltke, Roon, Bismarck — are there as well, but not the old women who would take away our joy in war. . . . *That is the heaven of young Germany.*" — *Jung Deutschland*, October, 1913 (the official organ of the "Young German League," an organization corresponding in a way to our Boy Scouts).

"Germany's mission is to rejuvenate exhausted Europe by a diffusion of Germanic blood." — *School and Fatherland*, 1913 (a school manual).

"Our fathers have left us much to do. . . . **To-day it is for Germany to arise from a European to a world power.** . . . Humanitarian dreams are imbecility. . . . Right and wrong are notions indispensable in *private* life. **The German people are always right, because they number 87,000,000 souls.**" — TANNENBERG, *Gross-Deutschland*, 1913.

"We are the salt of the earth. . . . God has called us to civilize the world. . . . We are the missionaries of human progress." — WILHELM II, speech at Bremen, March 22, 1900.

"Even in the distance, and on the farther side of the ocean, without Germany and the German Emperor, no great decision *dare* henceforth be taken." — WILHELM II, at Kiel, July 3, 1900.

"The world owes its civilization to Germany alone. . . . The time is near when the earth must be conquered by the Germans." — WIRTH, *Weltmacht in der Geschichte* (1901).

"Ye shall love peace as a means to new wars, and the short peace better than the long. . . . You say, a good cause hallows even war; but I tell you, **a good war hallows every cause.**" — NIETZSCHE, *Of Wars and Warriors.* (Nietzsche is a leader of German thought.)

"War is part of the divinely appointed order. . . . War is both justifiable and moral, and the idea of perpetual peace is not only impossible but also immoral." — TREITSCHKE, *Politics*, 1916, II, 597, 599. (Treitschke for many years had been a leader among German historians.)

"We must strenuously combat the peace propaganda. . . . War is a political necessity. . . . Without war there could be neither racial nor cultural progress.

"*Might is the supreme right*, and what is right is decided by war.

"It is presumptuous to think a weak nation is to have the same right to live as a powerful and vigorous nation.

"The inevitableness and . . . the blessedness of war, as the indispensable law of development, must be repeatedly emphasized." — BERNHARDI, a Prussian general, in his book, *The Next War*, in 1912.

"It is only by trust in our good sword that we shall be able to maintain that place in the sun which belongs to us, *and which the world does not seem very willing to allow us.*" — CROWN PRINCE, in *Deutschland in Waffen*, 1913.

"Do not forget the civilizing task which Providence assigns us. Just as Prussia was destined to be the nucleus of Germany, so the new Germany shall be the nucleus of a future Empire of the West. . . . We will successively annex Denmark, Holland, Belgium, . . . and finally northern France. . . . No coalition in the world can stop us." — SCHELLENDORF, Prussian War-Minister, in 1872.

"The salvation of Germany can be attained only by the annihilation of the smaller states." — TREITSCHKE, *Politics*.

And so on almost without end. Says Guy Stanton Ford in his Foreword to *Conquest and Kultur*,[1] a notable collection of these evil teachings:

[1] A volume of 171 pages that should be in every school library. Issued by the United States Committee on Public Information, and printed at Washington by the Government Printing Office.

"It is a motley throng who are here heard in praise of war and international suspicion and conquest and intrigue and devastation — emperors, kings, princes, poets, philosophers, educators, journalists, legislators, manufacturers, militarists, statesmen. Line upon line, precept upon precept, they have written this ritual of envy and broken faith and rapine. Before them is the war god to whom they have offered up their reason and their humanity; behind them, the misshapen image they have made of the German people, leering with bloodstained visage over the ruins of civilization."

True, in other lands, even in America, lonely voices are heard speaking this same doctrine of insolent and ruthless Might. But in these other lands any such occasional voice is smothered at once by storms of indignant rebuke. In Germany, for fifty years, this war-worship encountered almost no protest — except a feeble one from the Socialists. True again, no great country — not England or France or America — has been *wholly* free from greed for territory and for trade, — just such greed as lies at the root of most wars. But in these lands the time is past when public opinion will support an aggressive war, especially with a civilized people, waged *openly and avowedly* to satisfy such low ambitions. **Meanwhile, Germany, led by her war-besotted prophets, had been zealously making ready** for just such wars of greed.

No one must think that this teaching was mere talk. Said a member of the American Embassy in Belgium: "They [the Germans] fight, not because they are forced to, but because, curiously enough, they believe much of their talk. That is one of the dangers of the Germans to which the world is exposed: they really believe much of what they say." (Vernon Kellogg in the *Atlantic Monthly*, August, 1917.)

Testimony from a German Liberal

Ottfried Nippold, a Liberal professor in one of the German universities, shocked by the prevalence of this evil teaching, published a book against it in 1913. Said he: "A systematic stimulation of the war spirit is going on. . . . War is represented to us not merely as a possibility that might arise, but as a necessity that must come, and the sooner the better. . . . To them [the war party] war is quite a normal institution, not a means to be resorted to only in case of great necessity."

And from a French secret agent

And a French secret agent who had spent much time in studying opinion in Germany made an exhaustive report to his own government in a secret document in 1913. In a summary, he listed among the forces in Germany making for war:

> (1) The junkers, "who wish to escape the (new) taxes" that must be extended to their class if peace continues, and who "realize with dread the growing power of democracy and of the Socialists, and consider their own class rule doomed" without war.
>
> (2) The capitalist class — the manufacturers of big guns and armor plate; the merchants who demand bigger markets; all who regard war as good business, including those manufacturers who declare that the difficulties between them and their workmen originate in France, "the home of revolutionary ideas of freedom."
>
> (3) The universities, which teach war philosophy.

The same report declared: "There are forces making for peace, but they are unorganized, and have no popular leaders. They comprise *the bulk of the artisans and peasants;* but they have almost no influence. They are *silent* social forces, passive and defenseless against the infection of a wave of warlike feeling."

German hatred for England

And even those parts of the population not easily converted to the doctrine of aggressive war — the peasants and the Socialist city workers — were at least taught by constant iteration to hate England because of her leadership in trade, and to fear Russia's growing numbers, and so to accept the idea that war was unavoidable.

True, wherever the English flag floated, German traders and German ships were given freely every chance open to English traders, in honest accord with England's advanced doctrine of free trade and free seas. But English enterprise still led in world commerce. German conceit could explain this only by belief in some secret, gigantic trickery by their rivals. Moreover the molders of German opinion taught that England hated and feared Germany, and would welcome a chance to destroy her. Between 1912 and 1914, to be sure, the German ambassador to England, Prince Lichnowsky,[1] repeatedly assured his government of England's friendly and pacific feeling. English manufacturers and merchants, he said, felt no bitter envy of the swift advance of German prosperity, but saw instead that such advance made Germany a better customer for English products.

In 1912 English statesmen suggested that the two countries should cease their ruinous race in building warships. Lichnowsky wrote to Berlin that the proposal was made in perfect good faith. England, he said, would undoubtedly try to keep her lead in naval power, so absolutely necessary to her safety as an island state, but she had no desire to use her navy except to preserve peace. But these communications were out of tune with the purpose of the German government, and they never reached the German people.

English attempts to keep the peace

In 1912 there were other long negotiations between German and English governments, of which the people at that time knew nothing. The English statesmen offered to sign a declaration that England would not be a party to any *attack* upon Germany. This did not satisfy the Germans. They insisted that England should promise neutrality in a European war, no matter how it might come. To have done this would have been to desert France, and to make it more likely that Germany would attack. Very properly, and in the interests of peace, the English government refused such a shameful compact.

[1] This remarkable German, a cultivated and able Liberal, wholly free from the spirit of German jingoism, had been selected for the position apparently in order to blind English opinion as to Germany's warlike aims. When the war came, he found himself in disgrace with the Kaiser and the German court; and at the opening of the second year of the war (August, 1916) he wrote an account of his London mission for *private* circulation among his friends, to justify himself in their eyes. A copy fell into the hands of the Allies during the next year, and became at once one of the most valuable proofs of German guilt in forcing on the war.

Germany's preparedness

As Bismarck prepared his "Trilogy of Wars," of which he boasted so insolently, in order to make Prussia mistress of Germany, so after 1890, even more deliberately, Kaiser Wilhelm and his advisers prepared vaster war to make Germany mistress of the world. They hoarded gold in the war chest; heaped up arms and munitions, and huge stocks of raw materials, to manufacture more; secretly tried out new military inventions on a vast scale, — submarines, Zeppelins, poison gases, new explosives; created a navy in a race to best England's; bound other ruling houses to their own by marriage or by placing Hohenzollerns directly on the throne — in Russia, Greece, Bulgaria, Roumania; reorganized the Turkish Empire and filled offices in the army and navy there with Germans; permeated every great country, in the Old World and the New, with an insidious and treacherous system of spies in the guise of friendly business shielded by innocent hospitality; and secured control of banking syndicates and of newspapers in foreign lands, especially in Italy and America, so as to influence public opinion.

In June, 1914, the Kiel Canal was finally opened to the passage of the largest ships of war. Now Germany was ready, and her warlords were growing anxious to use their preparation before it grew stale — and before France and Russia, somewhat alarmed now, should have time to put into effect their new army laws (p. 574). Moreover war, better than anything else, would quiet the rising feeling in Germany, especially among the Socialists, against militarism.[1]

Why Germany did not fight sooner

Germany, we know now, had seriously considered precipitating war on several recent occasions connected with *colonial* questions[2] in Africa; but her leaders prudently preferred a first

[1] See C. Altschul's *German Militarism and Its German Critics*, No. 13 in the War Information Series.

[2] The two Morocco crises, 1905–1906 and 1911, were each caused by a brutal German show of force. War was averted the first time only by studious French moderation, and, the second time, by England's plain declaration that she would side with France. See War Encyclopedia under "Morocco," and Harding's *Great War*, Ch. ii, III.

war in which England would not be likely to join, so that the Teutonic empires might have only France and Russia to deal with at one time. Almost any colonial problem would concern England, who had been a chief party in the many European conferences that had adjusted colonial disputes. In the Balkans, however, England had shown no selfish interest for many years, and it was easy to believe that she would not fight upon a Balkan question.

The Serajevo murders, June 28, 1914

And now came just the kind of occasion the German warlords wished. Ever since its unjust seizure by Austria, Bosnia had been seething with conspiracies against Austrian rule. June 28, 1914, the heir to the Austrian throne, the Archduke Francis, and his wife were assassinated while in Bosnia by some of these conspirators — who, it is now known, included Serb officers.

Europe was aghast. Horror at the dastardly murder was mingled with fear of a great European war. Austria, it was known, was greedy for Serb territory. But if she used this murder as an excuse to attack Serbia, Russia would surely defend that country. And a conflict between Austria and Russia could not but draw in at once Germany and France, and perhaps others.

The month of quiet

Austria had long looked upon her unruly little neighbor to the south very much as some Americans look upon Mexico. Now Austrian papers loudly declared Serbia responsible for the murder, inasmuch as she had not suppressed societies of conspirators within her borders agitating for Bosnian liberation. But a month passed quietly before the Austrian government took any action, and European fears died down. That month, we know now on German evidence,[1] was used in ceaseless but

[1] July 5 there was held at Potsdam a secret conference of military authorities, bankers, and manufacturers of munitions, and so on; and a war program was decided upon. When the story leaked out, German papers denied it vehemently; but before the war closed, the truth of the meeting was well established by German evidence. The money kings asked a month's delay that they might "mobilize" their finances, turning foreign bonds into cash.

secret preparation to strike. Then, absolutely without warning, Austria sent to little Serbia an "ultimatum" harsh almost beyond belief, and in the next twelve days a world war was launched.

The Austrian ultimatum, July 23

Austria made ten demands, which may be summed up under three heads:

1. That Serbia suppress all agitation against Austria in newspapers, schools, and organizations of any sort.
2. That she agree to dismiss from her schools, from her army, and from her administration any teacher or official to whom Austria might object.
3. That she permit Austrian officials to become part of the Serbian government so far as necessary to attend to these foregoing provisions, and that she allow such officials to sit in Serbian courts to judge Serbians accused of connection with the murders of June 28.

The Austrian ambassador at Belgrade told the Serbian government that it must accept these terms without reservations *within 48 hours*. The German Socialist, Karl Liebknecht, at once said bravely that the demands "were more brutal than any ever made upon any civilized state in all human history" and that they were "intended to provoke war" (*Vorwärts*, July 25); but the German government stoutly supported Austria. Serbia, after trying vainly to get the time limit extended, made a humble and conciliatory reply, accepting the harsh Austrian terms except those under 3 above. These plainly would have reduced her to a mere vassal of Austria. But even these she offered to refer to longer negotiation or to arbitration. This reply the Austrian ambassador declared "dishonest and evasive," and he at once left Serbia.

Serbia's conciliatory reply

The Austrian demands had been sent to the Serbian government in the evening of July 23, too late to allow any consideration until the next day — especially as the Serbian ministers were scattered over the country in a political campaign. The Serbian reply was handed to the Austrian ambassador July 25, at 5:58 P.M. He and his whole staff left Belgrade from the railroad station at 6:30. He knew that his terms could not be accepted, and his staff must have been packed up, hat in hand.

Secret minutes of a meeting of the Austrian ministry of July 9 (just now published, in December 1919, by the new Government of Austria) prove that German aid had just been promised by the Kaiser. The Austrian ministry, except for one Hungarian, wished to invade Serbia at once without even a declaration of war. The Hungarian opposition resulted in this policy of sending an ultimatum, but one intended to be rejected.

England's attempt for peace balked by Germany

England, France, and Russia had been making every effort to get these extreme concessions from Serbia, in the interest of peace. Now England repeatedly asked Germany to help preserve peace by getting Austria to accept Serbia's submission or by referring the matter to arbitration, or at least to an informal discussion among representatives of the Great Powers, so as to try to come to an agreement. Germany professed to desire peace but found objections to each suggestion made by England, while she failed to accept England's request, that she herself suggest some plan.

The German ambassador at London, Lichnowsky, believed that if his country had wished peace, a settlement could easily have been secured, and, we know now, he "strongly backed" the English proposals, but in vain. "We insisted on war," he says in his account to his friends; "the impression grew that we wanted war under any circumstances. It was impossible to interpret our attitude in any other way." And again, "I had to support in London a policy the wickedness of which I recognized. That brought down vengeance upon me, because it was a sin against the Holy Ghost." [1]

The ten days, July 28–August 2

So passed the first four days, while the world held its breath. July 28, Austria declared war upon Serbia. Russia at once began to mobilize [2] troops on the Austrian frontier, — notify-

[1] Remember that this was written when the war was only a year old.

[2] In each European country "mobilization" was understood. Each of the millions of men in the Active Reserves would receive notice — through local authorities, who had been notified a few hours earlier by the central government, to report at a given hour at a given place. At that time and place the necessary officers would be present to organize the men, as

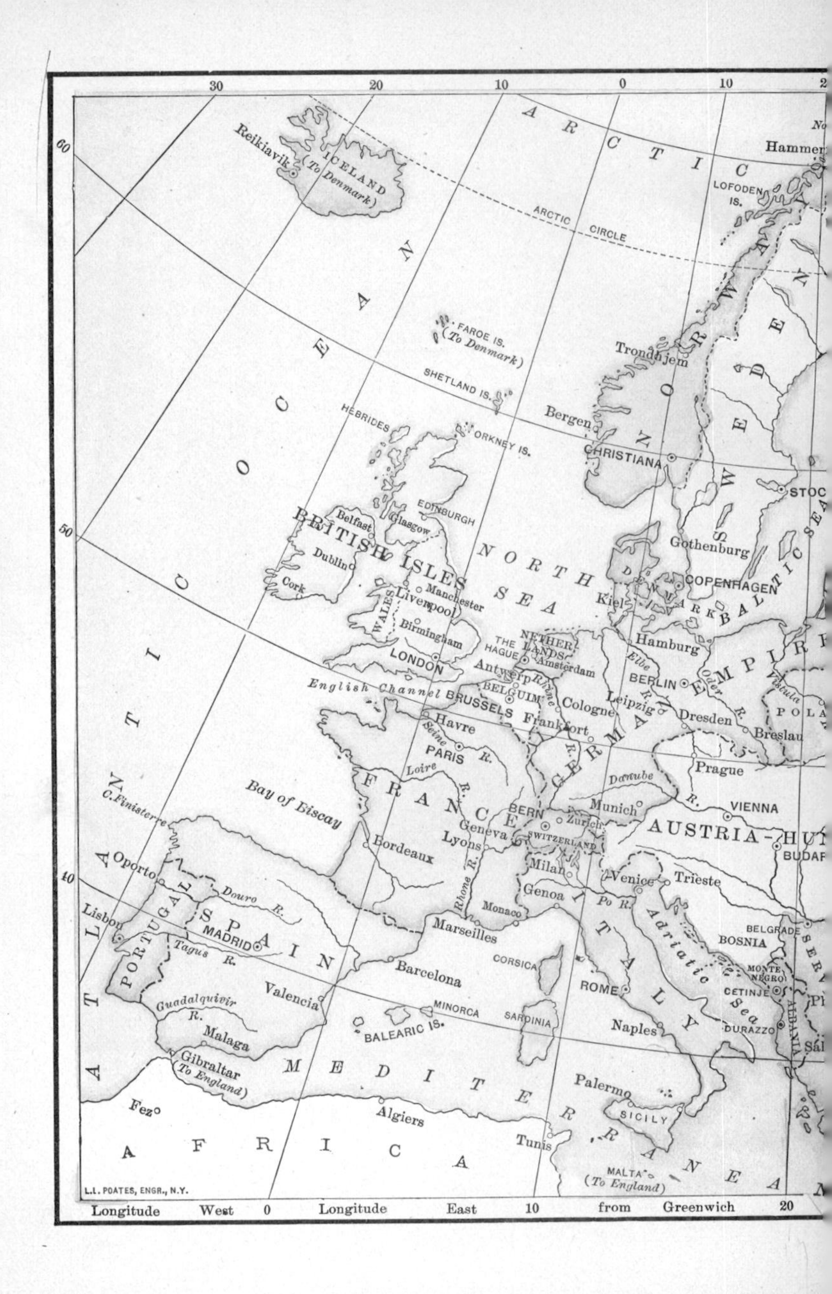

ATLANTIC OCEAN
ARCTIC
ARCTIC CIRCLE
Reikiavik
ICELAND (To Denmark)
FAROE IS. (To Denmark)
SHETLAND IS.
HEBRIDES
ORKNEY IS.
BRITISH ISLES
EDINBURGH
Glasgow
Belfast
Dublin
Cork
Manchester
Liverpool
WALES
Birmingham
LONDON
NORTH SEA
English Channel
Hammer
LOFODEN IS.
NORWAY
SWEDEN
Trondhjem
Bergen
CHRISTIANA
STOC
Gothenburg
DENMARK
COPENHAGEN
BALTIC SEA
Kiel
Hamburg
NETHERLANDS
THE HAGUE
Amsterdam
Antwerp
BELGIUM
BRUSSELS
Cologne
Frankfort
Elbe R.
BERLIN
Oder R.
Vistula
Leipzig
Dresden
Breslau
POLA
GERMAN EMPIRE
Prague
Havre
Seine R.
PARIS
Loire R.
FRANCE
Bay of Biscay
Bordeaux
Lyons
Rhone R.
Geneva
BERN
Zurich
SWITZERLAND
Munich
Danube R.
VIENNA
AUSTRIA-HU
BUDAP
Milan
Venice
Trieste
Genoa
Po R.
Monaco
Marseilles
C. Finisterre
Oporto
PORTUGAL
Douro R.
Lisbon
SPAIN
MADRID
Tagus R.
Guadalquivir R.
Malaga
Gibraltar (To England)
Valencia
Barcelona
CORSICA
BALEARIC IS.
MINORCA
SARDINIA
ITALY
ROME
Naples
Adriatic Sea
BELGRADE
BOSNIA
SERV
MONTENEGRO
CETINJE
ALBANIA
DURAZZO
MEDITERRANEAN
Palermo
SICILY
MALTA (To England)
Tunis
Algiers
Fez
AFRICA
L.L. POATES, ENGR., N.Y.
Longitude West 0 Longitude East 10 from Greenwich 20

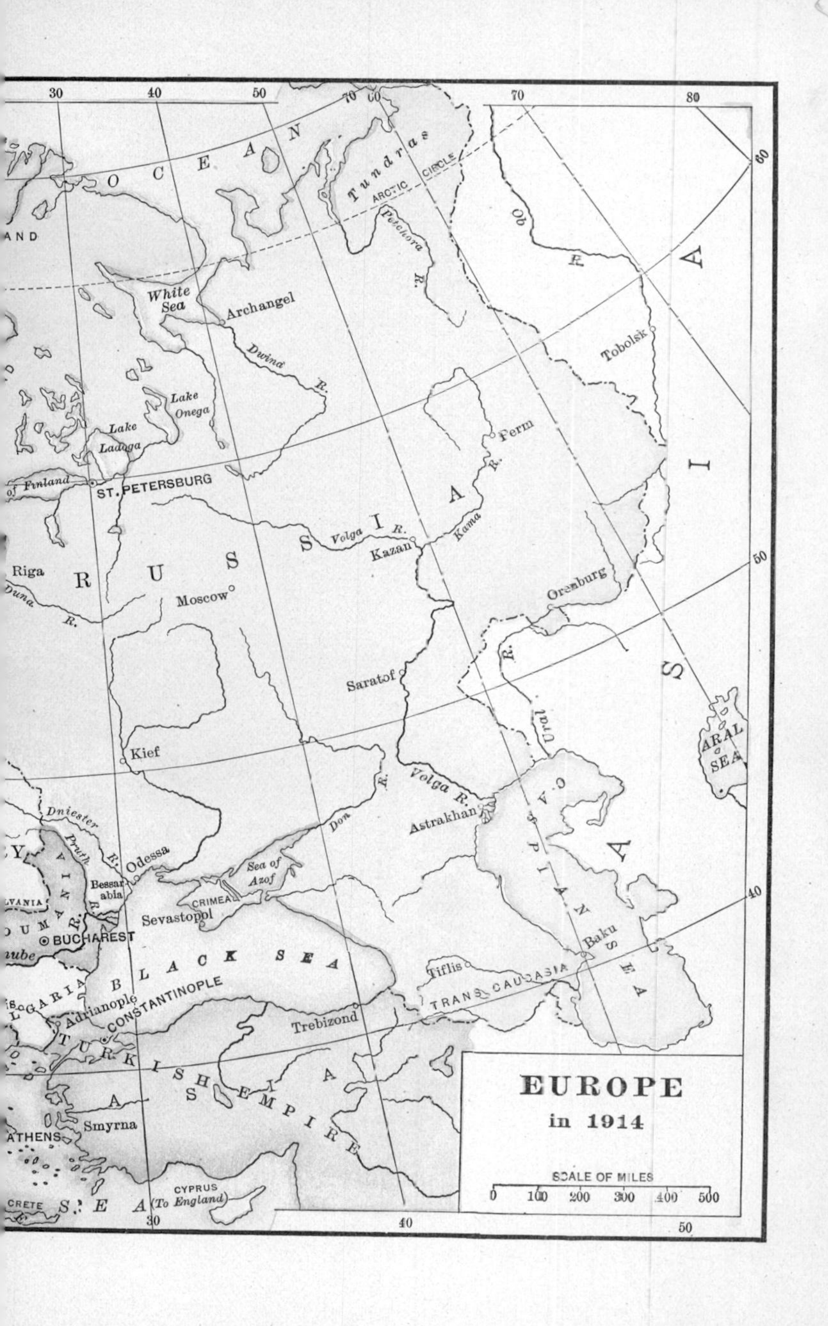
EUROPE
in 1914
SCALE OF MILES
0 100 200 300 400 500
OCEAN
Tundras
ARCTIC CIRCLE
Petchora R.
Ob R.
White Sea
Archangel
Dwina R.
Lake Onega
Lake Ladoga
Finland
ST. PETERSBURG
RUSSIA
ASIA
Tobolsk
Perm
Kama R.
Volga R.
Kazan
Riga
Duna R.
Moscow
Orenburg
Saratof
Ural R.
ARAL SEA
Kief
Volga R.
Astrakhan
Don R.
Dniester R.
Pruth R.
Odessa
Sea of Azof
CRIMEA
Sevastopol
Bessarabia
ROUMANIA
BUCHAREST
BLACK SEA
CASPIAN SEA
Baku
Tiflis
TRANS CAUCASIA
BULGARIA
Adrianople
CONSTANTINOPLE
Trebizond
TURKISH EMPIRE
ASIA
Smyrna
ATHENS
CRETE
SEA
CYPRUS (To England)

ing Germany that this act was in no way hostile to her, and also that no warlike action would be taken against Austria so long as that country permitted Serbia to continue negotiations for peace. Germany brusquely demanded that Austria be allowed her will with Serbia without Russian interference.

Austria hesitates

July 30 and 31, Russia offered, twice, to stop her slow preparations if Austria would promise to exact only a moderate punishment from Serbia and not to destroy that little country's independence. Now for the first time Austria seemed ready to yield somewhat. And so Germany, which all along had willed the war, had to come into the open to force it on. For some days (ever since July 21) she had secretly been concentrating troops on her western frontier, ready to strike France; and on the evening of July 29 a secret war council at Potsdam overruled the Kaiser's last eleventh-hour hesitation. August 1, Germany declared war upon Russia,[1] after an insulting twelve-hour ultimatum demanding instant demobilization.

Germany forces the war

At the same time Germany gave France 18 hours in which to promise to abandon Russia to her fate, and was ready further to demand that France surrender certain fortresses during the war as a guarantee of good faith. The next day (August 2)

they arrived, into military units; and transportation would be ready to move each unit to a larger rendezvous. Arms, munitions, cannons, machine guns, food, clothing, and transportation for all these things must also be in readiness.

[1] See Davis' *Roots of the War*, 510–512, for the story of a trick by which Germany had frightened the Tsar into a more warlike attitude. See also Harding, *Great War*, Ch. III. Liebknecht at the time declared the fact: "The decision rests with William II. . . . But the war-lords are at work . . . without a qualm of conscience . . . to bring about a monstrous world war, the devastation of Europe" (*Vorwärts*, July 30, 1914). A few months later, Liebknecht tried to distribute leaflets among the German people to tell them how the government had suppressed knowledge of the peaceful aims of Russia and England.

Week by week, as these lines are written, proof comes to light that leading Russian statesmen had been plotting for war as directly as the German government had (especially Sazanov, minister to France, and later the favorite of the Peace Congress). But as the crisis drew on, the Tsar seems to have clung to peace, either from his timidity or from a revival of his old attachment to peace.

German troops occupied neutral Luxemburg and began to mass upon the Belgian frontier; and the German government gave Belgium 12 hours (7 P.M. to 7 A.M.) to decide whether she would permit German troops to cross her territory so as to find an unguarded road into France. August 3, receiving no reply from France to her dishonorable proposals, Germany declared war upon that country and invaded Belgium, charging falsely that France had violated that territory — in face of the fact that, to avoid any clash through hotheadedness, France had withdrawn her troops everywhere six miles within her borders.

Hypocrisy of the German counter-charges

Reckless falsehood and hypocritical charges against others were the method used by Germany throughout to justify herself. Says Brand Whitlock, American ambassador to Belgium, recounting a long list of such pretended excuses in those days: — "When he (the German) wished to invade Belgium, he said (falsely) that French aviators had thrown bombs on Nuremberg [meaning that they had flown over Belgium to do so]. When he wished to sack and destroy Louvain, he said (falsely) that civilians had fired on him. When he wished to use asphyxiating gas, he said (falsely) the French were using it. The thing that vitiated the whole character of modern Germany . . . was the lie." Upright Germans themselves saw this. As early as 1909 the Socialist Scheidemann dared to say in the Reichstag that lying was "the most characteristic trait of the Hohenzollerns." And all will remember how Bismarck boasted of the forgery by which he tricked France into war in his day.

Belgium resists

Germany had promised, in case Belgium consented to the passage of her troops, to make good all damage, but had threatened the most savage consequences if her demand were refused. Belgium had replied with heroic dignity. Her neutrality had been solemnly and repeatedly guaranteed by the Great Powers, including Prussia,[1] and now she herself was ready to

[1] Prussia was a party to the original treaty of 1839, guaranteeing Belgium from invasion by any country, and also to its renewal in 1870; and the German Empire in 1871 accepted for itself all Prussia's international obligations.

suffer martyrdom to defend that neutrality, as she was in honor bound to do.

Belgium also at once appealed to England; and England (August 3) let Germany know that the invasion of Belgium must stop or England would declare war, as bound by the most solemn obligations. Chancellor Bethmann-Hollweg, was grievously chagrined. He had believed that "shop-keeping England" would refuse to fight; and he expressed bitterly to the departing English ambassador his amazement that England should enter the war "just for a scrap of paper."

The next day (August 4) in his address to the Reichstag, the Chancellor himself admitted Germany's guilt. "Necessity knows no law. Gentlemen, this [invasion of Belgium] is a breach of international law. . . . We knew France stood ready for an invasion [a false statement]. The wrong — I speak openly — the wrong we thereby commit, we will try to make good as soon as our military ends have been attained."

England "goes in"

The same day England "went in." England, it is to be hoped, would not in any case have looked on, to see France crushed, but she might have held off too long except for the German crime against Belgium. This was Germany's fatal blunder. And the consciousness that she had blundered called out among almost all classes a frenzy of hate for England — whose overthrow in a later war, it was now openly avowed, had been the real goal all along. France was to have been crushed first, to leave England alone and to enable Germany to launch her attack upon England from near-by French ports like Calais. From this time, too, the credulous German masses were taught zealously that England had willed the war from the first and had tricked a peace-loving Germany into it! "May God blast England" became the almost universal form of daily greeting.

Germany furious

Germany had indeed been tricked, but only by her own greed and conceit and her own silly contempt for others. After all, however, Germany was prepared "to the last shoe lace," and her opponents, with all the warning they had had, were not prepared. Least of all was England ready for war. She had no army worth mentioning — only a few scattered and distant garrisons; and, what was worse, she had no arms for her eager volunteers, and no factories worth mention to make munitions.

War aims of the two parties

Soon both parties claimed to be fighting for peace. But German leaders made it plain that they looked only to a sort of peace won by making Germany so supreme in the world that no other power could possibly dream of withstanding or disobeying her. The old balance of power theory was bad enough; but infinitely worse was this German theory of peace through slavery. Said Chancellor Bethmann-Hollweg (May 28, 1915): "We must endure till we have gained every possible guarantee so that none of our enemies — not alone, not united — will again dare a trial of strength with us."

Opposed to this ideal of a peace by force, English statesmen — like President Wilson later — set up at once the ideal of a peace of righteousness, and taught that the war was "a war to end war." Said Premier Asquith, November 9, 1914:

"We shall never sheathe the sword which we have not lightly drawn until Belgium recovers in full measure all and more than all that she has sacrificed, until France is adequately secured against the menace of aggression, until the rights of the smaller nationalities of Europe are placed upon an unassailable foundation, and until military domination of Prussia is wholly and finally destroyed."

And said Sir Edward Grey, the English Foreign Minister, January 26, 1916, in the House of Commons:

"The great object to be attained . . . is that there shall not again be this sort of militarism in Europe, which in time of peace causes the whole of the continent discomfort by its continual menace, and then, when it thinks the moment has come that suits itself, plunges the continent into war."

And again, six months later to an American newspaperman:

"What we and our allies are fighting for is a free Europe. We want a Europe free, not only from the domination of one nationality by another, but from hectoring diplomacy and the peril of war; free from the constant rattling of the sword in the scabbard, from perpetual talk of shining armor, and war lords. We are fighting for equal rights; for law, justice, peace; for civilization throughout the world, as against brute force."

For Further Reading. — In the flood of printed matter regarding the background of the war, the difficulty is to select. The following suggestions are made with particular view to their permanent value and at the same time to their suitability for the general reader: *I Accuse* (by an anonymous German), esp. 26–141; J. E. Barker's *Modern Germany*, 297–317, 798–829; W. S. Davis' *Roots of the War*, chs. xvii, xviii, xix; J. W. Gerard's *My Four Years in Germany*, chs. iv, v; Prince Lichnowsky's *Memoirs;* Gibbons' *New Map of Europe*, esp. pp. 1–367. For evidence that the German government was preparing for immediate war even before June 28, see S. B. Harding's *Great War*, ch. iii, **V, VI**; and on Belgium's neutrality, the same, ch. vi, **III**.

CHAPTER XLVI

THE FIRST YEAR, 1914

The German plan

The Germans had planned a short war. They expected (1) to go through Belgium swiftly with little opposition, and to take Paris within four weeks; (2) then to swing their strength against Russia before that unwieldy power could get into the war effectively, and crush her; and (3) with the Channel ports at command, to bring England easily to her knees, if she should really enter the war.

Foiled by Belgium

Thanks to Belgium, the first of these expectations fell through — and the others fell with it. The Germans had allowed *six* days to march through Belgium. But for *sixteen* days little Belgium, alone in her agony, under the command of her hero king, Albert, held back mighty Germany. When the French began mobilization, after August 2, they began it to meet an honest attack through Lorraine; but before the Belgians were quite crushed, the French managed to shift enough force to the north, along with a hurried and poorly equipped "Expeditionary Army" of 100,000 from England, to delay the German advance through northern France for three weeks more — ground that the German plan had allowed eight days to win. Tremendously outnumbered, outflanked, trampled into the dust in a ceaseless series of desperate battles, the thin lines of Allied survivors fell back doggedly toward the Marne. There Joffre, the French commander-in-chief, was collecting all resources for his final stand.

The battle of the Marne

The Germans drove on furiously, outrunning even their supply trains. September 3, the French government withdrew to Bordeaux. But September 6, when the boastful invaders were in sight of the towers of Paris, only 20 miles away, their guns thundering almost in the suburbs, the French and English turned at bay in a colossal battle along a two-hundred-mile front. Joffre issued to all corps commanders his famous order: "The hour has come to let yourselves be killed rather than to yield ground. Troops must let themselves be shot down where they stand rather than retreat." The crisis came on the fourth day when the Germans, anxious to use their superior numbers in an enveloping movement around both the Allied wings, had perilously weakened their center. With true military genius, General Foch, a trusted lieutenant of Joffre's, divined the situation, and hurled his exhausted troops desperately at that key-position. Even then, only splendid resolution won the day. Joffre had sent an anxious inquiry to ask Foch's situation. The dogged Foch telegraphed back hastily: "My right is beaten back; my center is crushed; my left has been repulsed. *Situation excellent.* I am attacking again with my left." And when a subordinate reported, "My men are exhausted," Foch replied curtly, "So are the enemy. Attack!" This time, the attack broke the invader's line.

To save themselves from destruction, the Germans retreated hastily to the line of the Aisne. Later attempts by them to resume the offensive failed; but the Allies were too exhausted to dislodge them. Both sides "dug in" along a 360-mile front, from Switzerland to the North Sea. Then began a "trench warfare," new in history. The positions stabilized, and, on the whole, in spite of repeated and horrible slaughter, were not materially altered on this Western front until the final months of the war four years later.

New methods of warfare

New and ever more terrible ways of fighting marked this warfare, with increasing ferocity and horror from month to month. Ordinary cannon were replaced by huge new guns whose high explosives blasted the whole landscape into indescribable and irretrievable ruin — burying whole battalions alive, and forming great craters where snipers found the best shelter in future advances. Ordinary defense works were elaborated into many lines of connected trenches beneath the earth, protected by mazy entanglements of barbed wire and strengthened at intervals by bomb-proof "dugouts" and underground chambers of heavy timbers and cement. To plow through these intrenchments, cavalry gave way to monstrous, heavily armored motor-tanks. New guns belched deadly poison gases, slaying whole regiments in horrible strangling torture when the Germans first used this devilish device, in April, 1915, — until English and French chemists invented gas masks that afforded fair protection if donned in time — and infernal "flame-throwers" wrapped whole ranks in liquid fire. Scouting was done, and gunfire directed, by airplanes equipped with new apparatus for wireless telegraphy and for photography; and daily these aërial scouts, singly or in fleets, met in deadly combat ten thousand feet above the ground, — combat that ended only when one or both went hurtling down in flames to crashing destruction. Worse than these terrors even, the soldiers dreaded the beastly filthiness of trench war; the never absent smell of rotting human flesh; the torture of vermin; the dreary monotony.

The East front in 1914

The original German plan had been wrecked at the Marne, and that name now ranks with Marathon. The Russians had mobilized more swiftly than friend or foe had believed possible, and were swarming into East Prussia, threatening Austria. August 26 they were defeated ruinously at Tannenberg by Hindenburg, a Prussian veteran of 1870, with the most fearful slaughter ever known in one battle in all history; but against the Austrians they fared better. After winning a great battle on the frontier, they forced their way into Austrian Galicia and captured Lemberg. Germany was forced to divert troops from France to succor her Austrian ally during the rest of the campaign, and when the year 1914 closed, the Russians were holding their own in Poland, with good prospects of renewing the invasion of the Austrian realms.

Austria had another pressing job. The story of the hatching of the war makes clear why she felt it necessary promptly to crush Serbia. That little country of fighters, however, supplied with necessary munitions by the other Allies through Saloniki, had repulsed two Austrian invasions, and now all Austrian soldiers were needed to meet the peril in Galicia.

Meantime Turkey had joined the Central Powers. We know now that Turkey made a formal war alliance with

MOSQUE OF SULEIMAN I and adjacent parts of Constantinople, in 1914.

Turkey joins the Teutonic empires

Germany at the opening of the struggle (August 4); but it was thought best to keep this secret for a time. In October, however, two German warships, fleeing from an English squadron, received shelter within the Dardanelles. The German ambassador then carried through a fictitious sale of these ships to "neutral" Turkey; and, flying the Turkish flag but manned by their old crew and officers, the two vessels raided Russian Odessa. Accordingly, in November, England, France, and Russia declared war on Turkey. At this time, the Ottoman state was still shut off from its Teutonic allies by a broad belt of neutral or hostile Balkan territory, and, isolated as it was, England and Russia hoped soon to crush it.

Germany turns back to the West front

In the West, after it became plain that a deadlock had developed, the German government realized the need of attacking England directly without waiting to annihilate France. In August and September, British sea-power had swept German shipping from the seas. If the war was to be a long one, this strangling of German commerce would be decisive. Hence the attack upon England must be tried at once if any possible base could be won. As a necessary step, the Germans turned to complete their conquest of the Belgian coast. King Albert of Belgium and the bulk of his heroic little army were still holding Antwerp. The huge German siege guns now beat to powder the protecting forts, and the invaders captured that city on October 9, — though in their exulting parade they foolishly permitted the Belgian army to escape towards France. Immediately after, they secured the port of Ostend and most of the rest of the Belgian coast.

To attack England successfully, however, against her unconquerable fleet, Germany needed better and nearer ports for a base, — at least Dunkirk and Calais; and October 16 they began the four weeks' *Battle of the Yser* in order to force the last natural barrier protecting those Channel ports. Checked by the cutting of the dykes, they next brought their force against the thin English lines near Ypres. The gallant resistance offered the magnificent "Prussian Guards" in the *First Battle of Ypres* by the outnumbered and ill-armed English makes one of the most heroic stories in all history. In vain, day after day for a long month, with slight intervals for preparation, did the overwhelming German forces deliver their reckless mass attacks upon the opponents whom they had styled "a contemptible little army." They wore themselves down upon that dying but unconquered line without ever becoming able to deliver a knock-out blow, losing more men than the total English force; and winter conditions set

But fails at the Yser and at Ypres

in, November 17, with the desired ports still in the hands of the Allies.

Close of the first season

Thus closed the first war-season. On the West front, Germany had failed. The French government had come back to Paris, and the French army was in perfect condition. England's gallant first army had died devotedly to gain her time; but the time had been fairly well used. England reorganized herself for war — built new munition factories — though not enough, time was to prove; poured forth gold lavishly for Russia and France; saved and suffered and toiled and drilled at home, and put into the field eventually a splendid fighting force of six million men, — a million ready for the second year. England had looked upon the war as a "beastly" interruption; but she was rapidly reorganizing her life on a war basis. True, deceived by a stupid censorship, she had not yet grasped the full danger, and was sadly behind, especially in the output of high explosives. But, from the first, her superb navy swept the seas, keeping the boastful German navy bottled up in harbor or in the South Baltic, and gradually running down the few German raiders that at first escaped to prey on British commerce. The blockade of Germany was not enforced rigidly, for fear of offending American opinion, but already it was creating a serious food problem for Germany. And on the other hand, America's resources in food and munitions, closed to Germany by the English navy, were all available to the Allies. Except for the English navy, Germany would have won the war in the second year.

The English navy

England's daughter-commonwealths join

Further, England's distant and peaceful daughter-commonwealths, — Canada, Australia, New Zealand, South Africa, and even her Indian Empire, — were rousing themselves splendidly to the defense of their common civilization. And Japan, England's ally in the Orient, had entered the war, to aggrandize herself by seizing Germany's holdings in China and many of her islands in the Pacific.

CHAPTER XLVII

THE SECOND YEAR, 1915

The danger of Russian collapse

At the opening of 1915, the chief danger to England and France was their too great trust in Russia, — their belief that the Russian "steam-roller," fully prepared, would now crush its way to Berlin or at least into Hungary. As a matter of fact, there was no ground for this expectation. Russia was near the end of her supply of munitions; and her industries were too primitive to cope with longer war. The minister of war, too, had secretly sold himself to Germany, and was doing his best to hinder military movements and to waste and misdirect the scanty supplies.[1] Similar treason permeated a large part of the official classes and the court circle, centering around the Hohenzollern wife of the Tsar.

The Germans, of course, understood this Russian situation — though the Allies did not. Accordingly they planned only to hold their trenches in the West, and to concentrate their energies in putting Russia quickly out of the war.

Necessity that the Allies secure the Dardanelles

Russia was almost isolated from the other Allies. Germany closed the Baltic; Turkey closed the Black Sea; Archangel was ice-closed during most of the year; and Vladivostok was so distant as to be almost negligible for the coming year. If Russia were to receive badly needed supplies, the Allies must force the Dardanelles and capture Constantinople. Success in this project in 1915 would have ended the war. The wavering Balkan states would have joined Russia. Turkey would

[1] Two years later this man was executed for high treason. Of Russia's four important munition factories, the largest was directly controlled, secretly, by Germany. And Ludendorff's Story of the War, now in print, discloses that the German victory at Tannenberg (p. 616) was due to the treason of a Russian general.

have been crushed. The conglomerate, ill-cemented Austrian Empire would have been open to invasion from the south; and the Allies must have won.

The attempt and failure

Thus both parties planned now to transfer the decisive struggle to the East front. The Allies were able to strike first. In February, the Allied navy attacked the Dardanelles. The outer forts were taken or battered down, but the inner fortresses resisted successfully. In March a more formidable attack all but succeeded. Had the Allies known how exhausted the Turkish ammunition was, they might have opened the straits. Not informed of this, however, and discouraged by heavy losses in ships, the navy now waited nearly two months for the arrival of land forces to coöperate in storming the Turkish defenses. When the British transports arrived, late in April, the Turks were perfectly prepared. British and Australian troops were landed, with horrible loss, under destructive fire; but the heroic attempts of the Anzacs[1] to storm the fortresses of the Gallipoli Peninsula failed deplorably. In August, the attempt was renewed, and came once more just short of decisive success. After this, there was no chance against the greatly strengthened Turkish positions.

The German drive against Russia

Meantime, in May, the Germans opened their drive against Russia in Galicia with the first enormous concentration of artillery in the war. The Russians were admirably commanded in the field, and they fought, as always, with reckless valor. But their cannon were useless from want of ammunition, and even with the infantry many a soldier had to wait until a comrade had fallen before he could get a gun to fight with. With amazing success, under the circumstances, their retreat was saved from becoming a rout. But the Austrians recaptured Lemberg in June, and the Germans took Warsaw early in August. The Teutonic armies then cleared most of eastern Poland of Russian garrisons before they halted their drive late in September, in order to attempt a more important drive on the southeast (below). Russia had lost an enormous

[1] *A*ustralian *N*ew *Z*ealand *A*uxiliary *C*orps.

number of lives, with a million and a half of prisoners; she had been driven out of a huge territory; and her offensive power had been destroyed for months to come.

Trench war on the West

On the West front, there was continuous trench fighting, with much loss of life, but the only important event of the year was the German offensive at Ypres (*Second Battle of Ypres*, April 17–May 17) where the English line was almost broken by the German asphyxiating gas, then first used in war. That the line held against this devilish attack was due largely to the splendid gallantry of the new Canadian divisions. Lack of high explosives kept the Allies from attempting a serious offensive until just before the season closed — in September — and the event proved that the supplies even then were insufficient to prepare the way for successful infantry attack, so that the only result was one more terrible lesson with pitiful sacrifice of lives.

Bulgaria joins the Central Empires

The Germans had stopped their triumphant progress into Russia only to avail themselves of a more attractive program. In October, Bulgaria finally joined the Central Powers (fear of Russia gone), hoping to wreak vengeance on Serbia for 1913 and to make herself the ruling state in the Balkans. Her secretly prepared army invaded Serbia from the east while a huge Teutonic force attacked from the north. Serbia had counted upon her treaty of 1913 with Greece for protection against possible Bulgarian attack. But King Constantine of Greece, brother-in-law of the German Kaiser, now repudiated that treaty and dismissed his prime minister, Venizelos, for desiring to keep Greece faithful to her ally. A Franco-British army had been sent to Saloniki, but, after the defection of Greece, it could accomplish nothing. In spite of their gallant resistance, the Serbs were overwhelmed. The survivors of their army made their way over the mountains of Albania to the coast, and were ferried across to Corfu by British ships. Serbia and Montenegro and much of Albania were occupied by the Bulgars and Teutons; and the Bulgarian atrocities toward the conquered populations during the next years exceeded anything those unhappy peoples had ever suffered from

Serbia is crushed

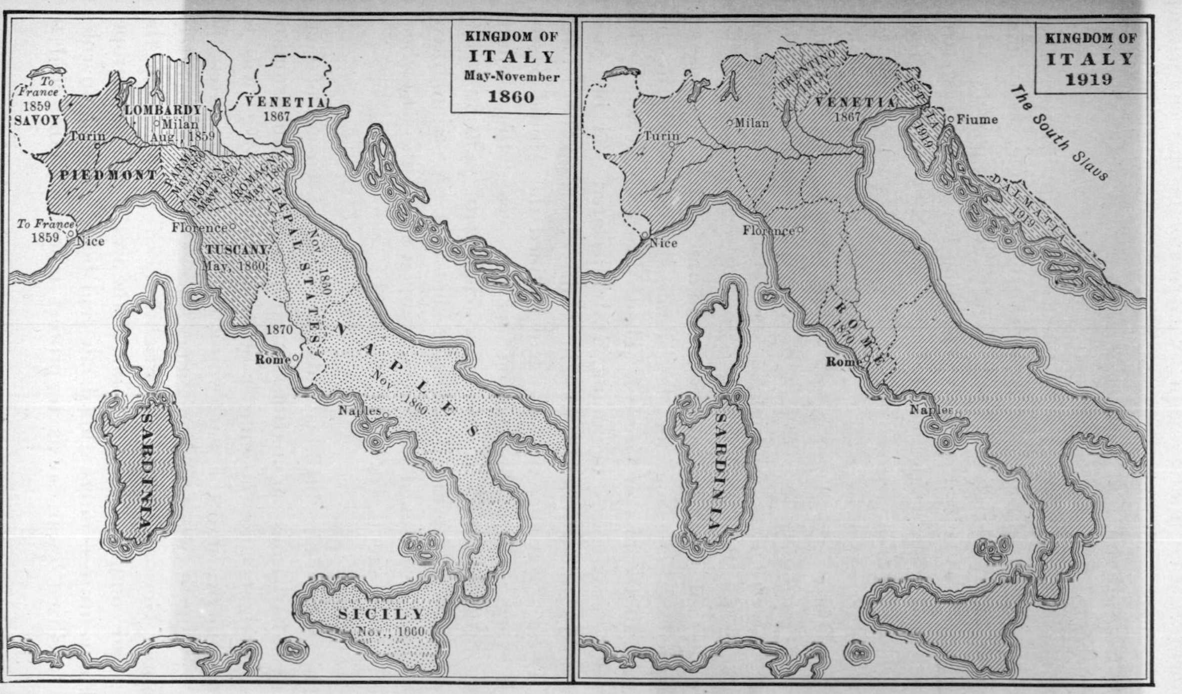

In July, 1859, Sardinia and Piedmont began to grow into the kingdom of Italy. For that growth before the World War, cf. pp. 398–401, 408–413, 417, 424. The additions marked 1919 were the price Italy demanded, and received, for joining the Allies — besides islands and Asiatic privileges not shown here.

the Turk. The military gain by Germany in this campaign was immense. She now dominated a solid broad belt of territory from Berlin and Brussels and Warsaw to Bagdad and Persia. (Cf. map. p. 655.)

Italy joins the Allies

This gloomy second year of the war brought to the Allies only one gain. From the outset of the struggle, Italy had repudiated the Triple Alliance. The Teutonic powers, who had forced on the war without consulting her in the least particular, had not expected help from her, but they did hope that she would remain neutral. The Italian government saw its opportunity to recover the "unredeemed" Italian territory about Triest and Trent — and more. When the Teutonic powers had refused its terms, it drove a hard bargain with the Allied governments, securing in a secret treaty (since known as the Secret Pact of London, April, 1915) promises for not only those districts but also for Dalmatia — at the expense of martyred Serbia — and for the islands she had seized in the Aegean, to the loss of Greece. Then May 23, just when the Russian retreat was beginning, Italy declared war on Austria, and launched her armies in a drive across the Isonzo for Triest. But the Austrians had fortified the Alpine passes with every modern device, and for two years the Italians made little advance, in spite of much gallant fighting. The threat of their advance, however, kept large Austrian forces busy, and so lessened the pressure upon the Allies elsewhere at critical moments. (Cf. maps, p. 623.)

Germany's "Frightfulness"

This same year, 1915, saw also a serious extension of Germany's barbarous submarine warfare, with the invasion of neutral rights and the murder of neutral lives. This was to bring America into the war two years later, and so hasten the close; but it was only one more phase of the deliberately adopted German policy of "Frightfulness," which from the first had compelled the attention of the world outside Europe.

For centuries, international law had been building up rules of "civilized" war, so as to protect non-combatants and to preserve some shreds of humanity among even the fighters. But German military rulers, for some years, had referred slurringly to such "moderation" as a deceitful attempt on the part of the weak to protect themselves against the strong. Humane considerations the official German War Manual referred to as flabby sentimentality.[1]

The first practical application of this German doctrine of Frightfulness had been given to the world in 1900. In that year a force of German soldiers set out to join forces from other European countries and from the United States in restoring order in China, after the massacre of Europeans there in the Boxer Rebellion. July 27 the Kaiser bade his troops farewell at Bremerhaven in a set address. In the course of that brutal speech he commanded them: "Show no mercy! Take no prisoners! As the *Huns* made a name for themselves which is still mighty in tradition, *so may you* by your deeds so *fix the name of German* in China that no Chinese shall ever again dare to look at a German askance. . . . Open the way for *Kultur*."[2]

The Kaiser's command to emulate the Huns

At the opening of the World War, this "Hun" policy was put into effect in Western Europe. Never since the ancient blood-spattered Assyrian monarchs stood exultingly on pyramids of mangled corpses had the world seen so huge a crime. Belgium and northeastern France were devastated. Whole villages of innocent non-combatants were wiped out, — men, women, children, burned in their houses or shot and bayo-

[1] Extracts in Harding, ch. vii, IV.

[2] The troops reached China too late to be of use. American, Japanese, French, and Italian troops had already restored order. But the Germans made a number of savage "punitive expeditions" for booty and rapine. In these they indulged not merely in indiscriminate murder of innocent non-combatants, but even in many indescribable outrages upon women. General Chaffee, the commander of the United States troops, and the senior officer among the Western forces, called together the commanders of the other allies, and then as their spokesman interviewed Von Waldersee, the German commander. Von Waldersee declared haughtily that there would be no change in his policy. His soldiers "must have some chance to indulge themselves." Said Chaffee: "We have not come to make requests, but to tell you that this sort of thing must stop." It stopped.

neted if they crept forth. All this by deliberate order of the "high command," like the frightfulness of the old Assyrians, to break the morale of the enemy, to make it easy to hold the conquered territory with a few soldiers, and to terrify neighboring small peoples — Dutch, Danes, Swiss — so that they might not dare risk a like fate.

Deliberate adoption of this policy in Belgium and France

War always develops brutes; and the terrible nerve strain of this war undoubtedly tended, more than ordinary war, to paralyze the moral sense and the will. The German soldiers, too, more than the soldiers of the Allies, had been brutalized by bestial treatment from their officers, and, without orders, they committed thousands of nameless outrages upon girls, and Sioux-Indian mutilations upon captives. But this, horrible as it was, leaves less stain upon Germany than the calm decision for this policy in cold blood by the polished and easy-living German rulers.

The Zeppelin raids

In like fashion, Zeppelins raided England, not mainly to destroy military depots, but to drop bombs upon resident parts of London and upon peaceful villages, murdering women and children. In the years 1915–1917, their aircraft raids murdered nearly 4000 non-combatants without accomplishing any military purpose.[1] So, too, German airplanes bombed hospitals and Red Cross trains, assassinating doctors and nurses along with the wounded soldiers; and soon the submarines began to torpedo hospital ships, clearly marked as such. Nor is it easy to find any imaginable crime against the war customs of all civilized nations that was not committed and boasted of by Germany within a few months after this war began. No wonder that even neutral lands began to know Germans no longer by the kindly "Fritz" but only by "Hun" or "Boche."[2]

[1] England long refused to adopt this barbarous policy, even for retaliation. She finally did so, somewhat later than France; but more efficient results were found in developing anti-aircraft guns and in the use of protecting airplanes, so that in the last years of the war a Zeppelin raid was too dangerous to be tried often.

[2] On all this, see *German War Practices* and *German Treatment of Conquered Territory*, volumes edited by Dana C. Munro and other well-known American historians, under the auspices of the Committee on Public Information.

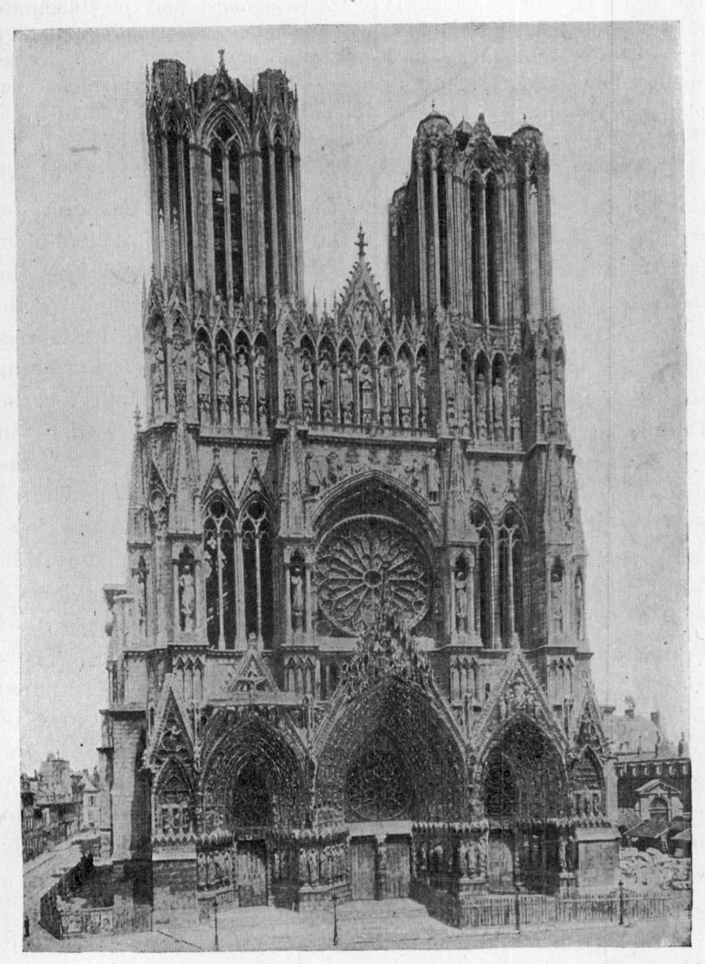

RHEIMS CATHEDRAL. This masterpiece of Gothic architecture was wantonly and seriously damaged by German shell fire in 1914 — in accordance with what seems a deliberate design to destroy art treasures that could not be carried away. This façade dates from the thirteenth century.

With German approval, and under the eyes of German officers, the Turks massacred a majority of the Armenians, and the Bulgarians massacred in wholesale fashion the non-combatant Serbian population. A word from Germany would have stopped these revolting excesses against humanity, which were upon a scale even huger than Germany's own crimes in the West, but which were committed by races from whom we do not expect "civilized" warfare.

America's long attempt at neutrality

To the United States, even more than to France or England, the war came as a surprise; and for some time its purposes and its origin were obscured by a skillful German propaganda in our press and on the platform. President Wilson issued the usual proclamation of neutrality, and followed this with unusual and solemn appeals to the American people for a real neutrality of feeling. For two years the administration clung to this policy. Any other course was made difficult for the President by the fact that many Democratic leaders in Congress were either pro-German or extreme pacifists. Moreover the President seems to have hoped that if the United States could keep apart from the struggle, it might, at the close, render mighty service to the world in a world-council to establish lasting world peace.

True, our best informed men and women saw at once that France and England were waging *our* war, battling and dying to save our ideals of free industrial civilization, and of common decency, from a militaristic despotism. Tens of thousands of young Americans, largely college men, made their way to the fighting line, as volunteers in the Canadian regiments, in the French "Foreign Legion," or in the "air service"; and hundreds of thousands more among us blushed with shame daily that other and weaker peoples should struggle and suffer in our cause while we stood idly by.

Forces for and against neutrality

But to other millions — long a majority — the dominant feeling was a deep thankfulness that our sons were safe from slaughter, our homes free from the horror of war. Nor was this attitude as strange or as grossly selfish then as it seems now. Vast portions of our people had neither cared nor known about the facts back of the war: to such, that mighty struggle between Wrong and Right was merely "a bloody *European* squabble." And even the better informed of our people found it not altogether easy to break with our century-long tradition of a happy aloofness from all Old-World quarrels.

Such indifference or apathy, however, needed a moral force to give it positive strength. And this moral force for neutrality was not wholly lacking. Many ardent workers, and some leaders, in all the great reform movements believed that in *any* war the attention of the nation would be diverted from the pressing need of progress at home. To them the first American gun would sound the knell, for their day, of all the reforms that they had long battled for. Still breathless from their lifelong wrestlings with Vested Wrongs, they failed to see that German militarism and despotism had suddenly towered into the one supreme peril to American life. And so many noble men, and some honored names, cast their weight for neutrality. And then, cheek by jowl with this misled but honorable idealism, there flaunted itself a coarse pro-German sentiment wholly un-American. Sons and grandsons of men who had fled from Germany to escape despotism were heard now as apologists for the most dangerous despotism and the most barbarous war methods the modern world had ever seen. Organized and obedient to the word of command, this element made many weak politicians truckle to the fear of "the German vote."

These forces for neutrality were strengthened by one other selfish motive. The country had begun to feel a vast business prosperity. Some forms of business were demoralized for a time; but soon the European belligerents were all clamoring to buy all our spare products at our own prices — munitions of war, food, clothing, raw materials. To be sure, the English navy soon shut out Germany from direct trade, though she long continued an eager customer, indirectly, through Holland and Denmark; but in any case the Allies called ceaselessly for more than we could produce. Non-employment vanished; wages rose by bounds; new fortunes piled up as by Aladdin's magic. A busy people, growing richer and busier day by day, ill-informed about the real causes of the war, needed some mighty incentive to turn it from the easy, peaceful road of prosperous industry into the stern, rugged paths of self-denial and war. A little wisdom, and Germany might readily have held us bound to neutrality in acts at least, if not always in feeling.

Germany makes neutrality impossible

But more and more Germany made neutrality impossible for us. From the first the German government actively stirred up bad feeling toward us among its own people because our people used the usual and legal rights of citizens of a neutral power to sell *munitions of war* to the belligerents. Germany had securely supplied herself in advance, and England's navy now shut her out from the trade in any case. So she tried, first by cajolery and then by threats, to keep us from selling to her enemies — which would have left them at her mercy, taken by surprise and unprepared as they were.

Quarrel over munitions

Our *legal* right to sell munitions she could not question seriously. Only two years before, she herself had been selling just such munitions freely to the warring Balkan nations. She demanded of us not that we *comply with* international law, but that we *change* it in such a way as to insure her victory — in such a way as would really have made us her ally. For our government to have yielded to her demands, and forbidden trade in munitions during the war, would have been not neutrality, but a plain breach of neutrality — and a direct and deadly act of war against the Allies.

Our government firmly refused to notice these arrogant German demands. And, says an authorized statement (in *How the War Came to America*):

"Upon the *moral* issue involved the stand taken by the United States was consistent with its traditional policy and with obvious common sense. For if, with all other neutrals, we refused to sell munitions to belligerents, we could never in time of a war of our own obtain munitions from neutrals, and the nation which had accumulated the largest reserves of war supplies in time of peace would be assured of victory. The militarist state that invested its money in arsenals would be at a fatal advantage over the free people who invested their wealth in schools. To write into international law that neutrals should not trade in munitions would be to hand over the world to the rule of the nation with the largest armament factories. Such a policy the United States of America could not accept."

The submarine controversy in its early stages

The submarine gave rise to a special controversy. The U-craft were not very dangerous to warships when such vessels were on their guard. Unarmed merchantmen they could destroy almost at will. But if a U-boat summoned a merchantman to surrender, the merchantman might possibly sink the submarine by one shot from a concealed gun, and in any case the U-boat had little room for prisoners. Thus it soon became plain that submarine warfare upon merchant ships was necessarily barbarous and in conflict with all the principles of international law. If it were to be efficient, the U-boat must sink without warning. In the American Civil War, a Confederate privateer, the *Alabama,* destroyed hundreds of Northern merchant ships, but scrupulously cared for the safety of the crews and passengers. But from the first the German submarines torpedoed English and French peaceful merchant ships without notice. Little chance was given even for women and children to get into the lifeboats, and of course many *neutral* passengers were murdered.

The new phase in 1915

And now, in February, 1915, Germany proclaimed a "submarine blockade" of the British Isles. She drew a broad zone in the high seas about Britain, declaring that any merchant ship, even of neutral nations, within those waters was liable to be sunk without warning.

The *Lusitania*

The world could not believe that Germany would really practice the crime she threatened. But May 7, 1915, the great English liner *Lusitania* was torpedoed without any attempt to save life. Nearly twelve hundred non-combatants were drowned, many of them women and children! With characteristic mendacity, the German government then asserted, falsely, that the *Lusitania* was really a war vessel, loaded with munitions.

One hundred and fourteen of the murdered Lusitania *passengers were American citizens;* and there at once went up from much of America a fierce cry for war; but large parts of the country, remote from the seaboard, were still indifferent to a "European struggle," and there were not lacking some shameless apologists for even this dastardly massacre. President Wilson, zealous to preserve peace, used every resource of diplomacy to induce

President Wilson's "notes"

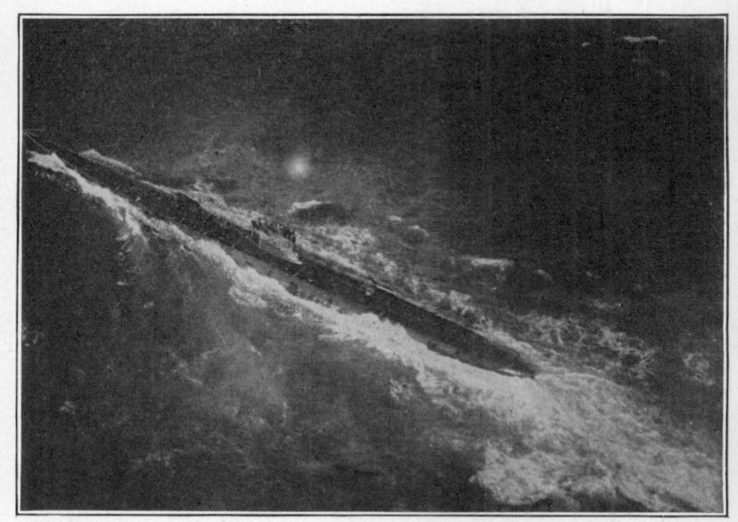

Copyright by Underwood and Underwood.

A German Submarine on the way to surrender at the end of the war. This view was taken from an English airplane at night with the aid of a searchlight.

Germany to give up its horrible submarine policy. At the same time he distinctly pointed out, in note after note, that a continuance in that policy would force America to fight.

The "First Lusitania Note" (after declaring that the use of submarines against merchant ships must *necessarily* endanger the lives of passengers and of neutrals, and after urging Germany to give up a practice so contrary to civilized warfare and to the law of nations) closed, —

"The Imperial German Government will not expect the government of the United States to omit any word *or any act* necessary to the performance of its sacred duty of maintaining the rights of the United States and its citizens, and of safeguarding their free exercise" (June 13, 1915).

The "Third Lusitania Note" (July 21) refused to consider the tissue of evasions put forward by Germany as in any way "relevant" to a discussion of "the grave and unjustifiable violations of the rights of American citizens," and uttered solemn warning, that if these "illegal and inhuman" acts were persisted in "they would constitute an unpardonable offense. . . .

"Repetition by the commanders of German naval vessels of acts in contravention of these rights must be regarded by the Government of the United States . . . *as deliberately unfriendly.*"

These well-meant efforts of the President were answered by the German government with quibbles, cynical falsehoods, and contemptuous neglect. Other merchant vessels were sunk, and finally (March, 1916) the sinking of the *Sussex*, an English passenger ship, again involved the murder of American citizens. President Wilson's note to Germany took a still sterner tone and specifically declared that *one* more such act would cause him to break off diplomatic relations. Germany now seemed to give way. She promised, grudgingly and with loopholes for future use, to sink no more passenger or merchant ships — unless they should attempt to escape capture — without providing for the safety of passengers and crews (May 4).

Wilson's seeming victory

This episode, running over into the *third* year, closed the first stage of this controversy. President Wilson's year of negotiation seemed to have won a victory for civilization. As he afterward complained, the precautions taken by the Germans to save neutrals and non-combatants proved distressingly meager, but for some time "a certain degree of restraint was observed."

CHAPTER XLVIII

THE THIRD YEAR, 1916

England fully aroused

The year 1916 brought the struggle back to the Western front. England had awakened from her complacency and was at last putting forth her full strength. The splendid volunteer army was now supplemented by conscription, wholly new to England, and the "work or fight" rule was applied to every able-bodied man between 18 and 45. The commander-in-chief, General French, a veteran of the Boer War, had been succeeded (October, 1915) at his own request by a younger man, Sir Douglas Haig. Haig would be ready to strike by midsummer.

The German Crown Prince attacks Verdun

Accordingly Germany planned to strike first and put France out before Britain was quite ready. February 21, weeks before campaigns would usually open in that region, she made a gigantic effort to deal a mortal blow by an attack on Verdun. The capture of that famous fortress, it was felt, would open the road to Paris. Certainly it would have been a terrific shock to the French morale.

For four days the Germans gained ground swiftly. A vast concentration of artillery prepared the way for each assault, and then huge masses of trained soldiery carried their objectives each day, — though with almost incredible losses. But France rushed in her reserves by thousands in motor busses,[1] and after February 25 her defense steadily tightened, meeting the haughty German boasts with the tight-lipped defiance — "They shall not pass." For two months more the Germans

[1] This method of transportation saved France. There was no time to construct military railroads, and human legs could not do the job. The motor bus won a new importance.

kept up the attack with some expectation of final success; and then for still two months more they renewed the assault from week to week, at a staggering cost of life, because the High Command dreaded the blow to its military prestige involved in a confession of failure.

France was saved. The German failure was generally ascribed to the Crown Prince, who had directed the campaign. Germany now put Hindenburg, the victor in the East, in supreme command of all her armies — though Ludendorff, Chief of Staff, was the real power behind him.

The British advance on the Somme

July 1 the new British armies began their carefully prepared drive along the Somme. Lloyd George himself had taken over the ministry of munitions some months before; and this time — for the first time during the war — the English had a superiority in guns and high explosives, while their tanks, now used first, wrought terrible havoc in the German lines. But the intended French drive, further south, did not come to a head — partly because of exhaustion from the Verdun campaign, partly, it was whispered, because at this moment the French legislative chamber, having already driven Joffre into retirement, saw fit again to interfere disastrously with the plans of the military staff. The English struggled on magnificently for four months, winning back a considerable extent of French soil, with many villages, and driving a deep dent into the German line. But that line was still *unbroken* when the unusually severe weather of November brought the campaign to a close. Two hundred thousand young Englishmen had given their lives, and six hundred thousand more lay mangled in hospitals. But they had proved that industrial England in two years had created and trained an army more than a match, unit for unit, for the veteran army of militaristic Germany.

Brief Russian revival

The war on the East front during this season furnished two surprises on the side of the Allies, but neither was of lasting value. (1) Russia showed a remarkable recovery. Early in June her armies took the offensive against the Austrians. For a month they won swift success — in great part because their opponents were largely subject Slavo-Czechs, who welcomed chances to surrender to a possible deliverer of their provinces from Austrian oppression. By July, however, the new supplies of Russian ammunition had again given out, and Germany had rushed to Austria's rescue a number of veteran divisions from the West front. Russia had been saved from complete collapse, the year before, by the desire of the Teutonic powers to crush Serbia and to consolidate their hold upon the Ottoman world. Now she was saved again for the moment by sacrificing Roumania.

Roumania enters the war — and is betrayed by Russia

(2) For now Roumania had entered the war. This story is still obscure. Roumania wished of course to recover from Austria the great Roumanian province of Transylvania, and apparently the Tsar had induced her to go in too soon by promises of support that was never given. The German traitorous court party at Petrograd, now in control over the weak Tsar, planned a separate peace with Germany, and seems to have intended deliberately to buy easy terms for Russia by betraying Roumania to the Central Powers. Bulgarians and Teutons entered doomed Roumania from south and west. December 16 the capital fell, and only the rigors of winter enabled the Roumanian army to keep a hold upon a narrow strip of its country. The large Allied army at Saloniki did not stir: why is not yet fully explained. No doubt if it left its base, it was in peril of being stabbed in the back by Constantine of Greece; and the Tsar vetoed all proposals of effective measures against that petty despot — from tenderness for a fellow monarch.

Conditions at the close of 1916

Thus the year 1916, too, ended gloomily. Germany had tremendously strengthened her position in the East, and had lost nothing in the West. Her supply of man-power, it was suspected, was running low, along with stocks of fats, rubber, cotton, and copper and other metals. Her poorer classes were suffering bitterly from undernourishment — especially the children, whose death-rate had tremendously increased. But her ruling classes felt no pinch and showed no discouragement;

and the world was uncertain how far her domination in the East might retrieve her markets. Russia was crumbling: transportation was broken down; the industrial system — always crude — was practically gone; hunger and despair ruled the peasantry; and only the stubborn resistance of the Duma and of a few great generals seemed to prevent a separate Russian peace, with complete victory for Germany on the East. On the other hand, England, France, and Italy were vastly better prepared for the struggle than ever before, and were about ready for their maximum effort. If they could make that effort before Russia collapsed, they still hoped for success.

And there were not wanting signs that the Allies were soon to receive long-delayed help from another quarter.

CHAPTER XLIX

THE FOURTH YEAR, 1917

America Enters and the War Spreads

Woodrow Wilson's reelection in 1916

In America, Woodrow Wilson had been reëlected President in November, 1916, after a peculiar campaign. Many of his followers, especially in the West and among the workingmen, shouted the slogan, "He kept us out of war." On the other hand, Mr. Wilson's firmness in defending American rights, and his plain drift toward the Allies, drew upon him the hatred of large organized pro-German elements. Neither party made the war a clear issue.

German plots against neutral America

But no sooner had the dust of this political campaign cleared away than the American people began to find indisputable proofs of new treacheries and new attacks upon us by Germany, *even within our own borders*. The official representatives of Germany in the United States, protected by their diplomatic position (and bound by every sort of international law and common decency not to interfere in any manner with our domestic affairs), had placed their hirelings as spies and plotters throughout our land. They had used German money, with the approval of the German government, to bribe our officials and even to "influence" our Congress. They had paid public speakers to foment distrust and hatred toward the Allies. They had hired agitators to stir up strikes and riots in order to paralyze our industries. They incited to insurrection in San Domingo, Haiti, and Cuba, so as to disturb our peace. They paid wretches to blow up our railway bridges, our ships, our munition plants, with the loss of millions of dollars of property and with the murder of hundreds of peaceful American workers. Each week brought fresh proof of such outrage —

more and more frequently, formal proof in the courts. The governments of the Central Powers paid no attention to our complaints, or to the evidence we placed before them regarding these crimes; and so finally President Wilson dismissed the Austrian ambassador (who had been directly implicated) and various guilty officers connected with the German embassy.[1]

German threats and hostility

All this turned our attention more and more to the hostility to our country plainly avowed for years by German leaders. Said the Kaiser himself to our ambassador (October 22, 1915) at a time when our government was showing extreme gentleness in calling Germany to account for her murder of peaceful American citizens on the high seas, — "*America had better look out. . . . I shall stand no nonsense from America after this war.*" Other representative Germans threatened more specifically that when England had been conquered, Germany, unable to indemnify herself in exhausted Europe for her terrible expenses, would take that indemnity from the rich and unwarlike United States. Our writers began to call our attention to the fact that this plan had been cynically avowed in Germany for years before the war began (*Conquest and Kultur*, 102–112). Slowly we opened our eyes to the plain fact that just as the conquest of France had been intended mainly as a step to the conquest of England, so now the conquest of England was to be a step to the subjugation of America. It came home to us that our fancied security — unprepared for war as we were — was due only to the protecting shield of England's fleet. If Germany came out victor from the European struggle, we must give up forever our unmilitaristic life, and turn our country *permanently* into a huge camp, on a European model, as our only chance for safety from invasion and rapine — and there was much doubt whether time would be given us to form such a camp. To live in peace, as we wished to live, we must help crush the militaristic power that hated and despised and attacked peace. German despotism and peace for free peoples

America forced to choose between temporary war and permanent militarism

[1] For proven guilt, see the notes to President Wilson's *Flag Day Address*, as published by the Committee of Public Information, Washington, D.C.

could not exist in the same world. We had long hoped to keep the peace by being peaceful. *But now peace had gone.* We could win peace back only by fighting for it.

Wilson's final attempts for peace

President Wilson strove still to avoid war. At the same time he had begun to speak solemn warning to our own people that we could not keep out of the struggle, or out of some like struggle, unless peace could be secured soon and upon a just basis. December 22, he sent to all the warring governments a note asking them to state their aims. The Allies demanded "restoration and reparation," with an adjustment of disputed territories according to the will of the inhabitants, and "guarantees" for future safety against German aggression. Germany replied evasively, making it plain that her own suggestion at this same time for a peace conference was merely sparring for time.

Then, January 22, 1917, the President read to Congress a notable address proposing *a League of Nations to enforce Peace,* and outlining the kind of peace which, he thought, the United States would join in guaranteeing, — not a Caesar's peace, not a peace of despotic and irresponsible governments, but a peace made by free peoples (*among whom the small nations should have their full and equal voice*) and "made secure by the organized major force of mankind."

Germany resumes "unrestricted" submarine warfare

Germany had ready a new fleet of enlarged submarines, and she was about to resume her barbarous warfare upon neutrals. She thought this might join the United States to her foes; but she held us impotent in war, and believed she could keep us busied at home. To this last end, through her ambassador at Washington — while he was still enjoying our hospitality — she had been trying secretly, as we learned a little later, to get Mexico and Japan to join in an attack upon us, *promising them* aid and *huge portions of our western territory.*

The United States breaks off diplomatic relations

January 31, the German government gave a two-weeks notice that it was to renew its "unrestricted" submarine policy, explaining to its own people with moral callousness, why it had for a time *appeared* to yield to American pressure —

and offering to America an insulting privilege of sending one ship a week to England provided it were painted in stripes of certain colors and width, and provided it followed a certain narrow ocean lane marked out by Germany. President Wilson at once dismissed the German ambassador, according to his promise of the preceding March, and recalled Ambassador Gerard from Berlin. By March 1, Germany had begun again actually to sink passenger ships and murder more Americans.[1] The temper of the nation was changing swiftly. Apathy vanished. Direct and open opposition to war there still was from extreme pacifists and from pro-Germans, including the organization of the Socialist party: but the great majority of the Nation roused itself to defend the rights of mankind against a dangerous government running amuck, and turned its eyes confidently to the President for a signal. And April 2 President Wilson appeared before the new Congress, met in special session, to ask it to declare that we were now at war with Germany. April 6, by overwhelming votes, that declaration was adopted.

Declaration of war, April 6, 1917

America went to war not to avenge slights to its "honor," or merely to protect the property of its citizens, or even merely to protect their lives at sea. America went to war not *merely* in self-defense. We did war for this, but more in defense of free government, in defense of civilization, in defense of humanity. Said President Wilson in his War Message:

American war aims

"The present German submarine warfare against commerce is a war against all mankind. . . . The challenge is to all. . . . Neutrality is no longer feasible or *desirable*, when the peace of the world

[1] Besides the eight American vessels sunk before March, 1916, eight had been sunk in the one month from February 3 to March 2, 1917. During the two months, February and March, 105 Norwegian vessels were sunk, with the loss of 328 lives. By April 3, 1917, according to figures compiled by the United States government, 686 neutral vessels had been sunk by Germany *without* counting American ships. When we turn to the still more important question of lives, we count up 226 American citizens slain by the action of German submarines before April, 1917. For details, see *The War Message and the Facts behind It:* published by the Committee on Public Information, Washington, D.C. Before the close of the war, 5000 Norwegian citizens were murdered in like manner.

is involved, and the freedom of its peoples, and when the menace to that peace and freedom lies in the existence of autocratic governments backed by organized force which is controlled wholly by their will, not the will of their people. . . . *We have no quarrel with the German people.* . . . A steadfast concert for peace can never be maintained except by a partnership of *democratic* nations. No autocratic government could be trusted to keep faith within it. Only free peoples . . . can prefer the interests of mankind to any narrow interests of their own. . . .

" We are now about to accept the gage of battle with the natural foe to liberty. . . . We are glad . . . to fight for the ultimate peace of the world and for the liberation of its peoples, *the German people included.* . . . .

" *The world must be made safe for democracy.* . . . We have no selfish ends. We desire no conquests, no dominion. We seek no indemnities for ourselves, no material compensations for the sacrifices we shall freely make.

" It is a fearful thing to lead this great, peaceful country into war, into the most terrible and disastrous of all wars, civilization itself seeming to be in the balance. But the right is more precious than peace; and we shall fight for the things which we have always carried nearest our hearts — for democracy, for the right of those who submit to authority to have a voice in their own governments, for the rights and liberties of small nations, for a universal dominion of right by such a concert of free peoples as shall bring peace and safety to all nations. . . .

" To such a task we can dedicate our lives and our fortunes, everything that we are and everything that we have, with the pride of those who know that the day has come when America is privileged to spend her blood and her might for the principles that gave her birth and happiness and for the peace which she has treasured. God helping her, she can do no other."

American unity

Splendid was the awakening of America, following quickly on the President's call. True, some misled pacifists and the positive pro-German forces still did their utmost to give aid and comfort to the Kaiser. Patriotic pacifists, however, like Mr. Bryan, recognized that to oppose our entering the war was a matter of judgment, but that now to hinder the success of America in the war was treason. Mr. Bryan had resigned from the Cabinet, in June of 1915, as a protest against the President's firmness in pressing the *Lusitania* matter: but now he promptly declared, "The quickest road to peace is through the war to victory"; and he telegraphed the President an offer of his services in any capacity. Henry Ford, who had led a shipload of peace enthusiasts to Europe the year before, to plead with the warring governments there, now placed his great automobile factories absolutely at the disposal of the government, and soon became a valued worker in one of the government's new War Boards. Charles Edward Russell, choosing to be an American rather than a Socialist if he could not be both, became one of a great Commission to Russia, and on his return supported and explained the war with voice and pen. Like action was taken by other leading Socialists, as by John Spargo and Upton Sinclair. And the oldest Socialist paper in America, *The Appeal to Reason,* soon declared itself convinced by President Wilson's statements, and came out as *The New Appeal* in support of the war. The great majority of Americans of German birth or descent also rallied promptly to the flag of the land they had chosen. Most important of all, the organized wage-earners spoke with emphasis and unity for America and democracy. Led by their president, Samuel Gompers, the delegates of the American Federation in November, by a vote of 21,579 local unions as against 402, organized the *Alliance for Labor and Democracy* to support the war.

The war spreads

And now the war spread more widely still. Cuba at once followed the example of the United States in declaring war against Germany, and most of the countries of South and Central America either took the same action within a few months or at least broke off diplomatic relations with the Central European Powers. Portugal had entered the war in 1916, because of her close alliance with England. Siam came in a little later, as did China *upon invitation from the United States.*

This lining up of the world had mighty moral value, and no small bearing upon the matter of supplies. In particular, the German ships which, since the beginning of the war, had been seeking refuge in the harbors of these new belligerents were now seized for the Allies, and helped to make good the losses due to submarines. Few of these Powers except America, however, had much direct effect upon military operations.

German success in 1917

And in spite of the entry of America, Germany continued to win great success in 1917. As the Germans had hoped, Russia dropped out. The Tsar's reactionary or incompetent ministers had maddened the Petrograd populace by permitting or preparing breakdown in the distribution of food. March 11, the populace rose. The troops joined the rioters, and the rising quickly became a political revolution. Absolutely deserted by all classes, Nicholas abdicated on March 15. The Liberal leaders of the Duma (Constitutional Democrats led by Miliukov) proclaimed a provisional government, which was promptly and peacefully accepted by the army and by the nation. Optimists among the Allies believed that Russia had merely passed from an inefficient autocracy to a sane and efficient republic. Keener-eyed thinkers warned (1) that, in the complete collapse of her industrial system, Russia would almost inevitably be forced into the hands of extremists; and (2) that the huge empire would probably break up into separate and possibly warring states — which in the past had had no real bond of union except the perished autocracy.

The Russian Revolution: the provisional government of Constitutional Democrats

These gloomy surmises proved correct. The provisional government of Miliukov could not stand the strain of foreign war and of internal dissolution, and in a few weeks (June, 1917) it was replaced by a Socialist-democratic government led by Kerensky. This interesting man was an emotional, well-meaning enthusiast, — a talker rather than a doer, altogether unfit to grapple with the tremendous difficulties before Russia. Finland, the Ukrainian districts, and Siberia were showing signs of breaking away from central Russia. Everywhere the peasants had begun to appropriate the lands of the great estates, sometimes quietly, sometimes with violence and outrage. The army was completely demoralized. The peasant soldiers, so often betrayed by their officers, were eager for peace, that

The Kerensky government

they might go home to get their share of the land. In all large cities, extreme Socialists began to win support for a further revolution, and in some places anarchists were taking the lead.

Kerensky battled against these conditions faithfully, and for a while with some show of success. He tried zealously to continue the war, and, in July, he did induce part of the demoralized army to take up the offensive once more. But after slight successes, the military machine collapsed. Whole regiments and brigades mutinied, murdered their hated officers, broke up, and went to their homes. The remaining army was intoxicated with the new political "liberty," and fraternized with the few German regiments left to watch it. Russia was really "out of the war." After a six-months rule, Kerensky fled from the extremists, and (November 7, 1917) these extreme Socialists (the Bolsheviki) seized the government and announced their determination to make peace.

The Bolshevik Revolution: Russia out of the war

During the chaos under Kerensky, the real power over nearly all Russia had fallen to new councils of workmen's delegates (with representatives also from the army and the peasantry). The Bolsheviki had seen that these "soviets," rather than the old agencies, had become the real government, and by shrewd political campaigning they captured these bodies, so securing control over the country.

It should be clearly recognized, however, that *no* Russian government could have continued the war. The Russian people had borne greater sacrifice than any other; they were absolutely without resources; they were unspeakably weary of war; and they failed to see that German victory would mean the return of the Tsar.

The campaign in the West

Nivelle's failure on the Aisne

In the West the Allies had begun the spring campaigns in high hopes. The French had borne the heaviest burden so far, but they were ready for one more supreme blow. Their new commander, Nivelle, was a brilliant general, but his plans became known to the enemy, probably by treachery, and his great offensive on the Aisne was heavily repulsed. He was superseded by Pétain, the hero of Verdun; but the army was so demoralized and discouraged that it could undertake no further important operations during the season. Whole regiments melted away, to go home; and Pétain found it unadvisable to punish even such wholesale desertion.

Very early in the season the Germans had executed an extended withdrawal in front of the British lines from their trenches of two years' warfare to a new "Hindenburg Line,"

General Pétain Decorating a French Soldier at Arches, in the Vosges.

The German "strategic retreat" to the "Hindenburg Line." The great British offensive

which, they boasted, had been prepared so as to be absolutely impregnable to any assault. This maneuver confessed a superiority in the English fighting machine — which the Germans had hitherto professed to despise — but it delayed Haig's attack for some weeks. His heavy guns had to be brought up to the new positions over territory rendered almost impassable by the Germans in their retreat, and new lines of communication had to be established. These things were accomplished, however, with a rapidity and efficiency wholly surprising to the German High Command; and in the subsequent British attack the Germans were saved only by the fact that now they were able to transfer all their best divisions from the Russian front to reinforce their troops pressed by the British. Even so, Haig continued to win important successes in Picardy and Flanders from April to November; but the failure of Nivelle and the collapse of Russia made it impossible for him to "break through" to stay.

Copyright by Underwood and Underwood.

FIELD MARSHAL HAIG.

German "propaganda," successful in Russia, now tried in Italy

The Russian military collapse had been caused in part by an exceedingly skillful German propaganda. Russian soldiers had been taught persistently by German emissaries that the war was the Tsar's war, or at least a capitalist war; and that their German brothers were quite ready to give the new Russia a fair peace. A little later the same tactics were repeated successfully against Italy. In August of 1917 the Italian armies seemed for a while to have overcome the tremendous natural difficulties confronting them. They had won important battles and had taken key positions commanding Triest, when suddenly their military machine, too, went almost to pieces. The Germans had been using with the Italian rank and file a skillful propaganda. England and France, the Italian soldiers were told, were looking only to their own selfish ambitions, and were leaving Italy an unfair share of the burden of the war. Peace could be secured at any moment if only Italy would cease to attack Austrian territory. Meanwhile the wives and children of Italian soldiers were in truth famishing for bread, and information to this effect — both reliable and exaggerated — was creeping through to the ranks.

The Italian collapse

While the Italian morale was so honeycombed, the Austrians, reinforced by German troops, suddenly took the offensive. They met at first with almost no resistance. They tore a huge gap in the Italian lines, took 200,000 prisoners and a great part of Italy's heavy artillery, and advanced into Venetia, driving the remnants of the Italian army before them in rout. French and British reinforcements were hurried in; and the Italians rallied when they saw how they had been tricked and how their country had been opened to invaders. The Teutons proved unable to force the line of the Piave River; and Venice and the rich Lombard plain were saved. Italy had not been put out of the war as Russia had been; but for the next six months, until well into the next year, the most that she could do, even with the help of Allied forces sadly needed elsewhere, was to hold her new line while she built up again her broken military machine.

The U-boat campaign fails

The brightest phase of the year's struggle for the Allies was at the point where there had seemed the greatest peril. Germany's new submarine warfare had indeed destroyed an enormous shipping tonnage, and for a few months had really promised to make good the threat of starving England into surrender. But the English navy made a supreme effort. An admirable convoy system was organized to protect important merchant fleets; shipbuilding was speeded up, to supply the place of tonnage sunk; submarine chasers and patrol boats waged relentless, daring, and successful war against the treacherous and barbarous craft of the enemy. America sent five battleships to reinforce the British Grand Fleet, and — more to the purpose — a much more considerable addition to the anti-submarine fleet; and newly created American shipyards had begun to launch new cargo ships in ever increasing numbers, upon a scale never before known to the world. The Allies were kept supplied with food and other necessaries enough to avert any supreme calamity. Before September, 1917, the menace — in its darkest form — had passed. Submarines remained a source of loss and serious annoyance; but it had become plain that they were not to be the decisive factor in the war.

America's man-power begins to count

Moreover, America was slowly getting into the struggle — slowly, and yet more swiftly than either friend or foe had dreamed possible. The general expectation had been that, totally unprepared as the United States was for war, her chief contribution would be in money, ships, and supplies. These she gave in generous measure (Chapter L, below). But, also, from the first the government wisely planned for military participation on a huge scale. Congress was induced to pass a "selective conscription" act; and as early as June a small contingent of excellent fighters was sent to France — mainly from the old regular army. In the early fall, new regiments were transported (some 300,000 before Christmas), and perhaps half a million more were in training. By 1920, it was then thought by the hopeful, America could place three million men in the field in Europe, or even five million, and so decide the war. But events were to make a supreme exertion necessary even sooner; and America was to meet the need.

CHAPTER L

THE LAST YEAR, 1918

French discontent and war-weariness

France could stand one year more of war, but she was very nearly "bled white," as Germany had boasted. Her working classes were war-weary and discouraged, and the Germans had infected all classes in that country more or less successfully with their poisonous and baseless propaganda to the effect that England was using France to fight her battles, and that she herself was bearing far less than her proper share of the burden. French morale was in danger of giving way, as Russian and Italian had given way. It was saved by two things: by the tremendous energy of the aged Clemenceau — "The Tiger" — whom the crisis had called from his retirement to the premiership; and by the encouraging appearance in France, none too soon, of American soldiers in large numbers.

Peace feeling in England

Even in England, peace talk began to be heard, not merely among the workers but here and there in all ranks of society. And among the laborers this dangerous leaning was fearfully augmented when the Russian Bolsheviki published the copies of the "Secret Treaties" between England, France, Italy, and the Tsar's government, revealing the Allied governments as purchasing one another's aid by promises of territorial and commercial spoils. For the first time the charge against the Allies that on their side too the war was "a capitalist and imperialist war" was given some color of presumption.

Conditions in Germany

In Germany, too, the masses of the people were war-weary. The entire generation of their young men was threatened with extinction, and their children were being pitifully stunted from lack of food. The "Independent Socialists," as Ludendorff now tells us, had spread among the people a peace propaganda which crippled seriously the efficiency of the army. The Reichstag actually adopted resolutions in favor of peace without annexations or indemnities — which from the German viewpoint was extremely conciliatory. But the junkers and great capitalists were still bent upon complete military victory, which they seemed to see within their grasp; and the German war lords at once made it plain that they recognized no binding force in the Reichstag resolutions. They had knocked out Russia, put out Italy temporarily at least, and might now turn all their strength as never before upon France and England. They were confident that they could win the war before American armies could become an important factor. The Allies, they insisted, had not shipping enough to bring the Americans in any numbers; still less to bring the supplies needful for them; and then the Americans "couldn't fight" anyway without years of training.

JOHN J. PERSHING, Commander of American troops in France.

A race between Germany and America

Thus in 1918 the war became a race between Germany and America. Could America put decisive numbers in action on the West front before Germany could deliver a knock-out blow? While winter held the German armies inactive, the British and American navies carried each week thousands of American soldiers toward the front, English ships carrying much the greater number.

And during these same months America and England won a supremely important victory in the moral field. In the sum-

Wilson's "diplomatic offensive"

mer of 1917 the Pope had suggested peace negotiation on the basis of July, 1914 — before the war began. Woodrow Wilson at once answered, for America and for the Allies, that there could be no safe peace with the faithless Hohenzollern government. This cleared the air, and made plain at least one of the "guarantees" the Allies must secure. Then Germany tried another maneuver: she put forward Austria to suggest peace negotiations — in hope, no doubt, of weakening the Allied morale. Instead, in two great speeches, Lloyd George and President Wilson stated the war aims of the Allies with a studious moderation which conciliated wavering elements in their own countries, and at the same time with a keen logic that put Germany in the wrong even more clearly than before in the eyes of the world. Lloyd George (January 6) demanded complete reparation for Belgium, but disclaimed intention to exact indemnities other than payment for injuries done by Germany in defiance of international law. President Wilson's address contained his famous Fourteen Points. These statements of America and England drove deeper the wedge between the German government and the German people, by convincing the masses that the Allies were warring only for freedom and for peace, and not for the destruction of Germany.

The Fourteen Points have had so much prominence in the months since, that it seems well to present here their important features.

1. "Open covenants of peace, openly arrived at, after which . . . diplomacy shall proceed always . . . in the public view."

2 and 3. [These "points" call for freedom of the seas and of trade.]

4. [Disarmament by international agreement.]

5. "An . . . absolutely impartial adjustment of all colonial claims . . . . The interests of the populations concerned to "*have equal weight* with the equitable claims of the government whose title is to be determined."

6. "The evacuation of all Russian territory and such a settlement of all questions affecting Russia as will secure the best and freest coöperation of the other nations of the world in obtaining for her an unhampered and unembarrassed opportunity for the independent determination of her own political development and national policy *and assure her of a sincere welcome into the society of free nations under institutions of her own choosing;* and, more than a welcome, assistance also of every

kind that she may need and may herself desire. *The treatment accorded Russia by her sister nations in the months to come will be the acid test of their good will. . . .*"

7. [Evacuation and "restoration" of Belgium.]

8. [Reparation for damages in France, and return of Alsace-Lorraine.]

9. "A readjustment of the frontiers of Italy . . . *along clearly recognizable lines of nationality.*"

10. [This point dealing with the subject peoples of Austria-Hungary, was soon made of little account by the progress of the war.]

11. . . . "Serbia [to be] accorded free and secure access to the sea; and the relations of the Balkan states to one another determined *by friendly counsel* along historically established lines of allegiance and nationality. . . ."

12. [Turkish Empire.]

13. [An independent Poland, to "*include the territories* inhabited by indisputably Polish populations. . . ."]

14. *A "general association of nations* must be formed under specific covenants [to afford] mutual guarantees of political independence and territorial integrity *to great and small states alike.*"

"For such arrangements and covenants we are willing to fight and to continue to fight until they are achieved; but only because we wish the right to prevail and desire a just and stable peace, such as can be secured only by removing the chief provocations to war. . . . We have no jealousy of German greatness, *and there is nothing in this program that impairs it.* We do not wish to injure her or to block in any way her legitimate influence or power. We do not wish to fight her either with arms *or with hostile arrangements of trade* if she is willing to associate herself with us and the other peace-loving nations of the world in covenants of justice and law and fair dealing. We wish her only to accept a place of equality among the peoples of the world — the new world in which we now live — instead of a place of mastery. . . ."

The Brest-Litovsk Treaty

And now Germany herself made plain how absolutely right the Allies were in their contention that the Hohenzollerns could be trusted to keep no promises. March 3, 1918, the German militarists, with the grossest of bad faith, shamelessly broke their many pledges to the helpless Bolsheviki and forced upon Russia the "Peace of Brest-Litovsk." By that dictated treaty, Germany virtually became overlord to a broad belt of vassal states taken from Russia — Finland, the Baltic Provinces, Lithuania, Poland, Ukrainia — and even the remaining "Great Russia" had to agree to German control of her industrial re-

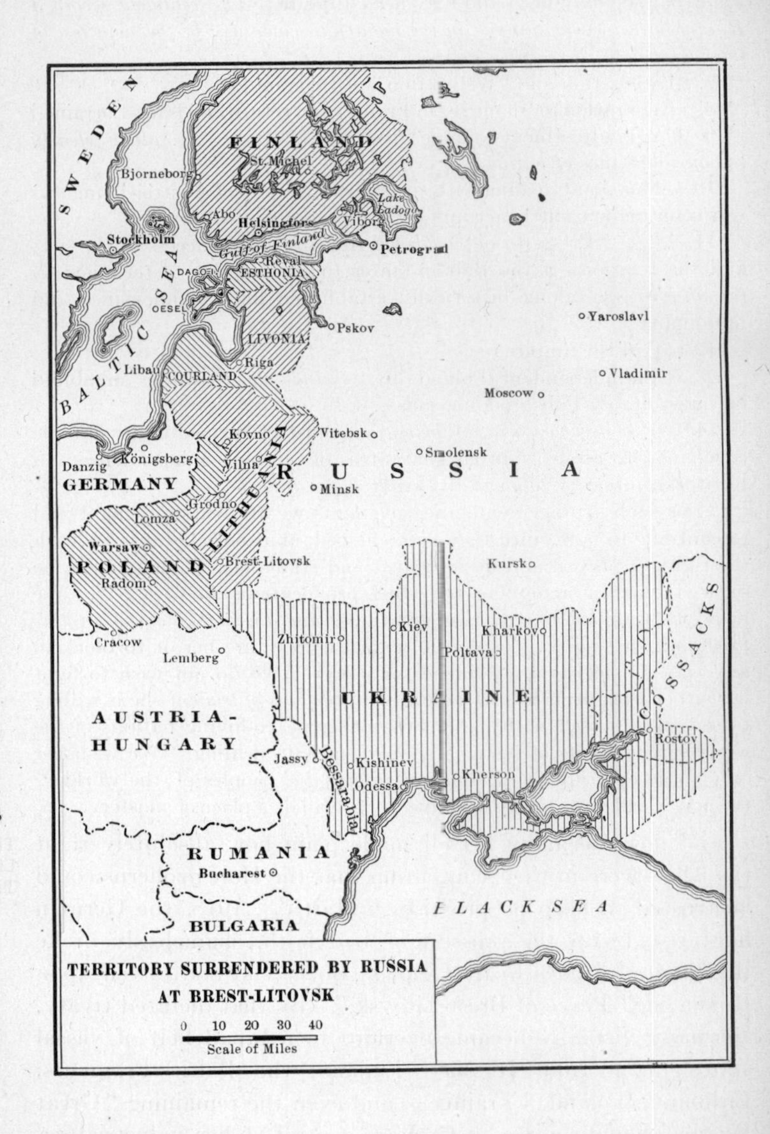

TERRITORY SURRENDERED BY RUSSIA AT BREST-LITOVSK

organization. When the German perfidy had revealed itself suddenly, after long and deceitful negotiations, the angered and betrayed Bolsheviki wished to break off, and renew the war. They were absolutely helpless, however, without prompt Allied aid upon a large scale. This aid they asked for, but urgent cablegrams brought no answer. The Allies apparently

THE MITTEL-EUROPA EMPIRE at its greatest extent in March, 1918. In Asia, only a few months before, it had reached to the Persian Gulf and the Red Sea (cf. p. 661).

had been so repelled by the Bolshevist industrial and political policy that they were unwilling to deal with that government, and preferred to leave Russia to its fate — and to the Germans.

At that moment the result was disastrous. Murmurs in Germany against the war were stilled by the immediate prospect of an empire stretching from the North Sea to the Pacific, and of large accumulated stores of Russian wheat — as soon as transportation systems could be restored to efficiency.

In all the Allied countries tremendous popular feeling was aroused against the Bolsheviki. In part this was because the Allied peoples — ignorant of the facts just mentioned — believed that government a mere tool of Germany. In part it was due to hatred and fear among propertied classes toward any Socialist régime. But more than all else, it was due to a false position adopted by the Bolsheviki in government — excluding all people living on their capital from political life.

This of course was not democracy: it was class rule. True, in Russia it was the rule of a large per cent of the whole population; but the example of a "proletarian dictatorship" was dreaded by the "upper" and "middle" classes everywhere. Moreover, the Bolsheviki announced a repudiation of the Russian national debt.[1] The Russian bonds were owned mainly in France; and that country persuaded the Allies to treat the Russian government as an enemy. Soon, too, various reactionary and middle-class movements against the Bolshevik tyranny found leaders for a vigorous civil war.

The great German offensive in Picardy in March

Naturally the Germans opened the campaign in the West at the earliest moment possible. They had now a vast superiority both in men and in heavy guns there. March 21 they attacked the British lines in Picardy with overwhelming forces. After five days of terrific fighting the British were hurled out of their trench lines and driven back with frightful losses nearly to Amiens, leaving a broad and dangerous gap between them and the French. It looked as though the Germans might drive the British into the sea, or the French back upon Paris, or both. But, as so often in their great offensives in this war, the Germans had exhausted themselves in their mass attack; and, while they paused, a French force threw itself into the gap, and British reserves reinforced the shattered front lines. For the first time since the First Battle of the Marne, the Germans had forced the fighting into the open, where they had always claimed

[1] They afterward offered to give up this policy if accorded recognition.

marked superiority; but they were unable to follow up their success decisively.

In April they struck again farther north, in Flanders, and again they seemed almost to have overwhelmed the British;

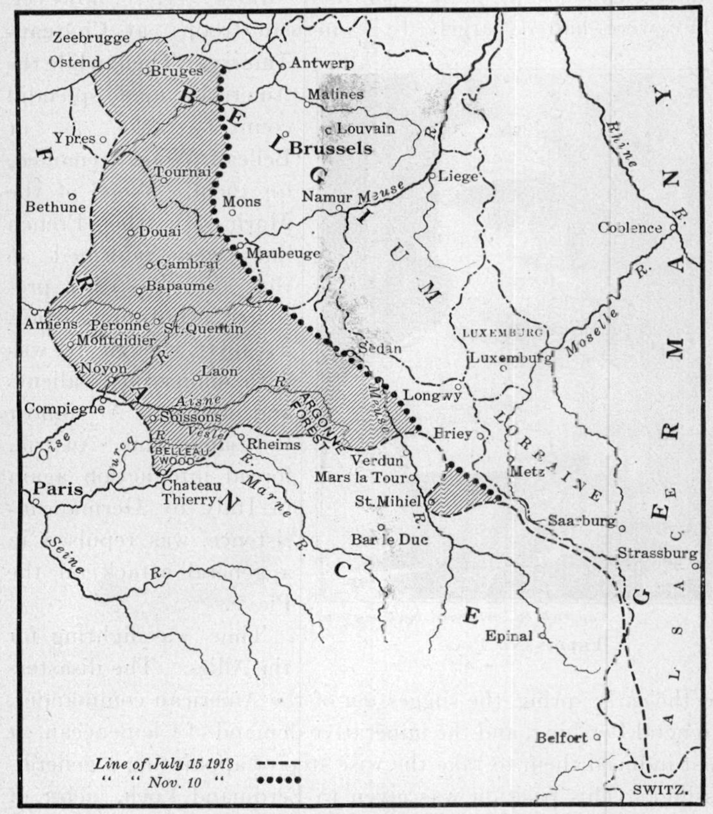

THE WAR ON THE WEST FRONT — German lines on July 15 and November 10, 1918.

but fighting desperately, "with our backs to the wall," as Haig phrased it in his solemn order to his dying army, and reinforced by some French divisions, the British kept their front unbroken, bent and thinned though it was.

The offensive in Flanders in April

The offensive on the Aisne in the last of May

The Germans took another month for preparation, and then struck fiercely in a general attack on the French lines north of the Aisne. Apparently the French were taken by surprise. The Germans broke through, for the moment, on an eighteen-mile front, and once more reached the Marne. Here, however, they were halted, largely by American troops, at **Château-Thierry**. Then, while the Americans made splendid counter-attacks, as at Belleau Wood (renamed, for them, "Wood of the Marines"), the French lines were reformed, so that still the Allies presented a continuous front, irregular though it was with dangerous salients and wedges. At almost the same time, Austria, forced into action again in Italy by German insistence, was repulsed in a general attack on the Piave.

Checked by Americans at Château-Thierry

Copyright by Underwood and Underwood.

FERDINAND FOCH.

Time given for the Americans to arrive

Time was fighting for the Allies. The disasters of the early spring, the suggestion of the American commander, General Pershing, and the imperative demand of Clemenceau, at last induced them to take the wise step of appointing a generalissimo. This position was given to Ferdinand Foch, victor of the First Marne. For the rest of the struggle, the Allied forces were directed with a unity and skill that had been impossible under divided commands, even with the heartiest desire to coöperate.

And now, too, America really had an army in France. Before the end of June, her effective soldiers there numbered 1,250,000.

Each month afterward brought at least 300,000 more. By September the number exceeded two million.

The last German offensive

The Germans could not again take up the offensive for five weeks (June 11–July 15), and in this interval the balance of available man-power seems to have turned against them. Hindenburg and Ludendorff believed only in mass attacks over wide fronts. When one of these gigantic onsets had once been stopped, with its tremendous losses and demoralization, a considerable interval had to elapse before another could begin. July 15 preparations were complete, and the Germans attacked again in great force along the Marne, expecting this time to reach positions that would command Paris. But the onset broke against a stone-wall resistance of French and American troops. *For the first time in the war*, a carefully prepared offensive failed to gain ground.

Foch's continuous offensive

The German failure was plain by the 17th. On the 18th, before the Germans could withdraw or reorganize, *Foch began his great offensive*, by counter-attacking upon the exposed western flank of the invaders. This move took the Germans completely by surprise. Their front all but collapsed along a critical line of twenty-eight miles. *Foch allowed them no hour of rest.* Unlike his opponents, he did not attempt gigantic attacks, to break through at some one point. Instead, he kept up a continuous offensive, threatening every part of the enemy's front, but striking now here, now there, on one exposed flank and then on another, always ready at a moment to take advantage of a new opening, and giving the Germans no chance to withdraw their forces without imperiling key positions. He took no intervals for rest — which would have allowed the enemy to attempt a new offensive — but kept the ball in his own hands.

The German retreat

By the end of July the invaders had been pushed out of the ground they had gained in May and June, between the Aisne and the Marne. Then the British, reorganized now, were brought again into action in Picardy, taking the burden of the offensive, while the French kept up activity enough to prevent any transfer of reinforcements to that district from the sector opposite them. For some weeks, the Americans, steadily growing in numbers and equipment, were held in reserve for the most part — after their gallant fighting in stopping the last German offensive — but before the end of August the British and French had won back all the ground lost in the German offensives of the spring.

The Americans at Sedan

The Germans had made their last throw — and lost. Foch's pressure never relaxed. In September American divisions began an offensive on a third part of the front, culminating in a drive toward Sedan, to cut one of the two main railways that supplied the German front. At the same time the British were wrenching great sections of the "Hindenburg Line" from the foe. In the opening days of October *the German commanders reported to Berlin that the war was lost,* and that it was necessary to get peace by negotiation. For the next month, while there went on an exchange of notes regarding an armistice, the German military situation grew steadily more critical.

Germany asks for an armistice

Bulgaria had already fallen

At the same time, it is true that Germany lasted longer than any of her allies and that her collapse was determined largely by *events in the East.* In September the Allied force, so long held inactive at Saloniki, suddenly took the offensive, crushing the Bulgarians in a great battle on the Vardar. Political changes had made this move possible. In 1917, now that the Tsar could no longer interfere, the English and French had deposed and banished King Constantine of Greece; and Venizelos, the new head of the Greek state, was warmly committed to the Allied cause. Moreover, the Bulgarians were war-weary and demoralized. They had failed to get from Germany and Austria the spoils they hoped for at the fall of Roumania; and now after their one great defeat they had neither spirit nor forces to continue the struggle. Foch's pressure made it impossible for the Germans to transfer reinforcements to them from the West. The Saloniki forces advanced swiftly into Bulgaria. Tsar Ferdinand abdicated, and (September 30) the Provisional Bulgarian government signed an armistice amounting to unconditional surrender and opening also the way for an attack upon Austria from the south.

And Turkey

And while these events were happening, a wholly independent series of movements were putting Turkey out of the war. In the spring of 1917 an English force from India worked its way up the Tigris and took Bagdad — after a romantic campaign that recalls the wars and marches of Alexander the Great in the Orient — and in the fall of the same year, another British force from Egypt took Jerusalem. But the Russian collapse endangered both these promising movements, and the pressure of the Germans on the West front made it unsafe for England then to send more men to either of these important Eastern districts. But by midsummer of 1918, reinforcements were sent at last to Palestine; and September 19, the British resumed a remarkable campaign north of Jerusalem. The Turks were utterly routed in a decisive battle, and the pursuit was so hot and so continuous that they never rallied in any force. Aleppo, the key to Northern Syria, surrendered October 26, without a blow — and with it fell the Ottoman Empire outside Asia Minor. The Turks saw that the collapse of Bulgaria had isolated them from any possible German succor — and in any case Germany was no more able to spare troops now for them than a month before for Bulgaria. The Turkish government at Constantinople fled. A new one was hastily constituted, and, October 30, Turkey surrendered as abjectly as Bulgaria. The Dardanelles were opened, and Constantinople admitted an Allied garrison.

And Austria

Austria too had dissolved. After the June repulse on the Piave, the Austrian army was never fit for another offensive. At home the conglomerate state was going to pieces. Bohemia on one side, and Slovenes, Croats, and Bosnians on the other were organizing independent governments — with encouragement from America and the Allies. Then, October 24, Italy struck on the Piave. The Austrian army broke in rout. Austria called frantically for an armistice, and when one was granted (November 4), the ancient Hapsburg Empire had vanished.

The Emperor Karl (recent successor to the old Francis Joseph) abdicated. Fugitive archdukes and duchesses crowded Swiss hotels. And each day or two saw a new revolutionary republic set up in some part of the former Hapsburg realms.

The Allies refuse to treat with the German autocracy

Germany had begun to treat for surrender a month earlier, but held out a week longer. October 5, the German Chancellor (now Prince Max of Baden) had asked President Wilson to arrange an armistice, offering to accept his "Fourteen Points" as a basis for peace. Wilson's replies to this and to a following communication made it plain that America and the Allies would not treat with the old despotic government, and that no armistice would be granted at that late moment which did not secure to the Allies fully the fruits of their military advantages in the field. The fighting went on, with terrific losses on both sides, but with daily increase in the military superiority of the Allies. The French and Americans, pushing north in the Argonne and across the Meuse, were threatening the trunk railway at Sedan, the only road open for German retreat except the one through Belgium. The British and Belgians pushed the discouraged invaders out of northern France and out of a large part of Belgium. The pursuit at every point was so hot that retreat had to be foot by foot, or in complete rout; and it was not clear that even that choice would long remain. As a last desperate throw, the German war lords ordered the Kiel fleet to sea, to engage the English fleet; but the common sailors, long on the verge of mutiny, broke into open revolt, while over all Germany the Extreme Socialists — all along opposed to the war — were openly preparing revolution.

German revolution

The armistice, November 11

Not till late in October did the War Council of the Allies make known to Germany the terms upon which she could have an armistice preliminary to the drafting of a peace treaty. By those terms Germany could save her army from destruction, and her territory would not suffer hostile conquest. But she was to surrender at once Alsace-Lorraine, and to withdraw her troops everywhere across the Rhine, leaving the Allies in possession of a broad belt of German territory. She was also to surrender her fleet, most of her heavy artillery, her aircraft, and her railway engines. Likewise she was at once to release all prisoners, though her own were to remain in the hands of the Allies. In March, Germany had treacherously and arrogantly set her foot upon the neck of prostrate Russia in the Brest-Litovsk treaty; November 11, she made this unconditional surrender to whatever further conditions the Allies might impose in the final settlement — though the Allies did pledge themselves to base their terms, with certain reservations, upon Mr. Wilson's Fourteen Points.

German revolution completed

Germany had already collapsed internally. November 7, Bavaria deposed her king and proclaimed herself a republic. State after state followed. In Berlin the Moderate Socialists seized the government — with the support of the aristocracy, who feared the rule of a more radical Socialist element. November 9, deserted by the army, the Kaiser had fled to Holland, whence he soon sent back to Germany his formal abdication. German autocracy and Prussian militarism had fallen forever.

CHAPTER LI

WAR EFFICIENCY OF A DEMOCRACY

No other war was ever so enormously destructive as was the World War, but neither did any other war ever give birth to so many healing and constructive forces. These forces the American student can most easily notice in America, but they were found also in other countries — in some respects, too, in more advanced forms even than here.

For this study there are two phases, more or less intertwined: (1) that phase which had to do mainly with greater efficiency in the war itself; and (2) that other phase which looked to a better and finer world after the war. The first phase is the theme of this chapter.

America's task

To our own surprise, and to that of the world, we proved that American democracy, utterly unready for war as it was, could organize for war, by *voluntary* coöperation, more efficiently and swiftly than any autocracy had ever done. The task was not merely to select and train three million soldiers, but to mobilize one hundred million people for "team work," so that every ability and every resource could be utilized with the utmost intelligence and harmony. After all, battles in modern war are won mainly *behind* the lines. The most important mobilization was mobilizing our civilian population to produce and transport munitions and supplies, to raise food, supply fuel, and furnish abundant funds.

Fitting each man to his job

At once the government put skilled brains at work: (1) to find out just what was needed in all these respects, and in what order, so as to be able to distribute effort wisely; (2) to find which men were best fitted for each job — often by systems of tests in the hands of educational experts; (3) to teach the nation, careless and wasteful by previous training, that *to save* food, clothing, and other supplies was just as useful and just as patriotic as *to produce* them; and (4) first of all, to educate the whole people as to what the war really meant and as to the best ways of coöperating in all these ways to win it.

The Committee on Public Information: American propaganda

The Committee on Public Information at Washington, created by President Wilson, was a new thing in human history. If a democracy was to turn away from all its ordinary ways of living in order to fight, it must be thoroughly posted on the danger that threatened it, and on the needs of the hour. Within a few months this Committee, at small expense, had published and circulated in every village in America more than a hundred different pamphlets, brief, readable, forceful, written by leading American scholars, and distributed literally by the million. These publications did a marvelous work in spreading information and arousing will power among the people, demonstrating that in war itself "the pen *is* mightier than the sword." Most of these studies are of permanent scholarly value, and some of them are referred to in footnotes and book lists in this volume.

The Four-Minute Men

With this Committee originated also the admirable organization of Four-Minute Men, — some 5000 volunteer speakers to explain the causes and needs of the war in their respective communities to audiences gathered at the movies and at other entertainments. Speakers and occasions were matters of local arrangement; but the central Committee put the plan in operation and made it effective by sending to all the thousands of local centers at frequent intervals suggestions and information on which to base the speeches.

War posters

The same Committee secured the chief of America's illustrators, with a strong staff of volunteer assistants, to design posters and placards, — which were plentifully distributed in every city and village in the land to arouse more determination to save food and to save money to be loaned to the government.

It is impossible to explain here the many other activities of the Committee — such as the cultivation of friendly feeling in South American lands, the uncovering of German plots, the driving a wedge between the German people and its government by shooting propaganda into Germany. And this Committee is only one instance out of many of the work of eminent American chemists, historians, engineers, heads of great business enterprises, who served at Washington during the war as volunteers with at best only a nominal money compensation, and often as "one dollar a year" men.

The United States formed no "alliance" by treaty with any of the Allies, but it recognized that they and we were "associated" as co-workers, and that we must give them every possible aid.

Raising funds for war

Money we furnished freely. To England, France, Italy, and Belgium (and to Russia before her collapse) we loaned nearly ten billions of dollars, most of which, it is true, was used by those governments in purchasing supplies in America. Within a few months after the war began, the special session of Congress in the spring and summer of 1917 appropriated the unparalleled sum of twenty-two billions of dollars for war purposes. Five billions of this were loaned to the government at once by citizens of all classes in the purchase of the first and second issue of Liberty Bonds (August and October, 1917). These bonds were sold mostly in small denominations, down to $50, and were taken largely by people of small means. During this first season one out of every ten people in the United States (children and all) became a bond-holder by so loaning to the government. During the next year and a half, by three more bond issues, the government borrowed of our people, including the earlier issues, 17 billions. For the fourth issue alone, the largest loan, there were 21 million subscribers, or one of every five inhabitants. Besides all this, vast sums were loaned to the government in even smaller amounts, by the purchase of Thrift Stamps (25 cents each) and War Savings Stamps ($5). This, too, is a way to encourage small savings that will surely be continued after the war (cf. p. 502).

Liberty Bonds

The amazing success of these loans — which for the most

part were heavily oversubscribed — is the more marked because the interest was low and because money at that time could earn much higher return in many other ways.

War taxes

But we had to raise money also by taxation. The first War Revenue bill provided for direct taxes to raise two and a half billions a year, and a subsequent bill increased the amount to more than four billions a year. Half of this came from a graduated income tax and allied taxes (an inheritance tax, and an "excess profits" tax). The income tax took 2 per cent of a small income [1] and rose by steep degrees to 65 per cent of very large incomes. Moreover, large amounts were raised by a "luxury tax," payable on a great variety of articles of clothing costing more than a certain price. In general, a serious effort was made by America to arrange the system of taxes so that for the first time in the world the cost of war should not fall mainly on the working classes.

Saving food and "doing without," to feed our Allies

England needed our cotton and wheat, and France and Italy could not fight longer without our iron and coal as well. These things we strove to send. But all the Allies, stripped of their own farm workers, needed American food; and *our poor harvest in 1917 left us no surplus above our ordinary consumption.*

This was an alarming condition. To meet it, Congress gave the President extraordinary powers over the nation's resources. The President created a Food Commission, headed by Herbert C. Hoover, an American business man and engineer, who for the three years preceding had shown signal administrative ability and devotion to humanity as head of the American Relief Commission in starving Belgium. When we entered the war, Mr. Hoover and his American associates in Belgium had been obliged to return to the United States.

This Commission, by spreading information broadcast and by skillful appeals kept everywhere before the eye, induced the American people voluntarily and cheerfully to limit its con-

[1] Each taxpayer was allowed $1000 income exempt from taxation; husband and wife, $2000; and $200 more was exempt for each minor child.

sumption, and especially to "save the waste." Wheatless and meatless days each week, agreed upon according to the Commission's "request" and enforced by public opinion, and a rigid limit on the amount of sugar allowed to any locality, made it possible for our government to export huge amounts of these three most essential foods for the peoples whose armies were fighting our battles in Europe.

By saving waste, and by using substitutes, we cut down our use of wheat for one year almost half; and the half so saved gave to every person in England, France, and Italy almost as much as we used at home. We had less than 20 millions of bushels to export in 1917, if we used as much as usual at home; but, *by doing without*, we did export 141 million bushels.

War saving a democratic voluntary movement

The statement regarding the savings brought about among the people by voluntary consent is by no means complete. The women's committees of the Defense Councils issued cook books to show the housewife how to save and how to use what had previously gone to the garbage can, and, through the action of local committees and Red Cross societies, these books received a wide welcome. In 1918, on the advice of the National Commercial Economy Board, manufacturers of clothing put forth fewer and simpler styles, omitting all needless buttons, frills, belts, collars, and so on. This alone saved millions of yards of cloth — fifteen per cent, it is estimated, of the cloth usually needed for men's clothing, and twenty-five per cent for women's.

Along with the saving, went also, of course, work for increased production. Farmers increased their acreage for the most needed crops, receiving from State or Nation necessary advances in money for seed or machinery. Needed farm labor was furnished by volunteer school boys — who were allowed school credits for the time so spent. And a vast amount of food was raised in new "war gardens" on small private grounds which before had been devoted, very rightfully, to beauty and pleasure.

To prevent the European demand from raising prices exorbitantly, and to check speculation in foodstuffs, the Commission took important steps in fixing fair prices and in regulating profits. This last, it must be said, was not wholly successful. Congress had not given the President power enough, vast as was his power, or else that power was not fully exercised. The price of wheat flour, for instance, was fixed; but the millers took advantage of the patriotic determination of the country to use less needed grain, like rye flour and oatmeal, by raising the prices of these flours exorbitantly. This was one instance of disgraceful "profiteering." There were others. Huge "war fortunes" sprang up by thousands. *And the government did not prove strong enough successfully to prosecute and punish any big profiteer.*

War profiteering largely held in check

To carry supplies to Europe in spite of the ravages of submarines, a new Shipping Board built ships on a scale beyond all precedent. First of all, new shipyards had to be built, and whole new cities to house the tens of thousands of new shipbuilders — who in turn had to be trained for their new work. Like much else in our haste, all this was not done without some sad blunders and much extravagance. But it *was done*, and done *swiftly*. In less than a year, America's new plants were turning out ships much faster than England's centuries-old yards had ever launched them. The new shipyards beat the submarine — and America could afford some extravagance in that work in return for speed.

Shipbuilding

Transportation at home had its own problems. The railroads began to break down almost at once under the increased business imposed upon them by the war; and the nation felt keenly the waste of so many non-coöperating systems. In December of the first year, Congress passed a law turning the railroads over to the government — for the period of the war — guaranteeing profits to the owners, and the government began to operate them as one system. Telegraph and express companies also passed into government hands.

The railroads

The mines were not ready on short notice to supply coal as fast as war needs called for it. Coal for ships and railroads and

Saving coal and gasoline

for many war industries we had to have. Accordingly the government regulated its private use. People learned to save fuel, to heat their houses and offices only to 65° instead of to 70° or 72°, and many changed their heating plants so as to use wood. For many weeks in 1918, at the request of the government, churches were closed, and stores, amusement halls, and

FLEET OF AIRPLANES over San Diego, California, suggesting on what a vast scale this country developed her aërial service during the war.

most industries were closed on certain days of the week, to save coal. People grumbled a little, but joked and assented. A little later, to save gasoline needed in France for tanks and auto-trucks and aëroplanes, "gasless Sunday" took its recognized place alongside the "heatless," "wheatless," and "meatless" days of each week — all essentially on government *recommendation* only.

The selective draft, and its success

It was necessary that America should give of her manhood as well as of her wealth. The results have been told in preceding pages. Here we may briefly note the method.

At the declaration of war, eager volunteers pressed forward for army and navy; but what was needed was more than *individual* volunteers. America needed a wise use of the whole nation's resources, each man being assigned the job he could do best. And so, May 18, 1917, the "selective draft" became law. Every man and youth from 18 to 45 (by the first law only from 21 to 31) was required to register in his county seat, giving, in answer to a questionnaire, full information about his character, training, health, and ability. All were *liable* for service: the President was to lay down principles upon which to *select* for service in the ranks those best fitted, or most easily spared from other service.

Before the end of the year, half a million soldiers were training in fifty swiftly built camps — each camp a new city — largely under officers who had been trained earlier in the year in new officers' training camps; and some 300,000 were already in France, receiving the finishing touches to their training just behind the trenches. When the armistice came, a year later, we had three million men under arms, of whom more than two million were doing splendid work in France. It is hard to say whether the Kaiser or we ourselves were the more astounded at the swift making of an American army.

Local activities

Along with this national activity, there was a vast volunteer activity by local democracies, always looking gladly to Washington for advice and direction, but also quite ready to trust to their own initiative if needful. Each State had its Council of Defense (modeled on the Council of National Defense). Most of these were well supplied with State funds; and many of them did exceedingly useful work in promoting unity, arousing interest, and suppressing possible treason within their States. Below each State Council, and in constant touch with it, were county and village councils of like character. In rural districts, the schoolhouse was usually the place for such bodies to meet, as well as for local chapters of the Red Cross and for war lectures.

Other organizations

Even more significant than these public organizations were the thousands of canvassing boards that served in the draft without pay; the examining boards of busy physicians, who gave their time freely to secure the physical fitness of the soldiers; the volunteer bodies of village teachers, working Saturdays, Sundays, and nights, to classify the results of draft questionnaires; the Red Cross societies in every neighborhood; and the volunteer canvassers for Liberty Bond sales, wherein the Boy Scouts had a fine share. Democracy proved that, when attacked, it could put aside its ordinary work and play, to take on war activities with resolution, efficiency, and unanimity unexcelled.

True, there were some blots on this splendid record. Here and there, selfish politicians sought personal popularity by wrapping their country's flag about them, or tried to discredit or destroy rivals by false accusations of lack of patriotism — a desecration of the flag that cannot be too severely condemned. In the heat of war passion, too, some grave injustices were committed by honest and intelligent patriots, and some foolish offenders were punished too severely. Mob violence, even, was permitted, and in some cases against thoroughly patriotic men falsely accused by personal enemies. The method by which poor people were sometimes intimidated into taking more bonds than they could afford did not suit well the name *Liberty* for those bonds. These things America will regret; but, spite of such blemishes, the history as a whole is a proud one.

The work of the women

In all good work, women had a part. Behind each man who took up a rifle there stood a woman to take up the work he laid down. Even in America, women ran elevators, street cars, and motor busses, and performed new and heavy work in factories, — especially in munition factories and in aircraft building; and in twenty states, college girls enlisted in the "Woman's

Land Army," for outdoor farm work. In England, as her men were drained away, five million women took up men's work, — an Earl's daughter sometimes toiling in a munition factory at the same bench with a working girl from the streets.

In all countries this war efficiency of women gave the final impetus to the movement for equal suffrage. The last "argument" against suffrage — the silly plea that a woman ought not to vote because she could not serve her country in war — was proven false.

CHAPTER LII

THE WORLD LEAGUE AND NEW EUROPE

January 18, 1871, the first German Emperor placed the new imperial crown upon his own head at Versailles, while his victorious armies were still besieging Paris (p. 423). January 18, 1919, the Peace Congress opened its meetings in the same room of the Versailles Palace, to reconstruct Europe after the fall of the German Empire.

Attempts at working-class rule in Central Europe

There was supreme need of reconstruction. Central Europe had broken into fragments, and each fragment was tossing helplessly on waves of revolution. In Germany an extreme wing of the Socialists, led by Karl Liebknecht and Rosa Luxemburg, was planning a second revolution to take power from the "Conservative Socialists" of the Provisional Government into the hands of the working class. The fearless Liebknecht had been foremost in all Germany in opposing Prussian militarism before the war,[1] and had spent most of the war years in prison as a traitor to German autocracy, because he had dared to oppose the war even after it began. That this work of his had given material aid to the Allies is proven by Ludendorff's story of the war (p. 650). Freed by the fall of autocracy, Liebknecht now taught that selfish capitalist and imperialist forces would try to make a peace of plunder. Only a workingman's government in Germany, he preached, and the spread of such a government into France and England, could secure a lasting peace based on justice and righteousness.

This mistaken doctrine, however honest in the leaders, was suited for use by selfishness, ignorance, and passion. Accord-

[1] See C. Altschul's *German Militarism and Its German Critics*, War Information Series, No. 13.

ingly in several large German cities, especially in Berlin, "Soldiers and Workingmen's Councils" seized the government in the interest of working-class rule. These bodies were attacked promptly by the regular troops, which for the most part remained true to the Provisional Government. Thousands fell in bloody street fights, marked by the use of poison gas, machine guns, and liquid fire. The superior equipment of the government forces in all such respects triumphed; and Liebknecht and Rosa Luxemburg were taken prisoners — and brutally murdered by their guards.[1]

German National Assembly of 1919

Then in January, 1919, Germany held an election for a National Assembly. By a new franchise law promulgated by the Provisional Government, all men *and women* over 19 years of age had been given the vote, and an excellent system of "proportional representation" secured due weight to minority parties. The result was a victory for a union of Moderate Socialists ("Majority Socialists") and "German Democrats" (the old Liberals).

To avoid revolutionary mobs, the Assembly met at Weimar instead of at Berlin. By an overwhelming vote, it chose Ebert (once a saddler) president of the German Republic (February 11), organized under a coalition cabinet led by Philip Scheidemann, and framed a new constitution while waiting for peace terms from the Allies.

The new Republic was a federation of the old states. Each state had already put off its monarchic government. Prussia, for instance, had also abolished its Upper House and had adopted universal suffrage (including women) for the election of its One-House legislature. But through the winter and spring, these republican governments were constantly threatened with anarchy. Factories could not open for lack of cotton, or rubber, or iron, or capital, or markets in which to sell goods. Germany's ships had been taken by the Allies, to

[1] Some of the assassins were obliged to go through the form of a trial. Two were sentenced *to two years' imprisonment;* but the next day one of these "escaped," — a fitting conclusion to the farce of the trial.

help replace those her submarines had sunk, and the Allied blockade had been lifted only far enough to permit the introduction of some foods, — not enough to restore any real trade with the world nor even to remove the pressure of hunger. Under these conditions, revolutions in some of the states put control for a time into the hands of the working classes. In the end, these revolutionary governments were all crushed by a union against them of all other parts of society, and their fall was followed too often by cruel and long-continued massacre of the more active and intelligent of the working class. These brutal and treacherous "White Terrors" have cast upon the middle-class Republicans of Germany a stain almost as black as marked the French Republic in 1871 (p. 489).

The Bavarian Revolution

For a few weeks even aristocratic Bavaria had a proletarian government, in which the leading ministers had been, one a blacksmith's apprentice, one a tailor, another a herd boy, while the president, Kurt Eisner, a gallant opponent of the war, had been until shortly before only a struggling Socialist newspaper man Eisner was soon murdered by an aristocratic officer, and the government was overthrown by a combination of military violence and treachery.

Revolutions in Hungary

Hungary had promptly become a republic under enlightened middle-class control. The president, the liberal Count Karolyi, turned over his princely domains for common use, and pleaded with the Allies for terms that might prevent further revolution. But the stupid Allied blockade, making impossible either work or food, put this government to such straits that it soon gave way, bloodlessly, to a proletarian rule under Bela Kun, similar to the Bolshevist rule in Russia.

Later (August, 1919), it may best be added here, the Allies brought about the overthrow of Bela Kun by secret promises of support to a more moderate Socialist and Trade-Union faction — and then betrayed this government of their own creation. Roumania had taken advantage of the woes of Hungary to declare war, and to invade that country even after every Hungarian government had declared its full willingness to cede all Roumanian lands. In spite of weak paper remonstrances from the Allies at Paris, the Roumanian army even occupied the Hungarian capital, and for months it ravaged the helpless country industriously and systematically. Under the influence of these conquerors, and with the shameful connivance of the Allies at Paris, a restoration of the Hapsburg monarchy was attempted in the person of the Archduke Frederick. Vigorous protest at Paris from Herbert Hoover prevented the lasting open success of this plot; but a reactionary aristocratic government was left in control.

New States in Europe

The other lands of the old "Central Empires" had already fallen away, but not into peace. A new and enlarged Bohemia (the Czecho-Slav Republic) was practically at war, not merely with Germany and Austria, but also with the new Polish Republic, over conflicting boundary claims; and this new Poland, under the leadership of Paderewski, the famous pianist, had other contests with Russian Bolsheviki on one side and with Germany on the remaining land frontier, besides being torn by internal factions and busied in massacring its own Jews. And Poland was only one of seven new states — all in equal anarchy — that had split off from the old Russian Empire, — Finland, Esthonia, Livia, Curland, Lithuania, Ukrainia. To the south conditions were little better. Below old Austria, there had appeared a Jugo-Slav state by the long-sought union of Serbians, Bosnians, Croatians, and Slovenes; but this enlarged Serbia and Italy were in battle array, daily in peril of war, over the Adriatic coast. Italy and Greece were at daggers' points regarding South Albania, the islands of the Aegean, and the shores of Asia Minor.

Take the case of one of these new small peoples. Livia contained a population of Letts and of German aristocrats.

At the armistice, the Allies left a German army in the country, to defend it from anticipated Bolshevist attack. A monarchic Russian faction raised another army of Germans and maintained it there in hopes of invading Russia and restoring Tsarism. And the German aristocrats

Central Europe in 1919.

of the country, who had been driven from power and from their estates when Livia became a free republic, formed a third army of 7000 Junkers. This last force waged open civil war upon the republic, and was secretly supported by the two other German forces, who, pretending to be allies of the government against Russia, proved really to be invaders. Not till the end of a bloody year of war (December, 1919), did the Letts really secure their freedom by driving these three enemies from their soil.

No one of these many countries felt any trust in the honor of any other. Each believed that every one would hold what it could lay hands on, and so sought to lay its own hands on as much as possible before the day of settlement. The Peace Congress had its work cut out for it.

The Peace Congress

That famous gathering contained the leading statesmen of the world. The United States, Great Britain, France, Italy, and Japan each sent five delegates. England's colonies, too, sent delegates, — two each from Canada, Australia, South Africa, and India, and one from New Zealand. Eighteen other governments, which had taken part in the war upon the side of the Allies, were allowed from one to three delegates each. Each delegation voted as a unit. Countries that had been neutral were also invited to send representatives to be called in whenever matters arose that specially concerned them. The four "enemy countries" and Russia were allowed no part. A striking feature of the gathering was the great number of expert assistants accompanying their representatives. The United States delegation alone was aided by more than a hundred prominent men, most of them eminent authorities on the history or geography or economic resources of European lands.

Woodrow Wilson at Paris

President Wilson himself headed the American delegation, — in spite of vehement opposition to his leaving his own country for so long a time. In like manner, Lloyd George and Orlando, the English and Italian premiers, represented their lands; and Clemenceau, head of the French delegation, was naturally chosen president of the Assembly. These men made up "the Big Four." Part of the time this inner circle became the "Big Five" by the inclusion of the Japanese representative.

From the first it was plain that even within the Big Four there were critical differences. Mr. Wilson had promised the world, Germany included, "a permanent peace based on unselfish, unbiased justice," and "a new international order based upon broad universal principles of right." To such ends he insisted, (1) that the first step must be the organization of a League of Nations, a World federation; and (2) that all negotiations should be public — "open covenants, openly arrived at."

Lloyd George and Clemenceau

At times, Lloyd George had seemed heartily to adopt this program; but he was seriously hampered by the fact that

THE "BIG FOUR" — Lloyd George — Orlando — Clemenceau — Wilson. (Radical criticism sometimes alludes to the four as "the four old men of Paris.")

in the campaign for parliamentary elections, in December, he had won by appeals to the worst war passions of the English people. The other leaders never had any real faith in the Wilson program. In Clemenceau's words, they looked upon President Wilson as a benevolent dreamer of Utopias, and they preferred to rest all rearrangements upon the old European methods of rival alliances to maintain a balance of power — a plan which had been tried, only to prove through bloody centuries a seed bed of war.

Governments and peoples in Europe

Moreover France was dissatisfied and panicky. Germany, prostrate for the moment, still bordered upon her, with a population and resources greater than her own. So it is easy to understand that many French statesmen should have wished above all things to deal with Germany by German methods — to make her helpless by dismembering her and by plundering her through indemnities, and to build up the new Poland and Bohemia by giving them enough German territory so that they might always be fearful of Germany and therefore hostile to her. Such states on the east, with France on the west, could then hold Germany in a vise between them — especially if the proposed League of Nations could be made a cover for a guarantee of this arrangement by America and England.

Such a program meant the perpetuation of the old European system of alliances, armed camps, and, sooner or later, of war. But by the war-weary *peoples,* if not by the governments of Europe, the Wilson program of a just peace and a world league was at first hailed with joy. Mr. Wilson had arrived in Europe several weeks before the opening of the Congress, for conferences with European statesmen; and everywhere in his journey — in England, France, Italy — he was welcomed by the working classes with remarkable demonstrations of respect and affection, as "the president of all of us," as the Italians put it, — as the apostle of world peace and of human brotherhood. For a time it looked possible for him, at a crisis, to override the hostile attitude of the governments by appealing over their heads to the people themselves: and indeed in a great speech at Milan — just after some slurring attacks upon him by French statesmen — he hinted pointedly at such a possible program.

Mr. Wilson weakened by events at home

But as months passed in wearisome negotiations, this popular fervor wasted away, and in each nation bitter animosities began to show toward neighboring and allied peoples. Moreover Mr. Wilson had been fatally weakened in Europe by events at home. Late in the campaign for the new Congressional elections in the preceding November, he had made a special and ill-judged appeal to the country for endorsement of his policies by a Democratic victory. But the elections instead gave both Houses to the Republicans; and the jubilant victors, charging vengefully that the President had set an example of political partisanship, entered upon a bitter course of criticism and obstruction. Mr. Wilson's European opponents made the most of this — if indeed they did not, as many thought, have a positive part in starting it.

Secret negotiations

Mr. Wilson's first defeat at Paris was in the matter of secret negotiation. To save time, it was necessary no doubt for the Peace Congress to do most of its work in small committees. But it would have been possible to lessen bargaining and intrigue by having such meetings open to representatives of the press, or by publishing stenographic reports of each meeting. Mr. Wilson, however, allowed the Old World diplomats — with their tradition of backstair intrigue — to outgeneral him into consenting to only one public and general meeting each week. The result was that, from the first, the real work was done by the inner circle of four or five in secret conclave (with the addition of several advisory *secret* committees on special matters); and instead of even the promised open meeting once a week there were during the entire five months to the signing of the Peace with Germany (January 18–June 28) only six such meetings — and these not for discussion but merely to ratify conclusions arrived at by the Big Four.

Agreement for a League of Nations

The next point Mr. Wilson won. It was agreed that the first business of the Congress should be to provide a League of Nations. With such a league to guarantee peace, to secure disarmament, and to punish any bully or robber state, it was hoped that France and Italy might trust to a just and merciful peace, instead of insisting upon a peace of vengeance and booty. Many voices, in France and in the United States Senate, had been raised in protest, urging that a league should come only *after* a treaty of peace. Some of these objectors were honest: some used the objection as a means to defeat any real league.

But Mr. Wilson argued that the League would expedite, not hinder, the peace treaty, since it was a necessary prelude to any right sort of peace; and this view prevailed.

Spoils or Justice

While a committee of fourteen nations, headed by Mr. Wilson, was preparing the covenant, or constitution, of the league, dark rumors crept out regarding the plans of European statesmen for spoils. France talked of the necessity that she acquire all German territory west of the Rhine, "her natural frontier," so that *in future wars* that great river might serve as a protective ditch. Marshal Foch supported this plea for military reasons. This of course would have transferred several millions of unwilling Germans to French rule. But Mr. Wilson, as recognized spokesman for the Allies at the Armistice and in earlier negotiations with Germany, had repeatedly renounced the principle of forcible annexations either to punish a foe or to secure "strategic frontiers" — or for any purpose except to satisfy the just claims of oppressed nationalities. To grant this French claim would have been the grossest of bad faith — as well as one more continuation of the discredited policy of the old Congress of Vienna in 1814 that had seeded Europe for a century of war.

Italy, too, demanded, *and received*, not only the Italian populations of the Trentino (p. 527) formerly held by Austria, but also a needless "strategic frontier" against now helpless Austria, involving the annexation of a purely German district in the Brenner Pass of the Alps with a quarter of a million inhabitants.[1] Italy also advanced new claims on the Adriatic at the expense of the new South Slav state. And it became plain that the imperfectly known "secret treaties," under which Italy and Japan had entered the war, had provided for a far-reaching division of spoils, not only at the expense of Germany but also to the danger of future wars. Enough news leaked out from the secret conclaves to make it certain that President Wilson

[1] If this region was to be made safe against possible military use by Austria — or Italy — it might have been given to Switzerland with the vote of its people.

denounced these projects, and declared he would have no part in a "Congress for booty." At one time, indeed, when the Italian delegates insisted strenuously upon Croatian Fiume (the natural door of the South Slavs to the Adriatic), he cabled to America for his ship — a plain threat that he would leave Paris rather than assent — and this particular act of plunder was avoided, for a time,[1] even though Orlando did for a while leave the Congress in protest. Unhappily in other cases Mr. Wilson was not always so resolute. Victory over Fiume was followed by defeat over Shantung (p. 688), and the French demand for the Rhine became a trading pretext for granting her the Saar Valley (pp. 686–687).

England and the German Colonies

England seemed to hold the key to the situation. The secret treaties had assumed that she would retain the great bulk of the German colonies. For this there would have been much excuse. She had proved her eminent fitness for control of tropical colonies; and some of the conquered districts — if a state of war was to be looked upon as probable in the future — were essential to the safety of her other dominions. Indeed the South African and Australian representatives at Paris faced political death if they returned home without German Southwest Africa and German New Guinea in their pockets. But unless England renounced her conquests for the general good, there was no escape from an old-fashioned peace of plunder : if she did renounce them, there seemed good hope that England and the United States together might persuade the other Allies to yield their selfish and injurious claims under the secret treaties. And Lloyd George did for a time restore the fainting hopes of the world by seeming to promise this splendid renunciation — though the promise was accompanied by the suggestion of mandatories, responsible to the coming League of Nations.

The Covenant of the League of Nations

In March, while other negotiations dragged along, the committee on the League of Nations made its report, and the Congress enthusiastically adopted the proposed constitution. The

[1] Special report — the Fiume incident and the final settlement.

chief opposition to the proposal appeared in the United States Senate, where certain Republicans tried to make it a party question. This was rendered difficult, happily, by the splendid work of ex-President Taft, head of the American League to Enforce Peace, who, with a group of leading Republicans, toured the United States to secure support for the covenant. The opposition was sufficient, however, so that after a few weeks the Peace Congress revised the document in a few details.

The revised covenant was clear and brief. The union is very loose, and its managing bodies are not really a government. The forty-five "charter members" may include all organized governments except Russia, the four "enemy countries," Costa Rica, San Domingo, and Mexico; and there is a way provided for admitting these in time. Amendments require the unanimous consent of the five big states with a majority of all states; and the unanimous consent of all nations in the League is demanded for any other action of consequence, except that no party to a dispute has a voice in its settlement. Among the most valuable provisions of the "Covenant" are the prohibition of all secret treaties in future, and the clauses providing for disarmament, for regulation of the manufacture of munitions of war, for compulsory arbitration, and for delay in recourse to war even if an arbitration is unsatisfactory. A reservation of the Monroe Doctrine, inserted in the second draft as a sop to American opposition, suggests, by its unfortunate phrasing, a continuation of the pernicious doctrine of "spheres of influence," and satisfies neither advocates nor opponents of the League. Much debated, too, is Article X, which guarantees to each state its territorial integrity against external attack. Mr. Wilson wrote the original of this Article, — but in a very different form, suggesting especially the desirability of future peaceful correction of territorial boundaries by the League of Nations. In the present form, the Article may be a serious barrier to needed readjustments. Its proposed guarantee of existing frontiers has certainly encouraged the various European states each to grab all it could, in the hope of being protected later by the League in ill-gotten gains.

The German treaty

And, meanwhile, to secure a League, at all, Mr. Wilson had "traded" many of his principles in the making of the peace treaties. June 28, the treaty of peace with Germany was signed by the helpless German delegates, who had been summoned to Paris for the purpose. The treaty makes a good-sized book.

Courtesy of Underwood and Underwood.

CLEMENCEAU (REPRESENTING THE PEACE CONGRESS) DELIVERING TO THE GERMAN DELEGATES THE TERMS OF PEACE, at Versailles, May 7, 1919, at the Trianon Hotel. The German delegates are sitting, directly opposite Clemenceau, on the left side of the room. Cf. p. 423.

Only a few points can be stated here. A typical one relates to the Saar Valley, a small strip of German territory just east of Alsace.

The Saar Valley

Germany is to cede the rich coal mines of this region to France, in rightful reparation of her wanton destruction of French coal mines. France insisted long upon political sovereignty over the territory and people, along with this property. This claim was not directly granted; but a "compromise" places the valley for fifteen years under an International Commission. At the end of that time the inhabitants are to vote whether they will return to Germany or join France. If they decide for their own country, Germany must at once buy up France's claim to the coal mines. This may be difficult for her to do; but if she fails to do it, the territory passes at once and permanently to France. And French capital, which is managing the mines, is already importing thousands of Polish miners to work them. It will be easy to "colonize" these workers and to use their votes for French purposes.

"Veiled annexation."

This "veiled annexation" of half a million Germans to a foreign power, against their will, is in sharp defiance of the principle of "self-determination," — and it was wholly unnecessary. France ought to have the coal; but title to that could have been guaranteed safely, under the League of Nations, without this transfer of political allegiance. And the Saar Valley arrangement is merely one of several like or worse arrangements. The new Poland gets not merely the Polish territory long held by Prussia, to which she is entitled, but also large strips of German territory, like Upper Silesia (with its two million people), which she wants solely because of its mines. Moreover, in order to give Poland easy access to the sea, by the route of the Vistula, German Dantzig is made a "free" city, against its will, with added roundabout arrangements that leave it really subject to Poland. Besides these displeasing provisions, Germany very properly not only returns Alsace-Lorraine[1] to France and (with a favorable vote of the inhabitants) Danish Sleswig to Denmark, but also cedes to Belgium three small pieces of territory populated mainly by people of Belgian blood. In addition to all this, if the inhabitants so vote, she is to cede to Poland considerable territory east of the Vistula. In all, Germany loses outright 35,000 square miles, with a *probable* loss (by plebiscites) of nearly 20,000 more — in all, a territory about the extent of Pennsylvania, and more than a fifth of the old Germany. Even this is not enough to satisfy the French government. That

Silesia and Dantzig

[1] French military authorities are already exercising (1919) over German inhabitants in Alsace-Lorraine a tyranny as bad or worse than Germany used toward French inhabitants there after 1871.

government has failed to get recognition for its claim to the Rhine districts of Germany; but attempts, which may yet succeed, have been fomented by French agents to induce this part of Germany to secede and form a separate state.

The old colonies of Germany

Besides all this, Germany has lost her vast colonial empire. This is well. But, instead of being placed under the guardianship of the League of Nations until they can walk alone, the former German colonies are turned over as plunder to the Allies. Those in the Pacific have gone part to England, part to Japan, according to the terms of a secret treaty of 1914 between those countries. True, England and Japan are "mandatories" of the League of Nations; but that arrangement is left so vague and loose that it looks like little more than a screen for the division of spoils — and Japan surely has shown herself (in Korea) as unfit to rule subject-peoples as ever Germany was. And German Africa has been divided between France, Belgium, and England with hardly a pretext of even the mandatory screen.

The Shantung matter

In this connection Americans are especially chagrined that Japan succeeds also to all Germany's indefinite "rights" in the Shantung Peninsula, against the futile protest of China. True, Japan has promised vaguely that her political occupation shall be "temporary"; but that word has been used too often as a prelude to permanent grabs of territory. To allow the one remaining despotic and military power in the world so to seize the door to China is not merely to betray a faithful ally, but also to renounce a plain and wise American policy in the Orient. Shantung has a population of 40 millions, it is the seat of Chinese civilization, the home of the philosopher and moral teacher, Confucius. It is China's Holy Land for the past and her chief hope for modern industrialism.

Very objectionable, too, are the economic provisions of the German treaty. Germany is to pay *fixed* reparations amounting to about 30 billions of dollars during the fifteen years, 1920–1934. This is severe, but on the whole it is just. However,

Germany is to pay further *indefinite* amounts, to be determined *in future* by a commission of her conquerors. This provision, along with accompanying rules regarding German taxation, leaves Germany's head in a noose which English or French commercial jealousy may tighten at will. With biting sarcasm, a radical critic represents a French statesman saying, —"Well, we fought a war to end war, and now we have made a Peace to end peace."

"Liberal" criticism of the treaty

The American delegation opposed practically all these vicious provisions; but Mr. Wilson proved utterly unable to cope with the European diplomats. He had believed with supreme confidence that he could bring them to his terms: in fact he proved a plaything in their hands. Not a vestige of the Fourteen Points survives in the Treaty — neither their details nor their spirit. And yet, unwilling to confess defeat, Mr Wilson claimed to be satisfied. But some of the experts attached to the American Commission were so disappointed that they resigned their positions in protest; and General Smuts, the hero of South Africa, and one of the noblest of the world's statesmen, when signing for his country, declared in a formal statement that he signed only because of the absolute necessity of immediate peace for Europe and because he hoped that the most objectionable provisions might be modified in future by the League of Nations. Organized labor in England, France, and Italy made earnest protests also against the violations of the principle of self-determination. China naturally refused to sign.

Such opposition to the Treaty had nothing to do with sympathy for Germany. A stern peace was to be expected; and, in the conflict of so many claims, some unsatisfactory results were sure to appear. But progressive men, the world over, believe that the treaty is dishonorable to the Allies — contradicting solemn pledges as it does — and bad for the world at large. It must breed wars. It breaks faith not alone with the beaten foe but also with the hundreds of thousands of splendid youth who gave their lives, in torment and suffering, to win the "war for democracy," "a war that should end war" and secure "peace and safety for all nations." Wrote one of these young heroes in Flanders just before his death in battle — as if in sad prophecy:

> "If ye break faith with us who die,
> We shall not sleep, though poppies blow in Flanders fields."

The treaty with Austria

Late in July, after the return of President Wilson to America, the treaty with Austria was completed at Paris. The disposition of most of the Empire has been described (pp. 676–677). Austria herself is left a petty state of 7,000,000 people, grouped around Vienna, shut off from the sea, with no excuse for a separate political existence and with little chance for industrial existence. Markets, materials, mines, are all gone. The Austrians very naturally wish incorporation with Germany. Germany also desires it; but at French insistence, the Peace Congress has forbidden this application of the principle of "self-determination." In economic matters this treaty has the same traits as does the treaty with Germany.

The treaty with Bulgaria

In December came the treaty with Bulgaria. It leaves the Balkans as before a seed plot for European wars. No attention is paid to lines of nationality, as promised in the Fourteen Points. Greece and Serbia each extend their holdings on the north Aegean coast, and Bulgaria is practically shut off from the sea except by the course of the Danube. As in other lands, too, punishment falls on the wrong party. When Tsar Ferdinand of Bulgaria forced his country into the war on Germany's side, one peasant leader in the legislature resisted to the last, even warning Ferdinand that such action would cost him his crown. For this brave service, the "unpatriotic" Stambulowski was thrown into prison. The revolution of 1918 made good his prophecy. Ferdinand was driven into exile; and Stambulowski, the friend of the Allies, now head of the new Bulgarian republic, receives the stern terms that Ferdinand earned.

Spoils in Asia

At this writing (December, 1919) the treaty with Turkey is not complete. It is plain, however, that France has seized

Syria for herself, despite the vehement protest of the Syrian people, and that England has taken Mesopotamia and the Euphrates district. In the selfish desire to grab such prizes, these Allies seem careless whether or not Turkey retains sovereignty over the ancient city of Constantinople. As a "by-product" of these arrangements, too, English imperialistic capital has at last virtually seized Persia, persuading the young Shah to betray his country. The whole arrangement in the East is a frank surrender to extreme and arrogant imperialism, French and English.

The United States

The United States is not yet a party either to the Peace or the League. Attempts to *amend* the League of Nations covenant in the United States Senate failed; but reservations were added to it to preserve freedom of action for the United States in quarrels that may arise out of the European rivalries. The President refused to accept these reservations, and final action is yet to be taken (December, 1919).

Bolshevist Russia

One more miserable mess must be recorded — concerning Russia. The Bolshevists are trying a new principle of citizenship. An able-bodied man or woman who does no useful work with hand or brain they look upon as a social parasite. Such people they exclude from voting. Political citizenship is based upon service to society. So far, the Bolshevist idea, in theory at least, may command some sympathy, — though we may not always agree with the Bolshevist judgment as to what social service is. (Lawyers, bankers, and all who live upon invested capital, are excluded by them from the list of useful workers; but actors, teachers, physicians, engineers, and industrial managers are included, along with all hand workers.) However that be, the world certainly would never have dreamed of interfering, by force, merely to correct such a limitation of the franchise in a land where the same world for a thousand years has tolerated the despotic rule of a Tsar.

But, for the first time in the world on a national scale, the

Bolshevists also *began to put into operation* an extreme kind of Socialism. If the Russian *people* really wish to try even this experiment, they undoubtedly have the right to do so. But the plan was put in operation, not by the deliberate will of the people: it was done by a "dictatorship of the proletariat." The real control lay — and still lies (December, 1919) — in the small but perfectly organized class of town workers. The much more numerous but less organized peasantry, fairly content with the ownership of their new lands (p. 645), *acquiesced* passively and perhaps ignorantly in the Bolshevist rule. The small capitalist class, and those "intellectuals" who oppose Socialism, were overruled and silenced. Still these non-Socialist forces might have got together before this time, and overthrown or modified Bolshevism, if the Allies, by a cruel, colossal, and despotic blunder, had not identified Bolshevism with patriotism for all Russians who love their country.

Like the French "emigrant" nobles of 1792, Russian courtiers and nobles in 1917, fleeing from the Revolution, levied war against the new government of their country from without or in the border provinces — with foreign aid. *Kolchak* for a time held most of Siberia; *Denekin* threatened invasion from the Ukraine; "Butcher" *Mannerheim*, commander of the Finnish "White Guards," after murdering 12,000 Finnish Socialists in cold blood, without trial, planned to attack Petrograd from the west. All these leaders claimed at first to desire some constitutional government for Russia; but more and more clearly their acts proved beyond doubt that they really plotted the restoration of despotism; and the unspeakable atrocities of the various "White Terrors" that followed their early temporary successes at least equaled the excesses charged to the Bolshevists in their hour of bloody Revolution. It must be added that hostile Roumania, Poland, and Japan, and small reactionary armies in the Baltic provinces (as in Livia; p. 678) made the cordon complete — except for the Archangel port on the north; and that one opening to the world was closed by an army of 12,000 English, French, and *Americans*.

These troops were sent to Archangel during the last of the war against Germany, on the ground that their presence was necessary to protect military stores there from German seizure. Soon, troops who had enlisted to fight the Kaiser were used — at the behest of French and English rulers — as an invading army against the workingman's government of Russia. They were told that the Russian people, freed, and encouraged by their presence, would rally to overthrow Bolshevist tyranny. But the Russians did not rally — or rather they did rally to the Bolshevists. The few who at first fought along with the Allies deserted rapidly to their countrymen. The service was hateful to multitudes of the English and American soldiers. And military necessity compelled the complete withdrawal of these troops from Russian soil before the end of 1919. The English fleet, however, continues the blockade (December, 1919).

One curious feature of the business is that democratic America found itself at war with Russia — and has continued at war for nearly two years — without action by Congress, and that requests even from United States senators like Hiram Johnson for information as to the reasons for President Wilson's action in sending American soldiers against Russia have received no reply from the administration.

The Allies at Paris, dominated by fear and hatred of Bolshevism, supported zealously all these invasions of Russia. No doubt they believe that only by blockade, and by final conquest, can Bolshevism be kept from spreading to their own lands. They think it needful to combat the Bolshevist theory, not by reason but by violence; and they do not think it safe to let it work out its own failure.

Kolchak and Denekin, supplied lavishly by the Allies and by the American government with arms, money, and other military stores, won some success during the early months while the

Bolshevists were busied in putting their house in order after the disorder of successive revolutions. But the invading armies continued to be merely selfish "emigrants" or paid mercenaries; the Russian peasants and townsfolk alike held aloof; and as soon as the Bolshevik government showed energy, these elements began to support it against foreign intervention. Russian "intellectuals," who had been contending against Bolshevism, even some who had suffered bitterly from that rule, now offered their services eagerly to the Russian government; and Kerensky himself, fugitive as he was in Paris, wrote in November of 1919 that foreign invasion had united all patriotic Russians in support of the Bolshevist government, and that the only hope for Russia lay in the prompt recognition of that government by the world.

For, although the Allies have not hurt Bolshevism, their blockade has probably slain more Russians by starvation than the Allied armies slew Germans during the war. And these victims have been largely undernourished mothers and young children, most commonly from just those classes that the Allies profess to desire to "free." Of course, the blockade has also kept Russian factories from getting cotton or rubber or other raw material not produced in their own land, and so has prevented a revival of Russian industrial life. In spite of all this, the Bolshevist armies have at this writing wrested peace from the Baltic states, and driven back in rout their invaders on all frontiers.

For Further Reading. — Arthur Ransom, *Russia in 1919.* (A statement of personal observation by a trained, fair-minded Englishman, without any sympathy for Bolshevist theory.) William Bullitt, *The Bullitt Mission to Russia.* (A story of an attempt to bring about peace by an attaché of the American Peace Delegation at Paris; with valuable documents.) Raymond Robins' *Colonel Robins' Story.* (Edited by William Hard. Raymond Robins was the head of the American Red Cross in Russia during the Revolution and after.)

CHAPTER LIII

HEALING FORCES

The war *was* a world war. Eight out of every nine men on the globe belonged to the warring nations. It cost nine million lives and 200 billion dollars. A vast portion of all the wealth stored up laboriously through centuries is consumed, and over wide areas all the machinery for *producing* wealth is gone. The *moral* losses are beyond all computation — sickening to the imagination.

The cost of the war

The United States had relatively small sacrifices to make. We entered late, and our borders were remote from the struggle. Still, eighty thousand American boys lie in French soil, and thrice as many were horribly maimed. As to money, aside from the immense sums raised by war taxes, our war debt is more than twenty-five billions, besides some nine billions more that our government borrowed from our people to loan to England, France, Belgium, and Italy. On these loans the Allied governments will perhaps pay the interest,[1] and possibly sometime they will be able to repay the principal; but on the remaining twenty-five billions the interest alone will each year exceed the total yearly expenditure of our government before the war. Our debt is ten times that with which we came out of our Civil War, *and it equals all the receipts of our government from George Washington's first presidency to our entrance into the war:* Without paying a cent of the principal, we will have to tax ourselves each year three times as much as ever before for our national government.

The cost still to be paid

[1] So far (December, 1919) no interest payment has been made by any foreign country on this debt; and we begin to hear voices to the effect that these loans should be regarded as part of America's payments for the war.

But we must also pay the principal. If we pay it in one generation (as probably we shall), that will mean one billion more of taxes a year. As we pay the principal, the interest will lessen; but, taking into account the increased cost of living for the government, it is safe to say that for the next twenty-five years we must raise three billion dollars a year, — or three fourths as much as in the war years themselves. We have boasted that in this country the war has been paid for by the wealthy classes, not by the poor. But so far (1919) we have hardly begun to pay that cost: if our boast is to be made good, we must raise more than two thirds of our taxes during the next years by income and luxury taxes.

Conditions in Europe

In Europe the burden is terrifying. Words cannot express the ruin there; and the huge totals of indebtedness in France, England, and Germany have little meaning to us. Factories are gone; shipping is sunk; raw materials for manufactures are not available; it seems almost impossible to start the wheels of industry again. Poverty and profound discouragement permeate the masses of the people. England has suffered less than the continent; but England's debt is enormous. *Without paying a penny of it,* merely to keep up the interest and her old annual expenditure, she must raise more than *five billions* of dollars a year in taxes. With her smaller population, that means that each family must pay some four times as much as an American family.

Some lasting gains

Still there is another side. The world is freed, we trust, from the perpetual cost of vast navies and crushing military establishments; and it has learned fruitful lessons. In the preceding chapters we surveyed some of the forces that made for *war efficiency.* Many of these, and others apart from these, make also for healing and reconstruction in peace. We can survey them best as they are seen in our own country.

The whole American people learned that when the rich family saved its fragments for a later meal, instead of casting them to the garbage can, some starving child in Europe had bread. We learned to do our daily work not so much for private gain as for the general good. We learned that every man who did not do work useful to society was a parasite, dangerous to society, whether he were a tramp or a millionaire. We learned that by coöperation, in place of wasteful competition, we could enormously increase the productiveness of our labor and machinery, and that by wise direction we could find useful work for every worker. Lessons like these, after growing into our life for two years of war, must leave a mighty effect upon our life in peace.

Lessons in human conservation

And many other lessons of the war will count for peace. The medical examination of our drafted men revealed tens of thousands of cases of inefficiency and of wasted lives due to defective eyes or teeth or feet. Our doctors, dentists, and surgeons cured most of these cases, and augmented tremendously our fighting power. Surely we will now find a way to use the same healing forces to augment our power for peaceful industry and to remove needless unhappiness. Indeed our schools in their new "health crusade" have already begun to remake our nation on a sounder basis of body.

The Vocational Board

Very fruitful of good was the work of our National Board of Vocational Education. Many soldiers, by the loss of arms or legs or eyes, were disabled from ever taking up again the only work they had ever known. The Vocational Board of skilled experts educated and trained these disabled men, at government expense, for some new occupation for which they showed interest and fitness, making them useful and happy members of society instead of leaving them dependents and beggars. Many a real genius was thus enabled to do some work he had always longed to do but which he had never before been able to get into. The results within even a few months were so incredibly beneficent that bills were introduced into both Houses of Congress in the winter of 1919 to preserve this Vocational organization for peace, that it might at public expense do the same invaluable and merciful work for the hundreds of thousands of our people who every year are maimed in accidents and in industry. The press of Congressional work at the end of the session prevented these bills from becoming law, but the attempt will be renewed.

New interest in child welfare

Still other features of this "human conservation" have promise for the future. In Europe there had been an alarming loss of man power due to slaughter in battle. Along with this was a falling off in the birth rate. These conditions threatened depopulation. Accordingly European governments were forced to legislate, more than ever before, for *child* welfare, — especially for the saving of the lives and health of babies and mothers, with the use of public funds. Even in the stress of war, laws provided for reasonable rest for working mothers before and after the birth of a child, without loss of wages. Such civilized legislation has long been called for by enlightened opinion, and now it is sure to become universal. It is already found in some degree in all large countries except the United States.

Housing movements

Very early, certain leaders sensed a danger that the tense passion of war might blind us unduly to the rights of the working classes. In fighting to make the world safe for democracy it was supremely necessary to keep it safe for labor. For one illustration, the vast army of new workers in the shipyards and munition factories found no houses fit for their families, and were threatened with slum conditions of disease and squalor, besides paying exorbitant rates to greedy landlords. Accordingly a government's Housing Commission expended millions of dollars in building model homes for such workers. This has given an impulse, not to be wholly lost, to an old movement for better housing by the nation for the workers.

The War Labor Board

More difficult to meet was another problem. Labor had to give up its usual weapon of strikes in disputes with employers. The public good demanded this. But labor could not be left to the mercy of employers. And so in America the Congress created a *War Labor Board.* This proved one of the most remarkable parts of the war government, exercising for two years an influence upon American life second only to that of the Supreme Court. Wages were rising rapidly; and the public, only partially informed, could not easily understand that wages after all failed to keep up with the rising cost of living, and that workingmen were in danger of losing the standards of living that they had won in long years of effort.

The War Labor Board acted as a compulsory arbitration board between Capital and Labor in those industries which concerned the carrying on of the war. President Wilson appointed ex-President Taft and Mr. Frank Walsh as joint chairmen, and the other members came in equal numbers from employers and labor representatives. The Board recognized the right of labor to organize and bargain collectively, the eight-hour day, a living wage, and the necessity of maintaining safeguards against accidents and disease, and it encouraged in many industries the organization of "shop committees" from the workmen to confer with the employers upon all shop conditions, — a great step toward democratizing industry.

In its arbitrations, the Board itself had no power to *enforce* a decision, though in nearly every case both sides submitted at once to its award. But in some cases President Wilson found it needful to make the decisions compulsory by seizing for public use the factories whose owners refused compliance, or on the other side, by threatening strikers, who had refused an award, with military service, by withdrawing their exemption as married men. The judicial temper of Mr. Taft and his legal training and open-mindedness made his services on this Board invaluable to the nation, and he won deep and lasting gratitude from organized labor for his understanding of their needs.

The demo-ratization of industr[y]

English employers and workers during the war agreed upon the principles of the famous Whitley Report,[1] providing for the joint management of industries by Capital and Labor through joint councils of many grades. In the few months since the armistice, much has been done in England to extend and confirm this principle, and to provide against unemploy-

[1] Printed in full in No. 135 (February, 1919) of the American Association for International Conciliation.

ment, to shorten the working day, and to guarantee a decent living wage to every man or woman willing to work.

In the winter of 1918 the English Labor Party adopted an even more comprehensive plan [1] for reconstruction after the war, along the same lines. This plan attracted wide and favorable attention, and in Minnesota a convention of Congregational Churches declared it "the one great *religious* utterance of the war." It is deeply significant that many larger religious bodies have made like declarations if somewhat less emphatic ones, — especially the Catholic Church through a report of its Advisory War Council, and the Methodist Church, both in Canada and the United States.

In general these plans agree on the following points:

1. Recognition that industry is designed for social service, not for private profiteering.

2. A *decent* wage (not a bare living) for each worker and his family.

3. Insurance against unemployment, with wise provision by the government for using idle labor in housing enterprises and in land reclamation, and, if necessary, for shortening the working day. (There is no excuse for a long working day, for any laborer, say many of these recent programs, as long as another willing but idle worker is standing by, asking for work.)

4. Democratizing industry, so as to give to the workers a share in management and some ownership in their jobs.

5. Limitation of the profits of capital to a reasonable amount.

6. The use of the surplus (above wages and "reasonable" profits) for the public good, — the surplus to be taken by extension of income taxes and by other new taxes on mining royalties, water power, and so on.

7. The need of greater production by Labor — for which these other changes must provide the best inducement.

Five years ago these principles would have sounded wildly revolutionary: to-day society in general quietly assents to them.

[1] Printed in the same.

Stirring times are before us — times once more to try men's souls. Europe is still in desperate peril of social dissolution; even America is not wholly free from danger that revolution may destroy the wholesome and progressive evolution of our society; and the world is not yet out of the peril of a frightful shortage of food. True, too, there is going on a dangerous reaction typified by the arrogant attitude of the Steel Company in 1919 toward its striking employees. And these reactionaries have known how to throw discredit upon all progressive movements by confusing them in the popular mind with Bolshevism. But men of faith believe that the outlook brightens, and that a new day is breaking. Just after the exhausting conflict, there was a let down, a slump in morale. Society was marked for a time by careless self-indulgence and by thoughtless indifference toward great issues. But already there surges up again in the masses of mankind a new wave of moral earnestness, promising a world — such as our leaders have pointed us toward through the war clouds — "safe for democracy" and "fit for heroes."

High school youth for years will remember vividly the war years and their regret that they were too young to play a part. Now theirs is perhaps a harder part. The challenge to them is to complete the work for which their elder brothers died — to strive in peace for freedom and human brotherhood.

> "If ye break faith with us who die,
> We shall not sleep, though poppies blow in Flanders fields."

APPENDIX

A LIST OF BOOKS IN MODERN HISTORY FOR HIGH SCHOOLS

The following titles are classified in two periods, and under each period, in two groups. In the judgment of the writer, all high schools should have access to Group I (or an equivalent), while large schools may well have Group II also. Works marked with a * should be present in more than single copies. Prices are so uncertain at this time (1919) that no attempt is made to state them.

A. TO THE FRENCH REVOLUTION

Group I

Source Material.

Anglo-Saxon Chronicle (Bohn edition).

Chronicles of the Crusades (Bohn Library).

* **Davis, W. S.**, *Readings in Ancient History*, II. Allyn and Bacon.

Einhard, *Charlemagne.* American Book Co.

English History from Contemporary Writers, edited by F. York-Powell. A series of ten small volumes, published from 1886 to 1894 by Putnam, as follows: **Archer**, *Crusade of Richard I;* **Ashley**, *Edward III and His Wars;* **Barnard**, *Strongbow's Conquest of Ireland;* **Hutton**, *Misrule of Henry III; Simon of Montfort; St. Thomas of Canterbury;* **Jacobs**, *The Jews of Angevin England;* **Powell**, *Alfred and the Danes;* **Smith**, *Troublous Days of Richard II.*

Hill, Mabel, *Liberty Documents.* Longmans.

Joinville, *Memoir of St. Louis.* (Various editions.)

Lanier (editor), *The Boy's Froissart.* Scribner.

Lee, *Source Book of English History.* Holt.

Marco Polo, *The Story of*, edited by Noah Brooks. Century Co.

Ogg, F. A., *Source Book of Medieval History.* Am. Book Co.

Pennsylvania Translations and Reprints from Original Sources. 7 vols. University of Pennsylvania.

* **Robinson, J. H.**, *Readings in European History.* 2 vols. Ginn.

Modern Accounts.

* **Adams, G. B.**, *Growth of the French Nation.* Macmillan.

* —— *Civilization during the Middle Ages.* Scribner.

* **Archer** and **Kingsford**, *The Crusades* (" Nations "). Putnam.
Balzani, *Popes and Hohenstaufen*. Longmans.
Beard, Charles, *An Introduction to English Historians* (extracts from leading authorities on interesting topics). Macmillan.
Beesly, E. S., *Elizabeth* (" English Statesmen "). Macmillan.
Boyeson, H. H., *Norway* (" Nations "). Putnam.
Bradley, *Wolfe*. Macmillan.
Brown, Horatio, *The Venetian Republic* (" Temple Primers "). Macmillan.
* **Bryce, James**, *Holy Roman Empire*. Macmillan.
* **Cheyney, E. P.**, *Industrial and Social History of England*. Macmillan.
Church, *Beginnings of the Middle Ages* (" Epochs "). Longmans.
Clemens (Mark Twain), *Joan of Arc*. Harper.
Cornish, F. W., *Chivalry*. Macmillan.
Cox, G. W., *The Crusades* (" Epochs "). Longmans.
Creighton, M., *Age of Elizabeth* (" Epochs "). Longmans.
Cunningham, *Western Civilization* (Vol. II, Medieval and Modern). Macmillan.
Cunningham and **McArthur**, *Outlines of English Industrial History*. Macmillan.
Davis, H. W. C., *Charlemagne* (" Heroes "). Putnam.
* **Emerton**, *Introduction to the Study of the Middle Ages*. Ginn.
—— *Medieval Europe*. Ginn.
Firth, *Cromwell* (" Heroes "). Putnam.
Gardiner, S. R., *Student's History of England*. Longmans.
—— *The Puritan Revolution* (" Epochs "). Longmans.
—— *The Thirty Years' War* (" Epochs "). Longmans.
Gibbins, *Industrial History of England*. Methuen; London.
Gilman, *The Saracens* (" Nations "). Putnam.
Gray, *The Children's Crusade*. Houghton.
* **Green, J. R.**, *History of the English People*. 4 vols. Burt; New York.
Or, in place of this last work,
* **Green, J. R.**, *Short History of the English People*. Am. Book Co.
Green, Mrs., *Henry II*. Macmillan.
Hughes, Thomas, *Alfred the Great*. Macmillan.
Jenks, *Edward Plantagenet* (" Heroes "). Putnam.
Jessopp, *The Coming of the Friars*. Putnam.
Jiriczek, *Northern Hero Legends*. Macmillan.
Johnston, C., and **Spencer, C.**, *Ireland's Story*. Houghton.
Lane-Poole, *Saladin* (" Heroes "). Putnam.
Lindsay, T. M., *Luther and the German Reformation*. Scribner.

Masterman, J. H. B., *Dawn of Medieval Europe* ("Six Ages"). Macmillan.
Motley, *The Student's Motley*, — the best history of the Dutch Republic in its heroic age; edited by Griffis. Harper.
Mullinger, *University of Cambridge*. Longmans.
Oman, C. W. C., *Byzantine Empire* ("Nations"). Putnam.
Pears, E., *Fall of Constantinople*. Harper.
Perry, F., *St. Louis* ("Heroes"). Putnam.
Pollard, *History of England* ("Home University"). Holt.
* **Shepherd**, W. R., *Historical Atlas*. Holt.
Stubbs, *Early Plantagenets* ("Epochs"). Longmans.
Tout, T. F., *Edward I*. Macmillan.
Van Dyke, *History of Painting*. New York.
Walker, W., *The Reformation*. Scribner.
Ward, *The Counter-Reformation*. Longmans.
Willert, *Henry of Navarre* ("Heroes"). Putnam.
Woodward, W. H., *Expansion of the British Empire, 1500–1902*. Putnam.
Zimmern, H., *The Hansa* ("Nations"). Putnam.

Group II

Ashley, *Introduction to English Economic History*. Vol. I, Part I. Longmans.
Beard, *Martin Luther*. London.
Beazley, *Prince Henry the Navigator* ("Heroes"). Putnam.
Bourne, E. G., *Spain in America* (Am. Nation Series). Harper.
Bradley, *Wolfe*. Macmillan.
Caldecott, Alfred. *English Colonization and Empire*. (University Extension Manuals.) New York.
Cutts, *Parish Priests and their People*. London.
—— *Scenes and Characters of the Middle Ages*. New York.
Du Chaillu, *The Viking Age*. 2 vols. Murray.
Fletcher, *Gustavus Adolphus* ("Heroes"). Putnam.
Fox-Bourne, *Sir Philip Sidney* ("Heroes"). Putnam.
Gasquet, F. A., *Parish Life in Medieval England*. New York.
Harrison, F., *William the Silent*. Macmillan.
Henderson, E., *Short History of Germany*. 2 vols. in one. Macmillan.
Hodgkin, T., *Charles the Great*. Macmillan.
James, G. P. R., *History of Chivalry*. Harper.
Jusserand, *English Wayfaring Life in the Middle Ages*. London.
Keary, *The Vikings in Western Christendom*. Putnam.

Lübke, *History of Art*. 2 vols. Dodd and Mead.
McCabe, *Abelard*. Putnam.
Morison, *Life and Times of St. Bernard*. Macmillan.
Parkman, Francis, *New France, Half Century of Conflict, Montcalm and Wolfe*. Little, Brown, and Co.
Putnam, Ruth, *Books and Their Makers in the Middle Ages*. Putnam.
Robinson and **Rolfe**, *Petrarch*. Putnam.
Sabatier, *St. Francis*. Scribner.
Saintsbury, *Flourishing of Romance*. Scribner.
Seeley, *Expansion of England*. Macmillan.
Smith, J. H., *The Troubadours at Home*. Putnam.
Stephens, W. R. W., *Hildebrand and His Times*. Longmans.
Storrs, *Bernard of Clairvaux*. Scribner.
Story of the Burnt Njal (Dassent, translator). New York.
Symonds, J. A., *Short History of the Renaissance in Italy* (Edited by Pearson). Scribner.
Vincent, *The Age of Hildebrand*. Scribner.
Wiel, *Venice* (" Nations "). Putnam.
York-Powell, *Alfred the Truth-Teller*. Putnam.

B. FROM THE FRENCH REVOLUTION TO THE PRESENT TIME

Group I

Source Material.

* **Anderson, F. M.**, *Constitutions and Other Documents Illustraive of the History of France, 1789–1907*. H. W. Wilson Co.; White Plains, N.Y.
Robinson and **Beard**, *Readings in Modern European History (1650–1908)*. 2 vols. Ginn.
Lee's *Source Book*, and *Pennsylvania Reprints*, as under first list above.

Modern Accounts.

Andrews, C. M., *Historical Development of Modern Europe*. (From 1815 to 1897.) Putnam.
Barker, J. E., *Modern Germany*. London.
Cesaresco, *Cavour*. Macmillan.
Crawford, *Switzerland To-day* (1911). New York.
* **Gardiner, Mrs. B. M.**, *French Revolution* (" Epochs "). Longmans.
Gibbons, H. A., *New Map of Europe* (1911–1914). The Century Co.
Hayes, Carlton, *Modern Europe*. 2 vols. Macmillan (Vol. II covers 1815–1915.)
** **Hazen, C. D.**, *Europe since 1815*. Holt.

Headlam, J. W., *Bismarck* ("Heroes"). Putnam.
Lowell, E. J., *Eve of the French Revolution*. Houghton.
McCarthy, Justin, *Epoch of Reform, 1830–1850* ("Epochs"). Longmans.
* **Mathews, Shailer**, *French Revolution*. Longmans.
Ogg, F. A. *Social Progress in Contemporary Europe.* (An admirable brief survey from 1789 to 1912.) Macmillan.
* **Phillips, W. A.**, *Modern Europe (1815–1900)*. Macmillan.
Ransome, Arthur, *Russia in 1919.*
Robins, Raymond, Colonel Robins' Story (of Bolshevist Russia); edited by William Hard.
Rose, J. H., *Life of Napoleon I.* 2 vols. in one. Macmillan.
* —— *Revolutionary and Napoleonic Era.* Cambridge Press.
* —— *Rise of Democracy in Great Britain.* New York.
Spargo, John, *Elements of Socialism.* Macmillan.
—— *Bolshevism.* Macmillan.

GROUP II

Carlyle, *The French Revolution.* 3 vols. Putnam.
Hannay, *Castelar.* Macmillan.
Kerr, P. H. and **A. C.**, *Growth of the British Empire.* Longmans.
King, Bolton, *History of Italian Unity, 1814–1871.* Scribner.
Kirkup, T., *History of Socialism.* Macmillan.
Lloyd, *A Sovereign People* (Switzerland). New York.
McCarthy, Justin, *England in the Nineteenth Century.* Putnam.
McCarthy, J. H., *England under Gladstone.* London.
Nevison, *Dawn in Russia.* New York.
Russell, *German Social Democracy.* Longmans.
Seignobos, *Europe since 1814.* Holt.
Skrine, *Expansion of Russia* ("Cambridge Series"). Cambridge Press.
Stephens, H. Morse, *The French Revolution.* Scribner.
—— *Revolutionary Europe, 1789–1815.* Macmillan.
Stillman, W. J., *The Union of Italy, 1815–1895* ("Cambridge Series"). Cambridge Press.
Wallace (and others), *Progress of the Century* (Nineteenth). Harper.
Willert, *Mirabeau.* Macmillan.

No attempt is made to list fiction, though some of the best works of that kind are referred to in footnotes or at the close of chapters above. Nor is any list of books given upon the World War. The footnotes and chapter bibliographies list many of the most important ones — as they rank at present — but the histories of the war are not yet (1919) written.

INDEX

Pronunciation, except for familiar names and terms, is shown by division into syllables and accentuation. When diacritical marks for English names are needed, the common marks of Webster's Dictionaries are used. German and French pronunciation can be indicated only imperfectly to those who are not familiar with the languages; but attention is called to the following marks: the soft aspirated guttural sound *g* of the German is marked G; the corresponding *ch* (as in *ich*) is marked K; the sound of the nasal French *n* is marked *ñ*; for the German *ä* and *äu* the equivalents are indicated, to prevent confusion with English *ä*; *ö* is always the German letter; and *ü* is the German diphthong or the equivalent French *u*. In French words with an accent on the final syllable, that accent only is marked; but it should be understood that in such words the syllables as a rule receive nearly equal stress.